S0-AZJ-736

12 19
STRAND PRICE
$5.00

Published by
The Kabbalah Centre International Inc.

155 E. 48th St., New York, NY 10017
1062 S. Robertson Blvd., Los Angeles, CA 90035

Director Rav Berg

First Printing 2001

Revised Edition 2003

Printed in USA

ISBN: 1-57189-185-4

At this time
in the history of mankind,
it is my duty, privilege and joy
to participate in spreading the
Light of Kabbalah
throughout the world.
I am certain that the Zohar
is what the world needs the most
right now to stop all the chaos.

May the Light of the Zohar
bring Mashiach mercifully
for all humankind.

May the merit of spreading the Zohar

bring all the blessing of the light

to my family

Yacov ben Eugene
Julia bat Anatoly

and my soulmate

Miriam bat Moshe

APPLYING THE POWER OF THE ZOHAR

The Zohar is a book of great mystical power and wisdom. It is Universally recognized as the definitive work on the Kabbalah – and it is also so Much more.

The Zohar is a wellspring of spiritual energy, a fountainhead of metaphysical power that not only reveals and explains, but literally brings blessing, protection, and well-being into the lives of all those who read or peruse its sacred texts. All that is required is worthy desire, the certainty of a trusting heart, and an open and receptive mind. Unlike other books, including the great spiritual texts of other traditions, The Zohar is written in a kind of code, through which metaphors, parables, and cryptic language at first conceal but ultimately reveal the forces of creation.

As electrical current is concealed in wire and cable before disclosing itself as an illuminated light bulb, the spiritual Light of the Creator is wrapped in allegory and symbolism throughout the Aramaic text of the Zohar. And while many books contain information and knowledge, the Zohar both expresses and embodies spiritual Light. The very letters on its pages have the power to bring spiritual wisdom and positive energy into every area of our lives.

As we visually scan the Aramaic texts and study the accompanying insights that appear in English, spiritual power is summoned from above – and worlds tremble as Light is sent forth in response.

It's primary purpose is not only to help us acquire wisdom, but to draw Light from the Upper Worlds and to bring sanctification into our lives. Indeed, the book itself is the most powerful of all tools for cleansing the soul and connecting to the Light of the Creator. As you open these pages, therefore, do not make understanding in the conventional sense your primary goal.

Although you may not have a knowledge of Aramaic, look first at the Aramaic text before reading the English. Do not be discouraged by difficulties with comprehension. Instead, open your heart to the spiritual transformation the Zohar is offering you.

Ultimately, the Zohar is an instrument for refining the individual soul – for removing darkness from the earth – and for bringing well being and blessing to our fellow man.

Its purpose is not only to make us intellectually wise, but to make us spiritually pure.

Glossary of Hebrew words

Torah

Also known as the Five Books of Moses, the Torah is considered to be the physical body of learning, whereas the Zohar is the internal soul. The literal stories of the Torah conceal countless hidden secrets. The Zohar is the Light that illuminates all of the Torah's sublime mysteries.

Beresheet	Genesis
Shemot	Exodus
Vayikra	Leviticus
Bemidbar	Numbers
Devarim	Deuteronomy

Prophets

Amos	Amos
Chagai	Haggai
Chavakuk	Habakkuk
Hoshea	Hosea
Malachi	Malachi
Melachim	Kings
Michah	Micah
Nachum	Nahum
Ovadyah	Obadiah
Shmuel	Samuel
Shoftim	Judges
Tzefanyah	Zephaniah
Yechezkel	Ezekiel
Yehoshua	Joshua
Yeshayah	Isaiah
Yirmeyah	Jeremiah
Yoel	Joel
Yonah	Jonah
Zecharyah	Zechariah

Writings

Daniel	Daniel
Divrei Hayamim	Chronicles
Eicha	Lamentations
Ester	Esther
Ezra	Ezra
Nechemiah	Nehemiah
Iyov	Job
Kohelet	Ecclesiastes
Mishlei	Proverbs
Rut	Ruth
Sir Hashirim	Songs of Songs
Tehilim	Psalms

The Ten Sfirot – Emanations

To conceal the blinding *Light* of the Upper World, and thus create a tiny point into which our universe would be born, ten *curtains* were fabricated. These ten *curtains* are called Ten Sfirot. Each successive Sfirah further reduces the emanation of *Light*, gradually dimming its brilliance to a level almost devoid of *Light* – our physical world known as *Malchut*. The only remnant of Light remaining in this darkened universe is a *pilot light* which sustains our existence. This Light is the life force of a human being and the force that gives birth to stars, sustains suns and sets everything from swirling galaxies to busy ant hills in motion. Moreover, the Ten Sfirot act like a prism, refracting the Light into many *colors* giving rise to the diversity of life and matter in our world.

The Ten Sfirot are as follows:

Keter	Crown
Chochmah	Wisdom
Binah	Understanding
Da'at	Knowledge
Zeir Anpin	Small Face,
	(includes the next six Sfirot):
Chesed	Mercy (Chassadim - plural)
Gvurah	Judgment (Gvurot - Plural)
Tiferet	Splendor
Netzach	Victory (Eternity)
Hod	Glory
Yesod	Foundation
Malchut	Kingdom

The Partzufim - Spiritual forms

One complete structure of the Ten Sfirot creates a *Partzuf* or Spiritual Form. Together, these forces are the building blocks of all reality. As water and sand combine to create cement, the Ten Sfirot combine to produce a Spiritual Form *[Partzuf]*. Each of the Spiritual Forms below are therefore composed of one set of Ten Sfirot.

These Spiritual Forms are called:

Atik	Ancient
Atik Yomin	Ancient of Days
Atika Kadisha	Holy Ancient
Atik of Atikin	Anceint of Ancients
Aba	Father
Arich Anpin	Long Face
Ima	Mother
Nukva	Female
Tevunah	Intelligence
Yisrael Saba	Israel Grandfather
Zachar	Male

These names are not meant to be understood literally. Each represents a unique spiritual force and building block, producing a substructure and foundation for all the worlds make up reality.

The Five Worlds

All of the above Spiritual Forms *[Partzufim]* create one spiritual world. There are Five Worlds in total that compose all reality, therefore, five sets of the above Spiritual Forms are required.

Our physical world corresponds to the world of: Asiyah – Action

Adam Kadmon	Primordial Man
Atzilut	Emanation
Briyah	Creation
Yetzirah	Formation
Asiyah	Action

The Five Levels of the soul

Nefesh	First, Lowest level of Soul
Ruach	Second level of Soul
Neshamah	Third level of Soul
Chayah	Fourth level of Soul
Yechidah	Highest, fifth level of Soul

Names of God

As a single ray of white sunlight contains the seven colors of the spectrum, the one Light of the Creator embodies many diverse spiritual forces. These different forces are called *Names of God.* Each Name denotes a specific attribute and spiritual power. The Hebrew letters that compose these Names are the interface by which these varied Forces act upon our physical world. The most common Name of God is the Tetragrammaton (the four letters, *Yud Hei Vav Hei* יהוה.) Because of the enormous power that the Tetragrammaton transmits, we do not utter it aloud. When speaking of the Tetragrammaton, we use the term *Hashem* which means, *The Name.*

Adonai, El, Elohim, Hashem, Shadai, Eheyeh, Tzevaot, Yud Hei Vav Hei

People

Er	The son of Noach
Rabbi Elazar	The son of Rabbi Shimon bar Yochai
Rabbi Shimon bar Yochai	Author of the Zohar
Shem, Cham, Yefet	Noach's children
Shet	Seth
Ya'akov	Jacob
Yishai	Jesse (King David's father)
Yitzchak	Isaac
Yosef	Joseph
Yitro	Jethro
Yehuda	Judah

Angels

Angels are distinct energy components, part of a vast communication network running through the upper worlds. Each unique Angel is responsible for transmitting various forces of influence into our physical universe.

Adriel, Ahinael, Dumah (name of Angel in charge of the dead), Gabriel, Kadshiel, Kedumiel, Metatron, Michael, Rachmiel,

Glossary of Hebrew words

Raphael, Tahariel, Uriel

Nations

Nations actually represent the inner attributes and character traits of our individual self. The nation of Amalek refers to the doubt and uncertainty that dwells within us when we face hardship and obstacles. Moab represents the dual nature of man. Nefilim refers to the sparks of Light that we have defiled through our impure actions, and to the negative forces that lurk within the human soul as a result of our own wrongful deeds.

Amalek, Moab, Nefilim

General

Aba	Father Refers to the male principle and positive force in our universe. Correlates to the proton in an atom.
Arvit	The Evening prayer
Chayot	Animals
Chupah	Canopy (wedding ceremony)
Et	The
Avadon	Hell
Gehenom	Hell
Sheol	Hell The place a soul goes for purification upon leaving this world.
Ima	Mother The female principle and minus force in our universe. Correlates to the electron in an atom.
Kiddush	Blessing over the wine
Klipah	Shell (negativity)
Klipot	Shells (Plural)
Kriat Sh'ma	The Reading of the Sh'ma
Mashiach	Messiah
Minchah	The Afternoon prayer
Mishnah	Study
Mochin	Brain, Spiritual levels of Light
Moed	A designated time or holiday
Negev	The south of Israel
Nukva	Female
Partzuf	Face
Shacharit	The Morning prayer
Shamayim	Heavens (sky)
Shechinah	The Divine presence, The female aspect of the Creator
Tefilin	Phylacteries
The Dinur river	The river of fire
Tzadik	Righteous person
Zion	Another name for Jerusalem
Yisrael	The land of Israel The nation of Israel or an individual Israelite
Zohar	Splendor

The Hebrew vowels

Chirik אִ, Cholam אוֹ אֹ, Kamatz אָ, Patach אַ, Segol אֶ, Sh'va אְ, Shuruk אוּ אֻ, Tzere אֵ.

The Twelve Tribes

Asher, Dan, Ephraim, Gad, Issachar, Judah, Levi, Menasheh, Naphtali, Reuben, Shimon, Zebulun

Jewish Holidays

Rosh Hashanah	The Jewish New Year
Yom Kippur	Day of Atonement
Sukkot	Holiday of the Booths
Shmini Atzeret	The day of Convocation
Simchat Torah	Holiday on which we dance with the Torah
Pesach	Passover
Shavout	Holiday of the Weeks

כרך יג

פרשת פיקודי

Vol. XIII

Pekudei

A Prayer from The Ari

To be recited before the study of the Zohar

Ruler of the universe, and Master of all masters, The Father of mercy and forgiveness, we thank You, our God and the God of our fathers, by bowing down and kneeling, that You brought us closer to Your Torah and Your holy work, and You enable us to take part in the secrets of Your holy Torah. How worthy are we that You grant us with such big favor, that is the reason we plead before You, that You will forgive and acquit all our sins, and that they should not bring separation between You and us.

And may it be your will before You, our God and the God of our fathers, that You will awaken and prepare our hearts to love and revere You, and may You listen to our utterances, and open our closed heart to the hidden studies of Your Torah, and may our study be pleasant before Your Place of Honor, as the aroma of sweet incense, and may You emanate to us Light from the source of our soul to all of our being. And, may the sparks of your holy servants, through which you revealed Your wisdom to the world, shine.

May their merit and the merit of their fathers, and the merit of their Torah, and holiness, support us so we shall not stumble through our study. And by their merit enlighten our eyes in our learning as it stated by King David, The Sweet Singer of Israel: “Open my eyes, so that I will see wonders from Your Torah” (Tehilim 119:18). Because from His mouth God gives wisdom and understanding.

“May the utterances of my mouth and the thoughts of my heart find favor before You, God, my Strength and my Redeemer” (Tehilim 19:15).

PEKUDEI

Names of the articles

Page No.

1. "All the rivers run into the sea" 4
2. "Oh how great is Your goodness, which You have laid up for those who fear You" 6
3. "And in mercy a throne was established" 10
4. "These are the accounts of the Tabernacle" 13
5. "Beautiful for situation, the joy of the whole earth" 27
6. "These are the accounts of the Tabernacle," part two 31
7. "And He shall be the faithfulness of your times" 35
8. The name Betzalel caused 38
9. "When the wicked sprout like grass" 43
10. The 42 sacrifices of Balak 46
11. "All the gold that was applied for the work" 48
12. "And he turned back, and looked at them" 51
13. Gold from below upwards and silver from above downwards 54
14. Counting and Numbers 59
15. "Unless Hashem builds the house" 68
16. "And the thousand seven hundred and seventy-five" 73
17. Each order contains three 86
18. Forty-five kinds of lights 93
19. "mountains of brass" 97
20. Sacred robes 100
21. Breastplate and Efod 105
22. "Lift up your eyes on high" 125
23. "Praise Hashem from the heavens" 128
24. "the Mountain of Hashem's house shall be established on top of the mountains" 132
25. Sometimes he praises himself and sometimes he humbles himself 136
26. Measuring line and measuring reed 140
27. The names of *Mem-Bet* (42) and *Ayin-Bet* (72) 153
28. "He asked life of you" 160
29. "And they brought the Tabernacle to Moses" 164
30. The traps 166
31. The letters of Yud Hei Vav Hei are like the letters of Adonai 169
32. "And Moses erected the Tabernacle" 171
33. The secret of the camel 175
34. The dross of gold 178
35. The calf 182
36. A red heifer 187

Page No.

37. The hair in the Tefilin 190
38. "And they brought the Tabernacle to Moses," part two 195
39. "This is the Torah of the burnt offering" 201
40. And Moses erected the Tabernacle" 212
41. "when I fall, I shall arise" 228
42. "When those moved, these moved" 230
43. The Tabernacle and the Temple 235
44. The six grades of the Other Side 240
45. The chambers of holiness 259
46. The chamber of a sapphire stone – Yesod 263
47. The chamber of the very heaven – Hod 278
48. The chamber of brightness – Netzach 291
49. The chamber of merit – Gvurah 316
50. The fifth chamber of love – Chesed 333
51. The chamber of desire – Tiferet 340
52. The chamber of the Holy of Holies 386
53. The seven chambers of the Other Side 428
54. The first chamber of the Other Side, Empty Pit – Satan of the Evil Inclination 432
55. Second chamber of the Other Side, Grave – unholy of the Evil Inclination 436
56. The third chamber of the Other Side, Dumah, corresponding to the name 'foe of the Evil Inclination' 442
57. The fourth chamber of the Other Side, Debt, corresponding to the gruesome mud and a stone of stumbling 450
58. The fifth chamber of the Other Side, Sheol, corresponding to the name 'uncircumcised' 457
59. The sixth chamber, Evil, corresponding to the name 'shadow of death' 464
60. The seventh chamber of the Other Side – the dregs of wine 473
61. "dust of the ground' 479
62. "the End of all Flesh" 481
63. The chamber of the secret of sacrifice 484

1. "All the rivers run into the sea"

A Synopsis

Rabbi Chiya opens with: "All the rivers run into the sea, yet the sea is not full...," saying that these rivers are the secret of the Sfirot that are the holy rivers that filled the great sea, Malchut. The sea then flows over and provides water for the animals in the field. The sea of Malchut takes in the springs, the lights of Zeir Anpin, and pours them out into the Holy Chariots below. All of these are named and counted by Malchut. We are told that 'the Tabernacle' in the opening verse is Malchut, and that the grades that she waters correspond to the utensils of the tabernacle, all of which are called by name.

1. אֵלֶּה פְקוּדֵי הַמִּשְׁכָּן מִשְׁכַּן הָעֵדוּת אֲשֶׁר פֻּקַּד עַל פִּי מֹשֶׁה וְגוֹ׳. ר׳ חִיָּיא פָּתַח, כָּל הַנְּחָלִים הוֹלְכִים אֶל הַיָּם וְהַיָּם אֵינֶנּוּ מָלֵא וְגוֹ׳. הַאי קְרָא אוּקְמוּהָ וְאִתְּמַר, אֲבָל כָּל הַנְּחָלִים אִלֵּין רָזִין דִּנְחָלִין וּמַבּוּעִין קַדִּישִׁין, דְּאִתְמַלְיָין, וְנָפְקִין לְאַנְהָרָא וּלְמַלְיָיא לְהַאי יַמָּא רַבָּא, וְכֵיוָן דְּהַאי יַמָּא רַבָּא אִתְמְלֵי מִסִּטְרָא דְּאִינּוּן נַחֲלִין כְּדֵין הוּא אַפִּיק מַיָּא, וְאַשְׁקֵי לְכָל חֵיוָון בָּרָא, כד״א יַשְׁקוּ כָּל חַיְתוֹ שָׂדָי.

1. "These are the accounts of the Tabernacle, the Tabernacle of the Testimony as they were counted, according to the commandments of Moses..." (Shemot 38:21). Rabbi Chiya opened the discussion with the verse: "All the rivers run into the sea, yet the sea is not full…" (Kohelet 1:7). This verse has already been elucidated and learned. Yet all these rivers are the secret of the holy rivers and springs, THE SFIROT OF ZEIR ANPIN, that filled and flowed to illuminate and fill this great sea, MALCHUT. And when the great sea is filled by these rivers, it flows over and waters the field animals as it is written – "they give drink to every wild beast" (Tehilim 104:11), WHICH ARE THE GRADES OF BRIYAH, YETZIRAH AND ASIYAH.

2. מַה כְּתִיב לְעֵילָּא, הַמְשַׁלֵּחַ מַעְיָנִים וְגוֹ׳, וּלְבָתַר, יַשְׁקוּ כָּל חַיְתוֹ שָׂדָי יְשַׁבְּרוּ פְרָאִים צְמָאָם. אִלֵּין אִינּוּן רְתִיכִין דִּלְתַתָּא, דְּכַד יַמָּא נָקִיט לוֹן, כֻּלְּהוּ נָקִיט לוֹן, וְשָׁאִיב לוֹן בְּגַוֵּיהּ, וּלְבָתַר אַפִּיק מַיִין לְסִטְרָא אַחֲרָא, דְּאִינּוּן רְתִיכִין קַדִּישִׁין דִּלְתַתָּא, וְאַשְׁקֵי לוֹן. וְכֻלְּהוּ אִתְמְנוּן וְאִתְפָּקְדוּן

בִּשְׁמָא, כד״א לְכֻלָּם בְּשֵׁם יִקְרָא. וּבְגִין כָּךְ, אֵלֶּה פְקוּדֵי הַמִּשְׁכָּן מִשְׁכַּן הָעֵדוּת.

2. The verse preceding, "THEY GIVE DRINK TO EVERY WILD BEAST," is "He sends the springs into the valleys..." and after it, "they give drink to every wild beast: the wild asses quench their thirst." These are the lower Chariots, OF BRIYAH, YETZIRAH AND ASIYAH, CALLED 'WILD BEASTS' AND 'WILD ASSES'. And when the sea, MALCHUT, receives THE SPRINGS, THE LIGHTS OF ZEIR ANPIN, it takes and swallows them inside, then lets water out on the other side, which is the Holy Chariots below IN BRIYAH, YETZIRAH AND ASIYAH, and waters them and all are counted and numbered by name. FOR ALL THE GRADES THAT MALCHUT WATERS, SHE CALLS BY NAME, as it is said, "He calls them all by names" (Yeshayah 40:26). Therefore it is written: "These are the accounts of the Tabernacle." FOR THE TABERNACLE IS MALCHUT, AND THE GRADES THAT SHE WATERS, NAMELY THE UTENSILS OF THE TABERNACLE, ARE ACCOUNTED, THAT ARE CALLED BY NAME.

2. "Oh how great is Your goodness, which You have laid up for those who fear You"

A Synopsis

Rabbi Yosi says that people should observe the ways of God, for every day a voice tells people to stay away from sin. He tells us that supernal judgment is a wheel that is constantly turning, lifting people up and bringing them down. The wicked are pushed from the wheel and fall into a pit; they will never see the light that has been stored up for the righteous in the World to Come. "Oh how great is Your goodness" refers to this light. We are told that "You have performed for those who trust in You," means that God created the world with that light. Rabbi Yosi next tells us that..." in the sight of the sons of men" means that the construction of the world by means of the light sustains people, people live by it. The building of the world is like the building of the Tabernacle: both of them came from the power of the stored light. The Tabernacle, Malchut, was created by left and right, and Moses, the Central Column, founded it.

3. רִבִּי יוֹסֵי פָּתַח, מָה רַב טוּבְךָ אֲשֶׁר צָפַנְתָּ לִּירֵאֶיךָ פָּעַלְתָּ לַחוֹסִים בָּךְ נֶגֶד בְּנֵי אָדָם. מָה רַב טוּבְךָ. כַּמָּה אִית לוֹן לִבְנֵי נָשָׁא, לְאִסְתַּכְּלָא וּלְמִנְדַּע בְּאוֹרְחוֹי דְּקוּדְשָׁא בְּרִיךְ הוּא, דְּהָא בְּכָל יוֹמָא וְיוֹמָא קָלָא נָפִיק, וְאַכְרִיז וְאָמַר, אִסְתַּמְרוּ בְּנֵי עָלְמָא, טְרוּקוּ גַּלֵּי חוֹבִין, אִסְתַּלָּקוּ מֵרִשְׁתָּא דְּתָפִיס, עַד לָא יִתָּפְסוּן רַגְלַיְיכוּ בְּהַאי רִשְׁתָּא. גַּלְגְּלָא סָחֲרָא תָּדִיר, סָלִיק וְנָחִית. וַוי לְאִינּוּן דְּדַחְיָין רַגְלַיְיהוּ מִגּוֹ גַּלְגְּלָא, דְּהָא נַפְלֵי לְגוֹ עוּמְקָא, דְּטָמִיר לְאִינּוּן חַיָּיבֵי עָלְמָא.

3. Rabbi Yosi opened the discussion with the verse: "Oh how great is Your goodness, which You have laid up for those who fear You, which You have performed for those who trust in You in the sight of the sons of men!" (Tehilim 31:20). "Oh how great is Your goodness" MEANS how much should people observe and know the ways of the Holy One, blessed be He, for every day a voice resounds and proclaims, saying, 'Beware you people, close the doors of sins, stay away from the net that captures PEOPLE, before your legs are caught in the net.' There is a wheel constantly turning in the world, THE SUPERNAL JUDGMENT. It goes up and down, LIFTS UP AND BRINGS DOWN PEOPLE. Woe to those whose legs are pushed from the wheel, for they fall into a pit kept for the wicked people of the world.

4. וַוי לְאִינּוּן דְּנָפְלִין וְלָא יְקוּמוּן, וְלָא יִנְהֲרוּ בִּנְהוֹרָא דְּגָנִיז לְצַדִּיקַיָּיא לְעָלְמָא דְּאָתֵי. זַכָּאִין אִינּוּן צַדִּיקַיָּיא לְעָלְמָא דְּאָתֵי, דְּכַמָּה נְהוֹרִין גְּנִיזִין לוֹן, כַּמָּה עִדּוּנִין בְּהַהוּא עָלְמָא טְמִירִין לוֹן, דִּכְתִּיב מָה רַב טוּבְךָ אֲשֶׁר צָפַנְתָּ לִּירֵאֶיךָ. מָה רַב טוּבְךָ, הָא אוּקְמוּהָ, דָּא הוּא אוֹר דְּגָנִיז לְצַדִּיקַיָּיא לְעָלְמָא דְּאָתֵי, דִּכְתִּיב וַיַּרְא אֱלֹהִים אֶת הָאוֹר כִּי טוֹב, וּכְתִיב אוֹר זָרוּעַ לַצַּדִּיק וּלְיִשְׁרֵי לֵב שִׂמְחָה. וְעַל דָּא מָה רַב טוּבְךָ.

4. Woe to those who fall INTO THAT SAID PIT, for they will never rise nor be illuminated by the light stored up for the righteous in the World to Come. Happy are the righteous in the World to Come, for many lights are stored up AND KEPT for them, many delights of that world are laid up for them as it is said, "Oh how great is Your goodness, which You have laid up for those who fear You." We already explained that, "Oh how great is Your goodness," refers to the light stored up for the righteous in the World to Come, as it is written, "And Elohim saw the light, that it was good" (Beresheet 1:4), and – "light is sown for the righteous, and gladness for the upright in heart" (Tehilim 97:11), "SOWN" MEANING STORED UP. Upon this IT IS WRITTEN, "Oh how great is Your goodness."

5. כְּתִיב הָכָא מָה רַב טוּבְךָ, וּכְתִיב הָתָם וַיַּרְא אֱלֹהִים אֶת הָאוֹר כִּי טוֹב. אֲשֶׁר צָפַנְתָּ, בְּגִין דְּאִסְתָּכַּל קוּדְשָׁא בְּרִיךְ הוּא בְּהַהוּא נְהוֹרָא, וְאִסְתָּכַּל בְּאִינּוּן חַיָּיבַיָּא דִּזְמִינִין לְמֶחֱטֵי בְּעָלְמָא, וְגָנִיז לֵיהּ לְהַהוּא נְהוֹרָא, לְמִזְכֵּי בֵּיהּ צַדִּיקַיָּיא לְעָלְמָא דְּאָתֵי, כְּמָה דְּאִתְּמַר.

5. It is written here, "Oh how great is Your goodness," and elsewhere, "And Elohim saw the light, that it was good." AS IT IS SAID, THERE UPON THE LIGHT THAT IT IS GOOD, SO HERE "YOUR GOODNESS" MEANS 'YOUR LIGHT'. "Which You have laid up," MEANS that when the Holy One, blessed be He looked at the light, He also looked at the wicked destined to commit sins in the world, and so He stored up that light to grant it to the righteous in the World to Come, as we learned.

2. "Oh how great is Your goodness, which You have laid up for those who fear You"

6. פָּעַלְתָּ, בְּקַדְמֵיתָא צָפַנְתָּ, וּלְבָתַר פָּעַלְתָּ. אֶלָּא צָפַנְתָּ כְּמָה דְּאִתְּמַר. פָּעַלְתָּ בְּגִין דְּהַהוּא נְהוֹרָא דְּגָנִיז, בֵּיהּ עָבִיד קוּדְשָׁא בְּרִיךְ הוּא אוּמָנוּתָא דְּעָלְמָא. מְנָלָן. דִּכְתִּיב, אֵלֶּה תוֹלְדוֹת הַשָּׁמַיִם וְהָאָרֶץ בְּהִבָּרְאָם, בְּאַבְרָהָם כְּתִיב, וְהַהוּא נְהוֹרָא דְּאַבְרָהָם, גָּנִיז לֵיהּ קוּדְשָׁא בְּרִיךְ הוּא, וּבֵיהּ עָבִיד אוּמָנוּתָא דְּעָלְמָא, דִּכְתִּיב פָּעַלְתָּ לַחוֹסִים בָּךְ, לְאִינּוּן דְּיַתְבֵי תְּחוֹת צִלָּא דְּקוּדְשָׁא ב"ה.

6. It is said, "You have performed for those who trust in You." HE ASKS: Why IS IT SAID first "laid up" and then "performed"? HE ANSWERS THAT "laid up" MEANS, as we said, STORED FOR THE RIGHTEOUS. "Performed" MEANS THAT by that stored light, the Holy One, blessed be He performed the workmanship of the world. We know this from the verse, "These are the generations of the heaven and of the earth when they were created" (Beresheet 2:4). It is written, 'Abraham', BECAUSE THE LETTERS OF "WHEN THEY WERE CREATED (HEB. *BEHIBAR'AM*)" ARE THE SAME LETTERS AS 'BY ABRAHAM' (HEB. BEABRAHAM). For the light of Abraham, WHICH IS CHESED, is stored up by the Holy One, blessed be He, who, by using it, performed the building of the world, as it is written – "You have performed for those who trust in You," NAMELY, for those who sit under the shade of the Holy One, blessed be He, WHO TAKE REFUGE IN HIS SHADE.

7. נֶגֶד בְּנֵי אָדָם, דְּהָא בְּהַאי אוּמָנוּתָא דְּאִתְעָבֵיד בְּהַאי נְהוֹרָא, קַיְימִין בְּנֵי נָשָׁא בְּעָלְמָא, וְקִיּוּמָא דִּילְהוֹן הֲוֵי. אַף עַל גַּב דְּאִיהוּ גָּנִיז, בֵּיהּ קַיְימִין בְּנֵי נָשָׁא בְּעָלְמָא דֵּין. פָּעַלְתָּ, אוּמָנוּתָא דְּעָלְמָא דָּא, דְּבֵיהּ אִתְעָבֵיד כֹּלָּא בְּחוּשְׁבְּנָא, אוּמָנוּתָא דְּעָלְמָא, כְּגַוְונָא דָּא אוּמָנוּתָא דְּמַשְׁכְּנָא, דְּאִיהוּ אוּמָנוּתָא כְּגַוְונָא דְּעָלְמָא, וְהָא אוֹקִימְנָא.

7. "...in the sight of the sons of men": THE MEANING OF THIS IS that this construction, done by that light, sustains people in the world and is their existence. And though the light is stored up, people live by it in this world. "Performed" refers to the building of this world according to an orderly plan. The building of the world is like the building of the Tabernacle, that was constructed in the same manner as the world, as we explained.

8. כְּתִיב הָכָא אֵלֶּה פְקוּדֵי הַמִּשְׁכָּן, וּכְתִיב הָתָם אֵלֶּה תוֹלְדוֹת הַשָּׁמַיִם וְהָאָרֶץ. בְּגִין דְּכָל אִינּוּן תּוֹלְדִין דְּעָבְדוּ וְאַפִּיקוּ שְׁמַיָּא וְאַרְעָא, כֻּלְּהוּ בְּחֵילָא דְּהַהוּא נְהוֹרָא דִּגְנִיז אִתְעֲבִידוּ וְנַפְקוּ. פְּקוּדֵי הַמִּשְׁכָּן בְּהַהוּא חֵילָא נַפְקוּ. מְנָלָן. דִּכְתִיב וּבְצַלְאֵל בֶּן אוּרִי בֶן חוּר לְמַטֵּה יְהוּדָה, דָּא אִיהוּ מִסְּטְרָא דִּימִינָא. וְאִתּוֹ אָהֳלִיאָב דָּא אִיהוּ מִסְּטְרָא דִּשְׂמָאלָא. וּמַשְׁכְּנָא מִסִּטְרָא דִּימִינָא וּשְׂמָאלָא אִתְּקַם וְאִתְעֲבִיד. וּמֹשֶׁה דַּהֲוָה בֵּינַיְיהוּ, אוֹקִים לֵיהּ.

8. It is written here, "These are the accounts of the Tabernacle" (Shemot 38:21), and elsewhere, "These are the generations of the heaven and of the earth." THIS INDICATES THAT THE ACTIONS ARE THE SAME IN BOTH CASES, for all the generations produced by the heaven and earth were formed and came out by the power of the stored light, and also the accounts of the Tabernacle came out by that power OF THE STORED LIGHT. From where do we know that? From the verse, "And Betzalel the son of Uri, the son of Chur, of the tribe of Judah" (Shemot 38:22), of the right side, WHICH IS ABRAHAM, THE STORED LIGHT AS SAID, and with him Aholiav, of the left side, and the Tabernacle, WHICH IS MALCHUT, was founded by Right and Left. And Moses, who was between them, THE SECRET OF THE CENTRAL COLUMN, founded it.

3. "And in mercy a throne was established"

A Synopsis

Rabbi Elazar opens with the verse: "And in Mercy a throne was established, and he sat upon it in truthfulness..." He says this means that the thought went up to join with the will and joy that come from the incomprehensible, Atik. The joy shone into the thought, Aba, and then united with the supernal Ima by the light of Chesed in a never-ending union. Rabbi Elazar talks about the supernal hidden temple called Yisrael-Saba and Tevunah where all the lights flow through, the lights of Chassadim, Chochmah and Da'at from the right, left and Central Columns. He speaks about 'the throne,' saying: "and he sat upon it in truthfulness" means that God sits upon the throne by right of the seal that is truth. He adds that "inside the tent of David" is the lower throne. Then Rabbi Elazar turns to ."..judging, and seeking judgment, and quick to do righteousness." This refers to the joining of the Left Column, the Central Column, and the Throne of Judgment that is the lower court, Malchut.

9. רִבִּי אֶלְעָזָר פָּתַח וְאָמַר, וְהוּכַן בַּחֶסֶד כִּסֵּא וְיָשַׁב עָלָיו בֶּאֱמֶת וְגוֹ'. וְהוּכַן בַּחֶסֶד כִּסֵּא, הָא אוֹקִימְנָא, כַּד מַחֲשָׁבָה סָלִיק, בִּרְעוּ דְּחֶדְוָה מִטְּמִירָא דְּכָל טְמִירִין דְּלָא אִתְיְידַע וְלָא אִתְדְּבַק, מָטֵי הַהוּא חֶדְוָה, וּבָטַשׁ גּוֹ מַחֲשָׁבָה, וּכְדֵין עָאל בַּאֲתָר דְּעָאל.

9. Rabbi Elazar opened the discussion with the verse: "And in mercy a throne was established, and He sat upon it in truthfulness…" (Yeshayah 16:5). "And in Mercy a throne was established" refers, as we explained, to the thought, THE SECRET OF CHOCHMAH, CALLED 'THE SUPERNAL ABA AND IMA'. It went up to BE ESTABLISHED by the will and joy from the most hidden of all that is never known nor conceived, WHICH IS ATIK. The joy FROM ATIK shone into the thought, ABA, and came to wherever it came, NAMELY, IT UNITED WITH THE SUPERNAL IMA BY THE LIGHT OF CHESED IN A NEVER ENDING UNION, IN THE SECRET OF THE VERSE, "BECAUSE HE DELIGHTS IN MERCY (HEB. *CHESED*)" (MICHAH 7:18).

10. עַד דְּאִתְגְּנִיז בְּחַד הֵיכָלָא עִלָּאָה, דְּאִיהוּ טָמִיר לְעֵיל. וּמִתַּמָּן נַגְדִּין וְאִתְמַשְׁכָן כָּל נְהוֹרִין, דִּימִינָא דְּנָטִיל בְּקַדְמֵיתָא, וּלְבָתַר נָטִיל כֻּלְּהוּ.

וּמֵהַהוּא סְטָר יְמִינָא, אִתְקַן כּוּרְסְיָּיא לְתַתָּא. דְּהָא קוּדְשָׁא בְּרִיךְ הוּא, אַתְקִין לְהַהוּא כּוּרְסְיָּיא בְּחֶסֶד, וְיָשַׁב עָלָיו בֶּאֱמֶת, דְּאִיהוּ תִּקּוּנָא דְּחוּתָמָא דְּכֹלָּא. וְלָא יָתִיב עַל הַהוּא כּוּרְסְיָּיא, אֶלָּא בְּחוּתָמָא דָּא דְּאִיהוּ אֱמֶת. בְּאֹהֶל דָּוִד, דְּאִיהוּ בֵּי כּוּרְסְיָּיא לְתַתָּא.

10. Until ABA AND IMA were concealed, THAT IS, ESTABLISHED AND CLOTHED in a supernal temple, BINAH, CALLED YISRAEL – SABA AND TEVUNAH. This temple is hidden above IN ITS PLACE, NAMELY, CHOCHMAH IS NOT REVEALED THERE IN ITS PLACE. But in that place are drawn and flow all the lights, THE LIGHT OF CHASSADIM FROM THE RIGHT COLUMN, THE LIGHT OF CHOCHMAH FROM THE LEFT COLUMN, AND THE LIGHT OF DA'AT FROM THE CENTRAL COLUMN. ONLY THE LIGHT OF CHASSADIM from the right travels first. Then all the lights travel, THE LIGHTS OF CHOCHMAH AND OF DA'AT. The lower throne, MALCHUT, is amended from the right side, because the Holy One, blessed be He, ZEIR ANPIN, made this throne with Chesed, DRAWN FROM THE RIGHT COLUMN OF YISRAEL – SABA AND TEVUNAH AND SUPERNAL ABA AND IMA. "and he sat upon it in truthfulness," for He establishes the universal seal. He does not sit upon the throne, MALCHUT, save by right of the seal which is truth, THE ESTABLISHING OF THE CENTRAL COLUMN CALLED 'TRUTH' "in the tabernacle of David" (Yeshayah 16:5), WHICH IS MALCHUT, the lower throne.

11. שׁוֹפֵט וְדוֹרֵשׁ מִשְׁפָּט וּמְהִיר צֶדֶק. שׁוֹפֵט מִסִּטְרָא דְּדִינָא. וְדוֹרֵשׁ מִשְׁפָּט, מִסִּטְרָא דְּרַחֲמֵי. וּמְהִיר צֶדֶק, אִיהוּ כּוּרְסְיָּיא דְּדִינָא, דְּאִיהוּ בֵּי דִּינָא לְתַתָּא. ת״ח, כְּגַוְונָא דָּא, מַשְׁכְּנָא לָא אִתְתָּקַּן אֶלָּא בְּסִטְרָא דָּא כְּגַוְונָא דָּא, דְּחֶסֶד כִּדְקָאָמְרָן לְעֵיל, וְע״ד אִתְמְנוּן תּוֹלְדִין וְאִתְתְּקָנוּ כֻּלְּהוּ לְתַתָּא.

11. "...judging, and seeking judgment, and quick to do righteousness" (Ibid.) IS THE END OF THE VERSE. He is judging, MEANING, by the side of Judgment, THE LEFT COLUMN, "and seeking Judgment" by the side of Mercy, THE CENTRAL COLUMN; "and quick to do righteousness" refers to the Throne of Judgment, which is the lower court, NAMELY MALCHUT. Come and see: In the same manner, the Tabernacle was established only by that side, RIGHT, like the Chesed we mentioned, IN THE SECRET OF "AND IN MERCY A THRONE WAS ESTABLISHED." And thereby, all the generations were numbered and set in order, THAT ARE DRAWN FROM MALCHUT.

4. "These are the accounts of the Tabernacle"

A Synopsis

Rabbi Shimon opens by saying that God created this world in the image of the higher one. When He wanted to create the world He looked at the Torah, and He looked at the Holy Name, Yud Hei Vav Hei. He created the world with Chochmah, Tevunah and Da'at, through wisdom, through understanding, and through knowledge. The Tabernacle was built from these as well. We are told that Moses was dumbfounded when told to create the Tabernacle, because he didn't know how until God showed him the spiritual form of each thing; then each of these forms reshaped itself to resemble the imagined form made on earth. Moses saw each of these forms in Malchut, the mirror that does not shine but only reflects, but he grew confused over which image to use, so God told him to use the imaginary image and He would use the spiritual image, thus combining the two. Another explanation for 'the accounts of the Tabernacle' is that the Holy Spirit, in the form of the Tabernacle, was a mirror that reflected to everyone the amount of gold and silver offered by Yisrael. After the work was completed Moses had to count everything up to prove his trustworthiness, and even the Other Side was able to find no fault with him. Rabbi Shimon turns to the meaning of 'testimony' in "the Tabernacle of the Testimony," and offers two explanations of why the Levites serve in the Tabernacle. Rabbi Aba introduces a new topic, that time when God will increase peace in the world and the root of the Tree of Life will prevail. We also learn that blessings only exist where they aren't being counted. Rabbi Chizkiyah offers his explanation of the title verse, saying that the 'holy ground' Moses stood on was the Shechinah, and that God made him ruler over Malchut. Whatever Moses decreed God performed. Moses was the voice, Zeir Anpin, that uttered the speech, Malchut, and he inventoried the Tabernacle so it could come out of exile.

12. אֵלֶּה פְקוּדֵי הַמִּשְׁכָּן מִשְׁכַּן הָעֵדוּת אֲשֶׁר פֻּקַּד עַל פִּי מֹשֶׁה. ר"ש פָּתַח, בְּרֵאשִׁית בָּרָא אֱלֹהִים אֵת הַשָּׁמַיִם וְאֵת הָאָרֶץ, הַאי קְרָא אוּקְמוּהָ וְאִתְּמַר בְּכַמָּה סִטְרִין. אֲבָל כַּד בָּרָא קוּדְשָׁא בְּרִיךְ הוּא עָלְמָא, בָּרָא לֵיהּ כְּגַוְונָא דִּלְעֵילָּא, לְמֶהֱוֵי עָלְמָא דָּא בְּדִיוּקְנָא דְּעָלְמָא דִּלְעֵילָּא. וְכָל אִינּוּן גַּוְונִין דִּלְעֵילָּא, אַתְקִין לוֹן לְתַתָּא, לְאִתְדַּבְּקָא וּלְאִתְקַשְּׁרָא עָלְמָא בְּעָלְמָא.

4. "These are the accounts of the Tabernacle"

12. "These are the accounts of the Tabernacle, the Tabernacle of the Testimony, as they were counted, according to the commandment of Moses" (shemot 38:21). Rabbi Shimon opened the discussion with the verse: "In the beginning Elohim created the heaven and the earth" (Beresheet 1:1). This was already explained and expounded upon in different manners, yet the Holy One, blessed be He created it resembling the higher one, so this world will be shaped like the higher world, WHICH IS MALCHUT. And all the supernal hues of above were installed below IN THIS WORLD, to join and connect world to world, THIS WORLD TO MALCHUT.

13. וְכַד בָּעָא קוּדְשָׁא בְּרִיךְ הוּא לְמִבְרֵי עָלְמָא, אַשְׁגַּח בְּאוֹרַיְיתָא וּבָרָא לֵיהּ. וְאִסְתַּכַּל בִּשְׁמָא קַדִּישָׁא, כְּלָלָא דְּאוֹרַיְיתָא, וְקַיֵּים עָלְמָא. בִּתְלַת סִטְרִין אִתְקַיָּים עָלְמָא, וְאִינּוּן חָכְמָה וּתְבוּנָה וָדַעַת. בְּחָכְמָה, דִּכְתִּיב יְיָ' בְּחָכְמָה יָסַד אָרֶץ. בִּתְבוּנָה, דִּכְתִּיב כּוֹנֵן שָׁמַיִם בִּתְבוּנָה. בְּדַעַת, דִּכְתִּיב בְּדַעְתּוֹ תְּהוֹמוֹת נִבְקָעוּ. הָא כֻּלְּהוּ בְּקִיּוּמָא דְּעָלְמָא. וּבְאִלֵּין תְּלָתָא אִתְבְּנֵי מַשְׁכְּנָא, דִּכְתִּיב וָאֲמַלֵּא אוֹתוֹ רוּחַ אֱלֹהִים בְּחָכְמָה בִּתְבוּנָה וּבְדַעַת.

13. And when the Holy One, blessed be He wanted to create the world, He looked at the Torah and then created it. And He looked upon the Holy Name, YUD HEI VAV HEI, which comprises the Torah, and gave existence to the world. The world was created by three sides – Chochmah, Tevunah, and Da'at. By Chochmah, as it is written – "Hashem by Wisdom founded the earth" (Mishlei 3:19); by Tevunah, as it is written – "by understanding (Heb. *Tevunah*) He established the heavens" (Ibid.); and by Da'at, as it is written – "by His knowledge (Heb. *Da'at*) the depths were broken up" (Ibid. 20). So all contribute to the existence of the world, and by these three, the Tabernacle was built, as it is written, "and I have filled him with the spirit of Elohim, in Wisdom, and in understanding, and in knowledge" (Shemot 31:3).

14. וְכֻלְּהוּ תְּלָתָא רְמִיזִין בִּקְרָא דָּא, בְּרֵאשִׁית, הַיְינוּ דִּכְתִּיב בְּחָכְמָה. בָּרָא אֱלֹהִים, הַיְינוּ דִּכְתִּיב בִּתְבוּנָה. אֵת הַשָּׁמַיִם, הַיְינוּ דִּכְתִּיב בְּדַעַת. וְכֻלְּהוּ כְּתִיבֵי בַּעֲבִידַת מַשְׁכְּנָא. וּבְרָזָא דָּא כְּתִיב, אֵלֶּה פְקוּדֵי הַמִּשְׁכָּן, דָּא רָזָא דְּחָכְמָה. מִשְׁכַּן הָעֵדוּת, דָּא רָזָא דִּתְבוּנָה, אֲשֶׁר פֻּקַּד עַל פִּי

מֹשֶׁה, דָּא רָזָא דְּדַעַת. וְכֹלָּא דָּא לָקֳבֵל דָּא, בְּגִין דְּכָל מַה דְּבָרָא קוּדְשָׁא בְּרִיךְ הוּא בְּעָלְמָא דֵּין, בָּרָא לֵיהּ כְּגַוְונָא דִּלְעֵילָּא. וְכֹלָּא אִתְרְשִׁים בַּעֲבִידַת מַשְׁכְּנָא.

14. All these three, CHOCHMAH, TEVUNAH AND DA'AT, were alluded to in this verse. "In the beginning" corresponds to "in Wisdom," FOR CHOCHMAH IS CALLED 'BEGINNING' AS IT IS WRITTEN, "THE BEGINNING OF WISDOM" (TEHILIM 111:10); "Elohim created" corresponds to Tevunah, FOR TEVUNAH IS CALLED 'ELOHIM'. "The heaven" is as written – "and in knowledge." FOR ZEIR ANPIN IS CALLED 'HEAVEN' AND IS THE INNER MEANING OF DA'AT. And all are mentioned in the building of the Tabernacle. In this secret it is written, "And these are the accounts of the Tabernacle," for this is the secret of Chochmah, AS ACCOUNTS AND NUMBERS ARE DRAWN FROM CHOCHMAH. "The Tabernacle of the Testimony," is the secret of Tevunah, FOR THE ILLUMINATION OF CHOCHMAH, REVEALED IN YISRAEL – SABA AND TEVUNAH, IS CALLED 'TESTIMONY'. "According to the commandment of Moses," is the secret of Da'at, FOR MOSES IS THE SECRET OF DA'AT. All is done the one corresponding to the other, for everything the Holy One, blessed be He, created in this world, He created it as the reflection of above. All this is shown in the building of the Tabernacle.

15. תָּא חֲזֵי, בְּשַׁעֲתָא דְּאָמַר לֵיהּ קוּדְשָׁא בְּרִיךְ הוּא לְמֹשֶׁה עֲבִיד מַשְׁכְּנָא, הֲוָה קָאִים מֹשֶׁה תּוֹהֵא, דְּלָא יָדַע מַה לְמֶעְבַּד, עַד דְּאַחְזֵי לֵיהּ קוּדְשָׁא בְּרִיךְ הוּא בְּעֵינָא, כְּמָה דִּכְתִּיב וּרְאֵה וַעֲשֵׂה בְּתַבְנִיתָם אֲשֶׁר אַתָּה מָרְאֶה בָּהָר. מַאי בְּתַבְנִיתָם. אֶלָּא אוּלִיפְנָא, דְּאַחְמֵי לֵיהּ קוּדְשָׁא בְּרִיךְ הוּא לְמֹשֶׁה, דְּיוּקְנָא דְּכָל מִלָּה וּמִלָּה, כְּהַהוּא דְּיוּקְנָא דְּאִיהוּ לְעֵילָּא, וְכָל חַד וְחַד הֲוָה עָבִיד דְּיוּקְנָא דִּילֵיהּ כְּדְיוּקְנָא דְּאִיהוּ אִתְעֲבִיד בְּאַרְעָא.

15. Come and see: When the Holy One, blessed be He told Moses to construct the Tabernacle, Moses was dumbfounded, for he did not know what to do, until the Holy One, blessed be He showed him how it looked, as it is written, "And look that you make them after their pattern, which was shown to you in the mountain" (Shemot 25:9). The meaning of "after their pattern" is as we learned, that the Holy One, blessed be He showed Moses the supernal form of each thing, THE SPIRITUAL FORM, and each one OF THE SPIRITUAL HIGHER FORMS shaped itself to RESEMBLE the IMAGINED form made on earth. IN THIS WAY MOSES KNEW.

16. אֲשֶׁר אַתָּה מָרְאֶה בָּהָר, אֲשֶׁר אַתָּה רוֹאֶה מִבָּעֵי לֵיהּ. אֶלָּא אוֹלִיפְנָא, דְּאַסְפַּקְלַרְיָא דְּלָא נַהֲרָא, הֲוָה אַחְמֵי לֵיהּ בְּגַוֵּיהּ כָּל אִינּוּן גַּוְונִין וְדִיוּקְנִין דְּאִתְעֲבִידוּ לְתַתָּא, כְּהַאי חֵיזוּ דְּאַחְזֵי בְּגַוֵּיהּ כָּל אִינּוּן דִּיוּקְנִין.

16. HE ASKS: It should have been written, 'which you see' instead of "which was shown to you," AND ANSWERS: We learned that the mirror which does not shine, WHICH IS MALCHUT, showed him within it all the wheels and shapes made below, like a mirror reflecting within itself every image.

17. מַשְׁמַע דִּכְתִּיב אֲשֶׁר אַתָּה מָרְאֶה, אַתָּה, רָזָא דְּאַסְפַּקְלַרְיָא דְּלָא נַהֲרָא, דְּאַחְזֵי לֵיהּ בְּגַוֵּיהּ כָּל אִינּוּן דִּיוּקְנִין. וַהֲוָה חָמֵי לוֹן מֹשֶׁה כָּל מִלָּה וּמִלָּה עַל תִּקּוּנֵיהּ, כְּמָה דְּחָמֵי גּוֹ עֲשָׁשִׁיתָא, וְגוֹ חֵיזוּ דְּאַחְזֵי כָּל דִּיוּקְנִין. וְכַד אִסְתָּכַּל בְּהוּ מֹשֶׁה, אִתְקָשֵׁי קַמֵּיהּ, אָמַר לֵיהּ קוּדְשָׁא בְּרִיךְ הוּא, מֹשֶׁה, אַתְּ בְּסִימָנִיךְ, וַאֲנִי בְּסִימָנִי כְּדֵין אִתְיַישַּׁב מֹשֶׁה בְּכָל עֲבִידְתָּא.

17. This is the meaning of the verse, "which was shown to you." "You" is the secret of the mirror which does not shine, MALCHUT, which reflected all those forms for Moses to see. And he saw each thing correctly, as if looking through a glass lamp, and within a mirror reflecting all the shapes. And when Moses beheld them, he found it difficult. FOR INSIDE MALCHUT THE SPIRITUAL SHAPE OF EVERY OBJECT STOOD OUT, ONLY EACH SHAPE RESEMBLED THE IMAGINARY SHAPE PERTAINING TO THIS WORLD IN THE TABERNACLE, SO THERE WERE TWO SHAPES TO EACH OBJECT: THE SPIRITUAL AND THE IMAGINARY SHAPE. THEREFORE, MOSES FOUND IT DIFFICULT, FOR HE KNEW NOT WHICH ONE TO GRASP. So the Holy One, blessed be He said to him, 'you follow your signs and I follow Mine,' THAT MOSES SHOULD GRASP THE IMAGINARY SIGNS OF EVERY OBJECT, AND

THE HOLY ONE, BLESSED BE HE WOULD GRASP THE SPIRITUAL SIGNS OF EVERY OBJECT. AND THEN THE SPIRITUAL SHAPE WOULD DWELL ON THE IMAGINARY SHAPE. Moses was then clear-minded as to the construction OF THE TABERNACLE.

18. כַּד אִתְעֲבֵיד כָּל עֲבִידְתָּא, אִצְטְרִיךְ מֹשֶׁה לְמִמְנֵי כֹּלָּא, בְּגִין דְּלָא יֵימְרוּן יִשְׂרָאֵל דְּאִשְׁתְּאַר כַּסְפָּא וְדַהֲבָא, וְאִסְתְּלִיק לְנַטְלָא לֵיהּ. וְעַל דָּא אִצְטְרִיךְ לְמִמְנֵי חוּשְׁבְּנָא קַמַּיְיהוּ דְּיִשְׂרָאֵל, בְּגִין דִּכְתִּיב וִהְיִיתֶם נְקִיִּים מֵיְיָ׳ וּמִיִּשְׂרָאֵל.

18. And when all the work was completed, Moses had to count everything, so Yisrael would not say that some gold and silver was left, and that he was planning to take it. Therefore, he counted before Yisrael, as it is written, "and be guiltless before Hashem and before Yisrael" (Bemidbar 32:22).

19. וּבְגִין דָּא כְּתִיב, אֵלֶּה פְקוּדֵי הַמִּשְׁכָּן מִשְׁכַּן הָעֵדוּת, דְּהָא רוּחָא דְּקוּדְשָׁא, הֲוָה אַחְזֵי לְכֹלָּא, חוּשְׁבְּנָא דְּכָל דַּהֲבָא וְכַסְפָּא דִּנְדִיבוּ יִשְׂרָאֵל, וְרוּחַ קוּדְשָׁא הֲוָה אָמַר וְכֶסֶף פְּקוּדֵי הָעֵדָה מְאַת כִּכָּר וְגוֹ׳, כָּל הַזָּהָב הֶעָשׂוּי לַמְּלָאכָה וְגוֹ׳. בְּגִין דְּקוּדְשָׁא בְּרִיךְ הוּא אִתְרְעֵי בְּהוּ, בְּאִינּוּן אוּמָּנִין, וּבָעָא לְאַפָּקָא מְהֵימְנוּתָא דִּילְהוֹן קַמֵּי כֹּלָּא.

19. The reason the verse states, "These are the accounts of the Tabernacle, the Tabernacle of the Testimony," is that the Holy Spirit, WHICH IS MALCHUT, CALLED 'TABERNACLE', was a mirror which reflected to everyone the amount of all the gold and silver offered by Yisrael. And the Holy Spirit would say, "and the silver of them that were numbered of the congregation was a hundred talents..." (Shemot 38:25), and "all the gold that was applied for the work..." (Ibid. 24), for the Holy One, blessed be He was pleased with all the craftsmen, and wanted to display their trustworthiness before all.

20. אֵלֶּה פְקוּדֵי הַמִּשְׁכָּן. ת״ח, בְּהַהִיא שַׁעֲתָא דַּעֲבִידְתָּא דְּמַשְׁכְּנָא אִתְעֲבֵיד, הֲוָה סִטְרָא אַחֲרָא אָזִיל וְשָׁאט לְאַסְטָאָה, וְלָא אַשְׁכַּחַת עִילָּה עַל מְהֵימְנוּתָא דְּאוּמָּנִין, עַד דְּקוּדְשָׁא בְּרִיךְ הוּא כָּפִיף לֵיהּ לְקַמֵּיהּ

דְּמֹשֶׁה, וְאִיהוּ עָבֵיד חוּשְׁבָּנָא דִּמְהֵימְנוּתָא בְּעַל כָּרְחֵיהּ, וְסָלִיק מְהֵימְנוּתָא דִּילְהוֹן לְגַבֵּי כֹּלָּא. וְרָזָא דָּא דִּכְתִּיב אֵלֶּה פְקוּדֵי הַמִּשְׁכָּן. וְהָא אוֹקִימְנָא, אֵלֶּה: כד"א, גַּם אֵלֶּה תִשְׁכַּחְנָה. וּכְתִיב, אֲשֶׁר פֻּקַּד עַל פִּי מֹשֶׁה, דְּתַמָּן אִתְמְנֵי וְאִתְפְּקִיד, עַד דְּאִתְעָבֵיד חוּשְׁבָּנָא דְּבֵי מַשְׁכְּנָא, קַמֵּי מֹשֶׁה וְיִשְׂרָאֵל כֻּלְּהוּ.

20. "These are the accounts of the Tabernacle." Come and see: At the time when the construction of the Tabernacle took place, the Other Side roamed about, to bring accusations. He found no flaw in the faithfulness of the craftsmen, so the Holy One, blessed be He caused him to yield before Moses. And he, the Other Side, had to check their worthiness in spite of himself and to acknowledge it before all. This is the mystery of the verse, "These are the accounts of the Tabernacle." And we explained that "These" is the same as in "even these may forget" (Yeshayah 49:15), REFERRING TO THE OTHER SIDE, FOR BOTH CASES ALLUDE TO THE OTHER SIDE. It is also written, "as they were counted according to the commandment of Moses." For there, ACCORDING TO MOSES, all was counted and numbered, until the accounting of the Tabernacle was complete before Moses and all of Yisrael.

21. אֵלֶּה פְקוּדֵי הַמִּשְׁכָּן מִשְׁכַּן הָעֵדוּת. מַאן עֵדוּת. אֶלָּא תְּרֵי זִמְנֵי כְּתִיב הָכָא מִשְׁכָּן, חַד לְעֵילָּא, וְחַד לְתַתָּא. וּמִשְׁכָּן אִקְרֵי מִשְׁכַּן הָעֵדוּת. וּמַאן עֵדוּת. כד"א שִׁבְטֵי יָהּ עֵדוּת לְיִשְׂרָאֵל. שְׁמָא דָּא, אִיהוּ עֵדוּת לְיִשְׂרָאֵל.

21. "These are the accounts of the Tabernacle, the Tabernacle of the Testimony." HE ASKS: What is "Testimony"? HE ANSWERS THAT the word 'Tabernacle' is written twice, "THE TABERNACLE, THE TABERNACLE OF THE TESTIMONY." One above, IN BINAH, THE TABERNACLE OF THE TESTIMONY, and one below, IN MALCHUT, THE TABERNACLE. And the Tabernacle is called "the Tabernacle of the Testimony." What is "the Testimony"? It is as in the verse, "the tribes of Yah (Heb. *Yud-Hei*), a testimony to Yisrael" (Tehilim 122:4), this name, *YUD-HEI*, WHICH IS CHOCHMAH AND BINAH, is a testimony to Yisrael.

22. כְּגַוְונָא דָּא עֵדוּת בִּיהוֹסֵף שָׂמוֹ, עֵדוּת שֵׁם יָהּ בִּיהוֹסֵף, אִיהוּ עֵדוּת

וַדַּאי, אִלֵּין תְּרֵין אַתְוָון סָהֲדִין סַהֲדוּתָא בְּכָל אֲתַר, וְהָכָא אִיהוּ עֵדוּת. וּבְגִין כַּךְ, מִשְׁכַּן הָעֵדוּת, מַשְׁכְּנָא דְּהַאי עֵדוּת. וְעַל דָּא מַשְׁכְּנָא אִקְרֵי, עַל רָזָא דִּשְׁמָא דָּא קַדִּישָׁא. וְהַיְינוּ דִּכְתִּיב, וְעֵדוֹתִי זוֹ אֲלַמְּדֵם, בְּגִין דְּהַאי אֲתַר, אִיהוּ סְתִימוּ וּגְנִיזוּ דְּכֹלָּא.

22. The verse, "This He ordained in Yehosef for testimony..." (Tehilim 81:6) is explained in the same manner. IT IS CALLED 'testimony' for the name Yah in Yehosef, WHICH STANDS FOR CHOCHMAH AND BINAH, is surely a testimony. These two letters, *YUD* AND *HEI*, give testimony everywhere, NAMELY, THEY SHINE WITH THE ILLUMINATION OF CHOCHMAH CALLED 'EDEN' OR 'TESTIMONY'. And there is testimony here IN *YUD-HEI*. For this reason IT IS WRITTEN, "the Tabernacle of Testimony" MEANING THAT it is the Tabernacle of that testimony, *YUD-HEI*, NAMELY BINAH. Therefore it is called a Tabernacle, after the secret of the Holy Name, *YUD-HEI*. This is the meaning of the verse, "and My testimony that I shall teach them" (Tehilim 132:12). Since that place *YUD-HEI* is the most hidden and concealed of all, THEREFORE IT IS SAID, "I SHALL TEACH THEM."

23. אֲשֶׁר פֻּקַּד עַל פִּי מֹשֶׁה, עַד הָכָא לָא יְדַעְנָא, אִי הַאי מַשְׁכְּנָא פֻּקַּד, אוֹ הַאי עֵדוּת. אֶלָּא פֻּקַּד וַדַּאי הַאי עֵדוּת. בְּגִין דְּמִן יוֹמָא דְּאִסְתַּלִּיקוּ אֲבָהָן מֵעָלְמָא, וְכָל אִינּוּן שְׁבָטִין בְּנוֹי דְּיַעֲקֹב, וְאִשְׁתָּאֲרוּ יִשְׂרָאֵל בְּגָלוּתָא, בְּאִינּוּן עָאקָן, אִתְנְשֵׁי מִנַּיְיהוּ יְדִיעָא דְּרָזָא דִּשְׁמָא קַדִּישָׁא עִלָּאָה דָּא, דְּאִיהוּ שְׁמָא דְּעֵדוּת, קִיוּמָא דִּשְׁמַיָּא וְאַרְעָא, דְּאִלֵּין תְּרֵין אַתְוָון, אוֹקִימוּ עִילָּאֵי וְתַתָּאֵי, וְכֻלְּהוּ סִטְרִין דְּעָלְמָא.

23. "As they were counted, according to the commandment of Moses." HE ASKS: I do not know yet whether the Tabernacle was counted or the Testimony, AS IT WAS SAID, "THE ACCOUNTS OF THE TABERNACLE, THE TABERNACLE OF THE TESTIMONY." HE REPLIES: Assuredly the Testimony was, WHICH IS THE SECRET OF *YUD-HEI* AS MENTIONED. For since the day the patriarchs and the tribes, the sons of Jacob, passed away from the world, Yisrael were left in exile, and because of all their troubles, they forgot the knowledge of the Supernal Holy Name, which is the name Testimony, that sustains heaven and earth, NAMELY, THE MOCHIN OF

MALE AND FEMALE. For these two letters, *YUD-HEI,* established the high and low worlds, and all the sides of the world, NAMELY, THEY GIVE THEM MOCHIN.

24. כֵּיוָן דְּאָתָא מֹשֶׁה, אִתְפְּקַד וְאִדְכַּר שְׁמָא דָא בְּעָלְמָא. דְּכַד הֲוָה בִּסְנֶה מִיַּד שָׁאִיל עַל שְׁמָא דָא, דִּכְתִּיב וְאָמְרוּ לִי מַה שְּׁמוֹ מָה אוֹמַר אֲלֵיהֶם. וְתַמָּן אִתְפְּקַד שְׁמָא דָא עַל פִּי מֹשֶׁה.

24. When Moses came, this name OF *YUD-HEI* was accounted and remembered in the world, and when he was in the thorn bush, he immediately asked about this name, as it is written, "and they shall say to me, what is His name? What shall I say to them?" (Shemot 3:13). There the name was entrusted to Moses. THIS IS THE SECRET OF THE VERSE, "AS THEY WERE COUNTED, ACCORDING TO THE COMMANDMENT OF MOSES."

25. עֲבֹדַת הַלְוִיִּם, מַאי עֲבֹדַת הַלְוִיִּם. אֶלָּא רָזָא דָא דִּכְתִּיב, וְעָבַד הַלֵּוִי הוּא. הוּא: דָא רָזָא דִּשְׁמָא קַדִּישָׁא, דְּאִקְרֵי הוּא, וְלָא אִקְרֵי אַתָּה. וּבְגִין דָא עֲבוֹדַת הַלְוִיִּם וַדַּאי. ד״א עֲבֹדַת הַלְוִיִּם, דְּאִינּוּן נַטְלִין מַשְׁכְּנָא עַל כִּתְפַיְיהוּ מֵאֲתַר לַאֲתַר, דִּכְתִּיב וְלִבְנֵי קְהָת לֹא נָתַן כִּי עֲבוֹדַת הַקֹּדֶשׁ עֲלֵיהֶם בַּכָּתֵף יִשָּׂאוּ.

25. HE ASKS: IT IS WRITTEN, "THE TABERNACLE OF THE TESTIMONY... the service of the Levites," What is "the service of the Levites?" HE ANSWERS this is a secret, as it is written, "and the Levite shall do the service (lit. 'serve him')" (Bemidbar 18:23). For HE is the secret of the Holy Name, BINAH, that is called 'he' and not 'you', NAMELY, THIRD PERSON AND NOT SECOND PERSON, LIKE MALCHUT, WHICH IS CALLED 'YOU'. That is the reason the Levites serve THE TABERNACLE OF THE TESTIMONY, WHICH IS BINAH. Another explanation: the service of the Levites is carrying the Tabernacle upon their shoulders from one place to another, as it is written, "But to the sons of Kehat he gave none, because the service of the sanctuary belongs to them, they bore it on their shoulders" (Bemidbar 7:9). THEREFORE THE TABERNACLE IS CALLED IN THEIR NAME, NAMELY "THE SERVICE OF THE LEVITES."

26. אֵלֶּה פְקוּדֵי הַמִּשְׁכָּן מִשְׁכַּן הָעֵדוּת וְגוֹ'. רִבִּי אַבָּא פָּתַח, וְהָיָה בַּיּוֹם

הַהוּא שֹׁרֶשׁ יִשַׁי וְגוֹ׳. וְהָיָה בַּיּוֹם הַהוּא, בִּזְמְנָא דְקוּדְשָׁא בְּרִיךְ הוּא יַסְגֵּי שְׁלָמָא בְּעָלְמָא, יִתְקַיֵּים שָׁרְשָׁא דְּאִילָנָא דְחַיֵּי, וְהַהוּא שָׁרְשָׁא, מִנֵּיהּ יִתְקָיְימוּ שְׁאַר שָׁרְשִׁין לְתַתָּא, דְּכֻלְּהוּ אִשְׁתָּרְשָׁן וְאִתְקַיְּימָן מִנֵּיהּ.

26. "These are the accounts of the Tabernacle, the Tabernacle of the Testimony." Rabbi Aba opened the discussion with the verse: "And in that day it shall be, that the root of Yishai..." (Yeshayah 11:10). "In that day" refers to the time when the Holy One, blessed be He will increase peace in the world, and then the root of the Tree of Life will prevail, WHICH IS THE SECRET OF THE CENTRAL COLUMN, THAT RECONCILES AND MAKES PEACE BETWEEN RIGHT AND LEFT. From this root all other roots will prevail below, NAMELY, THE GRADES IN MALCHUT AND IN BRIYAH, YETZIRAH AND ASIYAH, for they all are rooted and draw their strength from it.

27. אֲשֶׁר עוֹמֵד לְנֵס עַמִּים, דְּהַאי אִיהוּ קַיְּימָא לְנִסָּא וּלְאָת לְרָזָא דִּשְׁמָא קַדִּישָׁא. אֵלָיו גּוֹיִם יִדְרֹשׁוּ, דְּתַמָּן רָזָא דְקִיּוּמָא דִּשְׁמָא קַדִּישָׁא, וּבְגִין כַּךְ אֵלָיו גּוֹיִם יִדְרֹשׁוּ. כד״א, וְהָלְכוּ עַמִּים רַבִּים וְאָמְרוּ לְכוּ וְנַעֲלֶה אֶל הַר יְיָ׳ וְגוֹ׳, וְעַל דָּא, אֵלָיו גּוֹיִם יִדְרֹשׁוּ. וְהָיְתָה מְנוּחָתוֹ כָּבוֹד, מְנוּחָתוֹ, דָּא בֵּי מַקְדְּשָׁא. דִּכְתִּיב זֹאת מְנוּחָתִי עֲדֵי עַד. כָּבוֹד, דְּהָכִי אִקְרֵי כְּבוֹד יְיָ׳ בְּהַהוּא זִמְנָא, דִּכְתִּיב וְהָיָה אוֹר הַלְּבָנָה כְּאוֹר הַחַמָּה וְאוֹר הַחַמָּה יִהְיֶה שִׁבְעָתַיִם.

27. The verse continues, "...that stands for a banner of the peoples" (Yeshayah 11:10), for it is a banner and an ensign to the mystery of the Holy Name, YUD HEI VAV HEI. "To it shall the nations seek" (Ibid.) because there is found the secret of existence, THAT IS, MOCHIN, of the Holy Name. Therefore the nations shall seek it, IN ORDER TO RECEIVE CHOCHMAH AND DA'AT FROM THERE, "and many people shall go and say, 'come and let us go up to the Mountain of Hashem'" (Yeshayah 2:3). Therefore, "to it shall the nations seek." "And his resting place shall be glorious" (Yeshayah 11:10), "His resting place" is the Temple, WHICH IS MALCHUT, as it is written, "This is My resting place forever" (Tehilim 132:14); it will be "glorious" because it is thus called 'the Glory of Hashem,' when "the light of the moon shall be as the light of the sun" (Yeshayah 30:26), THE LIGHT OF MALCHUT SHALL BE AS THE LIGHT OF

ZEIR ANPIN, and the light of the sun shall be sevenfold" (Ibid.), AND THE LIGHT OF ZEIR ANPIN WILL BE SEVENFOLD WHAT IT WAS BEFORE.

28. וּמְנוּחָתוֹ דְּהַהוּא שֹׁרֶשׁ יִשַׁי, דְּאִתְקְרֵי כְּבוֹד יְיָ׳, לָא יִתְמְנֵי, וְלָא יְקוּם בְּחוּשְׁבְּנָא לְעָלְמָא. מַאי טַעֲמָא. בְּגִין דְּכָל מַה דְּקַיְימָא בְּחוּשְׁבְּנָא, לָא שַׁרְיָין תַּמָּן בִּרְכָאן בִּשְׁלִימוּ. וּבִרְכָּאן שַׁרְיָין בְּמַּה דְּלָא קַיְימָא בְּחוּשְׁבְּנָא. בְּזִמְנָא קַדְמָאָה קַיְימָא בְּחוּשְׁבְּנָא, דִּכְתִּיב אֵלֶּה פְקוּדֵי הַמִּשְׁכָּן.

28. And the resting place of the root of Yishai, WHICH IS MALCHUT, called 'the glory of Hashem' must never be counted or numbered. What is the reason? Because no blessing dwells wholly upon something counted. Blessings prevail only where there is no reckoning. And this is the first time MALCHUT was counted, as it is said, "These are the accounts of the Tabernacle."

29. תָּא חֲזֵי, מַשְׁכְּנָא דָּא קַיְימָא בְּחוּשְׁבְּנָא, וּבְגִין כַּךְ אִצְטְרִיךְ לִצְלוֹתָא דְּמֹשֶׁה, דְּיִשְׁרֵי עָלֵיהּ בִּרְכָאן, דִּכְתִּיב וַיְבָרֶךְ אוֹתָם מֹשֶׁה, וּמַה בְּרָכָה בָּרִיךְ לוֹן, יְהֵא רַעֲוָה דְּתִשְׁרֵי בְּרָכָה עַל עוֹבָדֵי יְדֵיכוֹן. וּבִרְכָּאן לָא שָׁרָאן עַל הַאי חוּשְׁבְּנָא עַד דְּאִקְשַׁר לֵיהּ מֹשֶׁה בְּמַשְׁכְּנָא דִּלְעֵילָא, דִּכְתִּיב אֵלֶּה פְקוּדֵי הַמִּשְׁכָּן מִשְׁכַּן הָעֵדוּת אֲשֶׁר פֻּקַּד עַל פִּי מֹשֶׁה. דְּאִי לָאו דְּאִתְעֲבַד חוּשְׁבְּנָא עַל יְדָא דְּמֹשֶׁה, לָא יַכְלִין אִינּוּן לְמֶעְבַּד חוּשְׁבְּנָא, דִּכְתִּיב אֲשֶׁר פֻּקַּד עַל פִּי מֹשֶׁה.

29. Come and see: The Tabernacle is now subject to an inventory, FOR MALCHUT THAT IS CALLED 'TABERNACLE' CORRESPONDS TO THE LEFT COLUMN, WHENCE COUNTING COMES. Therefore it needed the prayer of Moses, WHICH IS THE SECRET OF THE CENTRAL COLUMN JOINING RIGHT AND LEFT AND POURING BLESSING UPON THEM AS MENTIONED ABOVE, as it is written, "And Moses blessed them" (Shemot 39:43). What is the blessing he gave them? 'May blessing be upon the work of your hands.' There were no blessings upon that counting until Moses bound it to the upper Tabernacle, BINAH, as it is written, "These are the accounts of the Tabernacle, the Tabernacle of the Testimony, as they were counted according to the commandment of Moses." AND THE TABERNACLE OF THE TESTIMONY IS BINAH, and were it not for Moses who did the counting, they would not have been able to count as it is written, "according to the commandment of Moses."

30. פָּתַח וְאָמַר, וַיְהִי דְּבַר יְיָ׳ אֵלָיו לֵאמֹר קוּם לֵךְ צָרְפַתָה וְגוֹ׳ הִנֵּה צִוִּיתִי שָׁם אִשָּׁה אַלְמָנָה לְכַלְכְּלֶךָ. וְכִי אָן פָּקִיד לָהּ קוּדְשָׁא בְּרִיךְ הוּא. אֶלָּא עַד לָא יֵיתֵי לְעָלְמָא, פָּקִיד קוּדְשָׁא בְּרִיךְ הוּא בִּגְזֵירָה דִּילֵיהּ לְעֵילָּא עַל הָעוֹרְבִים, לְמֵיתֵי מְזוֹנָא לְאֵלִיָּהוּ, וּלְהַהִיא אִתְּתָא לְמֵיהַב לֵיהּ מְזוֹנָא.

30. He opened the discussion and said: "And the word of Hashem came to him (Elijah), saying, 'Arise, go to Zarephath…behold, I have commanded a widow woman there to sustain you'" (I Melachim 17:8-9). HE ASKS: Where did the Holy One, blessed be He, command her? AND HE REPLIES: Before entering the world, the Holy One, blessed be He decreed above that the crows should bring food to Elijah, and that woman should give food to Elijah.

31. מַה כְּתִיב, וַתֹּאמֶר חַי יְיָ׳ אֱלֹהֶיךָ אִם יֶשׁ לִי מָעוֹג כִּי אִם מְלֹא כַף קֶמַח בַּכַּד וּמְעַט שֶׁמֶן בַּצַּפַּחַת וְגוֹ׳. וְהָא הָכָא מְדִידוּ הֲוָה בְּהַהוּא קִמְחָא, דְּהָא הֲוָה בֵּיהּ מְלֹא כַף קֶמַח בַּכַּד, כַּף הוּא מְדִידוּ דִּילֵיהּ, וְאִתְחֲזֵי דְּלָא שַׁרְיָין בֵּיהּ בִּרְכָן, הוֹאִיל וְקָאֵים בְּמִדָּה. מַה כְּתִיב, כִּי כֹה אָמַר יְיָ׳ אֱלֹהֵי יִשְׂרָאֵל כַּד הַקֶּמַח לֹא תִכְלָה וְצַפַּחַת הַשֶּׁמֶן לֹא תֶחְסָר עַד יוֹם תֵּת יְיָ׳ גֶּשֶׁם.

31. It is written: "And she said, 'As Hashem your Elohim lives, I have nothing baked, but a handful of meal in a jar, and a little oil in the cruse…'" (Ibid. 12). The meal was counted, for the jar contained a handful of meal, and that was its quantity. Being measured, it was not worthy for a blessing to dwell in it. But it is written, "For thus says Hashem, the Elohim of Yisrael, 'The jar of meal shall not be spent, neither shall the cruse of oil fail, until the day that Hashem sends (Heb. *tet*) rain upon the earth'" (Ibid. 14), AND BECAUSE OF THAT BLESSING, THERE WERE BLESSINGS UPON IT THOUGH IT WAS MEASURED.

32. תֵּת, תִּתֵּן כְּתִיב, מַאי טַעֲמָא. בְּגִין דִּבְכָל דָּרָא לָא אִשְׁתְּכַח מַאן דְּיִזְכֵּי לְזָכוּ כְּהַאי אִתְּתָא, וְעַל דָּא כְּתִיב תִּתֵּן, אַנְתְּ תִּתֵּן מִטְרָא עַל עָלְמָא, בְּגִין דִּזְכוּתָךְ סַגִּי.

32. HE ASKS: It is pronounced '*tet*' BUT IS WRITTEN '*TITEN*' (ENG. 'GIVE'), why is this so? HE ANSWERS in all that generation there was no person who was meritorious like that woman. Therefore it was written: 'titen' (lit. 'she will give'), to say, you will give rain upon the world due to your great merit.

33. וּכְתִיב כַּד הַקֶּמַח לֹא כָלָתָה וְצַפַּחַת הַשֶּׁמֶן לֹא חָסֵר כִּדְבַר יְיָ' אֲשֶׁר דִּבֶּר בְּיַד אֵלִיָּהוּ. וְכִי אִם הַהוּא קִמְחָא דְּקַיְּימָא בִּמְדִידוּ, דַּהֲוָה מְלֹא כַּף קֶמַח, לָא פַּסְקוּ מִנֵּיהּ בִּרְכָאן בְּגִין מִלָּה דְּאֵלִיָּהוּ, דִּכְתִּיב כַּד הַקֶּמַח לֹא תִכְלָה, וּכְתִיב כַּד הַקֶּמַח לֹא כָלָתָה. מִשְׁכַּן הָעֵדוּת אע"ג דְּקַיְּימָא בְּחוּשְׁבָּנָא, הוֹאִיל וְאִתְפַּקַּד עַל יְדָא דְּמֹשֶׁה, כָּל שֶׁכֵּן וְכָל שֶׁכֵּן דְּשַׁרְיָין בֵּיהּ בִּרְכָאן. וְעַל דָּא כְּתִיב, אֵלֶּה פְקוּדֵי הַמִּשְׁכָּן מִשְׁכַּן הָעֵדוּת אֲשֶׁר פֻּקַּד עַל פִּי מֹשֶׁה.

33. It is written: "And the jar of meal was not consumed, neither did the cruse of oil fail, according to the word of Hashem which He spoke through Elijah" (Ibid. 16). And though the meal was measured, for it was a handful, NEVERTHELESS no blessings were stopped from it, because of what Elijah had said, that "the jar of meal shall not be spent." And it is written, "the jar of meal was not spent." Even though the Tabernacle of the Testimony was accounted, since this was decreed by Moses, blessings dwell in it all the more. Therefore it is written, "These are the accounts of the Tabernacle, the Tabernacle of the Testimony that were counted according to the commandment of Moses."

34. אֵלֶּה פְקוּדֵי הַמִּשְׁכָּן. ר' חִזְקִיָּה פָּתַח וְאָמַר, אַל תִּקְרַב הֲלוֹם שַׁל נְעָלֶיךָ מֵעַל רַגְלֶיךָ וְגוֹ'. הַאי קְרָא אוּקְמוּהָ, דְּפָרִישׁ לֵיהּ קוּדְשָׁא בְּרִיךְ הוּא מְאִתְּתֵיהּ, בְּגִין לְאִתְדַּבְּקָא בִּשְׁכִינְתָּא, דִּכְתִּיב כִּי הַמָּקוֹם אֲשֶׁר אַתָּה עוֹמֵד עָלָיו אַדְמַת קֹדֶשׁ הוּא. אַדְמַת קֹדֶשׁ, דָּא שְׁכִינְתָּא, אִתְדַּבְּקוּתָא קַדִּישָׁא אִתְדַּבַּק מֹשֶׁה בְּהַהִיא שַׁעֲתָא לְעֵילָּא.

34. "These are the accounts of the Tabernacle." Rabbi Chizkiyah opened the discussion and said: "Do not come near, put off your shoes from off your feet..." (Shemot 3:5). This verse was thus explained, that the Holy One, blessed be He separated Moses from his wife so he may cleave to the Shechinah, as it is written, "for the place on which you stand is holy ground" (Ibid.). The holy ground is the Shechinah, NAMELY, holy unity with the high world Moses held on to at that time.

35. דִּכְדֵין קוּדְשָׁא בְּרִיךְ הוּא קָשִׁיר לֵיהּ בַּחֲבִיבוּתָא דִּלְעֵילָּא, וְאִתְפְּקַד רַב מְמָנָא עַל בֵּיתָא, וְאִיהוּ גָּזִיר, וְקוּדְשָׁא בְּרִיךְ הוּא עָבֵיד, דִּכְתִּיב וּפָצְתָה הָאֲדָמָה אֶת פִּיהָ וְגוֹ׳, וּכְתִיב וַיְהִי כְּכַלּוֹתוֹ לְדַבֵּר וְגוֹ׳, וַתִּבָּקַע הָאֲדָמָה. וּכְתִיב, קוּמָה יְיָ׳. שׁוּבָה יְיָ׳. הֲדָא הוּא דִּכְתִּיב אֲשֶׁר פֻּקַּד עַל פִּי מֹשֶׁה. עַל פִּי מֹשֶׁה אִתְתָּקַן, וְאִתְפְּקַד בְּכֹלָּא. פְּקִידָא דְּמִשְׁכָּן הֲוָה עַל יְדָא דְּמֹשֶׁה, דִּכְתִּיב פָּקֹד פָּקַדְתִּי אֶתְכֶם, דְּאִיהוּ הֲוָה קוֹל, דְּאַפִּיק לְהַהוּא דִּבּוּר, וְעָבֵד לֵיהּ פְּקִידָה לְנָפְקָא מִן גָּלוּתָא. וְהַשְׁתָּא אִתְפָּקְדָא לְאַמְשָׁכָא קְדוּשָּׁה מֵעֵילָּא לְתַתָּא, כמד״א וְעָשׂוּ לִי מִקְדָּשׁ וְשָׁכַנְתִּי בְּתוֹכָם.

35. For then the Holy One, blessed be He connected him with the fondness of above, and he was appointed supernal chieftain in charge of the house, MALCHUT, MEANING THAT HE BECAME A CHARIOT OF ZEIR ANPIN, WHICH IS SUPERIOR TO MALCHUT. He decrees, and the Holy One, blessed be He performs, as it is written, "and the earth opens her mouth, and swallows them up..." (Bemidbar 16:30), and "as he had made an end of speaking all these words, that the ground split" (Ibid.). It is also written, "Rise up, Hashem...Return, Hashem" (Ibid. 10:35-36). That is why it is written, "as they were counted, according to the commandment of Moses," for according to Moses the Tabernacle was accomplished, and everything counted. The counting of the Tabernacle, MALCHUT, was done by Moses, as it is written, "I have indeed taken count of you" (Shemot 3:16). Moses was a voice, NAMELY ZEIR ANPIN that utters the speech, MALCHUT, and he took count of it so it may come out of exile. And now you are commanded to draw holiness from above downward, as it is written, "And let them make Me a sanctuary, that I may dwell among them" (Shemot 25:8).

36. וּבְצַלְאֵל בֶּן אוּרִי בֶן חוּר לְמַטֵּה יְהוּדָה וְגוֹ׳. א״ר יְהוּדָה, הָא

אִתְּמַר, דְּהָא בְּצַלְאֵל מִסִּטְרָא דִּימִינָא הֲוָה, וְאִיהוּ אַתְקִין תִּקּוּנָא דְּכֹלָּא. וְתוּ, דְּהָא יְהוּדָה אִיהוּ שַׁלִּיטָא וּמַלְכָּא עַל כָּל שְׁאַר שְׁבָטִין, וּמִנֵּיהּ נָפַק מַאן דְּאַתְקִין כָּל מַשְׁכְּנָא. בְּצַלְאֵל, הָא אוּקְמוּהָ, בְּצֵל אֵל, וּמַאן אִיהוּ בְּצֵל אֵל. דָּא יְמִינָא. וְתוּ, מִסִּטְרָא דָּא אַתְקִין כֹּלָּא, וְיָרִית חָכְמְתָא לְמֶעְבַּד כָּל עֲבִידְתָא.

36. "And Betzalel the son of Uri, the son of Chur, of the tribe of Judah…" (Shemot 38:22). Rabbi Yehuda said: We have already learned that Betzalel was of the right side, FROM CHESED, and arranged everything. Moreover, Judah was the king and ruler over the rest of the tribes. Therefore, he who accomplished the whole work of the Tabernacle issued from him. It was explained that BetzalEl means 'IN THE SHADOW' (HEB. *BETZEL*) OF EL. Who dwells in the shadow of El? The right side, AS CHESED IS CALLED 'EL'. From this side did he construct everything and he inherited the Wisdom to accomplish all the work.

37. וְאִתּוֹ אָהֳלִיאָב בֶּן אֲחִיסָמָךְ לְמַטֵּה דָן, דָּא אִיהוּ מִסִּטְרָא דִּשְׂמָאלָא, דָּא אִיהוּ מִסִּטְרָא דְּדִינָא קַשְׁיָא, וְהָא אוּקְמוּהָ, דְּהָא מִתְּרֵין סִטְרִין אִלֵּין, אִתְעֲבֵיד מַשְׁכְּנָא, וְאִתְתְּקַן בְּהוּ, לְאִתְקַשְׁרָא בְּהוּ, לְמֶהֱוֵי בֵּין יְמִינָא וּשְׂמָאלָא, וְהָא אִתְּמַר וְאוּקְמוּהָ.

37. "And with him was Aholiav, son of Achisamach, of the tribe of Dan" (Ibid. 23). He is of the left side, of rigorous Judgment, FOR DAN INDICATES JUDGMENT (HEB. *DIN*). We already explained that by these two sides, RIGHT AND LEFT, the Tabernacle was made, WHICH IS MALCHUT. It was built and tied to them, so it may be between right and left. And this was already taught and explained.

5. "Beautiful for situation, the joy of the whole earth"

A Synopsis

Rabbi Yehuda says that when God created the world He threw a precious stone down from underneath the throne of glory. It fell into the abyss and one end of it stuck out, this is now the foundation of the world. From this point are three circles of expansion. The first is clear and pure, and corresponds to the temple and Jerusalem. The second is delicate and clear, though not so pure as the innermost circle, and corresponds to all of Yisrael. The third is all the rest of the world. The ocean surrounds them all. This schema is also the secret of all the colors in the eye that surround the middle point that gives the power of vision to the whole eye. This is like the Holy of Holies, the Ark and the Seat of Mercy, this point is the means of sight for the whole world. The people who merit forgiveness and mercy go into the temple until they reach the middle point that is "Beautiful of situation, the joy of the whole earth, Mount Zion..."

38. פָּתַח וְאָמַר, יְפֵה נוֹף מְשׂוֹשׂ כָּל הָאָרֶץ הַר צִיּוֹן יַרְכְּתֵי צָפוֹן קִרְיַת מֶלֶךְ רָב. תָּא חֲזֵי, כַּד בָּרָא קוּדְשָׁא בְּרִיךְ הוּא עָלְמָא, אַשְׁדֵּי חַד אַבְנָא יַקִּירָא מִתְּחוֹת כֻּרְסֵי יְקָרֵיהּ, וְשָׁקַע עַד תְּהוֹמָא, וְרֵישָׁא חֲדָא דְּהַהוּא אַבְנָא נָעִיץ גּוֹ תְּהוֹמֵי, וְרֵישָׁא אַחֲרָא לְעֵילָּא, וְהַהוּא רֵישָׁא אַחֲרָא עִלָּאָה, אִיהוּ חַד נְקוּדָה דְּקַיְימָא בְּאֶמְצָעִיתָא דְּעָלְמָא, וּמִתַּמָּן אִתְפָּשַׁט עָלְמָא לִימִינָא וּשְׂמָאלָא וּלְכָל סִטְרִין, וְאִתְקָיָּים בְּהַהִיא נְקוּדָה אֶמְצָעִיתָא, וְהַהִיא אַבְנָא אִתְקְרֵי שְׁתִיָּה, דְּמִנָּהּ אִשְׁתִּיל עָלְמָא לְכָל סִטְרִין. תּוּ שְׁתִיָּ"ה, שָׁת יָ"הּ, קוּדְשָׁא בְּרִיךְ הוּא שַׁוֵּי לָהּ לְמֶהֱוֵי יְסוֹדָא דְּעָלְמָא וּשְׁתִילוּ דְּכֹלָּא.

38. He opened the discussion and said: "Beautiful for situation, the joy of the whole earth; Mount Zion, the sides of the north, the city of the great king" (Tehilim 48:3). Come and see: When the Holy One, blessed be He created the world, He threw one precious stone from beneath the throne of glory. It fell down to the abyss, where one edge was stuck, and the other edge of the stone was up. This other head which stood upward is the one point standing in the middle of the universe, whence it spreads right and left and in all directions. And THE WORLD exists by that middle point, called ‘foundation’ (Heb. *shtiyah*), as from it the world spreads in all directions. We have to explain further, that ‘*Shtiyah*’ consists of ‘shat Yah (Eng. ‘Yah has put’)’, and that the Holy One, blessed be He put (Heb. *shat*) it to be the foundation of the universe and the plant of everything.

39. בִּתְלַת גַּוְונִין אִתְפַּשְּׁטַת אַרְעָא סַחֲרָנֵיהּ דְּהַהוּא נְקוּדָה, אִתְפַּשְּׁטוּתָא קַדְמָאָה, סַחֲרָנֵיהּ דְּהַהוּא נְקוּדָה, כָּל צָחוּתָא וּזְכוּתָא דְּאַרְעָא קַיְימָא תַּמָּן, וְתַמָּן אִיהוּ. וְהַאי קַיְימָא לְעֵילָּא עַל כָּל אַרְעָא סַחֲרָנֵיהּ דְּהַהוּא נְקוּדָה. אִתְפַּשְּׁטוּתָא תִּנְיָינָא, סַחֲרָנֵיהּ דְּהַהוּא אִתְפַּשְּׁטוּתָא קַדְמָאָה, לָאו אִיהוּ צָחוּתָא וְזָכוּתָא כְּהַהוּא קַדְמָאָה, אֲבָל אִיהוּ דָּקִיק וְצַח בְּצָחוּתָא דְּעַפְרָא, יַתִּיר מִכָּל שְׁאַר עָפָר אַחֲרָא. אִתְפַּשְּׁטוּתָא תְּלִיתָאָה, אִיהוּ חָשׁוּךְ וְגַסוּ דְּעַפְרָא יַתִּיר מִכֻּלְּהוּ, וְסַחֲרָנֵיהּ דְּהַאי, קַיְימִין מַיִין דְּיַמָּא דְּאוֹקְיָינוּס, דְּאַסְחַר כָּל עָלְמָא. אִשְׁתְּכַח דְּהַהוּא נְקוּדָה קַיְימָא בְּאֶמְצָעִיתָא, וְכֻלְּהוּ גַּוְונִין דְּאִתְפַּשְּׁטוּתָא דְּעָלְמָא סַחֲרָנֵיהּ.

39. The earth was spread in three ways around the point, WHICH IS MALCHUT, FOUND IN THE INNERMOST PART OF THIS WORLD. In the first expansion around the point there is all the clarity and purity on earth; it is above the earth around that point. The second expansion is around the first one, it is not as clear and pure, but is delicate and clear REGARDING the transparency of the dust, more than any other dust. The third expansion is dark and its dust is thicker than the rest, around which are the waters of the ocean that surrounds the world. It is found that this point stands in the center, and all manners of world expansion encircle it.

40. אִתְפַּשְּׁטוּתָא קַדְמָאָה אִיהוּ בֵּי מַקְדְּשָׁא, וְכָל אִינּוּן הֵיכָלִין וַעֲזָרוֹת, וְכָל הַהוּא תִּקּוּנָא דִּילֵיהּ, וִירוּשָׁלַםִ, וְכָל מָתָא מִשּׁוּרָא וּלְגוֹ. אִתְפַּשְּׁטוּתָא תִּנְיָינָא, כָּל אַרְעָא דְּיִשְׂרָאֵל דְּאִתְקַדְּשַׁת בִּקְדוּשָּׁה. אִתְפַּשְּׁטוּתָא תְּלִיתָאָה, אִיהוּ כָּל שְׁאַר אַרְעָא, אֲתָר בֵּי מוֹתְבָא דִּשְׁאַר עַמִּין. וְיַמָּא דְּאוֹקְיָינוּס דְּסָחֲרָא כֹּלָּא.

40. HE EXPLAINS WHAT HE SAID: The first expansion is the Temple, all its chambers, enclosures, courts and all that appertains, also Jerusalem and the city inside the walls. THEREFORE IT IS CLEARER AND PURER THAN THE REST OF THE LAND. The second expansion is all of the land of Yisrael that was sanctified in holiness. The third expansion is the rest of the earth, the dwelling place of the other nations. And the ocean surrounds it all.

41. וְהָא אוּקְמוּהָ, דְּרָזָא דָּא גַּוְונִין דְּעֵינָא, דְּסַחֲרָן לְהַהוּא נְקוּדָה דְּאֶמְצָעִיתָא דְּעֵינָא, דְּאִיהוּ חֵיזוּ דְּכָל עֵינָא, כְּגַוְונָא דְּהַהִיא נְקוּדָה אֶמְצָעִיתָא דְּקָאָמְרָן, דְּאִיהוּ חֵיזוּ דְּכֹלָּא, וְתַמָּן קָאֵים בֵּית קֹדֶשׁ הַקֳּדָשִׁים, וְאָרוֹן וְכַפֹּרֶת, דְּאִינּוּן חֵיזוּ דְּכֹלָּא. אִשְׁתְּכַח, הַהוּא נְקוּדָה חֵיזוּ דְּכָל עָלְמָא. וְעַל דָּא כְּתִיב, יְפֵה נוֹף מְשׂוֹשׂ כָּל הָאָרֶץ הַר צִיּוֹן וְגוֹ'. יְפֵה: שַׁפִּיר הַהוּא חֵיזוּ וְחֶדְוָה דְּכֹלָּא. נוֹף: נוֹפָא דְּאִילָנָא דְּאִיהוּ שְׁפִירוּ דְּכֹלָּא.

41. It was already explained, that this is the secret of the colors in the eye, surrounding the middle point in the eye, which gives the power of vision to the whole eye. It is like the middle point, IN THE INNERMOST PART OF THE EARTH, regarding which we said, it is the sight of all, where stand the Holy of Holies, the Ark and the seat of Mercy, that are the vision to everything. It is found that the point is the means of sight to the world. Therefore, it is written of it, "Beautiful for situation, the joy of the whole earth – Mount Zion..." IT IS CALLED beautiful because this sight is beautiful. Situation (Heb. *nof*) is the branch (Heb. *anaf*) of the tree, ZEIR ANPIN, the beauty of all.

42. תָּא חֲזֵי, שְׁפִירוּ דְּעָלְמָא, וְחֵיזוּ דְּעָלְמָא, לָא אִתְחָזֵי בְּעָלְמָא, עַד דְּאִתְבְּנֵי וְאִתְּקַם מַשְׁכְּנָא, וְעָאל אֲרוֹנָא לְגוֹ קוּדְשָׁא. מֵהַהִיא שַׁעֲתָא, אִתְחָזֵי חֵיזוּ דְּכֹלָּא בְּעָלְמָא, וְאִתְתָּקַן עָלְמָא, וְאַזְלֵי בְּהַהוּא מַשְׁכְּנָא וּבְהַהוּא אֲרוֹנָא, עַד דְּמָטֵי לְהַהִיא נְקוּדָה דְּאִיהִי יְפֵה נוֹף חֶדְוָה דְּכֹלָּא. כֵּיוָן דְּמָטוּ לְהָתָם כְּדֵין פָּתַח אֲרוֹנָא וְאָמַר, זֹאת מְנוּחָתִי עֲדֵי עַד פֹּה אֵשֵׁב כִּי אִוִּיתִיהָ.

42. Come and look at the beauty of the world. And the sight thereof was never revealed to the world until the Tabernacle was constructed and erected, and the Ark was put in the sanctuary. From that time the sight of the whole world, THE SHECHINAH, was seen and the world stood firm. And THE MERITORIOUS go in the Tabernacle and the Ark until they reach the MIDDLE point IN THERE, which is “Beautiful of situation, the joy of all.” When they arrive, the Ark opens and says, “This is My resting place forever, here will I dwell, for I have desired it” (Tehilim 132:14).

43. רִבִּי יֵיסָא אָמַר, הַאי קְרָא כְּנֶסֶת יִשְׂרָאֵל אָמְרָה לֵיהּ, בְּשַׁעֲתָא דְּאִתְבְּנֵי בֵּי מַקְדְּשָׁא, וְעָאל אֲרוֹנָא לְאַתְרֵיהּ. ר׳ חִזְקִיָּה אָמַר, קוּדְשָׁא בְּרִיךְ הוּא אָמַר לֵיהּ, עַל כְּנֶסֶת יִשְׂרָאֵל, כַּד יִשְׂרָאֵל עַבְדִּין רְעוּתֵיהּ, דְּהָא כְּדֵין קוּדְשָׁא בְּרִיךְ הוּא יָתִיב עַל כּוּרְסֵי יְקָרֵיהּ, וְחָיֵיס עַל עָלְמָא, וּבִרְכָה וְשָׁלוֹם וַחֲבִיבוּתָא דְּכֹלָּא אִשְׁתְּכַח. וּכְדֵין אָמַר זֹאת מְנוּחָתִי עֲדֵי עַד.

43. Rabbi Yisa says: This verse was pronounced by the Congregation of Yisrael, when the Temple was built and the Ark was put in its place. Rabbi Chizkiyah said that the Holy One, blessed be He said this verse, referring to the Congregation of Yisrael, for when Yisrael do His bidding, the Holy One, blessed be He sits on His throne of glory, and has mercy on the world, and there are blessings and peace and love for all. Then He said: “This is My resting place forever.”

6. "These are the accounts of the Tabernacle," part two

A Synopsis

Rabbi Chizkiyah says that although the craftsmen began work on the temple, it was finished on its own, and although God began work on the creation of the heavens and the earth they were finished on their own. As evidence for this he points out that all the verses pertaining to these events are in the passive tense, and concludes that all holy work is completed of its own accord. He turns to the account of Betzalel and Aholiav working on the Temple, and reiterates that this was the union of right and left. Next Rabbi Yisa tells us that the accounts were taken of the Tabernacle because this confirmed the work when it was finished. This accounting supersedes all previous events in the world.

44. וְתָא חֲזֵי, בְּשַׁעֲתָא דְּכֻלְּהוּ אוּמָנִין שָׁארוּ לְמֶעְבַּד אוּמָנוּתָא, הַהוּא עוֹבָדָא מַמָּשׁ דְּשָׁרָאן, אִיהִי אִשְׁתְּלִימַת מִגַּרְמָהּ. אִינּוּן שָׁרָאן, וְאִיהִי אַשְׁלִימַת עֲבִידְתָּא, אִיהִי מַמָּשׁ, מְנָלָן, דִּכְתִּיב וַתֵּכֶל כָּל עֲבוֹדַת מִשְׁכַּן אֹהֶל מוֹעֵד.

44. Come and see: When all the craftsmen began their work, the very work they started was finished on its own. They started and it was finished on its own. From where do we know that? From the verse, "Thus was all the work of the Tabernacle of the Tent of Meeting finished" (Shemot 39:32), MEANING THAT IT WAS FINISHED ON ITS OWN.

45. כְּגַוְונָא דָּא וַיְכֻלּוּ הַשָּׁמַיִם וְהָאָרֶץ. וְאִי תֵּימָא, וַיְכַל אֱלֹהִים בַּיּוֹם הַשְּׁבִיעִי. וַדַּאי הָכִי הוּא, דְּכָל עָלְמָא, אע"ג דְּכָל עֲבִידָן אִשְׁתְּלִימוּ כָּל חַד וְחַד, עָלְמָא כֹּלָּא לָא הֲוָה שְׁלִים בְּקִיּוּמֵיהּ, עַד דְּאָתָא יוֹמָא שְׁבִיעָאָה, דְּכַד אָתָא יוֹמָא שְׁבִיעָאָה, כְּדֵין אִשְׁתְּלִימוּ כָּל עֲבִידָן, וְאַשְׁלִים בֵּיהּ קוּדְשָׁא בְּרִיךְ הוּא עָלְמָא, הה"ד וַיְכַל אֱלֹהִים בַּיּוֹם הַשְּׁבִיעִי מְלַאכְתּוֹ אֲשֶׁר עָשָׂה. בְּהַאי, אִשְׁתְּלִים בְּקִיּוּמָא כָּל עֲבִידְתָּא דְּעָבֵד, וְע"ד וַיְכַל אֱלֹהִים בְּיוֹם הַשְּׁבִיעִי.

45. In the same manner, "The heavens and the earth were finished" (Beresheet 2:1), MEANING THAT THEY WERE COMPLETED ON THEIR OWN.

You may say, IT IS WRITTEN, “And by the seventh day Elohim ended” (Ibid.), HENCE ELOHIM COMPLETED THEM, AND THEY DID NOT COMPLETE THEMSELVES. Assuredly this is so, for though the works were completed one by one, nevertheless, the world was not altogether complete before the arrival of the seventh day. For when the seventh day arrived, all the works were completed and the Holy One, blessed be He completed the universe. This is the meaning of “And by the seventh day Elohim ended His work, which He had done.” AND BY THE SEVENTH DAY, all the work He had done was complete. Therefore “by the seventh day Elohim ended His work .”

46. וְכַד אִתְבְּנֵי בֵּי מַקְדְּשָׁא, כָּל עֲבִידְתָּא דְּאִתְעֲבִיד, אִיהִי מִגַּרְמָהּ אִתְעֲבֵידַת אוּמָנִין שָׁרָאן, וַעֲבִידְתָּא אִתְחֲזִיאַת לוֹן לְמֶעְבַּד, וְאִתְרְשִׁימַת קָמַיְיהוּ, וְאִשְׁתְּלִימַת הִיא מִגַּרְמָהּ. וְהָא אוּקְמוּהָ, דִּכְתִּיב וְהַבַּיִת בְּהִבָּנוֹתוֹ. וְהַבַּיִת כַּאֲשֶׁר בָּנֲהוּ לָא כְּתִיב. אֶלָּא בְּהִבָּנוֹתוֹ. דְּאִיהִי אִשְׁתְּלִימַת מִגַּרְמָהּ. וּכְתִיב אֶבֶן שְׁלֵמָה מַסָּע נִבְנָה. בָּנוּהוּ לָא כְּתִיב. אֶלָּא נִבְנָה הוּא מִגַּרְמֵיהּ נִבְנָה, וְכֵן בְּכָל עֲבִידְתָּא דְּאִיהִי קַדִּישָׁא, אִיהִי אִשְׁתְּלִימַת מִגַּרְמָהּ.

46. When the Temple was built, all the work was done on its own. The craftsmen began and the work showed them, how it should be done. And it was traced and completed of its own accord. It was also written, “And the house, when it was built” (I Melachim 6:7), not ‘when they built it,’ but “when it was built, because it was built on its own.” It is further written, “was built of stone made ready before it was brought there” (Ibid.) – “was built” and not ‘they built it.’ So all work, which is holy, is completed on its own accord.

47. וּבְצַלְאֵל בֶּן אוּרִי בֶן חוּר. הַאי קְרָא אוֹלִיפְנָא, דְּרוּחַ קוּדְשָׁא אַכְרִיז עֲלֵיהּ לְעֵינֵיהוֹן דְּיִשְׂרָאֵל, וְאָמַר וּבְצַלְאֵל בֶּן אוּרִי בֶן חוּר לְמַטֵּה יְהוּדָה עָשָׂה אֶת כָּל אֲשֶׁר צִוָּה יְיָ' אֶת מֹשֶׁה. וְאִתּוֹ אָהֳלִיאָב בֶּן אֲחִיסָמָךְ. מַאי וְאִתּוֹ. אֶלָּא אוֹלִיפְנָא, דְּאָהֳלִיאָב לָא עֲבֵיד עֲבִידְתָּא בִּלְחוֹדוֹי, אֶלָּא עִם בְּצַלְאֵל, וְעִמֵּיהּ עָבֵד כָּל מַה דְּעָבֵד. הה"ד וְאִתּוֹ, וְאִתּוֹ וְלָא בִּלְחוֹדוֹי. מִכָּאן דִּשְׂמָאלָא אִיהִי בִּכְלַל יְמִינָא תָּדִיר. וְע"ד כְּתִיב וַאֲנִי הִנֵּה נָתַתִּי

אִתּוֹ אֵת אָהֳלִיאָב, דָּא יְמִינָא וְדָא שְׂמָאלָא.

47. "And Betzalel the son of Uri, the son of Chur..." (Shemot 38:22): we learned by this verse that the Holy Spirit proclaimed concerning this verse before the eyes of Yisrael, and said, "Betzalel the son of Uri, the son of Chur, of the tribe of Judah, did all that Hashem commanded Moses. And with him Aholiav, son of Achisamach." HE ASKS: What is the meaning of "And with him"? AND HE REPLIES: We learned that Aholiav did not do the work alone but with Betzalel he did what he did. This is the meaning of "with him" and not on his own. FOR BETZALEL IS RIGHT AND AHOLIAV IS LEFT. From here we learn that the left is always included in the right. Therefore it is written, "I have given with him Aholiav" (Shemot 31:6). The one is right and the other left. AND LEFT IS INCLUDED IN THE RIGHT.

48. אֵלֶּה פְקוּדֵי הַמִּשְׁכָּן מִשְׁכַּן הָעֵדוּת אֲשֶׁר פֻּקַּד עַל פִּי מֹשֶׁה וְגוֹ'. ר' יֵיסָא אָמַר, כֵּיוָן דְּעָבְדוּ כָּל חַכִּימַיָּיא יַת מַשְׁכְּנָא, אִצְטְרִיךְ לְמֶהֱדַר חוּשְׁבָּנָא, מִכָּל אִינּוּן עֲבִידָן דְּאִתְעֲבֵידוּ בֵּיהּ. מַאי טַעֲמָא. בְּגִין דְּכָל חוּשְׁבָּן וְחוּשְׁבָּן, כַּד הֲוָה אִתְעֲבִיד חוּשְׁבָּנָא, הָכִי אִתְקַיָּים הַהוּא עֲבִידָא, וְאִתְקַיָּים בְּאַתְרֵיהּ.

48. "These are the accounts of the Tabernacle, the Tabernacle of the Testimony, as they were counted, according to the commandment of Moses ..." (Shemot 38:21). Rabbi Yesa said: Since all the wise men made the Tabernacle, there was need of counting all the works done in it. What is the reason? Each account, by being made, confirmed the work done, and it remained in place.

49. וְיִשְׂרָאֵל כֻּלְּהוּ כְּמָה דְּאִתְרְעוּ בְּמָה דִּנְדִיבוּ בְּקַדְמֵיתָא, הָכִי נָמֵי אִתְרְעוּ בְּהַהוּא חוּשְׁבָּנָא, וּכְדֵין אִתְקַיָּים כָּל עֲבִידָא, בְּהַהוּא רְעוּתָא. וְעַל דָּא אִצְטְרִיךְ הָכָא חוּשְׁבָּנָא, בְּגִין דִּבְהַאי אִתְקַיָּים עֲבִידָא. אֵלֶּה כְּתִיב, וְלָא כְּתִיב וְאֵלֶּה. אֶלָּא דָּא אִיהוּ חוּשְׁבָּנָא דְּפָסִיל כָּל חוּשְׁבָּנִין דְּעָלְמָא, וְדָא אִתְקַיָּים יַתִּיר מִכֻּלְּהוּ, דִּבְהַאי אִתְקַיָּים מַשְׁכְּנָא, וְלָא בְּאַחֲרָא.

6. "These are the accounts of the Tabernacle," part two

49. And all Yisrael, as at first they wanted to donate, so they wanted that account, MEANING THAT BY THEIR WISH THEY DREW THE MOCHIN OF THESE ACCOUNTING, and all the work prevailed by that wish. Therefore, there was need of accounting IN THE TABERNACLE, since through it the work is confirmed. It is therefore written, "These," NAMELY, "THESE ARE THE ACCOUNTS," and not 'And these', BECAUSE WHEREVER IT IS WRITTEN "THESE," WHATEVER WAS WRITTEN BEFORE IS ANNULLED, and that account annuls all the previous accounts in the world, prevails more than the rest, and the Tabernacle exists by that and not by another.

7. "And He shall be the faithfulness of your times"

A Synopsis

Rabbi Yesa says that the faithful should tune themselves to the name of heaven so that Malchut will unite with Zeir Anpin. "Your times" refers to the time set aside for studying the Torah, and "faithfulness" refers to Malchut. "A strength of salvation" consists of both judgment and mercy. "Wisdom and knowledge" means that wisdom is only revealed through knowledge. "The fear of Hashem is his treasure" means that God lets out all his streams, accounting for them carefully. We hear of several reasons that Malchut is called 'faithfulness.' Rabbi Yesa concludes that God let Yisrael know the faithfulness of those who built the Tabernacle.

50. פָּתַח וְאָמַר, וְהָיָה אֱמוּנַת עִתֶּךָ חֹסֶן יְשׁוּעוֹת חָכְמַת וָדָעַת יִרְאַת יְיָ׳ הִיא אוֹצָרוֹ. הַאי קְרָא אוֹקְמוּהָ חַבְרַיָּיא, אֲבָל הָא תָּנֵינָן, כָּל ב״נ דְּאִתְעַסָּק בְּאוֹרַיְיתָא בְּהַאי עָלְמָא, וְזָכֵי לְמִקְבַּע עִתִּין לָהּ, אִצְטְרִיךְ בֶּאֱמוּנָה, דִּרְעוּתָא דִּילֵיהּ יִתְכַּוֵּין לְקוּדְשָׁא בְּרִיךְ הוּא, יִתְכַּוֵּין לְשֵׁם שָׁמַיִם, בְּגִין דֶּאֱמוּנָה לְהָכִי אִתְכְּוָון. חֹסֶן יְשׁוּעוֹת, לְאַכְלְלָא רַחֲמֵי בְּדִינָא. חָכְמַת וָדָעַת, דִּתְרֵין אִלֵּין שַׁרְיָאן דָּא עַל דָּא. דָּא טָמִיר וְגָנִיז, לְאַשְׁרָאָה דָּא עַל דָּא.

50. He opened the discussion and said: "And He shall be the faithfulness of your times, a strength of salvation, wisdom and knowledge, the fear of Hashem is his treasure" (Yeshayah 33:6). This verse was explained by the friends. But we learned that whoever is occupied in the Torah in this world and merits in setting times for it, should be in faithfulness, set his mind upon the Holy One, blessed be He, ZEIR ANPIN, and tune himself to the name of heaven, SO THAT MALCHUT CALLED 'NAME', WILL BE UNITED WITH HEAVEN, ZEIR ANPIN, because faithfulness, WHICH IS MALCHUT, is attuned to this, TO BECOME UNITED WITH ZEIR ANPIN. THIS IS THE SECRET OF THE VERSE, "THE FAITHFULNESS OF YOUR TIMES;" "YOUR TIMES" REFERS TO THE TIMES SET FOR THE STUDY OF THE TORAH, ZEIR ANPIN, AND "FAITHFULNESS" REFERING TO MALCHUT, SO THAT THE TWO MAY JOIN. "A strength of salvation" comprises Judgment and Mercy, FOR STRENGTH IS JUDGMENT AND SALVATION IS MERCY. "Wisdom and knowledge," the two dwell one upon the other, FOR

CHOCHMAH is hidden and concealed AND THEY SHOULD dwell one upon the other, NAMELY, CHOCHMAH IS NOT REVEALED SAVE BY DA'AT.

51. יִרְאַת יְיָ׳ הִיא אוֹצָרוֹ. אוֹצָרוֹ דְּכָל אִלֵּין, בְּגִין דְּהַאי יִרְאַת יְיָ׳, נָקִיט כָּל אִינּוּן נַחֲלִין, וְאִיהִי אִתְעֲבִידַת אוֹצָר לְכֻלְּהוּ. וְכַד נָפְקִין מִנָּהּ כָּל אִינּוּן גְּנִיזִין כֻּלְּהוּ, אַפִּיק לוֹן בְּחוּשְׁבָּנָא. מְנָלָן. דִּכְתִּיב עֵינַיִךְ בְּרֵכוֹת בְּחֶשְׁבּוֹן. בְּחֶשְׁבּוֹן וַדַּאי עָבִיד, וְאַפִּיק אִינּוּן בְּרֵכוֹת מַיִם, וְאַשְׁגַּח לְאַפָּקָא כֹּלָּא בְּחוּשְׁבָּנָא.

51. "The fear of Hashem is his treasure." It is the treasure of all those GRADES, since that fear of Hashem, WHICH IS MALCHUT CALLED 'FEAR OF HASHEM', receives all the streams, NAMELY, THOSE SAID GRADES, and becomes a treasure (store-house) to them all, and when all that were hidden in it issue, it lets them out by accounting. From where do we know that? From the verse, "your eyes like the pools in Heshbon (Eng. 'account')" (Shir Hashirim 7:5). For it does things by reckoning, and lets out pools of water, THE GRADES IT RECEIVED, carefully letting all out with account.

52. וְעַל דָּא אִקְרֵי אֱמוּנָה. וּבְכֹלָּא אִקְרֵי אֱמוּנָה, וְהָא אוֹקִימְנָא. וּמַה אִי הָכָא אִצְטְרִיךְ לְאַחֲזָאָה מְהֵימְנוּתָא, לִשְׁאַר מִלֵּי דְּעָלְמָא עאכ״ו. וְעַל דָּא, קוּדְשָׁא בְּרִיךְ הוּא הֲוָה אוֹדַע לְהוּ לְכָל יִשְׂרָאֵל, רָזָא דִּמְהֵימְנוּתָא דִּילְהוּ, בְּכָל מַה דְּעָבְדוּ, וְכֹלָּא אִתְמַר.

52. SINCE IN MALCHUT ALL IS DONE WITH RECKONING, WHICH IS THE SECRET OF CHOCHMAH THAT SUSTAINS EVERYTHING, she is called 'faithfulness', MEANING FIDELITY AND SUSTENANCE. THERE ARE MORE REASONS WHY MALCHUT IS CALLED 'FAITHFULNESS'. For all these reasons it is called 'faithfulness', as we already explained. If in here, IN THE SUPERNAL SFIROT AND GRADES THAT MALCHUT RECEIVES, one should see faithfulness, NAMELY, ILLUMINATE THEM ACCORDING TO THE SECRET OF ACCOUNT, ACCORDING TO THE SECRET OF THE VERSE, "THE FEAR OF HASHEM IS HIS TREASURE," AS WAS DISCUSSED, and in the matters of the world, BY THE CORRECTIONS OF MALCHUT HERSELF CALLED 'WORLD', IN THE SECRET OF THE VESSELS OF THE TABERNACLE; how much more so ONE NEEDS TO ACCOUNT AND TO SHOW FAITHFULNESS,

THAT ARE THE MYSTERY OF SUSTENANCE AS MENTIONED. Therefore, the Holy One, blessed be He let Yisrael know the secret of faithfulness of those who made the Tabernacle, in all that they did, IN THE SECRET OF THE VERSE, "THESE ARE THE ACCOUNTS OF THE TABERNACLE." And everything is already explained.

8. The name Betzalel caused

A Synopsis

Rabbi Yosi and Rabbi Yitzchak are walking together. Rabbi Yosi says that God chose Betzalel to build the temple because of his name, that means 'in the shadow of El,' 'El' being the name of Chesed. He adds that God made names on earth because they have significance. To further this argument he says that Judah started building the left side and the Tabernacle was constructed of left and right. In the same way the Torah, Tiferet, started on the left side, Gvurah, and joined the right, Chesed. Reuben started building on the right and turned to the left to bring in the tribes Shimon and Gad. We hear that God gave Betzalel wisdom because he was already wise-hearted. Rabbi Shimon turns to: "Like the apple tree among the trees of the wood, so is my beloved among the sons... I sat down under His shadow with great delight, and His fruit was sweet to my taste." He says that 'under His shadow' refers to Betzalel, and 'His fruit' refers to the souls of the righteous since they are the fruit of God's deeds. Finally the verse: "All the gold that was applied" is explained as meaning that the gold that was supplied for the Tabernacle already existed above. In each work that was holy there was gold.

53. ר׳ יוֹסֵי וְרִבִּי יִצְחָק הֲווֹ אַזְלֵי בְּאָרְחָא, אָמַר ר׳ יוֹסֵי, וַדַּאי דְּקוּדְשָׁא בְּרִיךְ הוּא אִתְרְעֵי בֵּיהּ בִּבְצַלְאֵל לַעֲבִידַת מַשְׁכְּנָא, יַתִּיר מִכָּל יִשְׂרָאֵל, אֲמַאי. אָמַר לֵיהּ, שְׁמָא גָּרִים, וְהָא אוֹקְמוּהָ, דְּקוּדְשָׁא בְּרִיךְ הוּא שַׁוֵּי שְׁמָהָן בְּאַרְעָא, לְאִתְעַטְּרָא בְּהוּ, וּלְמֶעְבַּד בְּהוּ עֲבִידְתָּא בְּעָלְמָא, הה״ד אֲשֶׁר שָׂם שַׁמּוֹת בָּאָרֶץ.

53. Rabbi Yosi and Rabbi Yitzchak were walking along the way. Rabbi Yosi said: Assuredly the Holy One, blessed be He wanted Betzalel to do the work of the Tabernacle more than the rest of Yisrael. HE ASKS: Why? He told him: It was because of his name, FOR HE WAS CALLED 'BETZALEL', BETZEL (ENG. 'IN THE SHADOW OF') EL, AND EL IS THE NAME OF CHESED. It was already explained that the Holy One, blessed be He placed names (Heb. *shemot*) on earth to be adorned by them and to do there the work of this world, as it is written, "who has made desolations (Heb. *shamot*) in the earth" (Tehilim 46:9), MEANING THAT IT IS INCUMBENT BY HASHEM UPON MEN TO CALL BY NAME ON EARTH.

54. אָמַר לֵיהּ, רָזָא אִיהוּ הָכָא, יְהוּדָה מִסְּטַר שְׂמָאלָא הֲוָה, וְאַהְדָּר וְאִתְדַּבָּק בִּימִינָא. וְעַל דָּא, בְּסִטְרָא דָּא אִתְעֲבִיד מַשְׁכְּנָא, שָׁארֵי מִסְּטַר שְׂמָאלָא, וְאִתְדַּבָּק בִּסְטַר יְמִינָא, וּלְבָתַר אִתְכְּלִיל דָּא בְּדָא, וְאִתְעֲבִיד כֹּלָּא יְמִינָא. כְּגַוְונָא דָּא אוֹרַיְיתָא, שָׁארֵי מִשְּׂמָאלָא, וְאִתְדַּבָּק בִּימִינָא, וְאִתְכְּלִיל דָּא בְּדָא, וְאִתְעֲבִיד כֹּלָּא יְמִינָא. רְאוּבֵן שָׁרָא מִימִינָא, וְסָטָא לִשְׂמָאלָא, וְנַטְלוּ עִמֵּיהּ אִינּוּן שְׁאַר שְׁבָטִין, דְּאִינּוּן שְׂמָאלָא, בְּגִין דְּשָׁארֵי מִימִינָא וְסָטָא לִשְׂמָאלָא.

54. He told him: There is a secret here. Judah is of the left side, BEING OF MALCHUT, WHICH IS CONSTRUCTED BY THE LEFT SIDE. Then he joined the right, ZEIR ANPIN, and therefore the Tabernacle was built on that side, starting on the left side and joining the right side. Afterwards they were combined together and all was done from the right. In the same manner the Torah, WHICH IS TIFERET, started on the left side, FOR TIFERET RECEIVES THE EMANATION OF GVURAH WHICH IS LEFT, and joins the right, CHESED. They were combined together and all became right. Reuben started on the right. FOR REUBEN WAS CHESED, and turned to the left to take UNDER HIS BANNER the rest of the tribes, SHIMON AND GAD, that are of the left. For he started on the right and turned left.

55. יְהוּדָה שָׁרָא מִשְּׂמָאלָא, וְסָטָא לִימִינָא, שָׁרָא מִשְּׂמָאלָא, בְּגִין דְּאָתֵי מִסְּטַר שְׂמָאלָא, וְאִתְדַּבַּק בִּימִינָא, וּמַשְׁכְּנָא בְּסִטְרָא דָּא אִתְעֲבֵיד. שָׁארֵי מִסְּטַר שְׂמָאלָא, וְאִתְדַּבַּק בִּסְטַר יְמִינָא, וְע״ד, בְּצַלְאֵל אִיהוּ דְּאָתֵי מִסִּטְרֵיהּ, עָבֵד מַשְׁכְּנָא וְאִתְתָּקַן לְגַבֵּיהּ. וְהָא אוּקְמוּהָ, דְּקוּדְשָׁא בְּרִיךְ הוּא אִתְרְעֵי בֵּיהּ, וּבָרִיר לֵיהּ מִכֹּלָּא לַעֲבִידְתָּא דָּא.

55. HE EXPLAINS WHAT HE SAID: Judah started from the left side, FOR HE IS OF MALCHUT WHICH IS BUILT BY THE LEFT SIDE. And he joined the right, so the Tabernacle was ALSO constructed on that side, starting on the left side and joining the right side, BECAUSE THE TABERNACLE IS ALSO MALCHUT, and therefore Betzalel, who comes from Judah, built the Tabernacle and was established thereby. FOR HE IS CONSIDERED IN THE SAME WAY AS THE TABERNACLE. And it was already expounded that the Holy One, blessed be He wanted him and preferred him above all Yisrael for the building OF THIS TABERNACLE.

8. The name Betzalel caused

56. וְיָהַב לֵיהּ חָכְמָה וּתְבוּנָה וָדַעַת, כְּמָה דְּאוּקְמוּהָ. בְּגִין דְּעִמֵּיהּ הֲוָה בְּקַדְמֵיתָא סָכְלְתָנוּ דְּלִבָּא, דִּכְתִּיב וּבְלֵב כָּל חֲכַם לֵב נָתַתִּי חָכְמָה. בְּגִין דְּקוּדְשָׁא בְּרִיךְ הוּא לָא יָהִיב חָכְמְתָא, אֶלָּא לְמַאן דְּאִית בֵּיהּ חָכְמְתָא, וְאוּקְמוּהָ חַבְרַיָּיא וְאִתְּמַר. וְכֵן כְּגַוְונָא דָּא בְּצַלְאֵל. ר' שִׁמְעוֹן אָמַר, בְּצַלְאֵל שְׁמֵיהּ גָּרִים לֵיהּ, וְעַל חָכְמָתֵיהּ אִקְרֵי הָכִי, וְרָזָא דְּמִלָּה בְּצַלְאֵל, בְּצֵל אֵל.

56. And he gave him Chochmah and Tevunah, and Da'at as was explained, because he already possessed intelligence of heart, as it is written, "and in the hearts of all that are wise-hearted I have put wisdom" (Shemot 31:6), MEANING THAT HE WAS GIVEN WISDOM FOR BEING ALREADY WISE-HEARTED. For the Holy One, blessed be He gives wisdom only to him who already has wisdom. The friends explained it and we learned. In the same manner Betzalel, WHO WAS WISE, THE HOLY ONE, BLESSED BE HE GAVE HIM WISDOM. Rabbi Shimon said: Betzalel, his name caused this to him, and was called by that name for his wisdom. And the secret of the word 'Betzalel' is "in the shadow of El."

57. פָּתַח וְאָמַר, כְּתַפּוּחַ בַּעֲצֵי הַיַּעַר כֵּן דּוֹדִי וְגוֹ'. בְּצִלּוֹ: הַיְינוּ בְּצַלְאֵל, דְּאִיהוּ אַתְקִין מַשְׁכְּנָא, וְעָבֵד לֵיהּ. דִּכְתִּיב חִמַּדְתִּי וְיָשַׁבְתִּי. דְּמַשְׁכְּנָא חֲמִידָא אִיהוּ לְמֵיתַב בֵּיהּ, דְּאִיהוּ עָבֵיד חֲמוּדָא לִכְנֶסֶת יִשְׂרָאֵל, וּכְנֶסֶת יִשְׂרָאֵל יָתְבָא בְּצִלָּא דְּאֵל. וְדָא אִיהוּ בְּצַלְאֵל.

57. He opened the discussion and said: "Like the apple tree among the trees of the wood, so is my beloved among the sons… I sat down under His shadow with great delight, and his fruit was sweet to my taste" (Shir Hashirim 2:3). "Under his shadow (Heb. *tzel*)" refers to Betzalel, who prepared the Tabernacle and constructed it, as it is written, "I sat down…with delight." For it is delightful to sit in the Tabernacle, and it delights the Congregation of Yisrael. And the Congregation of Yisrael sits under the shadow of El. This is the meaning of Betzalel.

58. וּפִרְיוֹ מָתוֹק לְחִכִּי, דְּדָא אִיהוּ דְּעָבֵיד פֵּירִין טָבִין בְּעָלְמָא, דִּכְתִּיב מִמֶּנִּי פֶּרְיְךָ נִמְצָא. מַאן הוּא פְּרִי. אִלֵּין אִינּוּן נִשְׁמָתְהוֹן דְּצַדִּיקַיָּיא,

דְּאִינּוּן אִיבָּא דְּעוֹבָדוֹי דְּקוּדְשָׁא בְּרִיךְ הוּא. דְּהַהוּא נָהָר דְּנָפִיק מֵעֵדֶן, אִיהוּ אַפִּיק וְזָרִיק נִשְׁמָתִין לְעָלְמָא, וְאִינּוּן פֵּרִין דְּקוּדְשָׁא בְּרִיךְ הוּא, וּבג״כ פִּרְיוֹ. דָּא אִיהוּ כִּדְקָאָמְרָן.

58. "And his fruit was sweet to my taste." ZEIR ANPIN produced good fruit to the world, as it is written, "from Me is your fruit found" (Hoshea 14:9). What is a fruit? It is the souls of the righteous that are the fruit of the deeds of the Holy One, blessed be He. For the river that went out of Eden, WHICH IS YESOD OF ZEIR ANPIN, pulls out and casts souls into the world, and they are the fruit of the Holy One, blessed be He. That is why IT IS WRITTEN, "His fruit was sweet to my taste," as we explained.

59. בְּצִלּוֹ: דָּא הוּא בְּצַלְאֵל. וְעַל דָּא תִּקּוּנָא דְּמַשְׁכְּנָא עַל יְדָא דִּבְצַלְאֵל הֲוָה. וּבג״כ וּבְצַלְאֵל בֶּן אוּרִי בֶּן חוּר. בֶּן אוּרִי, דָּא נְהוֹרָא דְּשִׁמְשָׁא דְּנָפִיק. בֶּן אוּרִי, דָּא יְמִינָא. בֶּן חוּר, דָּא אִיהוּ שְׂמָאלָא. בֶּן אוּרִי בֶּן חוּר, וְעַל דָּא אִשְׁתְּלִים בֵּיהּ דִּינָא דְּקוּדְשָׁא בְּרִיךְ הוּא בְּעוֹבָדָא דְּעֶגְלָא.

59. "In his shadow" refers to Betzalel. Therefore the Tabernacle was constructed by Betzalel. That is why IT IS WRITTEN, "Betzalel the son of Uri, the son of Chur" (Shemot 38:22). "The son of Uri" is of the light of the sun coming out. "The son of Uri" is the right: "The son of Chur" is of the left. Therefore, it was by him that the Judgment of the Holy One, blessed be He was completed during the golden calf. FOR HE WAS KILLED BY THE MIXED MULTITUDES.

60. כָּל הַזָּהָב הֶעָשׂוּי. מֵהַהִיא שַׁעֲתָא דְּיָהֲבוּ לֵיהּ יִשְׂרָאֵל, הֲוָה עָשׂוּי וְאִתְתָּקַן מִקַּדְמַת דְּנָא, בְּכֹל מְלֶאכֶת הַקֹּדֶשׁ, כָּל הַהוּא דַּהֲבָא, אִתְעֲבִיד וְאִתְתָּקַן בְּכֹל מְלֶאכֶת הַקֹּדֶשׁ. מַאי טַעֲמָא. בְּגִין דִּבְכָל דַּרְגָּא וְדַרְגָּא, הֲוָה אִתְתָּקַן בֵּיהּ דַּהֲבָא. דְּלֵית שְׁלִימוּ אֶלָּא רַחֲמֵי וְדִינָא, וְעַל דָּא דַּהֲבָא הֲוָה אָזִיל בְּכָל מְלֶאכֶת הַקֹּדֶשׁ, בְּכָל הַהִיא עֲבִידְתָּא דְּאִקְרֵי קֹדֶשׁ, הֲוָה אָזִיל בָּהּ דַּהֲבָא, דַּהֲבָא בְּכֹלָּא.

60. "All the gold that was applied" (Shemot 38:24). From the time Yisrael gave it, it was already prepared and worked ABOVE by the holy work. What is the reason? That on each grade gold was arranged, for there is no wholeness but by Judgment and Mercy. Therefore, the gold was present in all the work of the Tabernacle, NAMELY, IN ALL THE GRADES OF MALCHUT, and in each work that was holy, there was gold. And gold was in everything.

9. "When the wicked sprout like grass"

A Synopsis

Rabbi Aba, Rabbi Yosi and Rabbi Chizkiyah are studying the Torah together, and Rabbi Chizkiyah wonders why God is so patient in judging the wicked. He says that Rabbi Shimon told him this is because the judgment that God desires is a clear, loving and joyful judgment. He does not want the judgment of defilement; therefore he doesn't mix the two. He will refrain from judging the wicked until evil is lost from the World to Come. Then Rabbi Shimon talks about "When the wicked sprout like grass, and when all the workers of iniquity flourish; it is that they shall be destroyed forever," and explains that the wicked shall be severed from their roots. One more explanation of God's patience is that this world is part of the Other Side and it is opposed to the World to Come that is part of the side of holiness. One is destined for the wicked and the other for the righteous.

61. רִבִּי אַבָּא רִבִּי יוֹסֵי וְרִבִּי חִזְקִיָּה הֲווֹ יַתְבִין וְלָעָאן בְּאוֹרַיְיתָא, אָמַר לֵיהּ ר' חִזְקִיָּה לר' אַבָּא, הָא חֲמֵינָן דְּקוּדְשָׁא בְּרִיךְ הוּא אִתְרְעֵי בְּדִינָא בְּכֹלָּא, לְאִתְעָרְבָא דָּא בְּדָא, וְאִיהוּ אָרִיךְ דִּינָא בְּחַיָּיבֵי עָלְמָא, אִי אִיהוּ אִתְרְעֵי בְּדִינָא, אֲמַאי סָלִיק לֵיהּ מֵחַיָּיבַיָּא. אָמַר לֵיהּ, כַּמָּה טוּרִין אִתְעַקָּרוּ בְּמִלָּה דָּא, אֲבָל כַּמָּה מִלִּין גַּלֵּי בּוּצִינָא קַדִּישָׁא בְּהַאי.

61. Rabbi Aba and Rabbi Yosi and Rabbi Chizkiyah were sitting and studying the Torah. Rabbi Chizkiyah said to Rabbi Aba: Indeed we see that the Holy One, blessed be He desires to have Judgment upon everything, so the two will mix together, JUDGMENT AND MERCY. Nevertheless, He withholds Judgment from the wicked of the world. Why, if He is desirous of Judgment, remove it from the evil? NAMELY, WHY IS HE SO PATIENT? He said to him: How many mountains, WISE MEN, have been uprooted by this, NOT KNOWING THE TRUE MEANING THEREOF. But the holy luminary revealed several things concerning the matter.

62. וְת"ח, דִּינָא דְּקוּדְשָׁא בְּרִיךְ הוּא אִתְרְעֵי בֵּיהּ, אִיהוּ דִּינָא בָּרִיר, אִיהוּ דִּינָא דְּאִתְּעַר רְחִימוּ וְחֶדְוָה. אֲבָל חַיָּיבַיָּא כַּד אִינּוּן בְּעָלְמָא, כֻּלְּהוּ דִּינָא דְּזוּהֲמָא. כֻּלְּהוּ דִּינָא דְּלָא אִתְרְעֵי בֵּיהּ קוּדְשָׁא בְּרִיךְ הוּא

כְּלָל. וְע"ד, לָא בָּעֵי לְאִתְעָרְבָא דִּינָא קַדִּישָׁא בְּדִינָא מִסְאֲבָא דְּזוּהֲמָא, עַד דְּאִיהוּ אִשְׁתְּצֵי מִגַּרְמֵיהּ, וּלְאוֹבָדָא לֵיהּ מִן עָלְמָא דְּאָתֵי, וְהַהוּא דִּינָא דְזוּהֲמָא דְּבֵיהּ אִיהוּ אוֹבִיד לֵיהּ מֵעָלְמָא.

62. Come and see: The Judgment that the Holy One, blessed be He is desirous of, is a clear Judgment, that stirs love and joy, NAMELY, THE JUDGMENT OF THE LEFT COLUMN AFTER JOINING THE RIGHT COLUMN, TO BECOME THE SECRET OF THE WINE THAT MAKES GLAD ELOHIM AND MEN, AND IS ALSO THE SECRET OF GOLD. But the wicked, when in the world, are under Judgment of defilement, the Judgment which the Holy One, blessed be He does not want at all. Therefore, there must not be mixing of the holy Judgment with the defiled Judgment, until THE DEFILED JUDGMENT is exterminated of itself, and causes EVIL to be lost from the World to Come, for the defiled Judgment in it causes it to be destroyed.

63. פָּתַח וְאָמַר בִּפְרֹחַ רְשָׁעִים כְּמוֹ עֵשֶׂב וַיָּצִיצוּ כָּל פּוֹעֲלֵי אָוֶן לְהִשָּׁמְדָם עֲדֵי עַד, הַאי קְרָא אוּקְמוּהָ, אֲבָל ת"ח, בִּפְרֹחַ רְשָׁעִים כְּמוֹ עֵשֶׂב. כְּהַאי עִשְׂבָּא דְּאִיהוּ בִּיבִישׁוּ דְּאַרְעָא, וְאִיהוּ יְבֵישָׁא, כַּד שָׁרָאן בֵּיהּ מַיָּא אַפְרִיחַ, וְהַהוּא יְבִישׁוּ אִתְפְּרַח. וּכְהַאי אִילָנָא קְצִיצָא דְּנָצִיץ, וְלָא סָלִיק אֶלָּא אִינּוּן פֹּארוֹת, לִסְטַר דָּא וְלִסְטַר דָּא, דְּאִינּוּן עַנְפִין דְּסַלְּקִין, וּלְעָלְמִין לָא סָלִיק אִילָנָא, כַּד הֲוָה בְּקַדְמֵיתָא לְמֶהֱוֵי אִילָנָא. וְכָל דָּא, לְהִשָּׁמְדָם עֲדֵי עַד, לְאַעְקְרָא לוֹן מִשָּׁרְשִׁין וּמִכֹּלָּא.

63. He opened the discussion and said: "When the wicked sprout like grass, and when all the workers of iniquity flourish; it is that they shall be destroyed forever" (Tehilim 92:8). This verse was explained. Nevertheless, come and see: "the wicked sprout like grass" MEANS just as grass on dry land becomes dry. And when it is given water, it blooms and the dryness disappears. Like a cut tree, when it flourishes again, grows only side branches growing upwards, but never a whole tree, as was before, NAMELY "THE WORKERS OF INIQUITY FLOURISH." And all that happens so "they shall be destroyed forever," that is, they will be severed from their root and from everything else.

64. תּוּ רָזָא אַחֲרָא אִית בְּהַאי, עַד דְּקוּדְשָׁא בְּרִיךְ הוּא אָרִיךְ רוּגְזֵיהּ

בְּחַיָּיבַיָּא בְּהַאי עָלְמָא, בְּגִין דְּהַאי עָלְמָא, אִיהוּ חוּלָקָא דְּסִטְרָא אַחֲרָא. וְעָלְמָא דְּאָתֵי אִיהוּ סִטְרָא דִּקְדוּשָּׁה. וְאִיהוּ חוּלָקָא דְּצַדִּיקַיָּיא, לְמֶהֱוֵי צַדִּיקַיָּיא אִינּוּן בְּעִטְרָא דִּיקָרָא דְּמָארֵיהוֹן בֵּיהּ. וּתְרֵין סִטְרִין אִלֵּין, קַיְימִין דָּא לָקֳבֵל דָּא. דָּא סִטְרָא דִּקְדוּשָּׁה. וְדָא סִטְרָא אַחֲרָא דִּמְסָאֲבָא. דָּא קַיְימָא לְצַדִּיקַיָּיא, וְדָא קַיְימָא לְרַשִּׁיעַיָּיא, וְכֹלָּא דָּא לָקֳבֵל דָּא. זַכָּאִין אִינּוּן צַדִּיקַיָּיא, דְּלֵית לוֹן חוּלָקָא בְּהַאי עָלְמָא, אֶלָּא בְּעָלְמָא דְּאָתֵי.

64. There is yet another secret in this, why the Holy One, blessed be He is long-suffering with the wicked in this world. It is because this world is the portion of the Other Side, and the World to Come is part of the side of holiness, and the portion of the righteous, where they will be adorned by the crown of the glory of their Master. These two sides stand the one against the other, THE WORLD TO COME, the side of holiness and THIS WORLD, the Other Side of defilement. This is destined for the righteous and that for the wicked. And all this corresponds to all that. Happy are the righteous, who have no part in this world, but in the World to Come.

10. The 42 sacrifices of Balak

A Synopsis

When Balak made his sacrifice he intended to placate God because he had killed so many people. God did not accept this sacrifice, nor did the Other Side. Those who were to be punished were cursed in Hashem's name but until now they have not been punished, nor have the sacrifices been accepted by either side. The sacrifice offered was to propitiate the Other Side, but it has not done so, and nor has it met with God's blessing.

65. ת״ח כֹּלָּא אִתְתָּקַּן וְאִתְגְּלֵי קַמֵּי קוּדְשָׁא בְּרִיךְ הוּא. וְאע״ג דְּבָלָק וּבִלְעָם לָא אִתְכַּוְּונוּ לְגַבֵּי קוּדְשָׁא בְּרִיךְ הוּא, כֹּלָּא אִיהוּ מִתְתַּקַּן קַמֵּיהּ, וְלָא גָּרַע מֵאֲגַר דִּלְהוֹן כְּלוּם בְּהַאי עָלְמָא. בְּהַהוּא זִמְנָא שְׁלִיטוּ עַל יִשְׂרָאֵל, דְּגָרַם הַהוּא קוּרְבָּנָא, לְאִסְתַּלְּקָא מִיִּשְׂרָאֵל אַרְבָּעָה וְעֶשְׂרִין אַלְפִין, בַּר כָּל אִינּוּן דְּאִתְקְטָלוּ, דִּכְתִּיב הִרְגוּ אִישׁ אֲנָשָׁיו הַנִּצְמָדִים לְבַעַל פְּעוֹר, וּכְתִיב קַח אֶת כָּל רָאשֵׁי הָעָם וְהוֹקַע אוֹתָם לַיְיָ׳. וְעַד כְּעַן הַהוּא קָרְבָּנָא הֲוָה תָּלֵי לְאִתְפָּרְעָא מִנְּהוֹן דְּיִשְׂרָאֵל. שִׁבְעָה מַדְבְּחָן כְּחוּשְׁבָּן אַרְבְּעִין וּתְרֵין.

65. Come and see: All is predisposed and revealed before the Holy One, blessed be He. Though Balak and Bilaam did not mean to devote THEIR SACRIFICES for the Holy One, blessed be He, yet all is established before Him, and He does not reduce their reward at all in this world. At that time they had power over Yisrael, by their sacrifice which caused twenty-four thousand people from Yisrael to pass away, besides those who were killed, as it is written, "Slay every one of his men that have attached themselves to Ba'al Peor" (Bemidbar 25:5), and "Take all the chiefs of the people, and hang them up before Hashem" (Ibid. 4). And even now that sacrifice impends upon Yisrael to cause misfortune. They built seven altars, AND OFFERED SACRIFICES UPON THEM, 42 in all.

66. רִבִּי שִׁמְעוֹן אָמַר, תָּא חֲזֵי, אִינּוּן אַרְבְּעִין וּתְרֵין קָרְבָּנִין עָבְדוּ בִּלְעָם וּבָלָק, וְנַטְלוּ לוֹן מֵהַהוּא סִטְרָא אַחֲרָא לְגַבֵּי קוּדְשָׁא בְּרִיךְ הוּא, וְע״ד הֲוָה תָּלֵי הַהוּא קָרְבְּנָא, לְנַטְלָא לֵיהּ הַהוּא סִטְרָא אַחֲרָא דְּאִקְרֵי

קְלָלָה מִיִשְׂרָאֵל, וְעַד הַשְׁתָּא לָא גָּבָה מִנַּיְיהוּ. וְדָא אִיהוּ רָזָא וַיִּפֶן אַחֲרָיו וַיִּרְאֵם. וַיִּפֶן אַחֲרָיו, אֲחוֹרֵי שְׁכִינְתָּא, דְּקַיְּימָא סִטְרָא אַחֲרָא לַאֲחוֹרָא. וַיִּרְאֵם. אִסְתָּכַּל בְּהוּ הַהוּא סִטְרָא אַחֲרָא, וְחָמָא לוֹן דְּאִתְחָזוּן לְאִתְעַנְשָׁא, וְעַל דָּא וַיְקַלְלֵם בְּשֵׁם יְיָ׳. בְּשֵׁם יְיָ׳ לְאַפָּקָא הַהוּא שֵׁם יְיָ׳ מֵחִיּוּבָא דָּא. מֵהַהוּא חִיּוּבָא דְּהַהוּא קָרְבָּן דְּאַקְרִיב הַהוּא סִטְרָא לְגַבֵּיהּ. וְכֹלָּא אִיהוּ מִתְתַּקַּן קַמֵּיהּ דְּקוּדְשָׁא בְּרִיךְ הוּא, וְלָא אִתְאֲבִיד מִלָּה. כְּגַוְונָא דָּא, כֹּלָּא אִתְתָּקַּן קַמֵּיהּ דְּקוּדְשָׁא בְּרִיךְ הוּא, הֵן לְטָב הֵן לְבִישׁ.

66. Rabbi Shimon said, Come and see: Balak and Bilaam offered 42 sacrifices, and took them from the Other Side to the Holy One, blessed be He. Therefore, that sacrifice is impending until it is taken by the Other Side called 'curse from Yisrael'. Until now, he has not taken it from them. And this is the secret of, "And he turned back, and looked at them" (II Melachim 2:23), AT THE BOYS WHO JEERED AT HIM AND SAID TO HIM "GO UP, BALD HEAD." "And he turned back," NAMELY, to the back of the Shechinah, because the Other Side stands at the back. "And looked at them," he looked and saw IN THOSE 42 BOYS, the Other Side CALLED 'CURSE', and saw that they deserved to be punished. Therefore, "he cursed them in the Name of Hashem" (Ibid. 24), in order to remove the Name of Hashem from the debt, NAMELY the debt of the sacrifice, that the Other Side offered him, NAMELY, BY BALAK AND BILAAM. And all was made right before the Holy One, blessed be He, and nothing is lost before the Holy One, blessed be He. In the same manner, everything stands before the Holy One, blessed be He, both good and evil.

11. "All the gold that was applied for the work"

A Synopsis

Rabbi Shimon says that David sinned greatly when he ran from Saul, causing so many thousands to be killed including all the priests except Evyatar; this sin still goes unpunished. He tells us that the title verse means that God took the gold the people gave for the Tabernacle as expiation for their sin of creating the golden calf. Finally, he explains that Moses and Betzalel combined above and below, Tiferet with Yesod, while Betzalel and Aholiav combined right and left, Chesed and Gvurah, so that the Tabernacle was the union of upper and lower, left and right.

67. ת"ח, דָּוִד אִיהוּ הֲוָה דְּעָרַק קָמֵיהּ דְּשָׁאוּל. וְעַל דָּא גָּרִים, דְּאִתְאֲבִידוּ כָּל אִינּוּן כַּהֲנֵי דְּנוֹב, וְלָא אִשְׁתְּאַר מִכֻּלְּהוּ בַּר אֶבְיָתָר בִּלְחוֹדוֹי דְּעָרַק. וְדָא גָּרִים כַּמָּה בִּישִׁין בְּיִשְׂרָאֵל, וּמִית שָׁאוּל וּבְנוֹי, וְנָפְלוּ מִיִּשְׂרָאֵל כַּמָּה אַלְפִין וְרִבְבָן. וְעכ"ד, הַהוּא חוֹבָה הֲוָה תָּלֵי עַל דָּוִד לִגְבוֹת מִנֵּיהּ, עַד דְּכָל בְּנוֹי דְּדָוִד אִתְאֲבִידוּ בְּיוֹמָא חַד, וְלָא אִשְׁתְּאַר מִנַּיְיהוּ אֶלָּא יוֹאָשׁ בִּלְחוֹדוֹי, דְּאִתְגְּנִיב. כְּגַוְונָא דְּלָא אִשְׁתְּאַר מֵאֲחִימֶלֶךְ בַּר אֶבְיָתָר בִּלְחוֹדוֹי. וְעַד כְּעַן הַהוּא חוֹבָא הֲוָה תָּלֵי, לְמֶעְבַּד דִּינָא עַל נוֹב, עַל הַהוּא חוֹבָה דְּנוֹב, דִּכְתִּיב עוֹד הַיּוֹם בְּנוֹב לַעֲמוֹד וְאוּקְמוּהָ.

67. Come and see: When David ran from Saul, he caused all the priests in Nob to perish, all but Evyatar, who escaped. And he caused much misfortune to Yisrael, in that Saul and his sons died, and thousands and tens of thousands from Yisrael fell. But notwithstanding, that sin was hanging over David to cause him misfortune until the day all his sons perished in one day, and no one was left save Yoash, who was stolen BY YEHOSHEVA DAUGHTER OF YORAM. In the same manner, no one was left from Achimelech save Evyatar alone. Until this day that sin impends, to punish Nob for the sin of Nob, as it is written, "This very day he will halt at Nob" (Yeshayah 10:32). And this was already explained.

68. כְּגַוְונָא דָּא, כָּל הַזָּהָב הֶעָשׂוּי לַמְּלָאכָה. מַאי הֶעָשׂוּי. הָכָא אִסְתָּכַּל קוּדְשָׁא בְּרִיךְ הוּא, כַּד יָהֲבוּ יִשְׂרָאֵל דַּהֲבָא לְעֶגְלָא, וְקוּדְשָׁא בְּרִיךְ הוּא

אַקְדִּים לוֹן דַּהֲבָא דָּא לְאַסְוָותָא, דְּהַאי דַּהֲבָא דְּמַשְׁכְּנָא אַקְדִּים לוֹן, לְהַהוּא דַּהֲבָא דְּיָהֲבוּ לְעֶגְלָא, דְּכָל דַּהֲבָא דַּהֲוָה עִמְּהוֹן, וְאִשְׁתְּכַח עִמְּהוֹן, יָהֲבוּ לְאָרָמַת מַשְׁכְּנָא. ס״ד, דְּכַד עָבְדוּ יַת עֶגְלָא אִשְׁתְּכַח עִמְּהוֹן דַּהֲבָא, וְאִינּוּן פְּרִיקוּ אוּדְנַיְיהוּ לְנַטְלָא הַהוּא דַּהֲבָא, דִּכְתִּיב וַיִּתְפָּרְקוּ כָּל הָעָם אֶת נִזְמֵי הַזָּהָב אֲשֶׁר בְּאָזְנֵיהֶם. וְע״ד אַקְדִּים דַּהֲבָא דְּאָרָמוּתָא. לְכַפְּרָא עַל עוֹבָדָא דָּא.

68. Likewise, "All the gold that was applied for the work" (Shemot 38:24). What is the meaning of 'applied'? It means that here the Holy One, blessed be He saw Yisrael giving gold for the calf, and He applied the gold as a remedy beforehand, by putting the gold for the Tabernacle before the gold for the calf. For all the gold they had with them, and about them, they donated to the Tabernacle. FOR could you possibly imagine, that they had gold when they made the calf, and that they would take the gold off their ears, as it is written, "And all the people broke off the golden earrings which were in their ears" (Shemot 32:3)? He therefore took first the gold of the donation to expiate for the making OF THE CALF.

69. וּבְצַלְאֵל בֶּן אוּרִי בֶּן חוּר לְמַטֵּה יְהוּדָה, מִסִּטְרָא דְּמַלְכוּתָא עָשָׂה אֶת כָּל אֲשֶׁר צִוָּה יְיָ׳ אֶת מֹשֶׁה. דְּהָא כָּל אוּמָנוּתָא דְּמַשְׁכְּנָא אִתְתַּקְּנַת בְּהוּ, וְעַל יְדַיְיהוּ. בְּצַלְאֵל אִיהוּ עָבֵיד אוּמָנוּתָא, וּמֹשֶׁה אִיהוּ אַתְקִין כֹּלָּא לְבָתַר. מֹשֶׁה וּבְצַלְאֵל כַּחֲדָא הֲווֹ, מֹשֶׁה לְעֵילָּא, בְּצַלְאֵל תְּחוֹתֵיהּ, סִיּוּמָא דְּגוּפָא כְּגוּפָא. בְּצַלְאֵל וְאָהֳלִיאָב, הָא אוּקְמוּהָ, דָּא יְמִינָא, וְדָא שְׂמָאלָא, וְכֹלָּא חַד. וּבג״כ, וּבְצַלְאֵל בֶּן אוּרִי בֶּן חוּר לְמַטֵּה יְהוּדָה וְגוֹ׳, וְאִתּוֹ אָהֳלִיאָב בֶּן אֲחִיסָמָךְ לְמַטֵּה דָן וְגוֹ׳.

69. "And Betzalel the son of Uri, the son of Chur, of the tribe of Judah" (Shemot 38:22) of the aspect of Malchut, "made all that Hashem commanded Moses" (Ibid.). For all the craftsmanship of the Tabernacle was prepared through them, by their hands. Betzalel performed the work and Moses after him made all ready. Moses and Betzalel were as one, Moses above, IN TIFERET, and Betzalel below, IN YESOD, the end of the body being also a part thereof, FOR YESOD AND TIFERET ARE ONE. Betzalel and Aholiav, it has been established, that the one is of the right, CHESED, and the other is of the left, JUDGMENT, and all is one, FOR ONE INCLUDES THE OTHER. That is why it is written, "and Betzalel the son of Uri, the son of Chur, of the tribe of Judah…and with him was Aholiav, son of Achisamach, of the tribe of Dan…"

12. "And he turned back, and looked at them"

A Synopsis

Rabbi Yosi begins by telling how Elisha went out of the city and was followed by some small boys who mocked him. He says 'small' means that they had no faith and that they were guilty according to the laws of this world and the next. "And he turned back, and looked at them" means Elisha looked to see if they would repent, and he knew that they had been conceived on the night of Yom Kippur, so he "cursed them in the Name of Hashem." Rabbi Yosi adds that he saw the boys were destined to cause a great deal of evil in Yisrael. He compares the title verse to "but his wife looked back from behind him," saying it means 'behind' the Shechinah. Next he quotes: "And there came forth two bears out of the wood," meaning that there were female bears with male cubs. Lastly, he says that when the bears "tore 42 of the children" this counteracted the sacrifices of Balak.

70. כָּל הַזָּהָב הֶעָשׂוּי לַמְּלָאכָה בְּכֹל מְלֶאכֶת הַקֹּדֶשׁ וְגוֹ׳. ר׳ יוֹסֵי פָּתַח קְרָא בֶּאֱלִישָׁע, דִּכְתִּיב וַיַּעַל מִשָּׁם בֵּית אֵל וְהוּא עוֹלֶה בַּדֶּרֶךְ וְגוֹמֵר. וּנְעָרִים קְטַנִּים. הָא אוּקְמוּהָ, מְנוּעָרִים הֲווֹ מִכָּל מִלֵּי אוֹרַיְיתָא וּמִכָּל פִּקּוּדֵי אוֹרַיְיתָא. קְטַנִּים זְעִירֵי מְהֵימְנוּתָא, וְאִתְחַיְּיבוּ בְּחִיּוּבָא דְּהַאי עָלְמָא, וּבְחִיּוּבָא דְּעָלְמָא דְּאָתֵי. יָצְאוּ מִן הָעִיר, נַפְקוּ מֵרָזָא דִּמְהֵימְנוּתָא. כְּתִיב הָכָא יָצְאוּ מִן הָעִיר, וּכְתִיב הָתָם וְלֹא אָבֹא בְּעִיר.

70. "And all the gold that was applied for the work, in all the work of the holy place" (Shemot 38:24). Rabbi Yosi opened the discussion with the story of Elisha. It is written, "And he went up from there to Bethel and as he was going up by the way, some small boys" (II Melachim 2:23). It has been said that they were small (Heb. *ne'arim*), empty (Heb. *niurim*) of words of Torah or its precepts, "small," as they were of little faith, and they were guilty according to the law of this world and of the World to Come. They "came out of the city" (Ibid.), leaving the secret of the Faith, WHICH IS MALCHUT THAT IS CALLED 'CITY'. It is written here, "came out of the city," and there "and I will not enter the city" (Hoshea 11:9); IN BOTH CASES IT MEANS MALCHUT.

71. וַיִּפֶן אַחֲרָיו וַיִּרְאֵם, וַיִּפֶן אַחֲרָיו, דְּאִסְתַּכַּל לַאֲחוֹרָא, אִי יְהַדְרוּן

בְּתִיוּבְתָּא, וְאִם לָאו. וַיִּרְאֵם, מַאי וַיִּרְאֵם. אִסְתָּכַּל בְּהוּ, דְּהָא לֵית זַרְעָא מִתַּתְקְנָא זַמִּין לְנָפְקָא מִנַּיְיהוּ, וְאוּקְמוּהָ. וַיִּרְאֵם, הָא אוּקְמוּהָ, דְּאִתְעֲבִידוּ בְּלֵילְיָא דְּכִפּוּרֵי. מִיַּד וַיְקַלְלֵם בְּשֵׁם יְיָ'.

71. "And he turned back, and looked at them" (II Melachim 2:24): "turned back" MEANS he looked back, to see whether they would repent or not. "And looked at them" means he saw that it is not worthy that a good seed issue from them, and this was explained. "And looked at them" that they were conceived on the night of Yom Kippur (Day of Atonement), THAT THEIR MOTHER CONCEIVED THEN. Immediately, he "cursed them in the Name of Hashem" (Ibid.).

72. וְרָזָא אִיהוּ בְּהַאי קְרָא, וַיִּפֶן אַחֲרָיו, אִסְתָּכַּל בְּהוּ, אִי יִתְעֲנֵשׁ עֲלַיְיהוּ, וְאִתְפְּנֵי מֵהַאי. כד"א, וַיִּפֶן אַהֲרֹן, דְּאִתְפְּנֵי מִצָּרַעְתֵּיהּ. אוּף הָכָא אִתְפְּנֵי מֵעוֹנְשָׁא דִּלְהוֹן. וַיִּרְאֵם, דַּהֲווֹ קַיְימִין לְבָתַר לְמֶעְבַּד כַּמָּה בִּישִׁין בְּיִשְׂרָאֵל.

72. And there is a mystery in this verse: "And he turned back" MEANING THAT he looked at them whether he would be punished for them, and turned away from it. Also "Aaron turned" (Bemidbar 12:10) from leprosy. Here also "TURNED" MEANS he turned from their punishment. "And he looked at them," MEANING THAT HE SAW that they are destined to cause much evil in Yisrael.

73. וַיִּפֶן אַחֲרָיו, כד"א וַתַּבֵּט אִשְׁתּוֹ מֵאַחֲרָיו. מַאי מֵאַחֲרָיו. מֵאֲחוֹרֵי שְׁכִינְתָּא. אוּף הָכָא וַיִּפֶן אַחֲרָיו, אִסְתָּכַּל מֵאֲחוֹרֵי שְׁכִינְתָּא. וְחָמָא לְכֻלְּהוּ, דְּהָא בְּהַהוּא לֵילְיָא דְּשַׁלְטָא עַל כַּפָּרָה דְּחוֹבֵיהוֹן דְּיִשְׂרָאֵל, אִתְעֲבָּרוּ אִמְּהוֹן מִנַּיְיהוּ, מִיַּד וַיְקַלְלֵם בְּשֵׁם יְיָ'. וַתֵּצֶאנָה שְׁתַּיִם דוּבִּים מִן הַיַּעַר. שְׁתַּיִם דוּבִּים, שְׁנַיִם דוּבִּים מִבָּעֵי לֵיהּ, מַאי שְׁתַּיִם דוּבִּים. נוּקְבִין הֲווֹ, וּבְנַיְיהוּ. וַתְּבַקַּעְנָה מֵהֶם אַרְבָּעִים וּשְׁנַיִם יְלָדִים, הָא אוּקְמוּהָ לָקֳבֵל קָרְבָּנִין דְּבָלָק.

73. "And he turned back" is similar to "but his wife looked back from behind him" (Beresheet 19:26). What does "behind him" mean? It means behind the Shechinah. Here also "he turned back," behind the Shechinah and saw that their mothers all conceived at the night in charge of the atonement of the sins of Yisrael, NAMELY, AT THE NIGHT OF YOM KIPPUR. Immediately "he cursed them in the Name of Hashem." IT IS WRITTEN, "and there came forth two bears out of the wood" (II Melachim 2:24). HE ASKS: Why is it written "two (fem.) bears (masc.)"? Because they were female bears and their cubs WERE WITH THEM, AND THEREFORE, IT SAYS 'BEARS' (MASC.). "And tore 42 of the children." This was established, to counteract the sacrifices of Balak.

13. Gold from below upwards and silver from above downwards

A Synopsis

We learn that in, "Even the gold of the wave offering," 'wave' always means lifting upward, not drawing downward, and that this term applies to gold and brass but not silver. Silver is Chassidim and it can be drawn downward, but whenever gold descends its beauty and light are dimmed. Gold needs to be raised but silver needs to be spread downward, as in "And the silver of them that were numbered of the congregation." Rabbi Shimon turns to: "For Hashem Elohim is a sun and shield...," saying that the sun is the secret of Yud Hei Vav Hei and the shield is the secret of the Holy Name Elohim. Together 'a sun and shield' are the union of Zeir Anpin and Malchut. A similar meaning is deduced from "Hashem will give grace and honor." We are told that God conceals the primordial light from the wicked but never withholds it from those 'who walk upright.' Therefore the first light does not move upward; it spreads downward and is revealed to them. Rabbi Shimon says when the priest spreads his hands in blessing the Shechinah comes to him and fills his hands. Then the priest raises his right hand above his left and everything is blessed by the source of all, the World to Come. The candles are lit and all blessings are drawn from above.

74. וַיְהִי זְהַב הַתְּנוּפָה, אֲמַאי אִקְרֵי זְהַב הַתְּנוּפָה, וְלָא אִקְרֵי הָכִי כֶּסֶף הַתְּנוּפָה. אֶלָּא, תְּרֵין אִינּוּן דְּאִקְרוּן הָכִי. זְהַב הַתְּנוּפָה, וּנְחֹשֶׁת הַתְּנוּפָה. וְלָא אִקְרֵי הָכִי כֶּסֶף הַתְּנוּפָה, אֶלָּא אִלֵּין אִקְרוּן הָכִי, בְּגִין דְּאִיהוּ אִסְתַּלְקוּתָא לְעֵילָּא, דְּהָא אִית הָכִי לְתַתָּא. וְלָאו אִיהוּ זָהָב דְּאָרָמוּתָא. וּבְכָל אֲתָר תְּנוּפָה אִיהוּ אֲרָמוּתָא לְעֵילָּא וְלָא לְנַחְתָּא לְתַתָּא.

74. "Even the gold of the wave offering" (Shemot 38:24). HE ASKS why the term 'the gold of the wave offering' does not apply to silver? AND ANSWERS: Two are called thus, 'wave gold' and 'wave brass' but not 'wave silver'. Only these are so called, GOLD AND BRASS, for the term alludes to going upward. For what is down below, AMONG THE KLIPOT, is not wave gold, BECAUSE THE OTHER SIDE DRAWS CHOCHMAH OF THE LEFT FROM ABOVE DOWNWARD, AND IT IS NOT WAVED LIKE HOLINESS. Always wave MEANS lifting upward and not bringing downward. BUT

SILVER IS CHASSADIM AND IT IS PERMITTED TO DRAW IT DOWNWARD, THEREFORE, IT IS NOT WRITTEN 'WAVE SILVER.'

75. וְאִיהוּ רָזָא דְּחוּשְׁבְּנָא דָּא, דְּכָל אִלֵּין דַּרְגִּין וּרְתִיכִין כֻּלְּהוּ, קַיְימֵי בְּאָרָמוּתָא, וְאִיהוּ דְּהַב אֲרָמוּתָא, וְדָא אִיהוּ דַּהֲבָא. דְּכָל מַה דְּמִתְפַּשְּׁטָא לְתַתָּא, אַסְתִּים חֵיזוּ וְטִיבוּ וּנְהִירוּ דִּילֵיהּ, וְכַד אִיהוּ בְּאָרָמוּתָא, כְּדֵין אִיהוּ דְּהַב טָב בְּרָזָא דִּנְהִירוּ דִּילֵיהּ. וְכָל הַהוּא דִּלְתַתָּא, סוּסְפִיתָא דְּדַהֲבָא, וְאִיהוּ הִתּוּכָא דִּילֵיהּ.

75. This is the mystery of the reckoning, NAMELY, THE ILLUMINATION OF CHOCHMAH CALLED 'RECKONING': All the grades and Chariots are waving, THAT IS, ILLUMINATING FROM BELOW UPWARD. This is 'wave gold'. This gold IS THE ILLUMINATION OF CHOCHMAH – whenever it descends, its beauty and light are dimmed. But when the gold is waved, FROM BELOW UPWARD, it becomes good gold, in the mystery of its light. And all the gold, which is drawn down, is dross and refuse, NAMELY, A KLIPAH AND THE OTHER SIDE.

76. וְכֶסֶף פְּקוּדֵי הָעֵדָה, בְּגִין דְּהַאי, אִיהוּ כָּל מַה דְּאִתְפָּשַׁט לְתַתָּא הָכִי הוּא טָב, וְאַף ע״ג דְּלָאו אִיהוּ בְּהַאי אֲרָמוּתָא, כֹּלָּא הוּא לְטָב. אֲבָל דַּהֲבָא, כָּל מַה דְּאִתְפָּשַׁט לְתַתָּא, כֹּלָּא הוּא לְבִישׁ. דָּא, אִתְפָּשַׁט לְטָב. וְדָא אִתְפָּשַׁט לְבִישׁ. וּבְגִין כַּךְ, דָּא אִצְטְרִיךְ לְאָרָמָא אֲרָמוּתָא, וּלְאִסְתַּלְּקָא לְעֵילָּא. וְדָא, אִצְטְרִיךְ לְאִתְפָּשְׁטָא לְתַתָּא, וּלְכָל סִטְרִין, בְּגִין דְּכֻלְּהוּ קָאִים לְטָב.

76. "And the silver of them that were numbered of the congregation" (Ibid.). IT IS NOT WRITTEN 'WAVE SILVER' since SILVER, WHICH IS THE LIGHT OF CHASSADIM OF THE RIGHT COLUMN, in its descent, is also good. And though it is not waved FROM BELOW UPWARD, nevertheless it is good. But gold, THE ILLUMINATION OF CHOCHMAH OF THE LEFT COLUMN, whatever of it that descends, is worsened. For that reason, THE GOLD needs to be waved, and raised, and SILVER needs spreading downward in all directions, because it is all for the good.

77. פָּתַח וְאָמַר כִּי שֶׁמֶשׁ וּמָגֵן יְיָ׳ וְגוֹ׳. כִּי שֶׁמֶשׁ, דָּא קוּדְשָׁא בְּרִיךְ הוּא.

וּמָגֵן, דָּא קוּדְשָׁא ב״ה. שֶׁמֶשׁ: דָּא הוּא רָזָא דִּשְׁמָא קַדִּישָׁא יְדֹוָ״ד, דְּהָכָא קַיְימִין כָּל דַּרְגִּין לְנַיְיחָא. וּמָגֵן; דָּא אִיהוּ רָזָא דִּשְׁמָא קַדִּישָׁא דְּאִקְרֵי אֱלֹהִים. וְרָזָא דָּא דִּכְתִּיב, אָנֹכִי מָגֵן לָךְ. וְשֶׁמֶשׁ וּמָגֵן דָּא אִיהוּ רָזָא דִּשְׁמָא שְׁלִים. חֵן וְכָבוֹד יִתֵּן יְיָ׳, לְמֶהֱוֵי כֹּלָּא רָזָא חֲדָא.

77. He opened the discussion and said: "For Hashem Elohim is a sun and shield..." (Tehilim 84:12). The sun is the Holy One, blessed be He, and the shield is the Holy One, blessed be He. HE EXPLAINS: The sun is the secret of the Holy Name Yud Hei Vav Hei, ZEIR ANPIN, where all the grades stand at ease. And the shield is the secret of the holy name Elohim, MALCHUT. This is the secret meaning of the verse, "I am your shield" (Beresheet 15:1), AS 'I' WHICH IS MALCHUT CALLED 'I', IS YOUR SHIELD. "A sun and a shield" are the secret of a whole name, WHICH INDICATES THAT ZEIR ANPIN AND MALCHUT ARE UNITED. "Hashem will give grace and honor" (Tehilim 84:12), FOR ELOHIM WILL BE A SHIELD AND YUD HEI VAV HEI WILL GIVE GRACE AND HONOR, and so all will become one secret. NAMELY, THOUGH GRACE AND HONOR ARE DRAWN AT EASE, AND A SHIELD IS DRAWN VIGOROUSLY BY WHOEVER IS BESET BY ENEMIES, AND THEY MERGE INTO ONE PRINCIPLE, THE JOINING OF YUD HEI VAV HEI AND ELOHIM.

78. לֹא יִמְנַע טוֹב לַהוֹלְכִים בְּתָמִים, רָזָא דָּא דִּכְתִּיב וְיִמָּנַע מֵרְשָׁעִים אוֹרָם. וְדָא אִיהוּ נְהוֹרָא קַדְמָאָה, דִּכְתִּיב בֵּיהּ וַיַּרְא אֱלֹהִים אֶת הָאוֹר כִּי טוֹב, דְּגָנִיז וְסָתִים לֵיהּ קוּדְשָׁא בְּרִיךְ הוּא, כְּמָה דְּאוּקְמוּהָ, וּמִן חַיָּיבַיָּא גָּנִיז לֵיהּ, וּמָנַע לֵיהּ בְּהַאי עָלְמָא, וּבְעָלְמָא דְּאָתֵי. אֲבָל לְצַדִּיקַיָּיא מַה כְּתִיב, לֹא יִמְנַע טוֹב לַהוֹלְכִים בְּתָמִים. דָּא אוֹר קַדְמָאָה דִּכְתִּיב בֵּיהּ וַיַּרְא אֱלֹהִים אֶת הָאוֹר כִּי טוֹב.

78. "He withholds no goodness from these who walk upright" (Ibid.). This is the secret of the verse, "And from the wicked their light is withheld" (Iyov 38:15). THEREFORE, IT IS SAID THAT FROM THOSE WHO WALK UPRIGHT NO GOOD THING WILL HE WITHHOLD, referring to the first light, WHICH IS CHESED, of which it is written, "And Elohim saw the light, that it was good" (Beresheet 1:4). And the Holy One, blessed be He hid and covered it, as explained, from the wicked He concealed and withheld it in this world and in the World to Come. But it is written of the righteous, "no good thing will He withhold from those who walk upright." This refers to the primordial light, as it is written, "And Elohim saw the light, that it was good."

79. וְע"ד, לָא אִצְטְרִיךְ דָּא לְאִסְתַּלְּקָא וּלְאַרְמָא לֵיהּ, אֶלָּא לְאִתְפַּשְּׁטָא וּלְאִתְגַּלָּאָה, וְלָא לְאִסְתַּלְּקָא כְּהַהוּא אַחֲרָא, דְּאִיהוּ שְׂמָאלָא, וְע"ד אִקְרֵי הַהוּא תְּנוּפָה, וְלָאו הַאי. וּבג"כ וְכֶסֶף פְּקוּדֵי הָעֵדָה מְאַת כִּכָּר וְגוֹ'.

79. Therefore, it, THE FIRST LIGHT, needs not go up FROM BELOW and be waved, but rather to spread and be revealed, unlike the other one of the left, GOLD, AS DISCUSSED. For that reason GOLD is called 'wave', and not 'SILVER', and that is why IT IS WRITTEN, "and the silver of...the congregation was a hundred talents" (Shemot 38:25) AND NOT 'THE WAVE SILVER.'

80. ת"ח, סִטְרָא דִּימִינָא, אִיהוּ תָּדִיר קַיְּימָא לְקַיְּימָא בְּכָל עָלְמָא, וּלְאַנְהָרָא וּלְבָרְכָא לֵיהּ. וּבג"כ, כַּהֲנָא דְּאִיהוּ מִסִּטְרָא דִּימִינָא, אִזְדְּמַן תָּדִיר לְבָרְכָא עַמָּא, דְּהָא מִסִּטְרָא דִּימִינָא, אַתְיָין כָּל בִּרְכָאן דְּעָלְמָא, וְכַהֲנָא נָטִיל בְּרֵישָׁא, וְעַל דָּא אִתְמַנָּא אִיהוּ לְבָרְכָא לְעֵילָּא וּלְתַתָּא.

80. Come and see: The right side stands in readiness always to sustain the world, to shine and bless it. Therefore the priest, who is of the right side, CHESED, is always in readiness to bless the people, for all the benedictions in the world come of the right side. And the priest is the first to take. That is why the priest is appointed to bless above and below, NAMELY, CHESED ABOVE AND THE PRIEST BELOW.

81. תָּא חֲזֵי, בְּשַׁעֲתָא דְּכַהֲנָא פָּרִישׂ יְדוֹי לְבָרְכָא עַמָּא, כְּדֵין שְׁכִינְתָּא אַתְיָא וְשַׁרְיָא עָלוֹהִי, וְאַמְלֵי יְדוֹי, יְדָא דִּימִינָא זַקְפָא לְעֵילָּא עַל יְדָא דִּשְׂמָאלָא, בְּגִין לְסַלְּקָא יְמִינָא, וּלְאִתְגַּבְּרָא עַל שְׂמָאלָא. וּכְדֵין כֻּלְּהוּ דַּרְגִּין דְּקָא פָּרִישׂ בְּהוּ יְדוֹי, כֻּלְּהוּ אִתְבָּרְכָאן מִמְּקוֹרָא דְּכֹלָּא. מְקוֹרָא דְּבֵירָא מַאן אִיהוּ. דָּא צַדִּיק. מְקוֹרָא דְּכֹלָּא, דָּא אִיהוּ עָלְמָא דְּאָתֵי,

דְּאִיהוּ מְקוֹרָא עִלָּאָה דְּכָל אַנְפִּין נְהִירִין מִתַּמָּן, דְּהָא אִיהוּ מַבּוּעָא וּמְקוֹרָא דְּכֹלָּא. וְכָל בּוּצִינִין וּנְהוֹרִין, מִתַּמָּן אִתְדְלִיקוּ.

81. Come and see: When the priest spreads his hands to bless the people, the Shechinah comes and dwells upon him and fills his hands. He raises his right hand above the left hand, in order to raise the right above the left. Then all the grades over which he spreads his hands, are blessed by the source of all. What is the source of the well? It is the Righteous, WHICH IS YESOD. The source of all is the World to Come, BINAH, whence all faces, ALL MOCHIN, illuminate. For it is the source and spring of all, whence all the candles and lights are lit.

82. כְּגַוְונָא דָּא, מְקוֹרָא וּמַבּוּעָא דְּבֵירָא, כָּל אִינּוּן בּוּצִינִין דִּלְתַתָּא, כֻּלְּהוּ אִתְנְהֲרִין וְאִתְמַלְיָין נְהוֹרִין מִנֵּיהּ. וְדָא קַיְימָא לָקֳבֵל דָּא. וּבג״כ, בְּשַׁעֲתָא דְּכַהֲנָא פָּרִישׂ יְדוֹי, וְשָׁארֵי לְבָרְכָא עַמָּא. כְּדֵין שָׁרָאן בִּרְכָאן עִלָּאִין, מִמְּקוֹרָא עִלָּאָה, לְאַדְלְקָא בּוּצִינִין, וְנָהֲרִין כָּל אַנְפִּין. וּכְנֶסֶת יִשְׂרָאֵל אִתְעַטְּרַת בְּעִטְרִין עִלָּאִין. וְכָל אִינּוּן בִּרְכָאן נַגְדִּין וְאִתְמַשְׁכָן מֵעֵילָּא לְתַתָּא.

82. In the same manner, WHAT WAS SAID OF BINAH, is also said of the source and spring of the well, YESOD: That all the lower candles, NAMELY, THE SFIROT OF MALCHUT, are illuminated and filled with its lights. And it, YESOD, faces that, BINAH. AS BINAH IS A SOURCE THAT GIVES AFFLUENCE TO EVERYTHING, SO YESOD IS A SOURCE GIVING TO MALCHUT. For that reason, when the priest spreads his hands and starts to bless the people, high blessings dwell from the supernal source, BINAH, and candles are lit and all the faces illuminate, and the Congregation of Yisrael, WHICH IS MALCHUT, is adorned with high crowns, and all blessings come down and are drawn from above downward.

14. Counting and Numbers

A Synopsis

Rabbi Shimon returns in his discussion to the building of the Tabernacle, in itself the union of Tiferet and the holy covenant. Since all of this building was done in the secret of the right, the evil eye has no power whenever the right side is present. The 'silver' in "and the silver of them that were numbered of the congregation" is not written as 'wave silver', so it poured from above downward. Rabbi Yitzchak asks, since there are no blessings in anything that has been counted, why were the things in the Tabernacle counted? Rabbi Shimon answers that whenever the purpose of the counting is to sanctify, there is holiness in it, just as the tithe is blessed. Blessings are withheld from the other counted things so that no blessings can come to the Other Side, nor will any reach the evil eyed. Rabbi Shimon explains the implications of the fact that the evil eye has no power over the seed of Joseph. Then five rabbis meet together on the road and begin talking. Rabbi Elazar says: "The eyes of Hashem are toward the righteous, and His ears are open to their cry," yet many righteous people cannot even get enough food. Rabbi Shimon says that in the world above the holy side knows and protects all of its own, and the Other Side knows and controls all of its own. The Other Side cannot rule over the righteous. Rabbi Elazar wants to know why then there was a plague in Yisrael after David counted the people. Rabbi Shimon answers that everyone failed to pay a ransom for his soul to God to avoid having the plague among them. He speaks then of the holiness that is subject to counting and the holiness that is not, concluding that the ransom is subject to numbering but the people of Yisrael are not. Rabbi Shimon proffers two meanings for "like the sand of the sea." The first means that the sands break the power of the waves to flood the world, so Yisrael is like that sand, preventing the other nations from ruling the world. The second meaning is that neither the sand nor Yisrael can be counted. He talks about a secret and hidden measurement and a reckoning in a hidden place that is the secret of Yisrael Saba and Tevunah. Rabbi Shimon draws a parallel between the talents and the shekels donated for the Tabernacle, kept in two separate accounts, and superior beings numbered by a supernal account with the rest being numbered by a different account.

83. תָּא חֲזֵי, מֹשֶׁה פָּקִיד, וּבְצַלְאֵל עָבֵיד, לְמֶהֱוֵי כֹּלָּא בְּרָזָא דְּגוּפָא,
וְסִיּוּמָא דְּגוּפָא דְּאִיהוּ אָת קַיָּימָא קַדִּישָׁא, לְאַסְגָּאָה רְחִימוּ וְקִשּׁוּרָא

דְיִחוּדָא בְּמַשְׁכְּנָא. וְכֹלָּא בְּרָזָא דִּימִינָא קָא אִתְעָבִיד. וְעַל דָּא, בְּכָל אֲתָר דְּסִטְרָא דִּימִינָא אִשְׁתְּכַח, עֵינָא בִּישָׁא לָא שַׁלְטָא בֵּיהּ. וּבג״כ, וְכֶסֶף פְּקוּדֵי הָעֵדָה. וּבְגִין דְּהַהוּא כֶּסֶף מִסִּטְרָא דִּימִינָא קָא אַתְיָא. וְעַל דָּא אִתְמְנָא כֹּלָּא בְּמִנְיָינָא.

83. Come and see: Moses ordered and Betzalel executed, so that all may be in the secret of the body: THE SECRET OF MOSES, WHO IS TIFERET, and the final part of the body, the holy covenant, WHICH IS BETZALEL, so as to increase the love and bond of the unison in the Tabernacle, WHICH IS MALCHUT. All was done in the secret of the right, and therefore, wherever the right side is present, the evil eye has no sway. That is why IT IS WRITTEN, "and the silver of them that were numbered of the congregation" (Shemot 38:25), FOR IT WAS NUMBERED AND COUNTED, IN THE SECRET OF THE ILLUMINATION OF CHOCHMAH, AND IT WAS NOT WRITTEN, 'WAVE SILVER,' because this silver comes of the right side, CHESED, and therefore everything was numbered. THIS IS THE MYSTERY OF COMPRISING THE LEFT COLUMN, AND THE REASON IT IS POURED FROM ABOVE DOWNWARD.

84. רִבִּי יִצְחָק שָׁאִיל לְר״ש, א״ל, הָא אוּקְמוּהָ דְּבִרְכְתָא לָא שַׁרְיָא בְּמִלָּה דְּקָאִים בְּמִדִּידוּ, וּבְמִלָּה דְּקָאִים בְּחוּשְׁבָּנָא, הָכָא בְּמַשְׁכְּנָא אֲמַאי הֲוָה כֹּלָּא בְּחוּשְׁבְּנָא. אָמַר לֵיהּ הָא אִתְּמַר, אֲבָל בְּכָל אֲתָר דְּסִטְרָא דִּקְדוּשָׁה שַׁרְיָא עָלֵיהּ, אִי הַהוּא חוּשְׁבָּנָא אַתְיָא מִסִּטְרָא דִּקְדוּשָׁה, בִּרְכָתָא שַׁרְיָא עָלֵיהּ תָּדִיר, וְלָא אִתְעֲדֵי מִנֵּיהּ. מְנָלָן. מִמַּעֲשֵׂר. בְּגִין דְּאַתְיָא חוּשְׁבָּנָא לְקֻדְשָׁא. בִּרְכָתָא אִשְׁתְּכַחַת בֵּיהּ. כָּל שֶׁכֵּן מַשְׁכְּנָא דְּאִיהוּ קֹדֶשׁ, וְאַתְיָא מִסִּטְרָא דְּקֹדֶשׁ.

84. Rabbi Yitzchak asked Rabbi Shimon: We established that blessing does not dwell on anything that was measured or counted. If so, in relation to the Tabernacle, why was everything counted? He said to him: Indeed we learned this already. But any place, upon which there dwells the side of holiness, NAMELY, THAT IT IS DRAWN FROM THE CENTRAL COLUMN COMBINING RIGHT AND LEFT, if the counting is from the holy side, blessing will be upon it always, never to pass away. We know it from the tithe, because since the purpose of the counting is to sanctify, there is blessing in it. All the more so the Tabernacle, which is holy and pertains to the side of holiness.

85. אֲבָל כָּל שְׁאָר מִלֵּי דְּעָלְמָא, דְּלָא אַתְיָין מִסִּטְרָא דִּקְדוּשָּׁה, בִּרְכָתָא לָא שַׁרְיָא עֲלַיְיהוּ, כַּד אִינּוּן בְּחוּשְׁבְּנָא. בְּגִין דְּסִטְרָא אַחֲרָא, דְּאִיהוּ רַע עַיִן, יָכִיל לְשַׁלְטָאָה עָלֵיהּ. וְכֵיוָן דְּיָכִיל לְשַׁלְטָאָה עָלֵיהּ, בִּרְכָתָא לָא אִשְׁתְּכַחַת בֵּיהּ, בְּגִין דְּלָא יִמְטוּ בִּרְכָאן לְהַהוּא רַע עַיִן.

85. But the rest of worldly matters, not coming from the side of holiness, no blessing dwells upon them when counted. For the Other Side, which is evil eyed, can have power over it, and since it can have power over it, there is no blessing therein, in order that no blessings will reach that evil eyed.

86. וּמְדִידוּ דִּקְדוּשָּׁה, וְחוּשְׁבְּנָא דִּקְדוּשָּׁה, תָּדִיר בִּרְכָאן אִתּוֹסְפָאן בֵּיהּ. וְע"ד, וְכֶסֶף פְּקוּדֵי הָעֵדָה. פְּקוּדֵי הָעֵדָה בְּקוּשְׁטָא וַדַּאי, וְלָא דְּחִילוּ מֵעֵינָא בִּישָׁא, וְלָא דְּחִילוּ מִכָּל חוּשְׁבְּנָא דָּא, דְּהָא בְּכֹלָּא שָׁרְאן בִּרְכָאן מִלְּעֵילָּא.

86. Blessings are always added to measurement of holiness and counting of holiness, and therefore it is written, "And the silver of them that were numbered of the congregation," MEANING THAT IT WAS COUNTED by them that were numbered of the congregation in truth, and there should be no fear of the evil eye for that reckoning since blessings hover over all from above.

87. וְתָא חֲזֵי, בְּזַרְעָא דְּיוֹסֵף לָא שַׁלְטָא בֵּיהּ עֵינָא בִּישָׁא, בְּגִין דְּאָתֵי מִסִּטְרָא דִּימִינָא, וְעַל דָּא אִתְעֲבֵיד מַשְׁכְּנָא עַל יְדָא דִּבְצַלְאֵל, דְּהָא אִיהוּ בְּרָזָא דְּיוֹסֵף קָא שַׁרְיָא, דְּאִיהוּ רָזָא דִּבְרִית קַדִּישָׁא. וְע"ד, מֹשֶׁה פָּקִיד, וּבְצַלְאֵל עָבֵיד, לְמֶהֱוֵי כֹּלָּא בְּרָזָא דְּגוּפָא, וְסִיּוּמָא דְּגוּפָא, דְּאִיהוּ אָת קַיָּימָא קַדִּישָׁא, לְאַסְגָּאָה רְחִימוּ וְקִשּׁוּרָא דְּיִחוּדָא בְּמַשְׁכְּנָא, וְכֹלָּא בְּרָזָא דִּימִינָא קָא אִתְעֲבֵיד, וּבְגִין כַּךְ וְכֶסֶף פְּקוּדֵי הָעֵדָה, וְהַהוּא חוּשְׁבְּנָא, אִיהוּ חוּשְׁבַּן דְּדַרְגִּין רַבְרְבִין מִמָּנָן, דְּאִתְאַחֲדָן מִסִּטְרָא דִּימִינָא. וְעַל דָּא כְּתִיב מְאַת כִּכָּר וְגוֹ'.

87. Come and see: The evil eye has no power over the seed of Joseph, since it comes of the right side. Therefore the Tabernacle was constructed by Betzalel, who dwelt in the mystery of Joseph, being the secret of the Holy Covenant, NAMELY, HE WAS OF YESOD, AND YESOD IS CALLED 'JOSEPH'. Therefore Moses orders and Betzalel executes, so all may be in the secret of the body: MOSES, NAMELY TIFERET, and the final part of the body; BETZALEL, WHO IS YESOD, the sign of the Holy Covenant, so as to increase love and the bond of union in the Tabernacle, MALCHUT. And all was done according to the secret of the right, and that is why IT IS WRITTEN, "And the silver…numbered of the congregation," because that reckoning is the reckoning of the great grades in charge, NAMELY THE FIRST THREE SFIROT, combined on the right side. Therefore it is written, "a hundred talents…" (Ibid.) TO INDICATE THE TEN SFIROT, EACH INCLUDING TEN, TOGETHER WITH THE FIRST THREE.

88. רִבִּי אַבָּא, וְר' אֲחָא, וְרִבִּי יוֹסֵי, הֲווֹ אַזְלֵי מִטְּבֶרְיָה לְצִפּוֹרִי, עַד דַּהֲווֹ אָזְלֵי, חָמוּ לֵיהּ לְרִבִּי אֶלְעָזָר דַּהֲוָה אָתֵי, וְרִבִּי חִיָּיא עִמֵּיהּ. אָמַר רִבִּי אַבָּא, וַדַּאי נִשְׁתַּתֵּף בַּהֲדֵי שְׁכִינְתָּא. אוֹרִיכוּ לְהוּ, עַד דְּמָטוּ לְגַבַּיְיהוּ. כֵּיוָן דְּמָטוּ גַּבַּיְיהוּ, אָמַר רִבִּי אֶלְעָזָר, כְּתִיב עֵינֵי יְיָ' אֶל צַדִּיקִים וְאָזְנָיו אֶל שַׁוְעָתָם. הַאי קְרָא קַשְׁיָא, מַאי עֵינֵי יְיָ' אֶל צַדִּיקִים. אִי בְּגִין דְּאַשְׁגָּחוּתָא דְּקוּדְשָׁא בְּרִיךְ הוּא עֲלַיְיהוּ לְאוֹטָבָא לוֹן בְּהַאי עָלְמָא, הָא חֲמֵינָן, כַּמָּה זַכָּאִין אִינּוּן בְּהַאי עָלְמָא, וַאֲפִילוּ מְזוֹנָא כְּעוֹרְבֵי בָּרָא לוֹן יַכְלִין לְאַדְבְּקָא, אִי הָכִי מַאי עֵינֵי יְיָ' אֶל צַדִּיקִים.

88. Rabbi Aba and Rabbi Acha and Rabbi Yosi were walking from Tiberias to Tzipori. As they were walking, they saw Rabbi Elazar coming together with Rabbi Chiya. Rabbi Aba said: Surely we shall be joined with the Shechinah. They waited for them, and when they arrived, Rabbi Elazar said: It is written, "The eyes of Hashem are towards the righteous, and His ears are open to their cry" (Tehilim 34:16). This verse is hard to explain; what is the meaning of "The eyes of Hashem are towards the righteous"? If it means that the Holy One, blessed be He, takes care of them to help them in this world, yet we see so many righteous in this world, who cannot get as much food as the crows in the field. What is the meaning, then, of "The eyes of Hashem are towards the righteous"?

89. אֶלָּא רָזָא הָכָא, תָּא חֲזֵי, כָּל אִינּוּן בִּרְיָין דְעָלְמָא, כֻּלְּהוּ אִשְׁתְּמוֹדְעָאן לְעֵילָּא, בֵּין לְסִטְרָא דָא, וּבֵין לְסִטְרָא דָא. אִינּוּן דִּלְסִטְרָא דִּקְדוּשָׁה, אִשְׁתְּמוֹדְעָאן לְעֵילָּא לְגַבֵּיהּ, וְאַשְׁגָּחוּתָא דִּילֵיהּ תָּדִיר עֲלַיְיהוּ. וְאִינּוּן דִּלְסִטְרָא מִסְאֲבָא, אִשְׁתְּמוֹדְעָאן לְגַבֵּיהּ, וְאַשְׁגָּחוּתָא דִּילֵיהּ תָּדִיר עֲלַיְיהוּ. וּבַאֲתָר דְּשַׁלְטָא הַהִיא אַשְׁגָּחוּתָא דְּסִטְרָא דִּקְדוּשָׁה, לָא אַשְׁגַּח עָלֵיהּ סִטְרָא אַחֲרָא, וְלָא יִקְרַב לְגַבֵּיהּ לְעָלְמִין, וְלָא יָכִיל לְדַחְיָיא לֵיהּ מֵאַתְרֵיהּ, בְּכֹלָּא בְּכָל מַה דְּאִיהוּ עָבֵיד. וְעַל דָּא, עֵינֵי יְיָ׳ אֶל צַדִּיקִים וְגוֹ׳, בְּגִין דָּא סִטְרָא אַחֲרָא לָא יָכִיל לְשַׁלְטָאָה עָלֵיהּ. וְהַשְׁתָּא סַיַּיעְתָּא דִּשְׁמַיָּא הָכָא, וְכָל אַשְׁגָּחוּתָא טָבָא דִּלְעֵילָּא הָכָא, וְכָל סִטְרָא אַחֲרָא, וְכָל מִלָּה בִּישָׁא, לָא יָכִיל לְשַׁלְטָאָה עֲלַיְיכוּ.

89. HE ANSWERS: This is a secret. Come and see: All the creatures in the world are known above, either as of this side OF HOLINESS, or of that OTHER Side. Those who are known by the holy side, are always under its protection. And those that are known by the side of defilement, are always under its control. And where the holy side has sway, the Other Side has not, and may never approach, nor thrust him from his place or occupation by any means. About this IT IS WRITTEN, "The eyes of Hashem are towards the righteous," for which reason the Other Side cannot rule over them. And there is help from heaven and good providence from above. And the Other Side and all that is evil may not rule over you.

90. א״ר אַבָּא, הָא אוֹלִיפְנָא דִּבְכָל אֲתָר דְּסִטְרָא דִּקְדוּשָּׁה שַׁרְיָא עָלוֹי, אע״ג דְּקַיְימָא בְּחוּשְׁבְּנָא, בִּרְכָתָא לָא אִתְמְנַע מִתַּמָּן. א״ר אֶלְעָזָר, וַדַּאי הָכִי הוּא. א״ל, הָא יִשְׂרָאֵל אִינּוּן קֹדֶשׁ, וְאַתְיָין מִסִּטְרָא דְּקֹדֶשׁ, דִּכְתִּיב קֹדֶשׁ יִשְׂרָאֵל לַייָ׳, וּכְתִיב וִהְיִיתֶם קְדוֹשִׁים כִּי קָדוֹשׁ אָנִי, אֲמַאי כַּד עָבֵד דָּוִד חוּשְׁבְּנָא לְיִשְׂרָאֵל, הֲוָה בְּהוֹן מוֹתָנָא, דִּכְתִּיב וַיִּתֵּן יְיָ׳ דֶּבֶר בְּיִשְׂרָאֵל מִן הַבֹּקֶר וְעַד עֵת מוֹעֵד.

90. Rabbi Aba said: But we have learned, that wherever the holy side abides, though there is reckoning, still blessings are not withheld from that place. Rabbi Elazar said: Assuredly this is so. He said to him: Yisrael is holy, and come from the holy side, as it is written, "Yisrael is holy to Hashem" (Yirmeyah 2:3), and "You shall be holy, for I Hashem, your Elohim am holy" (Vayikra 19:2). Why then, when David counted Yisrael, was there death among them, as it is written, "So Hashem sent a pestilence upon Yisrael from the morning even to the time appointed" (II Shmuel 24:15)?

91. א"ל, בְּגִין דְּלָא נָטַל מִנַּיְיהוּ שְׁקָלִים, דְּאִיהוּ פּוּרְקָנָא. דִּכְתִּיב וְנָתְנוּ אִישׁ כֹּפֶר נַפְשׁוֹ לַיְיָ' בִּפְקוֹד אוֹתָם וְלֹא יִהְיֶה בָהֶם נֶגֶף בִּפְקֹד אוֹתָם. בְּגִין דְּאִצְטְרִיךְ קֹדֶשׁ, לְמֵיהַב פּוּרְקָנָא דְּקֹדֶשׁ, וְהַהִיא פּוּרְקָנָא דְּקֹדֶשׁ לָא אִתְנְטִיל מִנַּיְיהוּ. ת"ח, יִשְׂרָאֵל אִיהוּ קֹדֶשׁ, דְּקַיְימָא בְּלָא חוּשְׁבָּנָא, וְעַל דָּא אִצְטְרִיךְ פּוּרְקָנָא דְּיִתְנְטִיל מִנַּיְיהוּ, וְהַהוּא פּוּרְקָנָא קַיְימָא בְּחוּשְׁבָּנָא, וְאִינּוּן לָא קַיְימוּ בְּחוּשְׁבָּנָא.

91. He told him: It happened since David did not take shekels from them as ransom, as it is written, "then shall they give every man a ransom for his soul to Hashem when you number them that there be no plague among them when you number them" (Shemot 30:12). For holiness is in need of holy ransom, and that ransom of holiness was not taken from them. Come and see: Yisrael is holiness without numbering, and therefore a ransom should be taken from them. And that ransom is to be counted, while they are not.

92. מ"ט. בְּגִין דְּקֹדֶשׁ אִיהוּ רָזָא עִלָּאָה דְּכָל דַּרְגִּין, מַה הַהוּא קֹדֶשׁ אִיהוּ סָלִיק עַל כֹּלָּא, וְאִית לֵיהּ לְבַר קֹדֶשׁ אַחֲרָא לְתַתָּא דְּקַיְימָא תְּחוֹתֵיהּ, וְקָאֵים בְּחוּשְׁבָּנָא וּבְמִנְיָין. אוּף הָכִי יִשְׂרָאֵל אִינּוּן קֹדֶשׁ, דִּכְתִּיב קֹדֶשׁ יִשְׂרָאֵל לַיְיָ', וְאִינּוּן יַהֲבֵי קֹדֶשׁ אַחֲרָא, פּוּרְקָן דִּלְהוֹן, דְּקַיְימֵי בְּחוּשְׁבָּנָא, וְרָזָא דָּא, יִשְׂרָאֵל אִינּוּן אִילָנָא דְּקַיְימָא לְגוֹ, פּוּרְקָנָא אַחֲרָא קַיְימָא לְבַר, וְסָלִיק לְחוּשְׁבָּנָא, וְאָגִין דָּא עַל דָּא. אָזְלוּ.

92. What is the reason? Holiness is a secret, higher than all the grades, THE MYSTERY OF SUPERNAL ABA AND IMA. As this holiness is superior to all, and outside it there is another holiness beneath it, YISRAEL – SABA AND TEVUNAH COVERING SUPERNAL ABA AND IMA FROM OUTSIDE, subject to numbering and accounting, so is Yisrael holiness, as it is written, "Yisrael is holy to Hashem." And they give another holiness, their ransom, that is subject to numbering. This is a secret: Yisrael is a tree standing inside, OPPOSITE SUPERNAL ABA AND IMA, and the ransom given is another holiness standing outside and counted, CORRESPONDING TO YISRAEL–SABA AND TEVUNAH. The one is shielding the other. They went on.

93. פָּתַח רִבִּי אֶלְעָזָר וְאָמַר, וְהָיָה מִסְפַּר בְּנֵי יִשְׂרָאֵל כְּחוֹל הַיָּם אֲשֶׁר לֹא יִמַּד וְלֹא יִסָּפֵר וְגוֹ'. מַהוּ כְּחוֹל הַיָּם. תְּרֵין גַּוְונִין אִינּוּן הָכָא. חֲדָא כְּחוֹל הַיָּם, בְּגִין דְּיַמָּא כַּד סַלְּקִין גָּלוּי בְּזַעְפָּא וְרוּגְזָא, וְאִינּוּן גַּלִּין סַלְּקָאן לְשַׁטְּפָא עָלְמָא, כַּד מָטָאן וְחָמָאן חוֹלָא דְּיַמָּא, מִיַּד אִתְּבָּרוּ וְתָבִין לַאֲחוֹרָא, וְאִשְׁתְּכָכֵי, וְלָא יַכְלִין לְשַׁלְטָאָה וּלְשַׁטְּפָא עָלְמָא.

93. Rabbi Elazar opened the discussion and said: "And the number of the children of Yisrael shall be like the sand of the sea, which cannot be measured or numbered..." (Hoshea 2:1). HE ASKS: What is the meaning of "the sand of the sea"? AND HE ANSWERS: That there are two meanings. The first is that "the sand of the sea" MEANS when the sea raises its waves wrathfully and the waves rise to flood the world. When they reach and see the sand, they are broken immediately and return quietly, and have no power to have control over and flood the world.

94. כְּגַוְונָא דָּא, יִשְׂרָאֵל אִינּוּן חוֹלָא דְּיַמָּא, וְכַד שְׁאַר עַמִּין דְּאִינּוּן גַּלֵּי יַמָּא, מָארֵי דְּרוּגְזָא, מָארֵי דְּדִינִין קָשִׁין, בָּעָאן לְשַׁלְטָאָה וּלְשַׁטְּפָא עָלְמָא, חָמָאן לְהוּ לְיִשְׂרָאֵל דְּאִינּוּן מִתְקַשְּׁרָאן בְּקוּדְשָׁא בְּרִיךְ הוּא, וְתָבִין וְאִתְּבָּרוּ קַמַּיְיהוּ, וְלָא יַכְלִין לְשַׁלְטָאָה בְּעָלְמָא. גַּוְונָא אַחֲרָא, בְּגִין דְּחוֹלָא דְּיַמָּא לֵית לֵיהּ חוּשְׁבָּנָא, וְלָא קַיְימָא בְּחוּשְׁבָּנָא, וְלָא בִּמְדִידוּ, דִּכְתִּיב אֲשֶׁר לֹא יִמַּד וְלֹא יִסָּפֵר, אוּף הָכִי יִשְׂרָאֵל לֵית לְהוּ חוּשְׁבָּנָא, וְלָא קַיְימִין בְּחוּשְׁבָּנָא.

94. In the same manner Yisrael is like the sand of the sea. When the other nations, which are like the furious waves of the sea of severe Judgment, see Yisrael bound to the Holy One, blessed be He, they return BACK and are broken before them, and cannot rule the world. Another meaning is that like the sand of the sea, that cannot be numbered or measured, as it is written, “which cannot be measured or numbered” so is Yisrael, who is not numbered nor subject to reckoning.

95. תָּא חֲזֵי, אִית מְדִידוּ טָמִיר וְגָנִיז, וְאִית חוּשְׁבָּן דְּקַיְּימָא בִּגְנִיזוּ טָמִיר וְגָנִיז, וְהַאי קַיְּימָא בִּמְדִידוּ, וְהַאי קַיְּימָא בְּחוּשְׁבָּן. וְדָא אִיהוּ רָזָא וְקִיּוּמָא דְּכֹלָּא דִּלְעֵילָּא וְתַתָּא, בְּגִין דְּהַהוּא מְדִידוּ לָא אִתְיְידַע לְעָלְמִין, עַל מַה קַיְּימָא רָזָא דְּהַהוּא מְדִידוּ. וְעַל מַה קַיְּימָא רָזָא דְּהַהוּא חוּשְׁבָּנָא, וְדָא אִיהוּ רָזָא דִּמְהֵימְנוּתָא דְּכֹלָּא.

95. Come and see: There is a secret and hidden measurement, THE SECRET OF ABA AND IMA. And there is reckoning in a hidden place, concealed and stored, WHICH IS THE SECRET OF YISRAEL – SABA AND TEVUNAH. And it may be measured and numbered. This is the secret of sustenance above and below. For the measurement IN ABA AND IMA, NAMELY, THE AMOUNT OF CHASSADIM IN THEM, the secret of its execution is never known, AND ALSO WE MAY NOT KNOW the basis of the secret of the reckoning IN YISRAEL–SABA AND TEVUNAH. This is the secret of the Faith of all.

96. וְיִשְׂרָאֵל לְתַתָּא לָא קַיְימִין בְּחוּשְׁבָּנָא, אֶלָּא סִטְרָא דְּמִלָּה אַחֲרָא, וּפוּרְקָנָא אִיהוּ דְּקַיְּימָא בְּחוּשְׁבָּנָא. וּבְגִין כַּךְ יִשְׂרָאֵל כַּד עָאלִין בְּחוּשְׁבָּנָא נַטְלֵי מִנַּיְיהוּ פּוּרְקָנָא כְּמָה דְּאִתְּמַר. וְעַל דָּא בְּיוֹמוֹי דְּדָוִד, כַּד עָבֵד חוּשְׁבָּנָא בְּיִשְׂרָאֵל, וְלָא נָטִיל מִנְּהוֹן פּוּרְקָנָא, הֲוָה רוּגְזָא, וְאִתְאֲבִידוּ מִיִּשְׂרָאֵל כַּמָּה חֵילִין וְכַמָּה מַשִׁרְיָין.

96. Yisrael below are not subject to reckoning, but only in a different aspect, NAMELY, COVERED CHASSADIM. The ransom they give, CORRESPONDING TO YISRAEL–SABA AND TEVUNAH, is subject to accounting. And for that reason whenever Yisrael are counted, ransom is taken from them, as we said. Therefore, at the time of David, when he counted Yisrael, and did not take ransom, there was wrath and many hosts and legions of Yisrael perished.

97. וּבג״כ כְּתִיב בְּעוֹבָדָא דְּמַשְׁכְּנָא, וְכֶסֶף פְּקוּדֵי הָעֵדָה וְגוֹ׳, וְכֹל

הָעוֹבֵר עַל הַפְּקֻדִים. וְכֹלָּא אִתְקַדַּשׁ לַעֲבִידַת מַשְׁכְּנָא, וְהָא אוּקְמוּהָ כִּכָּרִין חוּשְׁבְּנָא חֲדָא. שְׁקָלִים חוּשְׁבְּנָא חֲדָא. בְּגִין דְּאִית עִלָּאִין דְּסַלְקָן לְחוּשְׁבְּנָא עִלָּאָה, וְאִית אַחֲרָנִין דְּסַלְקָן לְחוּשְׁבְּנָא אַחֲרָא. דָּא עִלָּאָה וְדָא תַּתָּאָה. וּבְגִין כַּךְ כְּתִיב וַיְהִי מְאַת כִּכַּר הַכֶּסֶף לָצֶקֶת אֵת אַדְנֵי הַקֹּדֶשׁ וְגוֹ'. אִלֵּין אֲדָנִים הָא אוּקְמוּהָ.

97. For that reason it is written concerning the building of the Tabernacle: "And the silver of them that were numbered of the congregation…for everyone that went to be numbered" (Shemot 38:25), NAMELY, IN THAT SAID RECKONING. All was consecrated to the construction of the Tabernacle. It was established that the talents, "A HUNDRED TALENTS" (Ibid. 27), belong to one account, and the shekels, "A THOUSAND SEVEN HUNDRED AND SEVENTY-FIVE" (IBID. 28), are another account. For the superior ones are numbered by a supernal account, NAMELY, THE LIGHTS OF YISRAEL – SABA AND TEVUNAH, THE SECRET OF BINAH, THE HIGH RECKONING, ARE THE SECRET OF TALENTS. Others are numbered by a different account, THAT IS, THE ACCOUNTS IN ZEIR ANPIN THAT SHINES UPON MALCHUT, the one above and the other below. That is why it is written, "And of the hundred talents of silver were cast the sockets (Heb. *adanim*) of the sanctuary…" And these sockets were already explained, TO BE THE SECRET OF THE WHOLE MALCHUT CALLED 'ADONAI', THAT RECEIVES FROM THE HIGH RECKONING, NAMELY, FROM BINAH.

15. “Unless Hashem builds the house”

A Synopsis

We are told that King Solomon saw that the work was finished by the hands of the craftsmen but was actually constructed by God. The most important part of the labor is what Binah made, and if this is not included the work is done in vain. Then he speaks about: “Behold it is His litter, that of Solomon, sixty valiant men are round it, the mighty men of Yisrael,” saying that the ‘litter’ is the secret of Malchut, and it is all guarded because of the fear of Gehenom. All the men stand around it, and they are all inside the illumination of the incomprehensible thought. Rabbi Shimon talks about the nine temples that emanate from that thought, saying that they are not lights nor spirits nor souls, and cannot be comprehended. He says that the head of Arich Anpin is called ‘thought’, but it is not known by whose light it shines. The secret of the offering is that it unites the grades and the lights, and the ‘thought’ is then crowned by the Endless Light. That ‘thought’ expanded in all directions and is the secret of the Supernal World, Binah, that is characterized by the question “Who?” as in: “Lift up your eyes on high, and behold who (Mi) has created these.” The ‘question’ then, created ‘these’ – the six Sfirot of Zeir Anpin. Then Mi expanded and became a sea, and built everything below in Malchut exactly as it was in the Supernal World, Binah.

98. תּוּ פָּתַח וְאָמַר, שִׁיר הַמַּעֲלוֹת לִשְׁלֹמֹה אִם יְיָ׳ לֹא יִבְנֶה בַיִת וְגוֹ׳, הַאי קְרָא שְׁלֹמֹה מַלְכָּא א״ל, בְּשַׁעֲתָא דַּהֲוָה בָּנֵי בֵּי מַקְדְּשָׁא וְשָׁארִי לְמִבְנֵי, וַהֲוָה חָמֵי דְּעוֹבָדָא אִתְתַּקְנַת בִּידַיְיהוּ, וַהֲוָה מִתְבְּנֵי מִגַּרְמֵיהּ, כְּדֵין שָׁארִי וְאָמַר אִם יְיָ׳ לֹא יִבְנֶה בַיִת וְגוֹ׳, הַיְינוּ רָזָא דִּכְתִּיב בְּרֵאשִׁית בָּרָא אֱלֹהִים, דְּהָא קוּדְשָׁא בְּרִיךְ הוּא, בָּרָא וְאַתְקִין לְהַאי עָלְמָא, בְּכָל מַה דְּאִצְטְרִיךְ, דְּאִיהוּ בַּיִת.

98. Again he opened the discussion and said: “A song of ascent of Solomon, unless Hashem builds the house…” (Tehilim 127:2). This verse was uttered by King Solomon when he built the Temple. When he started building, he saw that the work was finished by their hands, but was constructed on its own. Then he said: “Unless Hashem builds the house…” He referred to the secret of the verse, “In the beginning Elohim created” (Beresheet 1:1), for the Holy One, blessed be He created and furnished this world, NAMELY, MALCHUT, with all that is needed.

99. שָׁוְא עָמְלוּ בוֹנָיו בּוֹ, אִלֵּין רָזָא דְּאִינּוּן נַהֲרִין, דְּנָפְקִין וְעָאלִין כֻּלְּהוּ בְּגוֹ הַאי בַּיִת, לְאַתְקְנָא לֵיהּ בְּכָל מַה דְּאִצְטְרִיךְ. וְאע״ג דְּכֻלְּהוּ קָא אַתְיָין לְאַתְקְנָא לְמֶעְבַּד תִּקּוּנֵיהּ, וַדַּאי אִם יְיָ׳, דְּאִיהוּ רָזָא דְּעָלְמָא עִלָּאָה, דְּאַתְקִין וְעָבֵיד בֵּיתָא כַּדְקָא יֵאוֹת, אִינּוּן בּוֹנִין לְמַגָּנָא אִינּוּן, אֶלָּא מַה דְּאִיהוּ עָבֵיד וְאַתְקִין. אִם יְיָ׳ לֹא יִשְׁמָר עִיר, כְּמָה דִּכְתִּיב תָּמִיד עֵינֵי יְיָ׳ אֱלֹהֶיךָ בָּהּ מֵרֵשִׁית הַשָּׁנָה וְעַד אַחֲרִית שָׁנָה וְאוּקְמוּהָ. וּבְאַשְׁגָּחוּתָא דָּא, אִיהִי נְטִירָא בְּכָל סִטְרִין.

99. "They who build it labor in vain" (Tehilim 127:2). His builders are the secret of those rivers, THE SFIROT OF ZEIR ANPIN, going out of and into this house, MALCHUT, to prepare whatever is needed. And though all come to fix and construct it, surely, but for Hashem, who is the secret of the high world, BINAH, who prepared and made the house as it should be, all who build it labor in vain. For THE MOST IMPORTANT PART IS what BINAH made and prepared. "Unless Hashem keeps the city" (Ibid.) as it is written, "the eyes of Hashem your Elohim are always upon it, from the beginning of the year to the end of the year" (Devarim 11:12). It was explained, that by that watchfulness, it is kept on all sides.

100. וְאַף ע״ג דִּכְתִּיב הִנֵּה מִטָּתוֹ שֶׁלִּשְׁלֹמֹה שִׁשִּׁים גִּבּוֹרִים סָבִיב לָהּ מִגִּבּוֹרֵי יִשְׂרָאֵל. וְכֻלְּהוּ נַטְרֵי לָהּ. מ״ט נַטְרֵי לָהּ. בְּגִין דִּכְתִּיב מִפַּחַד בַּלֵּילוֹת, דָּא פַּחְדָּא דְּגֵיהִנָּם, דְּקָאִים לָקֳבְלָהּ, בְּגִין לְדַחְיָיא לָהּ, וּבְגִין דָּא כֻּלְּהוּ סַחֲרִין לָהּ.

100. And it is written, "Behold it is his litter, that of Solomon, sixty valiant men are round it, the mighty men of Yisrael" (Shir Hashirim 3:7). THE LITTER OF SOLOMON IS THE SECRET OF MALCHUT. And they all guard it. Why do they guard it? Because "of the fear by night" (Ibid. 8). This is the fear of Gehenom, that is before it. And so that it would be rejected, all are standing around it.

101. וְאע״ג דְּכֻלְּהוּ קַיְימֵי בִּנְהִירוּ דְּמַחֲשָׁבָה דְּלָא אִתְיְידַע. וּכְדֵין, הַאי נְהִירוּ דְּמַחֲשָׁבָה דְּלָא אִתְיְידַע, בָּטַשׁ בִּנְהִירוּ דִּפְרִיסָא וְנַהֲרִין כַּחֲדָא וְאִתְעָבֵידוּ תֵּשַׁע הֵיכָלִין.

15. "Unless Hashem builds the house"

101. All are inside the illumination of the incomprehensible thought. And that light of the not-known thought strikes the veil and they illuminate together and become nine temples.

102. וְהֵיכָלִין לָאו אִינּוּן נְהוֹרִין, וְלָאו אִינּוּן רוּחִין, וְלָאו אִינּוּן נִשְׁמָתִין, וְלָא אִית מַאן דְּקַיְימָא בְּהוּ. רְעוּתָא דְּכָל תֵּשַׁע נְהוֹרִין דְּקַיְימֵי כֻּלְּהוּ בְּמַחֲשָׁבָה, דְּאִיהִי חַד מִנַּיְיהוּ בְּחוּשְׁבְּנָא, דְּכֻלְּהוּ לְמִרְדַּף אֲבַתְרַיְיהוּ, בְּשַׁעֲתָא דְּקַיְימֵי בְּמַחֲשָׁבָה. וְלָא מִתְדַּבְּקָן, וְלָא אִתְיְידִיעוּ, אִלֵּין לָא קַיְימֵי, לָא בִּרְעוּתָא, וְלָא בְּמַחֲשָׁבָה עִלָּאָה. תָּפְסִין בָּהּ וְלָא תַּפְסִין. בְּאִלֵּין קַיְימִין כָּל רָזֵי מְהֵימְנוּתָא, וְכָל אִינּוּן נְהוֹרִין מֵרָזָא דְּמַחֲשָׁבָה עִלָּאָה. דִּלְתַתָּא כֻּלְּהוּ אִקְרוּן אֵין סוֹף. עַד הָכָא מָטוּן נְהוֹרִין וְלָא מָטוּן, וְלָא אִתְיְידִיעוּ. לָאו הָכָא מַחֲשָׁבָה וְלָאו רְעוּתָא.

102. These temples are not lights, nor Ruchot (Eng. 'spirits'), nor Neshamot (Eng. 'souls'), and there is no one to comprehend them. The will of these nine lights, all within the thought, that is counted as one of them, is to chase THE NINE TEMPLES AND GRASP THEM, while they are within the thought. But they do not grasp nor become known, because these pertain to neither will nor to supernal thought. They grasp them, FOR THEY GET MOCHIN FROM THEM, yet do not grasp them, FOR THEY CANNOT BE COMPREHENDED. All the secrets of the Faith are within them. And all the lights coming from the secret of the supernal thought that is underneath are called 'the Endless World', for this far do the lights reach yet do not reach nor become known, for there is no will nor thought in here.

103. כַּד נָהִיר מַחֲשָׁבָה, וְלָאו אִתְיְידַע מִמַּה נָהִיר כְּדֵין אִתְלָבַּשׁ וְאַסְתִּים גּוֹ בִּינָה, וְנָהִיר לְמַה דְּנָהִיר, וְעָאִיל דָּא בְּדָא, עַד דְּאִתְכְּלִילוּ כֻּלְּהוּ כַּחֲדָא, וְהָא אוּקְמוּהָ. וּבְרָזָא דְּקָרְבְּנָא, כַּד סָלִיק כֹּלָּא, אִתְקַשַּׁר דָּא בְּדָא, וְנָהִיר דָּא בְּדָא, כְּדֵין קַיְימִין כֻּלְּהוּ בִּסְלִיקוּ, וּמַחֲשָׁבָה אִתְעֲטַּר בְּאֵין סוֹף, הַהוּא נְהִירוּ דְּנָהִיר מִנֵּיהּ מַחֲשָׁבָה עִלָּאָה, אִקְרֵי אֵין סוֹף.

103. When thought shines, it is not known by whose light, FOR THE THOUGHT IS NOT GRASPED. Then ITS LIGHT is covered and closed inside

Binah, FOR BINAH CANNOT RECEIVE CHOCHMAH WITHOUT CHASSADIM, AND THEREFORE, THE LIGHT IS CONCEALED IN IT. LATER it shone upon whoever it shines, MEANING THAT CHASSADIM SHONE, and entered one another, FOR CHOCHMAH AND CHASSADIM WERE INCLUDED WITHIN ONE ANOTHER, until eveything was included together. This was already explained. And the secret of the offering is that when all goes up, everything is bound together and they shine the one within the other, FOR THE LOWER RISES TO THE HIGHER AND JOINS IT, AND BY THAT RECEIVES SUPERNAL MOCHIN. FOR ALL THAT IS LOW RISES TO THE HIGHER AND THE HIGHER SHINES UPON THE LOWER. Then all the grades rise TO THE HIGH ONE. And the thought MOUNTS AND is crowned by the Endless Light. And the light with which the supernal thought is shining, is called 'the Endless World'.

104. כֵּיוָן דְּאַנְהִיר וְאִתְפָּשְׁטוּ מִנֵּיהּ חֵילִין, הַהִיא מַחֲשָׁבָה אַסְתִּים וְאַגְנִיז וְלָא יְדִיעַ, וּמִתַּמָּן אִתְפָּשַׁט פְּשִׁיטוּתָא לְכָל סִטְרִין, וְאִתְפָּשַׁט מִנֵּיהּ חַד פְּשִׁיטוּ, דְּאִיהוּ רָזָא דְּעָלְמָא עִלָּאָה.

104. Once thought is shining and powers were expanded from it – NAMELY, BINAH, THAT WENT UP TO IT, RECEIVED CHOCHMAH FROM IT – AND EXPANDED DOWNWARD it became concealed, stored and unknown. BECAUSE OF ITSELF, IT IS CLOSED AND DOES NOT SHINE AT ALL UPON THE LOWER BEINGS. And there from it expanded in all directions and spread in the one expansion, which is the secret of the Supernal World, NAMELY, BINAH AS SAID.

105. וְדָא קַיְּימָא בִּשְׁאֶלְתָּא, וְאִיהוּ מַאֲמָר עִלָּאָה, וְאוּקְמוּהָ דְּאִקְרֵי מִי. דִּכְתִּיב שְׂאוּ מָרוֹם עֵינֵיכֶם וּרְאוּ מִי בָרָא אֵלֶּה. שְׁאֶלְתָּא הַהוּא דְּבָרָא אֵלֶּה. לְבָתַר אִתְפָּשַׁט וְאִתְעֲבִיד יָם, סוֹפָא דְּכָל דַּרְגִּין, דְּאִיהוּ לְתַתָּא. וּמִתַּמָּן שָׁארֵי לְמִבְנֵי לְתַתָּא. וְכֹלָּא עָבִיד בְּהַהוּא גַּוְונָא מַמָּשׁ דִּלְעֵילָּא דָא, לָקֳבֵל דָא. וְדָא כְּגַוְונָא דְּדָא. ובג״כ, נְטִירוּ דְּכֹלָּא מֵעֵילָּא וְתַתָּא.

105. And this SUPERNAL WORLD is subject to questioning, which is the supernal utterance, NAMELY, BINAH. It was established that it is called 'Who' (Heb. *mi*), as it is written, "Lift up your eyes on high, and behold who (Heb. *mi*) has created these" (Yeshayah 40:26). That is, that 'question' created 'these'. FOR 'WHO', BINAH, CREATED 'THESE', THE SIX SFIROT OF ZEIR ANPIN. And then *Mi* (*Mem-Yud*) expanded and became a sea (Heb. *yam*, Yud-Mem), the ending of all the grades, being below IN MALCHUT. And from there, BINAH, it started to build below IN MALCHUT, and all that it did IN MALCHUT was exactly as is done above, IN BINAH, the one corresponding to the other, because BINAH protects everything above and below.

106. וְהַאי פְּשִׁיטוּ, דְּמַחֲשָׁבָה אִיהוּ, דְּאִיהוּ עָלְמָא עִלָּאָה. וְדָא אִיהוּ אִם יְיָ' לֹא יִשְׁמָר עִיר שָׁוְא שָׁקַד שׁוֹמֵר, דְּאִיהוּ שׁוֹמֵר יִשְׂרָאֵל. דְּלָאו בֵּיהּ קַיְּימָא נְטִירוּ, אֶלָּא בְּעָלְמָא עִלָּאָה.

106. This expansion, the Supernal World, comes from thought, bECAUSE EVERYTHING THAT SPREADS FROM THOUGHT IS BINAH CALLED 'THE SUPERNAL WORLD'. This is the meaning of "unless Hashem keeps the city, the watchman stays awake in vain" (Tehilim 127:1), who is the keeper of Yisrael, NAMELY ZEIR ANPIN. For keeping does not proceed FROM ZEIR ANPIN but from the Supernal World, BINAH, AS WAS EXPLAINED BEFORE.

107. תָּא חֲזֵי, תִּכְלָא דְּמַשְׁכְּנָא, כֹּלָּא קַיְּימָא בְּרָזָא עִלָּאָה, וְאוּקְמוּהָ. תְּכֵלֶת וְאַרְגָּמָן חַד, לְאִתְקַשְּׁרָא בְּחַד. וְהָא אִתְּמַר בְּרָזָא דִּכְתִּיב, כִּי יְיָ' אֱלֹהֶיךָ אֵשׁ אֹכְלָה הוּא. וְהָא אִתְּמַר דְּאִית אֶשָּׁא אַכְלָא אֶשָּׁא, וְאָכִיל לֵיהּ וְשָׁצֵי לֵיהּ. בְּגִין דְּאִית אֶשָּׁא תַּקִּיפָא מֵאֶשָּׁא.

107. Come and see the blue in the Tabernacle; everything is sustained by a high mystery. Blue, MALCHUT, and purple, TIFERET, are bound to one another, SO THAT ZEIR ANPIN AND MALCHUT WILL BE UNITED. And we have learned the secret of the verse, "For Hashem your Elohim is a consuming fire" (Devarim 4:24), that there is a fire that consumes fire, eats and extinguishes it, the one fire being stronger than the other. (THE ENDING IS MISSING, IT MAY BE FOUND IN BERESHEET 248 -269).

16. "And the thousand seven hundred and seventy-five"

A Synopsis

Rabbi Shimon says that Moses forgot about the shekels in "And of the one thousand seven hundred and seventy-five shekels he made hooks for the pillars, and overlaid their capitals" until a resounding voice reminded him of them. Rabbi Chizkiyah opens with: "While the King was reclining at His board, my nard sent forth its fragrance." This refers to Binah when He gave the Torah to Yisrael and went to Sinai accompanied by many sacred Chariots. We hear about all the letters in the Torah soaring and rising up in the air, how they were formed and what their value is, and that the 'vav's were the one thousand seven hundred and seventy-five lights. The high Vav is the resounding voice since the Torah comes out of that inner voice; this 'great voice' is the secret of the Holy Name. Next Rabbi Chizkiyah turns to the great flood, where God told Noah: 'you should be careful not to show yourself to the destroyer, the Angel of Death, so he would not have power over you,' because there was no one to protect him. But when Noah offered the sacrifice the world became perfumed. This perfume was increased when Yisrael stood on Mount Sinai and the destroyer was no longer present in the world. God wanted at that time to do away with the destroyer forever, but in a few days Yisrael sinned by making the golden calf, thus allowing the destroyer to rule the world again. Rabbi Yosi asks who put the destroyer in the world, since everyone was destroyed in the flood. Rabbi Shimon answers that the presence of Judgment means that the destroyer must be there to walk among the Judgments. He says that the destroyer was named 'flood,' and this is why God told Noah to hide himself. Referring again to the title verse, Rabbi Elazar wonders why he made 'hooks', hearing then from Rabbi Shimon that they were in the shape of 'vav's, meaning that they came from the Central Column. Rabbi Yitzchak isn't certain whether the verse is talking about secular or supernal matters, and decides it must be secular. Rabbi Shimon disagrees, and adds that secular matters do not come from the side of holiness. It is important to know the difference between holiness and the mundane. Even so, profanity has a fraction of holiness in it from the left side. There is now quite a bit of discussion about 'thousand' in various meanings, leading to thoughts about how long Yisrael may be in exile. Rabbi Shimon adds that wherever there is Vav in the Holy Name there is Mercy, and gives some examples. He tells how Judgment was executed in the destruction of Sodom, but the whole world was not destroyed as it was in the flood. Wherever the name Elohim is used it means

Judgment alone, not tempered with Mercy. When the name Hashem is used it means Judgment tempered with Mercy. Only Elohim was present at the flood. We are told how God is both concealed and revealed, and how people draw blessings when their utterances are concealed. Then we hear that “While the King was reclining at His board,” means that He was reveling in the supernal Eden. “My nard sent forth its fragrance” alludes to the last sea that is filled from that Eden, and that created the lower world as a reflection of the higher one. When the nard sends an odor upwards the Holy Chariots receive the wonderful odor and send it further upward, it being in the nature of odors to rise. The Chariots, since they transmit the odors higher are called ‘maidens of song’, since the word ‘alamot’ derives from ‘not revealed’. Finally Rabbi Shimon explains the significance of all the numbers in the title verse, emphasizing 1000, 700, seventy, and five, all of them pertaining to various combinations of Sfirot.

108. וְאֶת הָאֶלֶף וּשְׁבַע הַמֵּאוֹת וַחֲמִשָּׁה וְשִׁבְעִים עָשָׂה וָוִים לָעַמּוּדִים וְצִפָּה רָאשֵׁיהֶם וְגוֹ׳. תָּא חֲזֵי, אוֹלִיפְנָא דְּאִינּוּן תִּקְלִין אַנְשֵׁי לוֹן מֹשֶׁה, וְלָא יָדַע מַה דְּאִתְעָבֵיד מִנַּיְיהוּ, עַד דְּנָפַק קָלָא וְאָמַר, וְאֶת הָאֶלֶף וּשְׁבַע הַמֵּאוֹת וַחֲמִשָּׁה וְשִׁבְעִים עָשָׂה וָוִים לָעַמּוּדִים.

108. “And of the one thousand seven hundred and seventy-five shekels he made hooks for the pillars, and overlaid their capitals” (Shemot 38:28). Come and see: We learned that Moses forgot these shekels and knew not what became of them, until a voice resounded, saying, “And of the one thousand seven hundred and seventy-five shekels he made hooks for the pillars.”

109. רִבִּי חִזְקִיָּה פָּתַח וְאָמַר, עַד שֶׁהַמֶּלֶךְ בִּמְסִבּוֹ נִרְדִּי נָתַן רֵיחוֹ. הַאי קְרָא אִתְּמַר, אֲבָל עַד שֶׁהַמֶּלֶךְ בִּמְסִבּוֹ, דָּא קוּדְשָׁא בְּרִיךְ הוּא, כַּד יָהַב אוֹרַיְיתָא לְיִשְׂרָאֵל, וְאָתָא לְסִינַי. וְכַמָּה רְתִיכִין הֲווֹ עִמֵּיהּ, כֻּלְּהוּ רְתִיכִין קַדִּישִׁין, וְכָל קְדוּשִׁין עִלָּאִין, דִּקְדוּשָּׁה דְּאוֹרַיְיתָא, כֻּלְּהוּ הֲווֹ תַּמָּן, וְאוֹרַיְיתָא אִתְיְיהִיבַת בְּלַהֲטֵי אֶשָּׁא, וְכֹלָּא בְּסִטְרָא דְּאֶשָּׁא, וּכְתִיבָא בְּאֶשָּׁא חִוָּורָא, עַל גַּבֵּי אֶשָּׁא אוּכָמָא. וְאַתְוָון הֲווֹ פַּרְחִין וְסַלְּקִין בַּאֲוִירָא.

109. Rabbi Chizkiyah opened the discussion with the verse: "While the king was reclining at his board, my nard sent forth its fragrance" (Shir Hashirim 1:12). This was already explained. Yet, "While the King was reclining at His board" refers to the Holy One, blessed be He, BINAH, when He gave the Torah to Yisrael and came to Sinai. Many Chariots were with Him, all of them sacred, THE SECRET OF THE LEFT COLUMN, and all the high sanctifications, from the sanctification of the Torah, THE SECRET OF THE RIGHT COLUMN. All were there. The Torah, WHICH IS THE SECRET OF THE CENTRAL COLUMN, was given with flaming fire, and all was of the side of fire, written by white fire, OF THE SIDE OF CHESED, upon black fire, OF THE SIDE OF GVURAH. FOR THE CENTRAL COLUMN IS COMPRISED OF CHESED AND GVURAH, RIGHT AND LEFT. And the letters were soaring and rising up in the air. IN THE MYSTERY OF THE AIR, THE LOWER GRADES SOARED AND ROSE TO THE HIGHER ONES.

110. וְאָת קַדְמָאָה דְּאוֹרַיְיתָא, אִתְפְּלִיג לְשַׁבַע מֵאָה וְשַׁבְעִים וַחֲמִשָּׁה לְכָל סְטָר, וְכֻלְּהוּ אִתְחָזוּן בַּאֲוִירָא דִּרְקִיעָא בְּאָת ו׳, ו׳ לְסִטְרָא דָּא, ו׳ לְסִטְרָא דָּא. וְכֵן לְכָל סִטְרִין.

110. And the first letter of the Torah was divided into 775 on each side, and all were seen in the air of the firmament by the letter *Vav*, *Vav* on each and every side.

111. וְאִלֵּין וָוִין הֲווֹ קַיְימִין עַל עַמּוּדִין, וְאִינּוּן עַמּוּדִין הֲווֹ קַיְימִין עַל נִיסָא, וְכֻלְּהוּ וָוִין עֲלַיְיהוּ. בְּגִין דְּרָזָא דְּאוֹרַיְיתָא עַל וָ״ו קַיְימָא. וְאִינּוּן וָוִין דְּאִינּוּן רָזָא דִּמְהֵימְנוּתָא דְּאוֹרַיְיתָא, כֻּלְּהוּ עַל אִינּוּן עַמּוּדִים קַיְימִין, דְּאִינּוּן רָזִין דְּנָפְקִין בְּהוּ נְבִיאִים, רָזָא דִּלְהוֹן בְּכָל סְטָר. וְעַל אִינּוּן קַיְימִין, קַיְימָן אִינּוּן וָוִין.

111. These hooks (Heb. *vavim*) were standing on pillars, WHICH ARE NETZACH AND HOD OF ZEIR ANPIN FROM THE CHEST DOWN. And these pillars are suspended by means of a miracle, NAMELY, THEY WERE SHINING TO MALCHUT CALLED 'BANNER', and all the hooks are upon them, ALL ARE SHINING UPON MALCHUT. AND HE EXPLAINS: Since the secret of the Torah abides by the *Vav*, WHICH IS THE CENTRAL COLUMN, THEREFORE, THE ONE THOUSAND SEVEN HUNDRED AND SEVENTY-FIVE LIGHTS

COMPRISED IN IT ARE CALLED *'VAV'S'*. These *Vav's* (Heb. *vavim*), which are the mystery of the Faith in the Torah, all stand upon these pillars, the secret from which the prophets come, NAMELY, NETZACH AND HOD OF ZEIR ANPIN, WHENCE THE PROPHETS ARE INSPIRED. And their secret is on every side, NAMELY, THEY ILLUMINATE THE FOUR DIRECTIONS CHESED, GVURAH AND TIFERET AND MALCHUT. On these pillars the hooks stand.

112. ו' עִלָּאָה, אִיהוּ רָזָא דְּקוֹל דְּאִשְׁתְּמַע, וְאִיהוּ רָזָא דְּקַיְּימָא בֵּיהּ אוֹרַיְיתָא, בְּגִין דְּאוֹרַיְיתָא נָפְקָא מֵהַהוּא קָלָא פְּנִימָאָה, דְּאִקְרֵי קוֹל גָּדוֹל. וְדָא קוֹל גָּדוֹל אִיהוּ רָזָא דְּאוֹרַיְיתָא. וְעַל דָּא כְּתִיב קוֹל גָּדוֹל וְלֹא יָסָף.

112. The high *Vav* is the secret of a resounding voice, WHICH IS ZEIR ANPIN. Upon this secret the Torah is established, since the Torah, WHICH IS ZEIR ANPIN, comes out of that inner voice, WITHIN BINAH, called 'a great voice'. And a great voice IN BINAH is the secret of the Torah, THAT ISSUES FROM IT. Therefore, it is written, "a great voice which was not heard again" (Devarim 5:19), FOR THE TORAH ISSUED FROM IT.

113. ת"ח, הַאי קוֹל גָּדוֹל, אִיהוּ עִקָּרָא דְּכֹלָּא, וְרָזָא דִּשְׁמָא קַדִּישָׁא עִלָּאָה, וְעַל דָּא אוּקְמוּהָ, דְּאָסִיר לֵיהּ לְבַר נָשׁ לְאַקְדְּמָא שְׁלָמָא לְחַבְרֵיהּ, עַד לָא יְצַלֵּי צְלוֹתֵיהּ. וְרָזָא דָּא אוּקְמוּהָ, דִּכְתִּיב מְבָרֵךְ רֵעֵהוּ בְּקוֹל גָּדוֹל בַּבֹּקֶר הַשְׁכֵּם קְלָלָה תֵּחָשֶׁב לוֹ וְלָאו אִיהוּ אָסוּר, עַד דִּמְבָרֵךְ לֵיהּ בְּרָזָא דְּקוֹל גָּדוֹל, דְּאִיהוּ עִקָּרָא דִּשְׁמָא קַדִּישָׁא.

113. Come and see: This great voice is the main part and the secret of the Holy Name, WHICH IS THE SECRET OF DA'AT OF BINAH. For that reason we established that a man must not greet his friend before praying. This secret was explained from the verse, "whoever greets his friend in a great voice early in the morning, it is considered as a curse upon him" (Mishlei 27:14). This is not forbidden as long as greeting is not said with a great voice, which is the main part of the Holy Name, FOR EXAMPLE, IF HE SAID TO HIM 'MAY HASHEM BLESS YOU.' BUT WHEN THE HOLY NAME IS NOT MENTIONED, IT IS NOT FORBIDDEN.

114. וְעַל דָּא, רָזָא דְּאוֹרַיְיתָא נָפְקָא מֵהַהוּא קוֹל גָּדוֹל, וְדָא אִיהוּ מֶלֶךְ. בִּמְסִבּוֹ: דָּא מַעֲמַד הַר סִינַי, וְאוּקְמוּהָ נִרְדִּי נָתַן רֵיחוֹ, דָּא כְּנֶסֶת יִשְׂרָאֵל. בְּגִין דְּאָמְרוּ יִשְׂרָאֵל, כֹּל אֲשֶׁר דִּבֶּר יְיָ׳ נַעֲשֶׂה וְנִשְׁמָע. שֶׁהַמֶּלֶךְ: דָּא אִיהוּ מֶלֶךְ עִלָּאָה, וְאוּקְמוּהָ.

114. Therefore, the secret of the Torah emerges from that great voice, INSIDE BINAH, and this is the King, NAMELY WHAT WAS SAID, "While the king was reclining at His board," that alludes to the revelation of Sinai. "My nard sent forth its fragrance," this is the Congregation of Yisrael, WHICH IS MALCHUT. And all this came about because Yisrael said: "Everything that Hashem spoke, will we do and obey" (Shemot 24:7) BY WHICH THEY MERITED ALL THIS REVELATION. And the King is the High King, NAMELY, BINAH, as was explained.

115. תָּא חֲזֵי, כַּד קוּדְשָׁא בְּרִיךְ הוּא אַיְיתֵי טוֹפָנָא עַל עָלְמָא, בְּגִין לְחַבְּלָא כֹּלָּא, אָמַר לֵיהּ קוּדְשָׁא בְּרִיךְ הוּא לְנֹחַ, בָּעֵי לָךְ לְאִסְתַּמְּרָא, וְלָא תֶּחֱזֵי גַּרְמָךְ קַמֵּיהּ דִּמְחַבְּלָא, דְּלָא יִשְׁלוֹט עֲלָךְ, בְּגִין דְּלָא הֲוָה מַאן דְּיָגִין עָלוֹי. כֵּיוָן דְּאִתְקְרִיב קָרְבְּנָא, דְּקָרִיב נֹחַ, כְּדֵין אִתְבְּסַם עָלְמָא, וְלָא אִתְבְּסַם כּוּלֵּי הַאי עַד דְּקַיְימוּ יִשְׂרָאֵל עַל טוּרָא דְּסִינַי. כֵּיוָן דְּקַיְימוּ יִשְׂרָאֵל עַל טוּרָא דְּסִינַי, כְּדֵין אִתְבְּסַם עָלְמָא, וּמְחַבְּלָא לָא אִשְׁתְּכַח בְּעָלְמָא.

115. Come and see: When the Holy One, blessed be He brought a flood upon the world to destroy everything, He told Noah, 'you should be careful not to show yourself to the destroyer, THE ANGEL OF DEATH, so he would not have power over you'. THE REASON IS THAT there was no one to protect him. And when the sacrifice was offered by Noah, the world became perfumed. But it was not perfumed so much until Yisrael stood on Mount Sinai. And when Yisrael stood on Mount Sinai, the world was perfumed and the destroyer was no longer present in the world.

116. וּבָעָא קוּדְשָׁא בְּרִיךְ הוּא בְּהַהוּא זִמְנָא, לְאַעֲבְרָא הַהוּא מְחַבְּלָא מֵעָלְמָא, בַּר דְּיִשְׂרָאֵל סָרְחוּ בְּהַהוּא זִמְנָא, לְיוֹמִין זְעִירִין, וְעַבְדּוּ יַת

עֶגְלָא. וּכְדֵין מַה כְּתִיב, וַיִּתְנַצְּלוּ בְנֵי יִשְׂרָאֵל אֶת עֶדְיָם מֵהַר חוֹרֶב. וְעֶדְיָם הֲוָה רָזִין דִּשְׁמָא קַדִּישָׁא, דְּאַעְטָר לוֹן קוּדְשָׁא בְּרִיךְ הוּא, וְאִתְנְטַל מִנַּיְיהוּ, כְּדֵין שַׁלְטָא מְחַבְּלָא עַל עָלְמָא, וְאַהְדָּר כְּמִלְּקַדְּמִין, כְּהַהוּא זִמְנָא דְּשַׁלְטָא בְּעָלְמָא, וְעָבֵיד דִּינָא.

116. The Holy One, blessed be He wanted at that time to remove the destroyer from the world, THAT DEATH WILL BE SWALLOWED FOREVER, but after a few days Yisrael sinned and made the calf. Then, it is written, "the children of Yisrael stripped themselves of their ornaments (Heb. *edyam*) from Mount Horeb" (Shemot 33:6). Edyam is the secret of the Holy Name that the Holy One, blessed be He adorned them with AT THE GIVING OF THE LAW, then was taken from them. Then the destroyer ruled the world, as before, when he was ruling the world and judging PEOPLE.

117. אָמַר רִבִּי יוֹסֵי, בְּיוֹמוֹי דְּטוֹפָנָא, מַאן יָהִיב תַּמָּן מְחַבְּלָא, דְּהָא מַיָּא הֲווֹ דְּאִתְגַּבָּרוּ, תָּא חֲזֵי, לֵית לָךְ דִּינָא בְּעָלְמָא, אוֹ כַּד אִתְמְחֵי עָלְמָא בְּדִינָא, דְּלָא אִשְׁתְּכַח הַהוּא מְחַבְּלָא בֵּינַיְיהוּ, דְּאָזִיל בְּגוֹ אִינּוּן דִּינִין דְּאִתְעֲבֵידוּ בְּעָלְמָא. אוּף הָכָא, טוֹפָנָא הֲוָה, וּמְחַבְּלָא אָזִיל בְּגוֹ טוֹפָנָא, וְאִיהוּ אִקְרֵי הָכִי. וְעַל דָּא אָמַר לֵיהּ קוּדְשָׁא בְּרִיךְ הוּא לְנֹחַ, לְטַמְּרָא גַּרְמֵיהּ, וְלָא יִתְחָזֵי בְּעָלְמָא. וְהָא אוּקְמוּהָ. תָּא חֲזֵי, אָמַר רִבִּי יוֹסֵי לָא אִתְיַישַּׁב עָלְמָא וְלָא נָפְקַת אַרְעָא מִזּוּהֲמָא וְכוּ'.

117. Rabbi Yosi said: At the time of the flood, who put the destroyer there? For the water went up, AND WIPED OFF ALL THE WORLD. WHY DID NOAH HAVE TO BE CAREFUL OF THE DESTROYER? HE REPLIES: Come and see, there is no Judgment in the world, or a world smitten with Judgment, where there will not be that destroyer, to walk among the Judgments in the world. Here also, there was a flood and the destroyer walked in its midst and was named 'FLOOD' after it. Therefore, the Holy One, blessed be He told Noah to hide himself and not be seen in the world. And this was already explained. Come and see: Rabbi Yosi said, The word was not yet in order again, and the earth not over the filth of the snake.

118. תָּא חֲזֵי, א"ר אֶלְעָזָר, וְאֶת הָאֶלֶף וּשְׁבַע הַמֵּאוֹת וַחֲמִשָּׁה וְשִׁבְעִים

עֲשָׂה וָוִים לָעַמּוּדִים. אֲמַאי וָוִים. אֶלָּא כְּמִין וָ״ו הֲווֹ, וְרֵישֵׁיהוֹן חָפָא בְּדַהֲבָא. אִינּוּן דִּכְסֶף, וְרֵישֵׁיהוֹן מְחֻפָּן בְּדַהֲבָא, בְּגִין דְּכָל וָ״ו בְּסִטְרָא דְּרַחֲמֵי קָא אַתְיָא, וְכֻלְּהוּ הֲווֹ אִשְׁתְּמוֹדְעָן לְעֵילָּא בְּחוּשְׁבָּנָא. וּבְגִין דְּאָתוּ מִסִּטְרָא דְּרַחֲמֵי, הֲווֹ אִקְרוּן וָוִים. וְכָל שְׁאַר תַּלְיָין בְּהוּ. וְלֵית וָ״ו אֶלָּא דַּהֲבָא וְכַסְפָּא כַּחֲדָא. וּבְגִין כָּךְ, כָּל אִינּוּן אִקְרוּן, וָוֵי דְּאִינּוּן עַמּוּדִים. מַאן עַמּוּדִים. כד״א וְהָעַמּוּדִים שְׁנַיִם וְגוֹ׳. בְּגִין דְּהָא אִלֵּין לְבַר מִגּוּפָא, לְתַתָּא הֲווֹ קַיְימִין.

118. Come and see: Rabbi Elazar said, "And of the one thousand seven hundred and seventy-five shekels he made hooks (Heb. *vavim*) for the pillars." HE ASKS: Why did he make hooks? AND HE ANSWERS: For they were in the shape of '*Vav*', NAMELY, THEY WERE DRAWN FROM THE CENTRAL COLUMN CALLED '*VAV*'. And he overlaid their capitals with gold, and they of themselves were silver, WHICH IS THE LIGHT OF CHASSADIM. And their capitals, THAT IS, THEIR FIRST THREE SFIROT, are overlaid with gold, THE SECRET OF THE ILLUMINATION OF CHOCHMAH CALLED 'GOLD'. HE EXPLAINS: Each *Vav* is of the side of Mercy, NAMELY, FROM ZEIR ANPIN, WHICH IS THE CENTRAL COLUMN, and all were known above through reckoning, IN THE SECRET OF THE ILLUMINATION OF CHOCHMAH. Since they come from the side of Mercy, WHICH IS THE CENTRAL COLUMN, they are called '*Vav's* (Heb. *vavim*)'. And the rest OF THE SFIROT IN THEM are suspended from them. The *Vav's* are made solely of silver and gold together, TO INCLUDE THE TWO COLUMNS RIGHT AND LEFT, CHASSADIM AND THE ILLUMINATION OF CHOCHMAH. For this reason they are called the '*Vavvim* of the pillars'. What are the pillars? They are explained in the verse, "The two pillars" (I Melachim 7:20), NETZACH AND HOD, since they are outside the body, TIFERET, downward.

119. אָמַר רִבִּי יִצְחָק, לָא יְדַעְנָא אִי דָּא עֲבִידְתָּא דְּקֹדֶשׁ, אוֹ חוֹל. בְּגִין דִּכְתִּיב וְאֶת הָאֶלֶף, דְּהָא כְּתִיב הָכָא הָאֶלֶף, וּכְתִיב הָתָם הָאֶלֶף לְךָ שְׁלֹמֹה, מַה לְהַלָּן הָאֶלֶף חוֹל, אוּף הָכָא הָאֶלֶף חוֹל.

119. Rabbi Yitzchak said: I am not sure whether this is a holy or a mundane work, since it is written, "And of the thousand," the same as in "you, Solomon, may have the one thousand" (Shir Hashirim 8:12). As in the latter, ‘thousand’ is secular, so here it pertains to mundane matters.

120. אָמַר לֵיהּ, לָאו הָכִי, דְּאִי הוּא הֲוָה חוֹל, לָא יִתְעֲבִיד מִנַּיְיהוּ וָוִים. וְתוּ, דְּהָא תַּמָּן כְּתִיב הָאֶלֶף וְלָא יַתִּיר, וְהָכָא כְּתִיב הָאֶלֶף וּשְׁבַע הַמֵּאוֹת וַחֲמִשָּׁה וְשִׁבְעִים. הָאֶלֶף דְּהָתָם אִינּוּן חוֹל, דִּכְתִיב הָאֶלֶף לְךָ שְׁלֹמֹה. וְדָא אִיהוּ חוֹל, בְּגִין דְּכָל חוֹל לָאו אִיהוּ בְּסִטְרָא דִּקְדוּשָּׁה כְּלָל. חוֹל אִיהוּ מִסִּטְרָא אַחֲרָא מְסַאֲבָא. וְעַל דָּא הַבְדָּלָה בֵּין קֹדֶשׁ לְחוֹל, בְּגִין דְּבָעֵינָן לְאַפְרְשָׁא בֵּין קֹדֶשׁ לְחוֹל. וְרָזָא דִּקְרָא הָכִי הוּא, וּלְהַבְדִּיל בֵּין הַקֹּדֶשׁ וּבֵין הַחוֹל וּבֵין הַטָּמֵא וּבֵין הַטָּהוֹר.

120. He said to him: This is not so, for if it were secular, no hooks would have been made from it. Also, there it is written “thousand” and no more, and here it is written, “And of the one thousand seven hundred seventy-five.” THEREFORE, THE TWO MAY NOT BE COMPARED. That thousand pertains to the secular, as it is written, “You, Solomon, may have the thousand.” It is secular, because all that is mundane is not of the side of holiness at all, but pertains to impurity. Hence, the Havdalah (Eng. ‘separation’) between holiness and the mundane. This is the secret of the words “and that you may differentiate between holy and secular, and between unclean and clean” (Vayikra 10:10).

121. וְעִם כָּל דָּא אַף עַל גַּב דִּפְרִישׁוּ אִית לַקֹּדֶשׁ מִן הַחוֹל, חוּלָקָא חֲדָא אִית לֵיהּ בִּקְדוּשָּׁה מִסִּטְרָא דִּשְׂמָאלָא. הה״ד הָאֶלֶף לְךָ שְׁלֹמֹה, דְּאִינּוּן אֶלֶף יוֹמֵי הַחוֹל. וְאִינּוּן יוֹמֵי דְּגָלוּתָא. כְּמָה דְּאִית אֶלֶף יוֹמִין דִּקְדוּשָּׁה, הָכִי נָמֵי אֶלֶף יוֹמִין לְסִטְרָא אַחֲרָא. וְע״ד אִתְּעֲרוּ חַבְרַיָּיא, אִינּוּן יוֹמִין דְּגָלוּתָא, אֶלֶף שְׁנִין הֲווֹ.

121. But though we separate holiness from unholiness (lit. ‘secular’), nevertheless PROFANITY has one portion of holiness, from the left side OF HOLINESS. Therefore, “you, Solomon, may have the thousand” refers to the thousand days of unholiness, the days of exile. As there are a thousand days of holiness, so there are a thousand days to the Other Side. The friends mentioned here that the days of exile amount to a thousand years.

122. וְע"ד, אִית אֶלֶף וְאִית אֶלֶף, וְאִינּוּן אֶלֶף שְׁנִין דְּגָלוּתָא, אַף עַל גַּב דְּיִשְׂרָאֵל יְהוֹן בְּגָלוּתָא, וְיִתְמַשְׁכוּן יַתִּיר, בְּהָנֵי אֶלֶף שְׁנִין יִתְמַשְׁכוּן, דְּאִינּוּן אֶלֶף יוֹמִין דְּקָאָמַרָן. וּבְגִין דָּא אוֹקְמוּהָ, כָּל שְׁלֹמֹה דְּאִית בְּשִׁיר הַשִּׁירִים קֹדֶשׁ, בַּר מֵהַאי דְּאִיהוּ חוֹל. הָאֶלֶף דְּהָכָא, קֹדֶשׁ אִיהוּ, וְכָל עוֹבָדוֹי קֹדֶשׁ, וְעַל דָּא עָשָׂה וָוִים לָעַמּוּדִים.

122. And therefore, there is a thousand and a thousand, A THOUSAND OF HOLINESS AND A THOUSAND OF DEFILEMENT, the thousand years of exile. And though Yisrael may be in exile longer THAN A THOUSAND YEARS, it is considered to continue for one thousand years SINCE THEY DO NOT CORRECT THEM, which are the thousand days we mentioned. For that reason it was said that every mention of Solomon in Shir Hashirim pertains to holiness save this verse, "YOU, SOLOMON, MAY HAVE THE THOUSAND." But the thousand mentioned here OF THE HOOKS FOR THE PILLARS is sacred and all that is made thereof is sacred. Therefore, he used them to make hooks for the pillars.

123. תָּא חֲזֵי, הָא אַמָרָן כָּל ו' בְּרָזָא דְּרַחֲמֵי אִיהוּ, וְכָל אֲתַר דְּאָתֵי ו' בִּשְׁמָא קַדִּישָׁא, רַחֲמֵי אִיהוּ. כְּגוֹן וַיְיָ' הִמְטִיר עַל סְדוֹם. וַיְיָ' אָמַר אֶל אַבְרָם. רַחֲמֵי וְדִינָא כַּחֲדָא. דְּמַאי שְׁנָא בְּטוֹפְנָא, דִּכְתִּיב אֱלֹהִים בְּכָל אֲתָר, אֲמַאי לָא כְּתִיב וַיְיָ'. אֶלָּא תָּנֵינָן, בְּכָל אֲתַר דִּכְתִּיב וַיְיָ', הוּא וּבֵית דִּינוֹ. אֱלֹהִים סְתָם, דִּינָא בִּלְחוֹדוֹי.

123. Come and see: We have said that each and every *Vav* is in the secret of Mercy, and wherever there is *Vav* in the Holy Name there is Mercy. For example "And (=*Vav*) Hashem (Yud Hei Vav Hei) rained upon Sodom" (Beresheet 19:24), "And (*Vav*) Hashem said to Abram" (Beresheet 13:14). This indicates the merging of Mercy and Judgment. The difference in the account of the flood is that the name Elohim is used instead of "And Hashem." And we learned that wherever it is written, "And Hashem," it is INDICATION OF Him, ZEIR ANPIN, and His courthouse, MALCHUT. And if it is written just Elohim, it is Judgment alone.

124. אֶלָּא בִּסְדוֹם, אִתְעָבִיד דִּינָא, וְלָא לְשֵׁיצָאָה עָלְמָא. ובג"כ

אִתְעֲרַב אִיהוּ בַּהֲדֵי דִּינָא. אֲבָל בְּטוֹפְנָא, כָּל עָלְמָא שֵׁיצֵי, וְכָל אִינּוּן דְּאִשְׁתְּכָחוּ בְּעָלְמָא. וְאִי תֵּימָא, דְּהָא נֹחַ וּדְעִמֵּיהּ אִשְׁתֵּזִיבוּ. הָא סָתִים מֵעֵינָא הֲוָה, דְּלָא אִתְחָזֵי. וְעַל דָּא כָּל מַה דְּאִשְׁתְּכַח בְּעָלְמָא שֵׁיצֵי לֵיהּ.

124. Rather in Sodom Judgment was executed, but not to destroy the world. That is why ZEIR ANPIN is mingled with Judgment, MEANING THAT IT IS TEMPERED BY MERCY. But at the time of the flood the whole world perished, together with its inhabitants. THAT IS WHY THE NAME ELOHIM IS MENTIONED THERE, TO INDICATE JUDGMENT ALONE, NOT TEMPERED BY MERCY. And if you say that Noah and those with him were saved, it is because he was hidden from sight, and was not seen IN THE WORLD FOR HE WAS INSIDE THE ARK. But all that was in the world perished.

125. וְעַל דָּא וַיְיָ' בְּאִתְגַּלְיָיא, וְלָא שֵׁיצֵי כֹּלָּא. אֱלֹהִים סָתִים, וּבָעֵי לְאִסְתַּמְּרָא, דְּהָא כֹּלָּא שֵׁיצֵי. וְעַל דָּא אֱלֹהִים בִּלְחוֹדוֹי הֲוָה, וְרָזָא דָּא יְיָ' לַמַּבּוּל יָשָׁב. מַהוּ יָשָׁב. אִלְמָלֵא קְרָא כְּתִיב, לָא יַכְלֵינָן לְמֵימַר. יָשָׁב יָשַׁב בִּלְחוֹדוֹי, דְּלָא אָתָא עִם דִּינָא. כְּתִיב הָכָא יָשָׁב, וּכְתִיב הָתָם בָּדָד יֵשֵׁב בִּלְחוֹדוֹי.

125. Therefore, "And Hashem" is revealed and does not destroy everything. And if it is written Elohim, it is concealed, and we should take care for it destroys everything. Therefore, AT THE FLOOD, only Elohim was present. This is the secret of "Hashem sat enthroned at the flood" (Tehilim 29:10). What is the meaning of "sat"? Were it not for that verse, we would not have been able to tell, for "sat" MEANS THAT He sat alone, ON HIS OWN, and was not united with the Judgment OF THE FLOOD. The word "sat" is the same as in "he shall sit alone" (Vayikra 13:46), IN THE ONE CASE HE SITS ALONE, AND SO IN THE OTHER.

126. וְרָזָא אוֹלִיפְנָא, קוּדְשָׁא בְּרִיךְ הוּא סָתִים וְגַלְיָא. גַּלְיָא הוּא בֵּי דִּינָא לְתַתָּא. סָתִים הוּא אֲתָר, דְּכָל בִּרְכָאן נַפְקֵי מִתַּמָּן, בְּגִין כַּךְ, כָּל מִלּוֹי דְּבַר נָשׁ דְּאִינּוּן בִּסְתִימוּ, בִּרְכָאן שַׁרְיָין עָלֵיהּ וְכָל דְּאִינּוּן בְּאִתְגַּלְיָיא, הַהוּא אֲתָר דְּבֵי דִּינָא שַׁרְיָא עֲלוֹי, בְּגִין דְּאִיהוּ אֲתָר בְּאִתְגַּלְיָיא. וְכֹלָּא אִיהוּ בְּרָזָא עִלָּאָה, כְּגַוְונָא דִּלְעֵילָּא.

126. And we learned a secret. The Holy One, blessed be He is concealed and revealed, NAMELY, CONCEALED FROM THE ILLUMINATION OF CHOCHMAH, FOR IT SHINES THROUGH CHASSADIM ALONE, AND REVEALED IN THE ILLUMINATION OF CHOCHMAH. Revealed is the court below, WHICH IS MALCHUT, WHEREIN CHOCHMAH ILLUMINATES; concealed is the place whence all blessings issue, WHICH IS ZEIR ANPIN. Therefore, when the utterances of man are in secrecy, blessings are upon him. And when they are revealed, that place of the court house is upon him, since he is in an open place, WHICH IS MALCHUT. And everything is in the high secret as above.

127. עַד שֶׁהַמֶּלֶךְ בִּמְסִבּוֹ, בְּהַהוּא חֲבְרוּתָא וְתַפְנוּקָא דְּעֵדֶן עִלָּאָה, בְּהַהוּא שְׁבִיל דְּסָתִים וְגָנִיז וְלָא אִתְיְידַע, וְאִתְמַלְיָא מִנֵּיהּ, וְנָפְקִין בְּנַחֲלִין יְדִיעָאן. נִרְדִּי נָתַן רֵיחוֹ, דָּא יָם בַּתְרָאָה, דְּבָרָא עָלְמָא תַּתָּאָה, כְּגַוְונָא דִּלְעֵילָּא, וְסָלִיק רֵיחָא טָבָא עִלָּאָה, לְשַׁלְטָאָה וּלְמֶעְבַּד, וְיָכִיל וְשָׁלִיט וְנָהִיר בִּנְהוֹרָא עִלָּאָה.

127. "While the king was reclining at his board" (Shir Hashirim 1:12), namely joining and delighting in the supernal Eden, THE SUPERNAL CHOCHMAH, DRAWN TO BINAH by that unknown and concealed path WHICH IS YESOD OF ABA. It is filled thereof and emerges into certain brooks, NETZACH, HOD AND YESOD OF BINAH. "My nard sent forth its fragrance" (Ibid.) alludes to the last sea, WHICH IS MALCHUT, that created the lower world, MALCHUT, as a reflection of above, BINAH, and diffused a sweet loft perfume, THE ILLUMINATION OF CHOCHMAH, by which to rule and act. And it is able and rules and shines by the supernal light.

128. תָּא חֲזֵי, בְּשַׁעֲתָא דְּהַאי נִרְדָּא סַלְקָא רֵיחָא לְעֵילָּא, כְּדֵין חֲבִיבוּתָא אִתְקַשְּׁרַת, וְסַלְקָא הַאי נִרְדָּא לְאִתְאַחֲדָא לְעֵילָּא. וְכֻלְּהוּ רְתִיכִין קַדִּישִׁין, כֻּלְּהוּ סַלְקִין רֵיחִין לְאִתְעַטְּרָא לְגַבֵּי דִּלְעֵילָּא. אִינּוּן רְתִיכִין כֻּלְּהוּ אִקְרוּן עֲלָמוֹת שִׁיר, כד"א עַל עֲלָמוֹת שִׁיר, וְהָא אוּקְמוּהָ. מַאי עֲלָמוֹת שִׁיר. אֶלָּא כד"א, וַעֲלָמוֹת אֵין מִסְפָּר. מַאי וַעֲלָמוֹת אֵין מִסְפָּר. כד"א הֲיֵשׁ מִסְפָּר לִגְדוּדָיו. וּבְגִין דְּלֵית לְהוּ חוּשְׁבְּנָא כְּתִיב וַעֲלָמוֹת אֵין מִסְפָּר.

128. Come and see: While the nard sends an odor upwards, THE SECRET OF THE ILLUMINATION OF CHOCHMAH, love is united, NAMELY, CONJUGAL LOVE COMING FROM THE LEFT. This nard rises to be joined above, THAT IS, TO SHINE FROM BELOW UPWARD. And all the holy Chariots RECEIVE FROM THAT NARD AND send forth odors to be adorned above, NAMELY, TO ILLUMINATE FROM BELOW UPWARD AS IS THE NATURE OF ODORS. These Chariots are called 'maidens of song', as it is written, "upon maidens of song" (Tehilim 46:1), and this was explained. What are these maidens of song? They are "maidens without number" (Shir Hashirim 6:8), as "Is there any number to His armies?" (Iyov 25:3), NUMBER MEANING THE ILLUMINATION OF CHOCHMAH. And because they are without number, WHICH IS CHOCHMAH, therefore, it is written, "and maidens without number" FOR THERE IS NO ILLUMINATION OF CHOCHMAH IN THEM. THEY ARE THEREFORE CALLED 'MAIDENS' (HEB. *ALAMOT*), DERIVED FROM 'NOT REVEALED' (HEB. *HE'ALEM*), AND ARE IN NEED OF RECEIVING THE ILLUMINATION OF CHOCHMAH FROM THE NARD.

129. וָוִים לָעַמּוּדִים, כֻּלְּהוּ דְּכוּרִין. כָּל אִינּוּן דְּסַלְּקִין בִּרְבוּ מְשַׁח לְעֵילָּא, כֻּלְּהוּ קַיְימִין בְּרָזָא דִּדְכוּרִין, וְלָא אִקְרֵי דְּכַר אֶלָּא ו׳, רָזָא דִּשְׁמַיָּא, דְּאִינּוּן דְּכוּרִין. וְכָל אִינּוּן דִּלְתַתָּא, אִקְרוּן נוּקְבֵי. ובג״כ כָּל אִינּוּן דְּאַתְיָין מִסִּטְרָא דִּשְׂמָאלָא, מִסִּטְרָא דְּנוּקְבָא, אִתְמָנָן עַל הַשִּׁיר, וְאַמְרֵי שִׁירָתָא תָּדִיר. וע״ד כְּתִיב, עַל עֲלָמוֹת שִׁיר. וְכֻלְּהוּ נַפְקוּ בְּרָזָא דְּה׳. ה׳ אַפִּיקַת כַּמָּה חֵילִין לְזִנַּיְיהוּ בְּרָזָא דְּו׳. ו׳, דָּא רָזָא דִּדְכוּרָא דְּקַיְּימָא לְמֵיהַב מְזוֹנָא לְנוּקְבָא.

129. The "hooks for the pillars" are all male, for they are drawn from ZEIR ANPIN, WHICH IS MALE. They ascend with the dignity of anointing oil upward, TO ZEIR ANPIN, where they stand in the secret of males. And only the *Vav* is considered male, which is the secret of heaven, ZEIR ANPIN, being male. And all those below, NAMELY IN MALCHUT are considered females. For that reason, those that come from the left, NAMELY from the female, WHICH IS MALCHUT, are assigned to sing, and they sing always. Therefore, it is written, "upon maidens of song." All are issued in the secret of '*Hei*', WHICH IS MALCHUT. *Hei* issued many kinds of armies by the secret of *Vav*, FOR THEY ARE MALE. *Vav* is the secret of the male who is to give food to the female, WHICH IS MALCHUT.

130. ובג"כ, כָּל אִינּוּן וָוִין עָבֵד בְּצַלְאֵל, לְמֵיהַב לוֹן לְאַשְׁרָאָה עַל נוּקְבֵי. וְנַפְקֵי מֵרָזָא דְאֶלֶף, דְּאִיהוּ חוּשְׁבָּן שְׁלִים. וּשְׁבַע מֵאוֹת, דְּאִיהוּ רָזָא שְׁלִים. וַחֲמִשָּׁה הָכִי נָמֵי. וְשִׁבְעִים כֹּלָּא רָזָא חֲדָא. וְעַל דָּא, מֵרָזָא דְּנָא, וְחוּשְׁבָּן דָּא, עָשָׂה וָוִים. וְכֻלְּהוּ בְּרָזָא דְּו', וּבְדִיוּקְנָא דְּו' אִתְעָבִידוּ, וְכֹלָּא בְּרָזָא עִלָּאָה, וּבְחוּשְׁבְּנָא נַטְלֵי.

130. For that reason, all the hooks made by Betzalel, WERE MADE to let them dwell upon the female, WHICH IS MALCHUT. They are issued by the secret of thousand, which is a complete reckoning, NAMELY, CHOCHMAH CALLED 'RECKONING'. The seven hundred are a whole secret, NAMELY, THE SEVEN SFIROT CHESED, GVURAH, TIFERET, NETZACH, HOD, YESOD AND MALCHUT OF BINAH WHOSE SFIROT ARE NUMBERED BY HUNDREDS. Five is also a whole secret, NAMELY CHESED, GVURAH, TIFERET, NETZACH AND HOD OF MALCHUT, WHOSE SFIROT ARE COUNTED BY SINGLE UNITS. Seventy ARE CHESED, GVURAH, TIFERET, NETZACH, HOD, YESOD AND MALCHUT OF ZEIR ANPIN, WHOSE SFIROT ARE COUNTED BY TENS. And all pertain to one mystery. From that secret and that counting he made the hooks, and all are according to the secret of the *Vav*, MEANING FROM THE ASPECT OF THE CENTRAL COLUMN, with the shape of *Vav*, and they were all formed according to the high mystery and counting.

17. Each order contains three

A Synopsis

Rabbi Yehuda and Rabbi Yosi talk about King Nebuchadnezzar who made the image that he saw in his dream, that had a head of gold and silver and brass. Rabbi Yosi says the mystery of the Tabernacle is in these three metals. Discussion ensues of the numbers three and four, some things being found in the tabernacle in groups of two or three or four or even one. But three is the most important, since there are three orders that spread into the four directions of the world. An extended explanation follows of the significance of all the 22 letters of the alphabet plus those 5 letters that are different at the end of words, and how they move and interact and represent various Sfirot. The letters are also divided into male and female letters, the males comprising the waters above and the females comprising the waters below, making a complete unity. The numbers three, nine and 27 are heavily emphasized, as are the four directions.

131. וּנְחֹשֶׁת הַתְּנוּפָה שִׁבְעִים כִּכָּר, אָמַר רִבִּי יְהוּדָה, כָּל דָּא נַחְתָּא לְתַתָּא, בְּדִיּוּקְנָא עִלָּאָה דְּרָזָא דִּמְהֵימְנוּתָא. כְּגַוְונָא דָּא עֲבַד נְבוּכַדְנֶצַּר הָרָשָׁע הַהוּא צַלְמָא דְּאַתְקִין. אָמַר רִבִּי יוֹסֵי, אִיהוּ לָא עָבִיד הָכִי, אֲבָל בְּחֶלְמֵיהּ חָמָא הָכִי, דְּהָא בְּחֶלְמֵיהּ חָמָא, רֵישָׁא דִּי דַּהֲבָא, וּלְבָתַר כַּסְפָּא, וּלְבָתַר נְחָשָׁא. וְאִי תֵּימָא פַּרְזְלָא וְחַסְפָּא אֲמַאי לָאו הָכִי. בְּגִין דְּלָאו אִינּוּן כְּדַאי לְאַעֲלָא לְקוּדְשָׁא, וְאִלֵּין תְּלָתָא אַחֲרָנִין עָאלוּ.

131. "And the brass of the offering was seventy talents" (Shemot 38:29). Rabbi Yehuda said: It all came down in the high shape of the secret of the Faith, WHICH IS MALCHUT. Evil Nebuchadnezzar did the same when he made the image, FOR "ELOHIM HAS MADE THE ONE AS WELL AS THE OTHER" (KOHELET 7:14). Rabbi Yosi said that he did not make it, only saw in his dream AN IMAGE WHOSE head was gold and then silver and then brass. And if you say that there were iron and clay IN THE IMAGE, but not in the Tabernacle, this is because they are not worthy to be a part of holiness. The other three, GOLD, SILVER, AND BRASS, CHESED, GVURAH AND TIFERET, were.

132. וְרָזָא דִּילֵיהּ דְּמַשְׁכְּנָא, בִּתְלַת תְּלַת בְּאִלֵּין מִתְּכָן. וּבִשְׁאָרָא

אַרְבַּע, כְּגוֹן תְּכֵלֶת וְאַרְגָּמָן וְתוֹלַעַת שָׁנִי וָשֵׁשׁ. וּכְגוֹן אַרְבָּעָה טוּרֵי אֶבֶן.

132. The mystery of the Tabernacle is in these three metals, GOLD, SILVER AND BRASS. In other THINGS there were four, CORRESPONDING TO CHESED, GVURAH, TIFERET AND MALCHUT. For example: blue, MALCHUT; purple, TIFERET; scarlet, GVURAH; and fine linen, CHESED, or the four rows of stones, CORRESPONDING TO CHESED, GVURAH, TIFERET AND MALCHUT.

133. אָמַר רִבִּי יְהוּדָה, מִנְּהוֹן בִּתְלַת. מִנְּהוֹן בְּד׳. מִנְּהוֹן בִּתְרֵין. מִנְּהוֹן בְּחַד. אֲבָל כָּל סִדְרָא וְסִדְרָא לָאו אִיהוּ אֶלָּא בִּתְלַת. תְּלַת סִדְרִין אִינּוּן דְּמִתְפָּרְשִׁין לְכָל סְטָר, לְאַרְבַּע סִטְרֵי עָלְמָא, וְכָל סִדְרָא וְסִדְרָא דְּאִיהוּ לְכָל סְטָר, תְּלַת סִדְרִין אִינּוּן. וְאוֹקִימְנָא.

133. Rabbi Yehuda said: Some of them are in three's, some in four's, some in two's and some in one's. Nevertheless, each order contains but three. There are three orders, spread to the winds, the four directions of the world. In each order in each direction there are other three orders. This was explained.

134. סִדְרָא קַדְמָאָה דִּלְסְטַר מִזְרָח, תְּלַת סִדְרִין אִינּוּן וְאִינּוּן תִּשְׁעָה סִדְרִין, בְּגִין דְּכָל סִדְרָא מֵאִינּוּן ג׳, אִית לֵיהּ תְּלַת סִדְרִין, וְאִשְׁתְּכָחוּ דְּאִינּוּן תִּשְׁעָה. וְכַמָּה אֶלֶף וְרִבְבָן תְּחוֹתַיְיהוּ. וְהָנֵי סִדְרִין תִּשְׁעָה, כֻּלְּהוּ מִתְנַהֲגֵי בְּאַתְוָון רְשִׁימָן. וְכָל סִדְרָא אִסְתְּכֵי לְאִינּוּן אַתְוָון רְשִׁימָן, וְהָא אוּקְמוּהָ. וְכֵן לְכָל סִדְרָא וְסִדְרָא, וְכֻלְּהוּ נַטְלֵי בְּאַתְוָון רְשִׁימָן. וְאִלֵּין עִלָּאֵי מֵאִלֵּין, וְקַיְימָן אִלֵּין עַל אִלֵּין.

134. HE EXPLAINS: The first order on the east side, WHICH IS TIFERET, consists of three orders, NAMELY, THE THREE COLUMNS. There are nine orders altogether since each of the three orders, THAT IS, EACH OF THE THREE COLUMNS, is comprised of three orders, THE THREE COLUMNS COMPRISED OF ONE ANOTHER. In all, there are nine, namely, THE NINE COLUMNS. And many thousands and tens of thousands of grades are found beneath them! These nine orders, THE THREE COLUMNS, EACH COLUMN CONSISTING OF THREE, all conduct themselves in accordance with the written letters, THE 27 LETTERS OF THE ALPHABET: THE 22 LETTERS TOGETHER WITH THE FIVE FINAL LETTERS (AT THE END OF WORDS) MEM, NUN, TZADY, PE AND CAF, THAT ARE DOUBLED. And every order, EACH COLUMN, looks upon those written letters TO RECEIVE PLENITUDE FROM THE 27 LETTERS CONNECTED TO IT. This is true for each and every order, EACH AND EVERY COLUMN, and all travel by the written letters, the ones above the others and standing the ones upon the others.

135. וְכַד אִינּוּן אַתְוָון פַּרְחִין, גּוֹ אֲוִירָא דְּרוּחָא, הַהוּא דִּמְמָנָא עַל כֹּלָּא, כְּדֵין כֻּלְּהוּ נַטְלֵי, וְהָא אוּקְמוּהָ. וְחַד אָת בָּטַשׁ מִתַּתָּא, וְהַהוּא אָת סַלְּקָא וְנַחְתָּא, וּתְרֵין אַתְוָון פַּרְחֵי עָלֵהּ. וְהַאי אָת מִתַּתָּא, סַלְּקָא מִתַּתָּא לְעֵילָּא, וְאִתְחַבַּר בְּהוּ, וְאִתְעֲבִידוּ תְּלַת אַתְוָון, כֻּלְּהוּ לְפוּם אַתְוָון יד״ו, דְּאִינּוּן תְּלַת גּוֹ אַסְפַּקְלַרְיָא דְּנַהֲרָא. מֵאִלֵּין אִתְפְּרָשׁוּ תְּלַת סִדְרִין. וְאִינּוּן אַתְוָון תְּרֵין, וְהַהוּא אָת דְּסַלְּקָא מִתְחַבְּרָא עִמְּהוֹן, וְאִינּוּן תְּלַת.

135. And when these letters soar in the air of the direction in charge, all the letters travel, as was explained. And one letter kicks from below, and goes up, and down. Two letters soar above it, ABOVE THE MIDDLE LETTER, and the MIDDLE letter below goes upward, THE SECRET OF ZEIR ANPIN RISING TO BINAH, AND JOINING THE RIGHT AND LEFT COLUMNS OF BINAH. It joins them and together they become three letters, according to the three letters *Yud*, *Hei*, *Vav*, within the shining mirror, WHICH IS ZEIR ANPIN, *YUD* BEING OF THE RIGHT, *HEI* OF THE LEFT AND *VAV* OF THE MIDDLE. They are divided into three orders, NAMELY, THREE COLUMNS, two letters and one letter rising, WHICH IS ZEIR ANPIN RISING TO BINAH. It rises and joins them so they become three.

136. תָּא חֲזֵי, אִינּוּן תְּרֵין אַתְוָון עִלָּאִין דְּסַלְּקִין בַּאֲוִירָא, אִינּוּן כְּלִילָן דָּא בְּדָא, רַחֲמֵי וְדִינָא, וּבְגִין כָּךְ אִינּוּן תְּרֵין, וְאִינּוּן מֵעָלְמָא דִּלְעֵילָּא. בְּרָזָא דִּדְכוּרָא. וְהַאי דְּסַלְּקָא וּמִתְחַבְּרָא עִמְּהוֹן, אִיהִי נוּקְבָא, וְאִתְכְּלִילַת בְּתַרְוַויְיהוּ.

136. Come and see: The two supernal letters rising in the air, THE RIGHT LETTER AND THE LEFT LETTER, are comprised the one within the other, Chesed and Judgment, THE RIGHT ONE BEING CHESED AND THE LEFT BEING JUDGMENT. That is the reason there are two, and they are from the Supernal World, NAMELY, RIGHT AND LEFT OF BINAH, in the secret of the male, FOR THEY ARE CONSIDERED TO BE MALE. FOR BINAH IS THE WORLD OF THE MALE, and the MIDDLE letter that rises and joins them, AND UNITES THE TWO, is a female. And it is included in both of them.

137. כְּגַוְונָא דְּנוּקְבָא אִתְכְּלִילַת בִּתְרֵין סִטְרִין, בִּימִינָא וּשְׂמָאלָא, וְאִתְחֲבָּרַת בְּהוּ. הָכִי נָמֵי, הַאי אָת נוּקְבָא, וְאִתְחֲבָּרַת בִּתְרֵין אַתְוָון אַחֲרָנִין, וְאִינּוּן בִּתְרֵין סִטְרִין, אִלֵּין עִלָּאִין, וְאִלֵּין תַּתָּאִין, וְכֹלָּא אִיהוּ חַד, דְּכַר וְנוּקְבָא.

137. As the female, WHICH IS MALCHUT, is comprised on both sides, right and left OF ZEIR ANPIN and joins them, IN THE SECRET OF "HIS LEFT HAND IS UNDER MY HEAD, AND HIS RIGHT HAND EMBRACES ME" (SHIR HASHIRIM 2:6), so the female MIDDLE letter is united with the other two letters, of the two sides, RIGHT AND LEFT. These TWO LETTERS are superior, FROM BINAH, and these, THE MIDDLE ONES THAT JOIN EVERY TWO SUPERIOR LETTERS, are from below, FROM ZEIR ANPIN. All is one, male and female, FOR ALL THE UPPER TWO LETTERS ARE MALES AND EACH LETTER UNITING THEM, RISING FROM BELOW IS FEMALE.

138. דְּכַד אִתְבְּרֵי עָלְמָא, אִינּוּן אַתְוָון מֵעָלְמָא עִלָּאָה נִינְהוּ, דְּאִינּוּן אוֹלִידוּ כָּל עוֹבָדִין לְתַתָּא, כְּגַוְונָא דִּלְהוֹן מַמָּשׁ. בג״כ, מַאן דְּיָדַע לוֹן, וְאִזְדְּהַר בְּהוּ, רָחִים לְעֵילָּא רָחִים לְתַתָּא.

138. For when the world was created, NAMELY, WHEN BINAH EMANATED ZEIR ANPIN CALLED 'WORLD', these TWO letters, THE RIGHT AND LEFT from the upper world, BINAH, issued all that is below, IN ZEIR ANPIN, in their very shapes. BUT THE MIDDLE LETTER HAS NO NEW SHAPE, EXCEPT THAT IT UNITES THE RIGHT AND LEFT. And whoever knows them and is careful about them, is beloved above and beloved below.

139. ר׳ שִׁמְעוֹן אָמַר, אִלֵּין אַתְוָון כֻּלְּהוּ דְּכַר וְנוּקְבָא, לְאִתְכַּלְּלָא

כַּחֲדָא, בְּרָזָא דְּמַיִין עִלָּאִין וּמַיִין תַּתָּאִין, וְכֹלָּא חַד, וְדָא הוּא יִחוּדָא שְׁלִים. וְעַל דָּא, מַאן דְּיָדַע לוֹן, וְאִזְדְּהַר בְּהוּ, זַכָּאָה אִיהוּ בְּהַאי עָלְמָא, וְזַכָּאָה אִיהוּ בְּעָלְמָא דְּאָתֵי. בְּגִין דְּאִיהוּ עִקָּרָא דְּיִחוּדָא שְׁלִים כַּדְקָא חָזֵי. תְּלַת תְּלַת מִסִּטְרָא דָּא וּמִסִּטְרָא דָּא, בְּיִחוּדָא חֲדָא, בִּשְׁלִימוּ דְּכֹלָּא. וְכֻלְּהוּ רָזָא דְּסִדְרָא עִלָּאָה כַּדְקָא חָזֵי כְּגַוְונָא דִּלְעֵילָּא, דְּהַהוּא סִדְרָא תְּלַת תְּלַת בְּרָזָא חֲדָא.

139. Rabbi Shimon said: All these letters, THE 27 LETTERS OF THE ALPHABET, are male and female, SOME ARE MALE, AND SOME FEMALE. THE MALES are comprised within the waters of above, and THE FEMALES ARE COMPRISED within the waters of below, and all is one. This is a complete unity. Therefore, whoever knows of and is careful about them, happy is he in this world and happy in the World to Come. This is the principal part of the unity, properly complete. There are three on each and every side, NAMELY, THE LETTERS ARE DIVIDED INTO GROUPS OF THREE, TWO MALES ABOVE AND ONE FEMALE BELOW IN THE MIDDLE. They are in one unity, FOR THE RIGHT AND LEFT SIDES ARE UNITED BY THE MIDDLE IN ONE UNITY, and so all is in wholeness. And all are the mystery of the supernal order, IN BINAH, as ought to be, a reflection of above, where there is one order consisting of three in one mystery.

140. סִדְרָא תִּנְיָינָא דִּלְסְטַר דָּרוֹם, תְּלַת סִדְרִין אִינּוּן לְהַהוּא סִטְרָא. וְכָל סִדְרָא וְסִדְרָא תְּלַת תְּלַת, וְאִינּוּן ט׳, כְּמָה דְּאִתְּמַר. וְאַתְוָון אִתְפָּלָגוּ הָכִי לְכָל סִטְרֵי, לְאִתְחַבְּרָא כֹּלָּא בְּחַד, בְּגִין דְּאִית אַתְוָון בְּרָזָא דְּנוּקְבָא, וְאַתְוָון בְּרָזָא דִּדְכוּרָא, וְאִתְחַבָּרוּ כֻּלְּהוּ כַּחֲדָא, וַהֲווּ חַד, בְּרָזָא דִּשְׁמָא קַדִּישָׁא שְׁלִים. וּלְגַבַּיְיהוּ סִדְרִין מְמָנָן, תְּלַת תְּלַת, כְּמָה דְּאִתְּמַר. וְכֹלָּא נָפְקָא מִסִּדְרָא דַּאֲבָהָן דִּלְעֵילָּא כְּסִדְרָא דְּאִתְתַּקַּן אַתְוָון דִּשְׁמָא קַדִּישָׁא יד״ו, כְּמָה דְּאִתְּמַר. הָנֵי סִדְרִין כֻּלְּהוּ, מִתְנַהֲגֵי בְּאִלֵּין אַתְוָון יְדִיעָן, וְנַטְלֵי בְּהוּ. וְכַמָּה חֵילִין וְרַבְרְבָן, כֻּלְּהוּ לְתַתָּא, דְּנַטְלֵי וְאִתְנַהֲגֵי בְּסִדְרָא דָּא.

140. The second order is on the south side, CHESED. There are three orders to that order, THE THREE COLUMNS, three in each, EACH COLUMN

CONSISTS OF THREE. Altogether there are nine, as was said ABOUT THE EAST SIDE. The letters are divided similarly among all the sides, RIGHT, LEFT AND MIDDLE, THE SAME AS IN THE EAST, in order to unite everything together. Since there are female letters and male letters and they all join to become as one, they are one in the mystery of the complete Holy Name, WHICH IS *YUD-HEI-VAV*. The appointed orders, THE GROUPS OF THREE, as was said ABOUT THE EAST SIDE, all issue from the order of the patriarchs above, THE THREE COLUMNS OF BINAH, according to the order of the letters *Yud-Hei-Vav* in the Holy Name, as we said. These nine orders are all according to certain letters, THE THREE GROUPS OF THREE LETTERS, RIGHT, LEFT AND MIDDLE AS ON THE EAST SIDE. And the letters drive them. And many armies and tens of thousands of angels below, all travel according to that order.

141. סִדְרָא תְּלִיתָאָה דִּלְסְטַר צָפוֹן, בִּתְלַת סִדְרִין אִינּוּן לְהַהוּא סִטְרָא, וְאִינּוּן תִּשְׁעָה. וּבִתְלַת סִטְרִין תְּלַת תְּלַת לְכָל סְטָר, וְאִינּוּן תִּשְׁעָה. וְאִינּוּן סִדְרִין מִתְּלַת סִטְרִין כְּמָה דְּאִתְּמַר.

141. The third order is on the north side, GVURAH. There are three orders to that direction, nine altogether, for in each of the three orders there are three, NAMELY, THREE COLUMNS FOR EVERY COLUMN COMPRISED OF THREE COLUMNS, and they are nine. These orders are on three sides, RIGHT, LEFT, AND MIDDLE, ALL, as we said, LIKE ON THE EAST AND SOUTH SIDES.

142. שִׁבְעָה וְעֶשְׂרִין בְּרָזָא דְּאַתְוָון, דְּאִינּוּן שִׁבְעָה וְעֶשְׂרִין. וְאע״ג דְּאִינּוּן תְּרֵין וְעֶשְׂרִים, שְׁלִימוּ דְּאַתְוָון שִׁבְעָה וְעֶשְׂרִין אִינּוּן. וְאִשְׁתְּכָחוּ, כְּמָה דְּאַתְוָון כ״ז, הָכִי סִדּוּרָא דְּסִדְרִין אִלֵּין, שִׁבְעָה וְעֶשְׂרִין, לִתְלַת תְּלַת סִדְרִין לְכָל סְטָר. וְאִשְׁתְּכָחוּ אִלֵּין תְּלַת דְּהַאי סִטְרָא דְּאִינּוּן ט׳. וְאִלֵּין תְּלַת דְּהַאי סִטְרָא דְּאִינּוּן ט׳. וְאִלֵּין תְּלַת דְּהַאי סִטְרָא דְּאִינּוּן תִּשְׁעָה. אִשְׁתְּכָחוּ כֻּלְּהוּ לְשִׁבְעָה וְעֶשְׂרִין.

142. There are 27 ORDERS in the mystery of the 27 letters. And though there are only 22 letters IN THE ALPHABET, in completeness, TOGETHER WITH FINAL MEM, NUN, TZADI, PE AND CAF, they are 27. It is found, then, that just as there are 27 letters, so is the order of these orders, 27, three orders in every direction, OF THE THREE DIRECTIONS, EAST, SOUTH AND NORTH. Hence, the three of the one direction, SOUTH, are nine, EACH OF THE THREE COLUMNS COMPRISED OF THREE, AND TOGETHER THERE ARE NINE. The three of another direction, NORTH, are nine, and the three of yet another direction, EAST, are nine. Thus, there are 27 altogether.

143. וְרָזָא דְּאִלֵּין שִׁבְעָה וְעֶשְׂרִין, אִינּוּן ט׳ אַתְוָון דְּאִינּוּן בְּרָזָא דְּנוּקְבָּא, לְאִתְחַבְּרָא עִם אִינּוּן תַּמְנֵיסַר אַחֲרָנִין בְּרָזָא דִּדְכַר, וְכֹלָּא אִיהוּ כַּדְקָא חֲזֵי.

143. The secret of there being 27 letters is, that nine letters are in the secret of the female. They are united with eighteen other letters in the secret of the male. And all is as should be.

144. תָּא חֲזֵי, כְּגַוְונָא דְּאַתְוָון עִלָּאִין דְּעָלְמָא עִלָּאָה, הָכִי נָמֵי אַתְוָון אַחֲרָנִין לְתַתָּא. אַתְוָון עִלָּאִין רַבְרְבִין, וְאַתְוָון תַּתָּאִין זְעִירִין. וְכֹלָּא דָּא כְּגַוְונָא דָּא. וְכָל הָנֵי רָזִין בְּרָזָא דִּדְכַר וְנוּקְבָּא כֹּלָּא חַד בִּשְׁלִימוּ. וְעַל דָּא כֹּלָּא אִיהוּ בְּרָזָא עִלָּאָה.

144. Come and see: Like the letters in the upper world, BINAH, so are the other letters below, IN MALCHUT. The upper letters IN BINAH are big, and the lower letters IN MALCHUT are small. The one is like the other, FOR ALL THAT APPLIES FOR THE LETTERS IN BINAH, APPLIES ALSO FOR THE LETTERS IN MALCHUT. ALSO, all the secrets of male and female OF THE LETTERS APPLY TO THEM. And all is a whole unity. Therefore, WHATEVER IS IN MALCHUT is in the high secret IN BINAH.

18. Forty-five kinds of lights

A Synopsis

From Beresheet we read about how the world is divided into 45 kinds of lights. It tells about the seven Sfirot divided into seven abysses, stones that roll into the abyss and are pierced by light and then filled with water. We read about the darknesses, the pipes, tendons and nets, two chairs, the black firmament and the colored firmament, the seven colors and the seven seas.

145. בְּאַרְבְּעִין וְחָמֵשׁ זִינֵי גְּוָונֵי נְהוֹרִין אִתְפְּלִיג עָלְמָא.

145. The world, MALCHUT, is divided into 45 kinds of lights. (This article is in Beresheet 269 – 280).

146. שִׁבְעָה מִתְפַּלְגִין לְשִׁבְעָה תְּהוֹמִין. כָּל חַד בָּטַשׁ בִּתְהוֹמָא דִּילֵיהּ, וְאַבְנִין מִתְגַּלְגְּלָן בְּגוֹ תְּהוֹמָא, וְעָיֵיל הַהוּא נְהוֹרָא, בְּאִינּוּן אֲבָנִין, וְנָקִיב לוֹן, וּמַיִין נָפְקִין בְּהוּ. וְשַׁקְעִין כָּל חַד וְחַד עַל תְּהוֹמָא, וְחַפְיָא לִתְרֵין סִטְרִין.

146. The seven SFIROT CHESED, GVURAH, TIFERET, NETZACH, HOD, YESOD AND MALCHUT are divided into seven abysses. Each strikes its abyss, and stones roll into it. A light penetrates those stones, WHICH ARE VEILS, and pierces them. Water penetrates them and they sink into the abyss. The water covers the two aspects OF THE ABYSS.

147. נַפְקֵי מַיָּא בְּאִינּוּן נוּקְבִין, וְעָאל נְהוֹרָא, וּבָטַשׁ לְאַרְבַּע סִטְרֵי תְּהוֹמָא, מִתְגַּלְגְּלָא נְהוֹרָא בַּחֲבֶרְתֵּיהּ, וְאִתְעֲרָעוּ בְּחָד, וּפַלְגִּין מַיָּא.

147. The water oozes through the holes, and light enters THROUGH THEM and strikes the four sides of the abyss. The lights are combined in each other and merge into one, and the water is divided.

148. וְאֲחִידָן כָּל אִינּוּן שִׁבְעָה, בְּשִׁבְעָה תְּהוֹמֵי, וְכַרְאַן בַּחֲשׁוֹכֵי תְּהוֹמֵי, וַחֲשׁוֹכֵי אִינּוּן מִתְעָרְבֵי בְּהוּ. סַלְקִין מַיִין, וְנַחְתִּין מִתְגַּלְגְּלָן בְּאִינּוּן

נְהוֹרִין, וְאִתְעָרְבָן כַּחֲדָא, נְהוֹרִין וַחֲשׁוֹכִין וּמַיִין, וְאִתְעֲבִידוּ מִנַּיְיהוּ נְהוֹרִין דְּלָא אִתְחַזְיָין חֲשׁוֹכָאן.

148. And the seven SFIROT OF ZEIR ANPIN grasp the seven abysses and dig into the darkness therein. The darknesses intermingles, and the waters come up, and go and roll down by means of the lights. The lights mingle with the darkness, to become unseen dark lights.

149. בָּטַשׁ כָּל חַד בְּחַבְרֵיהּ, וּמִתְפַּלְגִין לְשַׁבְעִין וְחָמֵשׁ צִנּוֹרֵי תְּהוֹמִין וּבְהוּ נַגְדִּין מַיָּא.

149. All the sides OF ZEIR ANPIN strike and are divided into 75 pipes of the abyss, wherein water is drawn.

150. כָּל צִנּוֹרָא וְצִנּוֹרָא סָלִיק בְּקָלֵיהּ, וְאִזְדַּעְזְעָן תְּהוֹמִין. וְכַד הַהוּא קָלָא אִשְׁתְּמַע, כָּל תְּהוֹמָא קָארֵי לְחַבְרֵיהּ, וְאָמַר פָּלִיג מֵימָךְ, וְאֵיעוּל בָּךְ, הה״ד תְּהוֹם אֶל תְּהוֹם קוֹרֵא לְקוֹל צִנּוֹרֶיךָ.

150. Every pipe OF ZEIR ANPIN raises its voice, and the abysses shudder. And when that voice is heard, each abyss calls its fellow, saying 'divide your waters so I may enter you'. This is the meaning of "Deep calls to deep at the noise of Your cataracts" (Tehilim 42:8).

151. תְּחוֹת אִלֵּין, תְּלַת מֵאָה וְשִׁתִּין וְחָמֵשׁ גִּידִין, מִנְּהוֹן חִוָּורִין, מִנְּהוֹן אוּכָמִין, מִנְּהוֹן סוּמָקִין, אִתְכְּלִילָן דָּא בְּדָא, וְאִתְעֲבִידוּ גָּוֶון חַד. אִינּוּן גִּידִין אִתְרְקִימוּ בְּשִׁבְעָ עֶשְׂרֵה רְשָׁתוֹת, וְכָל חַד רֶשֶׁת גִּידִין אִקְרֵי. אִתְרְקִימוּ דָּא בְּדָא, וְנַחְתִּין בְּשִׁפּוּלֵי תְּהוֹמָא. תְּחוֹת אִלֵּין, תְּרֵין רְשָׁתִין קַיְימִין בְּחֵיזוּ דְּפַרְזְלָא, וּתְרֵין רְשָׁתִין אַחֲרָנִין בְּחֵיזוּ דִּנְחָשָׁא.

151. Underneath THE PIPES, there are 365 tendons, some white, some black, and some red. They are mingled into one color. These tendons are woven into seventeen nets, and each net is called 'tendons'. They interweave and descend into the bottom of the abyss. Beneath them there are two nets, one of the appearance of iron, the other of copper.

152. תְּרֵין כּוּרְסָוָון קַיְימֵי עֲלַיְיהוּ, חַד מִימִינָא, וְחַד מִשְּׂמָאלָא. כָּל אִינּוּן רְשָׁתִין מִתְחַבְּרָן כַּחֲדָא, וּמַיִין נַחְתִּין מֵאִינּוּן צִנּוֹרִין, וְעָאלִין בְּאִלֵּין רְשָׁתִין. אִינּוּן תְּרֵין כּוּרְסְוָון, חַד כּוּרְסַיָּא דִּרְקִיעָא אוּכָמָא, וְחַד כּוּרְסַיָּיא דִּרְקִיעָא סַסְגוֹנָא. אִלֵּין תְּרֵין כּוּרְסְוָון, כַּד אִינּוּן סַלְּקִין, סַלְּקִין בְּהַהוּא כּוּרְסְיָיא דִּרְקִיעָא אוּכָמָא. וְכַד נַחְתִּין, נַחְתִּין בְּהַהוּא כּוּרְסְיָיא דִּרְקִיעָא סַסְגוֹנָא.

152. Two thrones stand upon them, one to the right and one to the left. All the nets are merged together, and the water goes down by the pipes and into the nets. Of these two thrones, one is of the black firmament and the other of the colorful firmament. When they ascend, they ascend by way of the chair of the black firmament and when they descend, they do so by way of the colorful firmament.

153. אִלֵּין תְּרֵין כּוּרְסְוָון, חַד מִימִינָא וְחַד מִשְּׂמָאלָא. הַהוּא כּוּרְסְיָיא דִּרְקִיעָא אוּכָמָא מִימִינָא. וְהַהוּא כּוּרְסְיָיא דִּרְקִיעָא סַסְגוֹנָא מִשְּׂמָאלָא. כַּד סַלְּקִין בְּכוּרְסְיָיא דִּרְקִיעָא אוּכָמָא. מָאִיךְ כּוּרְסְיָיא דִּרְקִיעָא שְׂמָאלָא וְנַחְתִּין בֵּיהּ.

153. These two thrones are one on the right and one on the left. The chair of the black firmament, NETZACH, is on the right, and the throne of the colorful firmament, HOD, is on the left. When THE LIGHTS mount by way of the throne of the black firmament, the throne of the left firmament descends, AND THE LIGHTS descend through it, FROM ABOVE DOWNWARD.

154. מִתְגַּלְגְּלָן כּוּרְסָוָון חַד בְּחַד. נַקְטִין כָּל אִינּוּן רְשָׁתִין בְּגַוַויְיהוּ, וְעָאלִין לוֹן בְּשִׁפּוּלֵי דִּתְהוֹמָא תַּתָּאָה.

154. The thrones are united, grasp all the nets and put them in the lowest part of the lowest abyss.

155. קָאֵים חַד כּוּרְסְיָיא, וְסָלִיק לְעֵילָּא מִכָּל אִינּוּן תְּהוֹמֵי, וְקָאֵים

כּוּרְסְיָיא אַחֲרָא, לְתַתָּא דְּכָל תְּהוֹמֵי. בֵּין תְּרֵין כֻּרְסָוון אִלֵּין מִתְגַּלְגְּלָן כָּל אִינּוּן תְּהוֹמֵי, וְכָל אִינּוּן צִנּוֹרִין, אִתְנְעִיצוּ בֵּין תְּרֵין כֻּרְסָוון אִלֵּין.

155. One throne stands and rises above all the abysses and the other throne stands down beneath the abysses. Between the two chairs all the abysses whirl and the pipes are fastened between the two thrones.

156. שַׁבְעִין וְחָמֵשׁ צִנּוֹרִין אִינּוּן, שִׁבְעָה אִינּוּן עִלָּאֵי דְּכֹלָּא. וְכָל אִינּוּן אַחֲרָנִין אֲחִידָן בְּהוּ, וְכֻלְּהוּ נְעִיצִין בְּגַלְגְּלוֹי דְּהַאי כּוּרְסְיָיא בְּסִטְרָא דָּא, וּנְעִיצִין בְּגַלְגְּלוֹי דְּהַאי כּוּרְסְיָיא בְּסִטְרָא דָּא.

156. There are 75 pipes, seven of which are superior to the others, and the rest are included in them. They are all fastened to the wheels of the throne on this side, and fastened to the wheels of the throne on that side.

157. בְּהוּ, מַיִין סַלְּקִין וְנַחְתִּין, אִינּוּן דְּנַחְתֵּי כָּרָאן בַּתְּהוֹמֵי, וּבַקְעֵי לוֹן. אִינּוּן דְּסַלְּקִין עָאלִין בְּאִינּוּן נוּקְבֵי אַבְנִין, וְסַלְּקִין וּמַלְיָין לְשִׁבְעָה יַמִּים. עַד כָּאן שִׁבְעָה גְּוָונֵי נְהוֹרִין בְּרָזָא עִלָּאָה.

157. The waters go up and down the thrones. On the way down, they dig into the abysses and cleave them asunder. On the way up, they enter the holes in the stones, rise and fill in seven seas. Thus far, the seven colors of lights in the supernal mystery.

19. "mountains of brass"

A Synopsis

Rabbi Shimon speaks about the brass that is used in the building of the Tabernacle for the sockets and the ministering vessels of the altar and the brass clasps. He says this is 'wave brass' that is called "mountains of brass," and that they are the male and female of brightness (Nogah). The 'brass sockets' are compared to sentries, who guard what is inside the gates yet stand outside the gates. The 'ministering vessels of the altar' are so called because they help the souls to serve. Rabbi Shimon also tells us about how the gold in the temple is connected to the gold above, Gvurah, the silver to the silver above, Chesed, and the brass to the brass above, Tiferet. The colors intermingle and become united, the gold clasps bind the curtains together and the brass clasps bind the Tabernacle together. The clasps shine like the blazing stars in the sky, and the fifty clasps of gold and the fifty clasps of brass face each other and shine.

158. תָּא חֲזֵי, נְחוֹשֶׁת הַתְּנוּפָה דְּקָא אֲמָרָן, אִלֵּין אִינּוּן טוּרֵי נְחֹשֶׁת, דְּאִקְרוּן הָרֵי נְחֹשֶׁת. וְאִינּוּן דְּאִקְרוּן אַדְנֵי נְחֹשֶׁת. וְאִלֵּין קַיְימִין תַּרְעִין, בְּכָל אִינּוּן פִּתְחִין, וְסַחֲרִין לְהוּ, לְכָל אִינּוּן דְּקַיְימִן לְגוֹ, בְּגִין דְּאִלֵּין אִינּוּן תַּרְעִין דְּקַיְימִין לְפִתְחִין לְבַר, וְאִלֵּין עָאלִין וְנַפְקֵי בְּבֵי מַלְכָּא.

158. Come and see: The wave brass we mentioned is the brass mountains, CALLED "mountains of brass" (Zecharyah 6:1), FOR THERE ARE TWO MOUNTAINS, MALE AND FEMALE. And they are called 'brass sockets'. There are sentries of the gates around all the gates. They guard those who are inside, and being sentries of the gates, they stand outside. They come and go out of the King's abode, NAMELY, MALCHUT.

159. וּמִן נְחֹשֶׁת דָּא, כָּל אִינּוּן מָאנִין דְּמַדְבְּחָא לְשַׁמְּשָׁא בָּהּ. וְאִלֵּין אִינּוּן מָאנִין לְמַדְבְּחָא, דְּכַד נִשְׁמָתִין מִתְקָרְבִין לְסַלְּקָא עַל גַּבֵּי מַדְבְּחָא, אִלֵּין אִינּוּן פַּלְחִין הַהוּא פּוּלְחָנָא דְּמַדְבְּחָא, וְכֻלְּהוּ מְסַיְּיעֵי לְשַׁמְּשָׁא הַהוּא שִׁמּוּשָׁא, וְאִקְרוּן כְּלֵי הַמִּזְבֵּחַ. וְכָל אִלֵּין מָאנִין, וְכָל אִינּוּן יְתֵדוֹת הַמִּשְׁכָּן, כֻּלְּהוּ בִּשְׁמָהָן אִקְרוּן, מָאנֵי דְּשִׁמּוּשָׁא לְשַׁמְּשָׁא בְּקוּדְשָׁא. וְעַל דָּא קַיְימִין כֻּלְּהוּ מְמָנָן יְדִיעָאן, וּרְתִיכִין יְדִיעָאן, וְרוּחִין

יְדִיעָאן, כָּל חַד וְחַד כַּדְקָא חֲזֵי לֵיהּ. וּבְהֵיכָלִין דְקוּדְשָׁא דְאִינּוּן הֵיכָלִין יְדִיעָאן, כֻּלְּהוּ בְּחוּשְׁבְּנָא.

159. Out of this brass, all the ministering vessels of the altar are made. They are ministering vessels of the altar, for when the souls approach the altar, WHICH IS MALCHUT, they minister the service of the altar. They all help THE SOULS to serve, and are called 'ministering vessels of the altar'. All the vessels and all the pegs of the Tabernacle, WHICH ARE ALSO OUTSIDE IT, are all called 'vessels of service' that serve the sanctuary. Upon them stand all the appointed chieftains, appointed Chariots, and appointed spirits. Each one is in its appropriate PLACE. The temples of holiness are all known and subject to accounting, NAMELY, IN THE SECRET OF THE VERSE, "THAT BRINGS OUT THEIR HOST BY NUMBER" (YESHAYAH 40:26).

160. קִשּׁוּרָא דְּדַהֲבָא בְּדַהֲבָא. כַּסְפָּא בְּכַסְפָּא. נְחָשָׁא בִּנְחָשָׁא. אִלֵּין דִּנְחֹשֶׁת דִּלְתַתָּא, נַטְלֵי חֵילָא מִנְּחֹשֶׁת דִּלְעֵילָּא, וְכֵן כֹּלָּא. כָּל אִינּוּן גַּוְונִין מִתְעָרְבֵי אִלֵּין בְּאִלֵּין, לְאַחֲדָא לְאִתְקַשְּׁרָא אִלֵּין בְּאִלֵּין.

160. The gold IN THE TABERNACLE is connected to the gold ABOVE, WHICH IS GVURAH; the silver to the silver ABOVE, WHICH IS CHESED; and the brass OF THE TABERNACLE to the brass ABOVE, WHICH IS TIFERET. FOR the brasses below, draw strength from the brass of above, WHICH IS TIFERET. And so all the colors intermingle and become united and bound to one another.

161. קַרְסֵי זָהָב אִינּוּן קַיְימִין לְקַשְּׁרָא אִינּוּן יְרִיעָן חַד בְּחַד. קַרְסֵי נְחֹשֶׁת אִינּוּן קַיְימָאן לְקַשְּׁרָא מַשְׁכְּנָא. וְאִלֵּין לְקָבֵל אִלֵּין. וְכֻלְּהוּ קַיְימִין כְּכֹכְבַיָּא אִלֵּין בִּרְקִיעָא, כְּמָה דִּנְהִירִין כֹּכְבַיָּא בִּרְקִיעָא וְאִתְחָזוּן, הָכִי נָמֵי נְהִירִין אִינּוּן קְרָסִים בְּמַשְׁכְּנָא. וְהָא אוֹקִימְנָא. וּנְהִרִין אִינּוּן קְרָסִים וְאִתְחָזוּן, כְּכֹכְבַיָּא דְּקַיְימֵי וּבַלְטֵי וְנַצְצֵי. וְאִינּוּן חַמְשִׁין דְּדַהֲבָא, וְחַמְשִׁין דִּנְחָשָׁא, וְנַהֲרִין אִלֵּין לְקָבֵל אִלֵּין.

161. The gold clasps bind the curtains OF BLUE, PURPLE...to one another, ONE COUPLING TO ANOTHER. The brass clasps bind together the

Tabernacle, THE CURTAINS OF GOATS' HAIR. These are facing these. They are all like the stars in the sky. As the stars shine and are seen in the sky, so the clasps shine within the Tabernacle. We have already explained that. And the clasps are shining like glittering stars that stand out. The fifty clasps of gold and the fifty of brass shine, facing each other.

20. Sacred robes

A Synopsis

Rabbi Shimon describes how the sacred robes of Michael, the High Priest, were made from the supernal light that sparked off purple and blue. In the same way that Michael does not enter the sanctuary until he is robed, Moses did not go up into the mountain before he donned the cloud, as in: "Moses went into the midst of the cloud, and went up into the mountain." These garments are called 'uniforms' since they were made from the residue of the supernal lights. It is because the High Priest wears the robe that he is allowed to enter the temple. Rabbi Shimon talks about "Yisrael is holy to Hashem, His 0first fruits of the increase," saying that "Yisrael is holy" because all the colors are in Yisrael and the colors are the Priests, the Levites and Yisrael itself. They are also the colors of Chesed, Gvurah and Tiferet – white, red and green. We learn that the soul does not ascend until it is worthy of donning the highest garments, and that the soul does not descend to earth until it wears the clothes of this world. This is also true of the holy angels when they have a mission here. When Adam and Eve were still in the Garden of Eden they wore clothes of celestial light, but when they were driven out they wore the clothes of this world: "Hashem Elohim made for Adam and for his wife coats of skins, and clothed them." Rabbi Shimon repeats that man's raiment of the next world is made from the good deeds he performs in this world, as they draw light from the supreme radiance. To summarize, the reason that the soul has special garments in the two worlds is so that it has wholeness, both in the world below and the world above.

162. מִגּוֹ נְהוֹרָא דִּלְעֵילָּא, נָפַק חַד נְצִיצוּ דְּנָצִיץ, וְאַנְהִיר בְּגוֹ אַסְפַּקְלַרְיָא דְּלָא נַהֲרָא, וְהַהוּא נְצִיצוּ כָּלִיל מִכָּל גַּוְונִין דִּנְהִירִין, וְאִקְרֵי אַרְגָּמָן. וְכַד בָּטַשׁ הַאי אַרְגָּמָן בְּהַהוּא נְהוֹרָא חֲשׁוֹכָא, כְּדֵין נָפַק חַד נְצִיצוּ אַחֲרָא דְּלָא לָהִיט, וְאִתְעָרְבוּ דָּא בְּדָא. וְאִינּוּן הֲווֹ לְבוּשִׁין דְּקוּדְשָׁא, דְּאִתְלָבַּשׁ בְּהוּ מִיכָאֵל כַּהֲנָא רַבָּא.

162. Out of the supernal light, NAMELY ZEIR ANPIN, a spark shines out and into the mirror, which does not shine, NAMELY, SHINES UPON MALCHUT. This spark is comprised of all the illuminating colors, and is called 'purple'. When purple strikes, GIVING PLENTY TO that darkened light, WHICH IS

MALCHUT, another spark, not as glowing, comes out, WHICH IS BLUE. They intermingle, and form the sacred robes which Michael, the High Priest, donned.

163. וְכַד אִתְלְבַּשׁ בְּהוּ בְּאִינּוּן לְבוּשֵׁי יְקָר, כְּדֵין עָאל לְשַׁמְּשָׁא בְּקוּדְשָׁא, וְעַד לָא לְבִישׁ בְּמַלְבּוּשִׁין אִלֵּין, לֹא עָאל לְקוּדְשָׁא. כְּגַוְונָא דָּא, וַיָּבֹא מֹשֶׁה בְּתוֹךְ הֶעָנָן וַיַּעַל אֶל הָהָר, וְאוּלִיפְנָא דַּהֲוָה מִתְלַבַּשׁ בַּעֲנָנָא. וְכַד הֲוָה מִתְלַבַּשׁ בַּעֲנָנָא, כְּדֵין וַיַּעַל אֶל הָהָר. וְעַד לָא אִתְלָבַּשׁ בֵּיהּ, לָא יָכִיל לְמֵיעַל לְגוֹ. כְּגַוְונָא דָּא כַּהֲנָא רַבָּא, לָא עָאל לְקוּדְשָׁא, עַד דְּאִתְלָבַּשׁ בְּאִלֵּין לְבוּשִׁין, בְּגִין לְאַעֲלָא לְקוּדְשָׁא.

163. AND WHEN MICHAEL is attired with these glorious robes, he enters to minister in the sanctuary. He does not enter the sanctuary before he is thus attired. In the same manner "Moses went into the midst of the cloud, and went up into the mountain" (Shemot 24:18). We learned that Moses donned a cloud, and then went up into the mountain, for he could not go up the mountain before he donned the cloud. The High Priest also did not enter the sanctuary before he put on these robes.

164. וּבְגִין דְּנַפְקוּ מֵרָזִין עִלָּאִין, וְאִינּוּן כְּגַוְונָא דִּלְעֵילָּא, אִקְרוּן בִּגְדֵי שְׂרָד. בְּגִין דְּאִשְׁתְּאָרוּ מֵאִינּוּן לְבוּשִׁין עִלָּאִין, בְּגִין דַּהֲווֹ מִמַּה דְּאִשְׁתְּאַר מִנְּהוֹרִין דִּזִיוִין עִלָּאִין. תְּכֵלֶת וְאַרְגָּמָן, גַּוְונִין דְּרָזָא דִּשְׁמָא קַדִּישָׁא, דְּאִקְרֵי שְׁמָא שְׁלִים, יְדוָ"ד אֱלֹהִים. וְדָא אִיהוּ רָזָא, לְאִתְלַבְּשָׁא כַּהֲנָא רַבָּא, לְמֵיעַל לְקוּדְשָׁא. תּוֹלַעַת שָׁנִי אִינּוּן גַּוְונִין סוּמָקָא, וְתִכְלָא וְאַרְגְּוָונָא, דְּאִיהוּ כָּלִיל בְּכָל אִינּוּן גַּוְונִין. וּמִגּוֹ דְּאִיהוּ אִתְלָבַּשׁ בְּהוּ בִּלְבוּשִׁין דִּגְוָונִין אִלֵּין, הֲוָה עָאל לְגוֹ וְלָא דַּחְיָין לֵיהּ לְבַר.

164. Since they emanate from high principles, and are a reflection of above, they are called 'uniforms' (Heb. *serad*), FROM RESIDUE (HEB. *SARID*). For they are the residue of the supernal garments, being made of what was left of the light of the supernal splendors. Blue, MALCHUT, and purple, ZEIR ANPIN, are the colors of the Holy Name, that is considered a full name, Yud

Hei Vav Hei Elohim. FOR YUD HEI VAV HEI IS THE SECRET OF PURPLE, AND ELOHIM THE SECRET OF BLUE. This is the secret of what the High Priest wears when he enters the sanctuary: the scarlet is the red color, CORRESPONDING TO GVURAH, and blue and purple, CORRESPONDING TO MALCHUT AND ZEIR ANPIN, which are comprised of all these colors. And since the High Priest wears garments of these colors, he enters inside and is not ejected outside.

165. ת״ח, כֹּלָּא אִתְעֲבֵיד בְּרָזָא דִּמְהֵימְנוּתָא, לְמֶהֱוֵי כֹּלָּא כְּגַוְונָא דִּלְעֵילָּא. וע״ד כְּתִיב, בִּגְדֵי הַשְּׂרָד לְשָׁרֵת בַּקֹּדֶשׁ. וְאִקְרוּן בִּגְדֵי קֹדֶשׁ בְּגִין דְּלָא אִקְרוּן קֹדֶשׁ, אֶלָּא כַּד שָׁרָאן בֵּיהּ אִינּוּן גַּוְונִין. דִּכְתִּיב בִּגְדֵי קֹדֶשׁ הֵם. וּכְתִיב קֹדֶשׁ יִשְׂרָאֵל לַיְיָ׳ רֵאשִׁית תְּבוּאָתֹה. קֹדֶשׁ יִשְׂרָאֵל: בְּגִין דְּבְיִשְׂרָאֵל אִתְחָזוּן כָּל גַּוְונִין. כֹּהֲנִים וּלְוִיִּם וְיִשְׂרָאֵל. וְאִלֵּין אִינּוּן גַּוְונִין לְאִתְחֲזָאָה לְגו.

165. Come and see: All is done in the secret of the Faith, NAMELY, IN THE GRADES OF MALCHUT CALLED 'FAITH', so as to reflect what is above. Therefore it is written, "the uniforms for service in the holy place" (Shemot 39:41). They are called 'holy garments' only when these colors are in them as it is written, "these are holy garment" (Vayikra 16:4), and, "Yisrael is holy to Hashem, the first fruits of His increase" (Yirmeyah 2:3). "Yisrael is holy" since all the colors are seen in Yisrael, WHICH ARE the Priests, Levites, and Yisrael. THEY ARE THE COLORS OF CHESED, GVURAH AND TIFERET, WHITE, RED AND GREEN. THE PRIESTS ARE WHITE, THE LEVITES RED AND YISRAEL GREEN. These are the colors that are seen inside THE SANCTUARY.

166. ת״ח, נִשְׁמְתָא לָא סַלְקָא לְאִתְחֲזָאָה קָמֵי מַלְכָּא קַדִּישָׁא, עַד דְּזָכָאת לְאִתְלַבְּשָׁא בִּלְבוּשָׁא דִּלְעֵילָּא לְאִתְחֲזָאָה תַּמָּן. וְכֵן כְּגַוְונָא דָּא לָא נַחְתָּא לְתַתָּא, עַד דְּאִתְלַבְּשַׁת בִּלְבוּשָׁא דְּהַאי עָלְמָא.

166. Come and see: The soul does not go up to be seen before the Holy King, before it is worthy of donning the garments of above so it may be seen there. In the same manner, it does not descend to below, until it wears the clothes of this world.

167. כְּגַוְונָא דָא מַלְאֲכִין קַדִּישִׁין דִּלְעֵילָּא, דִּכְתִּיב בְּהוּ עוֹשֶׂה מַלְאָכָיו רוּחוֹת מְשָׁרְתָיו אֵשׁ לוֹהֵט. כַּד עַבְדִּין שְׁלִיחוּתָא בְּהַאי עָלְמָא, לָא נַחְתִּין לְתַתָּא, עַד דְּמִתְלַבְּשִׁין בִּלְבוּשָׁא דְּהַאי עָלְמָא. וְכֹלָּא אִיהוּ כְּגַוְונָא דְּהַהוּא אֲתַר דְּאָזִיל תַּמָּן. וְהָא אוֹקִימְנָא, דְּנִשְׁמְתָא לָא סַלְקָא, אֶלָּא בִּלְבוּשָׁא דְּנָהִיר.

167. It is the same with the holy angels of above, of which it is written, "who makes the winds His messengers, the flames of fire His ministers" (Tehilim 104:4). When they have a mission in this world, they do not descend until they wear the clothes of this world. Everything is according to the place visited. And we explained that the soul does not ascend unless it dons the luminous garment.

168. וְתָא חֲזֵי, אָדָם הָרִאשׁוֹן כַּד הֲוָה בְּגִנְתָּא דְּעֵדֶן, הֲוָה מִתְלַבַּשׁ בִּלְבוּשָׁא כְּגַוְונָא דִּלְעֵילָּא, וְאִיהוּ לְבוּשָׁא דִּנְהוֹרָא עִלָּאָה. כֵּיוָן דְּאִתְתָּרַךְ מִגִּנְתָּא דְּעֵדֶן, וְאִצְטְרִיךְ לְגַוְונִין דְּהַאי עָלְמָא, מַה כְּתִיב וַיַּעַשׂ יְיָ׳ אֱלֹהִים לְאָדָם וּלְאִשְׁתּוֹ כָּתְנוֹת עוֹר וַיַּלְבִּישֵׁם. בְּקַדְמֵיתָא הֲווֹ כָּתְנוֹת אוֹר, אוֹר, דְּהַהוּא נְהוֹרָא עִלָּאָה, דְּשַׁמֵּשׁ בֵּיהּ בְּגַן עֵדֶן.

168. Come and see: When Adam was in the Garden of Eden, he wore a garment looking like the supernal garment, a clothing of celestial light. When he was driven away from there, he needed the colors of this world, as it is written, "Hashem Elohim made for Adam and for his wife coats of skins, and clothed them" (Beresheet 3:21). Before that they were coats of light, of the supernal light, which ministered in the Garden of Eden.

169. בְּגִין דְּהָא גִּנְתָּא דְּעֵדֶן, נְהוֹרָא עִלָּאָה דְּנָהִיר מְשַׁמֵּשׁ בֵּיהּ. וְעַל דָּא, אָדָם קַדְמָאָה כַּד עָאל לְגוֹ גִּנְתָּא, אַלְבִּישׁ לֵיהּ קוּדְשָׁא בְּרִיךְ הוּא בִּלְבוּשָׁא דְּהַהוּא נְהוֹרָא, וְאָעִיל לֵיהּ תַּמָּן. וְאִי לָא אִתְלַבַּשׁ בְּקַדְמֵיתָא בְּהַהוּא נְהוֹרָא, לָא יֵיעוּל לְתַמָּן. כֵּיוָן דְּאִתְתָּרַךְ מִתַּמָּן, אִצְטְרִיךְ לְמַלְבּוּשָׁא אַחֲרָא, כְּדֵין, וַיַּעַשׂ יְיָ׳ אֱלֹהִים לְאָדָם וּלְאִשְׁתּוֹ כָּתְנוֹת עוֹר. וְכֹלָּא כְּמָה דְּאִצְטְרִיךְ. וְהָכָא כְּגַוְונָא דָא, עָשׂוּ בִּגְדֵי שְׂרָד לְשָׁרֵת

בַּקֹּדֶשׁ, לְאַעֲלָא בְּקוּדְשָׁא.

169. Since in the Garden of Eden, the supernal shining light served him; therefore, when Adam entered the Garden of Eden, the Holy One, blessed be He gave him a raiment of that light and led him in. And he could not enter before wearing that raiment of light. Since he was driven thence, he needed another garment. Then "Hashem Elohim made for Adam and for his wife coats of skins, and clothed them." All is as it should be. In the same manner, the uniforms were made for the service in the holy place, to bring him there.

170. וְהָא אוּקְמוּהָ, דְּעוֹבָדִין טָבִין דְּבַר נָשׁ דְּעָבֵיד בְּהַאי עָלְמָא, אִינּוּן עוֹבָדִין מַשְׁכֵי מִנְּהוֹרָא דִּזְיוָא עִלָּאָה, לְבוּשָׁא, לְאִתְתַּקְנָא בֵּיהּ לְהַהוּא עָלְמָא, לְאִתְחֲזָאָה קָמֵי קוּדְשָׁא בְּרִיךְ הוּא. וּבְהַהוּא לְבוּשָׁא דְּלָבִישׁ, אִתְהֲנֵי וְחָמֵי גּוֹ אַסְפַּקְלַרְיָא דְּנַהֲרָא, כְּמָה דְּאַתְּ אָמֵר לַחֲזוֹת בְּנֹעַם יְיָ' וּלְבַקֵּר בְּהֵיכָלוֹ.

170. And we established that the good deeds man performs in this world draw light from the supreme radiance and fix him a raiment of that world so he may be seen before the Holy One, blessed be He. And by that clothing which he dons, he has pleasure and looks into the shining mirror, as it is said, "to behold the beauty of Hashem, and to inquire in His temple" (Tehilim 27:4).

171. וע"ד, נִשְׁמְתָא אִתְלַבְּשַׁת בִּתְרֵין עָלְמִין, לְמֶהֱוֵי לָהּ שְׁלִימוּ בְּכֹלָּא, בְּהַאי עָלְמָא דִּלְתַתָּא, וּבְעָלְמָא דִּלְעֵילָּא. וְעַל דָּא כְּתִיב, אַךְ צַדִּיקִים יוֹדוּ לִשְׁמֶךָ יֵשְׁבוּ יְשָׁרִים אֶת פָּנֶיךָ. אַךְ צַדִּיקִים יוֹדוּ לִשְׁמֶךָ בְּהַאי עָלְמָא, יֵשְׁבוּ יְשָׁרִים אֶת פָּנֶיךָ בְּהַהוּא עָלְמָא.

171. For that reason the soul dons special garments for the two worlds, so it may have wholeness in all, in this world below and in the world above. Therefore it is written, "Surely the righteous shall give thanks to Your Name, the upright shall dwell in Your Presence" (Tehilim 140:14) – "Surely the righteous shall give thanks to Your Name" in this world, and "the upright shall dwell in Your Presence" in that world.

21. Breastplate and Efod

A Synopsis

Rabbi Yosi says that the Efod and the breastplate are the combination of Malchut and Zeir Anpin. He talks about the twelve stones on the breastplate that have inscribed on them the names of the children of Yisrael, and the twelve combinations of Yud Hei Vav Hei along with the supernal twelve tribes above. We hear an explanation of the verse: "there went the tribes," and learn that 'tribes' refers to the supernal twelve tribes above; these are the tribes of Yah, for 'Yah' means 'testimony'. Rabbi Chiya draws a distinction between the tribes below and the tribes above. We hear that when Jacob went to Haran, "he took some of the stones of the place, and put them under his head." These are the twelve holy stones, and all of them became one stone as in: "and this stone, that I have set for a pillar." The High Priest carries the stones always on his heart, in order to remember them forever. The twelve supernal stones are the secret of the Torah. We learn that the Shechinah is being referred to as a "stone of Yisrael," that is rolled into exile, until "They...put the stone back upon the well's mouth in its place" at the time of redemption. We read a description of many kinds of stones and their relationship to the Sfirot and the directions and the tribes, followed by the information that in all the names of the tribes the letters Chet and Tet are not used because they are the letters in 'Sin'. Rabbi Shimon explains to Rabbi Aba about the meaning of 'Urim' and 'Tumim', comparing them to the Tfilin and the knot of Tfilin. He says the 'Urim' are the face, and 'Tumim' are the back, and this is the secret of sound and speech, for the speech completes the word, and they are inseparable as are the breastplate and the Efod. Rabbi Shimon tells how things are often hidden by mentioning the less significant part, so sometimes the Efod is mentioned without the breastplate. In the same way the hidden significant name of Yud Hei Vav Hei is not referred to, the name mentioned is Adonai. There is an internal hidden part to everything. Rabbi Shimon turns to the question of why Gabriel is depicted as "the man clothed in linen," and says that Gabriel was appointed as a messenger to this world and must therefore wear the clothing of this world. He uses the analogy of the breastplate in front and the Efod behind to clarify how God created male and female from Adam. We learn that Eve bore Cain as the offspring of the serpent, and that is why Cain was the first to bring death into the world. Rabbi Shimon says he found in ancient books that when Cain killed Abel he bit him with serpent bites, this drew out his soul until he died. When Adam saw that Cain had killed Abel he separated from his wife for a hundred and thirty years, saying that he didn't wish to be a father any longer. At that time unholy female spirits came and mated with him, and he produced spirits and demons called 'the plagues of men'. After this he learned jealousy, and returned to mate with Eve who produced Seth. Seth was the first of his children that was exactly like him. Rabbi Shimon then turns his explanation back to the breastplate and the Efod, and says that the High Priest's face shone and the letters on the stones stood out, illuminating his face. The four rings that connect the breastplate to the Efod are the secret of the Chariots that connect the side below to the side above. The two rings in the breastplate are the secret of the beasts while the two rings in the Efod are the secret of the wheels. As they are connected, so are Yetzirah and Asiyah, as in: "And when the living creatures moved, the wheels went by them: and when the living creatures were lifted up from the earth, the wheels were lifted up." Rabbi Shimon concludes by reiterating how the lower world is connected to the upper world in all things, and that this is the secret of the construction of the Tabernacle.

172. וַיַּעַשׂ אֶת הָאֵפוֹד זָהָב, הָא אוּקְמוּהָ. אָמַר רִבִּי יוֹסֵי, אֵפוֹד וְחֹשֶׁן כַּחֲדָא הֲווֹ, וְאוּקְמוּהָ דְּהָא בַּאֲתָר דְּהוּא קִיּוּמָא, קַיְּימָן כָּל אִינּוּן תְּרֵיסָר אֲבָנִין, כֻּלְּהוּ נַטְלֵי שְׁמָהָן בְּנֵי יִשְׂרָאֵל, וְכֻלְּהוּ תְּרֵיסָר תְּחוּמִין עִלָּאִין, כֻּלְּהוּ בְּרָזָא דְּשִׁבְטֵי יִשְׂרָאֵל אִינּוּן.

172. "And he made the Efod of gold" (Shemot 39:2), this was already explained. Rabbi Yosi said: The Efod (Eng. 'priestly garment') and the breastplate were as one. FOR THE EFOD IS THE SECRET OF MALCHUT, AND THE BREASTPLATE IS ZEIR ANPIN. It was established that in a place that maintains, NAMELY, WHERE THERE ARE WHOLE MOCHIN, are found the twelve stones, with the names of the children of Yisrael upon them. And they are the twelve high borders, NAMELY, THE TWELVE COMBINATIONS OF YUD HEI VAV HEI, THE SECRET OF CHESED, GVURAH, TIFERET AND MALCHUT EACH INCLUDING THREE COLUMNS, TWELVE ALTOGETHER. All of them are in the secret of the tribes of Yisrael. FOR THE TWELVE TRIBES OF YISRAEL ARE ALSO IN THE SECRET OF THE TWELVE COMBINATIONS OF YUD HEI VAV HEI, TRANSMITTED TO MALCHUT.

173. וְרָזָא דָּא כְּתִיב, שֶׁשָּׁם עָלוּ שְׁבָטִים שִׁבְטֵי יָהּ עֵדוּת לְיִשְׂרָאֵל

לְהוֹדוֹת לְשֵׁם יְיָ׳. שֶׁשָּׁם עָלוּ שְׁבָטִים, אִלֵּין אִינּוּן תְּרֵיסַר שְׁבָטִין עִלָּאִין לְעֵילָּא, דְּאִינּוּן שִׁבְטֵי יָהּ, דְּהָא שְׁמָא דָּא עֵדוּת לְיִשְׂרָאֵל.

173. This is the secret of the verse, "there went the tribes, the tribes of Yah, as a testimony of Yisrael, to give thanks to the Name of Hashem" (Tehilim 122:4). For "there went the tribes" refers to the supernal twelve tribes above, NAMELY THE TWELVE BORDERS OF ZEIR ANPIN, THE ROOTS OF THE TWELVE TRIBES, AS SAID. And these are the tribes of Yah, for this name *YUD-HEI* is a testimony of Yisrael, A TESTIMONY BEING THE SECRET OF THE FIRST THREE SFIROT.

174. אָמַר רַבִּי חִיָּיא, תְּרֵי זִמְנֵי כְּתִיב שְׁבָטִים. אֶלָּא, שֶׁשָּׁם עָלוּ שְׁבָטִים, אִלֵּין שְׁבָטִין דִּלְתַתָּא. שִׁבְטֵי יָהּ, אִלֵּין שְׁבָטִין דִּלְעֵילָּא. עֵדוּת לְיִשְׂרָאֵל, דָּא רָזָא דִּשְׁמָא קַדִּישָׁא עִלָּאָה דָּא, דְּאִקְרֵי עֵדוּת, כְּמָה דְּאַתְּ אָמֵר, וְעֵדוֹתִי זוֹ אֲלַמְּדֵם. וְאִינּוּן תְּרֵיסַר שְׁבָטִין קַדִּישִׁין עִלָּאִין, אִינּוּן תְּרֵיסַר אַבְנִין קַדִּישִׁין. וְעַל דָּא אִינּוּן קַיְימִין לְתַתָּא, כְּגַוְונָא דִּלְעֵילָּא, וְכָל אִינּוּן שְׁמָהָן דִּתְרֵיסַר שְׁבָטִין, כֻּלְּהוּ גְּלִיפָאן בְּאִינּוּן אַבְנִין, וְכַהֲנָא רַבָּא נָטִיל לוֹן.

174. Rabbi Chiya said: 'tribes' is written twice, "...THE TRIBES, THE TRIBES OF YAH." "There went the tribes" refers to the tribes below IN MALCHUT. "The tribes of Yah" are the tribes above IN ZEIR ANPIN. "A testimony of Yisrael" is the secret of the supernal Holy Name, YAH, called 'testimony', as it is said: "and My testimony that I shall teach them" (Tehilim 132:12). THEREFORE, THERE ARE THE NAMES OF THE TWELVE TRIBES IN THE BREASTPLATE, THE COUNTERPART OF ZEIR ANPIN, AND THERE ARE THE NAMES OF THE TWELVE TRIBES IN THE EFOD, THE COUNTERPART OF MALCHUT. The twelve supernal holy tribes IN ZEIR ANPIN are the twelve holy stones IN THE BREASTPLATE. They are therefore IN THE BREASTPLATE below, as the ones above, and the names of the twelve tribes are engraved upon the stones, carried by the High Priest.

175. תָּא חֲזֵי, יַעֲקֹב כַּד הֲוָה אָזִיל לְחָרָן, מַה כְּתִיב וַיִּקַּח מֵאַבְנֵי הַמָּקוֹם וַיָּשֶׂם מְרַאֲשׁוֹתָיו. אִלֵּין תְּרֵיסַר אַבְנִין קַדִּישִׁין, וְכֻלְּהוּ אִתְעֲבִידוּ חַד

אַבְנָא, דִּכְתִּיב וְהָאֶבֶן הַזֹּאת אֲשֶׁר שַׂמְתִּי מַצֵּבָה. וְקָרֵי לְהוּ אֶבֶן, מַאי טַעֲמָא. בְּגִין דְּכֻלְּהוּ תְּרֵיסָר אֲבָנִין, אִתְכְּלִילוּ בְּאַבְנָא חַד קַדִּישָׁא עִלָּאָה, דְּאִיהִי לְעֵילָּא מִנְּהוֹן, דִּכְתִּיב וְהָאֶבֶן הַזֹּאת אֲשֶׁר שַׂמְתִּי מַצֵּבָה יִהְיֶה בֵּית אֱלֹהִים.

175. Come and see: When Jacob went to Charan, "he took some of the stones of the place, and put them under his head" (Beresheet 28:11). These are the twelve holy stones, CORRESPONDING TO THE TWELVE TRIBES IN MALCHUT, NAMELY CHESED, GVURAH, TIFERET AND MALCHUT, EACH INCLUDING THREE COLUMNS, and all of them became one stone, as it is written, "and this stone, which I have set for a pillar" (Ibid. 22). Why does he call it a stone? Because the twelve stones became the one holy stone, superior to them, NAMELY MALCHUT CALLED 'A STONE', as it is written, "and this stone, which I have set for a pillar, shall be Elohim's house." THEREFORE, THE ASPECT OF THE TWELVE TRIBES IN IT IS ALSO CALLED 'STONES'.

176. וְעַל דָּא הָכָא, כַּהֲנָא רַבָּא שַׁוֵּי לוֹן עַל לִבֵּיהּ, לְדַכְרָא לְהוֹן תָּדִיר, דִּכְתִּיב וְנָשָׂא אַהֲרֹן אֶת שְׁמוֹת בְּנֵי יִשְׂרָאֵל עַל לִבּוֹ לִפְנֵי יְיָ' תָּמִיד. וּבְגִין כַּךְ, כֹּלָּא אִיהוּ בְּרָזָא דִּתְרֵיסָר, תְּרֵיסָר עִלָּאִין טְמִירִין לְעֵילָּא, דְּאִתְגְּנִיזוּ בְּרָזָא עִלָּאָה קַדִּישָׁא, וְאִינּוּן רָזָא דְּאוֹרַיְיתָא, וְנַפְקֵי מִקּוֹל חַד דָּקִיק וְהָא אוּקְמוּהָ. תְּרֵיסָר אַחֲרָנִין טְמִירִין לְתַתָּא, כְּגַוְונָא דִּלְהוֹן, וְנַפְקֵי גוֹ קָלָא אַחֲרָא, דְּאִיהִי אֶבֶן דִּכְתִּיב, מִשָּׁם רוֹעֶה אֶבֶן יִשְׂרָאֵל.

176. For that reason the High Priest carries it always on his heart, to remember them forever, as it is written, "And Aaron shall bear the names of the children of Yisrael...upon his heart, for a memorial before Hashem, continually" (Shemot 28:29). Everything is in the secret of twelve. There are twelve supernal STONES, hidden above, stored in the high and holy secret, ZEIR ANPIN. They are the secret of the Torah, NAMELY, ZEIR ANPIN CALLED 'TORAH', and emanate from one thin voice, WHICH IS BINAH. This was established, there are twelve other stones, stored below, IN MALCHUT. They resemble the ones above IN ZEIR ANPIN and emanate from another voice, stone, as it is written, "the shepherd, the Stone of Yisrael" (Beresheet 49:24), NAMELY, MALCHUT.

177. וע"ד אוּקְמוּהָ בְּרָזָא דִּקְרָא דִּכְתִּיב, וְנֶאֶסְפוּ שָׁמָּה כָל הָעֲדָרִים וְגָלְלוּ אֶת הָאֶבֶן. דָּא שְׁכִינְתָּא, דְּאִקְרֵי אֶבֶן בֹּחַן, אֶבֶן יִשְׂרָאֵל. דִּמְגַנְדְּרִין לָהּ, וְעָאלִין לָהּ בְּגָלוּתָא, וּכְתִיב וְהֵשִׁיבוּ אֶת הָאֶבֶן עַל פִּי הַבְּאֵר לִמְקוֹמָהּ, וְעַל שְׁמָהּ אִקְרוּן כֻּלְּהוּ אֲבָנִין.

177. The secret of this verse is explained by the scripture, "and there were all the flocks gathered: and they rolled the stone from the well's mouth" (Beresheet 29:3). This refers to the Shechinah called 'a tried stone', "a stone of Yisrael." It is rolled into exile, and "they…put the stone back upon the well's mouth in its place" (Ibid.), AT THE TIME OF REDEMPTION. THE GRADES ISSUING FROM IT are all named after it, stones.

178. וְכַמָּה אֲבָנִין לַאֲבָנִין. אִית אֲבָנִין וְאִית אֲבָנִין, אִית אֲבָנִין יְסוֹדֵי בֵּיתָא, דִּכְתִּיב וַיְצַו הַמֶּלֶךְ וַיַּסִּיעוּ אֲבָנִים גְּדוֹלוֹת אֲבָנִים יְקָרוֹת לְיַסֵּד הַבָּיִת אַבְנֵי גָזִית. וְאִית אֲבָנִין עִלָּאִין יַקִּירִין, וְאִינּוּן תְּרֵיסָר. וְאִינּוּן אַרְבַּע סִדְרִין, תְּלָתָא תְּלָתָא לְכָל סִדְרָא, לְאַרְבַּע רוּחֵי עָלְמָא. כְּגַוְונָא דָּא אִינּוּן אַרְבַּע דְּגָלִים, דַּהֲווֹ אָזְלֵי בְּמַדְבְּרָא, וְאִינּוּן תְּרֵיסָר שְׁבָטִין, תְּלָתָא תְּלָתָא לְכָל סִטְרָא, לְאַרְבַּע רוּחֵי עָלְמָא. וְכֹלָּא רָזָא חֲדָא וְהָא אוּקְמוּהָ.

178. There are many KINDS OF stones. There are stones and there are stones. Some stones are the foundation of the house, NAMELY, MALCHUT OF THE ASPECT OF CHOCHMAH CALLED 'HOUSE', THE SECRET OF THE VERSE, "THROUGH WISDOM A HOUSE IS BUILT" (MISHLEI 24:3), as it is written, "And the king commanded, and they carried great stones, costly stones to lay the foundation of the house with hewn stones" (I Melachim 5:31). THE CHOCHMAH AND BINAH IN IT ARE CALLED 'GREAT STONES', COSTLY STONES. And there are high precious stones, twelve in number, in four orders, three to each, towards the four directions. THEY ARE CHESED, GVURAH, TIFERET AND MALCHUT, EACH INCLUDING THREE COLUMNS, AND ALTOGETHER TWELVE. So there were four standards marching in the desert, the twelve tribes, three to each direction of the world, TO THE EAST WERE JUDAH, YISASCHAR, AND ZEBULUN. TO THE SOUTH, REUBEN, SHIMON, AND GAD. TO THE NORTH EPHRAIM, MENASHEH, AND

BENJAMIN. TO THE WEST DAN, ASHER AND NAFTALI. THE FOUR DIRECTIONS OF THE WORLD ARE THE SECRET OF CHESED, GVURAH, TIFERET AND MALCHUT, AND THE THREE TRIBES ON EACH DIRECTION ARE THE THREE COLUMNS. All is one secret, and it has been explained.

179. וְתָא חֲזֵי, בְּשַׁעְתָּא דְּכַהֲנָא רַבָּא הֲוָה שַׁוֵּי אִלֵּין תְּרֵיסָר אַבְנִין, וְלָבִישׁ לוֹן בְּחוֹשְׁנָא וְאֵפוֹדָא, כְּדֵין שַׁרְיָא עֲלֵיהּ שְׁכִינְתָּא. וְאִינּוּן תְּרֵיסָר אַבְנִין, גְּלִיפִין בִּשְׁמָהָן דְּכֻלְּהוּ שִׁבְטִין. וְכָל שִׁבְטָא וְשִׁבְטָא אִתְגְּלִיף עַל אַבְנָא חַד. מְשַׁקְּעָן הֲווֹ אַתְוָון עַל אַבְנִין. וְכַד נְהִירִין אַבְנִין, אַתְוָון הֲווֹ בַּלְטִין לְבַר, וְנָהֲרִין עַל מַה דְּאִצְטְרִיכוּ.

179. Come and see: When the High Priest wore these twelve stones on the breastplate and on the Efod, the Shechinah dwelt upon him. The names of all the tribes were engraved upon the twelve stones. Each tribe was engraved upon one stone, and the letters were set in the stones. When the stones shone, the letters stood out and illuminated whatever was to be illuminated.

180. וּבִשְׁבָטִין כֻּלְּהוּ, לָא הֲווֹ תְּרֵין אַתְוָון ח׳ ט׳, בְּגִין דְּלָא אִשְׁתְּכַח חוֹבָה בְּכֻלְּהוּ. אָמַר רִבִּי חִזְקִיָּה, אִי הָכִי ח׳ דִּשְׁמָא גָּרִים יָאוֹת. אֲבָל ט׳, דְּאִיהִי אָת טַב, וְתָנֵינָן מַאן דְּחָמֵי אָת ט׳ בְּחֶלְמֵיהּ, טַב לֵיהּ, בְּגִין דְּבֵיהּ פַּתְחָא אוֹרַיְיתָא כִּי טוֹב. דִּכְתִּיב וַיַּרְא אֱלֹהִים אֶת הָאוֹר כִּי טוֹב, וְהוֹאִיל וְהִיא אָת טָב, אַמַּאי לָא אִכְתּוּב בְּאִינּוּן שִׁבְטִין.

180. In all the names of the tribes there were not to be found the letters *Chet*, *Tet*, THE LETTERS OF SIN (HEB. *CHET*), because there was no sin to be found in them. Rabbi Chizkiyah said: If *Chet* causes this, FOR THE NAME '*CHET*' MEANS DESCENT OR CENSER (HEB. *MACHTA*), it is well FOR IT NOT TO BE WITHIN THE NAMES OF THE TRIBES, but '*Tet*' is a good letter. And we learned that whoever sees the letter *Tet* in his dream, it is a good sign, for the Torah commences with "that it was good," as it is written, "and Elohim saw the light, that it was (Heb. *tov*) good" (Beresheet 1:14). If it is a good letter, why is it not found in the names of the tribes?

181. אָמַר לֵיהּ, בְּגִין דִּסְמִיכִין תְּרֵין אַתְוָון אַהֲדָדֵי. וְתוּ, דְּהָא אָת ט׳

גָּנִיז וְטָמִיר. וְאִיהוּ נָהִיר נְהִירוּ דְּכֻלְּהוּ, דְּהָא אָת דָּא נְהִירוּ דְּכֻלְּהוּ הֲוֵי. וְלָאו נְהִירוּ אִשְׁתְּכַח בַּר מֵאָת דָּא, דִּכְתִּיב וַיַּרְא אֱלֹהִים אֶת הָאוֹר כִּי טוֹב. וְהוּא נְהִירוּ דְּהַהוּא נְהוֹרָא דְּגָנִיז וְטָמִיר. וְעַל דָּא כְּתִיב, לֹא יִמְנַע טוֹב לַהוֹלְכִים בְּתָמִים. וְדָא אִיהוּ נְהוֹרָא דְּכֻלְּהוּ שְׁבָטִין. וּבְגִין כַּךְ לָא אִתְגַּלְיָא בְּהוּ. וְתוּ, דְּכֻלְּהוּ תְּרֵיסָר נַפְקֵי מִגּוֹ אַכְסַדְרָא דָּא טְמִירָא, דְּאִיהִי בְּרָזָא דְּאָת ט׳, ובג״כ אִיהוּ טָמִיר וְגָנִיז, וְלָא אִתְחָזֵי בְּהוּ.

181. He said to him: It is because these two letters are adjacent [in the alphabet]. NAMELY, THEIR BEING ADJACENT IS INDICATION OF SIN (HEB. *CHET*), FOR THAT REASON THEY WERE NOT AMONG THE NAMES OF THE TRIBES. Also, the letter *Tet* is hidden and concealed, AS IT INDICATES YESOD OF BINAH. It illuminates with the light of all, and there is no light to be found except from this letter, BECAUSE ALL THE LIGHTS ISSUE FROM YESOD OF BINAH, as it is written, "and Elohim saw the light, that it was good," good being the illumination of that hidden and concealed light WITHIN THE LETTER *TET*. It is concerning THIS LETTER that is written, "no good thing will He withhold from those who walk upright" (Tehilim 84:12), referring to the light of all the tribes. SINCE IT IS SO CONCEALED IT IS NOT FOUND IN THE TRIBES. Also, all the twelve tribes come out of that concealed compartment, YESOD OF BINAH, in the secret of the letter *Tet* and therefore, it is hidden and concealed, and not seen IN THE TRIBES.

182. ת״ח, כָּל הָנֵי אַבְנִין, קַיְימֵי בְּאוֹרַח אָת וְנִיסָא. וְכֻלְּהוּ כַּד הֲווֹ נָהֲרִין, כְּדֵין כַּהֲנָא רַבָּא הֲווֹ נְהִירִין אַנְפּוֹי, וְאַתְוָון נְהִרִין וּבַלְטִין לְאִשְׁתְּמוֹדְעָא לְבַר. וְכַד הֲווֹ נָהֲרִין אַנְפּוֹי דְּכַהֲנָא כְּדֵין הֲווֹ אִשְׁתְּמוֹדְעָן בְּלִיטוּ דְּאַתְוָון, דְּאִיהוּ לְטָב. וּבְדָא אִשְׁתְּמוֹדַע כַּהֲנָא, אִי זַכָּאָה הוּא אִי לָאו. וְעַל דָּא כֹּלָּא אִיהוּ בְּאָת וְנִיסָא, וְהָא אוּקְמוּהָ.

182. Come and see: All the stones IN THE BREASTPLATE were standing in a miraculous way, and when they were shining, the face of the High Priest shone, and the lights illuminated and stood out to be visible FROM THE STONES. When the face of the High Priest shone, the protrusion of the letters was considered to be favorable. Thus the priest was known to be either righteous or not. All this was by way of miracle, as was explained.

183. רִבִּי אַבָּא הֲוָה שְׁכִיחַ קַמֵּיהּ דְּרִבִּי שִׁמְעוֹן, אָמַר לֵיהּ, הָא דִּכְתִּיב וְנָתַתָּ אֶל חֹשֶׁן הַמִּשְׁפָּט אֶת הָאוּרִים וְאֶת הַתּוּמִּים, וְתָנֵינָן, אוּרִים: דְּנָהֲרִין בְּמִלָּה דְּאִצְטְרִיכוּ. תּוּמִים: דְּאַשְׁלִימוּ בְּמִלַּיְיהוּ. תּוּ אֲנָן צְרִיכִין לְמִנְדַּע.

183. Rabbi Aba was before Rabbi Shimon. He said to him: It is written, "And you shall put in the breastplate of Judgment the Urim and the Tumim" (Shemot 28:30). We learned that Urim (Eng. 'lights') MEANS that they illuminated that which was required, NAMELY WHATEVER WAS ASKED. Tumim (Eng. 'complete') means that they fulfilled what was said. BUT THIS EXPLANATION IS NOT ENOUGH, we need to know more.

184. אָמַר לֵיהּ, וַדַּאי, וְהָכִי אִיהוּ, חֹשֶׁן וְאֵפוֹד לָקֳבֵל אוּרִים וְתוּמִים. וְדָא רָזָא, דִּתְפִלִּין, וְקִשְׁרָא דִּתְפִלִּין, לָקֳבֵל תְּרֵין אִלֵּין. פָּתַח וְאָמַר וְרָאִיתָ אֶת אֲחוֹרָי וּפָנַי לֹא יֵרָאוּ. וְרָאִיתָ אֶת אֲחוֹרָי, הָא תָּנֵינָן, דְּאַחְזֵי לֵיהּ קוּדְשָׁא ב"ה לְמֹשֶׁה, קֶשֶׁר שֶׁל תְּפִלִּין. וּפָנַי: אִלֵּין תְּפִלִּין מַמָּשׁ. וּפָנַי אִינּוּן תְּפִלִּין, דְּאִינּוּן רָזָא עִלָּאָה שְׁמָא קַדִּישָׁא. אֲחוֹרָי, אִיהוּ רָזָא דְּקִשְׁרָא דִּתְפִלִּין. וְהָא יְדִיעָא לְגַבֵּי חַבְרַיָּיא. בְּגִין דְּדָא אַסְפַּקְלַרְיָא דְּנַהֲרָא. וְדָא אִיהִי אַסְפַּקְלַרְיָא דְּלָא נַהֲרָא.

184. He said to him: Surely it is so. Thus, the breastplate and the Efod correspond to Urim and Tumim. This is a secret of Tefilin and the knot of Tefilin, that correspond to these two. He opened the discussion and said: "And you shall see My back, but My face shall not be seen" (Shemot 33:23). "And you shall see My back"; we learned that the Holy One, blessed be He showed Moses the knot of Tefilin. "My face" are the Tefilin themselves. HE EXPLAINS: "My face" are Tefilin, the high secret, the Holy Name. "My back," is the secret of the knot of Tefilin. It is known among the friends that TEFILIN are the shining mirror, WHICH IS ZEIR ANPIN, and this, THE KNOT OF TEFILIN, is the mirror which does not shine, WHICH IS MALCHUT.

185. לָקֳבֵל דָּא, אוּרִים: דְּנָהֲרִין בְּמִלַּיְיהוּ. תּוּמִים: דְּאַשְׁלִימוּ בְּמִלַּיְיהוּ. דָּא פָּנִים. וְדָא אָחוֹר. וְרָזָא דָּא קוֹל וְדִבּוּר. קוֹל אַנְהִיר לְדִבּוּר, לְמַלְּלָא.

דִּבּוּר אַשְׁלִים מִלָּה. וְתָדִיר דָּא בְּדָא סַלְקָן, וְלָא אִתְפָּרְשָׁן דָּא מִן דָּא לְעָלְמִין, ובג״כ, חֹשֶׁן וְאֵפוֹד, דָּא פָּנִים וְדָא אָחוֹר וְכֹלָּא רָזָא חֲדָא בְּלָא פְּרִישׁוּ כְּלַל.

185. Correspondingly, these are Urim for they shine (Heb. *meirim*) with their utterances, NAMELY, ZEIR ANPIN, THE SHINING MIRROR. And these are Tumim so called for completing with their utterances, NAMELY MALCHUT, SHINING BY THE ILLUMINATION OF CHOCHMAH IN THE SECRET OF "AND YOU SHALL SEE MY BACK," WHERE ALL PERFECTION LIES. URIM ARE the face, and TUMIM ARE the back. This is the secret of sound and speech. Sound, WHICH IS ZEIR ANPIN shines upon the speech, WHICH IS MALCHUT, so it may speak. For the speech completes the word, NAMELY, THE VOICE IS THE MAIN AND SUBSTANTIAL PART, AND THE SPEECH COMPLETES IT. They always rise together, and never separate, FOR YOU CAN NEVER SEPARATE SOUND AND SPEECH. Hence, the breastplate and the Efod, the one is the face and the other the back, and all pertain to the same principle with no separation whatsoever, LIKE SOUND AND SPEECH.

186. אָמַר לֵיהּ, אִי הָכִי דְּלָא מִתְפָּרְשָׁן לְעָלְמִין, וּמַאן דְּאַפְרִישׁ לוֹן, הָא תָּנִינָן, דִּכְתִּיב מַפְרִיד אַלּוּף, מַהוּ דִּכְתִּיב וַיְהִי כִּבְרוֹחַ אֶבְיָתָר בֶּן אֲחִימֶלֶךְ אֶל דָּוִד קְעִילָה אֵפוֹד יָרַד בְּיָדוֹ, וְאִלּוּ חֹשֶׁן לָא קָאָמַר.

186. He said to him: If this is so, THAT THE BREASTPLATE AND THE EFOD never separate, and whoever separates them, it is said about him that he "separates close friends" (Mishlei 16:28), FOR THEY ALLUDE TO ZEIR ANPIN AND MALCHUT AS MENTIONED, THEN how do you explain the verse, "And it came to pass, when Aviathar, the son of Achimelech, fled to David to Ke'ila, that he came down with an Efod in his hands" (I Shmuel 23:6), yet the breastplate is not mentioned. IT APPEARS AS IF HE SEPARATED THEM.

187. אָמַר לֵיהּ, וַדַּאי הָכִי הוּא, כָּל מַה דְּהוּא חָשִׁיב, אִיהוּ טָמִיר וְגָנִיז, וְלָא אִדְכַּר כָּל כַּךְ. כְּגַוְונָא דָּא נוֹשְׂאֵי אֵפוֹד בַּד, מַה דְּאִיהוּ בְּאִתְגַּלְיָיא יַתִּיר, אִיהוּ אַדְכַּר, בְּגִין דְּיִתְכַּסֵּי מַה דְּאִיהוּ בִּגְנִיזוּ וּטְמִירוּ. וע״ד אַדְכַּר מַה דְּאִיהוּ בְּאִתְגַּלְיָיא יַתִּיר.

187. He said to him: Assuredly this is so. All that is more significant is hidden and stored, it is not mentioned too much. In the same manner it is written, "that did wear a linen Efod" (I Shmuel 22:18), AND THE BREASTPLATE IS NOT MENTIONED DUE TO ITS IMPORTANCE. What is revealed is mentioned so as to cover what is hidden and concealed. Therefore that which is the more revealed, THE EFOD is mentioned.

188. ובג״כ, שְׁמָא עִלָּאָה אִיהוּ רָזָא בִּטְמִירוּ וּגְנִיזוּ, וְלָא אַדְכַּר אֶלָּא בִּשְׁמָא דְּאִיהוּ בְּאִתְגַּלְיָיא. דָּא אַדְכַּר, וְדָא אִגְנִיז. דָּא בְּאִתְגַּלְיָיא, וְדָא בִּסְתִּירוּ, וְכָל מַה דְּאִתְגַּלְיָיא אִיהוּ אַדְכַּר לְעָלְמִין. שְׁמָא דְּגָנִיז אִיהוּ יְדֹוָ״ד, שְׁמָא דְּאִיהוּ בְּאִתְגַּלְיָיא אִיהוּ אֲדֹנָ״י, וע״ד אִכְתּוּב בְּאַתְוָון טְמִירִין, וְאִקְרֵי בְּאַתְוָון אִלֵּין, וְאִתְכַּסֵּי דָּא בְּדָא, לְמֶהֱוֵי יְקָרָא עִלָּאָה טָמִיר וְגָנִיז לְעָלְמִין. דְּכָל אוֹרְחֵי דְּאוֹרַיְיתָא הָכִי הוּא, אִתְגַּלְיָיא וּסְתִימָא. וְכָל מִלִּין דְּעָלְמָא בֵּין דְּעָלְמָא דֵּין, וּבֵין דְּעָלְמָא דִּלְעֵילָּא, כֻּלְּהוּ אִיהוּ טָמִיר וְגַלְיָא.

188. For that reason, the high name, which is a secret concealed and stored, is mentioned only through the uncovered name. The one is mentioned and the other concealed. The concealed name is Yud Hei Vav Hei, and the mentioned name is Adonai. Therefore, it is written with hidden letters YUD HEI VAV HEI, and it is read with these letters, ADONAI. This covers that. THE NAME ADONAI COVERS THE NAME YUD HEI VAV HEI, so the high glory will be covered and concealed forever. For all the ways of the Torah are like that: covered and uncovered. And all the matters of the world, either of this world or the high world are covered and uncovered, MEANING THAT THERE IS AN INTERNAL PART TO EVERYTHING.

189. פָּתַח וְאָמַר, וַיֹּאמְרוּ אֵלָיו הַגִּידָה נָא לָנוּ בַּאֲשֶׁר לְמִי הָרָעָה הַזֹּאת לָנוּ וְגוֹ׳. הַאי קְרָא אִית לְאִסְתַּכְּלָא בֵּיהּ, כֻּלְּהוּ בְּרָזָא דְּחָכְמְתָא שָׁאִילוּ. דִּכְתִּיב הַגִּידָה נָא לָנוּ בַּאֲשֶׁר לְמִי, בַּאֲשֶׁר, רָזָא דְּחָכְמְתָא שָׁאִילוּ. הָכָא שָׁאִילוּ רָזָא דְּאִיהוּ בְּאִתְגַּלְיָיא, לְמִנְדַּע אִי מִזַּרְעָא דְּיוֹסֵף קָאָתֵי, דְּיַמָּא כֵּיוָן דְּחָמָא אֲרוֹנָא דִּילֵיהּ, מִיַּד אִתְבְּקַע, וַהֲוָה יַבֶּשְׁתָּא, דִּכְתִּיב הַיָּם רָאָה וַיָּנוֹס, הַיָּם רָאָה, הַהוּא דִּכְתִּיב בֵּיהּ וַיָּנָס וַיֵּצֵא הַחוּצָה. מִיַּד

הַיַּרְדֵּן יִסּוֹב לְאָחוֹר.

189. He opened the discussion and said: "Then they said to him, tell us, we pray you, inasmuch as to whose cause this evil is upon us..." (Yonah 1:8). We should look at this verse, for all they asked was in the secret of wisdom. It is written, "tell us, we pray you, inasmuch as to whose cause," they asked, "inasmuch" with deep wisdom. They asked for an uncovered secret, to know whether he was of the seed of Joseph, for the sea, when it saw his coffin, straightway divided itself and became dry land, as it is written, "the sea saw and fled" (Tehilim 114:3). The sea saw him of whom it is written, "and fled, and went outside" (Beresheet 39:15). Immediately IT SPLIT, "the Jordan turned backward" (Tehilim 114:3).

190. וְעַל דָּא שָׁאִילוּ לֵיהּ בַּאֲשֶׁר, דִּכְתִּיב בֵּיהּ בְּיוֹסֵף, בַּאֲשֶׁר אַתְּ אִשְׁתּוֹ. אִי מֵהַהוּא זַרְעָא קָא אָתִית, צַלֵּי דְּיִשְׁתּוֹק יַמָּא מִינָן. לְמִי, וְאִי מִזַּרְעָא דְּיַעֲקֹב קָא אָתִית, דִּכְתִּיב בֵּיהּ, לְמִי אַתָּה וְאָנָה תֵלֵךְ, וְאִינּוּן הֲווֹ מַלְאֲכִין קַדִּישִׁין, דְּשָׁדַר בִּשְׁלִיחוּתֵיהּ, וְאִשְׁתְּזִיב מֵהַהוּא עָאקוּ. צַלֵּי לְמָרָךְ, וִישַׁדֵּר מַלְאֲכֵיהּ, וְנִשְׁתְּזִיב מֵהַהוּא עָאקוּ.

190. That is why they asked him "inasmuch," NAMELY, PRAY TELL US "INASMUCH AS TO WHOSE CAUSE THIS EVIL," FOR it is said about Joseph, "inasmuch as you are his wife" (Beresheet 39:9). THEY HINTED AT HIM BY THIS WORD: if you are of that seed OF JOSEPH, pray that the sea will be quiet. BY THIS WORD "Whose" IN "WHOSE CAUSE THIS EVIL," THEY HINTED THUS: are you a descendant of Jacob, who said, "Whose are you? And whither do you go?" (Beresheet 32:18). They, WHOM JACOB ADDRESSED, were the holy messengers he sent TO ESAU on an errand and so he was saved from that trouble. Now YOU TOO pray to your Master to send His messengers so we would be saved from this trouble.

191. וְאִי לָאו, מַה מְּלַאכְתְּךָ, בְּמָה אִשְׁתַּדְּלוּתָךְ בְּכָל יוֹמָא. וּמֵאַיִן תָּבֹא, מַאן אִינּוּן אֲבָהֲתָךְ. מָה אַרְצֶךָ, אִי הִיא אַרְעָא דְּאִתְחַזְיָיא לְאִתְעַנְשָׁא. וְאִי מִזֶּה עַם אָתָּה, אִי הוּא עֲמָלֵק, אוֹ חַד מִשִּׁבְעָה עַמְמִין, דְּאִתְחָזוּן לְאִתְעַנְשָׁא. כֹּלָּא שָׁאִילוּ לֵיהּ כַּדְקָא יֵאוֹת.

191. If this is not so, THEN TELL US, "what is your occupation," namely, what is your daily business? "And where do you come from," who are your forefathers? "What is your country," NAMELY, does it deserve punishment? "And of what people are you," to see whether he is of Amalek or of one of the seven nations that deserve punishment. All was properly asked.

192. מַה אָתִיב לוֹן, וַיֹּאמֶר אֲלֵיהֶם עִבְרִי אָנֹכִי, מֵהַהוּא זַרְעָא דְּאַבְרָהָם הָעִבְרִי, דְּאַקְדִּישׁ שְׁמָא דְּמָארֵיהּ בְּכָל יוֹמָא בְּעָלְמָא. וְאֶת יְיָ' אֱלֹהֵי הַשָּׁמַיִם אֲנִי יָרֵא וְגוֹ', אִינּוּן לָא שָׁאִילוּ לֵיהּ אֶלָּא מִלָּה בְּאִתְגַּלְיָא וּבְאִתְכַּסְיָא לְמִנְדַּע בֵּיהּ. וְאִיהוּ אָתִיב לוֹן כֹּלָּא בְּאִתְגַּלְיָא.

192. What did Jonah answer? "And he said to them: 'I am a Hebrew,'" namely, from the seed of Abraham the Hebrew, who sanctified the Name of his Master every day, "and I fear Hashem, the Elohim of heaven…" (Yonah 1:9). They asked to know both openly and covertly. NAMELY, THEY ASKED BY HINTING BY THE WORDS "INASMUCH" AND "WHOSE," COVERTLY, THE REST OF THE QUESTIONS WERE OPEN. And he, JONAH, answered all their questions openly.

193. מַה כְּתִיב וַיִּירְאוּ הָאֲנָשִׁים יִרְאָה גְּדוֹלָה, כֵּיוָן דְּשַׁמְעוּ שְׁמָא דְקוּדְשָׁא בְּרִיךְ הוּא, מִיַּד דָּחִילוּ, בְּגִין דְּכֻלְּהוּ הֲווֹ יַדְעִין נִסִּין וּגְבוּרָאן דְּעָבֵד קוּדְשָׁא בְּרִיךְ הוּא בְּיַמָּא, וְכֵיוָן דְּאָמַר לוֹן שְׁמָא דְקוּדְשָׁא בְּרִיךְ הוּא, מִיַּד דָּחִילוּ קַמֵּיהּ דְּחִילוּ סַגִּיא. תּוּ אָמַר לוֹן, דְּאִיהוּ עָרַק מִקָּמֵי קוּדְשָׁא בְּרִיךְ הוּא. וְעַל דָּא אָמְרוּ לֵיהּ, מַה זֹּאת עָשִׂיתָ, דְּאַנְתְּ עַרְקַת מִקַּמֵּיהּ, וְלָא עַבְדַּת פִּקּוּדוֹי. וּבְגִין כַּךְ מַה זֹּאת עָשִׂיתָ דְּאַנְתְּ עָבַרְתָּ עַל פִּקּוּדֵי דְּמָארָךְ.

193. It is written, "then the men were exceedingly afraid" (Ibid. 10). When they heard the Name of the Holy One, blessed be He, they were afraid because they knew of the miracles and mighty deeds performed by the Holy One, blessed be He upon the sea. So when he mentioned the Name of the Holy One, blessed be He, they "were exceedingly afraid." He also told them that he flees the Holy One, blessed be He, so they asked him 'Why have you done this?' running away from Him and not obeying HIS commands.

Therefore, they asked: 'Why have you done this?' You are transgressing your Master's commands.

194. וְתָא חֲזֵי, כָּל אִלֵּין אִתְגַּיָּירוּ לְבָתַר, כַּד חָמוּ נִסִּין וּגְבוּרָן דְּעָבֵד לֵיהּ קוּדְשָׁא בְּרִיךְ הוּא לְיוֹנָה בְּיַמָּא. וְכֻלְּהוּ חָמוּ לֵיהּ כַּד נָפַל בְּיַמָּא, וְהַהוּא נוּנָא דְּסָלִיק וּבָלַע לֵיהּ קַמַּיְיהוּ. וְכַד אָתָא הַהוּא נוּנָא רַבָּא לְעֵינֵיהוֹן דְּכֹלָּא, וּפָלַט לֵיהּ לְיַבֶּשְׁתָּא, אָתוּ לְגַבֵּיהּ וְאִתְגַּיְּירוּ כֻּלְּהוּ. הה"ד, מְשַׁמְּרִים הַבְלֵי שָׁוְא חַסְדָּם יַעֲזוֹבוּ.

194. Come and see: All of them converted afterwards, when they saw the miracles and mighty deeds that the Holy One, blessed be He did to Jonah at sea. They all saw him falling into the sea, and the fish swallowing him in their presence. And when that great fish came before their eyes and vomited him onto the dry land, they came to Him and became proselytes. This is the meaning of "They that guard lying vanities forsake their loyalty" (Yonah 2:9).

195. וְתָא חֲזֵי, כֻּלְּהוּ אִלֵּין הֲווֹ גֵּרֵי צֶדֶק, וְאִתְחַכָּמוּ בְּאוֹרַיְיתָא, וַהֲווֹ חַכִּימִין עִלָּאִין, בְּגִין דְּהָא קוּדְשָׁא בְּרִיךְ הוּא אִתְרְעֵי בְּהוּ, וּבְכָל אִינּוּן דְּמִקָּרְבֵי לְגַבֵּיהּ, וּמְקַדְּשִׁין שְׁמֵיהּ בְּאִתְגַּלְיָא דְּכַד אִתְקַדָּשׁ שְׁמֵיהּ בְּאִתְגַּלְיָא, שְׁמֵיהּ דְּאִתְכַּסְיָא, אִסְתְּלִיק עַל כּוּרְסֵי יְקָרֵיהּ, דִּכְתִּיב וְנִקְדַּשְׁתִּי בְּתוֹךְ בְּנֵי יִשְׂרָאֵל.

195. Come and see: They were all proselytes by conviction and became knowledgeable in the Torah, and high sages, because the Holy One, blessed be He, favored them and all those who approach Him, to sanctify His Name openly. For when His Name is sanctified openly, His hidden Name, YUD HEI VAV HEI, rises on His throne of glory, WHICH IS ADONAI, SO THERE IS UNISON OF YUD HEI VAV HEI ADONAI, as it is written, "and I will be hallowed among the children of Yisrael" (Vayikra. 22:32).

196. וַיִּרְכְּסוּ אֶת הַחֹשֶׁן מִטַּבְּעֹתָיו אֶל טַבְּעֹת הָאֵפוֹד בִּפְתִיל תְּכֵלֶת. אֲמַאי בִּפְתִיל תְּכֵלֶת. אֶלָּא לְאַחֲזָאָה בְּהַאי תְּכֵלָא אִתְקַשַּׁר בְּכֹלָּא. וְעַל דָּא כֹּלָּא אִיהוּ בְּרָזָא עִלָּאָה.

196. "And they bound the breastplate by its rings to the rings of the Efod with a lace of blue" (Shemot 39:21). HE ASKS: Why "with a lace of blue"? AND HE ANSWERS: To show that this blue, THE JUDGMENT PART OF MALCHUT, BOUND WITH CHESED, is connected to all. Therefore, all is in the high secret, THE BLUE TYING THE BREASTPLATE, WHICH IS ZEIR ANPIN, TO THE EFOD, WHICH IS MALCHUT.

197. מַה כְּתִיב, פַּעֲמוֹן זָהָב וְרִמּוֹן, וְאוֹקִימְנָא, וְכֹלָּא אִיהוּ בְּרָזָא עִלָּאָה כִּדְקָאָמְרָן. מַה כְּתִיב, וְנִשְׁמַע קוֹלוֹ בְּבֹאוֹ אֶל הַקֹּדֶשׁ לִפְנֵי יְיָ'. בְּגִין דְּאִצְטְרִיךְ קָלָא דְּאִשְׁתְּמַע, וּבִרְכָּאן יִשְׁרוּן עַל עָלְמָא בְּגִינֵיהּ דְּכַהֲנָא, דְּאִיהוּ מְבָרֵךְ כֹּלָּא, וּפָלַח כֹּלָּא. פַּעֲמוֹן זָהָב, הָא אוֹקִימְנָא. רִמּוֹן, דְּאִתְמַלְיָיא כְּרִמּוֹנָא דָּא, דְּאִיהוּ אִתְמַלְיָיא מִכֹּלָּא, וְכֹלָּא אוֹקִימְנָא.

197. It is written, "a golden bell and a pomegranate" (Shemot 28:34). And we explained that all pertains to the high secret as we said. It is therefore written, "and its sound shall be heard when he goes in to the holy place before Hashem" (Ibid. 35). For he is in need of the sound that is heard, WHICH IS ZEIR ANPIN, and blessings dwell in the world for the priest's sake, who blesses all and performs everything. "The golden bell" we explained TO BE THE SOUND THAT IS HEARD, NAMELY ZEIR ANPIN. "A pomegranate" IS MALCHUT filled by all, RECEIVING FROM ALL THE HIGHER WORLDS. And we explained all.

198. וַיַּעַשׂ אֶת מְעִיל הָאֵפוֹד מַעֲשֵׂה אוֹרֵג כְּלִיל תְּכֵלֶת. הָא אִתְּמַר בְּרָזָא דְּחֹשֶׁן וְאֵפוֹד, וְכֹלָּא חַד. כְּלִיל תְּכֵלֶת, דְּהָכִי אִתְחָזֵי כְּמָה דְּאוֹקִימְנָא, דִּתְכֵלָא אִיהוּ רָזָא דִּנְהוֹרָא דְּכוּרְסְיָיא תִּכְלָא. דְּאִיהוּ בְּקִשּׁוּרָא דִּנְהִירוּ חִוָּורָא, כֹּלָּא כַּחֲדָא. וְעַל דָּא תִּכְלָא לְאֵפוֹדָא אִיהוּ.

198. "And he made the robe of the Efod of woven work, all of blue" (Shemot 39:22). We already explained the secret of the breastplate and the Efod, and all is one. THAT IS, THE ROBE OF THE EFOD PERTAINS TO THE SAME MYSTERY AS THE EFOD, NAMELY MALCHUT. It is "all of blue," as ought to be, for blue is the secret of the light of the throne, MALCHUT, WHICH IS THE BLACK LIGHT OF THE CANDLE BURNING AND CONSUMING WHATEVER IS BENEATH IT. Blue is connected to the white light IN THE

CANDLE, WHICH IS CHESED, and therefore, the Efod is of blue, BEING THE LIGHT OF MALCHUT.

199. אָמַר רִבִּי שִׁמְעוֹן, הָנֵי מָאנֵי דִּלְבוּשִׁין דְּכַהֲנָא, כֻּלְּהוּ בְּרָזָא עִלָּאָה אִיהוּ, לְמֶהֱוֵי לְבוּשִׁין דִּלְתַתָּא, כְּגַוְונָא דִּלְעֵילָּא. תָּא חֲזֵי, כֵּיוָן דְּמִיכָאֵל כַּהֲנָא רַבָּא אִיהוּ, וְאָתֵי מִסִּטְרָא דִּימִינָא, אֲמַאי כְּתִיב בְּגַבְרִיאֵל, הָאִישׁ לְבוּשׁ הַבַּדִּים, דְּהָא לְבוּשִׁין לְכַהֲנָא רַבָּא אִיהוּ, וּמִיכָאֵל אִיהוּ כַּהֲנָא, וְאָתֵי מִסִּטְרָא דִּימִינָא. אֶלָּא מֵהָכָא, דִּשְׂמָאלָא אִתְכְּלִיל בִּימִינָא תָּדִיר, וְאִתְלָבַּשׁ גַּבְרִיאֵל בִּלְבוּשִׁין אִלֵּין.

199. Rabbi Shimon said: These priestly garments all pertain to the high mystery, that the garments of below bear the likeness of those from above. Come and see: Since Michael is a High Priest, and of the right, why is Gabriel depicted as "the man clothed in linen" (Daniel 12:6), whereas these are the garments of the High Priest, and Michael is a priest of the right side? HE REPLIES: It is UNDERSTOOD from this, that left is always included in the right, and therefore Gabriel, WHO IS OF THE LEFT, was clothed in these garments OF THE RIGHT.

200. תּוּ, דְּהָא גַּבְרִיאֵל אִיהוּ אִתְמַנָּא שְׁלִיחָא בְּהַאי עָלְמָא, וְכָל שְׁלִיחָא דְּאִתְמַנָּא בְּהַאי עָלְמָא, אִצְטְרִיךְ לְאִתְלַבְּשָׁא בִּלְבוּשִׁין דְּהַאי עָלְמָא, וְהָא אוֹקִימְנָא בְּרָזָא דְּנִשְׁמְתָא, כַּד סָלְקַת לְעֵילָּא אִתְלַבְּשַׁת בִּלְבוּשָׁא כְּגַוְונָא דִּלְעֵילָּא, בְּגִין לְמֶהֱוֵי תַּמָּן. וְכֵן כַּד נַחְתַּת לְתַתָּא מִלְּעֵילָּא, כֹּלָּא אִיהוּ כְּגַוְונָא דְּהַהוּא אֲתַר דְּאַזְלַת תַּמָּן. כְּגַוְונָא דָּא כָּל אִינּוּן שְׁלִיחָן דְּאִתְמְנָן בִּשְׁלִיחוּתָא בְּהַאי עָלְמָא, וְהָא אוֹקִימְנָא.

200. Also, ANOTHER EXPLANATION IS, that Gabriel was appointed messenger to this world, and every appointed messenger to this world should wear the garments of this world. We also explained this in the secret of the soul, that when it goes up, it wears the clothing of above, to be there, and when it descends, IT WEARS A GARMENT. And all, AND ALL THE GARMENT, is according to where it goes. In the same manner, these appointed messengers, on an errand to this world, NEED CLOTHES OF THIS WORLD. And we established that.

201. ות"ח, הַאי מְעִילָא דְּאֵפוֹדָא, לְחַפְיָא עָלֵיהּ, כַּד לָבִישׁ לֵיהּ. כְּתִיב אָחוֹר וָקֶדֶם צַרְתָּנִי וַתָּשֶׁת עָלַי כַּפֶּכָה.

201. Come and see: The robe of the Efod covered him AROUND HIS BODY. When he wore it, it is written, "You have beset me behind and before, and laid Your hand upon me" (Tehilim 139:5), THE BREASTPLATE BEING BEFORE AND THE EFOD FROM BEHIND.

202. הַאי קְרָא הָא אוּקְמוּהָ. אֲבָל ת"ח, בְּשַׁעֲתָא דְּבָרָא קוּדְשָׁא בְּרִיךְ הוּא לאדה"ר. דְּכַר וְנוּקְבָּא אִתְבְּרִיאוּ, וַהֲווֹ תַּרְוַויְיהוּ דָּא עִם דָּא קְשׁוּרָא, נוּקְבָּא לַאֲחוֹרָא, וּדְכוּרָא לְקָמָא, עַד דְּנָסַר לוֹן קוּדְשָׁא בְּרִיךְ הוּא, וְאַתְקִין לָהּ, וְאָעִיל לָהּ לְקַמֵּיהּ דְּאָדָם, לְאִסְתַּכְּלָא אַנְפִּין בְּאַנְפִּין, וְכֵיוָן דְּאִסְתַּכְּלוּ אַנְפִּין בְּאַנְפִּין, כְּדֵין אִתְסַגֵּי רְחִימוּתָא בְּעָלְמָא, וְאוֹלִידוּ תּוֹלְדִין בְּעָלְמָא, מַה דְּלָא הֲוַות מִקַּדְמַת דְּנָא, וְהָא אוֹקִימְנָא.

202. This verse, "YOU HAVE BESET..." was already explained. Nevertheless, come and see: When the Holy One, blessed be He created Adam, male and female were created, bound to each other so the female was from behind and the male in front, until the Holy One, blessed be He sawed AND SEPARATED them. He prepared and put her in front of Adam so that they may see face to face. When they looked face to face, love was increased in the world, and they issued offspring, something that was not beforehand. And we explained.

203. וּלְבָתַר דְּחָב אָדָם וְאִתְּתָא, וְאָתָא נָחָשׁ עַל חַוָּה, וְאָטִיל בָּהּ זוּהֲמָא, אוֹלִידַת חַוָּה לְקַיִן, וַהֲוָה דִּיּוּקְנֵיהּ, דִּיּוּקְנָא דִּלְעֵילָּא וְתַתָּא, מֵרָזָא דְּזוּהֲמָא דְּסִטְרָא אַחֲרָא, וּמִסִּטְרָא דִּלְתַתָּא. וְעַל דָּא אִיהוּ הֲוָה קַדְמָאָה, דַּעֲבַד מוֹתָא בְּעָלְמָא, בְּגִין דְּסִטְרָא דִּילֵיהּ גָּרִים. חִוְיָא אוֹרְחֵיהּ הוּא לְמֶהֱוֵי כַּמִּין לְקַטוֹלָא, הַהוּא דְּאָתֵי מִנֵּיהּ אוֹרְחֵיהּ נָקִיט וְאָזִיל, וְעַל דָּא כְּתִיב וַיְהִי בִּהְיוֹתָם בַּשָּׂדֶה וַיָּקָם קַיִן אֶל הֶבֶל אָחִיו וַיַּהַרְגֵהוּ.

203. After Adam and his wife sinned, and the serpent had intercourse with

Eve and injected filth into her, Eve bore Cain. He had the shape from above and FROM below in the secret of the filth of the Other Side, and from the side below OF THE EXTERNAL FORCES. Therefore, he was the first to bring death into the world, caused by his side, AS HE CAME OF THE FILTH OF THE SERPENT. The nature of the serpent is to lurk so as to kill, and his issue, CAIN, learned his ways. And so it is written, "and it came to pass, when they were in the field, that Cain rose up against Abel his brother and slew him" (Beresheet 4:8).

204. אַשְׁכַּחְנָא בְּסִפְרִין קַדְמָאִין, דְּכַד קָטַל לֵיהּ קַיִן לְהֶבֶל, הֲוָה נָשִׁיךְ לֵיהּ נְשִׁיכִין, כְּחִוְיָא, עַד דְּאַפִּיק נִשְׁמָתֵיהּ, וְקָטַל לֵיהּ.

204. I have found in ancient books, that when Cain killed Abel, he bit serpentine bites, until he killed him.

205. וְכָל מִלִּין אָהַדְרוּ לִיסוֹדָא קַדְמָאָה, וְאִי לָאו דַּהֲוָה קַיִן מֵהַהוּא סִטְרָא, לָא אִשְׁתְּכַח הָכִי לְגַבֵּי אָחוּהּ. וע״ד, כֵּיוָן דְּחָזָא אָדָם דְּאִתְקְטִיל הֶבֶל, וְאִתְתְּרִיךְ קַיִן, אָמַר, מָה אֲנָא אוֹלִיד מִכָּאן וּלְהָלְאָה, אִתְפְּרַשׁ מֵאִתְּתֵיהּ מֵאָה וּתְלָתִין שְׁנִין, וְרוּחִין נוּקְבֵי מִסְּאֲבֵי, הֲווֹ אַתְיָין וּמִתְחַמְּמָן מִנֵּיהּ, וַהֲוָה אוֹלִיד רוּחִין וְשֵׁדִין, וְאִקְרוּן נִגְעֵי בְּנֵי אָדָם, וְאוֹקִימְנָא.

205. All things return to the element, FROM WHERE THEY CAME. Unless Cain came from that side OF THE SERPENT, he would have not behaved so towards his brother. Therefore, when Adam saw Abel killed and Cain expelled, he said, 'why shall I henceforth be a father?' He separated from his wife for a hundred and thirty years, and unholy female spirits would come and conceive from him, and he begot spirits and demons called 'the plagues of men'. This was established.

206. לְבָתַר קָנֵי וְאִתְלָבַּשׁ בְּקִנְאָה, וְאִתְחַבַּר בְּאִתְּתֵיהּ, וְאוֹלִיד לְשֵׁת. דִּכְתִּיב וַיּוֹלֶד בִּדְמוּתוֹ כְּצַלְמוֹ וַיִּקְרָא אֶת שְׁמוֹ שֵׁת. דָּא אִיהוּ בִּדְמוּתוֹ כְּצַלְמוֹ, מַה דְּלָא הֲוָה הָכִי בְּקַדְמֵיתָא, בְּאִינּוּן בְּנִין קַדְמָאֵי, דַּהֲווֹ מִקַּדְמַת דְּנָא.

206. After that, he was jealous, and wore jealousy. He united with his wife and begot Seth as written, "and begot a son in his own likeness, after his image; and called his name Seth" (Beresheet 5:3), which was not true for the first sons born before.

207. בְּגִין, דְּהָא בְּקַדְמֵיתָא, אִתְחַבְּרוּתָא אַחֲרָא הֲוַות לְגַבֵּיהּ, וְאוּקְמוּהָ, עַד דְּאָתַת חַוָּה, וְאַתְקִין לָהּ קוּדְשָׁא בְּרִיךְ הוּא לְגַבֵּיהּ דְּאָדָם, וְאִתְחַבָּרוּ אַנְפִּין בְּאַנְפִּין. וְעַל דָּא כְּתִיב, לְזֹאת יִקָּרֵא אִשָּׁה, דָּא אִיהִי אִתְּתָא, אֲבָל אַחֲרָא לָא אִקְרֵי הָכִי. וְהָא אוּקְמוּהָ.

207. For in the beginning, BEFORE EVE, he had another union, WITH LILITH, as explained, until Eve came. For the Holy One, blessed be He prepared her for Adam, and they were united face to face. Therefore it is written, "this one shall be called 'woman'" (Beresheet 2:23). But the other one, LILIT, is not so called, as was explained.

208. וּבְגִין דְּאָדָם וְחַוָּה כַּחֲדָא אִתְבְּרִיאוּ, כְּתִיב זָכָר וּנְקֵבָה בְּרָאָם וַיְבָרֶךְ אוֹתָם, תַּרְוַויְיהוּ כַּחֲדָא הֲווֹ. וְעַל דָּא כְּתִיב, אָחוֹר וָקֶדֶם צַרְתָּנִי.

208. Since Adam and Eve were created together, it is written, "male and female He created them, and blessed them" (Beresheet 5:2). The two of them were together, therefore it was written, "You have beset me behind and before."

209. ת"ח, אֵפוֹד וְחֹשֶׁן, אָחוֹר וָקֶדֶם הֲווֹ, וְכַד כַּהֲנָא אִתְלְבַּשׁ בְּהוּ, הֲוָה דָּמֵי בְּדִיוּקְנָא עִלָּאָה. וְהָא אִתְּמַר, דִּכְדֵין אַנְפּוֹי נְהִירִין, וְאַתְוָון בַּלְטִין, וְסַלְּקִין לְעֵילָּא מִנַּהֲרָן, וּכְדֵין הֲוָה יָדַע מִלָּה.

209. Come and see: The Efod and the breastplate were behind and before, THE BREASTPLATE BEFORE AND THE EFOD BEHIND. And when the priest wore them, he had the likeness of the higher image, ZEIR ANPIN AND MALCHUT, THE SECRET OF BEHIND AND BEFORE. And we have learned, that his face shone and the letters stood out, illuminating and rising up. Then he knew that WHICH WAS NEEDED.

210. וּבְגִין כַּךְ, תִּקּוּנָא דְּחוֹשְׁנָא, וְתִקּוּנָא דְּאֵפוֹדָא, כַּחֲדָא מִתְקַשְּׁרָן. ואע״ג דְּתִקּוּנָא דְּדָא לָאו אִיהוּ כְּתִקּוּנָא דְּדָא, וְכֹלָּא בְּרָזָא חֲדָא. קְשׁוּרָא דְּדָא בְּדָא, לְאִתְאַחֲדָא חוֹשְׁנָא בְּאֵפוֹדָא, בְּאַרְבַּע עִזְקָן, דְּאִתְקַשְּׁרוּ בְּהַאי אֲתָר, וּבְהַאי אֲתָר. וְאִינּוּן רָזָא דְּאִינּוּן רְתִיכִין, דְּמִתְקַשְּׁרָן בְּהַאי סִטְרָא דִּלְתַתָּא, לְאִינּוּן דִּלְעֵילָּא, וְכֹלָּא אִיהוּ בְּרָזָא דְּאוֹפַנִּין וְחַיּוֹת.

210. For that reason the function of the breastplate and the function of the Efod are closely connected. And though their functions are not the same, yet all is in the one secret. They are connected so the breastplate, WHICH IS ZEIR ANPIN, will be united with the Efod, WHICH IS MALCHUT, by four rings connected to this place and that place, NAMELY, TO THE BREASTPLATE AND THE EFOD. They are the secret of the Chariots connecting this side below to those above, all in the mystery of the wheels and the holy living creatures. FOR THE TWO RINGS IN THE BREASTPLATE ARE IN THE SECRET OF THE LIVING CREATURES, WHICH ARE YETZIRAH. AND THE TWO RINGS IN THE EFOD ARE IN THE SECRET OF THE WHEELS, WHICH ARE ASIYAH. AND THEY ARE INTERCONNECTED, AS SAID: "AND WHEN THE LIVING CREATURES MOVED, THE WHEELS WENT BY THEM: AND WHEN THE LIVING CREATURES WERE LIFTED UP FROM THE EARTH, THE WHEELS WERE LIFTED UP" (YECHEZKEL 1:19).

211. כְּתִיב, בְּרֵאשִׁית בָּרָא אֱלֹהִים אֵת הַשָּׁמַיִם וְאֵת הָאָרֶץ. וְאוּקְמוּהָ, דְּהָא כֹּלָּא כְּגַוְונָא דָּא אִתְעֲבִיד מַשְׁכְּנָא, כְּגַוְונָא דְּעָלְמָא תַּתָּאָה, עֲבַד כְּגַוְונָא דְּעָלְמָא עִלָּאָה, וְכָל עוֹבָדוֹי דְּעָבֵד כְּגַוְונָא דִּלְעֵילָּא. ה״נ מַשְׁכְּנָא, כָּל עוֹבָדוֹי אִינּוּן כְּעוֹבָדָא וּכְגַוְונָא דְּעָלְמָא עִלָּאָה.

211. It is written, "In the beginning Elohim created the heaven and the earth" (Beresheet 1:1). It was explained, THAT THE HEAVEN IS ZEIR ANPIN AND THE EARTH IS MALCHUT. The Tabernacle was made in the same manner, in the likeness of the lower world, WHICH IS MALCHUT, and in the likeness of the upper world, WHICH IS ZEIR ANPIN. And all the deeds OF THE HOLY ONE, BLESSED BE HE performed in this world are a reflection of above. So is the Tabernacle. All its works are as the deeds, and are reflections of the upper world.

212. וְרָזָא דָּא כָּל עוֹבָדִין דְּמַשְׁכְּנָא, כֻּלְּהוּ עוֹבָדִין וְתִקּוּנִין דִּלְעֵילָּא וְתַתָּא, בְּגִין לְאַשְׁרָאָה שְׁכִינְתָּא בְּעָלְמָא, בְּדִיוּרִין עִלָּאִין, וּבְדִיוּרִין תַּתָּאִין. כְּגַוְונָא דָּא, גַּן עֵדֶן לְתַתָּא, אִיהוּ כְּגַוְונָא עִלָּאָה. וּכְגַוְונָא תַּתָּאָה, כָּל צִיּוּרִין, וְכָל דִּיוּקְנִין דְּעָלְמָא כֻּלְּהוּ תַּמָּן. וְעַל דָּא, עֲבִידַת מַשְׁכְּנָא, וַעֲבִידַת שָׁמַיִם וְאֶרֶץ, כֻּלְּהוּ בְּרָזָא חֲדָא.

212. This is the secret of the construction of the Tabernacle. All are deeds and improvements of above and below, to let the Shechinah dwell upon the world, over the upper tenants, THE ANGELS, and the lower tenants, PEOPLE. In the same manner, the lower Garden of Eden is like the upper, BINAH, and the lower, MALCHUT. And all the images and forms of the world are found there. Therefore, the construction of the Tabernacle and of heaven and earth, ZEIR ANPIN AND MALCHUT, are in one secret.

22. "Lift up your eyes on high"

A Synopsis

Rabbi Shimon asks if anyone who lifts his eyes and looks up could see anything that he wasn't permitted to see. He answers that the title verse means that whoever wants to see and know about God's deeds should look up, and after seeing all the armies and legions of angels then he can ask "Who created these?" Rabbi Shimon says that 'who' is Binah, and that there is never an answer because Binah is always hidden and concealed and unknown. Next he talks about: "Who brings out their host by number," saying that Binah brings everything out with the sound of the Shofar. This is the secret of the divine faith, that extends through all the levels from Zeir Anpin and downward all the way to Malchut. The armies are then divided up and numbered and named. Rabbi Shimon extends another explanation for "Lift up your eyes on high," and that is that whoever looked at the Tabernacle saw in it both what was above and what was below. All the works of both worlds were contained in it.

213. כְּתִיב שְׂאוּ מָרוֹם עֵינֵיכֶם וּרְאוּ מִי בָרָא אֵלֶּה וְגוֹ'. הַאי קְרָא אוּקְמוּהָ, אֲבָל ת"ח, וְכִי בְּגִין דְּיִסְתָּכַּל ב"נ עֵינוֹי לְעֵילָּא, וְזָקִיף לוֹן לְעֵילָּא, יָכִיל לְמִנְדַּע וּלְאִסְתַּכְּלָא בְּמָה דְּלָא אִתְרְשׁוּ לְמִנְדַּע וּלְמֶחֱמֵי.

213. It is written, "Lift up your eyes on high, and behold who has created these..." (Yeshayah 40:26). This verse was already explained. Nevertheless Come and see: Could anyone who lifts up his eyes and looks up, know and behold what is not permitted for him to see?

214. אֶלָּא שְׂאוּ מָרוֹם עֵינֵיכֶם, מַאן דְּבָעֵי לְאִסְתַּכְּלָא וּלְמִנְדַּע בְּעוֹבָדוֹי דְקוּדְשָׁא בְּרִיךְ הוּא, יִזְקוֹף עֵינוֹי לְעֵילָּא, וְיֶחֱמֵי כַּמָּה חַיָּילִין, וְכַמָּה מַשִׁרְיָין, עוֹבָדִין מְשַׁנְיָין דָּא מִן דָּא, רַבְרְבִין אִלֵּין מֵאִלֵּין. וּכְדֵין תֶּחֱמוּן וְתִשְׁאֲלוּן וְתֵימְרוּן, מַאן בָּרָא אִלֵּין. מִי בָּרָא אֵלֶּה, הָא אוּקִימְנָא רָזָא דְּמִי, בָּרָא אֵלֶּה. דְּהוּא אֲתָר דְּקַיְּימָא מָרוֹם וְגָנִיז וְסָתִים וְלָא יְדִיעַ, וְקַיְּימָא תָּדִיר לְשָׁאֲלָה, בְּגִין דְּלָא אִתְגַּלְיָיא לְהַהוּא אֲתָר.

214. HE REPLIES: No, "Lift up your eyes on high" MEANS THAT whoever wishes to behold and know the deeds of the Holy One, blessed be He, let him lift up his eyes and see how many are the armies and legions, AND HOW MANY are the deeds, each different than the other, one mightier than the other. Then you may look and ask “Who created these?” We explained this mystery: ‘who’, WHICH IS BINAH, created ‘these’. FOR BINAH is a place located up high, hidden, concealed and unknown. It remains a constant question, because this place is not revealed.

215. הַמּוֹצִיא בְּמִסְפָּר צְבָאָם, מַאי הַמּוֹצִיא. אֶלָּא בְּגִין דְּהַהוּא אֲתָר דְּאִיהוּ טָמִיר וְגָנִיז, אִיהוּ אַפִּיק כֹּלָּא, בְּרָזָא דְּקוֹל דְּנָפִיק מִשּׁוֹפָר. וְהַהוּא קוֹל, אִיהוּ מִסְפָּר דְּכָל חֵילִין עִלָּאִין, וְחוּשְׁבְּנָא דְּכֹלָּא. וּמִתַּמָּן אִשְׁתְּכַח רָזָא דִּמְהֵימְנוּתָא עִלָּאָה, בְּכָל אִינּוּן סִטְרִין עִלָּאִין, עַד דְּנַגְדִּין דַּרְגִּין, וְאִתְמַשְׁכָאן לְתַתָּא, וְאִתְפָּרְשָׁאן כַּמָּה חֵילִין לְזַנַּיְיהוּ, וְכֻלְּהוּ קַיְימָן בְּחוּשְׁבְּנָא, וְאִקְרוּן בִּשְׁמָא. מֵרוֹב אוֹנִים, דָּא סִטְרָא דִּימִינָא. וְאַמִּיץ כֹּחַ, דָּא סִטְרָא דִּשְׂמָאלָא. אִישׁ לֹא נֶעְדָּר, סִטְרִין דְּנַגְדִּין מִתְּרֵין עִבְרִין.

215. “Who brings out their host by number.” HE ASKS: What does “that brings out” mean? HE ANSWERS: Since that place is hidden and concealed, NAMELY, BINAH, it brings out all by the secret of the sound coming out of the Shofar, ZEIR ANPIN CALLED ‘SOUND’ COMES OUT OF BINAH CALLED ‘SHOFAR’. That sound is the amount of all the supernal armies and the account of everything. Thence is found the secret of the divine Faith, WHICH IS MALCHUT, on all the supernal sides, CHASSADIM ON THE RIGHT AND CHOCHMAH ON THE LEFT, WHERE CHOCHMAH IS REVEALED. It extends in grades FROM ZEIR ANPIN downward TO MALCHUT. The armies are then divided after their kind, and all are numbered and called by name. “Because of the greatness of His might” (Ibid.) refers to the right side;“He is strong in power” (Ibid.) refers to the left side. “No one is missing” (Ibid.) from the sides drawn from the two directions, FROM THE TWO COLUMNS RIGHT AND LEFT, WHERE NOTHING IS MISSING, BECAUSE THEY COMPREHEND ALL OF REALITY. EVEN THE CENTRAL COLUMN ADDS NOTHING, ONLY COMPRISES WHAT IS IN THE TWO COLUMNS, RIGHT AND LEFT.

216. דָּבָר אַחֵר שְׂאוּ מָרוֹם עֵינֵיכֶם וּרְאוּ מִי בָרָא אֵלֶּה, הַאי קְרָא כַּד

אִתְּקַם מַשְׁכְּנָא. וַהֲוָה אִתְתָּקַּן, כָּל מַאן דְּחָמֵי לֵיהּ לְמַשְׁכְּנָא, אִסְתָּכַּל בֵּיהּ לְעֵילָּא וְתַתָּא, וְכֹלָּא חָמֵי בֵּיהּ בְּמַשְׁכְּנָא. בְּגִין דְּכָל עוֹבָדִין דְּעָלְמָא עִלָּאָה וְתַתָּאָה, כֻּלְּהוּ אִתְתָּקָנוּ בֵּיהּ בְּמַשְׁכְּנָא, וְהָא אוּקִימְנָא, כָּל מַאן דְּחָמֵי אִינּוּן קְרָסִים בְּמַשְׁכְּנָא, וְאִסְתָּכַּל בְּהוּ, הֲוָה מִסְתָּכַּל בִּנְהִירוּ דִּלְהוֹן, בִּנְהִירוּ דְּכֹכְבַיָּא, בְּגִין דְּהָכִי קַיְּימָן כֹּכָבַיָּא בִּרְקִיעָא.

216. Another explanation to the verse, "Lift up your eyes on high and behold, who has created these." This verse means that when the Tabernacle was constructed and completed, whoever saw the Tabernacle, beheld in it WHAT WAS above, and WHAT WAS below, and saw all that in the Tabernacle. For all the works of the upper world and the lower world were all contained in the Tabernacle. And we established that whoever looked at the clasps, could see in their illumination that of the stars, because this is how the stars are situated in the firmament.

23. "Praise Hashem from the heavens"

A Synopsis

Rabbi Shimon talks about two of the Psalms of praise and how they correspond to the Sfirot and the names of God and then the parts of the body. He says that "Praise Him, all His angels" refers to the two pillars Netzach and Hod that stand underneath and support the body, Tiferet. These pillars are also the secret of the angels, and the knees are the messengers. Speaking about "Praise Him, sun and moon," Rabbi Shimon tells us that the sun includes all the Sfirot of Zeir Anpin, and therefore it contains all the high stars and constellations. When it has finished shining it goes up to a high place from where Briyah, Yetzirah and Asiyah all emanate. He reveals that the stars below exist by virtue of what they can draw from the supernal pattern in Zeir Anpin, so all the stars and constellations from the highest firmament rule the world beneath them. From that high place there are levels all the way down to the stars below in this world that don't have anything under their command. Everything is ruled by the higher level.

217. פָּתַח וְאָמַר, הַלְלוּיָהּ הַלְלוּ אֶת יְיָ' מִן הַשָּׁמַיִם וְגוֹ', ת"ח תּוּשְׁבַּחְתָּא דָּא אָמַר דָּוִד, לְקָבֵל רָזָא דִּשְׁמָא קַדִּישָׁא, דְּאִיהוּ כְּלָלָא דְּתוּשְׁבַּחְתָּא דְּכֹלָּא. תְּרֵין תּוּשְׁבְּחָן אִינּוּן, כְּגַוְונָא דְּרָזָא דִּשְׁמָא קַדִּישָׁא עִלָּאָה, דְּאִיהוּ כְּלָלָא דְּתוּשְׁבַּחְתָּא דְּכֹלָּא. וְאִינּוּן: דָּא, וְתוּשְׁבַּחְתָּא בַּתְרָאָה, דְּאִיהִי כְּלָלָא דְּתוּשְׁבַּחְתָּא דְּכֹלָּא, דִּכְתִּיב הַלְלוּיָהּ הַלְלוּ אֵל בְּקָדְשׁוֹ וְגוֹ'. אֲבָל דָּא הֲוָה, עַל עֶשֶׂר מִינִים. וְדָא הוּא עַל שֶׁבַע, וְכֹלָּא רָזָא חֲדָא בִּשְׁמָא קַדִּישָׁא.

217. He opened the discussion and said: "Haleluyah, Praise Hashem from the heavens…" (Tehilim 148:1). Come and see: This praise was said by David in reference to the secret of the Holy Name, YUD HEI VAV HEI, NAMELY ZEIR ANPIN, which is comprised of all the praises. There are two praises reflecting the secret of the Holy Supernal Name, YUD HEI VAV HEI, which is comprised of all the praises. There is this one "PRAISE HASHEM FROM THE HEAVENS" and the last praise IN THE BOOK OF TEHILIM that is comprised of all of the praises, as it is written, "Haleluyah, praise Hashem in His sanctuary" (Tehilim 150:1). In the latter there are ten kinds, AS TEN TIMES IT IS MENTIONED, CORRESPONDING TO THE TEN

SFIROT OF ZEIR ANPIN. The former consists of seven, FOR SEVEN TIMES THE WORD "PRAISE" APPEARS, CORRESPONDING TO CHESED, GVURAH, TIFERET, NETZACH, HOD, YESOD AND MALCHUT OF ZEIR ANPIN. And everything is the one secret of the Holy Name.

218. הַלְלוּיָהּ הַלְלוּ אֶת יְיָ׳ מִן הַשָּׁמַיִם, אִיהוּ שֵׁירוּתָא דְּשִׁית סִטְרִין לְאִתְפַּשְּׁטָא לְתַתָּא, דְּדָא אִיהוּ רָזָא דְּקַיְימָא לִשְׁאֵלָה, כד״א, כִּי שְׁאַל נָא לְיָמִים רִאשׁוֹנִים אֲשֶׁר הָיוּ לְפָנֶיךָ וְגו׳, עַד הָכָא אִית רְשׁוּ לְשָׁאֲלָה, מִן הַיּוֹם אֲשֶׁר בָּרָא וְגו׳, וְעַד קְצֵה הַשָּׁמַיִם מִכָּאן וּלְהָלְאָה, לָאו קַיְימָא לִשְׁאֵלָא, בְּגִין דְּאִיהוּ אֲתָר טָמִיר וְגָנִיז.

218. "Haleluyah, praise Hashem from the heavens": this refers to the beginning from where the six directions, CHESED, GVURAH, TIFERET, NETZACH, HOD AND YESOD, emanate downward, for this secret may be examined, OR COMPREHENDED, NAMELY, ZEIR ANPIN, according to the verse, "For ask now of the days that are past, which were before you..." (Devarim 4:32). THEY ARE THE SEVEN DAYS CHESED, GVURAH, TIFERET, NETZACH, HOD, YESOD AND MALCHUT OF ZEIR ANPIN, up to which one may investigate, "From the day of creation until the end of heaven" (Ibid.), CHESED OF ZEIR ANPIN. From here and further, WHICH ARE KETER, CHOCHMAH AND BINAH OF ZEIR ANPIN, one may not inquire there, because that place is hidden and concealed.

219. וע״ד הַלְלוּ אֶת יְיָ׳ מִן הַשָּׁמַיִם הַלְלוּהוּ בַּמְּרוֹמִים, אִלֵּין תְּרֵין סִטְרִין, יְמִינָא וּשְׂמָאלָא. וּמֵהָכָא אִתְפַּשְּׁטָאן כֻּלְּהוּ אַחֲרָנִין לְתַתָּא, בְּרָזָא דְּדַרְגִּין לְאִתְתַּקְנָא כַּדְקָא יֵאוֹת. הַלְלוּהוּ כָל מַלְאָכָיו, אִלֵּין תְּרֵין קַיְימִין דְּקַיְימֵי תְּחוֹת גּוּפָא, לְמִשְׁעַן גּוּפָא עֲלַיְיהוּ.

219. Therefore, "Praise Hashem from the heavens, praise Him in the heights," allude to the two sides right and left, NAMELY, CHESED AND GVURAH OF ZEIR ANPIN, whence emanate all the other SFIROT downward in the mystery of the grades, to be properly corrected. "Praise Him, all His angels" (Tehilim 148:2): these are the two pillars, NETZACH AND HOD, standing underneath the body, TIFERET, so it may lean on them.

220. ת"ח, אִינּוּן קַיָּימִין דְגוּפָא אִשְׁתְּעָן עֲלַיְיהוּ, קַיְימֵי הָכָא בְּרָזָא דְמַלְאָכִין, בְּגִין דְּיַרְכִּין אִינּוּן שְׁלִיחָן, לְמֵיזַל מֵאֲתָר לַאֲתָר, וּמֵרָזָא דָא, נָפְקִין אִינּוּן דְּאִקְרוּן מַלְאֲכִין, דְּאִינּוּן שְׁלִיחָן לְמֵהַךְ בִּשְׁלִיחוּתָא דְמָארֵיהוֹן, מֵאֲתָר לַאֲתָר.

220. Come and see: These pillars upon which the body stands, pertain to the secret of the angels, ABOUT WHOM IT WAS SAID: "PRAISE HIM, ALL HIS ANGELS." For the knees are the messengers of the body to go from place to place. Of this secret are also those called 'angels', the messengers that go from place to place, at the behest of their Master.

221. הַלְלוּהוּ כָּל צְבָאָיו, דָּא אִיהוּ אֲתָר דְּנַפְקֵי מִנֵּיהּ כָּל חֵילִין קַדִּישִׁין עִלָּאִין, רָזָא דְּאָת קַיָּימָא קַדִּישָׁא, וְאִיהוּ רָשִׁים בְּכָל שְׁאַר רִבְוָון, כַּדְקָא אֲמָרָן, דִּכְתִּיב יְיָ' צְבָאוֹת שְׁמוֹ, אוֹת אִיהוּ בְּכָל שְׁאַר חֵילִין וְרִבְוָון.

221. "Praise Him, all His hosts" (Ibid. 2). This is the place from where all the holy high armies come out. It is the secret of the sign of the Holy Covenant, NAMELY, YESOD OF ZEIR ANPIN. It is marked upon all the tens of thousands ISSUING FROM IT, as it is written, "Hashem Tzevaot is His Name" (Yeshayah 48:2), MEANING THAT this sign is marked upon all the rest of the armies and multitudes.

222. הַלְלוּהוּ שֶׁמֶשׁ וְיָרֵחַ, בֵּיהּ קַיְּימָא רָזָא דָא, וְאִיהוּ שִׁמְשָׁא לְאַנְהָרָא, וּבֵיהּ קַיְימִין כֹּכְבַיָּיא עִלָּאִין דְּנַהֲרִין, וּמַזָּלֵי, וְהָא אוּקִימְנָא. לְבָתַר אַהְדָּר לְעֵילָּא, לְהַהוּא אֲתָר דְּקָאֵים בְּרוּמָא דִּמְרוֹמִים, וְתַמָּן תְּקִיעוּ דְּכֹלָּא, הַלְלוּהוּ שְׁמֵי הַשָּׁמָיִם. לְבָתַר הַלְלוּ אֶת יְיָ' מִן הָאָרֶץ, לְקָבֵל אִלֵּין אֵשׁ וּבָרָד וְגוֹ'.

222. "Praise Him, sun and moon" (Tehilim 148:3). The secret OF ALL THE SFIROT OF ZEIR ANPIN is based on THE SUN, BECAUSE THE SUN IS TIFERET OF ZEIR ANPIN, ITS MAIN PART, AND ALL THE REST OF THE SFIROT ARE BUT COMPRISED WITHIN TIFERET. So the sun shines and in it are the illuminating high stars and the constellations, as we explained.

Afterwards it returns up high to the place in the height of heights, BINAH, where all of them are stored, MEANING THAT THE MOCHIN OF ZEIR ANPIN AND MALCHUT AND BRIYAH, YETZIRAH AND ASIYAH EMANATE FROM THERE. This place is alluded to in "praise Him, heavens of heavens" (Ibid. 7), BECAUSE THE HEAVENS ARE ZEIR ANPIN AND THE HEAVENS OF HEAVEN ARE BINAH. Then "Praise Hashem from the earth" (Ibid.), WHICH IS MALCHUT OF ZEIR ANPIN, corresponding to the rest of the verse, "fire and hail..." (Ibid. 8)

223. ת״ח, אִינּוּן כֹּכָבִים לְתַתָּא, קַיְימִין בִּמְשִׁיכוּ דְּאִתְמַשְׁכָאן מֵרָזָא עִלָּאָה, בְּגִין דְּכֹלָּא קַיְימָא בְּדִיוּקְנָא עִלָּאָה, וְהָא אוּקִימְנָא. וּבְגִין כַּךְ כָּל אִינּוּן כֹּכָבַיָּא וּמַזָּלֵי, מֵרוּם רְקִיעָא, כֻּלְּהוּ קַיְימֵי לְאַנְהָגָא בֵּיהּ עָלְמָא דִּלְתַתָּא מִנֵּיהּ, וּמִתַּמָּן אִתְפַּשְׁטָאן דַּרְגִּין, עַד דְּקַיְימִין דַּרְגִּין לְאִינּוּן כֹּכָבַיָּא דִּלְתַתָּא, דְּכֻלְּהוּ לָא קַיְימֵי בִּרְשׁוּתַיְיהוּ כְּלוּם, וְהָא אוּקִימְנָא, וְכֻלְּהוּ קַיְימָאן בִּרְשׁוּתָא דִּלְעֵילָּא. וְעַל דָּא כְּתִיב, יַעַמְדוּ נָא וְיוֹשִׁיעֻךָ הוֹבְרֵי שָׁמַיִם הַחוֹזִים בַּכּוֹכָבִים, וְכֹלָּא אִיהוּ בִּרְשׁוּתָא וְאִתְּמַר.

223. Come and see: The stars below exist upon what they draw from the high secret IN ZEIR ANPIN, for their existence is based upon the supernal pattern, as was already explained. That is why all the stars and constellations from the height of the firmament, ZEIR ANPIN, rule the world beneath them. From that place grades are spread down to the stars below, IN THIS WORLD, which have nothing under their command. For we have already explained that all are ruled by a higher authority. About that speaks the verse, "let now the astrologers, the stargazers...stand up and save you" (Yeshayah 47:13). All is by permission FROM ABOVE, as explained.

24. "the Mountain of Hashem's house shall be established on top of the mountains"

A Synopsis

Rabbi Yosi explains that 'the end of days' refers to the time when God will visit the daughter of Jacob and raise her up from the dust, and the sun will be united with the moon. 'The mountain of Hashem's house' refers to the higher Jerusalem that will shine with the supernal light of Zeir Anpin, and it will be seven times brighter than before. He tells us that 'the light of the sun' is Zeir Anpin and 'the light of the moon' is Malchut. The 'top' of the mountains refers to the High Priest, Chesed, and 'the mountains' are Chesed, Gvurah and Tiferet. Rabbi Yosi reveals the inner meaning of "and they made the tunics of fine linen (shesh)...and the mitre of fine linen (shesh), and goodly turbans of fine linen (shesh)." When the priest awakens below in the Tabernacle, when he spreads his hands over the congregation and the candles are burning, a priest also awakens above. At the end of times God will depose all the chieftains in charge over the other nations; then only He shall be exalted. Lastly Rabbi Yosi speaks of the secret of six.

224. וַיַּעֲשׂוּ אֶת הַכָּתְנוֹת שֵׁשׁ וְגוֹ' וְאֵת הַמִּצְנֶפֶת שֵׁשׁ וְגוֹ'. ר' יוֹסֵי פָּתַח, וְהָיָה בְּאַחֲרִית הַיָּמִים נָכוֹן יִהְיֶה הַר בֵּית יְיָ' בְּרֹאשׁ הֶהָרִים וְגוֹ'. וְהָיָה בְּאַחֲרִית הַיָּמִים, כַּד יִפְקוֹד לָהּ קוּדְשָׁא בְּרִיךְ הוּא לִבְרַתָּא דְּיַעֲקֹב, וִיוֹקִים לָהּ מֵעַפְרָא, וְיִתְחַבַּר שִׁמְשָׁא בְּסִיהֲרָא, כְּדֵין נָכוֹן יִהְיֶה הַר בֵּית יְיָ', דָּא יְרוּשְׁלֵם לְעֵילָּא, דִּתְהֵא מִתְתַּקְּנָא בְּתִקּוּנָהָא לְאִתְנַהֲרָא בִּנְהוֹרָא דִּלְעֵילָּא, דְּכָל נְהוֹרָהָא לָאו אִיהוּ מִתְתַּקְּנָא, אֶלָּא בִּנְהוֹרָא דִּלְעֵילָּא. וּבְהַהוּא זִמְנָא יִתְנְהִיר עָלָהּ נְהוֹרָא עִלָּאָה, עַל חַד שִׁבְעָה מִמַּה דַּהֲוָת מִקַּדְמַת דְּנָא, כְּמָה דִּכְתִּיב, וְהָיָה אוֹר הַלְּבָנָה כְּאוֹר הַחַמָּה וְאוֹר הַחַמָּה יִהְיֶה שִׁבְעָתַיִם וְגוֹ'.

224. "And they made the tunics of fine linen…and the mitre of fine linen" (Shemot 39:27-28). Rabbi Yosi opened the discussion with the verse: "And it shall come to pass in the end of days, that the mountain of Hashem's house shall be established on the top of the mountains…" (Yeshayah 2:2). "And it shall come to pass in the end of days," refers to the time when the Holy One, blessed be He will visit the daughter of Jacob and raise her from the dust, and the sun will be united with the moon, NAMELY, ZEIR ANPIN AND MALCHUT. Then "the mountain of Hashem's house shall be established," referring to celestial Jerusalem, WHICH IS MALCHUT, which shall be constructed with all its establishments and shining with the supernal light. For all its lights are established only by the supernal light OF ZEIR ANPIN. At that time, the supernal light will illuminate it seven times what was before, as it is written, "and the light of the moon shall be as the light of the sun, and the light of the sun shall be sevenfold..." (Yeshayah 30:26). THE LIGHT OF THE SUN IS ZEIR ANPIN AND THE LIGHT OF THE MOON IS MALCHUT.

225. בְּרֹאשׁ הֶהָרִים. בְּרָאשֵׁי הֶהָרִים מִבָּעֵי לֵיהּ. מַאי בְּרֹאשׁ אֶלָּא נְהוֹרָא דָּא דִּיְהֵא לָהּ בְּרֹאשׁ הֶהָרִים אִיהוּ. וּמַאן אִיהוּ רֹאשׁ הֶהָרִים. דָּא כַּהֲנָא רַבָּא. דְּאִיהוּ רֹאשׁ הֶהָרִים. רֵישָׁא דְּכֹלָּא סְטַר יְמִינָא. וְדָא אִיהוּ דִּמְתַקֵּן לְבֵיתָא תָּדִיר, וּמְבָרֵךְ לָהּ לְאַנְהָרָא אַנְפָּהָא. וְעַל דָּא, יִהְיֶה נָכוֹן.

225. "On the top of the mountains." HE ASKS: Should it not be said, 'tops of the mountains'? What is "top"? HE ANSWERS: The light it will then have is on the top of the mountains. Who is the top of the mountains? The High Priest, NAMELY CHESED OF ZEIR ANPIN, is the top of the mountains. FOR CHESED, GVURAH AND TIFERET ARE CALLED 'MOUNTAINS', AND CHESED IS THEIR TOP. It is altogether of the right side, CHESED, and the one to build the house, WHICH IS MALCHUT, and bless it so its face may shine. Therefore it is written, it "shall be established."

226. וּבְמָּה יִתַקֵּן לָהּ. בְּאִינּוּן לְבוּשִׁין דְּאִינּוּן כְּגַוְונָא דִּלְעֵילָּא, כְּמָה דְּאוּקְמוּהָ. וְאִינּוּן לְבוּשִׁין כֻּלְּהוּ קַיְימָן בְּרָזָא דְּשִׁית. וְהַאי בֵּיתָא כַּד יְהֵא מִתְתַּקָּן בְּהַאי רֹאשׁ הֶהָרִים, דְּאִיהוּ כַּהֲנָא רַבָּא, כְּדֵין אִתְקַשַּׁר וְאִסְתַּלָּק לְעֵילָּא בְּקִיּוּמָא עִלָּאָה, וְיִתְנְהִיר עָלְמָא מֵהַהוּא נְהִירוּ עִלָּאָה, וְדָא הוּא וְנִשָּׂא מִגְּבָעוֹת, מִכָּל שְׁאַר חֵילִין וּמַשִׁרְיָין עִלָּאִין, וּכְדֵין וְנָהֲרוּ אֵלָיו כָּל הַגּוֹיִם.

226. With what shall he ready it? With garments resembling what is above, LIKE ZEIR ANPIN, as explained. These garments are all in the secret of six

(Heb. *shesh*), CHESED, GVURAH, TIFERET, NETZACH, HOD AND YESOD INCLUDED IN CHESED, THE SECRET OF THE HIGH PRIEST. THIS IS THE INNER MEANING OF “AND THEY MADE THE TUNICS OF FINE LINEN (HEB. *SHESH*)...AND THE MITRE OF FINE LINEN (HEB. *SHESH*), AND GOODLY TURBANS OF FINE LINEN (HEB. *SHESH*).” And when the house is built on the top of the mountains, the High Priest, CHESED OF ZEIR ANPIN, it will be elevated into the high existence, BINAH, and the world will be illuminated by that supernal light WITHIN BINAH. And “shall be exalted above the hills” (Yeshayah 2:22) MEANS above the rest of the supernal armies and legions. Then “all the nations shall flow to it” (Ibid. 2).

227. תָּא חֲזֵי, בְּשַׁעֲתָא דְּכַהֲנָא דִּלְתַתָּא פָּרִישׂ יְדוֹי, כְּדֵין רוּחָא עִלָּאָה אַנְהִיר, וְנָפִיק, וְכָל בּוּצִינִין נָהֲרִין, וּנְהוֹרִין אִתְמַשְׁכָאן וְאִתְנַהֲרָן וְאִתְקַשְּׁרָן אִלֵּין בְּאִלֵּין, עַד דְּיִתְנְהִירוּ אַנְפָּהָא דִּכְנֶסֶת יִשְׂרָאֵל, וְכֹלָּא עַל יְדָא דִּנְהוֹרָא קַדְמָאָה דְּאִיהוּ כַּהֲנָא. וְכַד כַּהֲנָא אַתְעַר לְתַתָּא, כַּהֲנָא אִתְּעַר לְעֵילָּא. וּבְעוֹבָדִין דִּלְתַתָּא, אַתְעַר אִתְּעָרוּתָא דִּלְעֵילָּא.

227. Come and see: When the priest below, IN THIS WORLD, spreads his hands, the upper spirit, BINAH, comes out to illuminate. Then all the candles, THE SFIROT OF ZEIR ANPIN, burn, and lights flow, shining and joining together until the face of the Congregation of Yisrael, MALCHUT, becomes radiant. All this is done by the first light, the priest, CHESED. When the priest awakens below, a priest awakens above. By the deeds below there is awakening above.

228. וְעַל דָּא נָכוֹן יִהְיֶה הַר בֵּית יְיָ׳ בְּרֹאשׁ הֶהָרִים וְגוֹ׳, וְנָהֲרוּ אֵלָיו כָּל הַגּוֹיִם. בְּגִין דְּהַשְׁתָּא, כָּל שְׁאַר עַמִּין, אִית לוֹן מְמָנָן בִּרְקִיעָא עֲלַיְיהוּ. וּבְהַהוּא זִמְנָא, יְבָעֵר לוֹן, וְיַפִּיל לוֹן קוּדְשָׁא בְּרִיךְ הוּא מִשּׁוּלְטָנֵיהוֹן, דִּכְתִּיב יִפְקוֹד יְיָ׳ עַל צְבָא הַמָּרוֹם בַּמָּרוֹם, וְכֵיוָן דְּכֻלְּהוּ יִתְעַבְרוּן מִשּׁוּלְטָנֵיהוֹן, כְּדֵין קוּדְשָׁא בְּרִיךְ הוּא יִתְתָּקַף בִּלְחוֹדֵיהּ, כד״א וְנִשְׂגַּב יְיָ׳ לְבַדּוֹ בַּיּוֹם הַהוּא, וּכְדֵין וְנָהֲרוּ אֵלָיו כָּל הַגּוֹיִם. והה״ד, וְהָלְכוּ עַמִּים רַבִּים וְאָמְרוּ לְכוּ וְנַעֲלֶה אֶל הַר יְיָ׳ אֶל בֵּית אֱלֹהֵי יַעֲקֹב וְגוֹ׳.

228. Therefore, "the mountain of Hashem's house shall be established on the top of the mountains...and all the nations shall flow to it." Whereas now, all the rest of the HEATHEN nations have a chieftain in charge over them in the firmament, at that time the Holy One, blessed be He shall set fire to them and depose them from their sovereignty, as it is written, "and it shall come to pass on that day, that Hashem shall punish the host of the high ones on high" (Yeshayah 24:21). Since they will fall from power, the Holy One, blessed be He alone shall be exalted, as says the verse, "and Hashem alone shall be exalted in that day" (Yeshayah 2:17). Then "all the nations shall flow to it, and many people shall go and say, come and let us go up to the mountain of Hashem, to the house of the Elohim of Jacob" (Ibid. 2-3).

229. וְכֹלָּא אִיהוּ, בְּשַׁעֲתָא דְּכַהֲנָא, דְּאִיהוּ רֹאשׁ הֶהָרִים יַנְהִיר לָהּ, וְכֹלָּא אִיהוּ בְּרָזָא דְּשֵׁשׁ, שִׁית אִינּוּן בְּכָל סִטְרִין דְּיַנְהִיר לָהּ, דְּהָא בְּרָזָא דְּשִׁית יַנְהִיר לָהּ.

229. All this happens when the priest, the top of the mountain, CHESED, will shine upon MALCHUT, in the secret of six. He will shine upon her through all the six DIRECTIONS, in the secret of six.

25. Sometimes he praises himself and sometimes he humbles himself

A Synopsis

Rabbi Elazar is walking with Rabbi Yitzchak and Rabbi Yehuda, and he begins with: “I am small and despised, yet have not forgotten Your precepts.” He says that at times King David used to praise himself when he was having success conquering his enemies, yet when he found himself in trouble he would humble himself before God. Because of this God elevated him over everyone and wants him to be king in the World to Come as well. In the same way that the moon is dark when the sun turns his face away from her, yet radiant when the sun turns his face toward her, David reflected the face of Zeir Anpin.

230. רִבִּי אֶלְעָזָר וְרִבִּי יִצְחָק וְרִבִּי יְהוּדָה הֲווֹ אָזְלֵי בְּאוֹרְחָא, א״ר אֶלְעָזָר, עִידָּן אִיהוּ לְמֵהַךְ בִּשְׁכִינְתָּא, בְּגִין דִּשְׁכִינְתָּא לָא תִּשְׁרֵי עֲלָן, אֶלָּא מִגּוֹ מִלֵּי דְּאוֹרַיְיתָא. אָמַר ר׳ יְהוּדָה, מַאן דְּאִיהוּ רֵישָׁא, לִיפְתַּח בְּרֵישָׁא.

230. Rabbi Elazar, Rabbi Yitzchak, and Rabbi Yehuda were walking on the way. Rabbi Elazar said: It is time to walk with the Shechinah, because the Shechinah will not hover above us unless we utter words of the Torah. Rabbi Yehuda said: Let the leader begin.

231. פָּתַח רִבִּי אֶלְעָזָר וְאָמַר, צָעִיר אָנֹכִי וְנִבְזֶה פִּקּוּדֶיךָ לֹא שָׁכָחְתִּי. צָעִיר אָנֹכִי וְנִבְזֶה, דָּוִד מַלְכָּא, לְזִמְנִין אִיהוּ קָא מְשַׁבַּח גַּרְמֵיהּ, דִּכְתִּיב, וְעוֹשֶׂה חֶסֶד לִמְשִׁיחוֹ לְדָוִד וּלְזַרְעוֹ עַד עוֹלָם. וּכְתִיב, נְאֻם דָּוִד בֶּן יִשַׁי וּנְאֻם הַגֶּבֶר הוּקַם עָל מְשִׁיחַ אֱלֹהֵי יַעֲקֹב. וּלְזִמְנִין עָבֵד גַּרְמֵיהּ מִסְכְּנָא, דִּכְתִּיב כִּי עָנִי וְאֶבְיוֹן אָנִי. וּכְתִיב צָעִיר אָנֹכִי וְנִבְזֶה. וְאִיהוּ אָמַר אֶבֶן מָאֲסוּ הַבּוֹנִים הָיְתָה לְרֹאשׁ פִּנָּה.

231. Rabbi Elazar opened the discussion and said: “I am small and despised, yet have not forgotten Your precepts” (Tehilim 119:141). “I am small and despised.” King David used to praise himself at times, as it is written, “and whose mercy to His anointed, to David and to his seed forevermore” (Tehilim 18:51), and “the saying of David, the son of Yishai, and the saying of the man raised on high, the anointed of Elohim of Jacob" (II Shmuel 23:1), and sometimes he would abase himself, saying "for I am poor and needy" (Tehilim 86:1), and "I am small and despised." He said: "The stone which the builders rejected is become the chief corner-stone" (Tehilim 118:22).

232. אֶלָּא, בְּזִמְנָא דַּהֲוָה סָלִיק בְּדַרְגָּא דִּשְׁלָמָא, וְאִסְתַּלַּק בְּדִינָא דִּקְשׁוֹט, וַהֲוָה שַׁלִּיט עַל שָׂנְאוֹי, הֲוָה קָא מְשַׁבַּח גַּרְמֵיהּ. וּבְזִמְנָא דְּחָמָא גַּרְמֵיהּ בְּעָקוּ, וְשָׂנְאוֹי קָא דַּחֲקִין לֵיהּ, כְּדֵין מָאִיךְ גַּרְמֵיהּ, וַהֲוָה קָרֵי גַּרְמֵיהּ מִסְכְּנָא, זְעִירָא לְכֹלָּא. מַאי טַעֲמָא. בְּגִין, דְּהָא לְזִמְנִין הֲוָה שַׁלִּיט, וּלְזִמְנִין הֲוָה בְּעָקוּ דְּשָׂנְאוֹי.

232. HE REPLIES: When he was rising in the grade of peace, elevated by true justice, and overpowering his enemies, he used to praise himself. And when he found himself in trouble, beset by enemies, he humiliated himself and called himself poor, the least of all. The sense in it is that sometimes he governed and sometimes he was harassed by his enemies.

233. ועב"ד אִיהוּ שַׁלִּיט עֲלַיְיהוּ תָּדִיר, וְלָא יָכִילוּ לֵיהּ. וְדָוִד מַלְכָּא, תָּדִיר אִיהוּ הֲוָה שָׁפִיל גַּרְמֵיהּ לְגַבֵּי קוּדְשָׁא בְּרִיךְ הוּא, דְּכָל מַאן דְּמָאִיךְ גַּרְמֵיהּ קָמֵי קוּדְשָׁא בְּרִיךְ הוּא, אִיהוּ זָקִיף לֵיהּ עַל כֹּלָּא. ובג"כ, אִתְרְעֵי בֵּיהּ קוּדְשָׁא בְּרִיךְ הוּא בְּהַאי עָלְמָא, וּבְעָלְמָא דְּאָתֵי. בְּעָלְמָא דֵּין, דִּכְתִּיב וְגַנּוֹתִי עַל הָעִיר הַזֹּאת לְהוֹשִׁיעָהּ לְמַעֲנִי וּלְמַעַן דָּוִד עַבְדִּי. וּבְעָלְמָא דְּאָתֵי, דִּכְתִּיב וּבִקְשׁוּ אֶת יְיָ' אֱלֹהֵיהֶם וְאֵת דָּוִד מַלְכָּם וּפָחֲדוּ אֶל יְיָ' וְאֶל טוּבוֹ בְּאַחֲרִית הַיָּמִים. דָּוִד אִיהוּ הֲוָה מַלְכָּא בְּהַאי עָלְמָא, וְדָוִד יְהֵא מַלְכָּא לְזִמְנָא דְּאָתֵי. וע"ד אָמַר, אֶבֶן מָאֲסוּ הַבּוֹנִים הָיְתָה לְרֹאשׁ פִּנָּה.

233. For all that, he always ruled over them and they did not prevail over him. King David always debased himself before the Holy One, blessed be He, for whoever does so, the Holy One, blessed be He elevates him above everything. And this is why He favored him, DAVID, in this world and in the World to Come. In this world, as it is written, "For I will defend this city to save it for My own sake, and for My servant David's sake" (Yeshayah 37:35), and in the World to Come, as it is written, "and seek Hashem their Elohim and David their king, and shall come trembling to Hashem and to His goodness in the end of days" (Hoshea 3:5). David is a king in this world, and David will be king in the World to Come. Therefore he said: "The stone which the builders rejected is become the chief corner-stone."

234. תָּא חֲזֵי, בְּשַׁעֲתָא דְּשִׁמְשָׁא מְהַדֵּר אַנְפּוֹי, וְלָא נָהִיר לְסִיהֲרָא, אִתְעֲבָר נְהוֹרָהָא וְלָא נְהִירַת, כְּדֵין אִיהִי בְּמִסְכְּנוּתָא בְּכָל סִטְרִין, וְאִתְקַדְּרַת. וְלֵית לָהּ נְהוֹרָא כְּלַל. וְכַד שִׁמְשָׁא אַהְדָּר לָקֳבְלָהּ, וְאַנְהִיר לָהּ, כְּדֵין אִתְנְהִירַת אַנְפָּהָא, וְאִתְקַשְּׁטָת לְגַבֵּיהּ, כְּנוּקְבָא דְּאִתְקַשְּׁטַת לְגַבֵּי דְּכוּרָא, וּכְדֵין אִיהִי שַׁלְטָא בְּשׁוּלְטָנוּ בְּעָלְמָא.

234. Come and see: When the sun, ZEIR ANPIN, turns his face away and shines not upon the moon, MALCHUT, the light passes from the moon and she does not shine. She is then poor on all sides and dark, without light at all. And when the sun faces her again and shines upon her, her face is radiant and she adorns herself for him, THE SUN, like a female adorning herself for a man, and then she rules the world.

235. וְעַל דָּא, דָּוִד הֲוָה מְעַטֵּר גַּרְמֵיהּ, בְּהַהוּא גַּוְונָא מַמָּשׁ. לְזִמְנִין אִיהוּ מִסְכְּנָא, וּלְזִמְנִין אִיהוּ בְּעוּתְרָא בַּעֲתִירוּ דְּכֹלָּא, ובג"כ הֲוָה אָמַר, צָעִיר אָנֹכִי וְנִבְזֶה. וְעִם כָּל דָּא, פִּקּוּדֶיךָ לֹא שָׁכָחְתִּי. כְּגַוְונָא דָּא, אִית לֵיהּ לב"נ לְמֶהֱוֵי נִבְזֶה בְּעֵינָיו, לְאַשְׁפְּלָא גַּרְמֵהּ בְּכֹלָּא, לְמֶהֱוֵי אִיהוּ מָאנָא דְקוּדְשָׁא בְּרִיךְ הוּא אִתְרְעֵי בֵּיהּ, וְהָא אוּקְמוּהָ, דִּכְתִּיב וְאֶת דַּכָּא וּשְׁפַל רוּחַ. הַשְׁתָּא אֲנָא אֶפְתַּח בְּרֵישָׁא.

235. Therefore, David used to adorn himself in the same way, LIKE THE MOON, FOR DAVID CORRESPONDS TO MALCHUT. Sometimes he is poor and sometimes rich in every way. That is why he says, "I am small and despised," and yet, "I have not forgotten Your precepts." Thus it behooves a man to consider himself lowly and debase himself in all, so as to become a vessel favored by the Holy One, blessed be He. This was already explained concerning the verse, "with him also that is of a contrite and humble spirit …"

(Yeshayah 57:15). AND AFTER THIS INTRODUCTION, I will be the first to utter words of the Torah. THUS, HE ANSWERED THE WORDS OF RABBI YEHUDA SAYING THAT THE LEADER WILL SPEAK FIRST.

26. Measuring line and measuring reed

A Synopsis

Rabbi Elazar opens with: "And He brought me there, and behold, there was a man, whose appearance was like the appearance of brass, with a thread of flax in his hand, and a measuring reed, and he stood by the gate." He explains that the 'appearance of brass' meant that the man, the messenger Gabriel, shone with brightness and holiness. He talks about the measuring reed and the measuring line and about how the measuring line was knotted to do the measurements for the Tabernacle when it was under construction. He reveals the meaning of how 'cubit' was used, and mentions the 32 paths of wisdom. He also emphasizes the numbers four, seven and 28. We are told that there is measurement both above and below, in Binah and in Malchut. He speaks of the ten curtains and their measurements, and the sacred colors alluding to Chesed, Gvurah, Tiferet and Malchut. The curtains allude to poverty and judgment and they cover and protect holiness so that nothing outside can derive nourishment from them. Holiness is kept inside and the Other Side is outside, therefore holiness is compared to a nut that has the fruit inside. Rabbi Elazar explains how adding to letters to numbers actually lessens their value. We hear that the measuring line was also used to measure the size of the boards that are the secret of the Seraphim in Briyah. He goes into great detail about the size of the proportions of the boards and the secret of the measurements. The curtains of the tabernacle are the secret of heaven, and their inner meaning comes out of the number 32. There are curtains of good and curtains of evil, so that people can learn to distinguish between good and evil and can begin to know the Wisdom in everything. They can learn to distinguish between something that is established by wisdom and something that is not. Next there is a description of the measurements of the ark, and we hear that it also enables the discernment of good and evil. Rabbi Elazar tells us that all the measuring done by Ezekiel for the mansion was with the measuring reed rather than the measuring line because he was working with stone and things that would not change. But in the future his mansion will expand on all sides and there will be no Judgment in the world. He concludes by saying that when God renews the world it will be finally connected to the upper world and all will be one.

236. פָּתַח וְאָמַר, וַיָּבֵא אוֹתִי שָׁמָּה וְהִנֵּה אִישׁ מַרְאֵהוּ כְּמַרְאֵה נְחֹשֶׁת וּפְתִיל פִּשְׁתִּים בְּיָדוֹ וּקְנֵה הַמִּדָּה וְהוּא עוֹמֵד בַּשָּׁעַר. הַאי חָמָא לֵיהּ

יְחֶזְקֵאל, בְּהַהוּא חֵיזוּ דִּנְבוּאָה, וְהַאי אִיהוּ אִישׁ, דְּאִיהוּ שְׁלִיחָא בְּאִינּוּן לְבוּשִׁין.

236. He opened the discussion with the verse: "And He brought me there, and behold, there was a man, whose appearance was like the appearance of brass, with a thread of flax in his hand, and a measuring reed, and he stood by the gate" (Yechezkel 40:3). What Ezekiel saw in the mirror of prophecy was that man, who was a messenger clothed in linen, NAMELY GABRIEL.

237. וְהָכָא לָא אָמַר אֶלָּא אִישׁ, וְלָא אָמַר אִישׁ לְבוּשׁ הַבַּדִּים. אֶלָּא, בְּשַׁעְתָּא דְּעָבֵיד שְׁלִיחוּתָא לְמֶעְבַּד דִּינָא, אוֹ לְאַחֲזָאָה דִּינָא, אִקְרֵי לְבוּשׁ הַבַּדִּים. וּבְשַׁעְתָּא דְּלָא אָתֵי לְהָכִי, אִשְׁתַּנֵּי לְגַוְונָא אַחֲרָא, כְּפוּם שְׁלִיחוּתָא, הָכִי שָׁנֵי חֵיזוּ דִּילֵיהּ בְּאִינּוּן לְבוּשִׁין, וְאִשְׁתַּנֵּי מִלְּבוּשִׁין לִלְבוּשִׁין, בְּגִין דְּאִיהוּ תָּדִיר בִּסְטַר שְׂמָאלָא, וְכַמָּה גַּוְונִין אִינּוּן דְּאִתְלָבַשׁ בְּהוּ, וְכָל אִינּוּן דְּאַתְיָין מִסִּטְרֵיהּ.

237. Here he says "man," not "the man clothed in linen" (Yechezkel 10:2), for when he is on errand to deal Judgment or show it IN A VISION, he is "clothed in linen," but on a different mission he is differently clothed. As the mission differs, so do his appearance and clothes, ACCORDING TO THE MISSION. Indeed, he is always of the left side, GABRIEL IS ON THE LEFT SIDE OF THE CHARIOT, dressed in various clothes, and his attendants of his side.

238. מַרְאֵהוּ כְּמַרְאֵה נְחֹשֶׁת, הָכָא אִתְלָבַּשׁ בְּהַהוּא לְבוּשָׁא דְּאִינּוּן טוּרֵי נְחֹשֶׁת, דְּאִקְרוּן הָרֵי נְחֹשֶׁת. וְדָא אַיְיתֵי מְדִידוּ, לְמֶעְבַּד מִשְׁחָתָא.

238. "Whose appearance was like the appearance of brass." Here he is clad with the garment of mountains of brass, called in the scripture "mountains of brass" (Zecharyah 6:1), and he, GABRIEL, brings measurement with him, with which to measure.

239. הַאי לָאו אִיהוּ בּוּצִינָא דְּקַרְדִּינוּתָא דְּטָמִיר וְגָנִיז, אֶלָּא מִתַּמָּן נַפְקַת הַאי קָנֶה לְתַתָּא, דְּאִתְגְּלִיד מִגּוֹ נְהִירוּ דְּאִשְׁתְּבִיק מִבּוּצִינָא

דְּקַרְדִינוּתָא, כַּד אִסְתַּלְּקַת לְעֵילָא, וְאִתְגְּלָפַת גּוֹ סְפִירוּ דְּנָצִיץ וְלָא אִתְיְידַע. וְעַל דָּא, הַהוּא קְנֵה הַמִּדָּה אִיהוּ קַיְּימָא בְּמְדִידוּ דְּמִשְׁחָתָא, דְּקַיְּימָא לְתַתָּא.

239. This MEASUREMENT, NAMELY THE MEASURING REED, is not the hard spark, stored, and concealed, but the measuring reed come down from THE HARD SPARK, coated by the light left by the holy spark when it was gone up to be engraved upon the scintillating, unknown sapphires. Therefore, this measuring reed is present in the measuring below, IN THIS WORLD.

240. וּלְזִמְנִין קְנֵה הַמִּדָּה, וּלְזִמְנִין קַו הַמִּדָּה, וְעַל דָּא פְּתִיל וְקָנֶה, וְכֹלָּא מִשְׁחָתָא לְמֶעְבַּד מְדִידוּ, כָּל מְדִידוּ דִּיחֶזְקֵאל, אִיהוּ הֲוָה בְּהַהוּא קְנֵה הַמִּדָּה, וּבְעוֹבָדָא דְּמַשְׁכְּנָא כֹּלָּא הֲוָה בְּקַו הַמִּדָּה.

240. Sometimes the measuring reed IS USED and sometimes the measuring line. Therefore, there is the thread of flax, WHICH IS THE MEASURING LINE, and the measuring reed with which to measure. All the measurements done by Ezekiel were made by the measuring reed, AND NOT BY THE THREAD OF FLAX, WHICH IS THE MEASURING LINE. At the construction of the Tabernacle, all the measurements were made by the measuring line.

241. בְּמַשְׁכְּנָא, בְּהַהוּא מְדִידוּ דִּלְתַתָּא, דְּאִיהוּ קַו הַמִּדָּה, כְּגַוְונָא דְּהַהוּא פְּתִיל, דְּכַד שָׁרֵי לְאִתְפַּשְׁטָא, בְּכָל אַמָּה חַד קִשְׁרָא, וּבְהַהוּא מִשְׁחָתָא מְדִיד, וְאִקְרֵי אַמָּה. וּבג״כ, שְׁמֹנֶה וְעֶשְׂרִים בָּאַמָּה, דְּדָא הוּא אַרְכָּא וְפוּתְיָא אַרְבַּע בָּאַמָּה, וְלָא כְּתִיב אַרְבַּע אַמּוֹת, בְּגִין דְּאַמָּה מְדִיד לְכָל סְטָר.

241. In the Tabernacle, in the lower measurement by the measuring line, they used the thread OF FLAX. When it expanded, there was a knot each cubit, UP TO EACH KNOT THERE WAS ONE CUBIT LENGTH. And he measured using the unit of cubit, AND THOUGH HE MEASURED A NUMBER OF CUBITS, IT IS TERMED CUBIT, IN THE SINGULAR. It is therefore written, "28 cubit, and the breadth four cubit" (Shemot 36:9), and not "four cubits," because he was measuring using one cubit on each side, MEANING HE WAS

NOT USING NEW CUBITS, BUT THE SAME CUBIT, MULTIPLYING IT ALONG THE SIDES.

242. וְהַאי נָפְקָא, מֵרָזָא דְּבוּצִינָא דִּלְעֵילָּא, דִּמְדִידוּ דְּהַאי לְתַתָּא מֵהַאי מְדִידוּ דִּלְעֵילָּא אִשְׁתְּכַח. מְדִידוּ דִּלְתַתָּא, אֶלֶף וַחֲמֵשׁ מֵאָה סִטְרִין, וְכָל סִטְרָא וְסִטְרָא תְּרֵיסַר אַלְפֵי אַמִּין, וְעַל דָּא אַמָּה חַד אָזִיל בְּכֻלְּהוּ, וְהַהוּא אַמָּה דִּמְדִיד דָּא, אִתְפְּשַׁט קַו מִשְׁחָתָא וְאִתְגַּלְיָיא אַמָּה וּמְדִיד, וְכֵן בְּכָל אִינּוּן מִשְׁחָתֵי.

242. THIS MEASUREMENT LINE comes out of the mystery of the high luminary, BINAH, and the measurement below IN MALCHUT IS DERIVED from the measurement above, BINAH. The measurement below contains one thousand five hundred aspects, twelve thousand cubits each, and they are all measured by the same cubit, AS EACH CUBIT EXPANDS TO GRASP THIS SIZE. This cubit OF THE MEASURING LINE measures it, and the measuring line expands to produce a second cubit, and measures ANOTHER CUBIT – the same in all measurements.

243. שְׁמֹנֶה וְעֶשְׂרִים בָּאַמָּה, אִיהוּ אַרְכָּא, דְּחַד אַמָּה, וּפוּתְיָהּ אַרְבַּע בְּהַהוּא אַמָּה. אִשְׁתְּכַח, אַמָּה חַד דְּאִיהוּ תְּלָתִין וּתְרֵין שְׁלִישִׁים. כד״א וְכָל בַּשָּׁלִישׁ עֲפַר הָאָרֶץ, וְאִינּוּן ל״ב, לָקֳבֵל ל״ב שְׁבִילִין דְּנָפְקִין מִלְּעֵילָּא.

243. "28 cubit" is the length of one cubit. "And the breadth four cubit," refers also to the same cubit. It is found that one cubit is the length of 32 measures, as it is said: "and comprehended the dust of the earth in a measure" (Yeshayah 40:12). These 32 MEASURES correspond to the 32 paths OF WISDOM going out from above.

244. וְכַד אִתְעֲבִיד מִשְׁחָתָא דְּאַרְכָּא בְּהַאי מְדִידוּ, אִיהוּ אַרְבַּע סִטְרִין הַהוּא אַרְכָּא. וְכָל סִטְרָא ז׳ אַמִּין, דִּלְהָכִי סַלְקָן אִינּוּן שִׁבְעָה אַמִּין, לְאַרְבַּע סִטְרִין, בְּרָזָא דְּשֶׁבַע, דְּאִינּוּן תְּמַנְיָא וְעֶשְׂרִים דְּאִינּוּן בְּאַרְכָּא, בְּגִין דְּשֶׁבַע אִיהוּ רָזָא עִלָּאָה בְּכֹלָּא. וְכָל אִינּוּן תְּלָתִין וּתְרֵין שְׁבִילִין כְּלִילָן בְּשֶׁבַע, בְּרָזָא דִּשְׁמָא קַדִּישָׁא.

244. When the length was measured, and was found to contain four sides, CORRESPONDING TO CHESED, GVURAH, TIFERET AND MALCHUT, seven cubits to each, CHESED, GVURAH, TIFERET, NETZACH, HOD, YESOD AND MALCHUT, thus seven cubits to each of the four sides, in the secret of seven, amounting to the length of 28, because seven is the most high mystery. FOR SEVEN IS THE SECRET OF MALCHUT, THE SECRET OF LOWER CHOCHMAH. And all the 32 paths OF WISDOM are included in the seven, in the secret of the Holy Name, NAMELY, THE SECRET OF MALCHUT CALLED 'HOLY NAME'.

245. וְאִי תֵּימָא, הָא כְּתִיב מִדָּה אַחַת לְכָל הַיְרִיעוֹת. וַדַּאי מִדָּה אַחַת אִיהוּ, אע״ג דְּאִתְפָּשַׁט אַמָּה בָּתַר אַמָּה, וְדָא בָּתַר דָּא, וְכֹלָּא בְּרָזָא דְּבוּצִינָא דִּלְעֵילָּא קָא אַתְיָא, לְמֶהֱוֵי עֵילָּא וְתַתָּא מִשְׁחָתָא חֲדָא.

245. You may say that it is written, "the curtains were all of one size" (Shemot 36:9), MEANING THAT THEY ARE MANY CUBITS PER CURTAIN, AND THE SCRIPTURE SHOULD SAY THERE WERE ALL OF ONE SIZE. TO THIS HE REPLIES: Assuredly they were all of one size, THAT IS, ONE CUBIT. And though the measuring line expands one cubit after another, IT ADDS NOTHING TO THE FIRST CUBIT. All is in the secret OF THE MOCHIN OF the luminary above, BINAH, so there will be one measurement above and below, IN BINAH AND IN MALCHUT.

246. וְדָא אִיהוּ מִשְׁחָתָא דְּאִיהוּ בִּקְדוּשָּׁה יַתִּיר, בְּגִין דְּאִית מִשְׁחָתָא אַחֲרָא, דְּאִיהִי לְחַפְיָא עַל דָּא דְּאִיהִי לְגוֹ. דְּהָא בְּמִשְׁחָתָא אַחֲרָא דְּחַפְיָא עַל דָּא, סָלְקָא בְּחוּשְׁבְּנָא בְּחוּשְׁבַּן ד״ל, וּלְגָאו בְּחוּשְׁבַּן ל״ב וְדָא אִיהוּ רָזָא דְּחַפְיָא דָּא עַל דָּא, ל״ב לְגוֹ, ד״ל לְבַר.

246. This is a measurement pertaining more to holiness, and there is another measurement that covers THE TEN CURTAINS, which is inside, NAMELY, THE COVERING OF THE CURTAINS OF GOATS' HAIR. One unit that covers the other is 34 in number. THE CURTAINS inside are 32 in number. This is the mystery of covering – 32 inside and 34 outside.

247. בְּגִין דְּהָא מִשְׁחָתָא קַדְמָאָה, דְּאִיהוּ קַדִּישָׁא בִּגְוָונִין קַדִּישִׁין,

דְּאִינּוּן שֵׁשׁ מָשְׁזָר וּתְכֵלֶת וְאַרְגָּמָן וְתוֹלַעַת שָׁנִי, אִלֵּין גַּוְונִין קַדִּישִׁין, וְכָל חוּשְׁבָּן דִּילֵיהּ סַלְּקָא לְחוּשְׁבָּן ל״ב. וּמַשְׁחֲתָא תִּנְיָינָא דְּאִיהוּ לְבַר לְחַפְיָיא עַל דָּא, אִיהִי סַלְּקָא לְחוּשְׁבָּן ד״ל. וְדָא אִיהוּ רָזָא דִּכְתִּיב, אַשְׁרֵי מַשְׂכִּיל אֶל דָּל בְּיוֹם רָעָה יְמַלְּטֵהוּ יְיָ׳. בְּיוֹם רָעָה מַמָּשׁ, יְמַלְּטֵהוּ יְיָ׳.

247. He explains: Since the former measurement is sacred, with the sacred colors "of fine twined linen, and blue, and purple, and scarlet" (Shemot 36:8). These are sacred colors, ALLUDING TO CHESED, GVURAH, TIFERET AND MALCHUT, LINEN BEING CHESED; SCARLET, GVURAH; PURPLE, TIFERET; AND BLUE, MALCHUT. Its whole sum amounts to 32, 28 IN LENGTH AND FOUR IN BREADTH, ALTOGETHER 32. The other measurement OF GOATS' HAIR CURTAINS, which is outside, covering the former, amounts to 34 in number (*Dalet-Lamed*), NAMELY, THIRTY IN LENGTH AND FOUR IN BREADTH. To this alludes the verse, "Blessed is he who considers the poor (Heb. *dal*), Hashem will deliver him in the day of evil" (Tehilim 41:2), MEANING THAT in the day of evil, OF JUDGMENT, Hashem will deliver him. FOR THE CURTAINS OF GOATS' HAIR ALLUDE TO POVERTY AND JUDGMENT, COVERING AND PROTECTING HOLINESS, WHICH IS CURTAINS OF FINE TWINED LINEN...SO THAT THE EXTERNAL FORCES WOULD NOT NOURISH FROM THEM.

248. רָזָא דְּחוּשְׁבָּנָא לְגוֹ, דְּאִיהוּ רָזָא ל״ב. וּבְהַהוּא חוּשְׁבָּנָא דִּלְבַר, מַה כְּתִיב, וְעָשִׂיתָ יְרִיעוֹת עִזִּים. יְרִיעוֹת עִזִּים, אֲמַאי עִזִּים. אֶלָּא רָזָא דְּגַוְונָא דִּילֵיהּ, לְמֵיהַב דּוּכְתָּא בְּרָזָא דְּקוּדְשָׁא, וּבג״כ יְרִיעוֹת עִזִּים וַדַּאי. כְּתִיב אֶל גִּנַּת אֱגוֹז יָרַדְתִּי וְגוֹ׳, הָא אוּקְמוּהָ, אֲבָל מַה אֱגוֹז אִית לֵיהּ קְלִיפָּה, דְּסַחֲרָא וְחַפְיָיא עַל מוֹחָא, וּמוֹחָא לְגוֹ, אוּף הָכִי בְּכָל מִלָּה דְּקוּדְשָׁא, קְדוּשָּׁה לְגוֹ, וְסִטְרָא אַחֲרָא לְבַר. וְרָזָא דָּא, רָשָׁע מַכְתִּיר אֶת הַצַּדִּיק. וְעַל דָּא אִקְרֵי אֱגוֹז, וְהָא אוּקְמוּהָ.

248. The secret of reckoning inside OF THE CURTAINS OF FINE TWINED LINEN...is the secret of the 32 PATHS OF WISDOM. Of the reckoning outside, it is said: "And you shall make curtains of goats' hair" (Shemot 26:7). Why goats (Heb. *izim*) IF THE NAME 'GOATS' INDICATES SEVERE

(HEB. *AZIM*) AND RIGOROUS JUDGMENT? HE ANSWERS: The secret of its color gives it a place in the secret of holiness, BY ITS COVERING THE HOLINESS. Hence THERE IS NEED OF curtains of goats' hair, FOR THE JUDGMENT IN THEM PROTECTS HOLINESS, SO THE EXTERNAL FORCES WOULD NOT BE UNITED WITH IT, NAMELY WITH THE CURTAINS OF FINE TWINED LINEN... It is written, "I went down into the garden of nuts..."(Shir Hashirim 6:11). This verse was explained. Nevertheless, as the nut has a shell encircling it and covering its fruit, and its fruit is inside, so is everything pertaining to holiness. Holiness is inside and the Other Side outside. This is the inner meaning of the verse, "for the wicked man surrounds the righteous" (Chavakuk 1:4). Hence, it is called 'a nut', as explained elsewhere.

249. ת״ח, בְּהַהוּא דִלְבַר, כָּל מַה דְּאוֹסִיף גָּרַע, וְסִימָנִיךְ פָּרֵי הֶחָג, דְּמִתְמָעֲטִין וְאָזְלִין. אוּף הָכָא נָמֵי, בְּמָה דִּלְגָאו כְּתִיב, וְאֶת הַמִּשְׁכָּן תַּעֲשֶׂה עֶשֶׂר יְרִיעוֹת. בְּמָה דִּלְבַר כְּתִיב, עַשְׁתֵּי עֶשְׂרֵה יְרִיעוֹת. אוֹסִיף אַתְוָון וְגָרַע מֵחוּשְׁבְּנָא. אוֹסִיף חוּשְׁבְּנָא וְגָרַע, אוֹסִיף חוּשְׁבְּנָא, דִּכְתִּיב אֹרֶךְ הַיְרִיעָה הָאַחַת שְׁלֹשִׁים בָּאַמָּה וְרֹחַב אַרְבַּע בָּאַמָּה הַיְרִיעָה. וְכַד סָלִיק לְחוּשְׁבְּנָא, סָלִיק לְחוּשְׁבָּן ד״ל. דְּלֵית בְּכָל אִינּוּן זִינֵי מִסְכְּנוּתָא, כְּהַהוּא דְּאִקְרֵי ד״ל, ובג״כ כַּד סָלִיק לְחוּשְׁבְּנָא יַתִּיר, סָלִיק בִּגְרִיעוּ.

249. Come and see: On the outside, THE CURTAINS OF GOATS' HAIR, whatever is added, lessens, an example of which are the bulls on Sukkot that diminish SINCE THEY ARE SACRIFICED ON BEHALF OF THE NATIONS, WHICH ARE EXTERNAL FORCES. Also, here it is written about the inside, "and you shall make the Tabernacle with ten curtains" (Shemot 26:1). Of the outside, "eleven (Aramaic *ashtei esreh*) curtains" (Ibid. 7), is spelled with an additional letter. THE LETTER *AYIN* IS ADDED TO THE WORD SHTEI ESREH (LIT. 'TWELVE'), this reducing the number. THE NUMBER TWELVE IS REDUCED BY ONE, DUE TO THE ADDED *AYIN* TO SHTEI ESREH (TO ASHTEI). Thus adding to reckoning is lessening. There is addition in number in the words: "the length of one curtain shall be thirty cubit, and the breadth of one curtain four cubit" (Ibid. 8), WHILE THE INNER CURTAINS WERE ONLY 28 CUBIT LONG. Adding in number is lessening, for it amounts to 34 (*Dalet-Lamed*), the most severe connotation of poverty being poor (Heb. *dal*). And that is why, what is added, lessens.

250. וְכַד אִיהוּ גָּרַע בְּחוּשְׁבְּנָא, סָלִיק בִּסְלִיקוּ, דְּסָלִיק לְרָזָא דל"ב, דְּאִיהוּ רָזָא דְּכָל מְהֵימְנוּתָא, וְאִיהוּ רָזָא דִּשְׁמָא קַדִּישָׁא, וְעַל דָּא, דָּא סָלִיק, וְדָא גָּרַע. דָּא סָלִיק וְגָרַע. וְדָא גָּרַע וְסָלִיק. דָּא לְגוֹ. וְדָא לְבַר.

250. But when it lessens the reckoning, it is elevated, rising to the secret of 32 PATHS OF WISDOM, the secret of the whole Faith, MALCHUT, the secret of the Holy Name. Therefore, DIMINISHING is rising and ADDING is diminishing. This one adds yet diminishes, and that one diminishes yet adds, the one inside IS THE CURTAINS OF FINE TWINED LINEN, THE SECRET OF DIMINISHING YET ADDING, and the other outside, NAMELY, THE CURTAINS OF GOATS' HAIR IS THE SECRET OF ADDING YET LESSENING.

251. הַאי קַו הַמִּדָּה, שָׁרֵי לְאִתְפַּשְּׁטָא, וּמְדִיד מִשְׁחָתָא לַקְּרָשִׁים, דִּכְתִּיב וַיַּעַשׂ אֶת הַקְּרָשִׁים לַמִּשְׁכָּן עֲצֵי שִׁטִּים עוֹמְדִים, וְאִלֵּין אִינּוּן רָזָא דִּשְׂרָפִים, וְהָא אוּקְמוּהָ, דִּכְתִּיב עֲצֵי שִׁטִּים עוֹמְדִים, וּכְתִיב שְׂרָפִים עוֹמְדִים.

251. The measuring line started to stretch and measured the size of the boards, as it is written, "And he made boards for the Tabernacle of acacia wood, standing up" (Shemot 36:20). These BOARDS are the secret of the Seraphim IN THE WORLD OF BRIYAH. It was established, that it is said: "acacia wood, standing up," and "Seraphim were standing up" (Yeshayah 6:2); BOTH VERSES REFER TO SERAPHIM.

252. מְדִידוּ דְּמִשְׁחָתָא דָּא, עֶשֶׂר אַמּוֹת אֹרֶךְ הַקָּרֶשׁ וְאַמָּה וַחֲצִי הָאַמָּה. הָכָא כְּתִיב עֶשֶׂר אַמּוֹת, וְלָא כְּתִיב עֶשֶׂר בָּאַמָּה. אִלֵּין תְּלַת תְּלַת תְּלַת, דְּאִינּוּן תֵּשַׁע, וְחַד דְּשַׁרְיָא עֲלַיְיהוּ, וְדָא אִיהוּ רוּחָא חֲדָא דְּשַׁרְיָא עֲלַיְיהוּ.

252. The measurements are – "The length of a board was ten cubits, and the breadth of a board one cubit and a half" (Shemot 36:21). It is written, "ten cubits" and not 'ten cubit', AS SAID OF THE CURTAINS. These TEN CUBIT are three times three, which are nine, CORRESPONDING TO CHOCHMAH, BINAH, DA'AT, CHESED, GVURAH, TIFERET, NETZACH, HOD AND

YESOD OF THE SERAPHIM, and one hovering above them, the spirit hovering over them.

253. וְהָא אַמָּרָן, כַּמָּה אִיהוּ שִׁיעוּרָא דְּאַמָּה. וְדָא אִיהוּ רָזָא דְּשִׁיעוּרָא חַד סְרֵי וּפַלְגָּא, דְּסַלְּקִין, וְלָא סַלְּקִין, בְּגִין דְּגַרְעִין מֵאִינּוּן אוֹפַנִּים. וְאוּקְמוּהָ בְּרָזָא דִּרְתִיכָא קַדִּישָׁא, וְאִינּוּן עֶשְׂרִין, לְהַאי סִטְרָא עֶשֶׂר, וּלְהַאי סִטְרָא עֶשֶׂר, עַד דְּסַלְּקִין לְרָזָא דִּשְׂרָפִים עִלָּאִין. וּלְבָתַר סָלִיק רָזָא דְּקוּדְשָׁא, עַד דְּאִתְּעָרוּ כֻּלְּהוּ, בְּרָזָא דְּהַהוּא בְּרִיחַ הַתִּיכוֹן, כְּמָה דְּאוּקְמוּהָ, וְעַל דָּא פַּלְגּ אִית בֵּיהּ בְּלָא שְׁלִימוּ.

253. We already mentioned the size of the cubit, 28 IN LENGTH, AND FOUR IN BREADTH, 32 IN ALL. In here, the proportions are eleven and a half, TEN IN LENGTH AND ONE CUBIT AND A HALF CUBIT IN BREADTH, ELEVEN AND A HALF CUBITS IN ALL, amounting TO TWELVE but do not amount BECAUSE THEY ARE ONE-HALF SHORT, for the wheels are missing. It was explained in relation to the mystery of the Holy Chariot, that there are twenty BOARDS, ten to the right side and ten to the left side, reaching up to the high Seraphim. Then the secret of holiness rises until all are awakened in the secret of the middle bar. That is why they have but an incomplete half, BEING ONLY ELEVEN AND A HALF INSTEAD OF THE COMPLETE TWELVE.

254. רָזָא דְּהַאי מִשְׁחֲתָא, לְעֶשְׂרִין דַּפִּין אִינּוּן מָאתָן וּתְלָתִין. וְכָל הַאי קַיְימָא בְּמְדִידוּ בְּחוּשְׁבָּנָא, וְהָכִי סָלִיק כָּל חוּשְׁבָּן דְּנָפְקָא מֵהַאי מְדִידוּ בְּרָזָא דְּאִינּוּן שְׂרָפִים.

254. The secret of this measurement, OF ELEVEN AND A HALF, multiplied by the twenty boards is 230. All this is subject to measuring and reckoning. Each number measured in the measuring pertains to the secret of the Seraphim.

255. יְרִיעוֹת דְּמַשְׁכְּנָא דְּאַמָרָן דְּאִינּוּן רָזִין עִלָּאִין. רָזָא דִּשְׁמַיָּא וְהָא אוּקְמוּהָ נוֹטֶה שָׁמַיִם כַּיְרִיעָה. וְרָזָא דְּהַאי בְּהַהוּא חוּשְׁבָּן דְּקָאַמְרָן. וְאִית יְרִיעָן דְּקָאַמְרָן בְּרָזָא חֲדָא וְאִית יְרִיעָן בְּרָזָא אַחֲרָא, וְכֹלָּא אִיהוּ

בְּרָזָא דִּלְעֵילָּא. וע״ד כֹּלָּא אִיהוּ לְמִנְדַּע חָכְמְתָא, דְּכָל סִטְרָא וְסִטְרָא, וְכָל מִלָּה וּמִלָּה. וע״ד אַבְחִין ב״נ בֵּין טַב לְבִישׁ, בֵּין רָזָא דְּחָכְמְתָא, וּבֵין מִלָּה דְּלָא קַיְימָא בְּחָכְמְתָא. וּבְרָזָא דִּמְדִידוּ קַדְמָאָה, הָא אִתְּמַר בְּכַמָּה סִטְרִין אִיהוּ.

255. The curtains of the Tabernacle, which we said to contain high mysteries, are the secret of heaven, NAMELY, ZEIR ANPIN. It was explained in the secret of the verse, "who stretches out the heavens like a curtain" (Tehilim 104:2). Their inner meaning comes of the said reckoning, 32. There are curtains pertaining to one principle, THE CURTAINS OF FINE TWINED LINEN…and there are curtains pertaining to another principle, THE CURTAINS OF GOATS' HAIR. All is within the secret of above, OF THE ASPECT OF HEAVEN, for us to know wisdom in each and every aspect and thing. Therefore, man distinguishes between good and evil, NAMELY, BETWEEN THE CURTAINS OF FINE TWINED LINEN, WHICH ARE GOOD, AND THE CURTAINS OF GOATS' HAIR, WHICH ARE EVIL, between the secret of Chochmah, and something not established by Chochmah, BUT BY CHASSADIM, NAMELY BETWEEN THE CURTAINS OF FINE TWINED LINEN …UNDER THE RULE OF CHASSADIM, AND THE BOARDS UNDER THE RULE OF CHOCHMAH. In the secret of the first measurement, IN THE SECRET OF CUBIT, it was explained how many aspects it embraced, NAMELY ONE THOUSAND FIVE HUNDRED ASPECTS, TWELVE THOUSAND CUBIT EACH.

256. רָזָא דָּא רָזָא דַּאֲרוֹנָא דְּקָאִים בְּחוּשְׁבְּנָא, מִמָּה דְּאִיהוּ נָטִיל, וּמִמָּה דְּאִיהוּ קַבִּיל, וּמִמָּה דְּאִית בֵּיהּ, וּמִמָּה אִיהוּ מְקַבֵּל: דְּאִיהוּ תְּרֵין סִטְרִין, וְנָטִיל מֵאִינּוּן תְּרֵין סִטְרִין. וְעַל דָּא אַמָּה אִיהוּ בְּסִטְרָא דָּא, וְאַמָּה בְּסִטְרָא דָּא, וּפַלְגָּא דִּילֵיהּ. ובג״כ אַמָּתַיִם וָחֵצִי אָרְכּוֹ, אַמָּתַיִם מִתְּרֵין סִטְרִין, וּפַלְגָּא דִּילֵיהּ, הַאי בְּאַרְכָּא. בְּפוּתְיָא וְרוּמָא, אַמָּה וָחֵצִי, חַד מֵהַהוּא סִטְרָא יַתִּיר, דְּקָא נָטִיל כְּגַוְונָא דִּימִינָא וּשְׂמָאלָא. וּפַלְגָּא דִּילֵיהּ. דְּהָא לָא שַׁרְיָא מִלָּה, אֶלָּא עַל מִלָּה ובג״כ, פַּלְגָּא בְּכָל חוּשְׁבָּן וְחוּשְׁבָּן, וּבְגִין כַּךְ, אֲרוֹנָא מְקַבְּלָא מִכֹּלָּא, וְקַיְימָא בְּרָזָא דְּחוּשְׁבְּנָא דְּכֹלָּא.

256. This is the secret of the Ark: which is reckoned whence it takes, whence it receives and what it possesses. HE EXPLAINS: It takes from the two sides, RIGHT AND LEFT. ALSO, WHATEVER it receives IS from the same two sides. Therefore, there is one cubit on this side, RIGHT, and one cubit on that side, LEFT, and a half cubit it has on its own. Hence it is written, "two cubits and a half was the length of it" (Shemot 37:1), two cubits from the two sides, RIGHT AND LEFT, and a half of its own, regarding length. It is one cubit and a half wide and high; one CUBIT from the side which takes more, the same as it took from right and left, and a half of its own, for a thing dwells but upon some substance, hence there is a half in each and every reckoning. And that is why the Ark, WHICH IS MALCHUT, receives from all, and is found to contain the secret of the reckoning of them all.

257. וְהָא אוּקְמוּהָ, עַל מָה אִיהוּ מְחַפְּיָיא בְּדַהֲבָא, לְגוֹ וּלְבַר, וְהַאי אִיהוּ שִׁיעוּרָא לְמֵיקַם בְּמְדִידוּ קַדְמָאָה, וְכֹלָּא קָאֵים בְּרָזָא חֲדָא. פַּתּוֹרָא, כְּהַאי גַּוְונָא דְּמָדִיד בְּהַהוּא שִׁיעוּרָא קַדְמָאָה.

257. It was explained why THE ARK was inlaid with gold inside and outside, WHICH IS THE SECRET OF THE INCLUSION OF THE ILLUMINATION OF CHOCHMAH THAT IS CALLED 'GOLD'. This is the dimension established in the first measurement OF THE SAID CURTAINS, and everything is based on the same principle. The table too fits the first measurements OF THE CURTAINS.

258. אֲבָל הַאי מְדִידוּ דַּאֲרוֹנָא, דְּקַיְימָא בְּרָזָא דְּאוֹרַיְיתָא, וּבְהַהוּא מִשְׁחָתָא קַדְמָאָה דְּקָאָמַר אַבָּא, לֵית בָּהּ לְמֶעְבַּד שִׁיעוּרָא יַתִּיר כְּמָה דְּאִיהוּ גַּלֵּי בְּרָזָא לְחַכִּימֵי עֶלְיוֹנִין, לְמִנְדַּע בָּהּ רָזָא דְּחָכְמְתָא, לְאַבְחֲנָא בֵּין טַב לְבִישׁ, בֵּין חָכְמְתָא עִלָּאָה, לְחָכְמְתָא אַחֲרָא. כֻּלְּהוּ עוֹבָדִין אַחֲרָנִין, כֻּלְּהוּ בְּמְדִידוּ דְּאַמָּה, בְּהַהוּא מִשְׁחָתָא, בַּר מִשְׁחָתָא דְּחֹשֶׁן, דְּאִיהוּ זֶרֶת, וְהָא אוּקְמוּהָ.

258. But the dimensions of the Ark, found in the secret of the Torah, and the first dimensions OF THE CURTAINS, mentioned by my father, RABBI SHIMON, were not to be made MORE USE of than he revealed to the superior wise men, so they may know from it the secret of wisdom and distinguish between good and evil, between supernal Wisdom and the other Wisdom IN MALCHUT. All the other constructions of the Tabernacle were measured by the cubit, LIKE THE CURTAINS, except for the measuring of the breastplate, which was made by the span, as was explained.

259. ת״ח, כְּתֹנֶת דְּכֻלְּהוּ אִתְעֲבִידוּ בְּרָזָא דְּקוּדְשָׁא, כֹּלָּא אִיהוּ בְּרָזָא דְּשֵׁשׁ, וּבְעוֹבָדָא דְּשֵׁשׁ, וְקַיְימָא בְּשֵׁשׁ. וְכֻלְּהוּ תִּקּוּנִין, לְאִתְלַבְּשָׁא וּלְאַתְקְנָא בְּהוּ שֵׁשׁ, וּבְרָזָא דְּשֵׁשׁ.

259. Come and see: All the tunics, OF AARON AND HIS SONS, were made in the mystery of holiness, AND THOUGH THERE ARE NO SIZES MENTIONED, it was all in the secret of six, CHESED, INCLUDING THE SIX DIRECTIONS CHESED, GVURAH, TIFERET, NETZACH, HOD AND YESOD, and made by six THREADS, THE SECRET OF CHESED, GVURAH, TIFERET, NETZACH, HOD AND YESOD OF ZEIR ANPIN, ESTABLISHED and existing by six. All that was made IN THE TABERNACLE was to be dressed by and corrected by the six, CHESED, GVURAH, TIFERET, NETZACH, HOD AND YESOD OF ZEIR ANPIN, and in the secret of six, CHESED.

260. וְכֹלָּא בְּרָזָא דְּקַו הַמִּדָּה. וּקְנֵה הַמִּדָּה בְּהַהוּא מְדִידוּ דִּיְחֶזְקֵאל, בְּגִין דְּאִיהוּ בֵּיתָא לְאִתְקַיְּימָא בְּאַתְרֵיהּ, בְּאִינּוּן כּוֹתָלִין, בְּאִינּוּן שׁוּרִין, בְּאִינּוּן פִּתְחִין, בְּאִינּוּן דְּלָתִין, בְּגִין לְמֶהֱוֵי כֹּלָּא בִּמְדִידוּ. אֲבָל לְזִמְנָא דְּאָתֵי, מְשִׁחְתָּא הַהוּא מַה כְּתִיב בָּהּ, וְרָחֲבָה וְנָסְבָה לְמַעְלָה לְמַעְלָה. בְּשַׁעֲתָא דִּיִשְׁרֵי לְמִבְנֵי בֵּיהּ הַאי קְנֵה הַמִּדָּה, סָלְקָא לְעֵילָּא לְעֵילָּא, לְאַרְכָּא וּלְפוּתְיָא, לְמֶהֱוֵי אִתְפַּשְּׁטוּתָא דְּבֵיתָא בְּכָל סִטְרִין וְלָא יִשְׁגְּחוּן עָלֵיהּ לְבִישׁ, כְּמָה דְּאוּקְמוּהָ, דִּכְתִּיב וְדַמֶּשֶׂק מְנוּחָתוֹ. דְּהָא בְּהַהוּא זִמְנָא דִּינָא לָא יִשְׁתְּכַח בְּעָלְמָא, בג״כ כֹּלָּא אִתְקַיָּים עַל קִיּוּמֵיהּ בְּקִיּוּמָא שְׁלִים, כד״א לֹא יִרְגַּז עוֹד וְלֹא יוֹסִיפוּ בְנֵי עַוְלָה לְעַנּוֹתוֹ וְגוֹ׳.

260. All THE MEASUREMENTS IN THE TABERNACLE WERE in the secret of the measuring line. The measurements made by Ezekiel were made by the measuring reed, because that house is destined to remain with the same walls, and stone walls, the same entrances and the same doors, everything according to measure. But in the future, BY THE MEASUREMENTS OF THE

MANSION OF EZEKIEL, WHICH WILL BE IN THE FUTURE, it is said of that measure "the side chambers were broader as they wound higher and higher" (Yechezkel. 41:7). For when they will start to build using the measuring reed, it will stretch higher and higher in length and breadth, the mansion will expand on all sides, and none will think ill of it, as explained by the verse, "and Damascus shall be His resting place" (Zecharyah 9:1). For at that time there will be no Judgment upon the world, and all will be established firmly and completely, as it is said: "and be troubled no more; neither shall the children of wickedness torment them any more..." (II Shmuel 7:10).

261. ות״ח, כָּל מִשְׁחָתִין, וְכָל מְדִידִין, כֻּלְּהוּ קַיְימִין בְּהַאי עָלְמָא, בְּגִין לְאִתְקַיְּימָא הַאי עָלְמָא, בְּרָזָא דְּגַוְונָא דִּלְעֵילָּא, לְאִתְקַשְּׁרָא הַאי עָלְמָא בְּעָלְמָא דִּלְעֵילָּא, לְמֶהֱוֵי כֹּלָּא חַד בְּרָזָא חֲדָא. וּבְהַהוּא זִמְנָא דְּקוּדְשָׁא ב״ה אִתְּעַר לְחַדְּתוּתֵי עָלְמָא, כְּדֵין יִשְׁתַּכְּחוּן כֻּלְּהוּ עָלְמִין בְּרָזָא חֲדָא, וִיקָרָא דקוּדְשָׁא בְּרִיךְ הוּא בְּכֹלָּא, וּכְדֵין כְּתִיב, בַּיּוֹם הַהוּא יִהְיֶה יְיָ׳ אֶחָד וּשְׁמוֹ אֶחָד.

261. Come and see: All the measuring and measurements, MENTIONED OF THE HOUSE OF EZEKIEL, are all present in this world, so it may be a reflection of above, to connect this world to the upper world so all will be one in one mystery. But at that time when the Holy One, blessed be He will bestir Himself to renew the world, then all the worlds will be in the secret of one, LIKE THE UPPER WORLD, and the glory of the Holy One, blessed be He WILL BE in them all. And "in that day shall Hashem be One, and His Name One" (Zecharyah 14:9). HIS NAME, THE SECRET OF MALCHUT, IS ONE ON ITS OWN LIKE YUD HEI VAV HEI.

27. The names of *Mem-Bet* (42) and *Ayin-Bet* (72)

A Synopsis

Rabbi Yehuda opens with: "The counsel (secret) of Hashem is with them that fear Him, and His covenant to make them know it." One of the explanations he offers is that people who fear sin are afraid of the sublime mysteries and therefore do not study them but they may know and understand the secrets. He talks about the world being engraved with 42 letters. 'Engraving' is explained as the light being covered and withheld. The letters create the world above and the world below, the world of unity and the world of duality, when the letters are then called 'mountains of separation'. Next Rabbi Yehuda returns to a discussion of 'the Urim' and 'the Tumim' that are described as the secret of 72 engraved letters that reveal the light of Chochmah. Rabbi Yehuda talks about the letters Hei and Vav and how the Tabernacle was created using these letters. When he built the Tabernacle, Betzalel combined the letters and did the work with different combinations of them, also using the combinations of the letters of the Holy Name. But when he started to erect the Tabernacle he couldn't do it because only Moses knew what the letters wanted, therefore the Tabernacle was erected by Moses.

262. פָּתַח ר׳ יְהוּדָה אֲבַתְרֵיהּ וְאָמַר, סוֹד יְיָ׳ לִירֵאָיו וּבְרִיתוֹ לְהוֹדִיעָם. הַאי קְרָא הָא אוּקְמוּהָ, אֲבָל סוֹד יְיָ׳ לִירֵאָיו, הַהוּא רָזָא עִלָּאָה דְּקַיְּימָא בִּגְנִיזוּ, לָא קַיְּימָא אֶלָּא לִירֵאָיו, דְּאִינּוּן דַּחֲלִין לְקוּדְשָׁא בְּרִיךְ הוּא תָּדִיר, וְאִינּוּן אִתְחָזוּן לְאִינּוּן רָזִין עִלָּאִין, וּלְמֶהֱוֵי אִינּוּן רָזִין עִלָּאִין בִּגְנִיזוּ וּבִסְתִּימוּ כַּדְקָא יֵאוֹת, בְּגִין דְּאִינּוּן רָזִין עִלָּאִין. אֲבָל וּבְרִיתוֹ לְהוֹדִיעָם, רָזָא דְּאִיהוּ קַיְּימָא בִּבְרִית קַיָּימָא, לְהוֹדִיעָם, בְּגִין דְּאִיהוּ אֲתַר דְּקַיְּימָא לְגַלָּאָה לְמִנְדַּע.

262. Rabbi Yehuda then opened the discussion with the verse: "The counsel (secret) of Hashem is with them that fear Him, and His covenant to make them know it" (Tehilim 25:14). It means that this sublime secret is stored and available only for them that fear Him, who fear the Holy One, blessed be He always. They are worthy of these sublime secrets to keep them, which are hidden and concealed, being supernal mysteries. But the secret of "and His covenant to make them know it" is that it refers to the Holy Covenant, "to make them know it," as this place may be revealed and known.

263. תּוּ סוֹד יְיָ' לִירֵאָיו, דְּאִינּוּן רָזִין דְּקַיְימָן בִּדְחִילוּ, וְאִינּוּן דַּחֲלֵי חַטָּאָה דַּחֲלִין בְּהוּ, בְּאִינּוּן רָזִין עִלָּאִין. אֲבָל וּבְרִיתוֹ לְהוֹדִיעָם: לְמִנְדַּע וּלְפָרְשָׁא מִלִּין, בְּגִין דְּאִינּוּן מִלִּין דְּקַיְימָן לְפָרְשָׁא.

263. There is another EXPLANATION OF, "The counsel (secret) of Hashem is with them that fear Him." These secrets have the aspect of fear. They who fear sin are afraid of these sublime mysteries, AND DO NOT STUDY THEM. But "and His covenant to make them know it" means they may know and understand the things, that will explain the secrets.

264. תָּא חֲזֵי, בְּאַרְבְּעִין וּתְרֵין אַתְוָון אִתְגְּלִיף עָלְמָא, וְאִתְקַיָּים. וְכֻלְּהוּ עִטְרָא דִּשְׁמָא קַדִּישָׁא. כַּד מִצְטָרְפִין, סַלְּקִין בְּאַתְווֹי לְעֵילָּא, וְנַחְתִּין לְתַתָּא, מִתְעַטְּרָן עִטְרִין, בְּאַרְבַּע סִטְרֵי עָלְמָא, וְיָכִיל לְאִתְקַיְּימָא.

264. Come and see: The world, MALCHUT, had been engraved with and exists by 42 letters. COVERING THE LIGHTS AND WITHHOLDING THEM IS ENGRAVING. REVEALING THEM IS EXISTING, NAMELY MOCHIN THAT SUSTAINS THAT GRADE. They are all a crown for the Holy Name, FOR THE NAME OF 42 IS THE SECRET OF THE FIRST THREE SFIROT, KETER, CHOCHMAH AND BINAH THAT ARE MADE A CROWN TO MALCHUT CALLED 'NAME'. When they are united, THE 42 LETTERS TO GIVE PLENTY, they go up with its letters TO BINAH, WHERE THEY WERE FIRST REVEALED, and go down TO ZEIR ANPIN and make themselves IN IT, into crowns to the four directions, WHICH ARE CHESED, GVURAH, TIFERET AND MALCHUT UP TO THE CHEST, THE SECRET OF THE THREE COLUMNS AND MALCHUT WHICH RECEIVES THEM. Thus it may exist. NAMELY TO RECEIVE THESE MOCHIN FROM BINAH, THAT EXISTS THROUGH THEM.

265. וּלְבָתַר נַפְקוּ אַתְוָון וּבָרוּ עָלְמָא לְעֵילָּא וְתַתָּא. בְּעָלְמָא דְּיִחוּדָא, וּבְעָלְמָא דְּפֵרוּדָא, וְאִתְקְרוּן הָרֵי בָתֶר, טוּרֵי דְּפִרוּדָא דְּמִשְׁתַּקְיָין. כַּד סִטְרָא דְּדָרוֹם שַׁארֵי לְקָרְבָא בַּהֲדֵיהּ, וּכְדֵין מַיָּא נַגְדִּין, וּבְחֵילָא דָּא דְּעֵילָּא, נָגִיד, כֹּלָּא הוּא בְּחֵידוּ.

265. Then these letters depart FROM THE NAME OF 42 WITHIN ZEIR

ANPIN, and create the world, MALCHUT above and below, the world of unity and the world of division. They are then called "mountains of separation" (Shir Hashirim 2:17). These mountains of separation are watered when the south, RIGHT side, approaches THE LEFT SIDE, and water flows, drawn by the power of above IN ZEIR ANPIN. Then all is in rejoicing.

266. כַּד מַחֲשָׁבָה, סָלִיק בִּרְעוּ דְּחֶדְוָה, מִטְּמִירָא דְּכָל טְמִירִין, מָטֵי וְנָגִיד מִגַּוֵּיהּ חַד זִיהֲרָא, מִתְקָרְבִין דָּא בְּדָא, וְהָא אוּקְמוּהָ.

266. And when thought, THE SECRET OF CHOCHMAH, mounts with willing joy from the most covered, KETER, one light flows from it, WHICH IS BINAH, and they approach each other, CHOCHMAH AND BINAH. This was already explained.

267. וְאִינּוּן אַרְבְּעִין וּתְרֵין אַתְוָון, אִינּוּן רָזָא עִלָּאָה, וּבְאִינּוּן אִתְבְּרֵי עָלְמָא עִלָּאָה וְעָלְמָא תַּתָּאָה. וְאִינּוּן קִיּוּמָא וְרָזָא דְּכָל עָלְמִין. וְעַל דְּאִיהוּ רָזָא דְּעָלְמִין, כְּתִיב סוֹד יְיָ׳ לִירֵאָיו וּבְרִיתוֹ לְהוֹדִיעָם. דָּא רָזָא, דְּאַתְוָון גְּלִיפִין, בְּגִלָּפוֹי בְּאִתְגַּלְיָיא.

267. These 42 letters are a high mystery, with which were created the upper world, ZEIR ANPIN, and the lower world, MALCHUT. They establish and contain the mystery of all the worlds, and for their being their secret it is written, "The secret of Hashem is with them that fear Him." This is a secret of the engraved letters IN THE NAME OF 42, which is revealed in its engravings.

268. כְּתִיב וְנָתַתָּ אֶל חֹשֶׁן הַמִּשְׁפָּט אֶת הָאוּרִים וְאֶת הַתּוּמִּים, וְהָא אוּקְמוּהָ. אֶת הָאוּרִים: דְּנַהֲרִין, רָזָא דְּאַסְפָּקַלַרְיָא דְּנַהֲרָא, וְדָא אִיהוּ גְּלִיפוּ דְּאַתְוָון דִּשְׁמָא קַדִּישָׁא, בְּרָזָא דְּאַרְבְּעִין וּתְרֵין, דִּבְהוּ אִתְבְּרוּן עָלְמִין, וַהֲווֹ מְשֻׁקָּעִין בֵּיהּ. וְאֶת הַתּוּמִּים: רָזָא דְּאִינּוּן אַתְוָון, דִּכְלִילָן בַּאֲתָר דְּאַסְפָּקַלַרְיָא דְּלָא נַהֲרָא. וְאִיהִי אִתְנַהֲרָא בְּע״ב אַתְוָון גְּלִיפִין, דְּאִינּוּן רָזָא דִּשְׁמָא קַדִּישָׁא, וְכֻלְּהוּ אִקְרוּן אוּרִים וְתוּמִּים.

268. It is written, "and you shall put in the breastplate of judgment the Urim and the Tumim" (Shemot 28:30). It was explained that the MEANING OF Urim (Eng. 'lights') is that they illuminate, in the secret of the shining mirror, NAMELY, ZEIR ANPIN, and this is the engravings of the letters of the Holy Name in the secret of 42, with which the worlds were created. The letters were sunken into it. "The Tumim" refer to the secret of the letters contained in the mirror which does not shine, WHICH IS MALCHUT, shining with the 72 engraved letters, in the secret of the Holy Name. THE NAME OF 72 IS THE SECRET OF REVEALING THE LIGHT OF CHOCHMAH THAT IS WITHIN MALCHUT. Together they are called 'Urim and Tumim'.

269. תָּא חֲזֵי, כַּד אִינּוּן אַתְוָון מִשְׁקָעָאן תַּמָּן, בְּהַהוּא חֵילָא, נָהֲרִין אַתְוָון אַחֲרָנִין, בִּגְלִיפוּ דְּאִינּוּן שְׁמָהָן דִּשְׁבָטִין, וְנַהֲרִין אוֹ אִתְחַשְׁכָאן, וְכֹלָּא בְּהַהוּא רָזָא דְּאִינּוּן אַתְוָון דִּשְׁמָהָן קַדִּישִׁין כִּדְקָאמְרָן. וְאִינּוּן אַתְוָון דִּשְׁמָהָן קַדִּישִׁין, אִינּוּן אַתְיָין עַל רָזָא דְּאוֹרַיְיתָא, וְכֻלְּהוּ עָלְמִין אִתְבְּרוּן, בְּרָזָא דְּאִלֵּין אַתְוָון. אִלֵּין שְׁמָהָן הֲווֹ גְּנִיזִין מְשֻׁקָּעִין תַּמָּן, וּשְׁמָהָן דִּשְׁבָטִין הֲווֹ בַּלְטִין אַתְוָון דִּלְהוֹן לְעֵילָּא. וְעַל דָּא כֹּלָּא מֵרָזָא דְּאִינּוּן אַתְוָון, וְכֹלָּא אוֹקִימְנָא.

269. Come and see: When the letters OF THE NAME OF 42 are sunken INTO THE BREASTPLATE OF JUDGMENT, by that power OF THE SUNKEN LETTERS other letters of the tribes shine, now illuminating, now darkening, according to the secret of the letters of the Holy Names we mentioned, THE NAME OF 42. These letters of the Holy Names OF 42 embrace the secret of the Torah, THEY ARE REVEALED WITHIN ZEIR ANPIN CALLED 'TORAH', and all the worlds were created in the secret of these letters. These names OF 42 were hidden and sunken IN THE BREASTPLATE, and the letters of the names of the tribes stood out above. Hence, everything springs from the secret of these letters. We already explained everything.

270. וְהָא אִתְּמַר בְּרָזָא דְּאַתְוָון דְּאוֹרַיְיתָא. ב', דְּאוֹרַיְיתָא שָׁרָאת בָּהּ, וְהָא אוּקְמוּהָ ב' בָּרָא וַדַּאי בְּחֵילָא עִלָּאָה, בְּתְקִיפוּ דְּרָזָא דְּאִינּוּן אַתְוָון. ב' נוּקְבָא, א' דְּכוּרָא. כְּמָה דְּב' בָּרָא, הָכִי נָמֵי א', אַפִּיק אַתְוָון, כְּלָלָא דְּעֶשְׂרִין וּתְרֵין אַתְוָון.

270. We learned, in relation to the secret of the letters in the Torah, that the letter *Bet* starts the Torah, THE LETTER *BET* OF "BERESHEET" (IN THE BEGINNING) – it has been explained, that it created with the supernal power, using the strength of the mystery of the 42 letters MEANING THE NAME 42. *Bet* is female, NAMELY MALCHUT, and *Aleph* is male, NAMELY ZEIR ANPIN. As *Bet* created, so did *Aleph* issue all the 22 letters, THE SECRET OF THE PARTICLE ET (*ALEPH-TAV*), INCLUDING ALL THE LETTERS FROM *ALEPH* TO *TAV*.

271. ה׳, זִוּוּגָא חֲדָא בַּשָּׁמַיִם, לְמֵיהַב לֵיהּ חַיִּין, וּלְאַשְׁרָאָה לֵיהּ. ו׳, הָאָרֶץ, לְמֵיהַב לָהּ מְזוֹנָא, וּלְאַתְקְנָא לָהּ סִפּוּקָא דְּאִתְחָזֵי לָהּ. וְרָזָא דָּא בְּרֵאשִׁית וְגוֹ׳, עַד הַשָּׁמַיִם וְאֵת הָאָרֶץ. ו׳ וְאֵת, כְּלָלָא דְּעֶשְׂרִין וּתְרֵין אַתְוָון, וּמִתְּזָן אַרְעָא, וְאַרְעָא כָּלִיל לוֹן לְגַוָּוהּ כְּמָה דְּאַתְּ אָמֵר, כָּל הַנְּחָלִים הוֹלְכִים אֶל הַיָּם, וְהַיְינוּ רָזָא, וְאֵת הָאָרֶץ, דְּכָנִישׁ לְכֹלָּא בְּגַוָּוהּ, וְקַבִּילַת לוֹן. הָאָרֶץ נַטְלַת ו׳, וְקַבִּילַת לָהּ לְאַתְזָנָא.

271. The letter *Hei* OF "THE (HEB. *HA)* HEAVEN" INDICATES uniting with the heaven, NAMELY THE INFLUENCE OF BINAH UPON THE HEAVEN, WHICH IS ZEIR ANPIN, to give it life and inspire it WITH MOCHIN. It is upon the letter *Vav* OF "AND (HEB. *VE*) THE EARTH," WHICH IS ZEIR ANPIN, to nourish MALCHUT CALLED 'EARTH' and supply it with what it needs. This is the secret of: "In the beginning…the heaven and the (Heb. *ve'et*) earth" (Beresheet 1:1). *VAV* ADJOINS THE PARTICLE ET, THOUGH IT SHOULD HAVE ADJOINED "THE EARTH." This indicates the set of 22 letters ISSUED BY *VAV*, FOR ET INCLUDES THE 22 LETTERS FROM *ALEPH* TO *TAV*, from which the earth, MALCHUT, is sustained. The earth then embraces them into itself, according to the verse, "all the rivers run into the sea, yet the sea is not full" (Kohelet 1:7), MEANING THAT ALL THE CHANNELS OF PLENTY OF ZEIR ANPIN FLOW INTO MALCHUT CALLED 'SEA'. This is the secret of "and the (Heb. *ve'et*) earth," as MALCHUT gathers all into her and receives them, the earth took the letter *Vav* and nourished UPON IT.

272. וְרָזָא דָּא, מַשְׁכְּנָא לָא אַתְקָן אֶלָּא עַל יְדָא דְּמֹשֶׁה, בְּגִין דְּמֵהַהוּא סִטְרָא, אַתְעַר דַּרְגָּא אַחֲרָא עִלָּאָה, לְקַיְּימָא לֵיהּ, לְמֶהֱוֵי קִיּוּמָא דְּכֹלָּא. וְרָזָא דָּא, וַיָּקֶם מֹשֶׁה אֶת הַמִּשְׁכָּן, קִיּוּמָא דִּילֵיהּ הֲוָה, בְּאִינּוּן אַתְוָון

דְּאִתְבְּרִיאוּ בְּהוּ שְׁמַיָּא וְאַרְעָא.

272. This is the mystery – why the Tabernacle was erected only by Moses, since from that side of Moses, ZEIR ANPIN, another high grade, BINAH, bestirred itself to establish the Tabernacle, MALCHUT, so there will be sustenance for all. This is the secret of "and Moses erected the Tabernacle" (Shemot 40:18), erecting it by these letters with which heaven and earth were created, REFERRING TO THE NAME OF 42.

273. וּבְגִין כַּךְ, כָּל עֲבִידָאן דְּמַשְׁכְּנָא, הֲוָה בְּצַלְאֵל עָבִיד לוֹן, בְּרָזָא דִּגְלוּפָא דְּאַתְוָון, דְּאִתְבְּרִיאוּ בְּהוֹן שְׁמַיָּא וְאַרְעָא. וְעַל דָּא אִקְרֵי בְּצַלְאֵל, בְּגִין דַּהֲוָה יָדַע בְּצַלְאֵל, גְּלוּפָא דְּאַתְוָון, דְּאִתְבְּרִיאוּ בְּהוּ שְׁמַיָּא וְאַרְעָא. וְאִי לָא דַּהֲוָה יָדַע לְהוּ בְּצַלְאֵל, לָא הֲוָה יָכִיל לְמֶעְבַּד אִיהוּ אִינּוּן עֲבִידָאן דְּמַשְׁכְּנָא. מַאי טַעֲמָא. אֶלָּא, כְּמָה דְּמַשְׁכְּנָא עִלָּאָה, לָא הֲוָה וְלָא אִתְקִינוּ כָּל עוֹבָדוֹי, אֶלָּא בְּהַהוּא רָזָא דְּאִינּוּן אַתְוָון, אוּף הָכָא מַשְׁכְּנָא דִּלְתַתָּא, לָא הֲוָה וְלָא אִתְתָּקַן, אֶלָּא בְּרָזִין דְּאִינּוּן אַתְוָון.

273. So Betzalel carried out all the work of the Tabernacle using the secret of the engraved letters, with which heaven and earth were created, NAMELY, THE NAME 42. He was therefore called 'Betzalel', since he knew the engraving of these letters, with which heaven and earth were created. Unless he knew them, he could not have done the work in the Tabernacle. The sense thereof is that as the upper Tabernacle was built, and all its actions done, only by the secret of these letters, OF THE NAME 42, so here in the Tabernacle below, nothing was built save by the secrets of these letters.

274. בְּצַלְאֵל הֲוָה מְצָרֵף אִינּוּן אַתְוָון, וּבְרָזָא דְּכָל צֵרוּפָא וְצֵרוּפָא הֲוָה עָבִיד אוּמָנוּתָא. וְכָל עֲבִידָא וַעֲבִידָא דְּמַשְׁכְּנָא, בְּכָל צֵרוּפָא הֲוָה עָבִיד חַד אוּמָנוּ, וְכָל מַה דְּאִתְחֲזֵי לֵיהּ. וְכֵן בְּכָל עֲבִידָאן דְּמַשְׁכְּנָא, וְכָל אִינּוּן שַׁיְיפִין וְתִקּוּנִין דְּמַשְׁכְּנָא, כֹּלָּא הֲוָה בְּצֵרוּפָא דְּאַתְוָון דִּשְׁמָא קַדִּישָׁא.

274. Betzalel was combining the letters, OF THE NAME 42, and did the various works with different combinations thereof. He used each combination to do one task, and all that pertains to it. And so with all the works in the Tabernacle, together with its parts and amendments, he used combinations of the letters of the Holy Name 42.

275. וְכַד אָתָא לְאַקָּמָא לֵיהּ, לָא הֲוָה יָכִיל לְמֵיקָם לֵיהּ. מ״ט. בְּגִין דִּרְעוּתָא דְּסָלִיק עַל אִינּוּן אַתְוָון, לָא אִתְמְסַר אֶלָּא לְמֹשֶׁה בִּלְחוֹדוֹי, וְאִיהוּ הֲוָה יָדַע הַהוּא רְעוּתָא דְּסָלִיק לְאִינּוּן אַתְוָון, וְעַל דָּא אִתְקַם מַשְׁכְּנָא עַל יְדֵיהּ, דִּכְתִּיב וַיָּקֶם מֹשֶׁה. וַיִּתֵּן מֹשֶׁה. וַיָּשֶׂם מֹשֶׁה. וּבְצַלְאֵל לָא הֲוָה יָדַע, וְלָא הֲוָה יָכִיל לְמֵיקָם לֵיהּ.

275. When he started to erect THE TABERNACLE, he could not set it up. Why? Because the will AND MEDITATION regarding coming from these letters OF THE NAME 42 was given to no one but Moses, who knew the wish concerning these letters, and therefore, the Tabernacle was erected by him, as it is written, "and Moses erected…and put…and set" (Shemot 40:18-19). But Betzalel did not know, and therefore could not build it.

28. "He asked life of you"

A Synopsis

Rabbi Yitzchak begins with: "The king joys in Your strength, Hashem, and in Your salvation how greatly he rejoices. You have given him his heart's desire... He asked life of You..." and tells us that David sang this in praise. 'Strength' is the joy of studying the Torah, and 'the king' refers to God. In "He asked life of You, and You did give it him; length of days for ever and ever," we learn that King David only lived 72 years, and that these years were actually taken from Adam, who had a thousand years but only used nine hundred and thirty. Lastly Rabbi Yitzchak talks about the time when the temple will be rebuilt again in the future.

276. פָּתַח ר׳ יִצְחָק אֲבַתְרֵיהּ וְאָמַר, יְיָ׳ בְּעָזְךָ יִשְׂמַח מֶלֶךְ וּבִישׁוּעָתְךָ מַה יָּגֶיל מְאֹד תַּאֲוַת לִבּוֹ וְגוֹ׳, חַיִּים שָׁאַל מִמְּךָ וְגוֹ׳, שִׁירָתָא דָּא לָא אָמַר לָהּ דָּוִד, אֶלָּא עַל תּוּשְׁבַּחְתָּא דִּכְנֶסֶת יִשְׂרָאֵל, דְּקוּדְשָׁא בְּרִיךְ הוּא חַדֵּי לָהּ בְּחֵידוּ דְּאוֹרַיְיתָא, דְּאִקְרֵי עֹז, דִּכְתִּיב יְיָ׳ עֹז לְעַמּוֹ יִתֵּן וְגוֹ׳. יִשְׂמַח מֶלֶךְ: דָּא קוּדְשָׁא בְּרִיךְ הוּא דְּאִתְקְרֵי מֶלֶךְ, דִּכְתִּיב וַיְהִי בִישֻׁרוּן מֶלֶךְ.

276. Rabbi Yitzchak then opened the discussion and said: "The king joys in Your strength, Hashem, and in Your salvation how greatly he rejoices. You have given him his heart's desire… He asked life of You…" (Tehilim 21:2-5). David sang this in praise of the Congregation of Yisrael, MALCHUT, which the Holy One, blessed be He gladdens with the joy of Torah called 'strength', as it is written, "Hashem will give strength to His people" (Tehilim 29:11). THIS IS THE MEANING OF "THE KING JOYS IN YOUR STRENGTH…" "The king joys" refers to the Holy One, blessed be He called 'king', as it is written, "and there was a king in Yeshurun" (Devarim 33:5).

277. וּבִישׁוּעָתְךָ מַה יָּגֶיל מְאֹד, דָּא יְשׁוּעָה דִּימִינָא, כד״א הוֹשִׁיעָה יְמִינְךָ וַעֲנֵנִי. וַתּוֹשַׁע לוֹ יְמִינוֹ. מַה יָּגֶיל מְאֹד, י׳ יְתֵירָה, וְדָא אִיהוּ רָזָא דִּבְרִית קַיָּימָא קַדִּישָׁא, דְּאִיהוּ חֶדְוָה דְּכֹלָּא, וְכֹלָּא עַל הַאי מֶלֶךְ אִתְּמַר.

277. "And in Your salvation how greatly he rejoices." This is the salvation of the right, WHICH IS CHASSADIM, as you say, "save with Your right hand" (Tehilim 60:7), and 'His right hand shall save him.' In "how greatly he rejoices (Heb. *yagil*)" an extra *Yud* IS WRITTEN, ('*YAGIL*' INSTEAD OF '*YAGEL*'). It is the secret of the sign of the Holy Covenant, in which all rejoice, NAMELY YESOD. 'All' is said of the King, WHO IS ZEIR ANPIN.

278. חַיִּים שָׁאַל מִמְּךָ נָתַתָּ לוֹ אֹרֶךְ יָמִים עוֹלָם וָעֶד. מֵהָכָא אוֹלִיפְנָא, דְּדָוִד מַלְכָּא לָא הֲוֵו לֵיהּ חַיִּים כְּלָל, בַּר דְּאָדָם קַדְמָאָה יָהַב לֵיהּ מִדִּילֵיהּ. וְהָא אוֹקְמוּהָ, דְּדָוִד דְּמַלְכָּא אִתְקַיָּים שַׁבְעִין שְׁנִין. וְאִינּוּן ע׳ שְׁנִין יָהַב לֵיהּ קוּדְשָׁא בְּרִיךְ הוּא מֵאִינּוּן שְׁנִין דְּאָדָם קַדְמָאָה, וּבְהוּ אִתְקַיָּים, וְאִתְיְיהִיב לֵיהּ אוֹרִיכוּ דְּיוֹמִין בְּהַאי עָלְמָא, וּבְעָלְמָא דְּאָתֵי, וְעַל דָּא חַיִּים שָׁאַל מִמְּךָ נָתַתָּ לוֹ.

278. "He asked life of You, and You did give it him; length of days for ever and ever" (Tehilim 21:5). We learned from here that King David had no life whatsoever, except what Adam gave him of his own. It was established that King David lived 72 years, the seventy years given him by the Holy One, blessed be He from the years of Adam, WHO HAD A THOUSAND YEARS TO LIVE, ACCORDING TO THE SECRET OF THE VERSE, "ON THE DAY THAT YOU EAT..." (BERESHEET 2:17). A DAY OF THE HOLY ONE, BLESSED BE HE LASTS A THOUSAND YEARS, BUT ADAM LIVED ONLY NINE HUNDRED THIRTY YEARS, AND THE SEVENTY HE GAVE TO KING DAVID. David lived upon them, and was given longevity in this world and in the World to Come. The verse, "He asked life of You, and You did give him" refers to this matter.

279. גָּדוֹל כְּבוֹדוֹ, בְּגִין דְּאִיהוּ גָּדוֹל, דִּכְתִּיב גָּדוֹל אֲדוֹנֵנוּ וְרַב כֹּחַ. וַדַּאי אִקְרֵי גָּדוֹל, וְרָזָא דָּא, וַיַּעַשׂ אֱלֹהִים אֶת שְׁנֵי הַמְּאוֹרוֹת הַגְּדוֹלִים, גְּדוֹלִים הֲווֹ וַדַּאי. ועב״ד, אִיהוּ אִקְרֵי גָּדוֹל, כְּמָה דְּאִתְּמַר גָּדוֹל אֲדוֹנֵינוּ וְרַב כֹּחַ. וְקוּדְשָׁא בְּרִיךְ הוּא לָא אִקְרֵי גָּדוֹל, אֶלָּא בְּהַאי, דִּכְתִּיב, גָּדוֹל יְיָ׳ וּמְהֻלָּל מְאֹד בְּעִיר אֱלֹהֵינוּ הַר קָדְשׁוֹ. בְּמָה אִיהוּ גָּדוֹל, בְּעִיר אֱלֹהֵינוּ הַר קָדְשׁוֹ.

279. "His glory is great" (Tehilim 21:6), because He is great, as it is written, “great is our Master, and of great power” (Tehilim 147:5). Assuredly, ZEIR ANPIN is called ‘great’. This is the secret of “And Elohim made the two great lights” (Beresheet 1:6). Surely they were great, EVEN MALCHUT, CALLED ‘MOON’, WAS AS GREAT AS ZEIR ANPIN, CALLED ‘SUN’. With all that ZEIR ANPIN is called ‘great’ as it is said, “great is our Master, and of great power,” BUT MALCHUT IS NOT CALLED ‘GREAT’, SINCE IT DIMINISHED. The Holy One, blessed be He is not called ‘great’, only by the words, “Great is Hashem, and highly to be praised in the city of our Elohim, in the mountain of His holiness” (Tehilim 48:2), MEANING THAT ZEIR ANPIN is great ONLY in the city of our Elohim, in the mountain of His holiness, WHICH IS MALCHUT.

280. כִּי תְשִׁיתֵהוּ בְרָכוֹת לָעַד. כִּי תְשִׁיתֵהוּ בְּרָכוֹת, בְּגִין דְּהַאי אִיהוּ בִּרְכָתָא דְּכָל עָלְמָא, וְכָל בִּרְכָאן דְּכָל עָלְמָא מֵהָכָא נַפְקֵי, וְדָא אִיהוּ בְּרָכָה. וְרָזָא דָּא, וֶהְיֵה בְּרָכָה. דְּהָא הָכָא שַׁרְיָאן כָּל בִּרְכָאן דִּלְעֵילָּא, וּמֵהָכָא נַפְקֵי לְכָל עָלְמָא, וְעַל דָּא אִקְרֵי בְּרָכָה.

280. “For You put blessings upon him forever” (Tehilim 21:7). For You put blessings upon him,” because MALCHUT is a blessing of the whole world, and all the blessings of the world emerge from here. And it is a blessing. This is the secret of “and you shall be a blessing” (Beresheet 12:2), because here, IN MALCHUT, dwell all the blessings of above and hence they go into the whole world. It is therefore called ‘a blessing’.

281. תְּחַדֵּהוּ בְשִׂמְחָה, כְּתִיב הָכָא תְּחַדֵּהוּ בְּשִׂמְחָה, וּכְתִיב הָתָם וַיִּחַדְּ יִתְרוֹ, בְּגִין דְּזַמִּין קוּדְשָׁא בְּרִיךְ הוּא לְאַקָּמָא לָהּ לִכְנֶסֶת יִשְׂרָאֵל מֵעַפְרָא, וּלְאִתְקְפָא בָּהּ בְּרָזָא דִּימִינָא, וּלְחַדְּתּוֹתֵי לָהּ חַדְתּוּתָא דְּסִיהֲרָא בְּשִׁמְשָׁא.

281. It is written here: “You make him glad” (Tehilim 21:7), and “Jethro rejoiced” (Shemot 18:9). IN THE LATTER VERSE THERE WAS JOY FOR THE REDEMPTION OF YISRAEL FROM EGYPT, IN THE FORMER ALSO FOR REDEMPTION, that the Holy One, blessed be He is destined to raise the Congregation of Yisrael, MALCHUT, from the dust, keep it in the secret of the right and renew it like the moon is renewed by the sun.

282. כְּתִיב תְּחַדֵּהוּ בְשִׂמְחָה אֶת פָּנֶיךָ, אֶת פָּנֶיךָ, לְמֶהֱוֵי קַמָּךְ, וּלְמֶהֱוֵי בְּחֵידוּ לָקֳבֵל אַנְפָּךְ, בְּהַהוּא שְׁלִימוּ דְּתִשְׁתְּלִים בְּהַהוּא זִמְנָא. דְּהָא בְּזִמְנָא דְּאִתְחָרַב בֵּי מַקְדְּשָׁא, אִתְרְקִינַת מִכָּל מַה דְּאִתְמַלְיָיא. כד״א אֻמְלְלָה יוֹלֶדֶת הַשִּׁבְעָה. וּכְתִיב אִמָּלְאָה הָחֳרָבָה.

282. It is written, "You make him glad with Your countenance" (Tehilim 21:7) MEANING THAT he will be before You, gladly in front of You with the perfection achieved at the time, NAMELY, IN THE FUTURE. For at the time the Temple was destroyed, MALCHUT emptied of her fullness, as it is said, "she that has borne seven languishes" (Yirmeyah 15:9), and, "I shall be filled with her that is laid waste" (Yechezkel 26:2), FOR IN THE FUTURE SHE WILL BE RENEWED AGAIN.

29. “And they brought the Tabernacle to Moses”

A Synopsis

We are told here of the time when Moses erected the Tabernacle and everything in it was brought before him. He was unable to enter into the Tent of Testimony because of the cloud that was in it. A comparison is drawn to a wife preparing herself and adorning herself for her husband, as Malchut comes to Zeir Anpin. We read of the prevalence of the color blue in the Tabernacle and are told of the ‘plate of pure gold’ that is inscribed “Holiness to Hashem.”

283. ת״ח, בְּהַהוּא זִמְנָא דְּאוֹקִים מֹשֶׁה יַת מַשְׁכְּנָא, אִסְתָּכַּל בְּכָל אִינּוּן עֲבִידָאן, דַּהֲווֹ כַּדְקָא יֵאוֹת, וּכְדֵין אוֹקִים לֵיהּ. וְכָל אִינּוּן עֲבִידָאן דַּהֲווֹ בֵּיהּ בְּמַשְׁכְּנָא, כָּל חַד וְחַד אַיְיתִיאוּ לֵיהּ לְמֹשֶׁה. וְרָזָא דָּא בְּתוּלוֹת אַחֲרֶיהָ רְעוֹתֶיהָ מוּבָאוֹת לָךְ. מוּבָאוֹת לָךְ דִּכְתִּיב. וַיָּבִיאוּ אֶת הַמִּשְׁכָּן אֶל מֹשֶׁה.

283. Come and see: When Moses erected the Tabernacle, he checked all the crafts, that they were done properly. Then he erected it. All the crafts of the Tabernacle were brought before Moses one by one. This is the secret of the verse, “the virgins, her companions that follow her, shall be brought to you” (Tehilim 45:15). “Brought to you” is the same as “brought the Tabernacle to Moses” (Shemot 39:33). IT IS THE SECRET OF THE SEVEN MAIDENS BRINGING MALCHUT CALLED ‘TABERNACLE’ TO MOSES, WHO IS THE SECRET OF ZEIR ANPIN.

284. אֲמַאי וַיָּבִיאוּ אֶת הַמִּשְׁכָּן. בְּגִין דְּהָא בְּהַהִיא שַׁעֲתָא, הֲוָה זִוּוּגָא דְּמֹשֶׁה לְאִזְדַּוְּוגָא, וְעַל דָּא וַיָּבִיאוּ אֶת הַמִּשְׁכָּן אֶל מֹשֶׁה, כְּמָה דְּאַיְיתֵי כַּלָּה לְבֵי חָתָן. בְּגִין דְּהָא בְּקַדְמֵיתָא אִצְטְרִיךְ לְאַעֲלָא לְכַלָּה לְגַבֵּי חָתָן, כד״א אֶת בִּתִּי נָתַתִּי לָאִישׁ הַזֶּה לְאִשָּׁה. וּלְבָתַר אִיהוּ יֵיתֵי לְגַבָּהּ, דִּכְתִּיב וַיָּבֹא אֵלֶיהָ. וּכְתִיב וַיָּבֹא מֹשֶׁה אֶל אֹהֶל הָעֵדוּת.

284. HE ASKS: Why did they bring the Tabernacle? AND HE ANSWERS it was then the time of espousals of Moses, ZEIR ANPIN, and therefore, they brought the Tabernacle, MALCHUT, to Moses, like a bride coming to the house of the groom. For first the bride should be brought to the groom, as it is written, "I gave my daughter to this man to wife" (Devarim 22:16). Then he comes to her, as said, "and went in to her" (Beresheet 38:2), and "Moses went into the Tent of Testimony" (Bemidbar 17:23), WHICH IS MALCHUT.

285. וְהָכָא מַה כְּתִיב, וְלֹא יָכֹל מֹשֶׁה לָבֹא אֶל אֹהֶל מוֹעֵד כִּי שָׁכַן עָלָיו הֶעָנָן וְגוֹ׳. מַאי טַעֲמָא. בְּגִין דַּהֲוַת אִיהִי מִתַּתְקְנָא, כְּהַאי אִתְּתָא דְּאִתְתַּקְּנַת וְאִתְקַשְּׁטַת לְגַבֵּי בַּעְלָהּ, וּבְהַהִיא שַׁעֲתָא דְּאִיהִי קָא מִתְקַשְּׁטָת, לָא אִתְחָזֵי לְבַעְלָהּ לְאַעֲלָא לְגַבָּהּ. וע״ד וְלֹא יָכֹל מֹשֶׁה לָבֹא אֶל אֹהֶל מוֹעֵד כִּי שָׁכַן עָלָיו הֶעָנָן בְּגִין כַּךְ וַיָּבִיאוּ אֶת הַמִּשְׁכָּן אֶל מֹשֶׁה. עוֹד מַה כְּתִיב וַיַּרְא מֹשֶׁה אֶת כָּל הַמְּלָאכָה וְגוֹ׳.

285. It is written, "and Moses was not able to enter into the Tent of Testimony, because the cloud rested on it…" (Shemot 40:35). The sense is that it adorned itself as a woman prepares and adorns herself for her husband. And when she does so, it is not fit that her husband should enter to her. Therefore, "Moses was not able to enter into the Tent of Testimony because the cloud rested on it." For this reason "they brought the Tabernacle to Moses." Also, "Moses saw all the work…" (Shemot 39:43).

286. תָּא חֲזֵי, בְּכָל עֲבִידָן דְּמַשְׁכְּנָא, בְּכֻלְּהוּ הֲוָה גַּוְונָא דִּתְכֵלָא. בְּגִין דִּתְכֵלָא אִיהוּ גַּוְונָא לְאִתְעַטְּרָא בְּרָזָא דְּכָל גַּוְונִין. מַה כְּתִיב וַיַּעֲשׂוּ אֶת צִיץ נֶזֶר הַקֹּדֶשׁ וְגוֹ׳, וַיִּתְּנוּ עָלָיו פְּתִיל תְּכֵלֶת וְגוֹ׳, וְהָא אוּקְמוּהָ, בְּרָזָא דִּכְתִּיב, וְעָשִׂיתָ צִיץ זָהָב טָהוֹר וּפִתַּחְתָּ עָלָיו פִּתּוּחֵי חוֹתָם קֹדֶשׁ לַה׳. וַיִּכְתְּבוּ עָלָיו מִכְתַּב פִּתּוּחֵי חוֹתָם קֹדֶשׁ לַה׳.

286. Come and see: In all the works of the Tabernacle the blue color was present, because it is adorned in the secret of all the colors, BEING THE SECRET OF THE BLACK LIGHT IN THE CANDLE UPON WHICH RESTS THE WHITE LIGHT. It is written, "and they made the plate of the holy crown of pure gold…and they tied to it a lace of blue" (Shemot 39:30). This we explained in the secret of the verse, "and you shall make a plate of pure gold, and engrave upon it, like the engravings of a signet, holiness to Hashem" (Shemot 28:36), "and wrote upon it a writing, like the engravings of a signet, Holiness to Hashem" (Shemot 39:30).

30. The traps

A Synopsis

This section tells about the turning wheels of light that are called 'traps'. They are described as the 'judgments of the Left Column' and they travel and turn around the world. There is one great pillar thrust into the abyss, and stones within the abyss, and many wheels revolving around the pillar. We read that above the pillar is a wheel that is present in twelve thousand worlds and it revolves within the Tabernacle, it both turns and does not turn. In the Tabernacle is a crier who proclaims: 'beware of the turning wheel'. Rabbi Shimon says that anyone who understands may have access to the high secrets and the keys hidden within the holy Tabernacle. He ends by saying how happy those people are who put their strength in God and who are chosen by Him.

תוספתא

287. בְּרָזִין עִלָּאִין. טַסְקוּרֵי קְמִיטִין שְׁכִיחִין, אִלֵּין סַלְּקִין וְנַחְתִּין, וְאִלֵּין קַיְימִין בְּקִיּוּמַיְיהוּ. גַּלְגַּלִּין דְּסַחֲרָאן, הֲווֹ קַיְימָן מֵהַהוּא זִמְנָא דְּעַפְרָא אִתְכְּבִישׁ. אִינּוּן גַּלְגַּלִּין סָחֲרִין עָלְמָא, בְּסָחֲרָנוּתָא.

Tosefta (addendum)

287. In the high mysteries, NAMELY, THE HIGH LIGHTS, there are traps, THE JUDGMENTS OF THE LEFT COLUMN. These LIGHTS go up and down, and THE TRAPS remain at their place. THESE LIGHTS are turning wheels. They exist from the time that the dust was gathered. And the wheels turn around the world and circle it.

288. סָחֲרָנוּתָא דְּסָחֲרִין מִדְבָּרִין, טִיפְסְרָא דְּקוּלְטָא בְּגַוַּויְיהוּ. חַד גַּלְגַּלָּא אִית בְּגַוַּויְיהוּ, הַאי גַּלְגַּלָּא סָחֲרָא וְלָא סָחֲרָא. קַיְּימָא בִּתְרֵיסַר אַלְפֵי עָלְמִין. בֵּינַיְיהוּ שְׁכִיחַ, סָלִיק וְנָטִיל בְּגַוַּויְיהוּ.

288. When they circle the deserts, the ruling of the receiving OF CHOCHMAH is within them. There is one wheel among them, which turns and turns not, present in twelve thousand worlds. It is in the midst OF THE WHEELS, rising and traveling among them.

289. תְּחוֹת הַהוּא גַּלְגַּלָּא, קַיְּימָא חַד עַמּוּדָא דְּנָעִיץ עַד תְּהוֹמָא רַבָּא. בֵּיהּ, מִתְגַּלְגְּלָאן אַבְנִין גּוֹ תְּהוֹמֵי, אִינּוּן סַלְּקִין וְנַחְתִּין. הַהוּא עַמּוּדָא קָאִים עֲלַיְיהוּ, נָטִיל וְלָא נָטִיל, נָעִיץ מֵעֵילָּא לְתַתָּא, סָחֲרָאן מָאתָן וְעֶשְׂרִין גַּלְגַּלִּין אַחֲרָנִין, סַחֲרָנֵיהּ דְּהַהוּא עַמּוּדָא.

289. Under that FOURTH wheel, stands one pillar, thrust into the great abyss. In THE GREAT ABYSS, stones roll within abysses, going up and down. That one pillar stands upon them, moving yet not moving, thrust from above to below. Two hundred and twenty other wheels are turning around that pillar.

290. הַהוּא גַּלְגַּלָּא אַחֲרָא דְּעָלֵיהּ, דְּקָאִים בִּתְרֵיסַר אַלְפֵי עָלְמָא, אִיהוּ סָחֲרָא גּוֹ מַשְׁכְּנָא, סָחֲרָא וְלָא סָחֲרָא. הַהוּא מַשְׁכְּנָא קָאִים עַל תְּרֵיסַר אַלְפֵי עָלְמִין, בֵּיהּ קַיְּימָא הַהוּא כָּרוֹזָא, דְּקָרֵי אִסְתָּמְרוּ מִגַּלְגַּלָּא דְּסָחֲרָא.

290. HE EXPLAINS: The other wheel above THE THRUST PILLAR, NAMELY THE FOURTH WHEEL, that is present in twelve thousand worlds, turns round within the Tabernacle, NUKVA OF ZEIR ANPIN, turning and turning not. That Tabernacle stands upon twelve thousand worlds. In it there is a crier proclaiming 'beware of the turning wheel'.

291. מַאן דְּאִיהוּ מָארֵי דְּעַיְינִין בְּסָכְלְתָנוּ, יִנְדַּע וְיִסְתַּכַּל בְּחָכְמְתָא דְּמָארֵיהּ, וְיִנְדַּע דְּאִינּוּן מִלִּין עִלָּאִין, דְּמַפְתְּחָן דְּמָארֵיהּ קַיְימָן תַּמָּן, דִּי אִינּוּן טְמִירָאן גּוֹ מַשְׁכְּנָא קַדִּישָׁא. זַכָּאִין אִינּוּן בְּהַאי עָלְמָא, וְזַכָּאִין אִינּוּן בְּעָלְמָא דְּאָתֵי, עֲלַיְיהוּ כְּתִיב אַשְׁרֵי אָדָם עוֹז לוֹ בָךְ מְסִלּוֹת בִּלְבָבָם. אַשְׁרֵי תִּבְחַר וּתְקָרֵב יִשְׁכּוֹן חֲצֵרֶיךָ נִשְׂבְּעָה בְּטוּב בֵּיתֶךָ קְדוֹשׁ הֵיכָלֶךָ.

(ע"ב תוספתא)

291. Whoever has understanding eyes, he may know and behold the Wisdom of his Master, and know most high matters, where the keys of his

Master are found, hidden within the holy Tabernacle. They are happy in this world, and happy in the World to Come. Of them it is written, "happy is the man whose strength is in You, in whose heart are Your highways" (Tehilim 84:6), and "happy is the man whom You choose, and causes to approach to You, that he may dwell in Your courts: we will be satisfied with the goodness of Your house, Your Temple" (Tehilim 65:5).

(End of Tosefta)

31. The letters of Yud Hei Vav Hei are like the letters of Adonai

A Synopsis

We are told that the mystery of the Tabernacle that is like the mystery of the Ark includes the secrets of the Holy Name Adonai, as can be seen in: "behold, the Ark of the Covenant of the Lord (Adon) of all the earth." Rabbi Shimon explains how the letters in Adonai are like the letters Yud Hei Vav Hei, and tells about their numerical significance. He says that the Tabernacle below on earth and the upper Tabernacle (Adonai) and the third Tabernacle that is even higher (Binah) are all comprised within each other "that the Tabernacle may be one."

292. בְּרָזָא דְּמַשְׁכְּנָא קַיְימָן רָזִין עִלָּאִין, בְּרָזָא דִּשְׁמָא קַדִּישָׁא אֲדֹנָ״י, הַאי אִיהוּ רָזָא דְּמַשְׁכְּנָא, כְּגַוְונָא רָזָא עִלָּאָה, רָזָא דַּאֲרוֹנָא, כְּמָה דִּכְתִּיב הִנֵּה אֲרוֹן הַבְּרִית אֲדוֹן כָּל הָאָרֶץ. אֲדוֹן כָּל הָאָרֶץ, דָּא הוּא רָזָא קַדִּישָׁא דִּשְׁמָא דְּאָלֶ״ף דָּלֶ״ת נוּ״ן יוּ״ד. וְדָא הוּא כְּגַוְונָא דְּרָזָא דִּשְׁמָא קַדִּישָׁא עִלָּאָה יְדֹוָ״ד. וְאַתְוָון אִלֵּין כְּגַוְונָא דְּאִלֵּין.

292. Within the mystery of the Tabernacle are found high secrets of the Holy Name Adonai. The mystery of the Tabernacle resembles the supernal mystery of the Ark, as it is written, "behold, the Ark of the Covenant of the Master (Heb. *adon*) of all the earth" (Yehoshua 3:11). "The Master of all the earth" is the holy secret of the name Adonai. It reflects the Holy Name Yud Hei Vav Hei, because THE LETTERS ADONAI are like the letters YUD HEI VAV HEI.

293. א׳ אִיהִי י׳, רָזָא דְּיוֹ״ד כְּגַוְונָא דָּא א׳, וְהָא אוּקְמוּהָ. ד׳, אִיהוּ רָזָא ה׳, וְדָא כְּגַוְונָא דְּדָא, וְכֹלָּא כְּגַוְונָא וְרָזָא חֲדָא. נ׳, אִיהִי רָזָא דְּאָת ו׳, ואע״ג דְּדָא דְּכַר, וְדָא נוּקְבָא. אֲבָל דָּא אִתְכְּלִיל בְּדָא, וְהָא אוּקְמוּהָ ן׳ ו׳ אִיהוּ בְּאֶמְצָעִיתָא, בְּגִין דְּאִיהוּ כְּלָלָא חֲדָא. ה׳ אִיהוּ רָזָא דְּאָת י׳, בְּגִין דְּהָכָא, דָּא אִיהִי חָכְמָה זְעֵירָא, דְּאִקְרֵי חָכְמַת שְׁלֹמֹה.

293. HE EXPLAINS: *Aleph* OF ADONAI is like *Yud* OF YUD HEI VAV HEI, WHICH IS ABA. The mystery of the *Yud* FULLY SPELLED is like *Aleph*, FOR IN THE SHAPE OF THE LETTER *ALEPH* THERE IS *YUD* ABOVE, *VAV* IN THE

MIDDLE AND *DALET* BELOW, NAMELY *YUD* (*YUD-VAV-DALET*). This was established. *Dalet* OF ADONAI is the secret of *Hei* OF YUD HEI VAV HEI, WHICH IS IMA, BECAUSE WHEN MALCHUT SERVES AS A GARMENT TO THE LEFT COLUMN OF IMA, IT IS CALLED '*DALET*'. The one resembles the other, all in one mystery and manner. IT WAS EXPLAINED THAT *Nun* OF ADONAI is the secret of the letter *Vav* OF YUD HEI VAV HEI, WHICH IS TIFERET, THE CENTRAL COLUMN. And though *VAV* is male, and *NUN* is female, they were combined within one another, TIFERET OF ADONAI, WHICH IS MALCHUT, THE SECRET OF *NUN*, IS INCLUDED WITHIN TIFERET OF YUD HEI VAV HEI, WHICH IS ZEIR ANPIN, THE SECRET OF *VAV*. It was explained that *Nun* and *Vav* are in the middle, combined together. *NUN* IS THE CENTER OF THE LETTERS NUMERICALLY COUNTED IN UNITS OF 'TENS', *YUD* (= 10), *CAF* (= 20), *LAMED* (= 30), *MEM*, *NUN*, *SAMECH*, *AYIN*, *PEI*, *TZADI*, AND *VAV* IS THE CENTER OF THE LETTERS NUMERICALLY COUNTED IN UNITS OF ONE: *ALEPH* (= 1), BET (= 2), *GIMEL*, *DALET*, *HEI*, *VAV*, *ZAYIN*, *CHET*, *TET*. *Hei* OF YUD HEI VAV HEI is the secret of *Yud* OF ADONAI, WHICH IS MALCHUT, since THE *YUD* in here is little Chochmah called 'the Wisdom of Solomon'.

294. וְאִתְכְּלִילוּ אַתְוָון אִלֵּין בְּאִלֵּין, וְכֹלָּא אִיהִי רָזָא חֲדָא, כְּלִילָן אִלֵּין בְּאִלֵּין, וְכֹלָּא חַד, וְכֹלָּא אִיהוּ רָזָא חֲדָא, בְּאַתְוָון קַדִּישִׁין. וְעַל דָּא מַשְׁכְּנָא דִּלְתַתָּא בְּאַרְעָא, קַיְּימָא בְּרָזָא דְּמַשְׁכְּנָא עִלָּאָה, וְהַהוּא מַשְׁכְּנָא עִלָּאָה, קַיְּימָא בְּרָזָא דְּמַשְׁכְּנָא אַחֲרָא עִלָּאָה עַל כֹּלָּא. וְכֹלָּא אִיהוּ כָּלִיל דָּא בְּדָא לְמֶהֱוֵי חַד, וְעַל דָּא כְּתִיב, וְהָיָה הַמִּשְׁכָּן אֶחָד.

294. The letters are comprised within one another, THE FOUR LETTERS OF ADONAI INCLUDED WITHIN THE FOUR LETTERS YUD HEI VAV HEI. They all belong to the same principle, including the one in the other, everything being one. Everything is one mystery by the holy letters. Therefore, the Tabernacle below on earth is based on the secret of the upper Tabernacle, WHICH IS MALCHUT CALLED 'ADONAI', and that upper Tabernacle is in the secret of yet another Tabernacle superior to all, WHICH IS BINAH. All are comprised within one another so as to form one whole. Hence it is written, "that the Tabernacle may be one" (Shemot 26:6).

32. "And Moses erected the Tabernacle"

A Synopsis

Rabbi Shimon tells us that there is another Tabernacle above like the one that Moses erected on the earth. The 'wise men' in "and all the wise men, that carried out all the work of the sanctuary..." who labor on the Tabernacle above are the directions of Zeir Anpin, these directions are the paths to the sea, Malchut. Betzalel worked from the right and Aholiav worked from the left, just as the higher Tabernacle is built from the right and left sides of Zeir Anpin. We learn that on the day the Tabernacle was finished death was removed from the world, or at least it lost its dominion. The angel of death will not be removed from the world altogether until the return of Messiah. Then "He will swallow up death forever." Rabbi Yehuda next tells us that when Yisrael made the golden calf, Moses pitched his tent outside the camp so that holiness would not be defiled by their unholy actions. He says that when Jerusalem is finally fulfilled the evil Tyre will be in ruins.

295. כְּתִיב רֵאשִׁית גּוֹיִם עֲמָלֵק וְאַחֲרִיתוֹ עֲדֵי אוֹבֵד. ת״ח, בְּיוֹמָא דְּאִתְקַם מַשְׁכְּנָא, דְּאָקִים לֵיהּ מֹשֶׁה, כְּמָה דְּאִתְּמַר, דִּכְתִּיב וַיָּקֶם מֹשֶׁה אֶת הַמִּשְׁכָּן, דְּלָא הֲוָה יָכִיל לְמֵיקָם, עַד דְּאוֹקִים לֵיהּ אִיהוּ. לְמַטְרוֹנִיתָא, דְּלֵית רְשׁוּ לְבַר נָשׁ אַחֲרָא לְמֵיקָם לָהּ אֶלָּא בַּעְלָהּ. אוּף הָכִי, כָּל אִינּוּן אוּמָנִין, כֻּלְּהוּ אָתֵי לְאַקָמָא מַשְׁכְּנָא, וְלָא יָכִיל לְמֵיקַם עַל יְדַיְיהוּ, עַד דְּאָתָא מֹשֶׁה, וְאוֹקִים לֵיהּ, בְּגִין דְּאִיהוּ מָארֵיהּ דְּבֵיתָא.

295. It is written, "Amalek was the first of the nations, but his latter end shall be everlasting perdition" (Bemidbar 24:20). Come and see: When the Tabernacle was erected, it was erected by Moses, as we learned from the verse, "And Moses erected the Tabernacle" (Shemot 40:18). No one could raise it up until MOSES raised it up. It is LIKE a queen, whom no one has permission to raise up save her husband. Also here, all the craftsmen came to erect the Tabernacle, but could not until Moses came, WHO IS A CHARIOT OF ZEIR ANPIN, THE HUSBAND OF THE QUEEN, and raised it up, for he is the landlord.

296. כֵּיוָן דְּאָקִים מֹשֶׁה יַת מַשְׁכְּנָא לְתַתָּא, אִתְקַם מַשְׁכְּנָא אַחֲרָא לְעֵילָּא, כְּמָה דְּאוּקְמוּהָ, דִּכְתִּיב הוּקַם, וְלָא פָּרִישׁ עַל יְדָא דְּמַאן, דְּלָא

אִתְּקַם אֶלָּא מֵרָזָא דְּעָלְמָא עִלָּאָה, דְּאִיהוּ סָתִים וְגָנִיז, עַל יְדָא דְּרָזָא דְּמֹשֶׁה, בְּגִין לְאִתְתַּקְּנָא בַּהֲדֵיהּ.

296. Since Moses erected the Tabernacle below, another Tabernacle was raised above. It is explained, that it is written, "was erected" (Shemot 40:17), not mentioning by whom, because it was erected out of the secret of the upper world, hidden and concealed, by the hands of the mystery of Moses, WHO IS ZEIR ANPIN, to be perfected together with him.

297. מַה כְּתִיב לְעֵילָּא, וַיָּבֹאוּ כָּל הַחֲכָמִים הָעוֹשִׂים אֵת כָּל מְלֶאכֶת הַקֹּדֶשׁ וְגוֹ', מַאן אִינּוּן חֲכָמִים הָעוֹשִׂים. אִלֵּין אִינּוּן יְמִינָא וּשְׂמָאלָא, וְכָל שְׁאַר סִטְרִין, דְּאִינּוּן אוֹרְחִין וּשְׁבִילִין לְאַעֲלָא גוֹ יַמָּא, וּלְמַלְיָא לֵיהּ, וְאִינּוּן עַבְדוּ מַשְׁכְּנָא לְעֵילָּא, וְאַתְקִינוּ לֵיהּ.

297. It is written above: "and all the wise men, that carried out all the work of the sanctuary…" (Shemot 36:4). HE ASKS: IF THIS REFERS TO THE TABERNACLE ABOVE, who then are the wise men that carry out THE WORK OF THE SANCTUARY THERE? HE ANSWERS: These are right, left, and all the rest of the directions OF ZEIR ANPIN, which are the paths and ways that gather in the sea, WHICH IS MALCHUT, THE SECRET OF THE TABERNACLE, to fill it up. It is they who built and prepared the Tabernacle above.

298. כְּגַוְונָא דָּא לְתַתָּא, וְעָשָׂה בְּצַלְאֵל וְאָהֳלִיאָב, דָּא בְּסִטְר יְמִינָא, וְדָא בְּסִטְר שְׂמָאלָא, בְּצַלְאֵל לִימִינָא, וְאָהֳלִיאָב לִשְׂמָאלָא, דָּא מִיהוּדָה, וְדָא מִדָּן, וּלְבָתַר וְכֹל אִישׁ חֲכַם לֵב, וַיָּבֹאוּ כָּל הַחֲכָמִים הָעוֹשִׂים, וְהָא אוֹקִימְנָא, וְכֹלָּא כְּגַוְונָא דִּלְעֵילָּא.

298. THE TABERNACLE BELOW was built in the same manner. Betzalel and Aholiav worked, one on the right side, CHASSADIM, and the other on the left side, CHOCHMAH. Betzalel was of the right and Aholiav of the left, this one of the tribe of Judah, THE RIGHT SIDE OF MALCHUT, and that one of the tribe of Dan, OF THE LEFT. THEY CORRESPOND TO THE RIGHT AND LEFT SIDES OF ZEIR ANPIN. After them, "every wise hearted man" (Ibid. 1), "and all the wise men, that carried out," CORRESPONDING TO THE

OTHER SIDES OF ZEIR ANPIN. And we explained that all IN THE TABERNACLE BELOW was like THE TABERNACLE above.

299. בְּהַהוּא יוֹמָא דְאִתְּקַם מַשְׁכְּנָא, אִתְבְּטַל מוֹתָא מֵעָלְמָא. אִתְבְּטַל לָא תֵימָא, אֶלָּא אִסְתַּלָּק מֵעָלְמָא, דְּלָא יָכִיל לְשַׁלְטָאָה. כְּמָה דְאוֹקִימְנָא. בְּגִין דְּלָא יִתְבְּטַל יֵצֶר הָרָע מֵעָלְמָא, עַד דְּיֵיתֵי מַלְכָּא מְשִׁיחָא, וְקוּדְשָׁא בְּרִיךְ הוּא יַחְדֵּי בְּעוֹבָדוֹי וּכְדֵין בִּלַּע הַמָּוֶת לָנֶצַח. כַּד אִתְּקַם מַשְׁכְּנָא ע״י דְּמֹשֶׁה, כְּדֵין אִתְפְּרַשׁ חֵילָא דְּיֵצֶר הָרָע, וְאִתְכַּפְיָא, וְלָא הֲוָה יָכִיל לְשַׁלְטָאָה. בְּהַהִיא שַׁעֲתָא, אִתְפְּרַשׁ סָמָאֵ״ל, תַּקִּיפָא רוּגְזָא דִּשְׂמָאלָא, מֵעַל תּוּקְפָּא דְּחִוְיָא בִּישָׁא, וְלָא יָכִיל לְשַׁלְטָא עַל עָלְמָא, וְלָא יָכִיל לְאִתְחַבְּרָא בֵּיהּ בְּבַר נָשׁ, וּלְמִסְטֵי לֵיהּ.

299. On the day the Tabernacle was erected, death was removed from the world. Do not say 'removed' but that death disappeared from the world and lost its dominion. And as we explained, the Evil Inclination, THE ANGEL OF DEATH, would not be removed from the world until King Messiah will come and the Holy One, blessed be He will rejoice in His doings. Then "He will swallow up death forever" (Yeshayah 25:8). When the Tabernacle was erected by Moses, the strength of Evil Inclination departed and became subdued, and lost its power. At that time, Samael separated the strength of the harshness of the left from the strength of the evil serpent, so it could not rule over the world, nor join man and lead him astray.

300. רִבִּי יְהוּדָה אָמַר, כַּד עָבְדוּ יִשְׂרָאֵל יַת עֶגְלָא, מַה כְּתִיב וּמֹשֶׁה יִקַּח אֶת הָאֹהֶל וְנָטָה לוֹ מִחוּץ לַמַּחֲנֶה. מַאי טַעֲמָא. בְּגִין דְּחָמָא יֵצֶר הָרָע דַּהֲוָה אָזִיל בֵּינַיְיהוּ. אָמַר מֹשֶׁה, סִטְרָא דִקְדוּשָּׁה לָא תִּשְׁרֵי בְּגוֹ סִטְרָא דִּמְסָאֲבָא. רִבִּי אֶלְעָזָר אָמַר, כָּל זִמְנָא דְּסִטְרָא דִּקְדוּשָּׁה שַׁלְטָא, סִטְרָא מְסָאֲבָא לָא יָכִיל לְשַׁלְטָאָה, וְאִתְכַּפְיָא קַמֵּיהּ. וְעַל דָּא תָּנֵינָן, כָּל זִמְנָא דִּירוּשְׁלֵם תִּהְיֶה מְלֵאָה, צוֹר חֲרֵבָא יְהֵא חֲרֵבָה.

300. Rabbi Yehuda said: When Yisrael made the golden calf, "Moses would take the tent, and pitch it outside the camp" (Shemot 33:7). The sense thereof is that he saw the Evil Inclination walking among them, and he said, 'the side of holiness shall not dwell within the side of defilement'. Rabbi Elazar said: As long as the side of holiness has dominion, the side of defilement does not, and is subdued before HOLINESS. From here we learn that when Jerusalem will be full, the evil Tyre shall be in ruins.

33. The secret of the camel

A Synopsis

Rabbi Yehuda wonders why Rebecca got down from the camel when she saw Isaac coming, and if it was because she saw how beautiful he was. Rabbi Shimon says that when she met Isaac it was Minchah time, during which there is a strict Judgment. She saw that this was symbolized by the camel as the secret of death. Rabbi Shimon explains how the camel (gamal) is like requital (gmulo), and says that the camel is all-devouring and all-exterminating, always ready to work against men, just like judgment and death. He says that the camel brought death into the world by inciting Adam and Eve to eat from the Tree of Knowledge. The camel's rider is Samael who came to confuse and bring death to everyone, Adam attracted him and then Samael led them all astray. Therefore Rivkah got off the camel because she saw that Isaac had strict Judgment attached to him. Rabbi Shimon also mentions the dross of gold that is another aspect of strict judgment.

301. פָּתַח וְאָמַר, וַתֹּאמֶר אֶל הָעֶבֶד מִי הָאִישׁ הַלָּזֶה הַהוֹלֵךְ בַּשָּׂדֶה לִקְרָאתֵנוּ וַיֹּאמֶר הָעֶבֶד וְגוֹ׳. מַה כְּתִיב לְעֵילָּא, וַתִּשָּׂא רִבְקָה אֶת עֵינֶיהָ וַתֵּרֶא אֶת יִצְחָק וַתִּפּוֹל מֵעַל הַגָּמָל. הַאי קְרָא אֲמַאי אִצְטְרִיךְ לְמִכְתַּב בְּאוֹרַיְיתָא. וְתוּ, וְכִי בְּגִין דְּחָמָאת שְׁפִירוּ דְּיִצְחָק אִתְרְכִינַת מִגַּמְלָא.

301. He opened the discussion with the verse: "and she said to the servant, 'What man is this that walks in the field to meet us?' And the servant said..." (Beresheet 24:65). In the preceding verse it is written, "And Rivkah lifted up her eyes, and when she saw Isaac, she alighted from the camel" (Ibid. 64). HE ASKS: Why is this verse in the Torah, and is it because she saw the beauty of Isaac that she alighted from the camel?

302. אֶלָּא, הַאי קְרָא רָזָא אִיהוּ. ת״ח, בְּשַׁעֲתָא דְּמָטָאת רִבְקָה לְגַבֵּי דְּיִצְחָק, שַׁעֲתָא דִּצְלוֹתָא דְּמִנְחָה הֲוָה, וּבְהַהוּא זִמְנָא דִּינָא אִתְּעַר בְּעָלְמָא, וְחָמָאת לֵיהּ בְּרוּגְזָא דְּדִינָא קַשְׁיָא, וְחָמָאת דְּהָא סִיּוּם דְּרוּגְזָא קַשְׁיָא אִיהוּ גָּמָל לְתַתָּא, וְדָא אִיהוּ רָזָא דְּמוֹתָא, וּבְגִין כַּךְ אִתְרְכִינַת וְאַשְׁמִיטַת גַּרְמָהּ מֵהַהוּא גָּמָל. דְּהָא כַּד אִסְתַּכַּל דִּינָא קַשְׁיָא, הַהוּא

גָּמָל אִתְתָּקַף. וּבְגִין כַּךְ אַשְׁמִיטַת גַּרְמָהּ מִינֵּהּ, וְלָא יַתְבַת תַּמָּן.

302. He responds: This verse contains a mystery. Come and see: When Rivkah met Isaac, it was Minchah time, and at that time, a strict Judgment bestirs itself in the world. She saw the rigor of harsh Judgment, and that its lower part ends in a camel. This is the secret of death. Hence she alighted from the camel, for when harsh Judgment is watching, that camel is strengthened. That is why she slipped off and did not remain seated.

303. תָּא חֲזֵי, הַאי גָּמָל, הַיְינוּ רָזָא דִּכְתִּיב וּגְמוּלוֹ יְשַׁלֶּם לוֹ, דָּא גְּמוּל דְּאִינּוּן חַיָּיבַיָּא, דִּכְתִּיב אוֹי לְרָשָׁע רָע כִּי גְּמוּל יָדָיו יֵעָשֶׂה לוֹ. וְהַאי אִיהוּ גָּמָל, דְּקַיְּימָא לְאַכְלָא כֹּלָּא, וּלְשֵׁיצָאָה כֹּלָּא. וְהַאי אִיהוּ זַמִּין תָּדִיר לְקַבֵּל בְּנֵי נָשָׁא. וּבְגִין כַּךְ הַאי מַאן דְּחָמֵי בְּחֶלְמֵיהּ גָּמָל, אַחְמִיוּ לֵיהּ מוֹתָא דְּאִתְגְּזָרַת עָלֵיהּ, וְאִשְׁתְּזִיב מִנֵּיהּ.

303. Come and see: This camel (Heb. *gamal*) is the secret of the verse, "and that which he has given (Heb. *gmulo*) He will pay him back" (Mishlei 19:17), for *Gamal* (Eng. 'camel') is similar to *Gmul* (Eng. 'requital'), which refers to the requital to the wicked, as said, "Alas! It shall be ill with the wicked, for according to the deserving (Heb. *gmul*) of his hands shall be done to him" (Yeshayah 3:11). This is a camel: all-devouring and all-exterminating, always ready against men. Therefore, whoever sees a camel in his dream, he is shown that death was decreed upon him, but he was saved.

304. תָּא חֲזֵי, הַאי סִטְרָא דִּמְסָאֲבָא אִקְרֵי הָכִי, דְּגָרִים מִיתָא לְכָל עָלְמָא, וְהַאי הֲוָה דְּאַסְטֵי לְאָדָם וּלְאִתְּתֵיהּ, וְהַהוּא דְּרָכִיב עָלֵיהּ אִיהוּ סָמָאֵ״ל, וְאִיהוּ אָתָא לְמִטְעֵי עָלְמָא, וְגָרַם מוֹתָא לְכֹלָּא. וּבְגִין כַּךְ אָתָא וְשָׁלִיט עַל כֹּלָּא. אָדָם אִיהוּ אַמְשִׁיךְ לֵיהּ לְגַבֵּיהּ, וְכֵיוָן דְּאִיהוּ אַמְשִׁיךְ לֵיהּ לְגַבֵּיהּ, כְּדֵין אִיהוּ אִתְמְשַׁךְ אֲבַתְרַיְיהוּ, עַד דְּאַסְטֵי לוֹן. וּבְגִין כַּךְ אָמַר שְׁלֹמֹה, וְאַל תִּקְרַב אֶל פֶּתַח בֵּיתָהּ, דְּכָל מַאן דְּאִתְקְרִיב לְבֵיתָהּ, כְּדֵין אִיהִי נָפְקַת וּמִתְקַשְּׁרַת וְאִתְמַשְּׁכַת אֲבַתְרֵיהּ.

304. Come and see: The side of defilement is called 'camel', because it brought death to the whole world, and instigated Adam and his wife TO THE TREE OF KNOWLEDGE OF GOOD AND EVIL. His rider is Samael, come to confuse the world and cause death to all. Hence, he became ruler over everything. It was Adam, who drew him, and once he did, he was drawn after them, until he led them astray. For that reason Solomon said: "and come not nigh the door of her house" (Mishlei 5:8), for whoever approaches her house, she comes out and attaches herself and is drawn to him.

305. וְעַל דָּא רִבְקָה, כַּד חָמָאת דַּהֲוָה לֵיהּ לְאִתְדַּבְּקָא בְּסִטְרָא דְּדִינָא קַשְׁיָא. כֵּיוָן דְּחָמָאת לֵיהּ לְיִצְחָק בְּרָזָא דְּדִינָא קַשְׁיָא, וְחָמָאת דְּמֵהַהוּא סִטְרָא נָפַק דִּינָא אַחֲרָא תַּקִּיפָא, מִזּוּהֲמָא דְּדַהֲבָא, כַּד חָמָאת הַאי, מִיַּד וַתִּפּוֹל מֵעַל הַגָּמָל, בְּגִין לְאִתְרַפּוּיֵי מִן דִּינָא מֵהַהוּא זוּהֲמָא. כְּתִיב קוֹל יְיָ' מְשַׁלֵּם גְּמוּל לְאוֹיְבָיו, מֵהַהוּא זוּהֲמָא.

305. Therefore, Rivkah saw ISAAC, with strict Judgment attached to him, and when she saw that he is in the secret of harsh Judgment, and that from that side another harsh Judgment comes from the dross of gold, she immediately "alighted from the camel" to break from the Judgment of that dross. It is written, "the voice of Hashem rendering recompense to His enemies" (Yeshayah 66:6), NAMELY, from that filth.

34. The dross of gold

A Synopsis

Rabbi Yehuda wonders why Yisrael chose a calf to make from the gold and not something else, and he wonders who chose it as an image for Elohim. Rabbi Shimon tells how the chieftain who is in charge of the strength of the sun looks like a calf and it is the sun that generates the red gold on earth. He says that red is the spirit of unholiness, and it is also the evil serpent that Samael rides on. He draws a distinction between 'this', referring to the Holy Spirit, and 'these', referring to the spirit of unholiness, 'this' and 'these' being found in many verses of the Torah.

306. תָּא חֲזֵי כַּד עָבְדוּ יִשְׂרָאֵל הַהוּא עוֹבָדָא, וְגָרְמוּ לְהַהוּא חוֹבָא, מַאי טַעֲמָא עֵגֶל, וְלָא סִטְרָא אַחֲרָא. וְאִי תֵּימָא, דְּאִינּוּן בְּרִירוּ עֶגְלָא, לָאו הָכִי. אֶלָּא אִינּוּן אָמְרוּ, קוּם עֲשֵׂה לָנוּ אֱלֹהִים אֲשֶׁר יֵלְכוּ לְפָנֵינוּ, וְאַהֲרֹן רְעוּתֵיהּ הֲוָה לְאַעְכְּבָא לוֹן.

306. Come and see: When Yisrael did what they did, and committed that sin, why did they choose a calf, and not something else? If you say they chose the calf, this is not so. They only said, "Arise, make us Elohim, which shall go before us" (Shemot 32:1), and Aaron wanted to detain them. WHO THEN CHOSE THE CALF?

307. אֶלָּא וַדַּאי עֲבִידְתָּא אִתְעָבֵיד כַּדְקָא חֲזֵי, דְּהָא מִסִּטְרָא דְּדַהֲבָא, נָפְקָא סוּסְפִיתָא, כַּד אִתְבְּרִיר דַּהֲבָא, וּמִתַּמָּן מִתְפַּשְּׁטֵי כָּל אִינּוּן סִטְרֵי שְׂמָאלָא, דְּאִינּוּן הִתּוּכָא דְּהַהוּא סוּסְפִיתָא דְּדַהֲבָא, וּמִתְפָּרְשָׁאן לְכַמָּה סִטְרִין. וְכָל אִינּוּן דְּאִית לוֹן חֵיזוּ סוּמָקָא, גָּוֶון דְּדַהֲבָא קַיְימָא בְּטוּרֵי, כַּד שִׁמְשָׁא בְּתוּקְפֵיהּ, בְּגִין דְּתוּקְפָּא דְּשִׁמְשָׁא אַחְזֵי דַּהֲבָא, וְאוֹלִיד לֵיהּ בְּאַרְעָא. וְהַהוּא דִּמְמָנָא בְּהַהוּא תּוּקְפָּא דְּשִׁמְשָׁא, חֵיזוּ דִּילֵיהּ כְּעֶגְלָא, וְאִקְרֵי קֶטֶב יָשׁוּד צָהֳרָיִם, וְדָא נָפְקָא מִגּוֹ עֶגְלָא הִתּוּכָא סוּמָקָא דְּדַהֲבָא, וְכָל הָנֵי אַתְיָין מֵהַהוּא סִטְרָא סוּמָקָא, רוּחַ מְסַאֲבָא, דְּכָל אִינּוּן דְּמִתְפָּרְשֵׁי מֵרוּחַ מְסַאֲבָא מִתְפַּשְּׁטֵי בְּעָלְמָא.

307. HE REPLIES: Assuredly this was done properly. For from the side of gold, THE LEFT COLUMN, the dross comes out when the gold is refined. From THE DROSS OF GOLD are spread all the aspects of the left, the fusion of the refuse, spread to different directions. They are all of a red color, the hue of gold found in the mountains, when the sun is strong. For the strength of the sun shines upon the gold and generates it on earth. The chieftain, in charge of the strength of the sun, resembles a calf in his looks, and is called "the destruction that wastes at noonday" (Tehilim 91:6). The red fusion of the gold is coming out of the calf, NAMELY, THAT CHIEFTAIN, AND ALSO all those coming from that red, which is the spirit of unholiness, AND ALSO all those issuing from that spirit of unholiness and spreading in the world. THEREFORE, THE CALF WAS MADE BY THE FUSION OF THE GOLD THAT AARON THREW INTO THE FIRE.

308. וְהַאי רוּחַ מִסְאֲבָא, אִיהוּ חִוְיָא בִּישָׁא. וְאִית מַאן דְּרָכִיב עָלֵיהּ, וְאִינּוּן דְּכַר וְנוּקְבָא. וְאִקְרוּן אֵלֶּה, דְּאִינּוּן מִזְדַּמְּנִין בְּעָלְמָא, בְּכָל אִינּוּן סִטְרִין דִּלְהוֹן. וְרוּחַ קוּדְשָׁא אִקְרֵי זֹאת, דְּאִיהִי רָזָא דִּבְרִית, רְשִׁימָא קַדִּישָׁא דְּאִשְׁתְּכַח תָּדִיר עִמֵּיהּ דב"נ. וְכֵן זֶה יְיָ', זֶה אֵלִי, אֲבָל אִלֵּין אִקְרוּן אֵלֶּה, וְעַל דָּא כְּתִיב, אֵלֶּה אֱלֹהֶיךָ יִשְׂרָאֵל. ובג"כ כְּתִיב, גַּם אֵלֶּה תִשְׁכַּחְנָה. וְאָנֹכִי רָזָא דְּזֹאת, לֹא אֶשְׁכָּחֵךְ. וּכְתִיב עַל אֵלֶּה אֲנִי בוֹכִיָּה, דְּהַהוּא חוֹבָה גָּרִים לְמִבְכֵּי לוֹן כַּמָּה בִּכְיָין.

308. The spirit of unholiness is the evil serpent, upon which rides SAMAEL, a male and a female called 'these', so called for appearing in the world in all their several aspects. The Holy Spirit is called 'this' (Heb. *zot*, fem.), the secret of the Covenant, the holy sign always found on men, NAMELY, THE CROWN OF YESOD. It is also CALLED 'this' (Heb. *ze*, masc.), as it is written, "this is Hashem" (Yeshayah 25:9), and "this is my El" (Shemot 15:2). But the others are called 'these', as it is written, "these are your Elohim, Yisrael" (Shemot 32:4), and "these may forget" (Yeshayah 49:15), REFERRING TO THE MAKING OF THE GOLDEN CALF, "yet I (the secret of 'this') shall not forget you" (Ibid.). It is also written, "for these I weep" (Eichah 1:16), because the sin OF THE CALF CALLED 'THESE' caused them much weeping.

309. ד"א עַל אֵלֶּה אֲנִי בוֹכִיָּה. מ"ט. בְּגִין דְּאִתְיְיהִיב רְשׁוּ לַאֲתָר דָּא לְשַׁלְטָאָה עַל יִשְׂרָאֵל, וּלְחַרְבָּא בֵּי מַקְדְּשָׁא. וּבְגִין דְּאִתְיְיהִיב לוֹן רְשׁוּ

לְשַׁלְטָאָה, כְּתִיב עַל אֵלֶּה אֲנִי בוֹכִיָּה, רָזָא דְּמִלָּה עַל אֵלֶּה דָּא סִטְרָא דְּמִסָּאֲבָא דְּאִתְיְיהִיב לוֹן רְשׁוּ לְשַׁלְטָאָה. אֲנִי בוֹכִיָּה דָּא רוּחַ קוּדְשָׁא דְּאִקְרֵי אֲנִי.

309. Another explanation OF THE VERSE "for these I weep": because the place CALLED 'THESE' was given permission to rule over Yisrael and destroy the Temple, it is written, "for these I weep." The secret of the matter is that "for these" is the side of defilement CALLED 'THESE', which was given permission to rule. "I weep" refers to the Holy Spirit, NAMELY MALCHUT, called 'I'.

310. וְאִי תֵּימָא, הָא כְּתִיב אֵלֶּה דִּבְרֵי הַבְּרִית. הָכִי הוּא וַדַּאי, דְּכָל אִינּוּן לָא מִתְקַיְּימִין, אֶלָּא מִגּוֹ אֵלֶּה, דְּתַמָּן כָּל לְווָטִין כְּמָה דְּאוֹקִימְנָא דְּאִיהוּ אָרוּר, דִּכְתִּיב אָרוּר אַתָּה מִכָּל הַבְּהֵמָה. ובג"כ, אַקְדִּים וְאָמַר אֵלֶּה, דְּקַיְּימָא לְמַאן דְּעָבַר דִּבְרֵי הַבְּרִית. אֵלֶּה הַמִּצְוֹת אֲשֶׁר צִוָּה יְיָ' אֶת מֹשֶׁה, בְּגִין דְּפִקּוּדַיָּא דְּאוֹרַיְיתָא לְאִתְדַּכְּאָה בַּר נָשׁ, וְלָא יִסְטֵי לְאוֹרְחָא דָּא, וְיִסְתָּמַר מִתַּמָּן, וְיִתְפְּרַשׁ מִנַּיְיהוּ.

310. And if you say, "these are the words of the covenant" (Devarim 28:69), is written AS CHASTISEMENT, HE ANSWERS: Assuredly so, FOR HERE ALSO THERE IS AN ALLUSION TO THE OTHER SIDE, because all these curses have existence only in 'these', where are all the curses are found as explained THAT THE OTHER SIDE is damned, as it is written, "you are cursed above...every beast" (Beresheet 3:14). For that reason 'these' precede, referring to whoever transgresses "the words of the covenant." ALSO, "these are commandments, which Hashem commanded Moses" (Vayikra 27:34), for the precepts of the Torah purify man so he would not stray to the path OF 'THESE', but beware of them, and stay away from them.

311. וְאִי תֵּימָא אֵלֶּה תּוֹלְדוֹת נֹחַ נֹחַ. הָכִי הוּא וַדַּאי, דְּהָא נָפַק חָם, דְּאִיהוּ אֲבִי כְּנַעַן, וּכְתִיב אָרוּר כְּנַעַן, וְאִיהוּ רָזָא דָּא דְּאֵלֶּה.

311. You may say "these are the generations of Noah, Noah..." (Beresheet 6:9). Assuredly, THE OTHER SIDE WAS THERE TOO, because he begot

Ham, the father of Canaan, upon which it is written, "cursed be Canaan" (Beresheet 9:25). This is the secret of writing 'these', THAT HE IS CURSED.

312. וְעַל דָּא כָּל הָנֵי הִתּוּכָא סוּסְפִּיתָא דְּדַהֲבָא. וְאַהֲרֹן קָרִיב דַּהֲבָא, דְּאִיהוּ סִטְרָא דִּילֵיהּ, דְּכָלִיל אִיהוּ בְּתוּקְפָּא דְּאֶשָּׁא, וְכֹלָּא חַד, וְסִטְרָא דָּא דַּהֲבָא וְאֶשָּׁא.

312. Hence they are all the fusion of the dross of gold. And Aaron offered gold, which is of his own side, THE ASPECT THEREOF included in the strength of fire, MEANING THAT RIGHT IS INCLUDED IN THE LEFT, AND THEREFORE, AARON, WHO IS RIGHT WAS COMPRISED WITHIN THE LEFT, WHICH IS THE STRENGTH OF FIRE. And all is one. This side, LEFT, is gold and fire.

35. The calf

A Synopsis

We learn that the golden calf gave the spirit of unholiness a place of focus in which it could strengthen. Furthermore, even though Yisrael had been free of death from the time they stood upon Mount Sinai they now brought death upon themselves and upon all future generations. We are told that Aaron had to be purified for seven days because if it were not for him the golden calf would not have existed. Rabbi Shimon says that the golden calf is from the left side. Yisrael had drawn upon itself the Evil Inclination with their worship of the calf, and when they wanted to become purified again they had to offer a goat, the goat being a part of the evil inclination. Next we are told that when the calf was made, as in: "I threw it into the fire, and there came out this calf," it was made by sorcerers. Rabbi Shimon tells us of successful and unsuccessful sorcerers, some men are fit for sorcery and some are not. In the event of the creation of the golden calf, everything that was necessary for the spirit of defilement was ready and waiting: a completely wasted desert, enough gold, and Aaron who was willing to sin in this way. Everything was ready for the Other Side, and the deed was done. When Aaron was ready to be redeemed he offered a calf on the altar, thus executing judgment and subduing the rulers of the Other Side.

313. וְרוּחַ מְסַאֲבָא דְּאִשְׁתְּכַח תָּדִיר בְּמַדְבְּרָא, אַשְׁכַּח אֲתָר בְּהַהוּא זִמְנָא לְאִתַּתְקְפָא בֵּיהּ. וּמַה דַּהֲווֹ יִשְׂרָאֵל דַּכְיָין, מֵהַהוּא זוּהֲמָא קַדְמָאָה, דְּאָטִיל בְּעָלְמָא, וְגָרִים מוֹתָא לְכֹלָּא, כַּד קַיְימוּ עַל טוּרָא דְּסִינַי, גָּרַם לוֹן כְּמִלְּקַדְּמִין, לְסָאֲבָא לוֹן, וּלְאִתַּתְקְפָא עֲלַיְיהוּ, וְגָרִים לוֹן מוֹתָא, וּלְכָל עָלְמָא, וּלְדָרֵיהוֹן בַּתְרֵיהוֹן, הֲדָא הוּא דִּכְתִּיב אֲנִי אָמַרְתִּי אֱלֹהִים אַתֶּם וְגוֹ׳. אָכֵן כְּאָדָם תְּמוּתוּן וְגוֹ׳. וּבְגִין כַּךְ, אַהֲרֹן אַהְדָּר לְבָתַר לְאִתְדַּכְּאָה, בְּרָזָא דִּמְהֵימְנוּתָא עִלָּאָה, בְּאִינּוּן שִׁבְעָה יוֹמִין קַדִּישִׁין, וּלְבָתַר לְאִתְדַּכְּאָה בְּעֶגְלָא.

313. The spirit of unholiness that forever dwells in the desert, then found a place in which to strengthen. And Yisrael, though purified from the first defilement, thrown BY THE SERPENT upon the world, bringing death to all, from the time they stood upon Mount Sinai. Now THE SIN OF THE CALF caused them to be defiled as before, and brought death upon them AGAIN and upon the whole world, and upon their generations after them. This is the secret meaning of the verse, "I had said, 'You are angels…' Nevertheless, you shall die like men" (Tehilim 82:6-7). Aaron therefore was purified again in the secret of divine Faith for seven holy days, THE CONSECRATED DAYS, and then purified by a calf FOR A SIN OFFERING.

314. וְתָא חֲזֵי, בְּכֹלָּא בָּעָא אַהֲרֹן לְאִתְדַּכְּאָה, דְּאִלּוּ אִיהוּ לָא הֲוָה, לָא נָפַק עֶגְלָא. מ״ט. בְּגִין דְּאַהֲרֹן אִיהוּ יְמִינָא. וְאִיהוּ תּוּקְפָּא דְּשִׁמְשָׁא, וְדַהֲבָא מִשִּׁמְשָׁא. רוּחַ מִסַּאֲבָא נָחַת, וְאִתְכְּלִיל תַּמָּן, וְאִסְתְּאָבוּ יִשְׂרָאֵל, וְאִסְתְּאַב אִיהוּ, עַד דְּאִתְדָּכוּ.

314. Come and see: Aaron had to be purified more, because had it not been for him, the calf would not have been made. Why? Because Aaron is the right, and the strength of the sun. Gold is from the sun, FOR THE SUN, WHICH IS TIFERET, IS COMPRISED OF RIGHT AND LEFT. HENCE GOLD COMES FROM THE LEFT, BUT THE STRENGTH AND RULING OF THE SUN IS RIGHT. The spirit of unholiness descended to be included IN THE GOLD, THAT MADE THE CALF, and so were Yisrael defiled and so was he, AARON, until they became purified.

315. מ״ט אִסְתְּאַב. בְּגִין דְּנָפַק עֵגֶל, דְּאִיהוּ מִסִּטְרָא דִּשְׂמָאלָא, דְּאִיהוּ שׁוֹר, וּמִימִינֵיהּ עֵגֶל. וְאִיהוּ שְׂמָאלָא, כְּמָה דְּאִתְּמַר, דִּכְתִּיב וּפְנֵי שׁוֹר מֵהַשְּׂמֹאל לְאַרְבַּעְתָּן. וְאַהֲרֹן דְּאִיהוּ יְמִינָא, אִתְכְּלִיל בֵּיהּ שְׂמָאלָא, וְנָפַק עַל יְדֵיהּ. וְעַל דָּא, אִתְיְיהִיב לֵיהּ עֵגֶל, כְּמָה דְּאִיהוּ גָּרִים.

315. Why was he defiled? HE ANSWERS: Because of the golden calf, which is of the left side. The bull is of the left side, whence the calf emerged. THERE ARE FOUR ASPECTS TO THE LEFT: A BULL, A COW, A CALF, AND A HEIFER, WHICH ARE CHOCHMAH AND BINAH, TIFERET AND MALCHUT OF THE LEFT. It is of the left, as it is written, "and they four had the face of an ox on the left side" (Yechezkel 1:10). And in Aaron, who is right, the left was included, whence it emerged. Therefore, he offered AS A SIN OFFERING a calf, as the one he made.

316. ובג״כ, כַּד הַאי רוּחָא מְסַאֲבָא אִתְתָּקַף, וְשָׁלִיט כְּמִלְּקַדְמִין עַל

עָלְמָא, דְּהָא בִּזְמְנָא דְּחָאבוּ יִשְׂרָאֵל, אַמְשִׁיכוּ עָלַיְיהוּ הַהוּא יֵצֶר הָרָע כְּמִלְּקַדְמִין. כַּד אִתְדָּכוּ יִשְׂרָאֵל, וּבָעוּ לְאִתְדַּכָּאָה, אִצְטְרִיכוּ לְקָרְבָא שָׂעִיר, בְּגִין דְּשָׂעִיר אִיהוּ חוּלָקָא דְּהַהוּא יצה״ר, הַהוּא רוּחַ מְסָאֲבָא כִּדְקַאמְרָן.

316. That is why the spirit of defilement became stronger and ruled AGAIN over the world as before. For when Yisrael committed the sin OF THE CALF, they drew upon themselves the Evil Inclination as before. And when Yisrael became purified, and wanted to purge themselves, they had to offer a goat, being a part of the Evil Inclination, the said spirit of defilement.

317. כְּתִיב וַיָּמִירוּ אֶת כְּבוֹדָם בְּתַבְנִית שׁוֹר אוֹכֵל עֵשֶׂב. מַאי תַּבְנִית שׁוֹר. דָּא עֵגֶל. שׁוֹר מִסִּטְרָא דִּשְׂמָאלָא, אַהֲרֹן יְמִינָא, אִתְכְּלִיל שְׂמָאלָא בֵּיהּ, וְאִתְתָּקַף בֵּיהּ, וְנָפַק עַל יְדֵיהּ. תָּא חֲזֵי, וַיָּמִירוּ אֶת כְּבוֹדָם, דָּא שְׁכִינְתָּא, דְּאָזְלַת קָמַיְיהוּ, וְאַחְלְפוּ לָהּ בְּדוּכְתָּא מְסָאֲבָא, אֵל אַחֲרָא. ובג״כ לָא אִתְעֲבָר זוּהֲמָא דָּא מֵעָלְמָא, עַד הַהוּא זִמְנָא דְּיִעֲבַר לֵיהּ קוּדְשָׁא בְּרִיךְ הוּא מֵעָלְמָא, כד״א וְאֶת רוּחַ הַטּוּמְאָה אַעֲבִיר מִן הָאָרֶץ, וְהָא אוּקִימְנָא.

317. It is written, "Thus they exchanged their glory for the likeness of an ox that eats grass" (Tehilim 106:20). "The likeness of an ox" is a calf. An ox is of the left side, and Aaron is of the right. The left was included in it, strengthened by it and came out of it. Come and see: "they exchanged their glory," referring to the Shechinah that went before them, for a place of defilement, another El. Therefore, defilement does not pass from the world until the time the Holy One, blessed be He will remove it thence. This is the meaning of, "and I will cause the unclean spirit to pass out of the earth" (Zecharyah 13:2), as explained.

318. כְּתִיב וַיַּעֲשֵׂהוּ עֵגֶל מַסֵּכָה, וּכְתִיב וָאַשְׁלִיכֵהוּ בָאֵשׁ וַיֵּצֵא הָעֵגֶל הַזֶּה, מַשְׁמַע דְּלָא עָבֵד לֵיהּ, אִי הָכִי מַאי וַיַּעֲשֵׂהוּ. אֶלָּא וַדַּאי כְּמָה דְּאוּקִימְנָא, דְּאִלְמָלֵא אַהֲרֹן, לָא אִתְתָּקַף רוּחָא מְסָאֲבָא לְאִתְכַּלְּלָא בְּדַהֲבָא, אֲבָל כָּל תִּקּוּנָא דְּאִצְטְרִיךְ, אַשְׁכַּח לְאִתְבְּנָאָה.

318. It is written, "and made it a molten calf" (Shemot 32:4), and "I threw it into the fire, and there came out this calf" (Ibid. 24), indicating that he did not make it, BUT IT WAS MADE BY ANOTHER. What does it mean, then, "and made it"? HE ANSWERS: Assuredly it is as we stated, that if it were not for Aaron, the spirit of defilement was not strong enough to become a part of the gold. But every work needs to be done, AND THIS ONE WAS DONE BY SORCERERS.

319. תָּא חֲזֵי, אִית מַאן דְּעָבֵיד חַרְשִׁין וְאַצְלַח בִּידוֹי. וְאִית מַאן דְּעָבֵיד לוֹן כְּהַהוּא גַּוְונָא מַמָּשׁ, וְלָא אַצְלַח בִּידוֹי, דְּהָא לְעוֹבָדִין אִלֵּין גַּבְרָא מְתֻקְּנָא אִצְטְרִיךְ.

319. Come and see: Some practice sorcery and do well, and some do not succeed, though they practice in the same manner, because for these practices there is need for a suitable man.

320. תָּא חֲזֵי מִבִּלְעָם, דְּאִיהוּ הֲוָה מְתֻקְּנָא, לְאִינּוּן חַרְשִׁין דִּילֵיהּ, לְאַצְלְחָא בִּידוֹי, בְּגִין דִּכְתִּיב וּנְאֻם הַגֶּבֶר שְׁתֻם הָעָיִן. שְׁתוּם הָעָיִן, סְתוּם הָעַיִן כֹּלָּא חַד. דְּחָד עֵינָא סָתִים תָּדִיר, וְחֵיזוּ דְּעֵינוֹי לָא הֲוָה בְּאֹרַח מֵישָׁר, מוּמָא הֲוָה בֵּיהּ בְּעֵינוֹי. כְּתִיב וְשִׁלַּח בְּיַד אִישׁ עִתִּי, זַמִּין בְּכֹלָּא, חֵיזוּ דְּעֵינוֹי דְּלָא יִתְכְּשַׁר. אֲבָל רוּחַ קוּדְשָׁא, מַאן דְּיִשְׁתַּמֵּשׁ בַּהֲדֵיהּ מַה כְּתִיב, כָּל אִישׁ אֲשֶׁר בּוֹ מוּם לֹא יִקְרָב אִישׁ עִוֵּר אוֹ פִסֵּחַ.

320. We know this from Bilaam who was suitable for sorcery, as it is written, "the speech of the man, whose eye is open (Heb. *satum*)" (Bemidbar 24:3). An open eye (Heb. *satum;* lit. 'covered') and a closed eye (Heb. *satum*) are the same, for he had one of his eyes always closed and was looking askance in the other. HE WAS THEREFORE SUITABLE FOR PRACTICING THE ART OF SORCERY. It is written, "and shall send him away by the hand of an appointed man" (Vayikra 16:22), MEANING THAT THE MAN is fit TO DO THIS ERRAND, in that he would not look straight before him. NAMELY, HE TOO SHOULD BE DEFORMED, BECAUSE THE OTHER SIDE CLINGS TO DEFORMITY AND WANT. But whoever serves the Holy Spirit, it is said, "for whatsoever he be that has a blemish, he shall not approach: a blind man nor a lame" (Vayikra 21:18).

321. וְהָכָא, כֹּלָּא אִתְקַן לְרוּחָא מְסָאֲבָא, לְמֵיהַב לֵיהּ דּוּכְתָּא לְשַׁלְטָאָה. אַשְׁכַּח מַדְבְּרָא דְּאִיהוּ חָרוּב מִכֹּלָּא, כְּמָה דִּכְתִּיב נָחָשׁ שָׂרָף וְעַקְרָב וְגוֹ', דְּמִתַּמָּן אִיהוּ שׁוּלְטָנוּתָא דִּילֵיהּ. אַשְׁכַּח דַּהֲבָא סִפּוּקָא כַּדְקָא יָאוֹת. אַשְׁכַּח אַהֲרֹן, לְאִתַּתְקְפָא בִּימִינָא, וּלְאִתְכַּלְלָא בֵּיהּ. כְּדֵין אַשְׁלִים דּוּכְתֵּיהּ כַּדְקָא יָאוֹת, וְנָפִיק וְאִשְׁתְּלִים עוּבְדָא.

321. In here, THE SIN OF THE GOLDEN CALF, everything was ready to give way to the spirit of defilement, so it may rule, for he found a desert completely wasted, as said: "venomous serpents, and scorpions…" (Devarim 8:15), whence his power issues. He found enough gold to fit, he found Aaron, through whom it may be strengthened by the right and be included into. Then the place OF THE OTHER SIDE was ready on all sides as fit. It came out and the deed was done.

322. וּמְנָלָן דְּרוּחַ מְסָאֲבָא הֲוָה. דִּכְתִּיב אָנָּא חָטָא הָעָם הַזֶּה חֲטָאָה גְּדוֹלָה, דָּא רוּחַ מְסָאֲבָא, נָחָשׁ קַדְמָאָה, כִּדְקָאמְרָן בְּכַמָּה דּוּכְתִּין. וּבְזִמְנָא דְּבָעָא אַהֲרֹן לְאִתְדַּכְּאָה, אַקְרִיב עֵגֶל, מֵהַהוּא סִטְרָא, לְמֶעְבַּד בֵּיהּ דִּינָא. בְּקַדְמֵיתָא עָבֵד לֵיהּ לְשַׁלְטָאָה, וְהַשְׁתָּא דְּיַעֲבִיד בֵּיהּ דִּינָא, לְאַכְפְּיָיא לֵיהּ, דְּהָא כַּד אִתְעֲבִיד דִּינָא בְּסִטְרָא דָּא, אִתְכַּפְיָין כָּל אִינּוּן דְּשַׁלְטִין מִסִּטְרֵיהּ.

322. Whence do we know the spirit of defilement was there? From what is written, "Oh, this people has sinned a great sin" (Shemot 32:31), referring to the spirit of defilement, the primordial serpent, we mentioned in several places. When Aaron wanted to be purged, he offered a calf AS A SIN OFFERING, to deal punishment to that side, BY SLAUGHTERING AND OFFERING IT ON THE ALTAR. At first, he let it rule, and now he deals it Judgment to subdue it, because when Judgment is executed upon that side, all its rulers are subdued.

36. A red heifer

A Synopsis

Rabbi Aba asks Rabbi Shimon why the 'red heifer' in "a red heifer, faultless without blemish" is compared to the calf and the lamb and why it should be cleansed just through roasting it. Rabbi Shimon says the essence of the message is that a clean thing can be brought out of an unclean thing. The heifer was unclean, but by burning her to ashes she became clean. She had to be burned to ashes because it is like the verse: "and you shall tread down the wicked, for they shall be ashes under the soles of your feet." When water was sprinkled on the ashes they became clean. The secret of the clean water is the verse: "water of purifying (sin)." After judgment was executed on the heifer she became clean and the Holy Spirit had dominion. The spirit of defilement was no longer found in the camp.

323. תָּא חֲזֵי, בְּמִצְרַיִם, בְּהַהוּא סִטְרָא דִּלְהוֹן כְּתִיב, אַל תֹּאכְלוּ מִמֶּנּוּ נָא וְגוֹ׳. צְלִי אֵשׁ, בְּגִין דְּיִסְלַק רֵיחוֹ נוֹדֵף. רֹאשׁוֹ עַל כְּרָעָיו, לְתַבְרָא לֵיהּ וּלְאַכְפְּיָיא לֵיהּ, וּכְדֵין כָּל אִינּוּן דְּאַתְיָין מִסִּטְרֵיהּ לָא שַׁלְטֵי. כְּגַוְונָא דָּא פָּרָה אֲדוּמָּה תְּמִימָה וְגוֹ׳ בְּגִין לְאַכְפְּיָיא כָּל אִינּוּן סִטְרֵי מִסְאֲבָא, דְּלָא יִשְׁלְטוּן.

323. Come and see: In Egypt, it was written of their side, THE LAMB THEY WORSHIPPED, "eat not of it raw…but roast with fire," so its odor will rise. "Its head with its legs" (Shemot 12:9), in order to break and subdue it, so all that issue from that side may not rule. In the same manner it is written, "a red heifer, faultless without blemish…" (Bemidbar 19:2), that may subjugate all the sides of defilement so they may not rule.

324. א״ל רִבִּי אַבָּא, וְהָא פָּרָה קַדִּישָׁא אִיהִי, דַּכְיָא אִיהִי, וַאֲמַאי. אָמַר לֵיהּ הָכִי הוּא, וְהָא אוּקְמוּהָ, כְּלָלָא דְּאַרְבַּע מַלְכְוָון הֲוַת. פָּרָה, כד״א כִּי כְּפָרָה סוֹרֵרָה סָרַר יִשְׂרָאֵל. אֲדוּמָּה, דָּא מַלְכוּת בָּבֶל, דִּכְתִּיב אַנְתְּ הוּא רֵישָׁא דִּי דַהֲבָא. תְּמִימָה, דָּא מַלְכוּת מָדַי. אֲשֶׁר אֵין בָּהּ מוּם, דָּא מַלְכוּת יָוָן. אֲשֶׁר לֹא עָלָה עָלֶיהָ עוֹל, דָּא מַלְכוּת אֱדוֹם, דְּלָא סָלִיק עָלֵיהּ עוֹל. וְרָזָא דְּמִלָּה דָּא, אַף עַל גַּב דְּכַמָּה מִלִּין אִתְיְיהִיבוּ לְמִדְרַשׁ

בַּקְרָאֵי, כֻּלְּהוּ חַד.

324. Rabbi Aba said to him: But the red heifer is pure; why THEN COMPARE IT TO THE CALF AND THE LAMB, WHICH THE EGYPTIANS WORSHIPPED, AND WHY WILL ITS BURNING SUBDUE THE ASPECTS OF UNCLEANLINESS? He told him: It is so, THAT THE HEIFER ALLUDES ALSO TO THEIR SIDE, as explained that the heifer is comprised of the four kingdoms. "A heifer" is as is written, "For Yisrael is stubborn like a stubborn heifer" (Hoshea 4:16). "Red" alludes to the kingdom of Babylon, as it is written, "you are the head of gold" (Daniel 2:38), GOLD BEING RED. "Faultless" is the kingdom of Media. It is "without blemish," referring to the Greek kingdom. "Upon which never came a yoke" alludes to the kingdom of Edom, which was never under any yoke. The secret meaning is that though this verse was given several explanations, they all pertain to the same mystery.

325. הָא אִתְּמַר, דִּכְתִּיב מִי יִתֵּן טָהוֹר מִטָּמֵא לֹא אֶחָד. מִי יִתֵּן טָהוֹר מִטָּמֵא, רָזָא דָּא, הָכִי הוּא, דְּדָא אִיהוּ טָהוֹר דְּנָפַק מִטָּמֵא. דְּהָא בְּקַדְמֵיתָא טָמֵא, וְהַשְׁתָּא דְּאִתְעֲבֵיד בֵּיהּ דִּינָא, וְאִתְיְיהִיב לִיקֵידַת אֶשָּׁא בְּנוּרָא דְּדָלִיק, וְאִתְעֲבֵיד עָפָר, הַשְׁתָּא אִיהוּ טָהוֹר מִטָּמֵא, טָהוֹר דְּנָפִיק מִטָּמֵא.

325. We have studied the verse: "who can bring a clean thing out of an unclean? Not one" (Iyov 14:4). The secret of this verse is that THE RED HEIFER is a clean thing brought out of an unclean, because at first she was unclean, INCLUDING THE FOUR SAID KINGDOMS. Now that Judgment was executed on her and she was cremated by burning fire to become ashes, she is a clean thing out of an unclean, a clean thing brought out of an unclean.

326. וּבְגִין כַּךְ, כָּל אִינּוּן דְּמִשְׁתַּדְּלֵי בָּהּ, כֻּלְּהוּ מִסְתַּאֲבֵי, דְּהָא הָכִי הוּא וַדַּאי, וְכֵיוָן דְּאִתְעֲבֵיד אֵפֶר, כְּדֵין עַד דְּיִתְכְּנִישׁ וְיִסְתָּלִיק מִתַּמָּן, מַסְאִיב לְכֻלְּהוּ, כְּמָה דְּאַתְּ אָמֵר וְכִבֶּס הָאוֹסֵף וְגוֹ' וְטָמֵא. אֵפֶר, מ"ט. כד"א וְעַסּוֹתֶם רְשָׁעִים כִּי יִהְיוּ אֵפֶר תַּחַת כַּפּוֹת רַגְלֵיכֶם. וְכֵיוָן דְּאִתְיְיהִיב עַל הַהוּא אֵפֶר מַיִם, כְּדֵין אִיהוּ טָהוֹר מִטָּמֵא.

326. Hence, all those who busied themselves with her became defiled indeed, BECAUSE SHE WAS UNHOLY. And though she turned into ashes, yet before being gathered and taken away, she defiles them all. And so it is written, "and he that gathers…shall wash his clothes, and be unclean…" (Bemidbar 19:10). Why DID SHE HAVE TO BECOME ashes? It resembles the verse, "and you shall tread down the wicked, for they shall be ashes under the soles of your feet" (Malachi 3:21), for when water was sprinkled upon the ashes, they became a clean thing out of an unclean.

327. וְרָזָא דְּמִלָּה, דִּכְתִּיב מֵי חַטָּאת, כד"א לַפֶּתַח חַטָּאת רוֹבֵץ. וּבְגִין דְּאִיהִי פֶּתַח חַטָּאת רוֹבֵץ וַדַּאי, בְּקַדְמֵיתָא כְּתִיב, וְהוֹצִיא אוֹתָהּ אֶל מִחוּץ לַמַּחֲנֶה. וּבְגִין כַּךְ אִתְיְיהִיבַת לַסְּגָן, וְלָא לְכַהֲנָא רַבָּא, וְדָא הוּא טָהוֹר מִטָּמֵא, בְּקַדְמֵיתָא טָמֵא, וְהַשְׁתָּא טָהוֹר. וְכָל סְטַר רוּחַ מְסַאֲבָא, כֵּיוָן דְּחָמָא דָּא, עָרַק, וְלָא יָתִיב בְּהַהוּא דוּכְתָּא.

327. The secret of this matter is the verse, "water of purifying (sin)" (Bemidbar 8:7), same as in "sin crouches at the door" (Beresheet 4:7). THE HEIFER IS ALSO A "SIN CROUCHES AT THE DOOR," and since she is a sin crouching at the door, it is written first, "that he may bring her outside the camp" (Bemidbar 19:3). Therefore, the work was given to the adjutant priest, and not to the High Priest. And a clean thing, out of an unclean, starts as impure and becomes pure. And all the aspects of the side of defilement, when they saw this, ran away and left that place. SHE THEREFORE PURIFIES THE UNCLEAN.

328. מֵי חַטָּאת וַדַּאי, מֵי נִדָּה, כֹּלָּא מְסַאֲבָא. וְעַל דָּא שַׁלְטָא רוּחַ קוּדְשָׁא, וְרוּחַ מְסַאֲבָא אִתְכַּפְיָא, דְּלָא שַׁלְטָא כְּלַל. וְדָא הוּא דִּינָא דְּרוּחַ מְסַאֲבָא, מִחוּץ לַמַּחֲנֶה. בְּגִין דְּאִיהִי רוּחַ מְסַאֲבָא, דִּכְתִּיב וְהָיָה מַחֲנֶיךָ קָדוֹשׁ. אָתָא רִבִּי אַבָּא וּנְשָׁקֵיהּ.

328. Therefore, she is of "water of purifying (sin)," and "water of sprinkling (unclean)," all of which is impure. Therefore, AFTER JUDGMENT WAS EXECUTED ON HER, the Holy Spirit had dominion. And the spirit of defilement surrendered all its power. The Judgment, EXECUTED on the spirit of defilement, was outside the camp. Since that spirit is defiled, it is written, "therefore shall your camp be holy" (Devarim 23:15). Rabbi Aba approached and kissed him.

37. The hair in the Tefilin

A Synopsis

Rabbi Shimon tells us that God gave the Other Side power to rule over the world in several areas. We should be careful to avoid the Other Side's judgment, and there are some secret means of doing this. In the Tfilin we enclose a small calf's hair, with a little bit of it poking out so that the Other Side can see it and leave us alone, seeing that we have given the Other Side its due. If the Other Side is not given its due, it may inflict harm and judgment on us. Yisrael knew this secret, so that when they were purifying themselves during Yom Kippur they gave the Other Side its share. Rabbi Aba is crying because he does not understand this explanation, and Rabbi Shimon comforts him, saying that on the day of Rosh Hashanah God sits in judgment over the world, while the Other Side watches carefully. But the Other Side gets distracted by the sound of the Shofar that awakens mercy, and then it forgets who has been condemned to death. People should protect themselves from the prosecutor's attention by sacrificing a he-goat once a month when the moon is new. He concludes by saying that Yisrael is blessed by the fact that God tells them how to be saved.

329. אר״ש, אַף עַל גַּב דְּכָל הָנֵי מִלִּין כִּדְקָאמְרָן, קוּדְשָׁא בְּרִיךְ הוּא יָהִיב לֵיהּ שׁוּלְטָנוּ. וְרוּחַ מְסַאֲבָא בָּעֵי לְאַכְפְּיָא לֵיהּ בְּכָל סִטְרִין. תָּא וְאֵימָא לָךְ רָזָא חֲדָא, וְלָא אִתְיְיהִיב לְגַלָּאָה בַּר לְאִינּוּן קַדִּישֵׁי עֶלְיוֹנִין.

329. Rabbi Shimon said: Though it is all as we said, yet the Holy One, blessed be He, lets THE OTHER SIDE rule, and we should subjugate the spirit of defilement on all sides. Come and I will tell you a high secret, that may not be revealed outside the circle of exalted saints.

330. ת״ח, לְהַאי אֲתַר דְּאִיהוּ רוּחַ מְסַאֲבָא. קוּדְשָׁא בְּרִיךְ הוּא יָהִיב לֵיהּ שׁוּלְטָנוּ, לְמִשְׁלַט בְּעָלְמָא, בְּכַמָּה סִטְרִין, וְיָכִיל לְנַזְקָא, וְלֵית לָן רְשׁוּ, לְאַנְהָגָא בֵּיהּ קְלָנָא, דְּבָעֵינָן לְאִסְתַּמְּרָא מִנֵּיהּ, דְּלָא יְקַטְרֵג עֲלָן בְּגוֹ קְדוּשָּׁה דִּילָן. וע״ד רָזָא חֲדָא אִית לָן, דְּבָעֵינָן לְמֵיהַב לֵיהּ דוּכְתָּא זְעֵיר, בְּגוֹ קְדוּשָּׁה דִּילָן דְּהָא מִגּוֹ קְדוּשָּׁה נָפִיק שׁוּלְטָנוּ דִּילֵיהּ.

330. Come and see: The Holy One, blessed be He gave that place, the spirit of defilement, power to rule over the world in several ways. It can inflict harm, and we may not treat it with contempt, but should be careful to avoid it so it may not denounce our holiness. Therefore, we have a secret means, that we give it a small place within that which is holy, for its power originates in holiness.

331. דְּבָעֵינָן גּוֹ רָזָא דִּתְפִלִּין, לְאַצְנְעָא חַד שַׂעֲרָא דְּעֶגְלָא, דְּיִפּוֹק לְבַר וְיִתְחָזֵי. דְּהָא חוּטָא דְּשַׂעֲרָא דָּא לָא מְסָאִיב, בַּר דְּאִי אִתְחַבָּר הַאי שַׂעֲרָא, וְאִתְעֲבֵיד כַּשִּׁעוּרָא, אֲבָל פָּחוּת מִן דָּא לָא מְסָאִיב. וְהַהוּא שַׂעֲרָא בָּעֵי לְאַעֲלָא לֵיהּ בְּגוֹ קְדוּשָּׁה עִלָּאָה דִּילָן, וּלְמֵיהַב לֵיהּ דּוּכְתָּא, בְּגִין דְּלָא יְקַטְרֵג לָן בִּקְדוּשָּׁן.

331. IT IS, in the secret of Tefilin we enclose a small calf's hair, jutting out to be seen. This hair does not defile, unless it is joins together and reaches the required size, less than that does not bring uncleanness. We should put this hair within our highest holiness, and give it place so it will not denounce us within our holiness.

332. וְיִפּוֹק מִן הַהוּא שַׂעֲרָא לְבַר, דְּיִתְחָזֵי, דְּכַד חָמֵי לְהַהוּא ב"נ בִּקְדוּשָּׁה עִלָּאָה, וְחוּלָקָא דִּילֵיהּ מִשְׁתַּתֵּף לְתַמָּן, כְּדֵין לָא יְקַטְרֵג לֵיהּ, וְלָא יָכִיל לְאַבְאָשָׁא לֵיהּ לְעֵילָּא וְתַתָּא, דְּהָא דּוּכְתָּא יְהַב לֵיהּ. וְאִי הַהוּא חוּלָקָא לָא יָהֲבִין לֵיהּ בְּהַאי קְדוּשָּׁה, יָכִיל לְאַבְאָשָׁא לֵיהּ לְתַתָּא, וְסָלִיק מְקַטְרְגָא לֵיהּ לְעֵילָּא, וְאָמַר פְּלוֹנִי דְּקָא מְקַדֵּשׁ הַשְׁתָּא, כַּךְ וְכַךְ עֲבַד יוֹמָא פְּלוֹנִי, וְכַךְ אִינּוּן חוֹבוֹי, עַד דְּיִמְטֵי דִּינָא עַל הַהוּא ב"נ, וְיִתְעֲנַשׁ עַל יְדוֹי.

332. SOME of the hair should jut out OF THE TEFILIN, to be seen, for when THE OTHER SIDE sees a man dwelling in upper holiness, with its own portion taking part, it would not denounce, nor be able to inflict harm above or below, for it was given place. But if it is not given a portion in holiness, it may inflict harm below and it goes up to prosecute above saying, 'a certain man, who now makes himself holy, did that and that on a certain day, and these are his sins.' So Judgment descends upon that man and he is punished by it.

333. וְכַךְ הֲווֹ יִשְׂרָאֵל עָבְדֵי, דַּהֲווֹ יַדְעֵי רָזָא דָּא, כַּד שָׁרָאן לְאִתְקַדְּשָׁא בִּקְדוּשָׁה עִלָּאָה בְּיוֹמָא דְּכִפּוּרֵי, הֲווֹ מִסְתַּכְּלֵי מִיַּד לְמֵיהַב חוּלָקֵיהּ לְהַאי אֲתָר, וּלְמֵיהַב לֵיהּ חוּלָקָא בֵּינַיְיהוּ, בְּגִין דְּלָא יִשְׁתְּכַּח מְקַטְרְגָא עֲלַיְיהוּ, וְלָא יֵיתוּן לְאַדְכְּרָא חוֹבֵיהוֹן דְּיִשְׂרָאֵל. דְּכַמָּה חֲבִילִין, וְכַמָּה מַשִׁרְיָין, אִינּוּן דְּאִזְדַּמְנָן לְנַטְלָא מִלָּה מִנֵּיהּ, כַּד אָתֵי לְקַטְרְגָא. זַכָּאָה חוּלָקֵיהּ, מַאן דְּיָכִיל לְאִסְתַּמְּרָא, דְּלָא יִדְכְּרוּן חוֹבוֹי לְעֵילָּא, וְלָא יַשְׁגְּחוּן עָלֵיהּ לְבִישׁ.

333. So did Yisrael do, who knew this secret: when they started to make themselves holy in the supernal holiness of Yom Kippur, they were careful to immediately give it its share and a portion among themselves so it would not denounce them, nor mention the sins of Yisrael. For how many are the bands and legions ready to take words of denouncements from it. Happy is the portion of he, who is able to guard himself so his sins may not be mentioned above, and he would not be noticed for the worse.

334. אַדְּהָכִי הֲווֹ זַלְגִין עֵינוֹי דְּרַבִּי אַבָּא. אָמַר לֵיהּ, אַבָּא אַבָּא, זִיל טַנְפִּיר קְטוּרָךְ, וְאַקְפִּיד בְּקוּלְטָךְ, דְּהָא רָזִין דְּאוֹרַיְיתָא לְזַכָּאֵי אִתְיְהִיבוּ דִּכְתִּיב סוֹד יְיָ' לִירֵאָיו.

334. Meanwhile, the eyes of Rabbi Aba were pouring tears, BECAUSE HE DID NOT UNDERSTAND THAT MYSTERY COMPLETELY. RABBI SHIMON told him: Aba, Aba, unloose your girdle, and see to it that you perceive, because the mysteries in heaven were revealed to the meritorious, as it is written, “the secret of Hashem is for them that fear Him” (Tehilim 25:14).

335. תָּא חֲזֵי, בְּיוֹמָא דְּרֹאשׁ הַשָּׁנָה, עָלְמָא אִתְדָּן, וְקוּדְשָׁא בְּ"ה יָתִיב, וְדָן כָּל עָלְמָא. וְהַהוּא סִטְרָא אַחֲרָא קָאִים מִסִּטְרָא דָּא, וְכָל אִינּוּן דְּאִתְדָּנוּ לְמוֹתָא אַשְׁגַּח עֲלַיְיהוּ, וְאִתְרְשִׁימוּ קָמֵּיהּ. וּבְשַׁעֲתָא דְּיִשְׂרָאֵל מִתְעָרֵי רַחֲמֵי, בְּהַהוּא קוֹל שׁוֹפָר, כְּדֵין אִתְעַרְבְּבָא לֵיהּ כֹּלָּא, דְּלָא יָדַע וְלָא מַשְׁגַּח, בְּאִינּוּן דְּאִתְדָּנוּ. עַד דִּלְבָתַר כָּל אִינּוּן דְּלָא מְהַדְּרֵי בִּתְיוּבְתָּא, וְאִגְזַר עֲלַיְיהוּ מוֹתָא, וַדַּאי נָפְקִין פִּתְקִין מִבֵּי מַלְכָּא,

וְאִתְמְסָרוּ לֵיהּ, כֵּיוָן דְּאִתְמְסָרוּ לֵיהּ, לָא אָהַדְרוּ פִּתְקִין, עַד דְּאִתְעָבֵיד דִּינָא.

335. Come and see: On the day of Rosh Hashanah (the Jewish New Year) the world is judged, and the Holy One, blessed be He, sits in Judgment over the world. The Other Side stands on one side, looking closely at and registering those condemned to death. When Yisrael awakens Mercy by the sound of the Shofar, it loses count, and does not know nor notices the condemned, until after those who do not repent are condemned to death, and the orders come out of the house of the King and delivered TO THE OTHER SIDE. Once THE ORDERS are delivered, they are not revoked until Judgment is executed.

336. וְיִשְׂרָאֵל כֻּלְּהוּ, בַּעְיָין לְאִסְתַּמְּרָא מִנֵּיהּ, כ״ש ב״נ בִּלְחוּדוֹי. דְּהָא בְּרָזָא עִלָּאָה דִּלְעֵילָּא, בָּעֵינָן לְאִסְתַּמְּרָא, וּלְמֵיהַב לֵיהּ בְּכָל יַרְחָא וְיַרְחָא, כַּד סִיהֲרָא בָּעֵי לְאִתְחַדְּתָא, חַד שָׂעִיר, בְּגִין דְּלָא יְקַטְרֵג חַדְּתּוּתָא וְיִטּוֹל חוּלָקֵיהּ כַּדְקָא חָזֵי לֵיהּ. וְסִיהֲרָא קַדִּישָׁא לְיָנְקָא בִּקְדוּשָׁה לְחַדְּתּוּתֵי כַּדְקָא יֵאוֹת.

336. Yisrael should beware of it, OF THE PROSECUTOR, all the more so a person alone, and they should be protected by means of the holy secret above, BECAUSE IT HAS ITS ROOT IN HOLINESS. They should give it monthly, when the moon, MALCHUT, is new, a he-goat, so it would not denounce the waxing, but will take its deserved portion from the he-goat, while the holy moon, MALCHUT, will suck from holiness and wax properly.

337. וְכַד מִתְחַדְּשָׁא בְּכָל יַרְחָא וְיַרְחָא, בְּגִין כַּךְ אִקְרֵי נַעַר, וְהָא אוּקִימְנָא. וְהַאי אַחֲרָא דָא, דְּאִיהוּ תָּדִיר בְּמִסְאֲבוּ, וְלָא נָפִיק מִנֵּיהּ, אִקְרֵי מֶלֶךְ זָקֵן וּכְסִיל. ובג״כ, יִשְׂרָאֵל קַדִּישִׁין דְּאִינּוּן עַמָּא חַד, בְּיִחוּדָא קַדִּישָׁא, קוּדְשָׁא בְּרִיךְ הוּא יָהִיב לוֹן עֵיטָא, לְאִשְׁתְּזָבָא מִכֹּלָּא. זַכָּאִין אִינּוּן בְּעָלְמָא דֵּין, וּבְעָלְמָא דְּאָתֵי, דִּכְתִּיב וְעַמֵּךְ כֻּלָּם צַדִּיקִים לְעוֹלָם יִרְשׁוּ אָרֶץ נֵצֶר מַטָּעַי מַעֲשֵׂה יָדַי לְהִתְפָּאֵר.

337. Since it waxes every month, it is called 'a youth', as we already explained. And that one, THE OTHER SIDE, always immersed in defilement, never to leave, is called "old and foolish king" (Kohelet 4:13). For that reason, holy Yisrael is the one nation in holy unison, to whom the Holy One, blessed be He, gives them advice on how to be saved from all. Happy are they in this world and in the World to Come, as it is written, "Your people also shall be all righteous, they shall inherit the land forever; they shall be the branch of My planting, the work of My hands, that I may be glorified" (Yeshayah 60: 21).

38. "And they brought the Tabernacle to Moses," part two

A Synopsis

Rabbi Shimon talks about the vision of Ezekiel, as in: "and above the firmament that was over their heads was the likeness of a throne, in appearance like a sapphire stone...," saying that the firmament is supported by the four animals. He tells how the creatures and the wheels are lifted up to Atzilut so that Malchut goes up to Zeir Anpin, as in: "and bore up the Ark, and it was lifted up above the earth." In the verse: "and they brought the Tabernacle to Moses," 'Tabernacle' is Malchut and 'Moses' is the secret of Zeir Anpin. "The likeness as the appearance of a man above upon it" is the secret of man, namely Moses. Here Rabbi Shimon says that Moses is Zeir Anpin. Next he offers several explanations for "And they brought the Tabernacle," all of which include the concept of Malchut joining with Zeir Anpin. When the wise men brought all the parts of the Tabernacle to Moses they were unable to join them all together, but he had no difficulty, this is the secret of "and Moses erected the Tabernacle." Rabbi Shimon says that as the holy side gets stronger the Other Side gets weaker; this is why Moses strengthened the holy side by constructing the Tabernacle.

338. וַיָּבִיאוּ אֶת הַמִּשְׁכָּן אֶל מֹשֶׁה וְגוֹ'. כְּתִיב וּמִמַּעַל לָרָקִיעַ, דָּא אִיהוּ רְקִיעָא, דְּקַיְּימָא עָלַיְיהוּ דְּאַרְבַּע חֵיוָון, דְּכַד מִסְתַּלְּקֵי בְּגוֹ חַד אֲוִירָא דְּבָטַשׁ בְּהוּ, לָא זַקְפִין רֵישָׁא לְאִסְתַּכְּלָא לְעֵילָּא.

338. "And they brought the Tabernacle to Moses" (Shemot 39:33). It is written, "and above the firmament THAT WAS OVER THEIR HEADS WAS THE LIKENESS OF A THRONE, IN APPEARANCE LIKE A SAPPHIRE STONE..." (Yechezkel 1:26). This firmament is supported by the four living creatures. When they are raised by a certain air that strikes them, TO RAISE THE THRONE, MALCHUT, they do not lift up their heads, TO BEHOLD THE SHECHINAH, WHICH IS THE THRONE, BECAUSE OF THE FIRMAMENT THAT IS ABOVE THEM.

339. בְּגִין דְּהַהוּא רוּחַ הַחַיָּה, בָּטַשׁ בְּכֻלְּהוּ, וּבְהַהוּא רוּחַ מִסְתַּלְּקֵי כֻּלְּהוּ, דִּכְתִּיב, וּבְהִנָּשֵׂא הַחַיּוֹת מֵעַל הָאָרֶץ יִנָּשְׂאוּ הָאוֹפַנִּים לְעֻמָּתָם. וּכְתִיב כִּי רוּחַ הַחַיָּה בָּאוֹפַנִּים.

339. Once the spirit of the animal, MALCHUT, strikes them all, THE ANIMALS AND THE WHEELS, ALL OF THEM IN THE WORLDS OF BRIYAH, YETZIRAH AND ASIYAH are raised by it, as it is written, "and when the living creatures were lifted up from the earth, the wheels were lifted up…along with them...for the spirit of the living creature was in the wheels" (Ibid.19-20), FOR THE SPIRIT OF THE ANIMAL, WHICH IS MALCHUT, RAISES THEM ALL.

340. אֲמַאי מִסְתַּלְּקֵי. אֶלָּא כַּד בָּטַשׁ הַהוּא אֲוִירָא עֲלַיְיהוּ, סָלִיק לְאִלֵּין אַרְבַּע דִּתְחוֹת הַאי חַיָּה, וְאִינּוּן סַלְּקֵי לָהּ לְעֵילָּא, עַד דְּמַתְיָין לָהּ לְגַבֵּי זִהֲרָא עִלָּאָה, וְהַיְינוּ רָזָא דִּכְתִּיב, בְּתוּלוֹת אַחֲרֶיהָ רֵעוֹתֶיהָ מוּבָאוֹת לָךְ, בְּגִין דְּהָנֵי אַרְבַּע אִקְרוּן הָכִי, וְלָא זָזוּ מִן חַיָּה דָּא, דְּאִיהִי כּוּרְסְיָיא, לְעָלְמִין. וְסָלְקִין לָהּ מִתַּתָּא לְעֵילָּא, לְאַתְקְנָא כּוּרְסְיָיא לְגַבֵּי עֵילָּא, וְרָזָא דָּא וַיִּשְׂאוּ אֶת הַתֵּבָה וַתָּרָם מֵעַל הָאָרֶץ. וְכַד אִסְתָּלְקַת לְעֵילָּא, וְאִלֵּין סַלְּקִין לָהּ, כְּדֵין כְּתִיב, וַיָּבִיאוּ אֶת הַמִּשְׁכָּן אֶל מֹשֶׁה.

340. HE ASKS: Why are they raised TO ATZILUT? AND HE ANSWERS that the air OF MALCHUT strikes THE FOUR LIVING CREATURES, raises the four living creatures beneath that living creature MALCHUT, and they raise it, until they bring it to the supernal splendor, ZEIR ANPIN. This is the secret meaning of the verse, "the virgins, her companions that follow her, shall be brought to you" (Tehilim 45:15), for the four LIVING CREATURES are thus called. They never budge from the animal, which is the throne, NAMELY, MALCHUT, and they raise it from below upward so as to fix the throne, MALCHUT, upward, TOWARDS ZEIR ANPIN. This is the secret of the verse, "and bore up the ark, and it was lifted up above the earth" (Beresheet 7:17). And when MALCHUT mounts up TO ZEIR ANPIN, and THE FOUR LIVING CREATURES raise it, then it is written, "and they brought the Tabernacle to Moses." FOR MALCHUT IS CALLED 'TABERNACLE', AND MOSES IS THE SECRET OF ZEIR ANPIN, AND IT IS THE FOUR LIVING CREATURES WHO BRING IT.

341. וַיָּבִיאוּ אֶת הַמִּשְׁכָּן, כד"א מוּבָאוֹת לָךְ, וּכְתִיב וַיִּשְׂאוּ אֶת הַתֵּבָה. אֶל מֹשֶׁה, כד"א דְּמוּת כְּמַרְאֵה אָדָם עָלָיו מִלְמָעְלָה, וְהַיְינוּ רָזָא דְּאָדָם. וּמְנָלָן דְּאִקְרֵי אָדָם, דִּכְתִּיב לָא יָדוֹן רוּחִי בָאָדָם לְעוֹלָם בְּשַׁגַּם

הוּא בָּשָׂר, וְהַיְינוּ מֹשֶׁה. ובג״כ, עַל הַאי כּוּרְסְיָיא, דְּיוּקְנָא דְּאָדָם קַיְימָא עָלֵיהּ, וְהַיְינוּ מֹשֶׁה.

341. "And they brought the Tabernacle to Moses" resembles the verse, "shall be brought to you," WHICH MEANS THAT THE LIVING CREATURES BRING MALCHUT. It is written, "and [they] bore up the ark," REFERRING TO THE LIVING CREATURES CARRYING MALCHUT to Moses, as it is said, "the likeness as the appearance of a man above upon it" (Yechezkel 1:26). This is the secret of man, ZEIR ANPIN. From where do we know that MOSES is called 'a man' (also: 'Adam')? From the verse, "My spirit shall not always strive on account of man, for that (Heb. *beshgam*) he also is flesh" (Beresheet 6:3). This alludes to Moses FOR BESHAGAM HAS THE SAME NUMERICAL VALUE AS MOSES. For that reason, upon the throne, WHICH IS MALCHUT, stands the appearance of man, namely, Moses, WHO IS ZEIR ANPIN. THEREFORE THE SCRIPTURE SAYS "AND ABOVE THE FIRMAMENT THAT WAS OVER THEIR HEADS" OF THE FOUR LIVING CREATURES, "IN APPEARANCE LIKE A SAPPHIRE STONE WAS THE LIKENESS OF A THRONE," WHICH IS MALCHUT. "AND UPON THE LIKENESS OF THE THRONE WAS THE LIKENESS AS THE APPEARANCE OF A MAN ABOVE UPON IT" (YECHEZKEL 1:26) REFERS TO ZEIR ANPIN.

342. וַיָּבִיאוּ אֶת הַמִּשְׁכָּן, אִלֵּין אַרְבַּע חֵיוָון, כַּד סַלְּקִין כִּדְקַאמְרָן. וַיָּבִיאוּ אֶת הַמִּשְׁכָּן, אִלֵּין כָּל שַׁיְיפִין דְּגוּפָא, דְּכֻלְּהוּ בְּתִיאוּבְתָּא קַדִּישָׁא, כֻּלְּהוּ אַחֲדִין בֵּיהּ, לְאִתְדַּבְּקָא דְּכַר וְנוּקְבָא כַּחֲדָא. וַיָּבִיאוּ אֶת הַמִּשְׁכָּן, לְמֵיעַל כַּלָּה לַחוּפָּה בְּקַדְמֵיתָא, אִינּוּן צְרִיכִין לְסַלְּקָא לָהּ, וּלְאַיְיתָאָה לָהּ לְגַבֵּיהּ, וּלְבָתַר אִיהוּ יֵיתֵי לְגַבָּהּ תָּדִיר, וְהָא אוֹקִימְנָא.

342. "And they brought the Tabernacle," "they," being the four living creatures BRINGING MALCHUT when they mount TO ATZILUT, as we said. ALSO, "they," in "And they brought the Tabernacle" refers to the members of the body, THE SFIROT OF ZEIR ANPIN, all with holy yearning, grasping THE TABERNACLE, WHICH IS MALCHUT, so male and female may be united. ANOTHER EXPLANATION FOR, "And they brought the Tabernacle" is bringing the bride, MALCHUT, under the Wedding Canopy. First they have to raise and bring her up to Him, then He will always come to her, as we already explained.

343. וַיָּבִיאוּ אֶת הַמִּשְׁכָּן, רָזָא דְּכָל אִינּוּן דְּקָשְׁרֵי קִשְׁרִין דְּיִחוּדָא, וְיַחְדֵי יִחוּדָא דְּרָזֵי דִּמְהֵימְנוּתָא כָּל יוֹמָא, אִינּוּן סַלְּקִין לָהּ לְכוּרְסְיָיא דָא, עַד דְּאַתְיָין לָהּ לְגַבֵּי מֹשֶׁה, וְכֵיוָן דְּדַבְקֵי לָהּ לְגַבֵּי מֹשֶׁה, כְּדֵין אִינּוּן הֲווֹ דְּרָוְוחֵי בִּרְכָאן מִמְּקוֹרָא דְּחַיֵּי, עַל רָזָא דָא, בְּקִשּׁוּרָא דְּיִחוּדָא דְּאִינּוּן קָשְׁרִין. וְרָזָא דָא, כַּד מִתְקַשְּׁרִין יִחוּדָא דְּכֹלָּא כַּדְקָא יֵאוֹת, וְרָזָא דָא כְּתִיב, וַיַּרְא מֹשֶׁה אֶת כָּל הַמְּלָאכָה וְגוֹ׳, וַיְבָרֶךְ אוֹתָם מֹשֶׁה, רַוְוחֵי בִּרְכָאן מֵאֲתַר דְּדַרְגָּא דְּמֹשֶׁה שַׁרְיָא בֵּיהּ, וְדָא אִיהוּ הַחֲכָמִים הָעוֹשִׂים אֶת כָּל מְלֶאכֶת הַקֹּדֶשׁ, בְּגִין דְּאִינּוּן יַדְעֵי לְסַדְּרָא עֲבִידְתָּא דְּקוּדְשָׁא כַּדְקָא חֲזֵי.

343. “And they brought the Tabernacle” refers to all those RIGHTEOUS, daily binding the knots of unison, and bringing together the unison of the secret of the Faith, MALCHUT CALLED ‘TABERNACLE’. Daily they raise the throne, WHICH IS MALCHUT, until it is brought before Moses, ZEIR ANPIN. THIS VERSE IS WRITTEN OF THEM. Once they connect it with Moses, these RIGHTEOUS MEN gain blessings from the source of life for this secret, for the knots of unison they bind. The secret lies in binding it properly. This is the recondite meaning of the verse, “And Moses saw all the work, NAMELY, THE UNISON…and Moses blessed them” (Shemot 39:43). For they gained the blessings from the place, where lies the grade of Moses, NAMELY, ZEIR ANPIN. They are “the wise men, that carried out all the work of the sanctuary” (Shemot 36:4), since they know how to properly carry out the work of the sanctuary, BY THE UNISONS THEY MAKE.

344. וְעַל דָּא, כָּל מַאן דְּצַלֵּי צְלוֹתָא, וְקָשִׁיר יִחוּדָא, מִסְתַּכְּלִין בֵּיהּ אִי אִיהִי צְלוֹתָא וְקִשּׁוּרָא כַּדְקָא יֵאוֹת, וְאִי הַהִיא צְלוֹתָא וְהַהוּא קִשּׁוּרָא כַּדְקָא יֵאוֹת, כְּדֵין אִתְבְּרַךְ אִיהוּ בְּקַדְמֵיתָא, מֵאֲתַר דְּכָל בִּרְכָאן נָפְקִין. הה״ד וְהִנֵּה עָשׂוּ אוֹתָהּ וְגוֹ׳, מִיַּד וַיְבָרֶךְ אוֹתָם מֹשֶׁה.

344. And so whoever says his prayer and ties the knot of union, he is checked to see whether the prayer and knot are in order. And if they are in order, he is then blessed first from the place from where all the blessings issue. This is the meaning of “they had done it…”; immediately, “and Moses blessed them” (Shemot 39:43).

345. ובג"כ, וַיָּבִיאוּ אֶת הַמִּשְׁכָּן אֶל מֹשֶׁה, דְּאִיהוּ מָארֵי דְּבֵיתָא, לְאַחֲזָאָה בְּתִקּוּנָא דְּבֵיתֵיהּ, וְלֵיהּ אִצְטְרִיךְ לְמֶחֱזֵי תִּקּוּנָהָא וְרָזִין דִּילָהּ, דְּלָא אִתְיְיהִיבוּ לְאַחֲרָא, לְאִסְתַּכְּלָא וּלְמֶחֱזֵי בָּהּ, בְּאִינּוּן סִתְרִין וּבְאִינּוּן רָזִין דִּילָהּ, בַּר מֹשֶׁה בִּלְחוֹדוֹי.

345. For that reason IT IS WRITTEN, "And they brought the Tabernacle to Moses," ZEIR ANPIN, the landlord, to see how the house, WHICH IS MALCHUT, is fixed. He should see all its constructions and secrets, for no one may look and behold its secrets and mysteries save Moses alone.

346. וְעַל דָּא וַיָּבִיאוּ אֶת הַמִּשְׁכָּן אֶל מֹשֶׁה אֶת הָאֹהֶל וְאֶת כָּל כֵּלָיו. וְכַד אַיְיתִיאוּ לֵיהּ לְמֹשֶׁה, כֹּלָּא אַיְיתִיאוּ לֵיהּ בְּשַׁיְיפִין יְדִיעָאן, כָּל חַד וְחַד לְאִתְקְנָא, שַׁיְיפָא בְּשַׁיְיפָא, לְאַעֲלָא דָּא בְּדָא, וְכַד הֲווֹ בָּעָאן לְתַקְּנָא דָּא בְּדָא, וּלְאַעְלָאָה דָּא בְּדָא, לָא הֲוָה סָלִיק בִּידַיְיהוּ. כֵּיוָן דְּאַיְיתִיאוּ לֵיהּ לְמֹשֶׁה, מִיַּד כֹּלָּא אִסְתְּלִיק בִּידֵיהּ, וְכָל שַׁיְיפָא וְשַׁיְיפָא הֲוָה אִסְתָּלִיק וְעָאל בְּדוּכְתֵּיהּ, הה"ד, וַיָּקֶם מֹשֶׁה אֶת הַמִּשְׁכָּן וּכְתִיב הוּקַם הַמִּשְׁכָּן, וְהָא אוֹקִימְנָא.

346. Therefore, "they brought the Tabernacle to Moses, the tent, and all its furniture" (Shemot 39:33). When they brought it all to Moses, they brought all its parts, so each may be joined one to the other. When they wanted to insert them one within the other THEMSELVES, they could not do it; only when they brought it to Moses, he straightway succeeded. Each part advanced and fit into its place. This is the mystery of "and Moses erected the Tabernacle" (Shemot 40:18), and "the Tabernacle was reared up" (Ibid. 17) which we already explained.

347. ת"ח, בְּהַהִיא שַׁעֲתָא כַּד שָׁארִי מֹשֶׁה לְאַקָּמָא מַשְׁכְּנָא, וְשָׁארֵי לְאִתְקְנָא תִּקּוּנָא דְּשַׁיְיפִין, לְאַעֲלָא דָּא בְּדָא. כְּדֵין, אִתְרְפִיוּ כָּל שַׁיְיפִין וְכָל תִּקּוּנִין דְּסִטְרָא אַחֲרָא מְסָאֲבָא, כַּד שָׁרֵי לְאִתְקְפָא הַאי סִטְרָא דְּאִיהִי קַדִּישָׁא, אִתְרַפֵּי סִטְרָא אַחֲרָא מְסָאֲבָא, אִתָּקַף דָּא וְאִתְרַפֵּי דָּא. וְהָא אוֹקִימְנָא, דְּכָל זִמְנָא דְּהִיא בְּתְקִיפוּ, סִטְרָא אַחֲרָא אִתְרַפָּן כָּל

שַׁיְיפוּי, דָא מַלְיָא, דָא חָרוּב, וְרָזָא דָא יְרוּשָׁלַם וְצוֹר חַיָּיבָא, כַּד מַלְיָא דָא, חָרוּב דָא. וע״ד, כַּד אִתְּקַף דָא אִתְרַפֵּי דָא.

347. Come and see: When Moses started to construct the Tabernacle, he started by fixing the parts and putting them together. Then all the parts and constructions of the Other Side became enfeebled. Once the holy side strengthens, the Other Side became weak. One gets stronger and the other gets weaker. We already explained that while HOLINESS is strong, all the members of the Other Side become enfeebled, the one becomes full, and the other dry. This is the secret of Jerusalem and the evil Tyre, when one is full the other is ruined. Therefore, when HOLINESS gets stronger, THE OTHER SIDE becomes weak.

348. וּבְגִין כַּךְ, וַיָּקֶם מֹשֶׁה אֶת הַמִּשְׁכָּן, לְאִתְתַּקְּפָא מֵרָזָא דִּלְעֵילָּא, וְלָא יִתְקַף מֵרָזָא דִּלְתַתָּא. וְעַל דָּא מֹשֶׁה דַּהֲוָה מֵרָזָא דְּגוֹ אַסְפַּקְלַרְיָא דְּנַהֲרָא, אִצְטְרִיךְ אִיהוּ לְאַקָּמָא מַשְׁכְּנָא, לְאַנְהָרָא מִנֵּיהּ, וְלָא מֵאַחֲרָא. סִיהֲרָא אִצְטְרִיךְ לְאַנְהָרָא מִן שִׁמְשָׁא, וְלָא מֵאַחֲרָא. תָּא חֲזֵי, כְּנֶסֶת יִשְׂרָאֵל אִצְטְרִיכַת לְאִסְתַּלְּקָא לְעֵילָּא, וּלְאִתְדַּבְּקָא גּוֹ שִׁמְשָׁא.

348. That is why "Moses erected the Tabernacle," so as to be strengthened by the mystery above, ZEIR ANPIN, FOR MOSES WAS A CHARIOT TO ZEIR ANPIN, and not to be strengthened from below. Therefore, Moses, who was of the secret of the shining mirror, ZEIR ANPIN, had to erect a Tabernacle that would shine by his light and not by another's. The moon, WHICH IS MALCHUT, must illuminate by the light of the sun, and not by that of another. Come and see: The Congregation of Yisrael, MALCHUT, must rise up to be joined with the sun, WHICH IS ZEIR ANPIN.

39. "This is the Torah of the burnt offering"

A Synopsis

Rabbi Shimon says that the burnt offering is called 'Holy of Holies' because it makes the connection between the congregation of Yisrael and Zeir Anpin. He compares it to the unity between male and female and the unity between the Oral Law and the Written Law. It also joins left and right and the Central Column. He reveals that the burnt offering consists of three spirits: 'the Holy Spirit', the spirit in the middle called 'the spirit of Chochmah and Binah' and the concealed upper spirit. After the offering, the Other Side takes sustenance from the fat and marrow, so the spirit of defilement is removed. Rabbi Shimon says that the offerings of men come from studying Torah and prayer, and the offerings of animals come from offering beasts on the altar. He explains that the numerical values of man, beast and Yud Hei Vav Hei show why offerings of both men and beasts are necessary. He talks about the phrase "and let birds fly above the earth" as it refers to the secret of the Chariot and to the two angels Michael and Gabriel. The two birds offered in sacrifice are a turtle-dove and a pigeon, this sacrifice raises the Holy Spirit. Rabbi Elazar wants to know how high the burnt offerings of the priests, the Levites and Yisrael rise. Rabbi Shimon answers that their devotion reaches all the way up to infinity. Infinity is not subject to comprehension, and there are no desires, no lights and no candles there. We hear about the odor of the supernal point and the World to Come, and the distinction between odor and smell. He tells about the meanings in "command Aaron and his sons, saying...," and says that one of them is that when the children of Yisrael do as God wishes, the Other Side cannot rule over them. He also explains the various meanings of the title verse. Through the burnt offering, we separate the Other Side from the Holy Spirit so that the Holy Spirit may rise up high.

349. פָּתַח וְאָמַר, זֹאת תּוֹרַת הָעוֹלָה הִיא הָעוֹלָה, אָמַר ר״ש, כְּתִיב, אָדָם וּבְהֵמָה תּוֹשִׁיעַ יְיָ׳. עוֹלָה סְלִיקוּ וְקִשׁוּרוּ דִּכ״י לְעֵילָּא, וְדִבּוּקָא דִּילָהּ בְּגוֹ עָלְמָא דְּאָתֵי, לְמֶהֱוֵי כֹּלָּא חַד. אִקְרֵי עוֹלָה קֹדֶשׁ קֳדָשִׁים. וּבְגִין כַּךְ אִקְרֵי עוֹלָה, דְּסַלְּקָא וְאִתְעַטְּרָא לְמֶהֱוֵי כֹּלָּא חַד. בְּקִשּׁוּרָא חֲדָא בְּחִדוּ.

349. He opened the discussion with the verse: "This is the Torah of the burnt offering; it is the burnt offering" (Vayikra 6:2). Rabbi Shimon said: It is written, "Hashem, You preserve man and beast" (Tehilim 36:7). A burnt offering (lit. 'ascension') is the ascension of and the bond between the Congregation of Yisrael, MALCHUT, AND ZEIR ANPIN above. It is its unity with the World to Come, BINAH, so that everything becomes one. The burnt offering considered the highest class of sacrifices (lit. 'Holy of Holies'), BECAUSE OF ITS CONNECTION TO BINAH. MALCHUT is therefore called 'burnt offering' (lit. 'ascension') for it ascends and adorns itself WITH ZEIR ANPIN AND BINAH, so all may be in one knot in joy.

350. וּבְגִין דְּסַלְּקָא לְעֵילָּא לְעֵילָּא, כְּתִיב זֹאת תּוֹרַת הָעוֹלָה. רָזָא דְּכַר וְנוּקְבָּא כַּחֲדָא, תּוֹרָה שֶׁבִּכְתָב וְתוֹרָה שֶׁבְּעַל פֶּה. הָעוֹלָה: דְּסַלְּקָא גּוֹ עָלְמָא דְּאָתֵי, לְאִתְקַשְּׁרָא בְּגַוֵּיהּ, דְּאִקְרֵי קֹדֶשׁ הַקֳּדָשִׁים וַדַּאי, וְעוֹלָה נָמֵי קֹדֶשׁ הַקֳּדָשִׁים הִיא.

350. Since it goes up and up, TO ZEIR ANPIN AND BINAH, it is written, "This is the Torah of the burnt offering," the secret of unity between male and female. FOR 'THIS' IS THE NUKVA CALLED 'THIS', 'TORAH' IS ZEIR ANPIN CALLED 'TORAH', NAMELY the Written Law, ZEIR ANPIN, and the Oral Law, MALCHUT. "The ascension" for it ascends to the World to Come, BINAH, to be connected to it, for BINAH is called 'the Holy of Holies', and ascension is also Holy of Holies.

351. וּבְגִין כַּךְ, סִדּוּרָא דִּנְכִיסוּ דִּילָהּ לְסְטַר צָפוֹן, דְּאִיהוּ סְטַר שְׂמָאלָא. דְּהַאי תּוֹרָה שבע"פ לָא סַלְּקָא בַּחֲבִיבוּתָא, אֶלָּא כַּד אִתְּעַר סִטְרָא דְּצָפוֹן, דִּכְתִּיב שְׂמֹאלוֹ תַּחַת לְרֹאשִׁי וִימִינוֹ תְּחַבְּקֵנִי, וּכְדֵין אִיהִי סַלְּקָא בַּחֲבִיבוּתָא, וְאִתְעַטְּרָא בִּימִינָא, וְאִתְחֲבָּרַת בְּאֶמְצָעִיתָא, וְאִתְנְהִיר כֹּלָּא, מֵרָזָא דְּקֹדֶשׁ הַקֳּדָשִׁים, וְדָא מִגּוֹ רָזָא דְּאָדָם, בִּרְעוּ דְּכַהֲנָא, וּבְשִׁירָתָא דְּלֵיוָאֵי, וּבִצְלוֹתָא דְּיִשְׂרָאֵל.

351. For that reason it is slaughtered on the north side, which is the left side, because the Oral Law, NAMELY MALCHUT, does not mount in love, unless the north side is awakened, WHICH IS THE SECRET OF THE LEFT SIDE, FROM WHERE IT IS BUILT, as it is written, "His left hand is under my head, and his right hand embraces me" (Shir Hashirim 2:6). Then it ascends in love, and is adorned with the right, THE LIGHT OF CHESED, and joins the Central Column, THAT COMBINES RIGHT AND LEFT, and shines upon everything from the secret of the Holy of Holies, WHICH IS BINAH, influenced by the mystery of man, the service of the priests, THE SECRET OF THE RIGHT COLUMN, the singing of the Levites, THE SECRET OF THE LEFT COLUMN, and the prayer of Yisrael, THE SECRET OF THE CENTRAL COLUMN.

352. וְהָא אוּקִימְנָא, דְּעוֹלָה קֹדֶשׁ הַקֳּדָשִׁים, בְּרָזָא דְּרוּחַ עִלָּאָה, בְּגִין דִּתְלַת רוּחִין קְשִׁירִין כַּחֲדָא, רוּחַ תַּתָּאָה, דְּאִקְרֵי רוּחַ הַקֹּדֶשׁ רוּחַ דִּלְגוֹ בְּאֶמְצָעִיתָא דְּאִקְרֵי רוּחַ חָכְמָה וּבִינָה. וְכֵן אִקְרֵי רוּחַ תַּתָּאָה, אֲבָל הַאי אִקְרֵי רוּחַ דְּנָפִיק מִגּוֹ שׁוֹפָר, כָּלוּל בְּאֶשָּׁא וּבְמַיָּא. רוּחַ עִלָּאָה, דְּאִיהוּ סָתִים בַּחֲשָׁאי, דְּבֵיהּ קַיְימָן כָּל רוּחִין קַדִּישִׁין, וְכָל אַנְפִּין נְהִירִין. וּבְגִין כַּךְ, אַהֲדְרַת עוֹלָה רוּחַ מַמָּשׁ.

352. We explained that the burnt offering is of the highest class of sacrifices, in the secret of the Supernal Spirit TO WHICH IT IS A GARMENT, for three spirits are connected together to THE BURNT OFFERING; THE FIRST IS a lower spirit called 'the Holy Spirit', NAMELY MALCHUT; THE SECOND IS the spirit in the middle, called 'the spirit of Chochmah and Binah', WHICH IS ZEIR ANPIN, BETWEEN CHOCHMAH AND BINAH, also called 'the lower spirit', IN COMPARISON WITH BINAH THAT IS SUPERIOR TO IT – but ZEIR ANPIN is called a spirit coming out of the Shofar comprising of fire and water; THE THIRD IS the upper spirit secretly concealed, WHICH IS BINAH, where all the Holy Spirits are and all faces shine. That is why the burnt offering returns to be the actual UPPER spirit.

353. וּלְבָתַר, מֵרָזָא דִּבְהֵמָה, מִסְתַּפְּקֵי וְאִתְּזָנוּ, לְאִתְקַשְּׁרָא רוּחַ אַחֲרָא דְּאִיהוּ גּוֹ מְסָאֲבוּ, מֵאִינּוּן תַּרְבִּין וְשַׁמְנוּנִין כְּמָה דְּאִתְּמַר. בג"כ, עוֹלָה קֹדֶשׁ הַקֳּדָשִׁים, שְׁאַר קָרְבָּנִין לְמֶעְבַּד שְׁלָמָא בְּעָלְמָא, כֻּלְּהוּ מִכַּמָּה סִטְרִין, וּמָארֵי דִּינִין לְאִתְעַטְרָא וּלְאִתְנַהֲרָא מִגּוֹ רְעוּתָא לְאִתְבַּסְמָא, אִקְרוּן קֳדָשִׁים קַלִּים, בְּגִין דְּלָא מִתְעַטְּרָא לְעֵילָּא בְּקֹדֶשׁ הַקֳּדָשִׁים, וְעַל דָּא אִינּוּן קֳדָשִׁים קַלִּים, וּנְכִיסוּ דִּילְהוֹן בְּכָל אֲתָר כְּמָה דְּאוּקִימְנָא. אֲבָל עוֹלָה דְּאִיהוּ רָזָא דְּקֹדֶשׁ הַקֳּדָשִׁים, לָאו אִיהוּ כִּשְׁאַר

קָרְבָּנִין, דְּכָל עוֹבָדָהָא קֹדֶשׁ.

353. Afterwards, from the secret of the beast OFFERED, THE EXTERNAL FORCES are sustained and nourished, so as to connect AND LET OUT THROUGH IT another spirit within defilement so it MAY BE LET OUT, NAMELY SO HOLY SPARKS MAY BE REMOVED FROM THE OTHER SIDE, by OFFERING fat and marrow, as we learned. The burnt offering is the highest class of sacrifices MEANT WHOLLY FOR THAT WHICH IS HIGH, AND THERE IS NO FOOD IN IT FOR THE EXTERNAL FORCES. But the rest of the offerings bring peace to the whole world, from the aspects of the forces of Judgment IN THE WORLD, by removing them, and shining in trying to mitigate them BY THE OFFERINGS. They are called 'lesser holy offerings,' because they are not adorned above in the Holy of Holies, BINAH. Therefore, they are 'lesser holy offerings' and may be slaughtered any place, as we explained. But the burnt offering, which is the secret of the highest class of sacrifices, is not like the rest of the offerings, for all of it is holy.

354. ת״ח, מַה כְּתִיב וְלָבַשׁ הַכֹּהֵן מִדּוֹ בַד, אִלֵּין לְבוּשִׁין מְיַיחֲדִין לִקְדוּשָּׁה. בַּד: יְחִידָאי, מְיַחֲדָא לִקְדוּשָּׁה. וּכְתִיב בִּגְדֵי קֹדֶשׁ הֵם וְרָחַץ בַּמַּיִם אֶת בְּשָׂרוֹ וּלְבֵשָׁם. מַאי טַעֲמָא. אֶלָּא רָזָא דְּמִלָּה כְּדְקָאַמְרָן, דְּאִיהִי קֹדֶשׁ הַקֳּדָשִׁים, דְּסַלְקָא כֹּלָּא וְאִתְעַטְּרָא בְּקֹדֶשׁ הַקֳּדָשִׁים, בְּקִשּׁוּרָא חֲדָא. וּלְבָתַר מִפְּנֵי וְאַעְבַּר רוּחַ מִסְאֲבָא דְּסָאִיב כֹּלָּא, דְּלָא שַׁלְטָא, וְלָא יִתְקְרִיב גּוֹ מַקְדְּשָׁא, וְאִתְעֲבָר מִכָּל סִטְרֵי קוּדְשָׁא, וְאִשְׁתְּאַר כֹּלָּא קֹדֶשׁ בִּקְדוּשָּׁה יְחִידָאי.

354. Come and see: It is written, "and the priest shall put on his linen garment" (Vayikra 6:3). This is a garment for holiness alone. 'Linen' (Heb. *bad*, *Bet-Dalet*) MEANS alone (Heb. *levad*, Lamed-Bet-Dalet), namely, it is for holiness alone. It is also written, "these are holy garments; therefore, shall he bathe his flesh in water, and so put them on" (Vayikra 16:4). Why DO WE NEED ALL THESE? The secret meaning of this is as we said, that THE BURNT OFFERING is of the highest class of sacrifices, since it ascends entirely and is bedecked in the Holy of Holies, WHICH IS BINAH, into one bond. Then the spirit of defilement that defiles everything, passes away and does not rule, nor approaches the Temples, and it is removed from all the sides of holiness, and all that is holy remains in holiness alone.

355. וְאָמַר ר׳ שִׁמְעוֹן, הָא אִתְּמַר דִּכְתִּיב אָדָם וּבְהֵמָה תּוֹשִׁיעַ יְיָ׳. וְהָכִי סָלְקָא רָזָא דְאָדָם, מִסִּטְרָא דְּאָדָם וַדַּאי. בְּהֵמָה, מִסִּטְרָא דִּבְהֵמָה. ובג״כ כְּתִיב, אָדָם כִּי יַקְרִיב מִכֶּם, אָדָם וַדַּאי, דְּדָא קָרְבָּנֵיהּ לְעֵילָּא, לְקַשְּׁרָא קִשְׁרָא בְּרָזָא דְאָדָם. וּלְבָתַר מִן הַבְּהֵמָה, וְכֹלָּא אִיהוּ בְּרָזָא דְאָדָם וּבְהֵמָה. וְדָא הוּא רָזָא דְּאִצְטְרִיךְ לְקָרְבָּנָא, אָדָם וּבְהֵמָה כִּדְקָאמְרָן. תָּא חֲזֵי, כַּד בָּרָא קוּדְשָׁא בְּרִיךְ הוּא עָלְמָא, הָכִי עֲבַד אָדָם וּבְהֵמָה.

355. Rabbi Shimon said: We studied the verse, "Hashem, You preserve man and beast" (Tehilim 36:7). The offering of man assuredly comes from the side of man, NAMELY, STUDYING TORAH AND PRAYER, and the beast comes from the side of the beast, NAMELY, OFFERING UPON THE ALTAR. It is therefore written, "If any man of you bring an offering" (Vayikra 1:2); assuredly this refers to a man, whose offering it is OF TORAH AND PRAYER, so it may tie above the knot in the secret of man, WHO IS ZEIR ANPIN, IN THE SECRET OF YUD HEI VAV HEI OF 45 IN NUMERICAL VALUE, THE NUMERICAL VALUE OF MAN (ADAM), and afterwards TO BE OFFERED ON THE ALTAR THEN ASCENDS TO MALCHUT, THE SECRET OF YUD HEI VAV HEI OF 52, IN NUMERICAL VALUE THE NUMERICAL VALUE OF BEAST (HEB. *BEHEMAH*). "Of the cattle" (Ibid.). All is in the secret of man and beast, as we said, this is the secret reason an offering of both man and beast is needed. Come and see: When the Holy One, blessed be He created the world, He made them so, man and beast.

356. וְאִי תֵּימָא, וְהָא כְּתִיב וְעוֹף יְעוֹפֵף עַל הָאָרֶץ, דְּהָא מִנַּיְיהוּ מְקָרְבִין קָרְבָּנִין, וַאֲפִילּוּ עוֹלָה, כְּמָה דִּכְתִּיב וְאִם מִן הָעוֹף עוֹלָה קָרְבָּנוֹ. ת״ח, מִכָּל אִינּוּן עוֹפֵי, לָא מְקָרְבִין אֶלָּא תּוֹרִים וּבְנֵי יוֹנָה, מַה דְּאִתְכְּשַׁר בְּדָא, פָּסִיל בְּדָא דָא יְמִינָא, וְדָא שְׂמָאלָא.

356. You may say, it is written, "and let birds fly above the earth" (Beresheet 1:20), from which sacrifices are offered, and even burnt offerings, as it is written, "and if his offering be a burnt offering of fowls" (Vayikra 1:14); Come and see: Of the fowls only the turtledove and young pigeons are offered, and what qualifies the one, disqualifies the other, RED QUALIFIES THE TURTLEDOVE AND DISQUALIFIES THE YOUNG PIGEON,

BECAUSE this one, THE YOUNG PIGEON is of the right, AND RED DISQUALIFIES IT, and that, TURTLEDOVE, is of the left, AND THAT IS WHY RED, THE COLOR OF THE LEFT, QUALIFIES IT.

357. אֲבָל רָזָא דָא הָא אוֹקִימְנָא, כְּתִיב וְעוֹף יְעוֹפֵף עַל הָאָרֶץ, דְּאִינּוּן רָזָא דִּרְתִיכָא, וּבְהוּ אִסְתַּלָּק רוּחַ הַקֹּדֶשׁ, לְסַלְּקָא לְעֵילָּא, דְּאִינּוּן תְּרֵי, חַד לִימִינָא, וְחַד לִשְׂמָאלָא, עוֹף לִימִינָא, וְדָא מִיכָאֵל. יְעוֹפֵף, לִשְׂמָאלָא, וְדָא גַּבְרִיאֵל. דָּא לִימִינָא וְדָא לִשְׂמָאלָא. ובג״כ, מְקָרְבִין תְּרֵין אִלֵּין, לְסַלְּקָא רוּחַ קוּדְשָׁא, וּשְׂמָאלָא מְעַטֵּר וְזָיֵין לְתַתָּא, לְהַהוּא סְטָר שְׂמָאלָא. וִימִינָא לִימִינָא וְאִתְקַשְּׁרָא אִתְּתָא בְּבַעְלָהּ, לְמֶהֱוֵי חַד, וְכֹלָּא אִסְתַּלָּק וְאִתְקָשַּׁר כַּחֲדָא לְעֵילָּא וְתַתָּא, וְקוּדְשָׁא בְּרִיךְ הוּא אִסְתַּלָּק בִּלְחוֹדוֹי וְאִתְקַף.

357. But we stated that, "and let birds fly above the earth" refers to the secret of the Chariot, NAMELY, THE ANGEL MICHAEL...UPON WHOM RIDES MALCHUT, AND THEY ARE CALLED 'BIRDS'. By them the Holy Spirit, MALCHUT, is raised up TO ZEIR ANPIN. They are two, one to the right and one to the left; "birds" to the right, referring to Michael and "fly" to the left, referring to Gabriel. Therefore, these two birds are offered: A TURTLEDOVE AND A YOUNG PIGEON, to raise the Holy Spirit, MALCHUT. The left OF ZEIR ANPIN crowns and arms the left side below OF MALCHUT. And the same happens with the right, and the wife, MALCHUT, is united with her husband, ZEIR ANPIN, to become one. And all is connected together above and below, and the Holy One, blessed be He alone is elevated and strengthened.

358. וּבְסִפְרֵי קַדְמָאֵי, מִסְכְּנָא, לָא יָהִיב חוּלְקָא לְאַתְזָנָא, אֶלָּא לְעֵילָּא לְאִתְקַשְּׁרָא, אֲבָל כֹּלָּא לְעֵילָּא וְתַתָּא מִתְקָשַּׁר, כָּל חַד וְחַד לְסִטְרֵיהּ כַּדְקָא יָאוֹת, וְהָא אוֹקִימְנָא.

358. In ancient books IT IS SAID THAT the poor man, WHO SACRIFICES TURTLEDOVES AND YOUNG PIGEONS does not give a portion TO SUSTAIN THE WORLDS, but only to the upper union. But everything above and below, is joined each to its side as deserved. And we already explained.

359. רִבִּי אֶלְעָזָר שָׁאִיל לְרִבִּי שִׁמְעוֹן, אָמַר, הָא קְשׁוּרָא דְּעוֹלָה, אִתְקָשַׁר בְּקֹדֶשׁ הַקֳּדָשִׁים, לְאִתְנַהֲרָא. אִתְדַּבְּקוּתָא דִּרְעוּתָא דְּכַהֲנָא וְלֵיוָאֵי וְיִשְׂרָאֵל לְעֵילָּא, עַד הֵיכָן אִיהוּ סַלְקָא.

359. Rabbi Elazar asked Rabbi Shimon: The burnt offering is bound to the Holy of Holies, BINAH, so it may shine. The devotion of the service of the priests, Levites, and Yisrael rises above, BY OFFERING SACRIFICE; how far does it go?

360. א״ל, הָא אוּקִימְנָא, עַד אֵין סוֹף, דְּכָל קְשׁוּרָא וְיִחוּדָא וּשְׁלִימוּ, לְאִצְנְעָא בְּהַהוּא צְנִיעוּ, דְּלָא אִתְדַּבָּק, וְלָא אִתְיְידַע, דִּרְעֲוָא דְּכָל רַעֲוִין בֵּיהּ, אֵין סוֹף לָא קַיְימָא לְאוֹדְעָא, וְלַאו לְמֶעְבַּד סוֹף, וְלָאו לְמֶעְבַּד רֹאשׁ, כְּמָה דְּאַיִן קַדְמָאָה אַפִּיק רֹאשׁ וְסוֹף. מַאן רֹאשׁ. דָּא נְקוּדָה עִלָּאָה, דְּאִיהוּ רֵישָׁא דְּכֹלָּא סְתִימָאָה, דְּקַיְימָא גּוֹ מַחֲשָׁבָה. וְעָבֵיד סוֹף, דְּאִקְרֵי סוֹף דָּבָר. אֲבָל לְהָתָם, אֵין סוֹף.

360. He told him: We stated that THEIR DEVOTION reaches the Endless World. The object of bond, unison, and completeness is to hide well that which cannot be perceived or known, where abides the will of all wills, NAMELY, THE ENDLESS WORLD. It is endless and not subject to knowledge, nor did it create an end or beginning, UNLIKE the first nought (Heb. *ayin*), WHICH IS KETER, that produced a beginning and an end. The beginning is the supernal point, the beginning of all that is concealed, existing within thought, WHICH IS CHOCHMAH, FOR CHOCHMAH ISSUED FROM KETER. IT IS THE SECRET MEANING OF THE VERSE, "BUT WHERE (HEB. *AYIN*) SHALL WISDOM BE FOUND?" (IYOV 28:12). It also produced an end, called "the end of the matter" (Kohelet 12:13), NAMELY, MALCHUT, THE END OF ALL THE LIGHTS. But there, IN THE ENDLESS WORLD there is no end.

361. לָאו רְעוּתִין, לָאו נְהוֹרִין, לָאו בּוּצִינִין, בְּהַהוּא אֵין סוֹף, כָּל אִלֵּין בּוּצִינִין וּנְהוֹרִין, תַּלְיָין לְאִתְקַיְּימָא בְּהוּ, וְלָא קַיְימָא לְאִתְדַּבְּקָא מַאן דְּיָדַע וְלָא יָדַע, לָאו אִיהוּ אֶלָּא רְעוּ עִלָּאָה, סְתִימָא דְּכָל סְתִימִין, אַיִן.

361. There are no desires, no lights and no candles, NAMELY, THE LIGHTS OF GVURAH, within that Endless World. All the candles and lights IN ATZILUT, are dependent upon THE ENDLESS WORLD for their existence. But it, in itself, is not subject to comprehension. That which is known but not known, NAMELY, THAT KNOWLEDGE PERTAINS TO IT BUT IT IS NOT KNOWN, is but the high desire most concealed of all, CALLED 'Ayin', THE SFIRAH OF KETER. BUT THERE IS NO WORD TO DESCRIBE THE ENDLESS WORLD BECAUSE THERE IS NO PERCEIVING IT.

362. וְכַד נְקוּדָה עִלָּאָה, וְעָלְמָא דְּאָתֵי, אִסְתְּלָקוּ, לָא יַדְעֵי בַּר רֵיחָא, כְּמַאן דְּאָרַח בְּרֵיחָא וְאִתְבְּסָם. וְלָאו דָּא נַיְיחָא נִחוֹחַ, דְּהָא כְּתִיב וְלֹא אָרִיחַ בְּרֵיחַ נִיחֹחֲכֶם, דְּהָא רֵיחַ נִיחֹחַ, רֵיחָא דִּרְעוּתָא דְּכָל הָנֵי רְעוּתָא דִּצְלוֹתָא, וּרְעוּתָא דְּשִׁירָתָא, וּרְעוּתָא דְּכַהֲנָא, דְּכֻלְּהוּ רָזָא דְּאָדָם. כְּדֵין כֻּלְּהוּ אִתְעָבִידוּ רְעוּתָא חֲדָא, וְהַהוּא אִקְרֵי נִיחֹחַ, רַעֲוָא, כְּתַרְגּוּמוֹ. כְּדֵין כֹּלָּא אִתְקָשַׁר וְאִתְנְהִיר כַּחֲדָא, כַּדְקָא יֵאוֹת, כְּמָה דְּאִתְּמַר.

362. When the supernal point, CHOCHMAH, and the World to Come, BINAH, mount BY THEIR ILLUMINATION, the odor alone is known, THE SECRET OF THE SIX ENDS OF THE ILLUMINATION OF CHOCHMAH CALLED 'ODOR', BUT NOT THE FIRST THREE SFIROT, AS KNOWN. It is as if they perfume themselves by that smell. This is not CONSIDERED the satisfaction (Heb. *nachat*) CALLED 'odor' (Heb. *nichoach*), as it is written, "and I will not smell the savor of your sweet odors" (Vayikra 26:31). FOR SMELL AND ODOR ARE TWO DIFFERENT THINGS. The smell of odor refers to the smell of desire, NAMELY, of all the desires, prayers, and songs, and the service of the priest, all in the mystery of man. They then all become one desire, AND THAT DESIRE is called 'odor', WHICH MEANS 'desire', according to the Aramaic translation. Then all is bound together and illuminates properly, as we learned.

363. וְעַל דָּא אִתְיְיהִיבַת הַאי סִטְרָא אַחֲרָא, בִּידָא דְּכַהֲנָא, דִּכְתִּיב צַו אֶת אַהֲרֹן וְאֶת בָּנָיו לֵאמֹר, רָזָא הָכָא, דְּהָא אוּקִימְנָא לֵית צַו אֶלָּא ע"ז, וְהָכָא אִתְיְיהִיבַת לֵיהּ, לְאִתּוֹקְדָא הַהִיא מַחֲשָׁבָה רָעָה, וּלְאַעְבְּרָא לָהּ מִגּוֹ קוּדְשָׁא, בְּהַאי רְעוּתָא דְּסַלְקָא לְעֵילָּא, וּבְהָא תְּנָנָא, וְתַרְבִּין דְּאִתּוֹקְדָן. בְּגִין לְאִתְעַבְּרָא מִן קוּדְשָׁא. וְהַאי צַו, בִּרְשׁוּתַיְיהוּ קַיְימָא,

לְאַפְרָשָׁא לָהּ מִן קוּדְשָׁא, מִגּוֹ הַאי קָרְבָּנָא. וְאִי תֵּימָא צַו אֶת בְּנֵי יִשְׂרָאֵל. הָכִי נָמֵי, דְּהָא בִּרְשׁוּתַיְיהוּ קַיְימָא, כָּל זִמְנָא דְּעַבְדֵי רְעוּתָא דְּמָארֵיהוֹן, דְּלָא יַכְלָא לְשַׁלְטָאָה עֲלַיְיהוּ.

363. By that the Other Side is handed to the priest, as it is written, "command Aaron and his sons, saying" (Vayikra 6:2). There is a mystery here, for we explained that "command" refers to idolatry, NAMELY, TO THE OTHER SIDE. Here it was handed to him so he could burn that wicked thought, and remove it from holiness, by that will rising upward, the smoke and the burning marrow, so they will pass away from holiness. That command is in their hands, to separate from holiness by sacrifice. And if you say, in the verse, "command the children of Yisrael" (Bemidbar 28:2), HOW WOULD YOU EXPLAIN THE WORD "COMMAND" SO IT WOULD REFER TO THE OTHER SIDE? HE ANSWERS: When Yisrael do the bidding of their Master, the Other Side cannot rule them.

364. וְהַאי קְרָא כֹּלָּא, אַתְיָא לְאַחֲזָאָה רָזָא דְּמִלָּה, לְאַעְטְרָא לְהַהוּא רוּחַ קוּדְשָׁא, לְעֵילָּא לְעֵילָּא, וּלְאַפְרְשָׁא לָהּ לְדָא רוּחַ טוּמְאָה, לְנַחְתָּא לָהּ לְתַתָּא לְתַתָּא, דָּא בִּרְעוּתָא וּבִצְלוֹתָא כִּדְקָאמְרָן, וְדָא בְּעוֹבָדָא, כֹּלָּא כִּדְקָחָזֵי לֵיהּ.

364. The whole verse shows the secret meaning of the matter: to adorn the Holy Spirit, MALCHUT, high above and to separate the spirit of defilement and bring it down below. YISRAEL do this by their desire and prayer, THE PRIESTS by offering sacrifices, each one as befits him.

365. וְהַאי קְרָא מוֹכַח עֲלַיְיהוּ, דִּכְתִּיב, צַו אֶת אַהֲרֹן וְאֶת בָּנָיו לֵאמֹר. צַו: דָּא ע"ז רוּחַ מִסְאֲבָא. לֵאמֹר: דָּא אִתְּתָא, דְּאִקְרֵי יִרְאַת יְיָ'. כְּתִיב הָכָא לֵאמֹר, וּכְתִיב הָתָם לֵאמֹר הֵן יְשַׁלַּח אִישׁ אֶת אִשְׁתּוֹ, וְהָא אוּקְמוּהָ. וּבג"כ, כֹּלָּא אִתְּמַר, וְכַהֲנָא קַיְימָא לְאַתְקְנָא כֹּלָּא, בְּרָזָא דְּאָדָם וּבְהֵמָה. זַכָּאָה חוּלָקֵיהוֹן דְּצַדִּיקַיָּיא, בְּעָלְמָא דֵּין, וּבְעָלְמָא דְּאָתֵי, לְאִינּוּן יַדְעֵי אָרְחֵי דְּאוֹרַיְיתָא, וְאַזְלֵי בָּהּ בְּאֹרַח קְשׁוֹט, עֲלַיְיהוּ כְּתִיב, יְיָ' עֲלֵיהֶם יִחְיוּ. מַאי עֲלֵיהֶם. אִלֵּין אָרְחוֹי דְּאוֹרַיְיתָא. יִחְיוּ,

יִתְקַיְימוּ בְּהַאי עָלְמָא, וּבְעָלְמָא דְאָתֵי.

365. This verse proves it. It is written, "command Aaron and his sons, saying." "Command" refers to idolatry, the spirit of defilement. "Saying" is a woman called, "who fears Hashem" (Mishlei 31:30), THAT IS, MALCHUT. It written here "saying" and it is written there "saying, if a man put away his wife" (Yirmeyah 3:1). IN BOTH CASES THERE IS REFERENCE TO WOMEN. And we already explained, that all was said, TO ADORN MALCHUT AND LOWER THE OTHER SIDE. It is for the priest to fix everything in the secret of man and beast. Happy is the portion of the righteous in this world and in the World to Come, for they know the ways of the Torah, and walk in it in the way of truth. Of them it is written, "Hashem, with these things men live" (Yeshayah 38:18). What are "these things"? They are the ways of the Torah. "Men live," namely, in this world and the World to Come.

366. תָּא חֲזֵי, כְּתִיב זֹאת תּוֹרַת הָעוֹלָה, אָמַר ר׳ חִיָּיא, הַאי קְרָא אוֹקִימְנָא לֵיהּ בְּהַאי גַּוְונָא, זֹאת תּוֹרַת: דָּא כְּנֶסֶת יִשְׂרָאֵל. הָעוֹלָה: דְּאִיהִי סַלְקַת וְאִתְעַטְּרַת לְעֵילָא לְעֵילָא, לְאִתְקַשְּׁרָא כַּדְקָא יֵאוֹת, עַד אֲתָר דְּאִקְרֵי קֹדֶשׁ הַקֳּדָשִׁים.

366. Come and see: It is written, "This is the Torah of the burnt offering" (Vayikra 6:2). Rabbi Chiya said: I explained this verse in this manner: "this is the Torah" refers to the Congregation of Yisrael, NAMELY, MALCHUT. It is a "burnt offering" (lit. 'ascension'), for it ascends and adorns itself up high, to be bound properly to the place called 'Holy of Holies', BINAH.

367. ד״א, זֹאת תּוֹרַת: דָּא כְּנֶסֶת יִשְׂרָאֵל. הָעוֹלָה: דָּא מַחֲשָׁבָה רָעָה, דְּאִיהִי סַלְקָא עַל רְעוּתָא דְּבַר נָשׁ, לְאַסְטָאָה לֵיהּ מֵאוֹרְחָא דִּקְשׁוֹט. הִיא הָעוֹלָה, הִיא הִיא דְּסַלְקָא, וְאַסְטִיאַת לֵיהּ לְבַר נָשׁ, בָּעֵי לְאוֹקְדָא לֵיהּ בְּנוּרָא, בְּגִין דְּלָא יִתְיְיהִיב לָהּ דּוּכְתָּא לְאַסְגָּאָה.

367. Another explanation: "This is the Torah" refers to the Congregation of Yisrael, WHICH IS MALCHUT. "The burnt offering" is an evil thought, taking over the desire of man to lead him astray from the way of truth. "The burnt offering" rises and denounces man. It should be burnt by fire, so it will not increase.

368. ובג"כ, עַל מוֹקְדָה עַל הַמִּזְבֵּחַ כָּל הַלַּיְלָה, מַאן לַיְלָה, דָּא כְּנֶסֶת יִשְׂרָאֵל. דְּאַתְיָא לְדַכְּאָה לֵיהּ לְבַר נָשׁ, מֵהַהוּא רְעוּתָא. עַל מוֹקְדָה. בְּגִין דִּי נְהַר דִּינוּר, אִיהוּ אֲתַר לְאוֹקְדָא לְכָל אִינּוּן, דְּלָא קַיְימֵי בְּקִיּוּמַיְיהוּ, דְּהָא עָאלִין לוֹן בְּהַהוּא נוּרָא דְּדָלִיק, וּמְעַבְרֵי שׁוּלְטָנֵהוֹן מֵעָלְמָא. וּבְגִין דְּלָא יִשְׁלוֹט, אִצְטְרִיךְ עַל מוֹקְדָה עַל הַמִּזְבֵּחַ כָּל הַלַּיְלָה, וְאִתְכַּפְיָיא וְלָא שַׁלְטָא.

368. It shall therefore, "be burning upon the altar all night" (Vayikra 6:2). The "night" is the Congregation of Yisrael, NAMELY, MALCHUT, that purifies man from that desire. It is "Upon the altar," because the river of fire is where those should be burnt who are not well established, ALL WHO ARE MADE DEFECTIVE BY THE OTHER SIDE. They are put in the burning fire, and their power is broken. It must be put "upon the altar all night" to subdue it, for then it is subdued and loses its power.

369. וְעַל דָּא, כַּד אִתְכַּפְיָיא הַאי, סַלְקָא כְּנֶסֶת יִשְׂרָאֵל, דְּאִיהִי רוּחַ קוּדְשָׁא, דְּסַלְקָא וְאִתְעַטְּרָא לְעֵילָא, דְּהָא סְלִיקוּ דִּילָהּ, כַּד אִתְכַּפְיָיא הַאי חֵילָא אַחֲרָא, וְאִתְפְּרְשָׁא מִינָּהּ. ובג"כ, בָּעֵינָן בְּרָזָא דְּקָרְבְּנָא, לְאַפְרְשָׁא לְהַאי סִטְרָא מֵרוּחַ קוּדְשָׁא, וּלְמֵיהַב לָהּ חוּלְקָא, בְּגִין דְּרוּחַ קוּדְשָׁא אִסְתַּלַּק לְעֵילָא.

369. Hence, when THE OTHER SIDE is subdued, the Congregation of Yisrael, which is the Holy Spirit, NAMELY MALCHUT, ascends to be adorned up high, because it ascends whenever the other force is subjugated and separated from it. Therefore, we need, by the secret of the offering, to separate that side from the Holy Spirit, WHICH IS MALCHUT, and give it a portion, so the Holy Spirit may rise above.

40. "And Moses erected the Tabernacle"

A Synopsis

Rabbi Shimon discusses the verse: "In that day will I raise up the Tabernacle of David that is fallen," and talks about how Moses raised the Tabernacle as if lifting someone who has fallen. He tells us that God lifted up Yisrael from the exile in Egypt. While God did not perform miracles to raise up Yisrael from the exile in Babylon, he will do so in future. Rabbi Shimon talks about the Tabernacle that Moses built and the upper Tabernacle (Binah) that Zeir Anpin built, saying that Zeir Anpin is the grade of Moses. We hear of the three aspects that went into the erection of the Tabernacle and how they subdued the Other Side. He turns to "and fastened its sockets," explaining that when the sockets were fastened Samael was flushed out and fled to hide himself in a hole in the dust. 'In that day' refers to the day that God will judge the world. Rabbi Shimon tells us how the ruins of the Tabernacle will be raised on that day and the breach against the wicked will be repaired. God will build the foundations of Jerusalem with sapphires because sapphires are full of the highest illumination and provide a firm foundation that the other nations will not be able to rule over. At that time a supernal illumination will be added to the sapphires as well. The original stones from the foundations of Zion and Jerusalem were hidden and treasured by God, and He will restore them to the new foundations. The angel of death will be swallowed up just as he swallowed the people for all these years. Rabbi Shimon tells us that when Moses fastened the sockets in the Tabernacle he bound the evil Samael up so he could not move. Rabbi Shimon tells Rabbi Yosi about "the heaven is My throne, and the earth is my footstool," saying that they are the firmaments where Jacob lives and the firmament where King David lives. He explains the difference between a Tabernacle and a temple or house, emphasizing that a Tabernacle travels from place to place, it is not an eternal resting place, it is a secret small place. We learn why Moses withdrew from the construction of the Tabernacle and why Betzalel and Aholiav built it, and are told that Moses is still considered to be the builder since he finished it.

370. וְתָא חֲזֵי, בְּזִמְנָא דְּאִתְבְּנֵי בֵּי מַקְדְּשָׁא, וְאִתְעֲבֵיד. אִתְכַּפְיָיא סִטְרָא אַחֲרָא, וְאִסְתַּלָּק מֵעָלְמָא. וְכַד אִסְתַּלָּק מֵעָלְמָא, וְאִתְּקַם מַשְׁכְּנָא עַל יְדָא דְּמֹשֶׁה, כְּדֵין אִתְּקַם לְעֵילָּא וְתַתָּא. הה"ד, וַיָּקֶם מֹשֶׁה אֶת הַמִּשְׁכָּן. מַאי וַיָּקֶם. אֶלָּא דְּאוֹקִים לָהּ, לְאִסְתַּלְּקָא לְעֵילָּא. וְעַל

דָא, וַיָּקֶם מֹשֶׁה, מַאן דַּהֲוָה מָאִיךְ אוֹקְמֵיהּ, כְּמַאן דְּאוֹקִים לְמַאן דְּנָפִיל. כְּגַוְונָא דָא, לְזִמְנָא דְּאָתֵי כְּתִיב אָקִים אֶת סֻכַּת דָּוִד הַנּוֹפֶלֶת.

370. Come and see: When the Temple was built and erected, the Other Side was subdued, and departed from the world. When it left the world, and the Tabernacle was raised by Moses, it was raised above and below. This is the meaning of "Moses erected (lit. 'raised') the Tabernacle" (Shemot 40:18). "Raised" means that he raised MALCHUT so she would rise up high. Therefore scripture says, "and Moses erected"; he raised what was low, as if lifting someone who fell. In the same manner it is written of the future, "In that day will I raise up the Tabernacle of David that is fallen" (Amos 9:11).

371. כְּתִיב, נָפְלָה לֹא תוֹסִיף קוּם בְּתוּלַת יִשְׂרָאֵל, מַאי לֹא תּוֹסִיף קוּם. אֶלָּא בְּזִמְנָא אַחֲרָא קָמַת. הִיא קָמַת מִגַּרְמָהּ, וְלָא אוֹקִים לָהּ קוּדְשָׁא בְּרִיךְ הוּא. דְּהָא בְּגָלוּתָא דְּמִצְרַיִם, קוּדְשָׁא בְּרִיךְ הוּא אוֹקִים לָהּ, וַעֲבַד כַּמָּה נִסִּין, בְּגִין לְאַקָּמָא לָהּ, וּבְגָלוּתָא דְּבָבֶל הוּא לָא אוֹקִים לָהּ, בְּגִין דְּלָא עֲבַד לוֹן נִסִּים, דְּגָרִים חוֹבָה, אֶלָּא הִיא קָמַת. וּסְלִיקוּ בְּנֵי גוֹלָה, כְּאִינּוּן דְּלָא הֲוָה לוֹן פּוּרְקָא, וְלָא הֲוָה תִּיאוּבְתָּא דְּקוּדְשָׁא בְּרִיךְ הוּא עֲלַיְיהוּ, בְּגִין דְּגָרַם הַהוּא חוֹבָא, דְּאִינּוּן נָשִׁים נָכְרִיּוֹת.

371. It is written, "The virgin of Yisrael is fallen; she shall no more rise" (Amos 5:2). HE ASKS: What is the meaning of "she shall no more rise"? HE ANSWERS: She rose on another time on her own and not raised by the Holy One, blessed be He. For from the exile in Egypt, she was raised by the Holy One, blessed be He, who performed many miracles in order to raise her. In exile in Babylon, THE HOLY ONE, BLESSED BE HE did not raise her. He did not perform miracles, because of the sin. So MALCHUT rose on her own, and the exiles went up TO JERUSALEM, as if they were not redeemed, and as if the Holy One, blessed be He had no interest in them. That was because they sinned with foreign women.

372. וע"ד, קוּדְשָׁא בְּרִיךְ הוּא לָא אוֹקִים לָהּ לִכְנֶסֶת יִשְׂרָאֵל, וְלָא עֲבֵד לָהּ נִסִּין וּגְבוּרָאן בְּהַהוּא זִמְנָא כִּדְקָא יֵאוֹת. אֲבָל לְזִמְנָא דְּאָתֵי, לֹא תוֹסִיף קוּם כְּתִיב, לָא תּוֹסִיף, קוּם מִגַּרְמָהּ, אֶלָּא קוּדְשָׁא בְּרִיךְ הוּא

יוֹקִים לָהּ, דִּכְתִּיב אָקִים אֶת סוּכַּת דָּוִד הַנּוֹפֶלֶת. וּכְתִיב וְאֵת דָּוִד מַלְכָּם אֲשֶׁר אָקִים לָהֶם. וּבְגִין כָּךְ כְּתִיב הָכָא, וַיָּקֶם מֹשֶׁה אֶת הַמִּשְׁכָּן. וַיָּקֶם מֹשֶׁה וְגוֹ'.

372. Therefore, the Holy One, blessed be He did not raise the Congregation of Yisrael, nor performed miracles and mighty deeds as fit at that time, WHEN THEY RETURNED FROM BABYLON. But in the future, it is written, "she shall no more rise," namely, on her own LIKE AFTER THE EXILE IN BABYLON, but the Holy One, blessed be He will raise her, as it is written, "In that day will I raise up the Tabernacle of David that is fallen" and "David their king, whom I will raise up for them" (Yirmeyah 30:9). That is why it is written, "and Moses erected the Tabernacle," MEANING THAT THE HOLY ONE, BLESSED BE HE ERECTED THE TABERNACLE. FOR MOSES IS A CHARIOT TO ZEIR ANPIN, AND AS MOSES ERECTED THE TABERNACLE BELOW, SO DID THE HOLY ONE, BLESSED BE HE ERECT THE TABERNACLE, WHICH IS MALCHUT, ABOVE.

373. ת"ח, כַּד אוֹקִים לֵיהּ מֹשֶׁה לְמַשְׁכְּנָא, אִתְּקַם מַשְׁכְּנָא אַחֲרָא עִמֵּיהּ. וּמַשְׁכְּנָא עִלָּאָה, אוֹקִים וְסָעִיד כֹּלָּא, בְּגִין דְּמַשְׁכְּנָא עִלָּאָה, סָתִים וְגָנִיז אִיהוּ לְעֵילָּא לְעֵילָּא. וּמַשְׁכְּנָא אַחֲרָא אִתְּקַם עַל מַשְׁכְּנָא דִּלְתַתָּא וְקַיְימָא עָלֵיהּ, בְּחֵילָא דְּהַהוּא מַשְׁכְּנָא עִלָּאָה עַל כֹּלָּא. וְכַמָּה דְּאִתְּקַם מַשְׁכְּנָא דִּלְתַתָּא עַל יְדָא דְּמֹשֶׁה, אוּף הָכִי לְעֵילָּא, ע"י דְּהַהוּא דַּרְגָּא דְּמֹשֶׁה. מְנָלָן. דִּכְתִּיב, וַיָּקֶם מֹשֶׁה אֶת הַמִּשְׁכָּן. אֶת דַּיְיקָא, לְאִתְחֲזָאָה דִּתְרֵי מַשְׁכְּנִין בְּרָזָא דְּמֹשֶׁה אִתְקָנוּ.

373. Come and see: When Moses erected the Tabernacle, another one was erected at the same time, NAMELY, MALCHUT. The upper Tabernacle, WHICH IS BINAH, establishes and supports everything, because it is concealed and stored high above, and another Tabernacle, MALCHUT, was erected above the Tabernacle below, THAT MOSES ERECTED, and stood upon it by the strength of the Tabernacle superior to all, BINAH. As the Tabernacle below was erected by Moses, so the one above, MALCHUT, was erected by the grade of Moses, ZEIR ANPIN. From where do we know that? From the verse, "and Moses erected the Tabernacle," the particle 'Et' (lit. 'the') indicating that two Tabernacles were established by the secret of

Moses, THE ONE BELOW, AND THE ONE ABOVE, WHICH IS MALCHUT, WHICH WAS ALSO BUILT BY THE GRADE OF MOSES, WHICH IS ZEIR ANPIN.

374. אָמַר רִבִּי יוֹסֵי, וְכִי וַיָּקֶם מֹשֶׁה, וְהָא כֹּלָּא עַד לָא אִתְתָּקַּן, וְקִימָה לָאו אִיהוּ אֶלָּא כַּד אִשְׁתְּלִים כֹּלָּא, וְעָאל שַׁיְיפָא בְּשַׁיְיפֵיהּ, מַאי וַיָּקֶם. א״ר יִצְחָק, בִּתְלַת סִטְרִין אוֹקִים מֹשֶׁה יַת מַשְׁכְּנָא, מַה כְּתִיב וַיָּקֶם מֹשֶׁה אֶת הַמִּשְׁכָּן, וַיִּתֵּן אֶת אֲדָנָיו, וַיָּשֶׂם אֶת קְרָשָׁיו. בְּהָנֵי תְּלַת סִטְרֵי, אוֹקִים מֹשֶׁה יַת מַשְׁכְּנָא. וּבְהָנֵי תְּלַת סִטְרֵי, אִסְתַּלָּק מַשְׁכְּנָא. וְאִתְכַּפְיָיא סִטְרָא אַחֲרָא. וע״ז, כַּד אוֹקִים מֹשֶׁה לְהַאי סִטְרָא, אִתְכַּפְיָיא סִטְרָא אַחֲרָא. בג״כ מֹשֶׁה אוֹקִים לֵיהּ וְלָא אַחֲרָא.

374. Rabbi Yosi said: When "Moses erected" not all was yet made, FOR THE FOLLOWING VERSE SAYS, "AND FASTENED ITS SOCKETS..." (SHEMOT 40:18). There is no raising up until all is completed and the parts intertwined. Why then is it written "erected"? Rabbi Yitzchak said: Moses erected the Tabernacle on three sides. The words "and Moses erected the Tabernacle" IMPLY THE CENTRAL COLUMN, CALLED 'MOSES'; "and fastened its sockets" IMPLY THE LEFT COLUMN, FOR SOCKETS (HEB. *ADANIM*) ARE SPELLED WITH THE LETTERS OF JUDGMENT (HEB. *DIN*), THAT PERTAINS TO THE LEFT; "and set up its boards" IMPLY THE RIGHT COLUMN. By these three aspects Moses erected the Tabernacle, and by these aspects the Tabernacle, MALCHUT, was erected and the Other Side subdued. Since Moses erected the side OF HOLINESS, the Other Side OF DEFILEMENT was subjugated. That is why Moses erected it and none other.

375. תָּא חֲזֵי, כְּתִיב וַיִּתֵּן אֶת אֲדָנָיו, בְּהַהִיא שַׁעֲתָא אִזְדַּעְזָע סָמָאֵ״ל מֵאַתְרֵיהּ, וְאַרְבְּעִין רְתִיכִין דְּעִמֵּיהּ, וְעָרַק אַרְבַּע מֵאָה פַּרְסֵי, גּוֹ טְסִירוּ דְּנוּקְבָּא דְּעַפְרָא. אָעִיל מֹשֶׁה אִינּוּן סַמְכִין, וְאִתְּקִיף סִטְרָא דָּא, כְּדֵין אִינּוּן סַמְכִין דְּסִטְרָא אַחֲרָא, נָפְלוּ וְאִתְרְפוּ.

375. Come and see: It is written, "and fastened its sockets." At that time, Samael was shaken from his place, together with his forty Chariots, and fled four hundred parasangs to hide himself in a hole in the dust. Moses brought the sockets, and that side was strengthened; the sockets of the Other Side were loosened and fell.

376. פָּתַח וְאָמַר, בַּיּוֹם הַהוּא אָקִים אֶת סֻכַּת דָּוִד הַנּוֹפֶלֶת וְגוֹ׳, מַאי בַּיּוֹם הַהוּא. בְּיוֹמָא דְקוּדְשָׁא ב״ה יַעְבִּיד דִּינָא בְּעָלְמָא, וְיִפְקוֹד עַל חַיָּיבֵי עָלְמָא כְּעוֹבָדֵיהוֹן. דְּהָא לֵית קִימָה לִכְנֶסֶת יִשְׂרָאֵל מֵעַפְרָא, בְּעוֹד דְּאִינּוּן חַיָּיבִין דְּיִשְׂרָאֵל יְקוּמוּן בְּעָלְמָא. מַה כְּתִיב לְעֵילָּא, בַּחֶרֶב יָמוּתוּ כֹּל חַטָּאֵי עַמִּי הָאוֹמְרִים לֹא תַגִּישׁ וְתַקְדִּים בַּעֲדֵנוּ הָרָעָה. מַה כְּתִיב בַּתְרֵיהּ, בַּיּוֹם הַהוּא אָקִים אֶת סֻכַּת דָּוִד הַנּוֹפֶלֶת וְגוֹ׳.

376. He opened the discussion and said, “In that day will I raise up the Tabernacle of David that is fallen” (Amos 9:11). HE ASKS: Which day? AND HE ANSWERS: On the day the Holy One, blessed be He will judge the world, and visit the deeds of the wicked, for the Congregation of Yisrael cannot rise from the dust, while the wicked still prevail. It is written above, “all the sinners of My people shall die by the sword, those that say, ‘The evil shall not overtake nor confront us’” (Ibid. 10). The following verse says, “In that day will I raise up the Tabernacle of David that is fallen.”

377. הַאי קְרָא אִית לְאִסְתַּכְּלָא בֵּיהּ, אֶת פִּרְצֵיהֶן, אֶת פִּרְצָהּ מִבָּעֵי לֵיהּ. וַהֲרִיסוֹתָיו, וַהֲרִיסוֹתֶיהָ מִבָּעֵי לֵיהּ. אֶלָּא וְגָדַרְתִּי אֶת פִּרְצֵיהֶן מִמַּאן, מֵאִינּוּן חַיָּיבִין, דִּכְתִּיב בַּחֶרֶב יָמוּתוּ כֹּל חַטָּאֵי עַמִּי, דְּהָא כְּדֵין יִתְעֲבִיד פִּרְצָן בְּיִשְׂרָאֵל, וע״ד וְגָדַרְתִּי אֶת פִּרְצֵיהֶן. וַהֲרִיסוֹתָיו אָקִים, הֲרִיסוֹתָיו דְּמַאן, הֲרִיסוֹתָיו דְּסוּכַּת דָּוִד. בְּגִין, דְּכַד אִתְּקַף מַלְכוּ חַיָּיבָא בְּעָלְמָא, כְּדֵין הַאי מַלְכוּ קַדִּישָׁא אִתְרַפֵּי, וְסֻכַּת דָּוִד אַסְתִּיר בִּנְיָינָא דִּילֵיהּ, וע״ד וַהֲרִיסוֹתָיו אָקִים.

377. We should look at this verse. IT IS WRITTEN, “their breaches” (Ibid. 11), which should have been ‘her (its) breaches,’ and “his ruins” (Ibid.) which should have been ‘her ruins,’ FOR THESE WORDS REFER TO “THE TABERNACLE (FEM.) OF DAVID.” HE ANSWERS: “I will…repair their breaches” (Ibid.) against the wicked, of whom it is written, “all the sinners of My people shall die by the sword.” Then the breach will be fixed, that THEY DID to Yisrael. It is therefore written, “I will…repair their breaches,” AND NOT ‘HER BREACHES’. “And I will raise up his ruins.” Whose ruins? Those of the Tabernacle of David, because WE LEARNED that when the evil kingdom is strengthened in the world, the holy kingdom is enfeebled, and the Tabernacle of David is ruined. Therefore it is written, "And I will raise up his ruins" (Ibid.).

378. דְּהָא תָּנֵינָן, כָּל זִמְנָא דְּהַאי אִתְּקָף, הַאי אִתְרַפֵּי. דָּא מַלְיָא, וְדָא חָרְבָה. ובג"כ, עַד הַהוּא יוֹמָא, מַלְכוּ חַיָּיבָא יִתְקָף. בְּהַהוּא יוֹמָא, יִתָּקַף וְיוֹקִים לָהּ קוּדְשָׁא בְּרִיךְ הוּא, לְהַאי מַלְכוּ קַדִּישָׁא. וע"ד וַהֲרִיסוֹתָיו אָקִים. וּבְנִיתִיהָ כִּימֵי עוֹלָם, מַאי וּבְנִיתִיהָ כִּימֵי עוֹלָם. הַיְינוּ דִּכְתִּיב, וְהָיָה אוֹר הַלְּבָנָה כְּאוֹר הַחַמָּה וְגו'.

378. We learned that when one is strengthened, NAMELY, DEFILEMENT, the other is enfeebled, NAMELY, HOLINESS. This one is full, and that is laid waste. Hence, until that SAID day, the evil kingdom shall get stronger. And on that day the holy kingdom will get stronger, and the Holy One, blessed be He will raise it. Therefore it is written, "and I will raise up his ruins, and I will build her as in the days of old" (Ibid.); the latter part is in accordance with the verse, "Moreover the light of the moon shall be as the light of the sun…" (Yeshayah 30:26).

379. וַיָּקֶם מֹשֶׁה אֶת הַמִּשְׁכָּן, בְּמַאי אוֹקִים לֵיהּ. דִּכְתִּיב וַיִּתֵּן אֶת אֲדָנָיו וְיָהַב אִינּוּן סַמְכִין דִּתְחוֹתֵיהּ, לְקִיּוּמָא עָלַיְיהוּ, וּלְאַסְחֲרָא בְּהוּ אִינּוּן צִירִים דְּפִתְחִין. בְּגִין דְּאִינּוּן סַמְכִין דִּתְחוֹתַיְיהוּ, אִינּוּן קִיוּמָא לְאַסְחֲרָא. אֲמַאי וַיִּתֵּן. אַתְקִיף וְאַתְקִין לוֹן בְּתוּקְפוֹי. בְּהַהִיא שַׁעֲתָא אַעְדִּיו אִינּוּן סַמְכִין אַחֲרָנִין דְּסִטְרָא אַחֲרָא.

379. "And Moses erected the Tabernacle." HE ASKS: With what did he erect it? AND HE ANSWERS: It is written, "and fastened its sockets" (Shemot 40:18). He laid the sockets underneath the boards, so that the hinges of the doors will revolve upon them, because the hinges underneath give support and firmness upon which they can revolve. Why is it WRITTEN "fastened"? Because he fixed and strengthened them with all his might. At that time the other sockets of the Other Side were removed.

380. תָּא חֲזֵי, כְּתִיב זְכוֹר יְיָ' לִבְנֵי אֱדוֹם אֵת יוֹם יְרוּשָׁלַםִ הָאוֹמְרִים עָרוּ עָרוּ עַד הַיְסוֹד בָּהּ. וְעַל דָּא זַמִּין קוּדְשָׁא בְּרִיךְ הוּא לְמִבְנֵי יְסוֹדֵי

יְרוּשְׁלֵם, מִיְסוֹדִין אַחֲרָנִין, דְּיִשְׁלְטוּן עַל כֹּלָּא. וּמַאן אִינּוּן. סַפִּירִין. דִּכְתִּיב, וִיסַדְתִּיךְ בַּסַּפִּירִים, דְּאִלֵּין אִינּוּן יְסוֹדִין, וְסַמְכִין תַּקִּיפִין וְעִלָּאִין, דְּלֵית לְהוּ חֲלִישׁוּ כְּקַדְמָאֵי. מַאי טַעֲמָא. בְּגִין דְּאַבְנִין קַדְמָאִין מֵאִינּוּן יְסוֹדֵי, יָכִילוּ שְׁאָר עַמִּין לְמִשְׁלַט עֲלַיְיהוּ. מַאי טַעֲמָא. בְּגִין דְּלֵית בְּהוּ נְהִירוּ עִלָּאָה, כַּדְקָא יָאוּת. אֲבָל אִלֵּין, יְהוֹן נְהִירִין מִגּוֹ נְהִירוּ עִלָּאָה, וּמִשְׁקְעָאן גּוֹ תְּהוֹמֵי, דְּלָא יַכְלִין לְשַׁלְטָאָה עֲלַיְיהוּ. וְאִלֵּין אִינּוּן סַפִּירִין, דְּיִנְהֲרוּן לְעֵילָּא וְתַתָּא. בְּגִין דִּבְהַהוּא זִמְנָא, יִתּוֹסַף נְהִירוּ עִלָּאָה, לְעֵילָּא וְתַתָּא.

380. Come and see: It is written, "Remember, O Hashem, against the children of Edom the day of Jerusalem; who said, Rase it, rase it, even to the foundation thereof" (Tehilim 137:7). Therefore, the Holy One, blessed be He will build the foundations of Jerusalem of other materials, that will have power over everything. What are they? They are sapphires, as it is written, "and lay your foundations with sapphires" (Yeshayah 54:11); which make strong and superior foundations, not weak as the first ones. What is the sense thereof? The other nations could rule over the stones of the first foundations. Why? Because there is no high illumination in them, as is fitting, BECAUSE THEIR ILLUMINATION IS NOT THEIR OWN, BUT DRAWN FROM BINAH. But these illuminate from the high illumination, NAMELY, THEY WILL ILLUMINATE ON THEIR OWN, AND WILL NOT NEED JOINING FROM BINAH. The illumination sinks into the abysses, so THE OTHER NATIONS will not be able to rule over them. These sapphires will illuminate above and below, for at that time, a supernal illumination will be added above and below.

381. וְאִי תֵּימָא אִינּוּן יְסוֹדֵי קַדְמָאֵי, יִתְבַּטְּלוּן. הָא כְּתִיב הִנֵּה אָנֹכִי מַרְבִּיץ בַּפּוּךְ אֲבָנָיִךְ. מַרְבִּיץ לְאַתְקְנָא תְּבִירָא. מַאי בַּפּוּךְ. כד"א וַתָּשֶׂם בַּפּוּךְ עֵינֶיהָ. אֲבָנִים אִית דְּאִקְרוּן פּוּךְ. מַאי טַעֲמָא הַאי. א"ר אֶלְעָזָר רָזָא אִיהוּ, וְרָזָא דָּא לְמַחֲצְדֵי חַקְלָא אִתְיְהִיב לְמִנְדַּע.

381. If you say that the first foundations, WHICH WERE IN USE BEFORE THE CORRECTION will be discarded, IT IS NOT SO, for it is written, "Behold, I will set your stones in antimony" (ibid.), "set" to fix what is broken. "With antimony," as it is said, "and she painted her eyes" (II Melachim 9:30). There are stones called 'antimony', BLACK BY COLOR, WHICH WOMEN USE TO PAINT THEIR EYES. Why DOES HE USE this? Rabbi Elazar said: This is a secret, known to the reapers of the field, NAMELY TO THOSE WHO HAD THE MERIT OF ESTABLISHING ALL THE CORRECTIONS OF THE FIELD, WHICH IS MALCHUT. THEY ALREADY REAP THE HARVEST OF THE FIELD AND ENJOY ITS FRUIT.

382. תָּא חֲזֵי, אִינּוּן אַבְנִין דִּיְסוֹדֵי צִיּוֹן וִירוּשָׁלַם, ח״ו דִּשְׁלִיטוּ עָלַיְיהוּ שְׁאַר עַמִּין, וְלָא אוֹקְדוּ לוֹן, וְלָא אִתּוֹקְדוּן, אֶלָּא כֻּלְּהוּ אִתְגְּנִיזוּ, וְגָנִיז לוֹן קוּדְשָׁא בְּרִיךְ הוּא, וְכָל אִינּוּן יְסוֹדֵי בֵּיתָא קַדִּישָׁא כֻּלְּהוּ אִתְגְּנִיזוּ, וְלָא אִתְאֲבִידוּ מִנַּיְיהוּ אֲפִילּוּ חַד. וְכַד יֶהְדַּר קוּדְשָׁא בְּרִיךְ הוּא וְיוֹקִים לָהּ לִירוּשְׁלֵם עַל אַתְרֵיהּ, אִינּוּן יְסוֹדֵי אַבְנִין קַדְמָאֵי, יַהַדְרוּן לְאַתְרַיְיהוּ, וְלָא יַשְׁלִיט בְּהוּ עֵינָא אַחֲרָא, בַּר בְּזִמְנָא דְּיִכְחוֹל בַּר נָשׁ עֵינוֹי בְּהַהוּא פּוּכָא, וְיִמְלֵי עֵינֵיהּ מִנֵּיהּ, וּכְדֵין יֶחֱמֵי כָּל אַבְנִין וְכָל יְסוֹדֵי יְרוּשָׁלַם, מִתְקְנָן עַל אַתְרַיְיהוּ, דְּלָא שָׁלִיטוּ בְּהוּ שְׁאַר עַמִּין, וְכָל אִינּוּן אַבְנִין יְקָרִין אַחֲרָנִין, וְכָל אִינּוּן בִּנְיָינֵי אַבְנִין, כֻּלְּהוּ קַיְימֵי עַל קִיּוּמַיְיהוּ.

382. Come and see: The stones of the foundation of Zion and Jerusalem, heaven forbid that other nations had power over them, or that they burned them. They were not burned but hidden and treasured by the Holy One, blessed be He. The foundations of the holy mansion were all stored, and not one was lost. And when the Holy One, blessed be He will restore Jerusalem again, these foundations of the first stones will be returned to their places, and no other eyes will rule them BY SIGHT, except when a man will paint his eyes with that antimony and fill his eyes with it. He will then see all the stones and all the foundations of Jerusalem, standing in their places, not ruled by other nations. And all the other precious stones, and stone buildings are all standing erect.

383. וּכְדֵין כִּי עַיִן בְּעַיִן יִרְאוּ בְּשׁוּב יְיָ׳ צִיּוֹן. מַאי בְּשׁוּב יְיָ׳. אֶלָּא כַּד שְׁלִיטוּ עָלָהּ שְׁאַר עַמִּין, קוּדְשָׁא בְּרִיךְ הוּא סָלִיק לָהּ לְעֵילָּא, וּבְהַהוּא זִמְנָא אִיהוּ יֶהְדַּר לָהּ לְאַתְרָהּ, דִּכְתִּיב בְּשׁוּב יְיָ׳ צִיּוֹן. בְּשׁוּב יְיָ׳ וַדַּאי.

383. Then, it is written, "for they shall see eye to eye, Hashem returning to Zion (also: 'Hashem causing Zion to return')" (Yeshayah 52:8). What does this mean? HE ANSWERS: When the other nations ruled over it, the Holy One, blessed be He raised it high, but at that time, He will return it to its place, as it is written, "Hashem causing Zion to return"; assuredly, HE WILL RETURN IT TO ITS PLACE.

384. וְתָא חֲזֵי, כָּל מַאן דְּאַסְתִּים מִן עֵינָא, וְלָא אִתְיְיהִיב רְשׁוּ לְשַׁלְטָאָה בֵּיהּ עֵינָא, לָא יַכְלִין לְמִשְׁלַט בֵּיהּ עֵינָא, בַּר בְּכַחְלָא דְּעֵינָא, בְּמִלִּין יְדִיעָאן. ובג״כ, הִנֵּה אָנֹכִי מַרְבִּיץ בַּפּוּךְ אֲבָנַיִךְ. ות״ח, כָּל אִלֵּין אַבְנִין יִתְקַיְּימוּן בְּאַתְרַיְיהוּ, וְלֶהֱווֹ יְסוֹדִין כְּקַדְמֵיתָא, וִיסוֹדֵי סַפִּירִין יִתְקַיְּימוּן בְּאַתָר אַחֲרָא סַחֲרָנָא, לְפוּתְיָא וּלְאַרְכָּא, הה״ד וִיסַדְתִּיךְ בַּסַּפִּירִים.

384. Come and see: All that was concealed to the eye, and that the eye had no permission to rule, NAMELY, WHEN THE LEFT IS WITHOUT THE RIGHT, the eye cannot control, except when kohl is APPLIED to the eye, NAMELY ANTIMONY. Then it may see certain things. That is why it is written, "Behold, I will set your stones in antimony" (Yeshayah 54:11). Come and see: All these stones, BEFORE THEY WERE MENDED, will be erected as foundations as before. And the sapphire foundations will stand around them. This is the meaning of "and lay your foundations with sapphires."

385. בְּזִמְנָא דְיוּקִים קוּדְשָׁא בְּרִיךְ הוּא לְבֵיתֵיהּ, בְּהַהוּא זִמְנָא מַה כְּתִיב, בִּלַּע הַמָּוֶת לָנֶצַח. בִּלַּע, כִּדְאָמְרִינָן בִּלַּע יְיָ׳ וְלֹא חָמַל, הַהוּא כּוֹס דְשָׁתָה הַאי, יִשְׁתֶּה הַאי.

385. When the Holy One, blessed be He will erect His house, MALCHUT, then, it is written, "He will destroy (also: 'swallow') death forever" (Yeshayah 25:8), swallow as in "Hashem has swallowed up without pity" (Eichah 2:2). As he drank of this cup, so he will drink of that. AS THE ANGEL OF DEATH SWALLOWED THE INHABITANTS OF THE WORLD, SO HE WILL BE SWALLOWED HIMSELF.

386. וְאִי תֵּימָא, הַהוּא בִּלַּע אִיהוּ לִזְמַן יְדִיעָא וְקָצִיב בְּיִשְׂרָאֵל, לָאו

הָכִי. כְּתִיב לָנֶצַח, מַאי לָנֶצַח. לְדָרֵי דָּרִין. וְלָאו כְּיִשְׂרָאֵל, וְלָאו כְּהַהוּא זִמְנָא דְּאוֹקִים מֹשֶׁה יַת מַשְׁכְּנָא. אֶלָּא לָנֶצַח לְעָלְמִין.

386. You may say that He swallowed him for a fixed time as Yisrael, WHO WERE IN EXILE FOR A FIXED PERIOD. This is not so, because it is written "forever." Forever is for all generations, unlike Yisrael and unlike that time that Moses erected the Tabernacle, FOR A FIXED PERIOD, but forever and ever.

387. וּכְדֵין קוּדְשָׁא בְּרִיךְ הוּא יוֹקִים לָהּ לִכְנֶסֶת יִשְׂרָאֵל, וְאִיהוּ יוֹקִים סַמְכִין, וְסִיפֵי, וְכָל אִינּוּן תִּקְרֵי בֵּיתָא, בְּתִקּוּנוֹי, לְעָלַם וּלְעָלְמֵי עָלְמַיָּא. וּכְתִיב הַרְחִיבִי מְקוֹם אָהֳלֵךְ וְגוֹ', בְּגִין דְּיִתְבְּלַע סִטְרָא אַחֲרָא, וְלָא יְקוּם לְעָלְמִין וּכְדֵין, וְחֶרְפַּת עַמּוֹ יָסִיר מֵעַל כָּל הָאָרֶץ כִּי יְיָ' דִּבֵּר.

387. Then the Holy One, blessed be He will raise the Congregation of Yisrael, WHICH IS MALCHUT, and set the sockets, the beams and the ceilings of the house in their proper settings forever and ever and ever. It is written, "Enlarge the place of your tent..." (Yeshayah 54:2), so that the Other Side will be swallowed never to rise again. Then "the insult of His people shall He take away from off all the earth, for Hashem has spoken it" (Yeshayah 25:8).

388. וַיָּקֶם מֹשֶׁה אֶת הַמִּשְׁכָּן, בְּהַהוּא זִמְנָא דְּאִלֵּין סַמְכִין אִתְּקָמוּ, וְאִתְיְיהִיבוּ בְּאַתְרַיְיהוּ, הַהוּא זִמְנָא אִתְרְפוּ וְאִתְעֲבָרוּ מֵאַתְרַיְיהוּ סַמְכִין בַּאֲתָר סִטְר אַחֲרָא, וְעַל דָּא, וַיִּתֵּן אֶת אֲדָנָיו.

388. "And Moses erected the Tabernacle." At the time when the sockets were made and put in their place, the sockets of the Other Side were loosened and removed from their place. Hence it is written, "and fastened its sockets."

389. מַאי וַיִּתֵּן. אֶלָּא אוֹלִיפְנָא, דְּחָמָא מֹשֶׁה לְקַמֵּיהּ לְסָמָא"ל חַיָּיבָא, דַּהֲוָה אָזִיל לְגַבֵּיהּ לְקַטְרְגָא לֵיהּ, וּכְדֵין אַתְקִיף בֵּיהּ מֹשֶׁה, וְקָשִׁיר לֵיהּ קַמֵּיהּ, וְאוֹקִים לֵיהּ לְמַשְׁכְּנָא, וְיָהַב לְסַמְכוֹי. דִּכְתִּיב וַיִּתֵּן אֶת אֲדָנָיו.

וְיִתֵּן: בִּתְקִיפוּ, דְּלָא יָכִיל ב״נ אַחֲרָא לְשַׁלְטָאָה עָלֵיהּ, וּלְמֵיהַב סַמְכִין בְּאַתְרַיְיהוּ, כְּמֹשֶׁה. דְּהָא בִּתְקִיפוּ רַב, אוֹקִים לֵיהּ מֹשֶׁה.

389. HE ASKS: What is the meaning of "fastened" IN "AND FASTENED ITS SOCKETS" (SHEMOT 40:18)? AND HE ANSWERS: We learned that when Moses saw the evil Samael before him, coming to accuse him, Moses attacked him and bound him, then erected the Tabernacle and fastened the sockets, as it is written, "and fastened its sockets." "Fastened" with force, for no one was able to rule over SAMAEL and fasten the sockets in their place like Moses, because he used great force to erect them.

390. בְּהַהוּא יוֹמָא דְּאִתְּקַם מַשְׁכְּנָא, כַּד שָׁארֵי מֹשֶׁה לְאַקָּמָא לֵיהּ, בְּחַד בְּנִיסָן הֲוָה, וּבְהַהוּא זִמְנָא, תְּקִיפוּ דסט״א הֲוָה בְּעָלְמָא, דְּהָא בְּיוֹמֵי דְּנִיסָן, רֵישׁ תּוֹרָא בְּדִיקוּלָא. תָּנֵינָן. וּבְנִיסָן שָׁארֵי מֹשֶׁה, וְחָמָא לֵיהּ לְסָמָאֵ״ל, אָזִיל סַחֲרָנֵיהּ, לְעַרְבְּבָא לֵיהּ, וְאִתְגַּבַּר עָלֵיהּ מֹשֶׁה, וּכְדֵין, וַיִּתֵּן אֶת אֲדָנָיו. שָׁארֵי הוּא וְיָהַב לְתַתָּא, וְשָׁארֵי מַאן דְּשָׁארֵי וְיָהַב לְעֵילָא דָּא לָקֳבֵל דָּא.

390. The day the Tabernacle was erected, when Moses started to erect it, was the first day of Nissan. At that time, the Other Side is loose in the world. For we learned that in the days of Nissan, THOUGH the head of a bull is in its fodder basket, RUN UP TO THE ATTIC, AND DROP THE LADDER DOWN, SO IT WILL NOT FOLLOW TO HARM YOU. Moses started TO ERECT THE TABERNACLE in Nissan, and saw Samael walking around him to confuse him. So Moses overpowered him, and then "fastened its sockets." He started below to fasten the sockets, and one started it, NAMELY THE HOLY ONE, BLESSED BE HE, to fasten the sockets above. The one corresponds to the other.

391. בְּיוֹמָא דְּאִתְּקַם הַאי מַשְׁכְּנָא לְתַתָּא, אִתְּקַם מַשְׁכְּנָא אַחֲרָא קַדִּישָׁא לְעֵילָא, וּמַשְׁכְּנָא עִלָּאָה טָמִיר וְגָנִיז, אַפִּיק נְהוֹרִין לְכָל סְטָר, וְאִתְנְהָרוּן עָלְמִין.

391. On the day the Tabernacle was erected below, another holy Tabernacle was erected above, WHICH IS MALCHUT, and the upper Tabernacle, hidden and concealed, WHICH IS BINAH, emitted lights in every direction, and the worlds illuminated.

392. רִבִּי יוֹסֵי שָׁאִיל לְרִבִּי שִׁמְעוֹן, א״ל, תְּלַת מַשְׁכְּנִין חָמֵינָן בִּקְרָא, דִּכְתִּיב וּבְיוֹם הָקִים אֶת הַמִּשְׁכָּן, כִּסָּה הֶעָנָן אֶת הַמִּשְׁכָּן לְאֹהֶל הָעֵדוּת, וּבָעֶרֶב יִהְיֶה עַל הַמִּשְׁכָּן כְּמַרְאֵה אֵשׁ עַד בֹּקֶר, הָא תְּלַת מַשְׁכְּנִין הָכָא. וַאֲמַאי מַשְׁכְּנָא, וְלָא בַּיִת, דְּהָא בַּיִת אִצְטְרִיךְ וְלָא מִשְׁכָּן.

392. Rabbi Yosi asked Rabbi Shimon, saying: Three Tabernacles are mentioned in the verse, "And on the day that the Tabernacle was erected the cloud covered the Tabernacle, even the tent of the Testimony, and at evening there was upon the Tabernacle as it were the appearance of fire, until the morning" (Bemidbar 9:15). Altogether there is mention of three Tabernacles. ALSO, why is it called 'a Tabernacle' and not 'a house'? For a house is needed rather than a Tabernacle.

393. פָּתַח וְאָמַר, כֹּה אָמַר יְיָ׳ הַשָּׁמַיִם כִּסְאִי וְגוֹ׳. תָּא חֲזֵי, קוּדְשָׁא בְּרִיךְ הוּא אִתְרְעֵי בְּהוּ בְּיִשְׂרָאֵל לְאַחֲסַנְתֵּיהּ וְעַדְבֵיהּ, וְקָרִיב לוֹן לְגַבֵּיהּ. וְהָא אוֹקִימְנָא דְּעָבַד מִנַּיְיהוּ דַּרְגִּין יְדִיעָן בְּהַאי עָלְמָא, כְּגַוְונָא דִּלְעֵילָּא, לְשַׁכְלְלָא עָלְמִין כֻּלְּהוּ כְּחַד, עֵילָּא וְתַתָּא. דִּכְתִּיב הַשָּׁמַיִם כִּסְאִי וְהָאָרֶץ הֲדוֹם רַגְלָי לְשַׁכְלְלָא עֵילָּא וְתַתָּא לְמֶהֱוֵי חַד.

393. He opened the discussion and said: "Thus says Hashem, 'The heaven is My throne…'" (Yeshayah 66:1). Come and see: The Holy One, blessed be He chose Yisrael as His inheritance and portion, and brought them near Him. We established that He formed from them certain grades, NAMELY, THE PATRIARCHS…reflecting those above, so as to make of all the worlds one unity, above and below, as it is written, "the heaven is My throne, and the earth is My footstool" (Ibid.) so the high and low would form one unity.

394. ת״ח, הַשָּׁמַיִם כִּסְאִי, דָּא רְקִיעָא דְּיַעֲקֹב שַׁרְיָא בֵּיהּ, דְּאִיהוּ דְּיוּקְנָא עִלָּאָה, לְכוּרְסְיָיא עִלָּאָה קַדִּישָׁא. וְהָאָרֶץ הֲדוֹם רַגְלָי, דָּא

רְקִיעָא דְּדָוִד מַלְכָּא שַׁרְיָא בֵּיהּ, לְאִתְהֲנָאָה מִזִּיוָא דְּאַסְפַּקְלַרְיָא דְּנַהֲרָא. וּבְגִין דְּבָעֵי לְאִתְפַּשְּׁטָא יַתִּיר לְתַתָּא אָמַר הֲדוֹם רַגְלָי. אֵיזֶה בַּיִת אֲשֶׁר תִּבְנוּ לִי, דָּא בִּנְיַן בֵּית מַקְדְּשָׁא. וְאֵיזֶה מָקוֹם מְנוּחָתִי, דָּא בֵּית קֹדֶשׁ הַקֳּדָשִׁים דִּלְתַתָּא.

394. Come and see: "the heaven is My throne" is the firmament where Jacob dwells, who is the supernal image of the supernal holy throne, NAMELY, CHESED, GVURAH AND TIFERET OF ZEIR ANPIN. "and the earth is My footstool," is the firmament where King David dwells, MALCHUT, to derive pleasure from the shining mirror, ZEIR ANPIN. And when He wanted to expand further down, FROM THE SUPERNAL THRONE, He said: "My footstool," WHICH IS MALCHUT. "the house that you would build for Me?" (Ibid.) is the Temple, "and where is the place of My rest?" (Ibid.) is the Holy of Holies in the lower Temple.

395. אֲבָל תָּא חֲזֵי, כָּל זִמְנָא דְּאָזְלוּ יִשְׂרָאֵל בְּמַדְבְּרָא, הֲוָה לְהוּ מִשְׁכָּן, עַד דְּאָתוּ לְשִׁילֹה, וַהֲוָה תַּמָּן. וְדָא אִיהוּ רָזָא, לְאַמְשָׁכָא דָּא בְּדָא, וּלְאַעֲלָא דָּא בְּדָא, לְאִתְקַשְּׁרָא דָּא בְּדָא, בְּגִין לְאַנְהָרָא. אֲבָל לָאו לְנַיְיחָא. דְּהָא לָאו נַיְיחָא, בַּר כַּד אִתְבְּנֵי בֵּי מַקְדְּשָׁא, בְּיוֹמוֹי דִּשְׁלֹמֹה מַלְכָּא, דְּהָא כְּדֵין אִיהוּ מְנוּחָה לְעֵילָּא וְתַתָּא. בְּגִין דְּתַמָּן תְּקִיפוּ דְּנַיְיחָא, וְלָא לְנַטְלָא מֵאֲתַר לַאֲתַר.

395. Yet Come and see: As long as Yisrael walked through the desert, they had a Tabernacle, until they reached Shiloh where there was A TABERNACLE already. And THIS TABERNACLE is the secret of continuation one from the other, unity between one and the other so as to spread light. But it was not meant for a resting place, because there was no rest, only when the Temple was built in the days of King Solomon. Then there is rest above and below, because rest stays there and does not travel from place to place LIKE THE TABERNACLE.

396. וּבְגִין כָּךְ אִית מִשְׁכָּן, וְאִית בַּיִת. מִשְׁכָּן: כְּמָה דְּאַתְּ אָמֵר, וְנָתַתִּי מִשְׁכָּנִי בְּתוֹכְכֶם וְלֹא תִגְעַל נַפְשִׁי אֶתְכֶם. מַאי מִשְׁכָּנִי. מִשְׁכְּנוֹתָיו

דְּקוּדְשָׁא בְּרִיךְ הוּא, דִּלְהֱווֹן גַּבַּיְיהוּ דְּיִשְׂרָאֵל. מַאי טַעֲמָא. בְּגִין דִּכְתִּיב וְלֹא תִגְעַל נַפְשִׁי אֶתְכֶם.

396. Therefore, there is a Tabernacle and a Temple, a Tabernacle, as in "and I will set My Tabernacle among you; and My soul shall not abhor you" (Vayikra 26:11). "My Tabernacle" means that the dwelling of the Holy One, blessed be He will be among Yisrael, because it is written, "and My soul shall not abhor you." FOR THE ILLUMINATION IS NOT SO STRONG, SINCE IT IS QUALIFIED BY "MY SOUL SHALL NOT ABHOR YOU."

397. מַה בֵּין הַאי לְהַאי. אֶלָּא מִשְׁכָּן, כְּמַלְכָּא דְּאָתֵי לְגַבֵּי רְחִימֵיהּ, וְלָא מַיְיתֵי כָּל אֻכְלוּסִין דִּילֵיהּ עִמֵּיהּ, בְּגִין דְּלָא לְאַטְרְחָא עָלֵיהּ, אִיהוּ אָתֵי לְגַבֵּיהּ בִּזְעֵיר חֵילִין. בַּיִת: דְּכָל חֵילִין וְכָל אֻכְלוּסִין דִּילֵיהּ, כֻּלְּהוּ אַיְיתֵי עִמֵּיהּ, לְדַיְּירָא בְּהַהוּא בֵּיתָא, וְדָא אִיהוּ בֵּין מִשְׁכָּן וּבֵין בַּיִת. בֵּית הַמִּקְדָּשׁ, אִיהוּ דִּיוּרָא דְּנַיְיחָא לְעָלְמִין, בְּכָל אִינּוּן רְתִיכִין, בְּכָל אִינּוּן דִּיוּקְנִין, בְּכָל אִינּוּן עוֹבָדִין, כְּגַוְונָא דִּלְעֵילָּא. לְחַבְרָא עוֹבָדִין דִּלְתַתָּא, כְּגַוְונָא דִּלְעֵילָּא. מִשְׁכָּן, בִּזְעֵיר דִּיוּקְנִין, בִּזְעִירִין עוֹבָדִין, לְנַטְלָא מֵאֲתָר לַאֲתָר, וְכֹלָּא בְּרָזָא דִּלְעֵילָּא.

397. HE ASKS: What is the difference between them, BETWEEN A TABERNACLE AND A TEMPLE? AND HE ANSWERS: In regard to the Tabernacle, IT IS AS IF a king comes to his friend without all his retinue, but in order not to trouble his friend, he brings with him only a small escort. In regard to a Temple, it is as if he brought all his army and retinue to live with him in that house. This is THE DIFFERENCE between a Tabernacle and a house. For a Temple house is an apartment for eternal resting place, with all the Chariots, with all images, all the deeds as above, so that deeds below may be connected as those above. A Tabernacle deals in small forms, few deeds, it travels from place to place. All is in supernal secret.

398. תָּא חֲזֵי, כַּד פָּקִיד קוּדְשָׁא בְּרִיךְ הוּא לְמֹשֶׁה עַל מַשְׁכְּנָא, לָא הֲוָה יָכִיל לְמֵיקַם בֵּיהּ, עַד דְּקוּדְשָׁא בְּרִיךְ הוּא אַחְמֵי לֵיהּ כֹּלָּא בְּדִיוּקְנֵיהּ, כָּל מִלָּה וּמִלָּה. בְּמָה אַחֲזֵי לֵיהּ. בְּאֶשָּׁא חִוָּורָא, וּבְאֶשָּׁא אוּכָמָא,

וּבְאֶשָּׁא סוּמָקָא, וּבְאֶשָּׁא יְרוֹקָא. מַה כְּתִיב, וּרְאֵה וַעֲשֵׂה כְּתַבְנִיתָם אֲשֶׁר אַתָּה מָרְאֶה בָּהָר. עִם כָּל דָּא אַקְשֵׁי לֵיהּ לְמֹשֶׁה.

398. Come and see: When the Holy One, blessed be He commanded Moses to erect the Tabernacle, he could not grasp it, until the Holy One, blessed be He showed him the shape of each and every thing. By what means did He show him? Namely, by a white fire, a black fire, a red fire, and a green fire, CORRESPONDING TO CHESED, GVURAH, TIFERET AND MALCHUT. It is written, "And see that you make them after their pattern, which is being shown to you in the mountain" (Shemot 25:40). With all that, it was difficult for Moses TO GRASP THEM.

399. תָּא חֲזֵי, אַף עַל גַּב דְּאַחְזֵי לֵיהּ עֵינָא בְּעֵינָא לָא בָּעָא מֹשֶׁה לְמֶעְבַּד. וְאִי תֵּימָא דְּאִיהוּ לָא יָדַע לְמֶעְבַּד, אוֹ חָכְמְתָא לָא הֲוָה עִמֵּיהּ. תָּא חֲזֵי, בְּצַלְאֵל וְאָהֳלִיאָב, וְכָל אִינּוּן שְׁאַר אַחֲרָנִין, אַף עַל גַּב דְּלָא חָמוּ כְּמֹשֶׁה, מַה כְּתִיב, וַיַּרְא מֹשֶׁה אֶת כָּל הַמְּלָאכָה וְהִנֵּה עָשׂוּ אוֹתָהּ וְגוֹ׳, אִי אִינּוּן דְּלָא חָמוּ, עָבְדוּ כַּךְ. מֹשֶׁה דְּחָמָא, עַל אַחַת כַּמָּה וְכַמָּה. אֶלָּא מֹשֶׁה, אַף עַל גַּב דְּאִסְתַּלַּק מִן מַשְׁכְּנָא מֵעֲבִידְתָּא, כֹּלָּא הֲוָה בִּידֵיהּ, וְעַל יְדֵיהּ, וְאִיהוּ אִקְרֵי עַל שְׁמֵיהּ, וע״ד כְּתִיב וּרְאֵה וַעֲשֵׂה.

399. Come and see: Though He showed him eye to eye, Moses did not want to do them. And if you say that he did not know how to do or did not have the skill, come and see: Betzalel, Aholiav and all the others, though they did not see THE SHAPES as Moses did, it is written, "and Moses saw all the work, and, behold, they had done it..." (Shemot 39:43). If those who did not see THE SHAPES, nevertheless did it, Moses, who saw ALL THE SHAPES ON THE MOUNTAIN, how more so WAS HE ABLE TO MAKE THEM. HE ANSWERS: Moses, though he retired from the construction of the Tabernacle, everything was under his supervision, and under him ALL WAS DONE. It was named after him, and therefore it is written, "and see that you make" (Shemot 25:40).

400. ד״א, מֹשֶׁה אִסְתַּלַּק מִן דָּא, וְיָהִיב דוּכְתֵּיהּ לְאַחֲרָא, עַד דְּאָמַר

לֵיהּ קוּדְשָׁא בְּרִיךְ הוּא רְאֵה קָרָאתִי בְשֵׁם בְּצַלְאֵל, וְאִתּוֹ אָהֳלִיאָב. וּכְתִיב וְעָשָׂה בְצַלְאֵל וְאָהֳלִיאָב וְכֹל אִישׁ חֲכַם לֵב. אִי יְקָרָא דָּא, הֲוָה דְּמֹשֶׁה, דְּאִיהוּ יַעְבִּיד לֵיהּ, יִתְקַיָּים בֵּיהּ תָּדִיר.

400. Another explanation: Moses withdrew FROM THE CONSTRUCTION OF THE TABERNACLE, and gave his place to another, BECAUSE HE WANTED OTHERS TO HAVE THE MERIT. So the Holy One, blessed be He told him, "See, I have called by name Betzalel...with him Aholiav" (Shemot 31:2). And it is written, "And Betzalel and Aholiav, and every wisehearted man" (Ibid. 36:1). And if that honor was reserved for Moses, that he will make THE TABERNACLE, AS IT IS WRITTEN, "AND SEE THAT YOU MAKE," it will be forever his. WHY THEN DID THE HOLY ONE, BLESSED BE HE ORDER, "AND BETZALEL AND AHOLIAV...DID"? BECAUSE FROM THIS WE UNDERSTAND AND MOSES HIMSELF WITHDREW FROM THE WORK TO GIVE MERIT TO OTHERS.

401. וְעִם כָּל דָּא, כֵּיוָן דְּאִיהוּ פָּקִיד, וּבְפִקּוּדֵיהּ יִתְעֲבִיד, אִיהוּ עָבֵיד כֹּלָּא. תּוּ, כָּל עֲבִידְתָּא לָא קַיְימָא, אֶלָּא בְּסִיּוּמָא דְּעוֹבָדָא, וְעַל דָּא, וַיָּקֶם מֹשֶׁה אֶת הַמִּשְׁכָּן. בָּעוּ לְאַקָּמָא לֵיהּ כָּל אִינּוּן חַכִּימֵי לִבָּא, וְלָא הֲוָה מִתְקַיֵּים, בְּגִין יְקָרֵיהּ דְּמֹשֶׁה, עַד דְּאָתָא מֹשֶׁה, וְאוֹקִים לֵיהּ. וְהָא אוּקְמוּהָ.

401. With all that, since he ordered, and all was done by his command, IT IS CONSIDERED as if he had done it all. Also, all the work is done, only when it is finished, AND NAMED AFTER WHOEVER FINISHED IT. Therefore, "Moses erected the Tabernacle." When the wisehearted men wanted to erect it, it did not stand, because of the honor of Moses, until Moses came and erected it. SINCE HE FINISHED THE WORK, IT IS CALLED AFTER HIM. This was explained.

41. “when I fall, I shall arise”

A Synopsis

Rabbi Yehuda begins with the verse: “Rejoice not against me, O my enemy: when I fall, I shall arise...” He says that this means the evil kingdom of the Other Side will not rise again, unlike the Congregation of Yisrael that will always rise again. Even though the other nations of the world have tried to exterminate Yisrael so many times, God always raised them up again. When Moses brought them out of Egypt God did many miracles to help them, and after that Moses erected the Tabernacle.

402. וַיָּקֶם מֹשֶׁה אֶת הַמִּשְׁכָּן רִבִּי יְהוּדָה פָּתַח, אַל תִּשְׂמְחִי אוֹיַבְתִּי לִי כִּי נָפַלְתִּי קָמְתִּי וְגוֹ׳. מַאן אוֹיַבְתִּי לִי. דְּבָבוּ דְּמַלְכוּ חַיָּיבָא בְּמַלְכוּת קַדִּישָׁא. וְהַאי קְרָא כְּנֶסֶת יִשְׂרָאֵל אָמַר לֵיהּ, אַל תִּשְׂמְחִי אוֹיַבְתִּי לִי כִּי נָפַלְתִּי קָמְתִּי, מַה דְּלֵית לָךְ הָכִי לְמַלְכוּ אַחֲרָא, דְּכֵיוָן דְּתִפּוֹל לָא תָּקוּם לְעָלְמִין. אֲבָל כְּנֶסֶת יִשְׂרָאֵל, אַף עַל גַּב דְּנַפְלַת, תָּקוּם וְקָמַת שְׁאַר זִמְנִין. דִּכְתִּיב כִּי נָפַלְתִּי קָמְתִּי.

402. “And Moses erected the Tabernacle” (Shemot 40:18). Rabbi Yehuda opened the discussion with the verse: “Rejoice not against me, O my enemy: when I fall, I shall arise…” (Michah 7:8). “My enemy” refers to the evil kingdom, the enemy of the holy kingdom. This verse is said by the Congregation of Yisrael, THE HOLY KINGDOM. “Rejoice not against me, O my enemy: when I fall, I shall arise,” not so the other, EVIL kingdom. Once it falls, it will never rise again. But the Congregation of Yisrael, though she fell, she rises, and has risen many times, as it is written, “when I fall, I shall arise.”

403. דְּהָא כַּמָּה זִמְנִין נַפְלַת כְּנֶסֶת יִשְׂרָאֵל בְּגָלוּתָא, וְיָתְבָא בֵּין אִינּוּן מָארֵי דְּבָבוּ, וּשְׁאַר עַמִּין קָמוּ עֲלַיְיהוּ דְּיִשְׂרָאֵל לְשֵׁיצָאָה לוֹן מֵעָלְמָא, כד״א, עַל עַמְּךָ יַעֲרִימוּ סוֹד, וּכְתִיב כִּי נוֹעֲצוּ לֵב יַחְדָּיו וְגוֹ׳, אָמְרוּ לְכוּ וְנַכְחִידֵם מִגּוֹי. וְעִם כָּל דָּא, אַף עַל גַּב דִּשְׁאַר עַמִּין קָמוּ עֲלַיְיהוּ, קוּדְשָׁא בְּרִיךְ הוּא לָא אֲנָח לוֹן בִּידַיְיהוּ, וְאִי נָפְלוּ קָמוּ, דִּכְתִּיב כִּי נָפַלְתִּי קָמְתִּי. דְּהָא קוּדְשָׁא בְּרִיךְ הוּא אָקִים לָהּ תָּדִיר.

403. How many times did the Congregation of Yisrael fall into exile, and sat in the midst of all these enemies. And the rest of the nations and idolaters, rose against Yisrael to exterminate them, as it is said, "They hold crafty converse against your people… For they have consulted together with one consent… They have said, 'Come, and let us cut them off from being a nation'" (Tehilim 83:4-6). With all that, and though the rest of the nations rose against them, the Holy One, blessed be He did not leave them in their hands, and if they fell, they arose, as it is written, "when I fall, I shall arise," as the Holy One, blessed be He always raises her.

404. וּזְמִינָא כְּנֶסֶת יִשְׂרָאֵל, לוֹמַר בְּהַהוּא זִמְנָא דְקוּדְשָׁא בְּרִיךְ הוּא יוֹקִים לָהּ מֵעַפְרָא דְּגָלוּתָא, וְתִסְתָּלַק מִנֵּיהּ, אַל תִּשְׂמְחִי אוֹיַבְתִּי לִי כִּי נָפַלְתִּי קָמְתִּי. כִּי נָפַלְתִּי בְּגָלוּתָא, וְאִשְׁתַּעְבְּדוּ בָּנַי, קָמְתִּי בְּהַאי זִמְנָא. וּבְגִין כַּךְ, בְּהַהוּא זִמְנָא דְּאַפִּיק מֹשֶׁה לוֹן לְיִשְׂרָאֵל, כַּד עָבֵד לוֹן קוּדְשָׁא בְּרִיךְ הוּא אִינּוּן נִסִּין וּגְבוּרָאן דְּעָבֵד לוֹן. כְּדֵין וַיָּקֶם מֹשֶׁה אֶת הַמִּשְׁכָּן כְּתִיב, דְּהָא עַל יְדָא דְּמֹשֶׁה אִתְקַם בְּכָל זִמְנָא.

404. And when the Holy One, blessed be He will raise her from the dust of exile, the Congregation of Yisrael, MALCHUT, will say, "Rejoice not against me, O my enemy: when I fall, I shall arise;" because "I fall" into exile, and my children became slaves, "I shall arise," now. For at the time when Moses brought Yisrael out OF EGYPT, and when the Holy One, blessed be He performed miracles and mighty deeds, then, it is written, "Moses erected the Tabernacle." Because through the hands of Moses, THE SECRET OF ZEIR ANPIN, the Tabernacle was erected, WHICH IS MALCHUT, each time.

42. “When those moved, these moved”

A Synopsis

Rabbi Shimon explores the verse: “When those moved, these moved, and when those stood still, these stood still.” He tells us that the living creatures move, and when they move the wheels move, the turnings of the wheels depend on the movement of the living creatures. The living creatures and the wheels move together. Rabbi Shimon turns to the 24 watches who guard the gates and who are hidden in the intensity of the flame surrounding the threshold. There are 24 thresholds and 24 sockets. These watches or guards of Zeir Anpin fly all over the world, watching things and listening to sounds and raising words up higher. Rabbi Shimon returns to the wheels moving and says “For the spirit of the living creature was in the wheels” meaning that the Holy Spirit, Malchut, makes the wheels move. He explains that ‘living creature’ means four living creatures, corresponding to Chesed, Gvurah, Tiferet and Malchut. They turn to the four directions of the world. He mentions the throne for the likeness of a man to sit on, and says the throne is Zeir Anpin. The higher throne has the image of Jacob, who is Zeir Anpin, while the lower throne has the image of David, who is Malchut. We learn that a spirit emerges from Binah above and flows down to the lower worlds where it has power over everything. Rabbi Shimon concludes by saying that in the same way Moses became a spirit in relation to the Tabernacle for the purpose of correcting everything below.

405. רִבִּי שִׁמְעוֹן פָּתַח וְאָמַר, בְּלֶכְתָּם יֵלֵכוּ וְגוֹ'. בְּלֶכְתָּם יֵלֵכוּ וּבְעָמְדָם יַעֲמֹדוּ. הַאי קְרָא אִית לְאִסְתַּכְּלָא בֵּיהּ. בְּלֶכְתָּם יֵלֵכוּ, וְכִי לָא יְדַעְנָא דְּהָא בְּלֶכְתָּם יֵלֵכוּ, וּבְעָמְדָם יַעֲמֹדוּ. אֶלָּא בְּלֶכְתָּם דְּמַאן. בְּלֶכְתָּם דְּחַיּוֹת. דְּכַד אִינּוּן אַזְלִין, אִינּוּן אוֹפַנִּים יֵלֵכוּ. כד"א וּבְלֶכֶת הַחַיּוֹת יֵלְכוּ הָאוֹפַנִּים אֶצְלָם. וע"ד בְּלֶכְתָּם יֵלֵכוּ וּבְעָמְדָם יַעֲמֹדוּ, בְּגִין דְּכָל מַטַּלְנֵיהוֹן דְּאִינּוּן אוֹפַנִּים, לָאו אִינּוּן אֶלָּא בְּמַטְלָנִין דְּחַיּוֹת, וְקִיּוּמָא דִילְהוֹן לָא קַיְימֵי בְּאַתְרַיְיהוּ, אֶלָּא כֹּלָּא תַּלְיָא בַּחַיּוֹת. וְכֵן כְּתִיב וּבְהִנָּשֵׂא הַחַיּוֹת מֵעַל הָאָרֶץ יִנָּשְׂאוּ הָאוֹפַנִּים לְעֻמָּתָם בְּגִין דְּחַיּוֹת וְאוֹפַנִּים כַּחֲדָא אַזְלִין.

405. Rabbi Shimon opened the discussion and said: “When those moved, these moved, and when those stood still, these stood still" (Yechezkel 1:21). We have to look at this verse: "When those moved, these moved." Now, do I not know that when those move, these move, and when those stand still, these stand still? HE ANSWERS: Who moves? The living creatures move, and when they move, the wheels move, as it is written, "and when the living creatures moved, the wheels went by them" (Ibid. 19). Therefore, "When those moved, these moved, and when those stood still, these stood still," for all the goings of the wheels depend upon the going of the living creatures. They do not exist INDEPENDENTLY on their own, but depend upon the living creatures. It is further written, "and when the living creatures were lifted up from the earth, the wheels were lifted up...along with them" (Ibid.), because the living creatures and the wheels move together.

406. ות״ח, עֶשְׂרִין וְאַרְבַּע מַשְׁקוֹפִין, דְּמַטְרָנִין עִלָּאִין קַיְימִין גּוֹ מַשְׁקוֹפָא חֲדָא דִּבְסִטַר מִזְרָח. לְהַאי פִּתְחָא, נַטְרִין אַרְבַּע וְעֶשְׂרִין מִשְׁמָרוֹת, טְמִירִין גּוֹ תּוּקְפָּא דְּשַׁלְהוֹבָא, דְּעַטְרָא וְסַחֲרָא לְגוֹ הַהוּא מַשְׁקוֹפָא מֵהַהוּא סִטְרָא דְּמִזְרָח.

406. Come and see: There are 24 thresholds, THE OPEN SPACES WITHIN THE DOOR PANES, of the supernal watches, within the one opening on the east side. Twenty-four watches stand guarding at that gate, hidden within the intensity of the flame surrounding that threshold on the east side.

407. וְאַרְבַּע וְעֶשְׂרִין סַמְכִין תְּחוֹתַיְיהוּ, וְעַל אִלֵּין סַמְכִין קַיְימִין עֶשְׂרִין וְאַרְבַּע עַמּוּדִין, וְאִלֵּין אִינּוּן דְּקַיְימִין תָּדִיר, וְלָא פַּרְחִין גּוֹ אֲוִירָא כְּאִינּוּן אַחֲרָנִין, וְאִלֵּין אִינּוּן דְּאִקְרוּן עוֹמְדִים, כד״א, וְנָתַתִּי לְךָ מַהְלְכִים בֵּין הָעוֹמְדִים הָאֵלֶּה. וְאִלֵּין עַמּוּדִים, קַיְימִין עַל אִינּוּן סַמְכִין, בְּהוּ סָחֲרָן לְאִתְקַיְּימָא בְּדוּכְתַּיְיהוּ.

407. There are 24 sockets beneath them, and upon the sockets 24 pillars. These always stand, and do not soar in the air like the others. They are called "standing ones," according to the verse, "I will give you access among these who stand by" (Zecharyah 3:7). The pillars stand upon the sockets, and turn in them, so they may remain in their places.

408. כַּד אִלֵּין עַמּוּדִים קַיְימִין עַל קִיוּמַיְיהוּ, כֻּלְּהוּ שַׁלִּיטִין דְּקַיְימִין עֲלַיְיהוּ, מְעַפְּפֵי וְטָסִין כָּל עָלְמָא, וְאַשְׁגְּחָן עַיְינִין. וְאִינּוּן דְּצַיְיתֵי קָלִין, סַלְּקִין מִלִּין לְעֵילָּא, כְּמָה דְּאַתְּ אָמֵר כִּי עוֹף הַשָּׁמַיִם יוֹלִיךְ אֶת הַקּוֹל. וּבְגִין כָּךְ, אִינּוּן סַמְכִין קַיְימִין בְּקִיּוּמָא תָּדִיר.

408. When these pillars stand firm, all the rulers standing above them, NAMELY, THE SAID GUARDS OF ZEIR ANPIN, soar and fly over the world, surveying with their eyes. Those who listen to sound, raise words above, as it is written, "for a bird of the sky shall carry the sound" (Kohelet 10:20). Therefore, all these sockets are always firm.

409. תָּא חֲזֵי, בְּלֶכְתָּם יֵלֵכוּ כִּדְקָאמְרָן. וּבְהִנָּשְׂאָם מֵעַל הָאָרֶץ יִנָּשְׂאוּ הָאוֹפַנִּים לְעוּמָּתָם. דְּהָא כְּמָה דְּאִלֵּין חַיוֹת נַטְלִין וְסַלְּקִין, הָכִי אִינּוּן. מַאי טַעֲמָא. בְּגִין, כִּי רוּחַ הַחַיָּה בָּאוֹפַנִּים. רוּחַ הַחַיָּה, רוּחַ קוּדְשָׁא, דְּנָשִׁיב וּבָטַשׁ בְּכֻלְּהוּ אוֹפַנִּים, לְמֵהַךְ. אִשְׁתְּכַח, דְּכָל מַאן דְּאִיהוּ בְּדַרְגָּא עִלָּאָה, אִיהוּ נָטִיל לְמַאן דְּנָטִיל לֵיהּ. תָּא חֲזֵי, דְּאָרוֹן אִיהוּ הֲוָה נָטִיל לְמַאן דְּנָטִיל לֵיהּ. אוּף הָכָא, חַיוֹת, אִינּוּן נַטְלִין לָאוֹפַנִּים.

409. Come and see: The meaning of "When those moved, these moved" (Yechezkel 1:17) is as we said, WITH THE MOVEMENT OF THE LIVING CREATURES. "And when the living creatures were lifted up from the earth, the wheels were lifted up…along with them" (Ibid. 19) because as the living creatures move and are lifted up, so do THE WHEELS. Why? "For the spirit of the living creature was in the wheels" (Ibid. 20). The spirit of the living creature is the Holy Spirit, MALCHUT, blowing and striking the wheels to make them move. Thus, whatever is in a higher grade, carries whatever carries it. Come and see: The Ark was carrying whoever carried it. Here also, the living creatures were carrying the wheels.

410. וְאִי תֵּימָא כִּי רוּחַ הַחַיָּה בָּאוֹפַנִּים כְּתִיב. הָכִי נָמֵי, דָּא חַיָּה, דְּאִיהוּ לִסְטַר יְמִינָא, לִסְטַר שְׂמָאלָא, וְלִסְטַר קָמָא, וְלִסְטַר אֲחוֹרָא, וְדָא אִיהִי חַיָּה, וְאִלֵּין אִינּוּן חַיוֹת.

410. You may say, that it is written, "The spirit of the living creature was in the wheels" AND NOT 'THE SPIRIT OF THE LIVING CREATURES.' FROM

WHERE DO WE UNDERSTAND THAT THE LIVING CREATURES CARRY THE WHEELS? HE ANSWERS: It also means that A LIVING CREATURE MEANS FOUR LIVING CREATURES, because it is in the right side, the left side, in front, and at the back. THAT IS, THE FOUR SFIROT CHESED, GVURAH, TIFERET AND MALCHUT OF THE LIVING CREATURE, CORRESPONDING TO RIGHT, LEFT, FRONT AND BACK, ARE CONSIDERED FOUR LIVING CREATURES. Therefore, a living creature and living creatures ARE THE SAME THING.

411. כְּתִיב הִיא הַחַיָּה אֲשֶׁר רָאִיתִי תַּחַת אֱלֹהֵי יִשְׂרָאֵל בִּנְהַר כְּבָר, דָּא הִיא חַיָּה דִּמְרַבַּע לְאַרְבַּע סִטְרִין דְּעָלְמָא. וְדָא אִיהִי דְּקַיְּימָא כּוּרְסְיָיא, לְדִיוּקְנָא דְּאָדָם. כְּמָה דִּכְתִּיב, וְעַל דְּמוּת הַכִּסֵּא דְּמוּת כְּמַרְאֵה אָדָם עָלָיו מִלְמָעְלָה. וְכֹלָּא לְהַהוּא דַּרְגָּא עִלָּאָה קַדִּישָׁא סְתִימָאָה, דְּאִקְרֵי אֱלֹהֵי יִשְׂרָאֵל.

411. It is written, "This is the living creature I saw under the Elohim of Yisrael by the river K'var" (Yechezkel 10:20). This is the fourfold living creature, turning to the four directions, NAMELY CHESED, GVURAH, TIFERET AND MALCHUT AS EXPLAINED BEFORE. There is a throne, MALCHUT, for the likeness of man, NAMELY ZEIR ANPIN, as it is written, "and upon the likeness of the throne was the likeness as the appearance of a man above upon it" (Yechezkel 1:26). And all that is for that high, holy and concealed grade called "the Elohim of Yisrael," WHICH IS BINAH, AS THE VERSE STATES, "THIS IS THE LIVING CREATURE I SAW" (YECHEZKEL 10:20) IS MALCHUT, UPON WHICH RIDES ZEIR ANPIN, THE SECRET OF MAN, AND BOTH "UNDER THE ELOHIM OF YISRAEL" (IBID.), BINAH.

412. וְדָא חַיָּה דִּלְתַתָּא, דְּקַיְּימָא תְּחוֹת כֻּלְּהוּ חֵיוָון עִלָּאִין קַדִּישִׁין. בְּגִין דְּאִית חֵיוָון עִלָּאִין אִלֵּין עַל אִלֵּין. כּוּרְסְיָיא דִּתְחוֹת אֱלֹהֵי יִשְׂרָאֵל, דָּא דִּיוּקְנָא דְּיַעֲקֹב. וְכוּרְסְיָיא דִּלְתַתָּא, דָּא דִּיוּקְנָא דְּדָוִד. אִיהִי דִּמְרַבְּעָא לְאַרְבַּע סִטְרִין דְּעָלְמָא. וּבְגִין כָּךְ רוּחָא נָפִיק מִלְּעֵילָּא, וְנָגִיד וְאִתְמְשַׁךְ מִדַּרְגָּא לְדַרְגָּא, עַד דְּבָטַשׁ בְּכֻלְּהוּ תַּתָּאֵי דִּלְתַתָּא, וְהַהוּא רוּחָא אַנְהִיג לְכֹלָּא, וְאַתְקִין תִּקּוּנָא דְּכֻלְּהוּ לְאַתְקְנָא.

412. THE LIVING CREATURE IN THE VERSE, "THIS IS THE LIVING

CREATURE I SAW" IS the lower living creature, MALCHUT, which stands upon all the supernal holy living creatures, CHESED, GVURAH, TIFERET AND MALCHUT OF ZEIR ANPIN, THE SECRET OF MAN, since there are supernal beasts, the ones over the others, AS ABOVE THOSE LIVING CREATURES OF MALCHUT THERE ARE SUPERNAL LIVING CREATURES OF ZEIR ANPIN. The throne under the Elohim of Yisrael has the image of Jacob, WHO IS ZEIR ANPIN, A THRONE TO BINAH CALLED 'THE ELOHIM OF YISRAEL'. And the lower throne, UNDER ZEIR ANPIN, has the image of David, MALCHUT. It is square to the four sides, and therefore, a spirit emerges from above, FROM BINAH, and goes out, flowing from one grade to another, FROM BINAH TO ZEIR ANPIN, AND FROM ZEIR ANPIN TO MALCHUT, until it strikes the lower beings below, IN BRIYAH, YETZIRAH AND ASIYAH. This spirit has power over everything, and it establishes everything so they will keep.

413. וּבְהַהוּא גַּוְונָא מַמָּשׁ, אִתְתָּקַּן לְתַתָּא. מַה כְּתִיב לְעֵילָּא, כִּי רוּחַ הַחַיָּה בָּאוֹפַנִּים. וּכְתִיב אֶל אֲשֶׁר יִהְיֶה שָׁמָּה הָרוּחַ לָלֶכֶת יֵלְכוּ. לְתַתָּא מַה כְּתִיב, וַיָּקֶם מֹשֶׁה אֶת הַמִּשְׁכָּן. בְּמָה. לְמֶהֱוֵי רוּחַ דְּהַהוּא דַּרְגָּא דִּלְתַתָּא, בְּהַהוּא דְּיוּקְנָא דְּהַהוּא רוּחַ עִלָּאָה, הִיא הַחַיָּה אֲשֶׁר רָאִיתִי תַּחַת אֱלֹהֵי יִשְׂרָאֵל, וּמֵהַאי חַיָּה נָפְקָא רוּחָא לְאַתְקְנָא כֹּלָּא. הָכִי נָמֵי מֹשֶׁה. הִיא הַחַיָּה דְּיָהַב רוּחָא לְתַתָּא, לְאַתְקְנָא כֹּלָּא. בג"כ כְּתִיב, וַיָּקֶם, וַיִּתֵּן, וַיָּשֶׂם. וּבְכֹלָּא שַׁוֵּי רוּחָא, לְאַתְקְנָא כֹּלָּא.

413. In exactly the same manner, things have been fixed below, IN THE TABERNACLE. It is written of above, "For the spirit of the living creature was in the wheels" (Yechezkel 1:20), and "Wherever the spirit was minded to go, they moved" (Ibid.). It is written concerning that which is below, "And Moses erected the Tabernacle." With what DID HE ERECT IT? THAT MEANS, he became a spirit in relation to that level below, THE TABERNACLE, assuming the shape of the Supernal Spirit, OF WHICH IT HAS BEEN SAID, "This is the living creature I saw under the Elohim of Yisrael" (Yechezkel 10:20), as from that living creature a spirit emerges, for the purpose of establishing everything AS MENTIONED. Moses was like that, he is the living creature that produces a spirit below, IN THE TABERNACLE, to fix everything. Therefore it is written, "erected," "And he put," "And he set," as by all of these he put a spirit that would correct everything.

43. The Tabernacle and the Temple

A Synopsis

Rabbi Shimon talks in this section about Moses building the Tabernacle and Solomon building the temple. The Temple was built in the spirit of peace, Yesod, that is rest. The Tabernacle was built in the spirit of love but not that of rest, so the Tabernacle was moved around as the people moved. Moses began his construction by starting in the middle, that was dark, and he raised his first point there. Then that point shone and all the other parts settled into place as they should. Rabbi Shimon adds more information about the sockets, that are connected with 'giving' since they support the boards. When Moses erected the point the Other Side sank but was not altogether destroyed, that will happen only in the future. The side of holiness began to strengthen and then the Other Side entered the hole in the great abyss. If Yisrael had not sinned the Other Side would not have been able to rule the world, but since they did they must always give a portion of the sacrifices to the Other Side. Finally we hear that the erection in the beginning was to weaken the Other Side, but the erection in the end will be the erection of the holy side so it will be elevated higher. Whenever holiness rises up, defilement is lowered.

414. ת"ח, בְּקַדְמֵיתָא, בְּמַשְׁכְּנָא דְּעֲבַד מֹשֶׁה, אִיהוּ אַתְקִין לֵיהּ, בְּרָזָא דְּהַהוּא דַּרְגָּא עִלָּאָה דְּאִיהוּ קַיְּימָא בֵּיהּ. בְּמַקְדְּשָׁא דְּעָבֵד שְׁלֹמֹה, אִיהוּ תַּקִּין לֵיהּ, בְּרָזָא דְּהַהוּא נָהָר דְּנָפִיק מֵעֵדֶן, דְּאִיהוּ שְׁלָמָא דְּבֵיתָא, וְאִיהוּ נַיְיחָא דְּבֵיתָא. וע"ד בְּרָזָא דְּמַשְׁכְּנָא, אִיהוּ קוּרְבָא דַּחֲבִיבוּתָא, בְּרָזָא דְּגוּפָא, הַהוּא דַּרְגָּא דְּמֹשֶׁה, קַיְּימָא בֵּיהּ קוּרְבָא דַּחֲבִיבוּתָא, וְלָאו דְּנַיְיחָא. כַּד אָתָא שְׁלֹמֹה, וְאַתְקִין מַקְדְּשָׁא, הַהוּא מַקְדְּשָׁא אִתְתָּקַן, בְּרָזָא דַּחֲבִיבוּ דְּנַיְיחָא. וע"ד כְּתִיב בִּשְׁלֹמֹה, הוּא יִהְיֶה אִישׁ מְנוּחָה.

414. Come and see: First Moses erected the Tabernacle, and fixed it in the secret of the high grade, where he was, NAMELY, ZEIR ANPIN. Then Solomon built the Temple, and constructed it in the secret of the river going out from Eden, named household peace, NAMELY, YESOD, which is household rest, MALCHUT. Therefore, in the secret of the Tabernacle is the closeness of love, in the secret of the body, TIFERET, MEANING THAT

Moses was of the grade where is closeness of love, but not that of rest; THEREFORE, THE TABERNACLE WAS ALWAYS MOVED BY TRAVELING. When Solomon constructed the Temple, it was built in the secret of the love of rest. Therefore it is written of Solomon, "who shall be a man of tranquillity" (I Divrei Hayamim 22:9).

415. ובג"כ, דָּא אַתְקִין בְּחַד דַּרְגָּא, וְדָא אַתְקִין בְּחַד דַּרְגָּא, דִּיוּקְנָא דְּהַאי בְּהַאי, וְרָזָא דָּא, אֵלֶּה תּוֹלְדוֹת יַעֲקֹב יוֹסֵף.

415. Hence MOSES corrected one grade, TIFERET, and Solomon corrected another grade, YESOD. Their shapes are interconnected, THAT OF TIFERET IS THAT OF YESOD. This is the secret of the verse, "These are the generations of Jacob, Joseph" (Beresheet 37:2), THE FORM OF JACOB, TIFERET, RESEMBLES THE FORM OF JOSEPH, YESOD.

416. שֵׁירוּתָא דְּשָׁאֲרִי מֹשֶׁה, לְאַתְקְנָא בְּהַאי אֲתָר, דְּאִיהוּ סִטְרָא דִּקְדוּשָּׁה אוֹקִים קִימָה דִּנְקוּדָה דְּקַיְּימָא בְּאֶמְצָעִיתָא, דַּהֲוָה חָשׁוּךְ וְשָׁקוּעַ בְּאַתְרֵיהּ, וְלָא אִתְחָזֵי, וְלָא נָהִיר כְּלַל, וְשֵׁירוּתָא דְּכֹלָּא אוֹקִים לָהּ לְהַאי נְקוּדָה, דְּאִשְׁתְּקָעַת בְּאַתְרָהָא. וּלְבָתַר לְכָל אַחֲרָא, דְּאִיהוּ בִּנְיָינָא דְּהַאי נְקוּדָה.

416. Moses started to repair that place of holiness by erecting the point standing in the middle, MALCHUT, which was dark and sunken in its place, unseen and not shining at all. He first raised that point that was sunken in its place, then CONSTRUCTED all the rest, that are based on this point.

417. וְאִם הַאי נְקוּדָה לָא אִתְתַּקַּן בְּקַדְמֵיתָא, כָּל מַאן דְּאִתְפָּשַׁט מִנָּהּ, לָא יָכִיל לְאִתְתַּקְנָא. וְכֵיוָן דְּהַאי נְקוּדָה אִתְקָמַת וְאִתְנְהִירַת, כְּדֵין, כָּל שְׁאַר תִּקּוּנָא אַחֲרָא אִתְתָּקַּן, וְאִתְיְישָׁבַת בְּדוּכְתָּהּ. וע"ד, וַיָּקֶם מֹשֶׁה אֶת הַמִּשְׁכָּן. דָּא נְקוּדָה דַּהֲוַות חֲשׁוּכָא וּשְׁקִיעָא בְּאַתְרֵיהּ. וּלְבָתַר, וַיִּתֵּן אֶת אֲדָנָיו, אִינּוּן סַמְכִין דְּאִינּוּן מִכָּאן וּמִכָּאן. וְכֻלְּהוּ הֲווֹ מֵאָה לְחֻשְׁבְּנָא, וְכֻלְּהוּ אִתְפְּלָגוּ לְאַתְרַיְיהוּ, דִּכְתִּיב, מְאַת אֲדָנִים לִמְאַת הַכִּכָּר כִּכָּר לָאָדֶן.

417. Unless that point, MALCHUT, were corrected first, all that spread from it could not have been corrected. Once that point was erected and made to shine, all the other corrections were made, and it was settled in its place. Therefore IT WAS FIRST WRITTEN, "And Moses erected the Tabernacle" (Shemot 40:18) referring to the point, dark and sunken in its place. He then "fastened the sockets" (Ibid.) the sockets of several places, ON ALL SIDES OF THE TABERNACLE, amounting to a hundred, and divided them each to its place, TO THE SIDES OF THE TABERNACLE, as it is written, "hundred sockets of the hundred talents, a talent for a socket" (Shemot 38:27).

418. וְאִלֵּין אֲדָנִים הָא אוֹקִימְנָא, אֲבָל לָא כְּתִיב בְּהוּ קִימָה, אֶלָּא וַיִּתֵּן, נְתִינָה לְשַׁוְּואָה עֲלַיְיהוּ מַה דְּאִצְטְרִיךְ, בְּגִין דְּאִית תַּתָּאִין וְעִלָּאִין, רְכִיבִין דָּא עַל דָּא. וְעַל דָּא כְּתִיב בְּהוּ נְתִינָה.

418. We already explained about these sockets. It was not written that they were erected, but that he fastened them (lit. 'he gave'), because they are connected with giving, so as to put upon them that which is needed, NAMELY, THE BOARDS. This is because there are lower beings, and higher ones set upon them. Therefore, the word 'give' is used in relation to them.

419. בְּהַהִיא שַׁעֲתָא דְּהַאי נְקוּדָה אִתְקָמַת, אִשְׁתְּקָעַת סִטְרָא אַחֲרָא. וְלָא אִתְמָחַת כְּלַל, דְּהָא לָא אִתְמְחֵי, אֶלָּא לְהַהוּא זִמְנָא דְּאָתֵי, דְּאִתְמְחֵי מֵעָלְמָא, כְּמָה דְּאִתְּמַר, אִתְּקַם דָּא וְאִשְׁתְּקַעַת דָּא.

419. At the time when the point was erected, the Other Side sank, BUT was not altogether wiped away. That will happen only in the future, when it will be wiped out, as we explained. Now, this was erected and that, THE OTHER SIDE, sank.

420. וַיִּתֵּן אֶת אֲדָנָיו, כְּדֵין שָׁארֵי לְאִתַּתְקְפָא הַאי סִטְרָא דִּקְדוּשָּׁה וְכַד אִתְיְיהִיבוּ אִלֵּין סַמְכִין, אִשְׁתְּקָעוּ כֻּלְּהוּ דְּסִטְרָא אַחֲרָא, וְעָאלוּ בְּנוּקְבָּא דִּתְהוֹמָא רַבָּא. בְּגִין דְּאִסְתַּלָּק הַאי סִטְרָא דִּקְדוּשָּׁה עִלָּאָה, וְאִיהוּ חוּלָקָא לְאִסְתַּלְּקָא, וּכְדֵין הַאי סִטְרָא אַחֲרָא אִשְׁתְּקַע, וְעָאל בְּהַהוּא נוּקְבָּא דִּתְהוֹמָא.

420. "and fastened its sockets" (Shemot 40:18): Then the side of holiness began to strengthen. And when these sockets were fastened, all THE SOCKETS of the Other Side sank and entered the hole in the great abyss. For when the side of high holiness was elevated, and partly REACHED exaltation, the Other Side sank and entered that hole in the abyss, BECAUSE WHEN THE ONE WAS ERECTED, THE OTHER SANK.

421. וְאִלְמָלֵא דְּיִשְׂרָאֵל חָאבוּ, לָא יָכִיל לְשַׁלְטָאָה בְּעָלְמָא יַתִּיר. וּלְבָתַר אוּף הָכִי חָאבוּ, וְאַמְשִׁיכוּ לֵיהּ עָלַיְיהוּ כְּקַדְמֵיתָא. וּמֵהַהוּא יוֹמָא, לָא הֲוָה עֵיטָא, אֶלָּא לְמֵיהַב חוּלָקָא לְהַהוּא סִטְרָא אַחֲרָא בְּכֹלָּא, בְּרָזָא דְּקָרְבְּנִין וּנְסָכִין וְעָלָוָון. ות"ח בג"כ עוֹלָה אִתּוֹקְדָא כֹּלָּא בְּאֶשָּׁא, לְאַכְפְּיָיא הַאי סִטְרָא, וּלְאִסְתַּלְקָא סִטְרָא דִּקְדוּשָּׁה, וּבְגִין כַּךְ כַּד מֹשֶׁה אוֹקִים לַאֲתַר דָּא. אִשְׁתְּקַע אֲתַר דָּא.

421. If it were not for Yisrael who sinned, THE OTHER SIDE could not have ruled the world. Then they sinned, and drew upon them THE OTHER SIDE as before. From that day, there is no remedy, but to give a portion to the Other Side from everything, from the secret of the sacrifices, libation offerings, and the burnt offerings. Come and see: The burnt offering is therefore burnt by fire completely, to subjugate that side, and raise the side of holiness. Once Moses erected this place OF HOLINESS, that place OF DEFILEMENT sank.

422. ת"ח וַיָּקֶם מֹשֶׁה, הַאי סִטְרָא דִּקְדוּשָּׁה. וְאִשְׁתְּקַע סִטְרָא אַחֲרָא מְסַאֲבָא. וַיִּתֵּן. לְהַאי סִטְרָא דִּקְדוּשָּׁה, וְאִתְרַפְּיָא הַאי סִטְרָא אַחֲרָא מְסַאֲבָא. וַיָּשֶׂם, לְהַאי סִטְרָא דִּקְדוּשָּׁה, וְאִתְכַּפְיָא הַאי סִטְרָא אַחֲרָא דִּמְסָאֲבָא. וּלְבָתַר אַהְדָּר וַיִּתֵּן אֶת בְּרִיחָיו.

422. Come and see: "Moses erected" (Shemot 40:18) the side of holiness, and the Other Side of defilement sank, "and fastened ITS SOCKETS" of the side of holiness, and that side of defilement was enfeebled. He "set up ITS BOARDS" (Ibid.) of the side of holiness, and the Other Side of defilement was subjugated. Then he "put up its bars" (Ibid.).

423. וּלְבָתַר וַיָּקֶם. מ"ט. בְּגִין דִּיְהֵא שֵׁירוּתָא וְסִיּוּמָא בְּקִימָה, שָׁארֵי

בְּקִימָה, וְסִיֵּים בְּקִימָה. בְּגִין דִּבְכֹלָּא בָּעֵי קִימָה, שֵׁירוּתָא וְסִיּוּמָא. קִימָה בְּשֵׁירוּתָא דְּסִטְרָא אַחֲרָא אִתְרַפֵּי. וְדָא, אִיהוּ קִימָה לְסִטְרָא דִּקְדוּשָּׁה, בְּגִין לְאִתְקַיְּימָא וּלְאִסְתַּלְּקָא לְעֵילָּא, לְמֶהֱוֵי אִתְקַשְּׁרוּתָא חֲדָא כַּדְקָא יֵאוֹת. בְּגִין דְּכָל זִמְנָא דִּקְדוּשָּׁה שַׁלְטָא וְסַלְקָא, מְסָאֲבוּ שָׁפִיל, וּמָאִיךְ לְתַתָּא.

423. Then IT IS WRITTEN AGAIN, "and he erected" (Ibid. 33) What is the sense? That the beginning and the end will be marked by erecting; therefore, he started by erecting and finished by erecting, for all, BOTH OF THEM, are in need of erection, in the beginning and in the end. For the purpose of the erection in the beginning was to weaken the Other Side. The one IN THE END, is the erection of the holy side, so it will be established and elevated above to be one knot as is proper. For whenever holiness goes up to rule, defilement is lowered and sinks down.

44. The six grades of the Other Side

A Synopsis

Rabbi Shimon explains the levels and grades of darkness, rage and judgment. We learn of 'the shadow of death' and 'death' and then of the color of smoke, the color of fire and the black color. The color of smoke goes down into the world and instigates people to anger. The color of fire descends to the world and causes killings and bloodshed. The color of black descends into the world and is in charge over the hanged and the strangled; it always harms people. Rabbi Shimon describes the four types of rage, and then talks about the second grade, where all the fiends come out. They roam around the world and are always ready to take revenge for the hidden sins that people do. We learn how the second and third grades spread until they reach the black firmament. Rabbi Shimon talks about the three 'joints' of the 'right arm'. The first is called 'transgression', and only weakens when Yisrael offers sacrifices. The second is called 'ire', that brings sorrow and hardship into the world. The third is called 'trouble' because it sends out the power to oppress and give trouble to men. The secret of these three joints is the verse: "wrath, and indignation, and trouble." Then he moves to the joints of the left arm, saying that when they join they get stronger, as in: "an embassy of evil messengers." From the left arm all the evil demons are sent down. The fourth grade of the Other Side sends out a force that gives permission in the world to shed blood. In all the grades and in each joint there are chieftains with battalions of fiends. Rabbi Shimon turns to the fourth grade, where fiends are sent down to execute the evil judgments against people. We hear that the fifth grade is divided into right and left called 'thighs', Netzach and Hod. This is where the power of pursuing every evil comes from. We learn that the joints of the Other Side all turn backward rather than forward, and are told about the right and left joints of the fifth grade. They harm anyone who is meritorious but has no ancestral merit to protect him and they chase the wicked who have been marked by the angel so that they get diseases. All the same Rabbi Shimon explains that diseases do not come from the Other Side: they are called 'sufferings of love', because the Torah says: "But it pleases Hashem to crush him by disease." Rabbi Shimon describes the sixth and last grade as 'foreskin' because it is the secret of the piercing serpent and pertains to the meaning of circumcision.

424. רֵישָׁא דִּנְקוּדָה, דְּקַיְּימָא תְּחוֹת דַּרְגִּין דִּי בְּסִטְרָא אַחֲרָא, אִיהוּ

רֵישׁ דַּרְגָּא דִּלְבַר, רֵישָׁא דִּדְכוּרָא, וְקַיְּימָא רָכִיב עַל חַד גָּמָל, אִיהוּ רֵישָׁא לְבַר דְּחַד עִרְבוּבָא דְּחֹשֶׁךְ דְּאִתְפָּשַׁט.

424. The source of the point underneath the grades of the Other Side, MALCHUT OF THE OTHER SIDE, BENEATH ALL THE GRADES OF THE OTHER SIDE, ITS BEGINNING (LIT. 'HEAD') is at the head of the grades OF THE OTHER SIDE, outside HOLINESS. It is the head of the male OF THE OTHER SIDE, riding on a camel. THIS IS THE SECRET OF SAMAEL, RIDING ON A CAMEL. It is the head outside HOLINESS, expanding from a mixture of darkness, NAMELY, SMOKE INTERMINGLED WITH DARKNESS AND THEY SPREAD TOGETHER.

425. דְּכַד תְּנָנָא נָפְקָא מִגּוֹ רוּגְזָא תַּקִּיף, אִתְפָּשַׁט הַהוּא תְּנָנָא, וְאָזִיל רוּגְזָא בָּתַר רוּגְזָא, דָּא עַל דָּא, וְדָא רָכִיב וְשָׁלִיט עַל דָּא, בְּחֵיזוּ דִּדְכַר וְנוּקְבָא לְמֶהֱוֵי כֹּלָּא רוּגְזָא תַּקִּיף.

425. For when smoke was issued from violent rage, that smoke expands and goes from rage to rage, the one atop the other, riding on and ruling upon the other, appearing like male and female, so as to make all into violent rage.

426. וְכַד שָׁארֵי תְּנָנָא לְאִתְפַּשְּׁטָא, דָּחִיק מִגּוֹ רוּגְזָא בִּדְחִיקוּ דְּחָד נְקוּדָה לְאִתְפַּשְּׁטָא, וּלְבָתַר אִתְפָּשַׁט תְּנָנָא דְּרוּגְזָא בְּעַקִּימוּ, כְּחַד חִוְיָא חַכִּים לְאַבְאָשָׁא.

426. When smoke started to expand, it pressed from within the rage, to expand through the pressure of one point. Then the smoke of rage spread aslant like a certain serpent, sly and dangerous.

427. רֵישָׁא דְּנָפְקָא לְאִתְפַּשְּׁטָא, אִיהוּ דַּרְגָּא דְּאִיהוּ חָשׁוּךְ, סָלִיק וְנָחִית, אָזִיל וְשָׁאט, וְנָח בְּדוּכְתֵּיהּ, וְקַיְּימָא דַּרְגָּא לְאִתְיַישְּׁבָא, מֵהַהוּא תְּנָנָא דְּנָפִיק מִגּוֹ רוּגְזָא, וְאִיהוּ צֵל. צִלָּא, עַל אֲתַר אַחֲרָא דְּאִקְרֵי מָוֶת. וְכַד מִתְחַבְּרָן תַּרְווַייְהוּ כַּחֲדָא, אִקְרֵי צַלְמָוֶת, וְהָא אוּקִימְנָא, תְּרֵין דַּרְגִּין אִינּוּן דְּמִתְחַבְּרָאן כַּחֲדָא.

427. The head, THE HEAD OF A MALE, which started to spread, is a grade of darkness. It goes up and down, roaming and hovering and resting in its place, FOR IT FINDS NO PLACE IN WHICH TO SETTLE, UNTIL that grade settles, BY CONNECTING with the smoke coming out of the rage. It is then called 'shadow'. It shadows a place called 'death'. When the two are combined, they are called 'the shadow of death.' We already stated that these are two grades joined together.

428. הַאי צֵל, אִיהוּ שֵׁירוּתָא דִּנְקוּדָה תַּתָּאָה דִּלְבַר, חֲשׁוֹכָא דִּמְרַחֲקָא מִנְקוּדָה קַדִּישָׁא, דְּקַיְימָא בְּאֶמְצָעִיתָא. וְהַאי אִיהוּ נְקוּדָה, דְּלָא קַיְימָא, וְלָא אִתְרְשִׁימַת בְּגַוְונָהָא. וּמִינָהּ אִתְפַּשְּׁטַת פְּשִׁיטוּ לְבַר וּלְתַתָּא. וְאִיהִי אִשְׁתְּקָעַת וְלָא אִתְחֲזִיאַת, וְלָא אִתְרְשִׁימַת.

428. That shadow is the beginning of the lowest point OF THE OTHER SIDE outside, NAMELY, OUT OF ITS FEMALE. THAT SHADOW, darkness, is far away from the holy point standing in the middle. The point does not exist, nor it is seen, nor inscribed with colors, BECAUSE IT IS ONLY A BEGINNING AND NO JUDGMENT IS FELT IN IT. From it, an expansion spread outward and downward, AND THE POINT ITSELF was sunk, not to be seen nor inscribed.

429. הַאי אִתְפַּשְּׁטַת לְתַתָּא, לִימִינָא וְלִשְׂמָאלָא, וְאִתְפַּשְּׁטַת בְּאֶמְצָעִיתָא, גּוֹ חָשׁוּךְ, קָבֵל אֶלֶף וּמֵאָה. תְּרֵין סַמְכִין מִתְגַּלְּפִין לְסִטְרָא דָּא, וּלְסִטְרָא דָּא, אִתְפַּשַּׁט חֲשׁוֹכָא, בְּגוֹ גָּוֶון אוּכָם וְלָא אוּכָם, דְּהָא לֵית לֵיהּ גָּוֶון לְאִתְקַיְּימָא בֵּיהּ. וּבְהַהוּא פְּשִׁיטוּ, קַיְימִין חֲשׁוֹכִין אִינּוּן דְּשַׁמְּשׁוּ בְּמִצְרַיִם, דִּכְתִּיב לֹא רָאוּ אִישׁ אֶת אָחִיו וְלֹא קָמוּ אִישׁ מִתַּחְתָּיו שְׁלֹשֶׁת יָמִים. וּכְתִיב וְיָמֵשׁ חֹשֶׁךְ.

429. THAT POINT expanded downward, left, and right, and spread in their midst inside the darkness, NAMELY, CHESED, GVURAH AND TIFERET OF THE OTHER SIDE, corresponding to a thousand one hundred. Two pillars are engraved on the two sides, CORRESPONDING TO NETZACH AND HOD, and the darkness was spread into a color, which is black yet not black, because no color prevails in it. Inside the expansion of darkness, there are darknesses that were in use in Egypt, as it is written, "they saw not one another, neither rose any from his place for three days" (Shemot 10:23), and "darkness which may be felt" (Ibid. 21).

430. הַאי פְּשִׁיטוּ, אִתְפָּשַׁט בְּכַמָּה זִינִין, מְשַׁנְיָין אִלֵּין גּוֹ אִלֵּין. גּוֹ הַהוּא פְּשִׁיטוּ, נָפְקָא חַד זְהָרָא דְּאִצְטְבַע בְּדַהֲבָא, וְדָא אִיהוּ דַּהֲבָא סוּמָקָא. אִתְפָּשַׁט הַאי זְהָרָא, וְחָפֵי חָשׁוּךְ דְּרֵישָׁא, וְאִיהוּ דַּהֲבָא, דְּאִתְכְּלִיל בֵּיהּ חֲשׁוֹכָא.

430. This said expansion expands in several different ways. HE EXPLAINS: From within that expansion one light comes out, painted gold. This is red gold. This color spreads, and covers the darkness in its head, NAMELY, IT INTERMINGLES WITH IT. THEREFORE it is gold, in which darkness is included.

431. הַאי חֲשׁוֹכָא אִתְפָּשַׁט לִימִינָא וְלִשְׂמָאלָא. וּמִגּוֹ אִלֵּין תְּרֵין סִטְרִין, נָפְקָא חַד גַּוְונָא דְּכַסְפָּא, דְּלָא זָהִיר. אִתְפָּשַׁט הַאי גָּוֶון דִּכְסַף, וְחָפֵי חֲשׁוֹכָא, וְאִתְכְּלִיל דָּא בְּדָא, וְנָחִית לְתַתָּא.

431. This darkness spreads right and left. From these two sides, a certain silver hue comes out, WHICH IS CHESED, that doesn't shine. This silver hue spreads to cover the darkness, NAMELY, IT MINGLED WITH IT. They were included, DARKNESS AND SILVER, within one another, and it went down.

432. אִתְפָּשַׁט חֲשׁוֹכָא, וְקַיְימָן תְּרֵין חֲשׁוֹכִין, רֵישׁ אוּכְמָא דְּקַיְימִין, וּמִתַּמָּן מִתְפָּשַׁט וְנָפִיק חַד גָּוֶון דִּנְחֹשֶׁת.

432. The darkness spread FROM CHESED, NAMELY THE SILVER HUE, and became two darknesses, ON THE RIGHT AND ON THE LEFT, standing on the beginning of blackness, whence another hue of brass comes out, WHICH IS TIFERET OF THE OTHER SIDE.

433. וּמִתַּמָּן אִתְפָּשַׁט לְתַתָּא, הַהוּא חָשׁוּךְ, וְקָאֵים קַיְימָא, וְנָפִיק חַד גָּוֶון אוּכָם חֵיזוּ דְּפַרְזְלָא. וְכֹלָּא בְּרָזָא דַּחֲשׁוֹכָא.

433. From that place, FROM TIFERET, this darkness spreads downwards, TO MALCHUT where it is established in its existence. Another color comes out, black looking like iron CALLED 'DEATH'. All is in the secret of darkness. FOR THE OTHER SIDE IS NAMLY BUILT ON THE PRINCIPLE OF DARKNESS.

434. מִבֵּין תְּרֵין קַיְימִין, נָפִיק קַיְּימָא חַד, חָשׁוּךְ בַּחֲשׁוֹכָא, וְכָל אִלֵּין גַּוְונִין אִתְחָזוּן בֵּיהּ. וְהַאי אִיהוּ עָרְלָה, דְּאַנְהִיג דְּכַר לְנֻקְבָּה, לְאִזְדַּוְּוגָא כַּחֲדָא, לְמֶהֱוֵי חַד.

434. From between the two pillars, NETZACH AND HOD OF THE OTHER SIDE, comes out a pillar of darkness in the dark, NAMELY, IT CONTAINS THE TWO KINDS OF DARKNESS OF EGYPT. All the hues, GOLD, SILVER…are seen in it. FOR IT IS THE ASPECT OF YESOD, CONSISTING OF THE FIVE SFIROT CHESED, GVURAH, TIFERET, NETZACH AND HOD. This is the foreskin, BECAUSE YESOD OF THE OTHER SIDE IS A FORESKIN, as the male leads the female to mate and to become one.

435. הָנֵי קַיְימִין, בְּז' דַּרְגִּין רַבְרְבִין יְדִיעָאן. דַּרְגָּא קַדְמָאָה, אִיהוּ דַּרְגָּא דְּקָאֵים בְּסִטְרָא דְּהַאי חֲשׁוֹכָא. דָּא חֲשׁוֹכָא סַלְקָא, גוֹ טְמִירוּ דִּתְנָנָא דְּאֶשָּׁא, הַאי כָּלִיל בְּגַוְון תְּנָנָא, וּבְגַוְון אֶשָּׁא, וּבְגַוְון אוּכָם. אִלֵּין תְּלַת גַּוְונִין, מִתְפָּרְשָׁן לְכַמָּה סִטְרִין, לְאִתְעַקְמָא בְּעִמְקֵי עָלְמָא.

435. These SEVEN GRADES are within seven certain great grades. The first grade is the grade inside that darkness. That darkness comes out of the hiding place of the smoke of fire, comprising the color of smoke, the color of fire and the black color. These three colors are different in their several manners of bending the crooked of the world, NAMELY, TO PUNISH THEM.

436. גַּוְון תְּנָנָא הַאי, נַחְתָּא לְעָלְמָא, וְאָעִיל לְכַמָּה סִטְרִין, וְדָא אִתְפָּשַׁט בְּעָלְמָא, וְאַסְטֵי לְרוּחֵי בְּנֵי נָשָׁא בִּרְגִּיזוּ, לְאַסְטָאָה אָרְחַיְיהוּ, וּלְאִתְתַּקְפָא בְּרוּגְזַיְיהוּ. וע"ד כְּתִיב, לֹא יִהְיֶה בְךָ אֵל זָר וְלֹא תִשְׁתַּחֲוֶה לְאֵל נֵכָר. לֹא יִהְיֶה בְךָ אֵל זָר דָּא דְּכוּרָא. וְלֹא תִשְׁתַּחֲוֶה לְאֵל נֵכָר דָּא

נוּקְבָּא. הַאי אִיהוּ רוּגְזָא דְּשַׁלְטָא וְאִתָּקַף בְּעָלְמָא, וְעָאל בְּגוֹ בְּנֵי נָשָׁא, וְאַתְקִיף לוֹן לְאַבְאָשָׁא.

436. HE EXPLAINS: The color of smoke goes down into the world and affects it in several ways. It spreads in the world, instigating the spirits of people, causing them to be angry, and leading them astray so they would become angry. Therefore it is written, "there shall be no strange El among you, nor shall you worship a foreign El" (Tehilim 81:10). "There shall be no strange El among you" refers to the male OF THE OTHER SIDE, and "nor shall you worship a foreign El" refers to the female OF THE OTHER SIDE. THE SMOKE is the anger ruling and gathering strength in the world, walking amongst men and assailing them to cause them harm.

437. גָּוֶון אֶשָּׁא, הַאי גַּוְונָא נַחְתָּא לְעָלְמָא, וְעָאל לְכַמָּה סִטְרִין, לְאַבְאָשָׁא, לְקַטְלָא, וּלְאוֹשְׁדָא דָּמִין, וּלְקַפְּחָא לִבְנֵי נָשָׁא. וְעַל דָּא כְּתִיב, אִם יֹאמְרוּ לְכָה אִתָּנוּ נֶאֶרְבָה לְדָם נִצְפְּנָה לְנָקִי חִנָּם. בְּגִין דְּאִית אוֹשְׁדֵי דָּמִין לְמַגָּנָא, וְקַטְלֵי לְמַגָּנָא. וְאִית דְּאוֹשְׁדֵי דָּמִין וְקַטְלֵי בִּקְרָבָא, וְהַאי מִסִּטְרָא דִּדְכוּרָא וְהַאי מִסִּטְרָא דְּנוּקְבָּא. סִטְרָא דִּדְכוּרָא אוֹשִׁיד דָּמִין לְמַגָּנָא, כִּדְקַאמְרָן. סִטְרָא דְּנוּקְבָּא, לְאַגָּחָא קְרָבִין, וּלְאִתְקַטְּלָא אִלֵּין בְּאִלֵּין, וְכָל קְרָבִין וְקַטוּלִין אִלֵּין בְּאִלֵּין, מֵהַהוּא סִטְרָא דְּנוּקְבָּא קָא אַתְיָין.

437. The color of fire descends into the world, and in several ways causes harm, killings, bloodshed, and perdition to men. It is therefore written, "If they say, come with us, let us lie in wait for blood, let us lurk for the innocent without cause" (Mishlei 1:11). For some shed blood and kill without cause, and some shed blood and kill in war. This comes from the male side OF THE OTHER SIDE, and that from the female side OF THE OTHER SIDE. The male side sheds blood without cause, as we said. The side of the female, causes wars, and makes people kill each other. All the wars and killings come from the side of that female.

438. גָּוֶון אוּכָם, הַאי גַּוְונָא נַחְתָּא לְעָלְמָא, וְנַחְתָּא לְאִתְמַנָּאָה עַל כָּל פְּצוּעִין, וּמַחְיָין, וּתְפִיסוּ דְּגוּפִין, וּצְלִיבוּ, וַחֲנִיקוּ, לְאַבְאָשָׁא תָּדִיר לִבְנֵי

נָשָׁא. אִלֵּין תְּלַת גַּוְונִין, מִתְפָּרְשָׁן לְכַמָּה סִטְרִין דְּעָלְמָא, וְאִתְפַּשְׁטָן גּוֹ בְּנֵי עָלְמָא.

438. The black color descending into the world, is in charge over the wounded and the dead, catching bodies TO PUT THEM IN JAIL, the hanged and the strangled. It always harms people. These three colors, SMOKE, FIRE, AND BLACK, spread in the world in several ways and spread amongst the inhabitants of the world.

439. גַּוֶון תְּנָנָא נַחְתָּא בְּעָלְמָא, וְהַאי אִיהוּ גַּוֶון קַדְמָאָה, דְּנָפְקָא מִגּוֹ נְקוּדָה דְּשָׁקִיעַ מֵהַהוּא צֵל דְּקָאָמַרָן, דְּאִיהוּ סָמָאֵ״ל, דְּקָא רָכִיב עַל גָּמָל, כְּמָה דְּאִתְּמַר, וְהַאי גַּוֶון תְּנָנָא אִקְרֵי קַצְפִּיאֵ״ל רַבְרְבָא. וְהַאי אִיהוּ רוּגְזָא דִּבְנֵי נָשָׁא, דְּאַתְקִיפוּ לִבָּא בְּרוּגְזָא.

439. The color of smoke descending into the world is the first color to come out of the point sunken in the shadow. It is Samael riding on a camel, as we said. The color of smoke is called 'Katzpiel the great', whence comes the anger of men, who harden their hearts in anger. HE IS THEREFORE CALLED 'KATZPIEL', NAMELY THE ANGER (HEB. *KETZEF*) OF EL.

440. תְּחוֹת הַאי, מִמָּנָן אֶלֶף וְשִׁית מְאָה חֲבִילִין, דְּאִינּוּן רוּגְזָא דְּגוּפַיְיהוּ דִּבְנֵי נָשָׁא. בְּגִין דְּאִית רוּגְזָא דְּשַׁלְטָא בְּעָלְמָא לְמֶעְבַּד דִּינָא. אֲבָל הַאי אִיהוּ רוּגְזָא, דְּשַׁלְטָא וְעָאל בְּגוּפַיְיהוּ דִּבְנֵי נָשָׁא, דְּאִתְרְגִיזוּ בְּהַאי רוּגְזָא. וְהַאי רוּגְזָא, אִיהוּ יְסוֹדָא דְּכָל שְׁאַר גַּוְונֵי, לְמֶעְבַּד בְּהוּ, בִּנְיָינָא לְאַבְאָשָׁא, בְּגִין דְּהַאי תְּנָנָא, נָפְקָא מִגּוֹ רוּגְזָא דְּאֶשָּׁא עִלָּאָה, דְּמִלַהֲטָא, וְהַאי אִיהוּ קַדְמָאָה לְהַהוּא אֶשָּׁא.

440. Under KATZPIEL there are one thousand six hundred battalions OF FIENDS. They are the anger FOUND within the bodies of men. For there is anger ruling over the world to do justice, but this anger is the anger ruling over and entering inside the bodies of men who are angry in this way. This anger is the foundation for all the rest of the HARMFUL colors, built from it to harm, since that smoke comes out of the rage of the supernal blazing fire. This type of rage is the first one of the fire.

441. אַרְבַּע רוּגְזֵי מִתְפָּרְשָׁאן מֵהַהוּא רוּגְזָא. רוּגְזָא קַדְמָאָה, אִקְרֵי רֹגֶז וְדָא אִיהוּ דְּאַרְגִּיז לְבַיְיהוּ דִּבְנֵי נָשָׁא, וְדָא אִיהוּ דְּנַחְתָּא וְאַזְלָא וְסַטְיָא לִבְנֵי נָשָׁא, וְאִתְרְגִיזוּ בְּרוּגְזַיְיהוּ. וְדָא אִיהוּ דְּאַמְשִׁיךְ מְחַבְּלָא עַל עָלְמָא.

441. That rage is divided into four rages. The first rage is called ‘rage’. It causes the hearts of people to be enraged. It descends and instigates people, and they become furious in their anger. This draws fiends upon the world.

442. רוּגְזָא תִּנְיָינָא, הַאי אִיהוּ נַחְתָּא לְעָלְמָא, וְשָׁאט וְאִתְפַּשַּׁט לְכָל סִטְרִין, וְהַאי אִקְרֵי שִׂנְאָה. וְהַאי נַחְתָּא וְעָאל בִּבְנֵי נָשָׁא, וְהַאי כֵּיוָן דְּעָאל, אִקְרֵי מְחַבְּלָא שְׁתִיקָא וְהַאי אִיהוּ רָגְזָא דִּשְׁתִיק, וְהַאי אִיהוּ דְּאִשְׁתַּתֵּף בְּהַהוּא אֲתָר דְּנוּקְבָא. וְהַאי אִיהוּ רוּגְזָא דִּשְׁתִיקָה, דְּקַיְּימָא בְּעַקִּימוּ. הַאי קַשְׁיָא מִכֻּלְּהוּ, בְּגִין דְּאִיהוּ כְּגַוְונָא דְּחִוְיָא, דִּשְׁתִיק תָּדִיר, וְקָטִיל לְבָתַר.

442. The second rage descends into the world, roaming and expanding into all sides. It is called ‘hatred’. This one, once it enters man, is called ‘a silent fiend’. It takes part in the place of the female. This is the silent rage, standing aslant. It is the strongest of them all, because it is like the serpent that keeps silent and then kills.

443. רוּגְזָא תְּלִיתָאָה, הַאי אִיהוּ רוּגְזָא בְּהִפּוּכָא מִקַּדְמָאָה, דְּאַזְלָא וְאִתָּקַף וְלָא שָׁתִיק, אֶלָּא אִתְגַּלֵּי הַהוּא רוּגְזָא, וְכָל מַאן דְּאִתְגַּלֵּי הָכִי אִתְּבַר כָּל מַה דְּאִתְגַּלֵּי וְלָא שָׁתִיק, הָכִי אִתְּבַר, וְהָכִי אִקְרֵי רוּגְזָא תְּבִירָא.

443. The third rage is the inverse of the first one, because it gets stronger, and does not keep silent. It is revealed, and as it is revealed, it is broken. NAMELY, all that is revealed and is not silent, is called ‘broken rage’.

444. רוּגְזָא רְבִיעָאָה, שֵׁירוּתָא תַּקִּיף, סוֹפָא תָּבִיר. וע״ד הַאי אִיהוּ

רוּגְזָא, דְּמִתְהַפְּכָא מִן קַדְמֵיתָא. בְּגִין כַּךְ, הַאי אִיהוּ סִטְרָא תְּבִירָא מִכֻּלְּהוּ. וע"ד, כֹּלָּא אִיהוּ בְּדַרְגָּא קַדְמָאָה.

444. The fourth rage is at first a strong RAGE, and in the end it is broken. Therefore, it is in opposition to the last one. For that reason it is the most broken aspect of them all. Hence, they all pertain to the first grade.

445. דַּרְגָּא תִּנְיָינָא, אִיהוּ דַּרְגָּא דְּנָפִיק מֵחֲשׁוֹכָא, וְהַאי אִיהוּ גָּוֶון חָשׁוּךְ, דְּקַיְּימָא מִגּוֹ הַאי חֲשׁוֹכָא בְּגִין דְּכֹלָּא קַיְימָא מִגּוֹ חֲשׁוֹכָא. וְקַיְּימָא בְּדַרְגִּין יְדִיעָאן. וְהַאי אִתְפָּשַׁט לְתַתָּא בִּגְוָונִין יְדִיעָאן.

445. AFTER EXPLAINING THE ASPECT OF THE HEAD OF THE OTHER SIDE, WHICH IS THE FIRST GRADE, HE NOW EXPLAINS THE SECOND GRADE, WHICH IS CHESED OF THE OTHER SIDE. HE SAYS: The second grade is a grade coming out of darkness OF THE HEAD. This grade is dark in color, AND THOUGH IT IS CHESED, AND A GRADE OF THE RIGHT, NEVERTHELESS IT IS ALSO DARK, for all THE SFIROT OF THE OTHER SIDE come from darkness. It is established in certain grades, and expands downward into certain colors.

446. בְּדַרְגָּא דָּא, קַיְימִין תְּלַת מְאָה סִטְרִין, מִתְפָּרְשִׁין דָּא מִן דָּא, וְכֻלְּהוּ כְּלִילָן דָּא בְּדָא. וְאַף עַל גַּב דְּמִשַּׁנְיָין דָּא מִן דָּא, וְאִתְגַּבְּרָן דָּא מִן דָּא, כֹּלָּא כָּלִיל דָּא בְּדָא. וּבְגִין כַּךְ, כָּל דַּרְגִּין יְדִיעָאן בְּהַאי סִטְרָא לְאַבְאָשָׁא.

446. Within this grade there are three hundred aspects separated from one another. IT IS THE RIGHT HAND, WHICH HAS THREE JOINTS, EACH CONSISTING OF A HUNDRED, ALTOGETHER THREE HUNDRED. And though they are different from each other, they strengthen and include one another. For that reason, all the grades of this side are known as harmful.

447. מֵהָכָא נַפְקֵי כָּל אִלֵּין מְחַבְּלִין דְּשַׁטְיָין בְּעָלְמָא, וְעַבְדֵי דִּינָא בְּאִתְגַּלְיָיא, עַל עוֹבָדִין סְתִימִין דְּאִתְעֲבִידוּ גּוֹ חָשׁוּךְ בִּטְמִירוּ, וְאִינּוּן שַׁטְיָין בְּעָלְמָא, וְעַבְדֵי דִּינָא בְּאִתְגַּלְיָיא בְּהוּ. וּבְגִין כַּךְ, כָּל אִלֵּין

דְּשַׁטְיָין בְּעָלְמָא, וְעַבְדֵי דִּינָא בְּאִתְגַּלְיָיא, כֻּלְּהוּ קַיְימִין בְּקִבְלַיְיהוּ דִּבְנֵי נָשָׁא, לְאִתְעַתְּדָא תָּדִיר, גַּבֵּי אִינּוּן חוֹבִין טְמִירִין דְּקָאָמַרָן, וְאִינּוּן דְּאִקְרוּן אַף וְחֵמָה, מִתְחַבְּרָן עִמְּהוֹן וְעַבְדֵי דִּינָא עֲלַיְיהוּ דִּבְנֵי נָשָׁא. הַאי אִתְעָבִיד בְּעָלְמָא, מֵאִלֵּין מָארֵי דְּדִינָא כִּדְקָאמְרָן.

447. From here, all the fiends come out. They roam about the world and execute Judgment openly, upon secret deeds done in hiding in the dark. They roam in the world, and execute judgment upon them openly. For that reason, all those who hover about the world, who execute Judgment openly are against people, always ready TO TAKE REVENGE for all the hidden sins. And those called 'wrath' and 'fury' join them and execute judgment upon people. This is done in the world by the complainants we mentioned, OF THE SECOND GRADE.

448. דַּרְגָּא דָּא קַיְּימָא גּוֹ חֲשׁוֹכָא וְאֶשָּׁא, דְּאִיהוּ רָזָא חֲדָא, וּמִגּוֹ דַּרְגָּא דָּא, מִתְפָּרְשָׁן כַּמָּה דַּרְגִּין תַּקִּיפִין דְּקַיְימָן תְּחוֹת סִטְרָא דִּרְקִיעָא חֲדָא, דְּאִקְרֵי רְקִיעָא אוּכָמָא. דַּרְגָּא תְּלִיתָאָה, הַאי אִיהוּ רְקִיעָא, דְּמִתְפַּשְּׁטָא עַל כָּל אִינּוּן דַּרְגִּין, דְּאִינּוּן סוּמָקִין כְּוַורְדָּא. וְאִלֵּין אִקְרוּן דְּרוֹעִין דְּהַאי סִטְרָא.

448. This grade is in darkness and fire, which form one secret. From this grade several strong grades are divided, standing under one of the aspects of the firmament called 'black color'. A third grade, GVURAH OF THE OTHER SIDE is a firmament spreading over all the grades that are red as a rose. These TWO GRADES, THE SECOND AND THE THIRD, are called 'the arms of this side', THE SECOND GRADE BEING THE RIGHT ARM, CHESED, AND THE THIRD GRADE BEING THE LEFT ARM, WHICH IS GVURAH.

449. תְּחוֹת אִלֵּין, מִתְפַּשְּׁטִין לְתַתָּא דַּרְגִּין, עַד דְּמָטוּ לְגוֹ הַהוּא רְקִיעָא אוּכָמָא בְּגִין דְּאִלֵּין דִּי בְּדַרְגָּא תִּנְיָינָא, נַפְקֵי מִגּוֹ הַהוּא רְקִיעָא אוּכָמָא, וְשַׁטְיָין בְּעָלְמָא.

449. Beneath these TWO ARMS, grades spread until they reach the black firmament; EVEN THOUGH THE GRADES OF THE LEFT ARM ARE RED,

THEY ALSO SPREAD INTO THE BLACK FIRMAMENT, for those of the second grade, WHICH IS THE RIGHT ARM, go out of the black firmament and hover about the world. THEREFORE, THEY TAKE WITH THEM THE GRADES OF THE THIRD GRADE, WHICH IS THE LEFT ARM.

450. אִלֵּין מִימִינָא, וְאִלֵּין מִשְּׂמָאלָא. אִלֵּין דִּימִינָא, מִתְפָּרְשָׁן לִתְלַת סִטְרִין, דְּאִינּוּן תְּלַת קִשְׁרִין. וְאִלֵּין דִּשְׂמָאלָא, מִתְפָּרְשָׁן לִתְלַת סִטְרִין, דְּאִינּוּן תְּלַת קִשְׁרִין אַחֲרָנִין.

450. There are those of the right and those of the left. Those of the right, NAMELY, OF THE SECOND GRADE, are divided into three aspects, the three joints OF THE RIGHT ARM. And those of the left, THE THIRD GRADE, are divided into three aspects, the three other joints OF THE LEFT ARM.

451. קִשְׁרָא קַדְמָאָה, קַיְימָא לְעֵילָּא. וּתְנָנָא חֲשׁוֹכָא בְּרוּגְזָא, אִתְקְשַׁר בֵּיהּ. הַאי קִשְׁרָא, אִית בָּהּ תְּלַת גַּוְונִין חֲשׁוֹכִין, וּמְשַׁנְיָין דָּא מִן דָּא, וְאִתְכְּלִילוּ דָּא בְּדָא. וְהַאי קִשְׁרָא, אִיהוּ כָּפִיף, וְלָא אִתְפָּשַׁט, בַּר לִזְמְנִין יְדִיעָאן, הַאי אִקְרֵי עֶבְרָ"ה.

451. The first joint OF THE RIGHT ARM is above, NAMELY, AT THE JOINT CONNECTED TO THE SHOULDER. Smoke darkened with rage is connected to it. This joint has three dark hues, different from each other, intermingled in each other. That joint is crooked, and does not expand, save at certain times. It is called 'wrath'.

452. וְאִיהוּ קַיְימָא בְּלָא שְׁכִיכוּ, בְּגִין דְּלָא שָׁכִיךְ, בַּר בִּזְמְנָא דְּיִשְׂרָאֵל מְקָרְבִין קָרְבָּנָא לְתַתָּא, בְּגִין דִּבְהַהוּא זִמְנָא אִשְׁתְּכַךְ הַהוּא רוּגְזָא, וְאִתְכַּפְיָיא לְתַתָּא, וְאִתְחַלָּשׁ רוּגְזֵיהּ. וְלָא יָכִיל לְשַׁלְטָאָה וּלְאַתְקְפָא. וְכַד אִתְחֲלָשׁ הַאי, כְּדֵין קִשְׁרָא תִּנְיָינָא, דְּאִיהוּ בְּאֶמְצָעִיתָא לָא יָכִיל לְנַטְלָא וּלְאַנְהָגָא.

452. That joint remains in rage, that does not abate, save when Yisrael offer sacrifices below. For at that time rage abates, and is subdued below, so it cannot have power to strengthen. When it is weakened, the other joint in the middle OF THE ARM cannot travel or conduct.

453. קְשְׁרָא תִּנְיָינָא, דָּא הוּא דְּאִקְרֵי זַעַם, הַאי קְשְׁרָא אִיהוּ דְּנָטִיל מֵאֲתָר לַאֲתָר, וְאַנְהִיג לְכָל שְׁאַר קִשְׁרִין, וְכָל שְׁאַר קִשְׁרִין כֻּלְּהוּ, אִתְנַהֲגָן בֵּיהּ, וְכֻלְּהוּ אִתְּקָפוּ בְּהַאי קְשְׁרָא. הַאי אִיהוּ דְּמַנְהִיג כָּל צַעֲרִין לְעָלְמָא, בְּגִין דְּכַד אִתְחַבַּר בְּדַרְגָּא אַחֲרָא, לְחַבְקָא לְנוּקְבָּא, כְּדֵין נַחְתֵּי לְעָלְמָא, כָּל צַעֲרִין, וְכָל דַּחֲקִין, וְכָל עָאקוּ, דְּהָא לָא יָכִילוּ לְשַׁלְטָאָה דָּא בְּלָא דָּא. וְכֻלְּהוּ דַּרְגִּין, אִתְיְיהִיבוּ לְנוּקְבָּא, לְשַׁלְטָאָה, וּלְמִסְטֵי עָלְמָא, וְאִי לָאו דְּרָכִיב דָּא עַל דָּא, וְאִתְחַבַּר דָּא בְּדָא, לָא יַכְלִין לְשַׁלְטָאָה.

453. The second joint OF THE RIGHT ARM, is called 'ire'. This joint travels from place to place, leading all the other joints. The rest of the joints are led by it, and strengthened by it. This is the one that brings sorrow into the world, because when it is connected on another level, and embraces the female, all kinds of sorrow, hardship, and trouble descend into the world, for they cannot rule the one without the other, THE MALE WITHOUT THE FEMALE. And all the grades are given to the female OF THE OTHER SIDE so she may rule, and mislead the world. Unless they were riding on each other and connected with each other, they could not have ruled.

454. תָּא חֲזֵי, כַּד הֲוָה אָדָם בְּגִנְתָּא דְּעֵדֶן, לְאִשְׁתַּדְּלָא בְּפוּלְחָנָא דְּמָארֵיהּ. נָחַת הַאי סָמָאֵ"ל, וְכָל אִינּוּן דַּרְגִּין דְּבֵיהּ, וַהֲוָה רָכִיב עַל הַהוּא חִוְיָא בִּישָׁא, בְּגִין לְאַסְטָאָה לוֹן. בְּגִין דְּהַהוּא חִוְיָא דַּהֲוָה קָאֵים תְּחוֹתֵיהּ, אִיהוּ עֲקִימָא לְאַסְטָאָה, בְּנֵי נָשָׁא, וּלְפַתָּאָה לוֹן. בְּגִין דִּכְתִּיב כִּי נֹפֶת תִּטֹּפְנָה שִׂפְתֵי זָרָה וְחָלָק מִשֶּׁמֶן חִכָּהּ. וְדָא יָהִיב חֵילָא, וְדָא עָבֵיד אוּמָנוּתָא בְּעָלְמָא, וְדָא בְּלָא דָא לָא יַכְלֵי לְשַׁלְטָאָה.

454. Come and see: When Adam was in the Garden of Eden and was occupied in worshipping his Master, Samael went down with all the grades in him, and was riding on the evil serpent, HIS FEMALE, to deviate them. As the serpent underneath SAMAEL was subtle, and led astray and seduced people, as it is written, "For the lips of a strange woman drip honey, and her mouth is smoother than oil" (Mishlei 5:3), SO THE MALE gives power and THE FEMALE practices the art OF SEDUCTION AND INSTIGATION in the world, and they cannot rule the one without the other.

455. בג"כ, כַּד הַהוּא קִשְׁרָא דְּאֶמְצָעִיתָא, אִתְחַבָּר בְּנוּקְבָּא, כְּדֵין נַחְתֵּי דִּינִין, וְכָל דַּחֲקִין לְעָלְמָא וְכַד הַאי לָא אִתְתָּקַף דְּלָא נָטִיל, כֹּלָּא אִתְּבַר וְאִתְכַּפְיָיא, דְּלָא יָכִיל לְשַׁלְטָאָה. וע"ד, כֹּלָּא אִתְּבַר וְאִתְכַּפְיָיא, בְּרָזָא דְּקָרְבְּנִין דִּלְתַתָּא. וְסַלְקָא מַאן דְּסַלְקָא, לְאִתְעַטְרָא לְעֵילָּא, וּלְאִתְבָּרְכָא מֵעִמְקָא עִלָּאָה, דְּנָהִיר לְכָל אַנְפִּין.

455. That is why when the middle joint OF THE ARM is united with the female, then Judgments and all sorts of hardships descend into the world. But when it is not strengthened, and does not travel, everything is broken and subjugated, and they cannot have sway. Hence, all is broken and subdued by the secret of the offering below, and one ascends, NAMELY MALCHUT OF HOLINESS, to be bedecked above, and be blessed by the highest depth, BINAH, that illuminates upon all faces.

456. קִשְׁרָא תְּלִיתָאָה הַאי אִיהוּ תַּקִּיפָא בְּתְקִיפוּ יַתִּיר, וְהַאי אִקְרֵי צָרָ"ה, בְּגִין דְּמֵהַאי נַפְקֵי שׁוּלְטָנוּ, לְאַשְׁרָאָה דַּחֲקִין, וּלְמֶעְבַּד עָאקוּ לִבְנֵי נָשָׁא. וְרָזָא דִּתְלַת קִשְׁרִין אִלֵּין, דִּכְתִּיב עֶבְרָה וָזַעַם וְצָרָה. אִלֵּין תְּלַת קִשְׁרִין דִּימִינָא.

456. The third joint OF THE RIGHT ARM is much stronger THAN THE REST. It is called 'trouble', because from it emerges the power to oppress and give trouble to men. The secret of these three joints is the verse, "wrath, and indignation, and trouble" (Tehilim 78:49). These are the three joints of the right ARM, WHICH IS THE SECOND GRADE.

457. תְּלַת קִשְׁרִין דִּשְׂמָאלָא, כַּד מִתְתַּקְפֵי כַּחֲדָא, כְּדֵין הַהִיא שְׂמָאלָא אִקְרֵי, מִשְׁלַחַ"ת מַלְאֲכֵי רָעִים. בְּגִין דְּמֵהַאי שְׂמָאלָא, אִשְׁתַּדְּרוּ לְתַתָּא, וְנַטְלֵי תּוּקְפָּא, כָּל אִינּוּן מַלְאֲכִין בִּישִׁין, אִינּוּן דְּנַפְקֵי מִסִּטְרָא דִּלְתַתָּא, כִּדְקַאמְרָן. וְכָל דָּא מִגּוֹ דַּרְגָּא תִּנְיָינָא וְדַרְגָּא תְּלִיתָאָה.

457. When the three joints of the left ARM, WHICH ARE THE THIRD GRADE, get stronger together, then the left is called, "an embassy of evil messengers" (Ibid.). For from that left all those evil demons are sent below, and draw their strength. They come out of the lower side, as we said. All that COMES out of the second and the third grades, FOR THE SECOND GRADE IS THE RIGHT ARM AND THE THIRD GRADE IS THE LEFT ARM.

458. דַּרְגָּא רְבִיעָאָה, הַאי דַּרְגָּא קַיְּימָא, מִגּוֹ עֲקִימוּ דְּרוּגְזָא, גָּוֶון אֶשָּׁא. וְהַאי אִקְרֵי אֶמְצָעִיתָא. דְּאִיהוּ גּוּפָא, דְּקַיְימָא בֵּין תְּרֵין דְּרוֹעִין. הָכָא אִית לַהֲטָא, דִּמְלַהֲטָא בְּסוּמָקָא כְּוַורְדָּא. מֵהָכָא נַפְקֵי תְּקִיפוּ לְנַחְתָּא לְתַתָּא, לְאַתְקְפָא לְאוֹשְׁדָא דָּמִין. בְּגִין דְּהַאי אִיהוּ דְּיָהִיב רְשׁוּ וְשׁוּלְטָנָא לְתַתָּא, לְאַתְקְפָא וּלְאוֹשְׁדָא דָּמִין. הַאי נְבִיעַ לְנוּקְבָא, וְדָא אִצְטְרִיךְ לְדָא, כְּמָה דְּאִצְטְרִיךְ גּוּפָא לְנַפְשָׁא, וְנַפְשָׁא לָא עָבֵיד אוּמָנוּתָא, אֶלָּא בְּגוּפָא. וע״ד, כָּל חֵילָא, וְכָל תְּקִיפוּ, מֵהָכָא נָפִיק, לְאַתְקְפָא, וּלְמֶעְבַּד אוּמָנוּתָא בְּעָלְמָא, לְאַבְאָשָׁא. כְּנוּקְבָא דִּמְקַבְּלָא מִן דְּכוּרָא תָּדִיר.

458. The fourth grade OF THE OTHER SIDE is within the crookedness of rage, fiery in color. It is called 'middle one', which is the body, TIFERET, that is between the two arms, CHESED AND GVURAH. There is a blazing FIRE here, glowing with a color red like a rose. From here comes out a force, going down to assault and shed blood, since this grade gives permission and ability down below IN THE WORLD to assault and shed blood. This grade is the source OF the female. This needs that, THE FEMALE NEEDS THE MALE, as the body needs a soul. And the soul practice its art only within the body. Therefore, all forces and every might emerge from here, FROM THIS GRADE, WHICH IS THE MALE, to attack and practice the art of inflicting harm, as a female that always receives from the male.

459. בְּכָל דַּרְגָּא וְדַרְגָּא, וּבְכָל קִשְׁרָא וְקִשְׁרָא, אִית כַּמָּה מִמָּנָן, וְכַמָּה טְרִיקֵי חֲבִילִין, דְּכֻלְּהוּ אִתְנָהֲגָן בְּגִינַיְיהוּ, וְכֻלְּהוּ דְּאִתְנָהֲגָן בְּגִינַיְיהוּ, כֻּלְּהוּ לְתַתָּא, דְּאִינּוּן חַיָּילִין דִּי בְּנוּקְבָא, וְכֻלְּהוּ אִית לוֹן דַּרְגָּא יְדִיעָא לְעֵילָּא לְאִתְנַהֲגָא בֵּיהּ.

459. In each and every grade, in each joint, there are chieftains, and battalions of fiends led by them. All those led by them are below IN THE WORLD. These are the armies of the female OF THE OTHER SIDE, all of whom have a certain grade above, by which they are led.

460. כְּמָה דְּאִית לְסִטְרָא עִלָּאָה קַדִּישָׁא, הֵיכָלִין יְדִיעָאן, לְגַבֵּי דַּרְגִּין עִלָּאִין, לְאִתְכַּלְלָא אִלֵּין בְּאִלֵּין, ה״נ לְתַתָּא בְּהִפּוּכָא, בְּסִטְרָא אַחֲרָא, אִית דַּרְגִּין, לְגַבֵּי אִינּוּן הֵיכָלִין דְּנוּקְבָּא, לְאִתְכַּלְלָא אִלֵּין בְּאִלֵּין.

460. As there are on the supernal side of holiness certain chambers OF THE FEMALE, facing the supernal grades OF THE MALE, comprising each other, so below, opposite TO HOLINESS, there are in the Other Side grades OF THE MALE facing the chambers of the female, comprising each other.

461. בְּהַאי דַּרְגָּא, דְּאִיהוּ רְבִיעָאָה, קַיְימָן דִּינִין בִּישִׁין, לְנַחְתָּא לְתַתָּא, וּלְאִתְמַסְרָא לְאִינּוּן דְּעַבְדִּין דִּינָא בִּישָׁא תַּקִּיפָא. מֵהָכָא יַנְקֵי תּוּקְפָּא דִּילְהוֹן, לְאַתְקְפָא, וּלְאַשְׁלְמָא הַהוּא דִּינָא דְּעַבְדֵי. ובג״כ, כָּל הָנֵי דַּרְגִּין כְּלִילָן בְּהוּ, בְּכָל אִינּוּן הֵיכָלִין תַּתָּאִין, דְּלִסְטַר נוּקְבָּא דִּלְתַתָּא. זַכָּאָה חוּלָקֵהוֹן דְּצַדִּיקַיָּיא, דְּסָטוּ אָרְחַיְיהוּ מֵאוֹרְחָא דָּא, וְאַזְלֵי בָּתַר דַּחַלְתָּא דקוּדְשָׁא בְּרִיךְ הוּא, לְאִתְקַדְּשָׁא בִּקְדוּשָׁה דְּמָארֵיהוֹן, זַכָּאִין אִינּוּן בְּעָלְמָא דֵּין, וּבְעָלְמָא דְּאָתֵי.

461. In this grade, the fourth one, there are evil Judgments gone down to be delivered to these FIENDS, who execute evil and stark Judgment UPON THE WICKED. Here they suck their strength to attack and carry out the justice they execute. Therefore, all these grades are included within the lower chambers from the side of the female down below. Happy is the portion of the righteous, who stay away from this way, and follow the fear of the Holy One blessed be He, to be sanctified by the sanctity of their Master. They are happy in this world and in the World to Come.

462. דַּרְגָּא חֲמִישָׁאָה. הַאי דַּרְגָּא אִתְפְּלִיג לִתְרֵין דַּרְגִּין יְמִינָא, וּשְׂמָאלָא. וְאִלֵּין אִקְרוּן שׁוֹקִין, מִתְדַּבְּקָן לְאַבְאָשָׁא וּלְמִרְדַּף. בְּגִין דְּהָכָא תְּקִיפוּ דִּרְדִיפוּ. דְּכָל מַרְעִין, וְכָל בִּישִׁין, דְּרַדְפֵי בַּתְרַיְיהוּ

דְּחַיְּיבַיָּא. וְכַד דִּינָא דָּא אִתְקְרִיב, כְּדֵין הָרָצִים יָצְאוּ דְּחוּפִים. וְאִינּוּן רָצִים אִינּוּן לְתַתָּא, לְמִרְהַט לְאַבְאָשָׁא. וְכָל אִינּוּן אִקְרוּן רוֹדְפִים, וע״ד כְּתִיב קַלִּים הָיוּ רוֹדְפֵנוּ מִנִּשְׁרֵי שָׁמָיִם.

462. The fifth grade is divided into two grades, right and left. They are called 'thighs', NAMELY, NETZACH AND HOD. They pursue and chase to harm, for here abides the power of pursuing of every illness and evil, which comes after the wicked. When this Judgment approaches, "the couriers went out in haste" (Ester 3:15). These couriers are below, hastening to cause harm. All these are called 'pursuers', as it is written, "Our pursuers were swifter than the vultures in the sky" (Eichah 4:19).

463. הַאי דַּרְגָּא אִתְפְּלַג לִתְרֵין סִטְרִין, לִימִינָא וְלִשְׂמָאלָא. תְּלַת קִשְׁרִין אִינּוּן לִימִינָא. וּתְלַת קִשְׁרִין אִינּוּן לִשְׂמָאלָא, וְאִלֵּין קִשְׁרִין, וְאִינּוּן קִשְׁרִין דְּקָאָמַרָן, כֻּלְּהוּ מִסְתַּכְּלָן לַאֲחוֹרָא. בְּגִין דְּאִינּוּן קִשְׁרִין עִלָּאִין קַדִּישִׁין, כֻּלְּהוּ מִסְתַּכְּלָן לְגוֹ פְּנִימָאֵי לְגוּפָא, כד״א וְכָל אֲחוֹרֵיהֶם בָּיְתָה. וְאִלֵּין כֻּלְּהוּ מִסְתַּכְּלָן לַאֲחוֹרָא.

463. This grade is divided into two sides, right and left. There are three joints on the right, and three joints on the left. FOR EACH LEG HAS THREE JOINTS, LIKE THE ARMS. The joints OF THE LEGS AND ARMS all face backward, because all the high and holy joints all face inward, towards the body, as it is written, "and all their hinder parts were inward" (I Melachim 7:25). And those of the Other Side face backward, FROM THE BODY OUT.

464. מַה בֵּין הַאי לְהַאי. אֶלָּא אִלֵּין קִשְׁרִין, עִלָּאִין קַדִּישִׁין כֻּלְּהוּ בְּרָזָא דְּאָדָם, וּבְגִין דְּכֹלָּא אִיהוּ בְּרָזָא דְּאָדָם, כָּל אֲחוֹרֵיהֶם בָּיְתָה כְּתִיב. וְאִלֵּין קִשְׁרִין אַחֲרָנִין דְּקָאָמַרָן, אִינּוּן קִשְׁרִין דְּאֶמְצָעִיתָא, כֻּלְּהוּ מִסְתַּכְּלָן לַאֲחוֹרָא, וְאִלֵּין אִינּוּן בְּרָזָא דִּבְהֵמָה. ובג״כ כָּל אֲחוֹרֵיהֶם לַאֲחוֹרָא. וְרָזָא דָּא כְּמָה דְּאוֹקִימְנָא, אָדָם וּבְהֵמָה תּוֹשִׁיעַ יְיָ׳. דָּא בְּסִטְרָא דְּאָדָם, וְדָא בְּסִטְרָא דִּבְהֵמָה. וְקָרְבְּנָא הָכִי סָלְקָא, אָדָם וּבְהֵמָה.

464. HE ASKS: What is the difference between them, BETWEEN THE

JOINTS OF HOLINESS AND THE JOINTS OF THE OTHER SIDE. HE ANSWERS: The supernal, holy joints are all in the secret of man, and since they are all in the secret of man, "all their hinder parts were inward." But the other joints OF THE OTHER SIDE, are, as we said, the ones in the middle, NAMELY, THE SECOND JOINT OF EACH, are all facing backward, in the secret of the beast. For that reason all their backs turn backward. This secret is as we explained, "Hashem, You preserve man and beast" (Tehilim 36:7). This one is of the side of man and that, of the side of the beast. Thus the offering rises in the aspect of man and beast.

465. קִשְׁרָא קַדְמָאָה, בֵּיהּ קַיְימָא גַּוְונָא דַּחֲשׁוֹכָא גּוֹ עוּרְפְלָא, דְּצָמַח בְּאִתְלַטְיָיא תְּחוֹת אַבְנָא דְּקַיְימָא עָלֵיהּ, דְּלָא צָמַח. וְהַאי קַיְימָא עָלַיְיהוּ דְּזַכָּאֵי, דְּאִית בְּהוּ זַכְיָין, וְלָא אִית בְּהוּ זְכוּ דַּאֲבָהָתָא לְאִתַּתְקְפָא בְּהוּ, וּלְאַגָּנָא עָלַיְיהוּ.

465. The first joint, OF THE FEET OF THE OTHER SIDE, is of a hue dark in the mist. LIKE a cursed plant cannot grow underneath a stone which stands on it, SO IS THIS JOINT ready to harm the meritorious, who has merits but no ancestral merits to protect him. HE RESEMBLES THE PLANT GROWING UNDERNEATH A STONE, AND SO CANNOT GROW, FOR IT GROWS UNDER CURSE.

466. וְקִשְׁרִין אַחֲרָנִין, רַדְפֵי בָּתַר חַיָּיבַיָּא דְּסָטוּ אָרְחַיְיהוּ מִקַּדְמַת דְּנָא, וְרַדְפֵי אֲבַתְרַיְיהוּ, וְכָל אִינּוּן דִּרְשִׁימוּ אִתְחָזֵי בְּהוּ לְאִשְׁתְּמוֹדְעָא. בְּגִין דְּכָל אִינּוּן דְּאִתְחָזוּן לְאִתְעַנְשָׁא, חַד מַלְאָכָא, שְׁלִיחָא קַדִּישָׁא, דִּי מִסִּטְרָא דִּגְבוּרָה, נָחִית וְרָשִׁים בְּהוּ רְשִׁימָא, וְהַהוּא רְשִׁימָא אִשְׁתְּמוֹדָע לְעֵילָּא, לְגַבֵּי כָּל אִינּוּן מָארֵיהוֹן דְּדִינָא. וְכַד הַהוּא רְשִׁימָא אִשְׁתְּמוֹדַע לְגַבַּיְיהוּ, מַאן דְּאִתְחָזֵי לְמַרְעִין, אַלְקֵי לֵיהּ בְּמַרְעִין. מַאן דְּאִתְחָזֵי לְמַכְאוֹבִין, וְלִשְׁאַר עוֹנָשִׁין, כֹּלָּא חָמָאן בְּהַהוּא רְשִׁימוּ.

466. The other joints OF THE FEET OF THE OTHER SIDE chase the wicked who have strayed from the path earlier. They chase these and those recognized by a mark, for an angel, a holy messenger of the side of Gvurah, descends and marks all those worthy of punishment. This mark is seen above by the complainants, and when it is known to them, all those fit for disease are hit by disease, and those fit to be in pain and other blows, RECEIVE THEM. And they see everything in the mark.

467. וּבְגִין דָּא, אִינּוּן קִשְׁרִין כֻּלְּהוּ קַיְימוּ לַאֲחוֹרָא, וּבַעֲטֵי בְּאִינּוּן דְּבַעֲטֵי בְּמָארֵיהוֹן, וּבְכָל אִינּוּן דְּאִתְחָזוּן לְבַעֲטָא בְּהוּ. בַּר צַדִּיקֵי וַחֲסִידֵי וְאִית לוֹן זְכוּ דַּאֲבָהָן, דְּמַרְעִין רַדְפִין אֲבַתְרַיְיהוּ, דְּאִלֵּין לָא שַׁלְטֵי בְּהוּ, וְלָא אָתֵי לוֹן מַרְעִין מִסִּטְרָא דָּא.

467. These joints all face backward, and kick those who kick their Master, and those worthy of being kicked, save the righteous and the pious, who have ancestral merits. These are pursued by diseases, which are not governed BY THE JOINTS. No diseases are come upon them from that side.

468. וְאִי תֵּימָא, מֵאָן אֲתַר אָתֵי לוֹן מַרְעִין. ת"ח כְּתִיב, וַיְיָ' חָפֵץ דַּכְּאוֹ הֶחֱלִי. וַיְיָ' חָפֵץ, דַּכְּאוֹ, אִתְרְעֵי לְמַחֲאָה לֵיהּ, וּלְמֵיהַב לֵיהּ מַרְעִין, בְּגִין לְזַכָּאָה לוֹן לְעָלְמָא דְּאָתֵי, וְלָא מִסִּטְרָא אַחֲרָא, וְאִלֵּין אִקְרוּן יִסּוּרִין דְּאַהֲבָה, וְכֹלָּא בְּחַד מַתְקְלָא דְּקוּדְשָׁא סַלְּקָא.

468. You may ask, from where do these diseases that come upon them, come from? Come and see: It is written, "But it pleases Hashem to crush him by disease" (Yeshayah 53:10). "It pleases Hashem to crush him," meaning that He desires to strike him and cause him illnesses, to grant him merits in the World to Come. But they do not come from the Other Side. They are called 'sufferings of love'. And they all flows from holiness.

469. דַּרְגָּא שְׁתִיתָאָה. הַאי אִקְרֵי עָרְלָה. וְדָא, וְכָל אִינּוּן דַּרְגִּין תַּתָּאִין, לְתַתָּא, כֻּלְּהוּ אִקְרוּן עָרְלָה, בְּגִין דְּיַנְקֵי מִסִּטְרָא דָּא. וְהַאי אִיהוּ גּוֹ רָזָא דְּנָחָ"שׁ בָּרִיחַ. וְהַאי יָנִיק, לְהַהוּא נָחָ"שׁ עֲקַלָּתוֹ"ן. וְכֻלְּהוּ דַּרְגִּין אַחֲרָנִין, דְּאִתְאַחֲדָן בְּהַאי סִטְרָא, אִקְרוּן גּוֹהַרְקֵי דְּעָרְלָה. וְכֹלָּא בְּרָזָא חֲדָא קָא אַזְלֵי.

469. The sixth grade, YESOD OF THE OTHER SIDE, is called 'foreskin' (Heb. *orlah*), because it sucks from this side. It is based on the secret of the piercing serpent, THE MALE, which suckles the slanted serpent, ITS FEMALE.

All the other grades, holding to each other are called 'unripe *orlah*' (lit. 'fruit of a tree not above three years old'). All this pertains to the same principle.

470. ות"ח, עַל דָּא, כָּל אִינּוּן אִילָנִין דְּאִתְנְטָעוּ בְּאַרְעָא, עַד לָא אִשְׁתְּרָשׁוּ, שַׁרְיָא עֲלַיְיהוּ רוּחָא מִסִּטְרָא דְּהַאי עָרְלָה, וְעַל דָּא כְּתִיב, וַעֲרַלְתֶּם עָרְלָתוֹ אֶת פִּרְיוֹ שָׁלֹשׁ שָׁנִים יִהְיֶה לָכֶם עֲרֵלִים לֹא יֵאָכֵל. בְּגִין דְקוּדְשָׁא בְּרִיךְ הוּא, חֲבִיבוּתָא דְּיִשְׂרָאֵל תָּדִיר לְגַבֵּיהּ, וְרָחִיק לוֹן, מִכָּל אוֹרְחִין בִּישִׁין, וְסִטְרִין בִּישִׁין וּמְסָאֲבִין, לְאִתְדַּבְּקָא בְּסִטְרָא דִּקְדוּשָּׁה. זַכָּאִין אִינּוּן בְּהַאי עָלְמָא וְזַכָּאִין אִינּוּן בְּעָלְמָא דְּאָתֵי.

470. Come and see: This is why the spirit of the side of the foreskin hovers above all the trees planted in the land of Yisrael, before they strike roots. It is therefore written, "then you shall reckon their fruit as uncircumcised, three years shall it be as uncircumcised to you, it shall not be eaten" (Vayikra 19:23). For the Holy One, blessed be He always loves Yisrael, and keeps them away from evil ways, and bad and defiling ways, so they may join the side of holiness. Happy are they in this world and in the World to Come.

45. The chambers of holiness

A Synopsis

Rabbi Shimon describes for us the chambers where praises to God are arranged, one of them is for words, and the is other according to the wordless desire and intention of the heart. The chambers are arranged for one purpose, and that is to unite above and below. He tells us that when Moses prayed for Yisrael he made his prayer long, for it is a prayer that ascends to Zeir Anpin, but when he prayed for his sister he made his prayer short, for it remains below. He said: "Heal her now, O El, I pray you," and did not need to pray further because he was the master of this level. Rabbi Shimon tells us that all the arrangements for the chambers were made to allow the Shechinah to live in the world. He then discusses Adam, and the delight that he had in living in the Garden of Eden where there were seven canopies for his pleasure. He speaks of the supernal beauty that Adam could see and that refer to the seven firmaments above and below. Rabbi Shimon says to Adam that he was given both the seven supernal holy canopies that are the secret of Chassadim and the seven lower firmaments of Malchut, and that God gave him everything for his completion. He had all these things until he was driven out of the garden by being drawn to unholy desires called 'poison of asps'. After this Abraham came and repaired the world by rejoining the firmaments above and the firmaments below. We are told that the lower firmaments of Malchut are chambers for the upper firmaments of Zeir Anpin.

471. אָמַר רִבִּי שִׁמְעוֹן, הָא תָּנֵינָן בְּאִינּוּן הֵיכָלִין, דְּאִינּוּן קַיְימִין, לְסַדְּרָא סִדּוּרָא דִּשְׁבָחָא דְקוּדְשָׁא בְּרִיךְ הוּא בֵּין סִדּוּרָא דְקַיְּימָא בְּמִלָּה בֵּין סִדּוּרָא דְקַיְימָא בִּרְעוּתָא. בְּגִין דְּאִית סִדּוּרָא דְקַיְּימָא בְּמִלָּה, וְאִית סִדּוּרָא דְקַיְּימָא בִּרְעוּתָא וְכַוָּונָה דְלִבָּא, לְמִנְדַּע וּלְאִסְתַּכְּלָא, בְּגִין לְאִסְתַּכְּלָא לְעֵילָּא לְעֵילָּא עַד אֵין סוֹף, דְּתַמָּן תְּקִיעוּ דְּכָל רְעוּתִין וּמַחֲשָׁבִין, וְלָא קַיְימִין בְּמִלָּה כְּלַל, אֶלָּא כְּמָה דְּאִיהוּ סָתִים, הָכִי כָּל מִלּוֹי בִּסְתִימוּ.

471. Rabbi Shimon said: We learned of the chambers, where praises to the Holy One, blessed be He are arranged, the one by words, another composed of will. For there is the arrangement of words, and there is an arrangement according to desire and the meditation of the heart, with which to know and look toward the Endless World, where all desires and thoughts are put, but no words at all. As it is concealed, so are all matters concealed.

472. ת״ח הַאי דְּאַמָרָן בְּאִינּוּן הֵיכָלִין כֻּלְּהוּ, כָּל אִינּוּן סִדּוּרִין אִינּוּן כְּלָלָא חֲדָא, בְּגִין לְאִתְכַּלְּלָא תַּתָּאֵי בְּעִלָּאֵי.

472. Come and see: What we explained about all the chambers, all these arrangements are for one purpose, namely, to include the lower chambers within the upper chambers.

473. אֲבָל תָּא חֲזֵי, מֹשֶׁה כַּד סִדֵּר צְלוֹתֵיהּ בְּגִינֵיהוֹן דְּיִשְׂרָאֵל, אָרִיךְ בְּהַאי צְלוֹתָא, בְּגִין דְּאִיהִי צְלוֹתָא דְּקַיְּימָא לְעֵילָּא. וְכַד סִדֵּר צְלוֹתֵיהּ בְּקְצִירוּ דְּאַחְתֵיהּ, לָא אָרִיךְ בָּהּ, בְּגִין דְּקַיְּימָא לְתַתָּא. דִּכְתִּיב, אֵל נָא רְפָא נָא לָהּ, וְלָא אָרִיךְ יַתִּיר, בְּגִין דְּאִיהוּ מָארֵי דְּבֵיתָא, וּפָקִיד בֵּיתֵיהּ כַּדְקָא חֲזֵי, ובג״כ לָא אָרִיךְ יַתִּיר בְּבָעוּתֵיהּ. וְכֻלְּהוּ סִדּוּרִין, לְאַשְׁרָאָה שְׁכִינְתָּא בְּעָלְמָא, כְּמָה דְּאוֹקִימְנָא בְּכָל אִינּוּן הֵיכָלִין דְּקָאָמַרָן.

473. But Come and see: When Moses arranged his prayer for the sake of Yisrael, he made this prayer long, for it is a prayer abiding above, IN ZEIR ANPIN, and when he composed a short prayer, IN PRAYING for his sister, he did not lengthen it, because it abides below, IN MALCHUT, as it is written, "Heal her now, O El, I pray You" (Bemidbar 12:13). He did not pray further, since he is the master of the house, WHICH IS MALCHUT CALLED 'HOUSE', AND MOSES WAS A CHARIOT OF ZEIR ANPIN, HER MASTER. He therefore commanded the house properly, and did not prolong his prayer. All the arrangements CONCERNING THE CHAMBERS were made to allow the Shechinah to dwell in the world, as we already expounded upon in relation to the said chambers.

474. ר״ש קָם וְאָמַר, זַכָּאָה חוּלָקָא דִּילָךְ אָדָם קַדְמָאָה, בְּרִירָא דְּכָל נִבְרָאִין, דְּקַיְימִין בְּעָלְמָא, דְּרַבֵּי לָךְ קוּדְשָׁא בְּרִיךְ הוּא עַל כֹּלָּא, וְאָעִיל לָךְ בְּגִנְתָּא דְּעֵדֶן, וְאַתְקִין לָךְ ז׳ חוּפּוֹת בֵּיהּ, לְאִשְׁתַּעְשְׁעָא בְּעִנּוּגָא דְּנֹעַם עִלָּאָה, כד״א לַחֲזוֹת בְּנֹעַם יְיָ׳ וּלְבַקֵּר בְּהֵיכָלוֹ. לַחֲזוֹת בְּנֹעַם יְיָ׳ לְעֵילָּא. וּלְבַקֵּר בְּהֵיכָלוֹ לְתַתָּא. לַחֲזוֹת בְּנוֹעַם יְיָ׳, בְּאִינּוּן שִׁבְעָה

רְקִיעִין לְעֵילָּא, וּלְבַקֵּר בְּהֵיכָלוֹ בְּאִינּוּן שִׁבְעָה רְקִיעִין דִּלְתַתָּא, וְאִלֵּין קַיְימִין אִלֵּין לָקֳבֵל אִלֵּין.

474. Rabbi Shimon stood up and said: Happy is your portion, Adam, chosen of all the creatures in the world, for the Holy One, blessed be He raised you above all, put you in the Garden of Eden, and prepared seven canopies for your pleasure, to delight in the supernal beauty, as it is said: "to behold the beauty of Hashem, and to inquire in His temple" (Tehilim 27:4). "To behold the beauty of Hashem" above IN ZEIR ANPIN, "and to inquire in His temple" below IN MALCHUT. HE FURTHER EXPLAINS: "To behold the beauty of Hashem" refers to the seven firmaments above OF ZEIR ANPIN, and "to inquire in His temple" refers to the seven firmaments below, IN MALCHUT. The ones correspond to the others.

475. וּבְכֻלְּהוּ קָמֵת בְּגִנְתָּא דְעֵדֶן. אִינּוּן שִׁבְעָה חוּפּוֹת עִלָּאִין קַדִּישִׁין, קַיְימוּ עֲלָךְ לְעֵילָּא, לְאִתְעַטְּרָא בְּהוּ. וְאִינּוּן ז׳ תַּתָּאִין, קָמֵת בְּהוּ לְאִשְׁתַּעְשְׁעָא בְּהוּ, וּבְכֻלְּהוּ אַשְׁלִים לָךְ מָארָךְ, לְמֶהֱוֵי שְׁלִים בְּכֹלָּא.

475. You stood within all THE SEVEN FIRMAMENTS OF ZEIR ANPIN AND THE SEVEN OF MALCHUT, in the Garden of Eden. The seven supernal holy canopies, NAMELY, THE SEVEN FIRMAMENTS OF ZEIR ANPIN stood above you for your adornment, FOR THEY ARE THE SECRET OF CHASSADIM. You stood within the lower seven FIRMAMENTS, OF MALCHUT, to take pleasure in, FOR THEY ARE THE SECRET OF THE ILLUMINATION OF CHOCHMAH CALLED 'PLEASURE'. And your Master gave you all for your perfection, NAMELY, BOTH BY CHASSADIM AND BY CHOCHMAH.

476. עַד דְּאִתְדְּחוּ רַגְלָךְ, בָּתַר עֵיטָא דְּהַהוּא חִוְיָא בִּישָׁא, וְאִתְתָּרְכַת מִגִּנְתָּא דְעֵדֶן, וְגַרְמַת מוֹתָא לָךְ, וּלְכָל עָלְמָא, בְּגִין דְּשַׁבְקַת אִלֵּין עִדּוּנִין דִּלְעֵילָּא וְתַתָּא, וְאִתְמַשְּׁכַת בָּתַר אִינּוּן כְּסוּפִין מִסְאָבִין, דְּאִקְרוּן רֹאשׁ פְּתָנִים, דְּגוּפָא מָשִׁיךְ בְּהוּ, וְלָא רוּחָא. כד״א, וְרֹאשׁ פְּתָנִים אַכְזָר. וּכְתִיב עֲנָבֵימוֹ עִנְּבֵי רֹאשׁ. עַד דְּאָתָא אַבְרָהָם חֲסִידָא, וְשָׁארֵי לְאַתְקְנָא עָלְמָא, וְעָאל גּוֹ מְהֵימְנוּתָא קַדִּישָׁא, וְאַתְקֵן לְעֵילָּא וְתַתָּא, בְּאִינּוּן רְקִיעִין עִלָּאִין, וּבְאִינּוּן רְקִיעִין תַּתָּאִין.

476. Until your legs were tempted to follow the counsel of the evil serpent, and you were driven out of the Garden of Eden, thus bringing death to you and to the whole world, by leaving all the delicacies of above and below. You were drawn to unholy desires called, "poison of asps" (Iyov 20:16), to which the body was drawn and not the spirit, as it is said, "and cruel venom of asps" (Devarim 32:33), THAT IS CRUEL TO THE SPIRIT, AND ALSO "their clusters are bitter" (Ibid. 32). Then came Abraham the pious, and started to amend the world, and entered the holy Faith, fixing above and below, in the firmaments above, and in the firmaments below.

477. אִינּוּן תַּתָּאִין, הֵיכָלִין לְאִינּוּן רְקִיעִין עִלָּאִין, לְאִתְאַחֲדָא דָּא בְּדָא, וּלְאִתְקַשְּׁרָא דָּא בְּדָא, כְּמָה דְּאוֹקִימְנָא בְּאִינּוּן הֵיכָלִין דְּקָאָמַרָן. ואע"ג דְּאוֹקִימְנָא הָתָם גּוֹ כְּלָלָא, הָכָא אִית לָן לְפָרְטָא מִלִּין, וּלְאַתְקְנָא לְיִחוּדָא כַּדְקָא יֵאוֹת, בְּגִין דְּלָא יִטְעוּן חַבְרַיָּיא, וְיֵהָכוּן בְּאֹרַח מֵישָׁר, כְּמָה דִּכְתִּיב כִּי יְשָׁרִים דַּרְכֵי יְיָ' וְצַדִּיקִים וְגוֹ'.

477. The lower firmaments OF MALCHUT are chambers for the upper firmaments OF ZEIR ANPIN, to be united and joined together, as we explained elsewhere in relation to the chambers. And though we explained it there in a general way, it behooves us to explain here in detail, and fix the unison properly, so the friends will not be misled, but walk the right way, as it is written, "for the ways of Hashem are right, and the just do walk in them…" (Hoshea 14:10).

46. The chamber of a sapphire stone – Yesod

A Synopsis

Rabbi Shimon tells us that the first chamber marks the beginning of the faith and is the light of wisdom or 'sight'. Although it is the first or lowest of the grades of holiness it is also the last of the descending grades of the Other Side. Therefore when Hosea looked into it he saw the levels of defilement, and we are told that people should not enter these chambers of defilement so that they won't be drawn to them. Hosea looked into the chamber because he wanted to know why Yisrael left the secret of the faith, he wanted to know what the defilement was like that they were always drawn to, and he saw these things in the first chamber. This chamber is the start of all the grades of ascent, and it is governed by a chieftain called Tahariel. He and his other chieftains guard the gate that each soul has to pass through after death. If the soul is not good enough to enter, another chieftain of the Other Side is summoned and the soul is moved to the chambers of defilement from where it is taken to Gehenom and judged for twelve months. Tahariel also decides that prayers are worthy to be passed upward through his gate. If a public prayer comes along he opens the gate and brings it in. If it is a solitary prayer he opens the door and lets it in if it is good enough for the Holy King, but if it is unworthy he pushes it out and it goes back down to the lowest of the firmaments below. Here a chieftain called Sahadiel keeps all the rejected prayers until the person repents. When he repents and prays a better prayer Sahadiel takes the unfit prayer and elevates it to meet the good one, then they both rise to stand before the Holy King. We hear about the 'gate of tears', and Rabbi Shimon talks about the Holy Spirit named Staturiyah who rejoins male souls with female souls in the seventh chamber above. Similarly a spirit named Adiriyah Snugiya rejoins female souls with male souls. After describing the marriage of the souls Rabbi Shimon describes the wheels and the living creatures and the flash of lightning. We hear how Sandalphon takes the finished prayers of the people of Yisrael and brings them up to their Master. The words of the rising prayers and the words of the Torah rise up to the place in the firmament where the stars and constellations and sun and moon are, and this place is called 'the book of remembrance'. We are told more about the wheels and pillars and the secret of the letters of the name Adonai. The name Ya'ahadonahi is shown to comprise two spirits, Yud Hei Vav Hei and Adonai, and to cause the unification of everything, so that "they have all one spirit."

478. הֵיכָלָא קַדְמָאָה. שֵׁירוּתָא גּוֹ מְהֵימְנוּתָא, וְהַאי אִיהוּ שֵׁירוּתָא לְרָזָא דִּמְהֵימְנוּתָא, וּבְדַרְגִּין דְּחֵיזוּ דִּמְהֵימְנוּתָא. נְבִיאֵי קְשׁוֹט, הֲווֹ חָמָאן מִגּוֹ דָּא אַסְפַּקְלַרְיָא דְּאֵינָהּ מְאִירָה, וּבְגִין דְּהַאי אִיהוּ שֵׁירוּתָא דִּמְהֵימְנוּתָא, כְּתִיב תְּחִלַּת דִּבֶּר יְיָ׳ בְּהוֹשֵׁעַ. דְּחָמָא מִגּוֹ דַּרְגָּא דָּא, דְּאִיהוּ שֵׁירוּתָא דְּכָל דַּרְגִּין לְסַלְּקָא לְעֵילָּא, וְסוֹפָא דְּכָל דַּרְגִּין לְנַחְתָּא לְתַתָּא.

478. The first chamber, NAMELY, YESOD AND MALCHUT, IS THE FIRST FROM BELOW UPWARD. It marks the beginning of the Faith, NAMELY, THIS CHAMBER IS MALCHUT OF THE CHAMBERS CALLED 'FAITH'. It is the start of the secret of the Faith, NAMELY, OF THE MYSTERY OF MALCHUT OF ATZILUT, and is of the grade of sight within Faith, NAMELY, THE ILLUMINATION OF CHOCHMAH IN IT IS CALLED 'SIGHT'. The true prophets used to look from within the mirror, which does not shine, MALCHUT, for that CHAMBER is the beginning of the Faith, MALCHUT OF ATZILUT. It is written, "When Hashem spoke at first with Hosea" (Hoshea 1:2), for he looked from this grade, NAMELY, THE FIRST CHAMBER, the beginning of all the ascending grades, and the end of all the descending grades OF THE OTHER SIDE.

479. וּבְגִין דְּהוֹשֵׁעַ חָמָא מִגּוֹ שֵׁירוּתָא דָּא, סוֹפָא דְּכָל דַּרְגִּין, אִצְטְרִיךְ לְנַטְלָא הַאי אֵשֶׁת זְנוּנִים, בְּגִין דְּיִשְׂרָאֵל אִתְדָּחוּ וְאִתְמְשָׁכוּ מִתַּמָּן לְתַתָּא, לְגַבֵּי הַהוּא אֲתַר דְּאִקְרֵי אֵשֶׁת זְנוּנִים, בְּגִין דְּשַׁבְקוּ, וְלָא אִתְדַּבָּקוּ בְּהַאי אֵשֶׁת חָיִל. וְחָמָא מִתַּמָּן כָּל אִינּוּן הֵיכָלִין דְּאִינּוּן בְּסִטְרָא מְסָאֲבָא.

479. Since Hosea saw, in this beginning, NAMELY, OF THE CHAMBERS OF DEFILEMENT, the end of all the grades, he had to take "a wife of harlotry" (Hoshea 1:2). This is because Yisrael were tempted and drawn away FROM THE FIRST CHAMBER downward to the place called "a wife of harlotry," MALCHUT OF DEFILEMENT, by leaving behind, instead of joining, the "woman of worth" (Mishlei 31:10), MALCHUT OF HOLINESS. From there he saw all the chambers on the side of defilement.

480. הֵיכָלִין דִּמְסָאֲבָא, כֻּלְּהוּ מְסָאֲבִין לְמַאן דְּאִתְדַּבַּק בְּהוֹן, וְעַל דָּא

כְּתִיב, קַח לְךָ אֵשֶׁת זְנוּנִים וְגו'. וְכִי נְבִיאָה דִּקְשׁוֹט אִצְטְרִיךְ לְדָא. אֶלָּא, בְּגִין דְּאָסִיר לֵיהּ לְבַר נָשׁ לְאַעֲלָא בְּאִינּוּן הֵיכָלִין, בְּגִין דְּלָא יִתְמְשַׁךְ אֲבַתְרַיְיהוּ, כְּגַוְונָא דְּעָבֵד נֹחַ, דִּכְתִּיב וַיֵּשְׁתְּ מִן הַיַּיִן וַיִּשְׁכָּר וַיִּתְגַּל.

480. The chambers of defilement defile whoever clings to them. Hence, SINCE HOSEA HAD TO LOOK AT THE CHAMBERS OF DEFILEMENT, it is written, "take to you a wife of harlotry…" IT IS DIFFICULT TO UNDERSTAND why a true prophet should need that. But a man should not enter these chambers OF DEFILEMENT, lest he be drawn to them, as was Noah, as it is written, "and he drank of the wine, and was drunk, and he was uncovered within his tent" (Beresheet 9:21), MEANING THAT HE CLUNG TO THE OTHER SIDE, WHICH IS THE INTOXICATING WINE.

481. וְהוֹשֵׁעַ דָּחִיל לְאִסְתַּכְּלָא בְּאִינּוּן הֵיכָלִין דְּאִסְתְּאָבוּ בְּהוּ יִשְׂרָאֵל וְאִתְדַּבָּקוּ, דְּלָא יִתְמְשַׁךְ אֲבַתְרַיְיהוּ, כְּמָה דִּכְתִּיב בְּנֹחַ וַיֵּשְׁתְּ מִן הַיַּיִן וַיִּשְׁכָּר וַיִּתְגַּל. עַד דְּאָמַר לֵיהּ, קַח לְךָ אֵשֶׁת זְנוּנִים וְיַלְדֵי זְנוּנִים. וּכְתִיב וַיֵּלֶךְ וַיִּקַּח אֶת גֹּמֶר בַּת דִּבְלָיִם. לְמִנְדַּע בְּמָה דְּאִתְדַּבָּקוּ וְאִסְתְּאָבוּ, וְשָׁבְקוּ רָזָא דִּמְהֵימְנוּתָא, בְּגִין אֵל נֵכָר. וְעַל דָּא, חָמָא מִגּוֹ הֵיכָלָא דָּא, שֵׁירוּתָא דְּכָל דַּרְגִּין.

481. Hosea was afraid to look at the chambers, where Yisrael clung to, to be defiled, IN FEAR of being drawn after them, as it is written of Noah "and he drank of the wine, and was drunk: and he was uncovered." Then He said to him "take to you a wife of harlotry, and children of harlotry," THE WIFE OF HARLOTRY BEING MALCHUT OF THE OTHER SIDE, AND THE CHILDREN OF HARLOTRY HER GRADES. It is also written, "So he went and took Gomer the daughter of Divlayim" (Hoshea 1:3), to know what Yisrael clung to and were defiled with and why they left the secret of the Faith, MALCHUT OF HOLINESS, for a strange El, MALCHUT OF DEFILEMENT. And he saw THIS within the first chamber, the opening of all the grades. THEREFORE, IT IS SAID OF HER "SIN CROUCHES AT THE DOOR" (BERESHEET 4:7), FOR AT THE VERY OPENING OF THIS CHAMBER, THE OTHER SIDE CROUCHES, WHICH IS A WIFE OF HARLOTRY. AND THE CHIEFTAIN OF THE OTHER SIDE IS STANDING AT THE GATE.

482. הֵיכָלָא דָּא, שֵׁירוּתָא דְּכֹלָּא, לְסַלְקָא בְּדַרְגִּין. הַאי הֵיכָלָא, אִיהוּ מָדוֹרָא דְּקַיְימָא בִּנְהִירוּ. לְאִתְעַטְּרָא בְּדַרְגּוֹי, לְאִסְתַּכְּלָא בְּאִינּוּן דַּרְגִּין עִלָּאִין, דִּכְתִּיב וַיִּרְאוּ אֵת אֱלהֵי יִשְׂרָאֵל.

482. This chamber is the start for all who ascend the grades. It is a compartment within the light, to be adorned with its grades, through which to look at the supernal grades, as it is written, "and they saw the Elohim of Yisrael" (Shemot 24:10). BECAUSE THIS CHAMBER IS AN ASPECT OF MALCHUT, SIGHT PERTAINS TO IT, FOR SIGHT IS ONLY IN MALCHUT.

483. בְּהַאי הֵיכָלָא, חַד מְמָנָא שַׁמָּשָׁא טָהֲרִיאֵ״ל שְׁמֵיהּ. וְאִיהוּ קַיְּימָא עַל פִּתְחָא דְּהַהוּא הֵיכָלָא, וְכָל נִשְׁמָתִין דְּסַלְקִין, קַיְּימָא הַאי מְמָנָא בְּהַאי פִּתְחָא, וְכַמָּה מְמָנָן אַחֲרָנִין עִמֵּיהּ, כֻּלְּהוּ אֶשָּׁא דְּמִלַהֲטָא, וְשַׁרְבִיטִין דְּאֶשָּׁא בִּידַיְיהוּ, וְכֻלְּהוּ מָארֵי דְּעַיְינִין. הַאי מְמָנָא קַיְּימָא בְּסִטְרָא דָּא, אִי זָכַאת הַאי נִשְׁמְתָא לְמֵיעַל, הַאי מְמָנָא פָּתַח פִּתְחָא וְעָאלַת.

483. There is a chieftain appointed over this chamber, by the name of Tahariel. He stands at the gate of the chamber, and all the souls, AFTER PASSING FROM THIS WORLD, mount AND WISH TO ENTER THIS FIRST CHAMBER. This chieftain stands at the gate, together with other chieftains, they are wholly ablaze with fire, with scepters of fire in their hand, all eyed. FOR THERE IS SIGHT IN THIS CHAMBER, IN THE SECRET OF CHOCHMAH CALLED 'EYES', SINCE CHOCHMAH IS REVEALED ONLY WHEN JUDGMENT IS IN THE OPEN. THEREFORE, THEY ARE OF BLAZING FIRE... This chieftain stands on this side, and if the soul, AFTER PASSING FROM THIS WORLD, has the merit to enter, he opens the gate and THE SOUL enters.

484. וְאִי לָא זַכָּאת, הַהוּא מְמָנָא אַחֲרָא דְּקַיְימָא בְּסִטְרָא אַחֲרָא, זַמִּין, וְכַמָּה אֶלֶף וְרִבְבָן גַּרְדִּינֵי נִימוּסִין עִמֵּיהּ. דָּחֵי לָהּ הַהוּא מְמָנָא אַחֲרָא קַדִּישָׁא, וְנָקִיט לָהּ הַאי אַחֲרָא, דִּי בְּסִטְרָא דִּמְסָאֲבָא, וְאָעִיל לָהּ גּוֹ אִינּוּן הֵיכָלֵי מִסְאֲבֵי. וְכָל אִינּוּן גַּרְדִּינֵי נִימוּסִין אַחְדֵי לָהּ, עַד דְּנַחְתֵּי לָהּ לַגֵּיהִנָּם, וְאִתְדָּנַת תַּמָּן תְּרֵיסַר יַרְחֵי. תִּקּוּנָא דְּהַהוּא סִטְרָא אַחֲרָא,

בֵּי דִינָא לְאִתְדְּנָא בְּהוּ חַיָּיבַיָּא.

484. And if the soul has not the merit to enter, BECAUSE IT SINNED IN THIS WORLD, then another chieftain OF THE OTHER SIDE standing at another side, is summoned, together with thousands and myriad of guardians of law and accusers. The other, holy chieftain, pushes it and the other of the side of defilement receives it, and puts it in the chambers of defilement. All the guardians of law and accusers hold it, and bring it down to Gehenom, where it is judged for twelve months. This is the place of correction of the Other Side, a court to judge the wicked.

485. כְּגַוְונָא דָא, הַהוּא מְמָנָא קַדִּישָׁא, דְּקַיְּימָא עַל הַהוּא פִּתְחָא, כָּל אִינּוּן צְלוֹתִין, דְּבַקְעֵי אֲווירִין וּרְקִיעִין, לְמֵיעָאל קָמֵי מַלְכָּא, אִי צְלוֹתָא דְּסַגִּיאִין אִינּוּן פָּתַח פִּתְחָא, וְאָעִיל הַהוּא צְלוֹתָא עַד דְּאִתְעֲבִידוּ כָּל צְלוֹתִין דְּעָלְמָא, עֲטָרָא בְּרֵישָׁא דְּצַדִּיק חַי עָלְמִין, כְּמָה דְּאוּקְמוּהָ.

485. In the same manner is the holy chieftain that stands at the entrance. When all the prayers that cleave airs and firmaments come before the King. If this is a public prayer he opens the gate and brings it in, WHERE IT WAITS until all the prayers in the world become a crown on the head of the righteous who lives forever, YESOD, as we already explained.

486. וְאִי צְלוֹתָא דְּיָחִיד, סַלְקָא עַד דְּמָטֵי לְפִתְחָא דְּהֵיכָלָא דָא, דְּהַאי מְמָנָא קַיְּימָא בֵּיהּ. אִי יָאָה הַהִיא צְלוֹתָא, לְאַעֲלָא קָמֵי מַלְכָּא קַדִּישָׁא, מִיַּד פָּתַח פִּתְחָא, וְאָעִיל לָהּ. וְאִי לָא יָאָה, דָּחֵי לָהּ לְבַר, וְנַחְתָּא וְאִתְשַׁטְיָא בְּעָלְמָא, וְקַיְּימָא גּוֹ רְקִיעָא תַּתָּאָה מֵאִינּוּן רְקִיעִין דִּלְתַתָּא, דְּמִדַּבְּרֵי גּוֹ עָלְמָא, וּבְהַהוּא רְקִיעָא, קַיְּימָא חַד מְמָנָא דִּי שְׁמֵיהּ סָהֲדִיאֵ״ל, וּמְמָנָא עַל הַאי רְקִיעָא. וְנָטִיל כָּל הָנֵי צְלוֹתִין דְּאִתְדַּחְיָין, דְּאִקְרוּן צְלוֹתֵי פְּסִילָאן וְגָנִיז לוֹן, עַד דְּתָב הַהוּא ב״נ.

486. If the prayer is solitary, it rises until it reaches the entrance of this chamber, where the chieftain stands. If it is good enough to be presented before the Holy King, he immediately opens the door and lets it in. If it is not worthy, he pushes it out, and it goes down and hovers about the world, standing at the lowest of the firmaments in the world below, where there is a chieftain by the name of Sahadiel, in charge over that firmament. He takes all the rejected prayers, called 'unfit prayers', and stores them until that person repents.

487. אִי תָּב לְגַבֵּי מָארֵיהּ כַּדְקָא יָאוֹת, וְצַלֵּי צְלוֹתָא אַחֲרָא זַכָּאָה, הַהִיא צְלוֹתָא זַכָּאָה כַּד סַלְקָא, נָטִיל הַהוּא מְמָנָא סַהֲדִיאֵ״ל הַאי צְלוֹתָא, וְסָלִיק לָהּ לְעֵילָּא, עַד דְּאִעְרַע בְּהַהִיא צְלוֹתָא זַכָּאָה, וְסַלְקִין וְאִתְעָרְבוּן כַּחֲדָא, וְעָאלִין קָמֵי מַלְכָּא קַדִּישָׁא.

487. If he properly repents before his Master, and prays another, good prayer then when the good one rises, the chieftain Sahadiel take the UNFIT prayer and elevates it, until it meets the good prayer and they both rise and intermingle and come before the Holy King.

488. וּלְזִמְנִין אִתְדַּחְיָא הַהִיא צְלוֹתָא, בְּגִין דְּהַהוּא ב״נ אִתְמְשַׁךְ בָּתַר סִטְרָא אַחֲרָא, וְאִיהוּ אִסְתְּאַב בְּהַהוּא סִטְרָא, וְנָטִיל לָהּ הַהוּא מְמָנָא דִּי בְּהַהוּא סִטְרָא אַחֲרָא מְסָאֲבָא. וּכְדֵין קַיְּימָא הַהוּא סִטְרָא אַחֲרָא מְסָאֲבָא. סָלִיק וְאַדְכַּר חוֹבוֹי דְּהַהוּא ב״נ קָמֵי קוּדְשָׁא בְּרִיךְ הוּא, וְאַסְטֵי עָלֵיהּ לְעֵילָּא. וְעַל דָּא, כָּל צְלוֹתִין, וְכָל נִשְׁמָתִין, כַּד סַלְקִין, כֻּלְּהוֹן סַלְקִין וְקַיְימָן קָמֵי הֵיכָלָא דָּא. וְהַאי מְמָנָא קַיְּימָא עַל פִּתְחָא דְּהֵיכָלָא דָּא, לְאַעֲלָא נִשְׁמָתִין וּצְלוֹתִין, אוֹ לְדַחְיָיא לוֹן לְבַר.

488. Sometimes the prayer is rejected because that man is drawn to the Other Side, where he is defiled. The chieftain of the defiled Other Side takes the prayer, and the defiled Other Side mentions the sins of that man before the Holy One, blessed be He and accuses him above. Therefore, all the prayers and the ascending souls, all stand in front of the FIRST chamber, where the chieftain stands at the gate to show them in or reject them.

489. לְעֵילָּא מֵהַאי פִּתְחָא, אִית פִּתְחָא אַחֲרָא, דְּקוּדְשָׁא בְּרִיךְ הוּא חָתִיר לָהּ וְאִתְפְּתַח תְּלַת זִמְנֵי בְּיוֹמָא, וְלָא אַנְעִיל, וְקַיְּימָא לְאִינּוּן מָארֵיהוֹן דִּתְיוּבְתָּא, דִּי אוֹשְׁדִין דִּמְעָה בִּצְלוֹתְהוֹן קָמֵי מָארֵיהוֹן. וְכָל

תַּרְעִין וּפִתְחִין נִנְעָלוּ, עַד דְּעַיְילֵי בִּרְשׁוּתָא, בַּר תַּרְעִין אִלֵּין, דְּאִקְרוּן שַׁעֲרֵי דִּמְעָה.

489. Above this gate OF THE CHAMBER, there is another opening dug by the Holy One, blessed be He. It is opened three times a day, NAMELY, THE THREE COLUMNS SHINE IN IT. It is never closed, but stands OPEN for those who repent and shed tears in their prayers before their Master. All the gates and openings are closed, until given permission, save the gates called 'the gates of tears', THAT DO NOT NEED PERMISSION TO BE OPENED.

490. וְכַד הַאי צְלוֹתָא דְּדִמְעָה סַלְקָא לְעֵילָּא, לְאַעֲלָא בְּאִינּוּן תַּרְעִין, אִזְדַּמַּן הַהוּא אוֹפָן דְּקַיְּימָא עַל שִׁית מְאָה חֵיוָון רַבְרְבָן, וְרַחֲמִיאֵ״ל שְׁמֵיהּ, וְנָטִיל הַהִיא צְלוֹתָא, בְּאִינּוּן דִּמְעִין, צְלוֹתָא עָאלַת וְאִתְקַשְּׁרַת לְעֵילָּא. וְאִינּוּן דִּמְעִין אִשְׁתָּאֲרוּ הָכָא, וּרְשִׁימִין בְּהַאי פִּתְחָא.

490. When the tearful prayer rises through these gates, a wheel chances, NAMELY, AN ANGEL OF THE ASPECT OF MALCHUT CALLED 'WHEEL', standing on six hundred large living creatures, called 'Rachamiel'. He takes the tearful prayer, the prayer enters to be united above, and the tears stay, engraved upon the opening DUG BY THE HOLY ONE, BLESSED BE HE.

491. וְאִית דִּמְעִין אַחֲרָנִין, וּרְשִׁימִין תָּדִיר עַל כֹּל אִינּוּן רְתִיכִין עִלָּאִין, דְּלָא אִתְמְחוּן. אִלֵּין אִינּוּן דִּמְעִין, דְּאוֹשְׁדוּ לְעֵילָּא וְתַתָּא, כַּד אִתְחָרַב בֵּי מַקְדְּשָׁא, דִּכְתִיב הֵן אֶרְאֶלָּם צָעֲקוּ חוּצָה מַלְאֲכֵי שָׁלוֹם מַר יִבְכָּיוּן. וְאִינּוּן דִּמְעִין דְּאוֹשְׁדִין עַל צַדִּיקַיָּיא, וְזַכָּאִין, כַּד מִסְתַּלְּקֵי מֵעָלְמָא. כֻּלְּהוּ נַטְלֵי לוֹן אִינּוּן רְתִיכִין, וְעַרְבֵי לוֹן בְּאִינּוּן דִּמְעִין, דְּאִתּוֹשְׁדוּ עַל חָרִיבוּ דְּבֵי מַקְדְּשָׁא וְעַל דָּא כְּתִיב, וּמָחָה יְיָ׳ אֱלֹהִים דִּמְעָה מֵעַל כָּל פָּנִים. מַאן פָּנִים. אִלֵּין רְתִיכִין עִלָּאִין קַדִּישִׁין. וּלְבָתַר וְחֶרְפַּת עַמּוֹ יָסִיר מֵעַל כָּל הָאָרֶץ כִּי יְיָ׳ דִּבֵּר.

491. There are other tears, forever engraved upon the supernal Chariots, and they are not wiped. These are the tears shed above and below when the Temple was destroyed, as it is written, "Behold, the mighty ones shall cry outside: ambassadors of peace shall weep bitterly" (Yeshayah 33:7). And those are the tears shed for the righteous and meritorious who pass from this world. They are all taken by these Chariots to be mingled with the tears shed for the destruction of the Temple. Therefore it is written, IN THE FUTURE TENSE, "and Hashem Elohim will wipe away tears from off all faces" (Yeshayah 25:8). What are "all faces"? they are the holy supernal Chariots. Then "the insult of His people shall He take away from off all the earth: for Hashem has spoken it" (Ibid.). THIS WILL HAPPEN AT THE END OF THE CORRECTION.

492. בְּהַאי הֵיכָלָא, אִית רוּחַ דְּאִקְרֵי סְטוּטְרִיָּ"ה, וְהַאי אִיהוּ חֵיזוּ סַפִּירָא, דְּנָצִיץ לְכָל עֵיבַר, וְהַאי אִיהוּ דְּקַיְּימָא לִתְרֵין סִטְרִין, וּמֵאִלֵּין מִתְפָּרְשָׁאן נְצִיצִין כִּנְצִיצוּ דְּשַׁרְגָא, כְּמָה דְּאוֹקִימְנָא בְּכַמָּה סִטְרִין. וְכַמָּה גַּוְונִין מְלַהֲטָן מֵהַאי בְּסִטְרָא דִּימִינָא.

492. In this chamber there is one spirit called 'Situt'riyah', looking like a sapphire glittering on all sides. It is facing both sides, ILLUMINATING RIGHT AND LEFT. From them spreads a glow, like that of a candle, as we explained. IT SHINES upon several sides, NAMELY, FOUR SIDES. Some colors are blazing from this LIGHT of the right side.

493. כַּד הַהוּא רְקִיעָא עִלָּאָה, נָהָר דְּנָגִיד וְנָפִיק מֵעֵדֶן, אַפִּיק נִשְׁמָתִין, לְאַעֲלָא גוֹ הֵיכָלָא שְׁבִיעָאָה לְעֵילָּא, הַהוּא הֵיכָלָא שְׁבִיעָאָה נָקִיט לוֹן. וְכַד נָפְקֵי אִינּוּן נִשְׁמָתִין קַדִּישִׁין, מִגּוֹ הַהוּא הֵיכָלָא שְׁבִיעָאָה, נַחְתִּין עַד דְּמָטוּן לְהַאי הֵיכָלָא, וְנָקִיט לוֹן הַאי רוּחָא קַדִּישָׁא סְטוּטְרִיָּ"ה שְׁמֵיהּ, דְּאִיהוּ לִימִינָא. וְכָל אִינּוּן נִשְׁמָתִין דְּכוּרִין, דְּאִינּוּן זְמִינִין לְאִתְפָּרְחָא בְּזַכָּאִין דְּכוּרִין, לִימִינָא כֻּלְּהוּ נָקִיט לוֹן, וּמִתְעַכְּבֵי תַּמָּן, עַד דְּאִתְכְּלִילוּ בְּנִשְׁמָתִין דְּנוּקְבֵי.

493. When the upper firmament, the river that goes and flows from Eden, YESOD OF ZEIR ANPIN, brings out souls to take them to the seventh chamber above, BINAH OF THE CHAMBERS, this seventh chamber receives them. When the holy souls go out of the seventh chamber, they descend until they reach this FIRST chamber, where this holy spirit named Situt'riyah of the right, takes them. And all the male souls, destined to flourish and be clothed by male righteous, WHICH ARE OF the right, are taken BY THAT SPIRIT, and detained until they are comprised with female souls.

494. מֵהַאי רוּחָא נָפְקָא רוּחָא אַחֲרָא, לִשְׂמָאלָא. דְּאִתְחָזֵי וְאִתְגְּנִיז וְאִתְכְּלִיל בְּהַאי רוּחָא קַדְמָאָה, וְאִינּוּן חַד, כְּלִילָן דָּא בְּדָא. וְהַאי רוּחָא אַחֲרָא, אִקְרֵי אַדִּירִיָּ"ה סָנוּגְיָ"א. הַאי אִיהוּ רוּחָא לִשְׂמָאלָא. וְהַאי קַיְּימָא, דְּכַד תִּיאוּבְתָּא דְּהֵיכָלָא שְׂבִיעָאָה לְאִתְדַּבְּקָא בְּהַהוּא נָהָר דְּנָגִיד וְנָפִיק, הַהוּא רְעוּתָא דְּסַלְּקָא מִתַּתָּא לְעֵילָּא, עַבְדָּא נִשְׁמָתִין בִּרְעוּתָא דִּילֵיהּ, וְאִינּוּן נוּקְבֵי.

494. From this spirit, CALLED 'SITUT'RIYAH', another spirit issues, of the left, which is seen FIRST BY ITSELF, then concealed, included within the first spirit, so they become one, comprising each other. The other spirit is called 'Adiriyah Sanug'ya'. This is a spirit of the left side. Its business is TO RECEIVE FEMALE SOULS, when the seventh chamber yearns to cling to the river that is drawn and goes out, WHICH IS YESOD OF ZEIR ANPIN OF ATZILUT. This desire that mounts from below upwards, produces souls according to its pleasure, and they are female. SINCE THIS SPIRIT IS OF GVURAH AND THE LEFT COLUMN, IT IS CALLED 'ADIRIYAH' (FROM HEB. *ADIR*, LIT. 'GREAT'), FOR HE IS IMMENSE.

495. וְכַד רְעוּתָא דְּהַהוּא נָהָר, נַחְתָּא וְאִתְדַּבְּקָא מֵעֵילָּא לְתַתָּא, עַבְדִּין נִשְׁמָתִין דְּכוּרִין. רְעוּתָא דִּלְעֵילָּא עָבֵיד דְּכוּרִין. רְעוּתָא דִּלְתַתָּא עָבֵיד נוּקְבִין.

495. When the desire of that river, YESOD OF ZEIR ANPIN, descends and joins from above downward, it creates male souls. The desire OF YESOD above creates male souls, and below, IN MALCHUT, IN WHICH THE SEVENTH CHAMBER IS INCLUDED, it creates female souls.

496. וְכַד אִלֵּין נִשְׁמָתִין נוּקְבִין נָפְקִין מִגּוֹ הַהוּא הֵיכָלָא שְׂבִיעָאָה, נַחְתִּין עַד דְּמָטוּ לְהַאי רוּחָא שְׂמָאלָא, דְּאִקְרֵי אַדִּירִיָּ"ה. וְאִקְרֵי לִבְנַ"ת הַסַּפִּי"ר. כְּמָה דְּאוֹקִימְנָא בְּסִתְרִין אַחֲרָנִין.

496. When the female souls depart from the seventh chamber, they descend until they reach the spirit of the left called 'Adiriyah'. It is ALSO called "sapphire stone" (Shemot 24:10). FOR THE FIRST SPIRIT, SITUT'RIYAH, IS CALLED 'SAPPHIRE' AND THE SPIRIT OF THE LEFT IS CALLED "SAPPHIRE STONE," as we explained in other ways THE SECRET MEANING OF THE VERSE, "AND THERE WAS UNDER HIS FEET A KIND OF PAVED WORK OF A SAPPHIRE STONE" (IBID.).

497. כֵּיוָן דְּמָטוּ לְהַאי רוּחָא אִינּוּן נִשְׁמָתִין נוּקְבִין, נַקְטָא לוֹן הַאי רוּחָא, וְקַיְימָאן בֵּיהּ. וּלְבָתַר אִתְכְּלִילוּ רוּחָא דָּא דִּשְׂמָאלָא, בְּרוּחָא דָּא דִּימִינָא. וּכְדֵין אִתְעָבִידוּ אִינּוּן נִשְׁמָתִין, כְּלִילָן דְּכַר וְנוּקְבָא כַּחֲדָא וּפַרְחָאן מֵהַאי הֵיכָלָא וְאִתְפָּרְשָׁן בִּבְנֵי נָשָׁא. כָּל חַד כְּפוּם אָרְחֵיהּ, וּלְבָתַר מִזְדַּוְּוגָן כַּחֲדָא.

497. Once the female souls reach that spirit, ADIRIYAH, he takes them and they remain there. Then the spirit of the left is included within the spirit of the right, and the souls are completed, male and female together, and soar from this chamber, to be again divided within people, WHEN THEY COME TO BE CLOTHED, each according to their disposition, A MALE SOUL WOULD BE CLOTHED BY A MALE, AND A FEMALE SOUL BY A FEMALE. Then they GET MARRIED AND come together.

498. כַּד אָתָא לְאִתְכַּלְלָא רוּחָא דָּא דִּשְׂמָאלָא בִּימִינָא, בָּטַשׁ דָּא בְּדָא לְאִתְכַּלְלָא. וְנַפְקֵי נְצִיצִין דְּמִתְפַּשְּׁטֵי לְכָל עֵיבָר, וְאִתְעֲבִידוּ אִינּוּן אוֹפַנִּים מִנַּיְיהוּ, מֵאִינּוּן נְצִיצִין דְּנַפְקֵי מִגּוֹ רוּחָא שְׂמָאלָא, דִּכְתִּיב בְּהוּ, מַרְאֵה הָאוֹפַנִּים וּמַעֲשֵׂיהֶם כְּעֵין תַּרְשִׁישׁ. וְאִלֵּין אִינּוּן אוֹפַנִּים דְּמִלַּהֲטָן אֶשָּׁא, וְקַיְימִין בְּשִׁירָתָא.

498. When the spirit of the left comes to be included within the spirit of the right, they strike each other to be included, and sparks spread on all sides. Wheels are made from the sparks coming from the spirit of the left, as it is written, "the appearance of the wheels and their work was like the color of an emerald" (Yechezkel 1:16). These are the wheels, which blaze in the fire, singing.

499. כֵּיוָן דְּאִתְבְּסָמוּ רוּחָא בְּרוּחָא, וְאִתְכְּלִילוּ כַּחֲדָא, כְּדֵין נָפְקָא חַד נְהִירוּ דְּסַלְּקָא וְנַחְתָּא, וּמִתְיַשְּׁבָא עַל אַרְבַּע שׁוּרִין דְּאוֹפַנִּים, וְאִיהוּ חַד חֵיוָתָא דְּשַׁלְטָא עֲלַיְיהוּ, וְאִקְרֵי בָּזָק, הַאי בָּזָק נָהִיר בִּנְהוֹרָא דְּנָצִיץ גּוֹ שַׁלְהוֹבָא, וְשַׁלְטָא עַל כָּל אִינּוּן אוֹפַנִּים.

499. Once they were perfumed, a spirit by its fellow spirit, LEFT AND RIGHT, they were included together. Then one light was born and came out, went up and down, and settled upon the four rows of the wheels. It is the one living creature controlling them, ABOUT WHICH WAS SAID: "THE SPIRIT OF THE LIVING CREATURE WAS IN THE WHEELS" (IBID. 20). It is called "a flash of lightning" (Ibid. 14). This flash of lightning illuminates as a gleaming light of a flame, and rules over the wheels.

500. וְאִתְפָּשַׁט מִנֵּיהּ חַד רְקִיעָא, דְּקַיְּימָא עַל תְּרֵין סָמְכִין, וְאִינּוּן תְּרֵין סָמְכִין אִינּוּן תְּרֵין כְּרוּבִין, חַד מִסִּטְרָא דָּא, וְחַד מִסִּטְרָא דָּא. וְהַאי רָקִיעַ עַל רֵישַׁיְיהוּ, כְּמָה דִּכְתִּיב וָאֶרְאֶה וְהִנֵּה אֶל הָרָקִיעַ אֲשֶׁר עַל רֹאשׁ הַכְּרוּבִים. וְלָאו הַאי רָקִיעַ דְּעַל רֵישׁ חֵיוָתָא. וְהַאי בָּזָק מְמָנָא עָלֵיהּ, וְרוּחָא עִלָּאָה דְּאִתְכְּלִיל, עַל כֹּלָּא.

500. From THE FLASH OF LIGHTNING one firmament expanded, standing upon two pillars. These two pillars are two Cherubs, METATRON AND SANDALPHON, the one on this side and the other on that side, with a firmament above their heads, as it is written, "Then I looked, and, behold, in the firmament that was above the head of the Cherubs" (Yechezkel 10:1). This is not the firmament above the heads of the living creatures. And the flash of lightning is in charge over THE FIRMAMENT and the high spirit SITUT'RIYAH, included IN ADIRIYAH, in charge over all.

501. כָּל אִינּוּן צְלוֹתִין, דְּמַקְדְּמֵי עַל לָא סַיְּימֵי יִשְׂרָאֵל כֻּלְּהוּ צְלוֹתֵהוֹן, מִתְעַכְּבֵי בְּהַאי רְקִיעָא, וְהַאי בָּזָק דְּשַׁלְטָא עַל הַאי רְקִיעָא, מְתַקֵּן לוֹן. עַד דְּאָתָא סַנְדַּלְ"פוֹן רַב מְמָנָא, רוּחַ עִלָּאָה, דְּשַׁלִּיט עַל כֹּלָּא, וְכַד סַיְּימֵי יִשְׂרָאֵל כֻּלְּהוּ צְלוֹתִין, נָטִיל לוֹן מֵהַאי רְקִיעָא, וְסַלְּקָא וְקָשִׁיר לוֹן קִשְׁרִין לְמָארֵיהּ כְּמָה דְּאוּקְמוּהָ.

501. All the first prayers, before the rest of Yisrael finished theirs, wait in that firmament, and this flash, the ruler of this firmament, prepares them. Then comes the great minister Sandalphon, the high spirit and ruler over all, and when Yisrael finished saying their prayers, he takes them from this firmament, rises with them and ties them as knots to their Master, as we explained.

502. הַאי בָּזָק, קָאֵים לְמִמְנֵי כָּל אִינּוּן צְלוֹתִין דְּסַלְקָן, וְכָל אִינּוּן מִלֵּי דְּאוֹרַיְיתָא דְּמִתְעַטְּרָן בְּלֵילְיָא, כַּד רוּחָא דְּצָפוֹן אַתְעַר, וְלֵילְיָא אִתְפְּלַג כָּל מַאן דְּקָאֵים בְּהַהִיא שַׁעֲתָא, וְאִתְעֲסָק בְּאוֹרַיְיתָא, כָּל אִינּוּן מִלִּין סַלְקִין, וְנָטִיל לוֹן הַאי בָּזָ"ק, וְאָנַח לוֹן בְּהַאי רְקִיעָא, עַד דְּסַלְקָא יְמָמָא.

502. This flash counts all the rising prayers, and the words of the Torah bedecked at night, when the spirit of the north awakens at the middle of the night. Whoever is occupied in the Torah at that time, his studies rise, and this flash takes them and puts them in the firmament until daybreak.

503. וּלְבָתַר דְּסָלִיק יְמָמָא, סַלְקָן אִינּוּן מִלִּין, וְשָׁארָן בַּאֲתָר דִּרְקִיעָא, דְּבֵיהּ תַּלְיָין כֹּכָבַיָּא וּמַזָּלֵי שִׁמְשָׁא וְסִיהֲרָא. וְהַאי אִקְרֵי סֵפֶר הַזִּכָּרוֹן, דִּכְתִּיב וַיִּכָּתֵב סֵפֶר זִכָּרוֹן לְפָנָיו. לְפָנָיו, בְּגִין דְּסֵפֶר וְזִכָּרוֹן כְּתָב בְּקִשּׁוּרָא חֲדָא.

503. When the day breaks, the words rise and dwell in the place at the firmament where the stars and constellations, sun and moon abide. THIS IS YESOD OF ZEIR ANPIN, BY WHICH NAME ITS GRADES ARE CALLED. This is called 'the book of remembrance', as it is written, "and a book of remembrance was written before Him" (Malachi 3:16), BOOK BEING MALCHUT AND REMEMBRANCE YESOD. IT IS WRITTEN, "before Him" because the book of the remembrance is written by one knot, NAMELY BY UNITY FACE TO FACE.

504. אִינּוּן אַרְבַּע גַּלְגַּלִּין, אִינּוּן נַטְלִין עַל תְּרֵיסָר סַמְכִין. אִלֵּין ד', אַהֲנִיאֵ"ל. קְדוּמִיאֵ"ל מַלְכִּיאֵ"ל יְאֲהַדוֹנָהִ"י, יְהֲדוֹנִיָּ"ה. דִּי מַפְתְּחָאן דִּשְׁמָא קַדִּישָׁא בִּידַיְיהוּ.

504. The four wheels are traveling upon twelve pillars, AS FOR EACH WHEEL THERE ARE FOUR WHEELS, AND EACH WHEEL IS ON THREE STRUTS. The four WHEELS ARE, Ahaniel, K'dumiel, Malkiel, Ya'hadonahi, Yehadoniyah, who have the keys of the Holy Name in their hands.

505. וְאִלֵּין אַרְבַּע אִינּוּן כְּלִילָן בְּרָזָא דְּאַתְוָון אֲדֹנָ"י, דִּי סַנְדַּלְפוֹ"ן מָארֵי רְתִיכִין. מִשְׁתַּמֵּשׁ בְּהוּ. אִלֵּין אַרְבַּע אַתְוָון פַּרְחִין בַּאֲוִירָא, דְּהַהוּא אֲוִירָא כָּלִיל בְּאַתְוָון דִּשְׁמָא קַדִּישָׁא, יְהֹוָ"ה, יוֹ"ד הֵ"א וָא"ו הֵ"א. וְהַהוּא אֲוִירָא כָּלִיל לוֹן, וְאִתְכְּלִילוּ אִלֵּין בְּאִלֵּין. וְאִלֵּין ד' נַטְלִין לוֹן, בְּרָזָא דְּהַהוּא בָּזָק.

505. These four are included in the secret of the letters of THE NAME Adonai, which Sandalphon, the owner of the Chariots, uses. These four letters soar in the air, which includes the letters of the Holy Name Yud Hei Vav Hei FULLY SPELLED WITH *ALEPH*'S *Yud-Vav-Dalet*, *Hei-Aleph*, *Vav-Aleph-Vav*, *Hei-Aleph*. That air comprises THE FOUR LETTERS ADONAI, and they are included within one another, ADONAI IN YUD HEI VAV HEI. The four letters OF YUD HEI VAV HEI take THE FOUR OF ADONAI, in the secret of that flash of lightning.

506. וְאִלֵּין ד' עָאלִין בְּד', אִלֵּין בְּאִלֵּין, דִּכְתִּיב מַקְבִּילוֹת הַלּוּלָאוֹת אֶחָת אֶל אֶחָת. וְהָא אוֹקִימְנָא, וְרָזָא אִיהוּ לְאִתְכַּלְּלָא אִלֵּין בְּאִלֵּין, וּלְשַׁלְּבָא אִלֵּין בְּאִלֵּין, בְּרָזָא דְּהַהוּא רוּחָא דְּכָלִיל בְּרָזָא דִּשְׁמָא קַדִּישָׁא. דְּכָלִיל שְׁמָא דָּא בִּשְׁמָא דָּא.

506. These four LETTERS OF ADONAI enter the four LETTERS OF YUD HEI VAV HEI, the ones within the others, as it is written, "the loops opposite one another" (Shemot 26:5), as was explained. It is the mystery of combining them and interlacing them together, according to the secret of that spirit, FLASH, which includes the secret of the Holy Name FROM BOTH, FOR IT COMES FROM THE SPIRIT ADIRIYAH, THE SECRET OF ADONAI, JOINED BY THE SPIRIT SITUT'RIYAH, THE SECRET OF YUD HEI VAV HEI. THEREFORE, it includes the name ADONAI in the name YUD HEI VAV HEI.

507. וְכֹלָּא בְּהַאי הֵיכָלָא מִתְנַהֲגֵי, וְנַטְלֵי בְּהַהוּא רוּחָא, בְּרָזָא דִּשְׁמָא

קַדִּישָׁא דְּשַׁלִּיט עַל כֹּלָּא. בְּהַאי הֵיכָלָא אִיהוּ יְאַהֲדוֹנָהִ״י, כְּלָלָא דִּתְרֵין שְׁמָהָן, מִגּוֹ דְּאִיהוּ רוּחָא רוּחָא בְּרוּחָא. וְכַד שְׁמָא דָּא, דְּכָלִיל בְּרָזָא דְּרוּחָא בְּרוּחָא, וְכָלִיל דָּא בְּדָא. נָהִיר דָּא בְּדָא, כְּדֵין נָהִיר כֹּלָּא, וְסַלְקָא נְהוֹרָא וְנַחְתָּא, כִּנְהוֹרָא דְּשִׁמְשָׁא גּוֹ מַיָּא וְאוֹקִימְנָא.

507. Everything in this chamber is conducted and travels by the spirits, in the secret of the Holy Name, which rules over all. Within this chamber is THE HOLY NAME Ya'ahadonahi, comprising the two names, YUD HEI VAV HEI ADONAI INTERLACED, since it is a spirit within spirit, AS THERE ARE TWO RULING SPIRITS, SITUT'RIYAH, WHICH IS MALE, AND ADIRIYAH, WHICH IS FEMALE. THE NAME YUD HEI VAV HEI IS OF THE SIDE OF THE MALE SPIRIT, AND THE NAME ADONAI IS OF THE SIDE OF THE FEMALE. Since the name YA'AHADONAHI comprises THE TWO SPIRITS, in the secret of spirit in spirit, that are including each other, and shining within one another; then everything illuminates, and the light goes up and down, as the light of the sun upon the water.

508. וּכְדֵין הַאי רוּחָא נָטִיל, כֹּלָּא נַטְלִין בְּגִינֵיהּ, דִּכְתִּיב אֶל אֲשֶׁר יִהְיֶה שָׁמָּה הָרוּחַ לָלֶכֶת יֵלֵכוּ לֹא יִסַּבּוּ בְּלֶכְתָּן. וְכַד רוּחָא דָּא נָהִיר בִּשְׁמָא דָּא, כְּדֵין עָאלִין כֻּלְּהוּ דָּא בְּדָא, וְאִתְקַשְּׁרוּ כֻּלְּהוּ כַּחֲדָא, לְסַלְקָא לְעֵילָּא, בְּרָזָא דִּשְׁמָא דָּא קַדִּישָׁא.

508. When this spirit travels, NAMELY, SITUT'RIYAH, WHO IS INCLUDED IN ADIRIYAH, everything travels because of it, as it is written, "wherever the spirit was minded to go, they went; they turned not when they went" (Yechezkel 1:12). And when the spirit illuminates with the light of the name, YA'AHADONAHI, all intermingle and bind as one to mount above in the mystery of this Holy Name.

509. בְּאֶמְצָעִיתָא דְּהֵיכָלָא דָּא, קַיְּימָא חַד עַמּוּדָא, נָעִיץ מֵהֵיכָלָא דָּא לְהֵיכָלָא תִּנְיָינָא, בְּהַאי סָלִיק רוּחָא דִּלְתַתָּא לְגַבֵּי רוּחָא דִּלְעֵילָּא, לְאִתְאַחֲדָא רוּחָא בְּרוּחָא, וְכֵן עַד לְעֵילָּא מִכֻּלְּהוּ, לְמֶהֱוֵי כֻּלְּהוּ רוּחָא חֲדָא, כד״א וְרוּחַ אֶחָד לַכֹּל.

509. In the middle of this chamber stands one pillar, fastened from this chamber to the second, UPPER chamber. Through this PILLAR mounts the lower spirit to the upper spirit OF THE SECOND CHAMBER, so the spirits may be united. Also THROUGH THIS PILLAR IT GOES UP to the spirit that is above them all, IN THE SEVENTH CHAMBER, FOR IN EACH CHAMBER, THIS PILLAR IS IN THE MIDDLE, so that all may become one spirit, as it is written, "they have all one spirit" (Kohelet 3:19).

510. עַמּוּדָא דָּא דְּקַיְּימָא בְּאֶמְצָעִיתָא, אַדְרָהַנִי״אֵל שְׁמֵיהּ, וְרָזִין דְּמַפְתְּחָן דִּשְׁמָא קַדִּישָׁא בִּידֵיהּ. כַּד צְלוֹתִין סַלְקָאן וּמָטָאן לְהַאי עַמּוּדָא, כְּדֵין נַטְלֵי כֻּלְּהוּ דְּאִינּוּן בְּהֵיכָלָא דָּא, לְגוֹ הֵיכָלָא תִּנְיָינָא, לְאִתְאַחֲדָא דָּא בְּדָא, לְמֶהֱוֵי כֹּלָּא בְּרָזָא חֲדָא, לְאִתְיַיחֲדָא עֵילָּא וְתַתָּא כַּחֲדָא לְמֶהֱוֵי שְׁמָא קַדִּישָׁא שְׁלִים כִּדְקָא יָאוּת.

510. The pillar in the middle is called 'Adrahaniel'. It has the keys of the Holy Name in its hands, and when the prayers mount and reach that pillar, all that are in that chamber travel to the second chamber, to join each other, all in one secret, to be united above and below together, so the Holy Name will be complete as it should.

47. The chamber of the very heaven – Hod

A Synopsis

Rabbi Shimon tells us that the second chamber is more hidden than the first, but that it also pertains to faith. He says the chieftain in charge of this chamber is Urfaniel, and that he deals with all the souls who were executed or killed by other nations. We are told about the 'cup of consolation' and the 'cup of bitterness'. This second chamber is called 'chamber of splendor' and it is lit from above and below. We are told that all the cherubim come from Hadarniel, the spirit of the left. Next we hear that in this second chamber is a chieftain called Tzidkiel who is appointed over the garments, and when the souls of the righteous ascend he takes them to the river of fire. After their cleansing Tzidkiel clothes the righteous souls with their garments and brings them to the Angel Michael as sacrifice to Atik Yomim. Rabbi Shimon says that by the mating of Urfaniel and Hadarniel all the other rulers appointed over the world were created. These are the six winged Seraphim. We also learn of an living creature that rules over the Seraphim, he is called Yofiel, and has all the keys of Wisdom. He rewards all people who pursue Wisdom. Rabbi Shimon tells us of pillars that are in charge of singing and pillars that are in charge of chanting. He explains that it is from the second chamber that prophets who achieve their wisdom through visions or through dreams draw their inspiration, but Moses drew his prophecies from a higher level.

511. הֵיכָלָא תִּנְיָינָא הֵיכָלָא דָּא, קַיְימָא גּוֹ רָזָא דִּמְהֵימְנוּתָא, לְאִתְאַחֲדָא בְּרָזָא דִּלְעֵילָּא. הַאי הֵיכָלָא, טָמִיר וְגָנִיז יַתִּיר מִן קַדְמָאָה. בְּהֵיכָלָא דָּא, אִית תְּלַת פִּתְחִין, וְחַד שַׁמָּשָׁא מְמָנָא עֲלַיְיהוּ, אוּרְפָּנִי"אֵל שְׁמֵיהּ. הַאי מְמָנָא, שַׁלִּיט עַל תְּלַת סִטְרֵי עָלְמָא, דָּרוֹם וְצָפוֹן וּמִזְרָח. דָּרוֹם מֵהַאי סִטְרָא, וְצָפוֹן מֵהַאי סִטְרָא, וּמִזְרָח בְּאֶמְצָעִיתָא.

511. The second chamber pertains to the secret of the Faith, so as to be united within the mystery above. This chamber is more recondite and concealed than the first. There are three openings to this chamber, and one chieftain in charge over them, named Urfaniel, DERIVED FROM 'THE LIGHT (HEB. *OR*) OF THE FACE (HEB. *PANIM*)', BECAUSE HE STANDS ON THE EAST SIDE CALLED 'FACE'. This chieftain rules over the three directions south, north and east – south on this side, RIGHT, CHESED; north on that side, LEFT, GVURAH; and east in the middle, THE SECRET OF TIFERET, THE MEDIATING COLUMN.

512. אִלֵּין תְּלַת פִּתְחִין, לִתְלַת סִטְרִין אִלֵּין. תְּרֵין סְתִימִין, וְחַד בְּאֶמְצָעִיתָא פָּתִיחַ, בְּרָזָא דִּכְתִיב, וּכְעֶצֶם הַשָּׁמַיִם לָטֹהַר. הַאי מְמָנָא אִתְפְּקַד וְקַיְּימָא בְּהַהוּא פִּתְחָא דְּאִיהוּ פָּתִיחַ, וּתְחוֹת יְדֵיהּ תְּרֵין מְמָנָן אַחֲרָנִין, דִּמְמָנָן עַל אִינּוּן פִּתְחִין אַחֲרָנִין סְתִימִין.

512. Of the three openings to the three Columns, the two are closed, and THE OPENING in the middle is open, in the secret of the verse, “as it were the very heaven for clearness” (Shemot 24:10), REFERRING TO THE SECRET OF THE OPEN GATE IN THE MIDDLE, TIFERET, CALLED ‘HEAVEN’. The chieftain URFANIEL stands at the open gate, TO THE EAST. Under him there are two other chieftains, in charge over the other two closed openings, OF THE SOUTH AND NORTH.

513. וְכָל אִינּוּן נִשְׁמָתִין, דְּאִינּוּן קְטוּלֵי בֵּית דִּין, אוֹ אִינּוּן קְטוּלֵי שְׁאַר עַמִּין, כֻּלְּהוּ אִתְמְנָן תְּחוֹת יְדֵיהוֹן, וְהַאי מְמָנָא דְּעָלַיְיהוּ, חָקִיק לוֹן לְדִיוּקְנֵיהוֹן בִּלְבוּשׁוֹי, דְּאִינּוּן נוּר דָּלִיק, וְסָלִיק לוֹן לְעֵילָּא, וְאַחְמֵי לוֹן לְמָארֵיהּ, וּכְדֵין נָטִיל לוֹן, וְחָקִיק לוֹן בְּפוּרְפּוּרוֹי, לְאִינּוּן קְטוּלֵי שְׁאַר עַמִּין.

513. All the souls executed by court order or killed by other nations, are all numbered by THE THREE CHIEFTAINS, and the chief above them engraves their forms upon his garments of burning fire. He raises them above, and shows them to his Master. THE HOLY ONE, BLESSED BE HE then takes them, and engraves those killed by other nations on His garments.

514. וְאִינּוּן קְטוּלֵי בֵּית דִּין, נָחִית לוֹן הַאי מְמָנָא, וְאָעִיל לוֹן בָּתַר אִינּוּן תְּרֵין פִּתְחִין סְתִימִין, דְּאִינּוּן תְּרֵין מְמָנָן אַחֲרָנִין קַיְימִין עָלַיְיהוּ, וְתַמָּן חָמָאן יְקָרָא דְּכָל אִינּוּן דְּקַיְימוּ אוֹרַיְיתָא, וְנָטְרוּ פִּקּוּדוֹי, וְאִינּוּן כְּסִיפִין בְּגַרְמַיְיהוּ, וְנִכְוִין מֵחוּפָּה דִּלְהוֹן. עַד דְּהַאי מְמָנָא דְּקַיְּימָא

עֲלַיְיהוּ, פָּתַח לוֹן תַּרְעָא דְּמִזְרָח, וְנָהִיר לוֹן, וְיָהִיב לוֹן חַיִּים דְּאִתְפַּתְּחוּ בְּהַהוּא תַּרְעָא דְּמִזְרָח. וּבִידָא דְּהַהוּא מְמָנָא חַד כַּסָּא דְּחַיִּין, דְּאִיהוּ מַלְיָא נְהוֹרִין, וְהַאי אִקְרֵי כּוֹס תַּנְחוּמִין, כַּסָּא דְּחַיֵּי. דְּהָא בְּגִין כַּסָּא אַחֲרָא דְּשָׁתוּ בְּקַדְמֵיתָא, זָכוּ לְהַאי.

514. Those executed by court order are lowered by the chieftain and put behind the two closed gates, where two other chiefs stand. From there THE SOULS see the glory of those who kept the Torah and His precepts. They are ashamed of themselves and get burned by their canopies. Then the chieftain in charge opens the east gate before them, lights their way, and gives them life starting at the east gate. In his hand there is a cup of life, full of lights, called 'the cup of consolation', the cup of life. It is because they drank first of another cup, OF DEATH, FOR THEY WERE KILLED, that they now deserve this one.

515. כְּגַוְונָא דָּא אִית בְּסִטְרָא אַחֲרָא, בְּהֵיכָלָא דִּמְסָאֲבָא, מְמָנָא אַחֲרָא, וּבִידֵיהּ כּוֹס דְּאִקְרֵי כּוֹס תַּרְעֵלָה, כּוֹס חֲמָתוֹ. כְּמָה דְּתָנֵינָן, אִית יַיִן וְאִית יַיִן, הָכִי נָמֵי אִית כּוֹס וְאִית כּוֹס, וְכֹלָּא, דָּא לְטָב, וְדָא לְבִישׁ. יַיִן לְטָב, דִּכְתִּיב וְיַיִן יְשַׂמַּח לְבַב אֱנוֹשׁ. וְיַיִן לְבִישׁ, דִּכְתִּיב וְיַיִן חָמַר מָלֵא מֶסֶךְ וְגוֹ'. כּוֹס לְטָב, דִּכְתִּיב, כּוֹס יְשׁוּעוֹת אֶשָּׂא. כּוֹס לְבִישׁ, דִּכְתִּיב כּוֹס חֲמָתוֹ כּוֹס הַתַּרְעֵלָה.

515. In the same manner, there is, in the chamber of defilement of the Other Side, another chieftain, with a cup in his hands called 'a cup of bitterness', a cup of His fury. We learned that there is wine and wine. Here also, there is a cup and a cup. Of all, some is for the better and some for worse. HE EXPLAINS: Wine is for the better, as it is written, "and wine that makes glad the hearts of men" (Tehilim 104:15), and there is wine for the worse, as it is written, "a cup, with foaming wine; it is full of mixture" (Tehilim 75:9). A good cup is as it is written, "I will raise a cup of salvation" (Tehilim 116:13). An evil cup is as it is written, "the cup of His fury…the cup of bitterness" (Yeshayah 51:17).

516. כְּמָה דְּאִית בְּסִטְרָא דִּקְדוּשָּׁה, הֵיכָלִין וּמְמָנָן כֹּלָּא לְטָב, וְרוּחִין קַדִּישִׁין וְכָל סִטְרִין קַדִּישִׁין. הָכִי נָמֵי אִית בְּסְטַר מְסָאֲבָא, הֵיכָלִין

וּמִמְּנָן כֻּלְּהוּ לְבִישׁ, וְרוּחִין מְסָאֲבִין, מְמָנָן, וְכָל סִטְרִין מְסָאֲבִין. וְדָא לָקֳבֵל דָּא, כְּגוֹן יֵצֶר הַטּוֹב וְיֵצֶר הָרָע, וְכֹלָּא בְּרָזָא חֲדָא.

516. As there are on the side of holiness chambers and chieftains, all for the good, holy spirits and holy aspects, so there are on the side of defilement, chambers and chieftains all for the evil, spirits of defilement in charge, and all aspects of unholiness. These are against those, like the Good Inclination and the Evil Inclination, all part of one mystery.

517. הֵיכָלָא דָּא אִקְרֵי הֵיכַל זוֹהַר, בְּגִין דְּאִית בֵּיהּ רוּחָא, דְּאִקְרֵי אוּרְפָּנִיאֵ״ל. וְאִיהוּ זוֹהַר דְּלָא אִשְׁתַּנֵּי, וְקַיְּימָא בִּנְהִירוּ סְתִימָא, דְּנָהִיר מֵעֵילָּא, וּבִנְהִירוּ דְּנָהִיר לְתַתָּא. וְכַד בָּטַשׁ נְהִירוּ דִּלְתַתָּא בִּנְהִירוּ עִלָּאָה, נָהִיר הַאי רוּחָא, כְּגַוְונָא דְּחֵיזוּ דְּעֵינָא, דְּכַד מִתְגַּלְגְּלָא, כְּדֵין אַפִּיק נְהוֹרָא דְּנָצִיץ וְזַהֲרָא, הָכִי נָמֵי הַאי רוּחָא. וְעַל דָּא, הֵיכָלָא דָּא אִקְרֵי זוֹהַר.

517. This chamber is called 'chamber of splendor', since in it there is a spirit called 'Urfaniel', a never changing splendor, ILLUMINATING CONSTANTLY ONLY WITH THE WHITE LIGHT IN IT, WHICH IS CHESED. It stands within the concealed light shining from above, FROM THE THIRD CHAMBER, and within the light illuminating from below, COMING FROM THE SPIRIT OF THE FIRST CHAMBER THAT ASCENDED HERE. And when the light of below OF THE FIRST CHAMBER, strikes the upper light HERE, then this spirit shines as sight in the eyes. And when it rolls, it spreads a glowing light, full of splendor. Therefore, this chamber is called 'splendor'.

518. הַאי רוּחָא דְּאִקְרֵי אוּרְפָּנִי״אֵל, הַאי אִיהוּ דְּנָהִיר לְהֵיכָלָא דָּא, וְנָהִיר לְהֵיכָלָא קַדְמָאָה, בְּגִין דְּהַהוּא רוּחָא דְּהֵיכָלָא קַדְמָאָה, נָהִיר בְּאִתְגַּלְיָיא, מֵהַאי רוּחָא דְּאִיהוּ סְתִימָאָה. דָּא רוּחָא נָטִיל לְעֵילָּא וְנָטִיל לְתַתָּא, בְּרָזָא דִּכְתִּיב חַמּוּקֵי יְרֵכַיִךְ כְּמוֹ חֲלָאִים. וּמַה דְּאָמַר חַמּוּקֵי יְרֵכַיִךְ. בְּגִין דְּאִית רוּחָא אַחֲרָא דְּנָפִיק מִנֵּיהּ לִסְטַר שְׂמָאלָא, וְאִתְקָשַׁר בַּהֲדֵיהּ. וְעַל דָּא כְּתִיב חַמּוּקֵי תְּרֵין. וְהַאי רוּחָא שְׂמָאלָא אִקְרֵי הֲדַרְנִיאֵ״ל, וְאִתְכְּלִילוּ דָּא בְּדָא, כְּלִילָן כַּחֲדָא, וְאִינּוּן עֶצֶם הַשָּׁמַיִם,

דִּכְלִילָא בְּאֵשׁ וּמַיִם.

518. The spirit called 'Urfaniel' shines upon this chamber and upon the first chamber, as the spirit of the first chamber illuminates openly, from the spirit HERE that is concealed. Therefore, this spirit travels up and down, in the secret of the verse, "your rounded thighs are like jewels" (Shir Hashirim 7:2), FOR THIS IS THE CHAMBER OF HOD, AND NETZACH AND HOD ARE CALLED 'THIGHS'. SINCE THE LIGHT IS CONCEALED, IT IS CALLED 'ROUNDED' (HEB. *CHAMUKEI*), HINTING AT CONCEALMENT, LIKE IN THE VERSE, "BUT MY BELOVED HAD TURNED AWAY (HEB. *CHAMAK*) AND WAS GONE" (SHIR HASHIRIM 5:6). "Rounded (thighs)" IS IN THE PLURAL, because there is another spirit here, on the left side, who came out OF URFANIEL, and joined him. Therefore it is written, "rounded thighs," referring to the two. The spirit of the left is called 'Hadarniel', FROM HOD AND HADAR (ENG. 'MAJESTY'). They are included and joined together, being "the very heaven" (Shemot 24:10) comprising fire and water, NAMELY, THE TWO SPIRITS, RIGHT AND LEFT. RIGHT IS WATER AND LEFT IS FIRE.

519. כְּתִיב כְּמַרְאֵה הַקֶּשֶׁת אֲשֶׁר יִהְיֶה בֶעָנָן בְּיוֹם הַגֶּשֶׁם וְגוֹ'. הַאי רוּחָא קַדְמָאָה אוּרְפָנִיאֵ"ל, דְּאִיהוּ סָתִים בֵּין עֵילָּא וְתַתָּא, וְנָהִיר, אִיהוּ כְּעֵין חַשְׁמַל, הַאי אִיהוּ כְּעֵין חַשְׁמַל, וּלְזִמְנִין אִיהוּ חַשְׁמַל. בְּגִין דְּמִנֵּיהּ קַיְימִין כָּל אִינּוּן שְׂרָפִים חֵיוָון אֶשָּׁא מְמַלְּלָן, חֵיוָון דְּקַיְימֵי וְלָא קַיְימֵי, וְעַל דָּא אִיהוּ חַשְׁמַל.

519. It is written, "As the appearance of the bow that is in the cloud in the day of rain..." (Yechezkel 1:28). The first spirit, Urfaniel, is concealed both above and below, shining. It is "something like the color of electrum" (Ibid. 27), NOT EXACTLY ELECTRUM (HEB. *CHASHMAL*), THE SECRET OF 'CHAYOT ESH MEMALELOT' (LIT. 'MOTTERING FIERY LIVING CREATURES') BECAUSE IT CANNOT BE UTTERED, THE SECRET OF THE ILLUMINATION OF CHOCHMAH. But sometimes it is electrum, WHEN IT COMPRISES HADARNIEL, from which come all the Seraphim. FOR ELECTRUM (HEB. *CHASHMAL*) COMPRISES THE LETTERS "*Cha*-yot e-*sh* me-*mal*-et"; ALSO the living creatures exist and exist not, MEANING THAT THEY SOMETIMES TALK AND SOMETIMES ARE QUIET. Therefore it is electrum.

520. אוּרְפָּנִיאֵ״ל דְּקָאָמַרָן, בְּדָא אִשְׁתְּמוֹדְעָן חַיִּין לְעָלְמָא. כַּד אִתְּדָן עָלְמָא לְטָב, כְּדֵין נָהִיר רוּחָא דָּא, וְכָל חַיִּין וְכָל חֶדְוָה אִשְׁתְּכַח, דְּהָא כֵּיוָן דִּזְכוּתָא נָפְקָא, וּנְהִירוּ, דִּינִין כְּדֵין רוּחָא דָּא אַנְהִיר. וְסִימָנָךְ בְּאוֹר פְּנֵי מֶלֶךְ חַיִּים.

520. Through Urfaniel, life is made known to the world. When the world is acquitted, this spirit shines, and there are life and joy, for with acquittal, the Judgments ARE ANNULLED AND shine. Then this spirit shines, as seen by the verse, "In the light of the king's countenance (Heb. *or pnei*) is life" (Mishlei 16:15), ALLUDING TO THE LETTERS OF URFANIEL.

521. וְכַד אִתְּדָן עָלְמָא בְּדִינָא, כְּדֵין הַהוּא סִטְרָא אַחֲרָא מְסָאֲבָא, שַׁלְטָא וְאִתְּקַף, וְהַאי רוּחָא אִגְנִיז וְאִתְחֲשַׁךְ, וּכְדֵין כָּל עָלְמָא קַיְּימָא בְּדִינָא וְאִתְּדָן. וְכֹלָּא קַיְּימָא בְּהַאי רוּחָא. וְסִימָנֵיךְ וְאַרְכֻּבָּתֵיהּ דָּא לְדָא נָקְשָׁן.

521. When the world is condemned, the unholy Other Side has sway and rules. The spirit URFANIEL is stored and darkened, and the whole world is sentenced, under Judgment. All depends upon this spirit, as seen in the verse, "and his knees smote one against the other" (Daniel 5:6), FOR FEAR OF JUDGMENT IS FELT IN THE KNEES, THE SECRET OF NETZACH AND HOD, AND THIS CHAMBER IS THE CHAMBER OF HOD.

522. הָכָא קַיְימָן, כָּל אִינּוּן מַלְבּוּשִׁין דְּנִשְׁמָתְהוֹן דְּצַדִּיקַיָּא, דְּסַלְּקִין לְאִתְחֲזָאָה קַמֵּי מָארֵיהוֹן, וּלְקַיְּימָא קַמֵּיהּ. וְכַד נִשְׁמְתָא סַלְּקָא וּמָטֵי לְהַאי הֵיכָלָא, כְּדֵין אִזְדָּמַן חַד מְמָנָא, דְּאִתְפְּקַד עַל אִינּוּן לְבוּשִׁין, וְצַדְקִיאֵ״ל שְׁמֵיהּ. דְּהָא בְּזִמְנָא דְּבַ״נ עָבֵיד פִּקּוּדִין דְּאוֹרַיְיתָא בְּהַאי עָלְמָא, כְּגַוְונָא דְּאִיהוּ אִשְׁתָּדַּל גַּרְמֵיהּ, הָכִי אִתְעֲבֵיד לֵיהּ בְּהַאי הֵיכָלָא לְעֵילָּא, מַלְבּוּשָׁא לְאִתְלַבְּשָׁא בֵּיהּ, בְּהַהוּא עָלְמָא.

522. Here are found all the garments of the souls of the righteous, who rise to be presented before their Master, and stand before Him. When the soul ascends and reaches this chamber, a chieftain comes, appointed over these garments. His name is Tzidkiel, FROM JUSTICE (HEB. *TZEDEK*). For when a man abides by the precepts of the Torah in this world, as he labored, AND STROVE TO ABIDE BY THEM, a garment is prepared for him accordingly in this chamber, for him to wear in that world.

523. וְכַד נִשְׁמְתָא סַלְקָא, הַהוּא מְמָנָא נָטִיל לְבוּשָׁא דִּילָהּ, וְאָזִיל עִמָּהּ עַד דִּי מָטָא לְנָהָר דִּינוּר, דִּי נִשְׁמְתָא אִצְטְרִיכָא לְאִתְסַחְיָיא וּלְאִתְלַבְּנָא תַּמָּן, וּלְזִמְנִין דְּטַבְעָא הַהִיא נִשְׁמְתָא תַּמָּן וְאִתּוֹקְדָא, וְלָא סַלְקָא כֹּלָּא יוֹמָא, עַד בְּצַפְרָא, כַּד אַתְעַר רוּחָא דִּסְטְרָא דְּדָרוֹם, כְּדֵין קַיְימֵי כֻּלְּהוּ וּמִתְחַדְשָׁן, וְאַמְרֵי שִׁירָתָא, וּמְזַמְּרָן כְּגַוְונָא דְּאִינּוּן מַלְאֲכִין דְּאִתְעֲבַר שׁוּלְטָנֵהוֹן וְאִתּוֹקְדָן, וְקַיְימָן וּמִתְחַדְּשָׁן כְּמִלְּקַדְמִין, וְאַמְרֵי שִׁירָתָא, הָכִי נָמֵי אִלֵּין נִשְׁמָתִין.

523. When the soul mounts, that chieftain takes its garment and walks with it, until they reach the river of fire, where the soul has to bathe and be cleansed. Sometimes it drowns and get burned, and does not rise all day until morning, when the spirit of the south is awakened. They all become renewed then and sing, and chant like the angels, who lost their power, were burnt and then regenerated, and they chant. So do these souls.

524. וְאִי זַכָּאת הַאי נִשְׁמְתָא וְסַלְקַת. הַאי מְמָנָא צִדְקִיאֵ״ל, נָטִיל לָהּ לְהַאי נִשְׁמְתָא, וְאַלְבִּישׁ לָהּ בְּהַהוּא לְבוּשָׁא, וְאִתַּקְנַת בֵּיהּ, וְסַלְקָא לְקָרְבְּנָא עַל יְדָא דְּמִיכָאֵל כַּהֲנָא, לְקַיְּימָא תָּדִיר כָּל יוֹמִין קָמֵי עַתִּיק יוֹמִין, זַכָּאָה חוּלָקָא דְּהַאי נִשְׁמְתָא, דְּקַיְּימָא וְזָכְאת לְהַאי.

524. If the soul has the merit to ascend, the chieftain Tzidkiel takes it, and clothes it with that garment. It is prepared by it and offered as sacrifice by THE ANGEL Michael the priest, to stand always before Atik Yomin. Happy is the portion of that soul who merits this.

525. וּבְכֹּלָּא, אִתְמְנָא הַאי רוּחָא אוּרְפָּנִיאֵ״ל דְּקָאֲמָרָן, וְאִיהוּ שַׁלִּיט עַל הַאי הֵיכָלָא. מִכְּלָלָא דָּא, כַּד אִתְכְּלִיל רוּחָא בְּרוּחָא, וּבָטַשׁ דָּא בְּדָא לְאִתְכַּלְּלָא כַּחֲדָא, אִתְבְּרִיאוּ אִינּוּן שַׁלִּיטִין אַחֲרָנִין דְּאִתְמְנָן עַל

עָלְמָא, וְאִלֵּין אִינּוּן שְׂרָפִים דְּשִׁית גַּדְפִּין. דִּמְקַדְּשֵׁי לְמָרֵיהוֹן תְּלַת זִמְנִין בְּיוֹמָא. וְאִלֵּין אִינּוּן דִּמְדַקְדְּקֵי עִם צַדִּיקַיָּיא, אֲפִילּוּ כְּחַד נִימָא דְּשַׂעֲרָא. וְאִלֵּין אִינּוּן דְּקַיְימֵי לְאַעַנְשָׁא, בְּהַאי עָלְמָא וּבְעָלְמָא דְּאָתֵי. וּלְאִינּוּן דִּמְזַלְזְלֵי לב"נ דְּאוֹלִיפוּ מִנֵּיהּ אֲפִילּוּ מִלָּה חֲדָא בְּאוֹרַיְיתָא, וְלָא מְנָהֲגֵי בֵּיהּ יְקָר. וּלְכָל אִינּוּן דְּמִשְׁתַּמְשֵׁי, בְּמַאן דְּקָארִי שִׁית סִדְרֵי מִשְׁנָה, לְיַחֲדָא יִחוּדָא דְּמָארֵיהוֹן.

525. The spirit Urfaniel is in charge over the whole process, and rules over this chamber. From this unity of spirit within spirit, URFANIEL AND HADARNIEL, by their striking each other to become united, NAMELY, THEIR JOINING, were created all the other rulers, appointed over the world. These are the six winged Seraphim who sanctify their Master three times a day. It is they who are strict with the righteous to a hairbreadth. It is they who punish in this world and in the World to Come, those who slight a man from whom they learned even one thing of the Torah, and treat him with disrespect, and those who make use of a person who learned the six orders of the Mishnah, and studied them for the purpose of declaring the unity of their Master.

526. כַּד מִתְיַשְּׁבָן רוּחָא בְּרוּחָא, וְאִתְנְהָרָן כַּחֲדָא. מֵהַהוּא נְהִירוּ נָפְקָא חֵיוָתָא חֲדָא, דְּשַׁלְטָא עַל אִינּוּן שְׂרָפִים, וְאַרְבַּע תְּחוֹתָהּ, דְּאַנְפַּיְיהוּ אַנְפִּין דְּנֶשֶׁר, הַאי חֵיוָתָא יוֹפִיאֵ"ל שְׁמֵיהּ, וְאִיהִי קַיְימָא בְּכָל רָזֵי דְּחָכְמְתָא, לְכָל אִינּוּן מַפְתְּחָאן דְּחָכְמְתָא קַיְימִין בֵּיהּ.

526. When they are settled a spirit within spirit, URFANIEL WITH HADARNIEL, and illuminate together, there emerges from that light a living creature that rules over the Seraphim, beneath which there are four eagle-faced LIVING CREATURES. The living creature's name is Yofiel, who is familiar with all the mysteries of Wisdom, and has all the keys of Wisdom.

527. הַאי חֵיוָתָא, קַיְימָא לְמִתְבַּע אַגְרָא מֵעִם קוּדְשָׁא בְּרִיךְ הוּא, לְמֵיהַב לְכָל אִינּוּן דְּרַדְפֵי בָּתַר כָּל מָארֵיהוֹן דְּחָכְמָה, וַאֲפִילּוּ מִכָּל ב"נ, וְאוֹלְפֵי חָכְמָה לְמִנְדַּע לְמָארֵיהוֹן, וְהַהוּא אַגְרָא דְּיָהִיב לִבְנֵי נָשָׁא

דִּרְדְּפֵי בָּתַר חָכְמָה לְמִנְדַּע לְמָארֵיהוֹן.

527. This living creature claims reward from the Holy One, blessed be He, to give to all who go after the initiated in Wisdom, and after any man, to learn Wisdom and know their Master. This reward is for people who pursue Wisdom to know their Master.

528. דְּכַד נָפַק ב"נ מֵהַאי עָלְמָא, הַאי חֵיוָתָא נָפְקָא עַל ד' שְׂרָפִים מְעֹפְפִין, וְטָאסַת קַמֵּיהּ, וְלָא שָׁבִיק כָּל אִינּוּן גַּרְדִּינֵי נִימוּסִין דִּי בְּסִטְרָא אַחֲרָא, לְמִקְרַב בַּהֲדֵיהּ, וְכַמָּה אִינּוּן שְׁלִיחָן דִּשְׁלָם, סַחֲרָנֵיהּ. וְאִלֵּין שְׂרָפִים כַּד נַטְלִין וְאִתְחַזְיָין, אִתְכַּפְיָין אִינּוּן שְׂרָפִים נְחָשִׁים, דְּנַפְקָן מֵהַהוּא נָחָשׁ דְּגָרִים מוֹתָא לְכָל עָלְמָא.

528. When a man passes away from this world, this living creature goes out riding on four flying Seraphim, and they fly before that person. It does not let the accusers who seek justice approach him. Many are the messengers of peace around him. And when the Seraphim travel and are seen, all the fiery serpents, who came out of the serpent which brought death to the world, are subjugated.

529. הַאי חֵיוָתָא קַדִּישָׁא קַיְימָא כַּד נִשְׁמְתָא סַלְקָא וּמָטָאת לְגַבֵּיהּ, כְּדֵין שָׁאַל לָהּ בְּרָזָא דְּחָכְמְתָא דְּמָארֵיהּ, וּכְפוּם הַהִיא חָכְמְתָא דְּרָדִיף אֲבַתְרָהּ וְאַדְבַּק, הָכִי יַהֲבֵי לֵיהּ אַגְרֵיהּ. וְאִי יָכִיל לְאַדְבְּקָא וְלָא אַדְבַּק, דָּחֵי לֵיהּ לְבַר, וְלָא עַיְילָה, וְקַיְימָא תְּחוֹת הַהוּא הֵיכָלָא בִּכְסִיפוּ, וְכַד נַטְלֵי גַּדְפַיְיהוּ, אִלֵּין שְׂרָפִים דִּתְחוֹתָהּ, כְּדֵין כֻּלְּהוּ בַּטְשֵׁי בְּגַדְפַיְיהוּ, וְאוֹקְדוּן לָהּ וְאִתּוֹקְדַת וְלָא אִתּוֹקְדַת, וְקַיְימָא וְלָא קַיְימָא, וְהָכִי אִתְדָּנַת בְּכָל יוֹמָא, נְהִירַת וְלָא נְהִירַת.

529. This holy living creature stands ready, and when the soul rises and reaches it, it asks THE SOUL the secret of its Master's Wisdom. It is given its due according to the Wisdom it pursued and acquired. If THAT PERSON could have gained Wisdom but did not, the soul is rejected outside. It does not enter, but stands under that chamber in shame. When the Seraphim under THE LIVING CREATURE raise their wings, and flap them, they burn

THE SOUL. It burns and burns not, exists and exists not, shines and shines not. So it is sentenced each day.

530. וְאַף ע״ג דְּעוֹבָדִין טָבִין אִית לָהּ, בְּגִין דְּלֵית אַגְרָא בְּהַהוּא עָלְמָא, כְּאִינּוּן דְּמִשְׁתַּדְּלֵי בְּחָכְמְתָא, לְאִסְתַּכְּלָא בִּיקָרָא דְּמָארֵיהוֹן, וְלֵית שִׁיעוּרָא לְאַגְרָא, דְּאִינּוּן דְּיַדְעֵי חָכְמְתָא, לְאִסְתַּכְּלָא בִּיקָרָא דְּמָארֵיהוֹן. זַכָּאָה חוּלָקֵיהוֹן בְּעָלְמָא דֵּין, וּבְעָלְמָא דְּאָתֵי, דִּכְתִּיב אַשְׁרֵי אָדָם מָצָא חָכְמָה וְאָדָם יָפִיק תְּבוּנָה.

530. Though it has done good deeds, IT IS REJECTED OUTSIDE. For there is no greater reward in that world, as for those who strove after wisdom, to behold the glory of their Master. There is no limit to the reward for the initiated in the Wisdom of beholding the glory of their Master. Happy are they in this world and in the World to Come, as it is written, "Happy is the man who finds wisdom, and the man who gets understanding" (Mishlei 3:15).

531. רוּחָא דָּא, שַׁלְטָא עַל כֹּלָּא. כֹּלָּא כְּלִילָן בָּהּ, כֹּלָּא אִסְתַּכְּיָין לְגַבָּהּ. הַאי חֵיוָתָא, שַׁלְטָא עַל אַרְבַּע אַחֲרָנִין, וְאַרְבַּע גַּלְגַּלִּין לְכָל חַד וְחַד. גַּלְגַּלָּא חֲדָא אִסְתָּכֵי לִסְטַר מִזְרָח. וְגַלְגַּלָּא חֲדָא אִסְתָּכֵי לִסְטַר צָפוֹן. וְגַלְגַּלָּא חֲדָא אִסְתָּכֵי לִסְטַר דָּרוֹם. וְגַלְגַּלָּא חֲדָא אִסְתָּכֵי לִסְטַר מַעֲרָב. וְכָל חַד וְחַד בִּתְלַת סַמְכִין. גַּלְגַּלָּא דִּלִסְטַר מִזְרָח. חַנִיאֵ״ל שְׁמֵיהּ. גַּלְגַּלָּא דִּלִסְטַר צָפוֹן, קַרְשִׁיאֵ״ל שְׁמֵיהּ. גַּלְגַּלָּא דִּלִסְטַר דָּרוֹם, עַזְרִיאֵ״ל שְׁמֵיהּ. גַּלְגַּלָּא דִּלִסְטַר מַעֲרָב, עָנִיאֵ״ל שְׁמֵיהּ. וְאִינּוּן תְּלַת סַמְכִין דְּאִינּוּן לְכָל חַד וְחַד, כֻּלְּהוּ אִסְתַּכְּיָין לְאֶמְצָעִיתָא. בְּגִין דְּאֶמְצָעִיתָא אִיהוּ נָטִיל לוֹן, וְכֻלְּהוּ נַטְלוּ בְּגִינֵיהּ דְּאֶמְצָעִיתָא.

531. The spirit URFANIEL rules over everything, and everything is included in him, and looks at him. The living creature YOFIEL rules over four other living creatures, with four wheels to each. One wheel faces east, one wheel faces north, one wheel faces south, and one wheel faces west. Each WHEEL has three struts. The wheel to the east, TIFERET, is called 'Chaniel', DERIVED FROM GRACE (HEB. *CHEN*). The wheel to the north, GVURAH, is called 'Karshiel', DERIVED FROM CONGELATION (HEB. *KRISHAH*),

BECAUSE THE LIGHTS ON THE LEFT SIDE ARE CONGEALED, NAMELY, FROZEN. The wheel to the south, CHESED, is called 'Azriel', DERIVED FROM HELP (HEB. *EZRA*). The wheel to the west, MALCHUT, is called 'Aniel', FROM POOR (HEB. *ANI*), FOR MALCHUT HAS NOTHING OF ITS OWN, AND IS THEREFORE POOR. The three pillars in each WHEEL are facing the middle, TIFERET, since they are carried by the middle one and they travel with it, FOR WITHOUT IT THEY WOULD BE DARKENED WITHOUT LIGHT.

532. אִלֵּין דְּקַיְימֵי בְּאֶמְצָעִיתָא, כֻּלְּהוּ מְמָנָן בְּשִׁירָתָא. וְאִלֵּין דִּימִינָא אָמְרֵי שִׁירָתָא, דְּסַלְּקָא רְעוּתָא לְעֵילָּא, וְאָמְרֵי קָדוֹשׁ. וְאִלֵּין דִּשְׂמָאלָא אָמְרֵי שִׁירָתָא, וְסַלְּקֵי רְעוּתָא לְעֵילָּא, וְאַמְרֵי בָּרוּךְ. קָדוֹשׁ לְעֵילָּא, וּבָרוּךְ לְתַתָּא. אִלֵּין דְּקַיְימֵי לְעֵילָּא לִסְטַר יְמִינָא, נַטְלֵי קְדוּשָּׁה, וּמִתְחַבְּרָאן בִּקְדוּשָּׁה, בְּכָל אִינּוּן דְּיָדְעֵי לְקַדְּשָׁא לְמָארֵיהוֹן, בְּיִחוּדָא בְּרָזָא דְּחָכְמְתָא. וְאִלֵּין דְּקַיְימֵי בִּשְׂמָאלָא, נַטְלֵי קְדוּשָּׁה, וּמִתְחַבְּרָאן בְּכָל אִינּוּן דְּלָא יַדְעֵי לְקַדְּשָׁא לְמָארֵיהוֹן כַּדְקָא יֵאוֹת. וְכֻלְּהוּ כְּלִילָן אִלֵּין בְּאִלֵּין בְּיִחוּדָא חֲדָא, וּמִתְקַשְּׁרָאן דָּא בְּדָא, עַד דְּכֻלְּהוּ אִתְעֲבִידוּ קְשׁוּרָא חֲדָא, וְרוּחָא חֲדָא, וּמִתְקַשְּׁרָן בְּאִינּוּן דִּלְעֵילָּא, לְמֶהֱוֵי כֹּלָּא חַד, לְאִתְכַּלְּלָא דָּא בְּדָא.

532. The ones standing in the middle, THE SECRET OF TIFERET, are in charge of singing. Those of the right, THE SECRET OF CHESED, chant; the desire rises up high, and they say the prayer 'holy'. Those of the left, GVURAH, chant; the desire rises high and they say the prayer 'Blessed be He', FOR He IS holy above, IN CHESED, GVURAH AND TIFERET, and blessed below IN MALCHUT. THEREFORE, those who stand above to the right take the sanctification, join it and all those who know how to sanctify their Master, in the SECRET OF unison in the mystery of wisdom. Those who stand to the left take the sanctification, and join all those who do not know how to sanctify their Master properly. All are included in one another in one unison, joining each other, to become one knot and one spirit. They are connected to THE CHAMBERS above, to make all into one, joined together.

533. מֵאֲתַר דָּא, יַנְקֵי כָּל אִינּוּן מָארֵיהוֹן דְּחָכְמְתָא, דְּקַיְימָן לְמִנְדַּע

בְּמַרְאָה, אוֹ בְּרָזָא דְּחֶלְמָא, בְּגִין דִּנְבִיאִים יַנְקֵי מִלְעֵילָּא. וְאִלֵּין מָארֵי דְּחֶלְמָא, אוֹ דְּמַרְאָה, יַנְקֵי מֵהָכָא. וְכַד מִתְחַבְּרָא אַתְרָא דָּא בְּאַתְרָא דִּלְעֵילָּא בְּקִשּׁוּרָא חֲדָא, כְּדֵין נְבִיאִים, יַנְקֵי מֵעֵילָּא וּמִתַּתָּא, בְּקִשּׁוּרָא חֲדָא.

533. From this place nourish all the initiated in Wisdom, who are able to know by vision, or by the secret of the dream. The prophets nourish from above, NETZACH AND HOD OF ZEIR ANPIN OF ATZILUT, and those who look at dreams or in visions nourish from here, THE CHAMBER OF HOD, and when this place is united with the upper place IN NETZACH AND HOD OF ZEIR ANPIN, then the prophets nourish from above and below in one knot.

534. ובג״כ, אִית מָשָׁל בְּמִלַּיְיהוּ, דְּלָא צַחְצְחָא נְבוּאַתְהוֹן כַּדְקָא יֵאוֹת, כְּמָה דַּהֲוָה בֵּיהּ בְּמֹשֶׁה, דַּהֲוָה צַחְצוּחָא בִּנְבוּאָתֵיהּ בְּכֹלָּא. בְּגִין דִּנְהִירוּ נָפִיק מֵעֵילָּא, מֵאֲתָר דְּכָל נְהוֹרִין נָפְקִין מִנֵּיהּ, וּמָטָא לְדַרְגֵּיהּ, וּמִתַּמָּן יָנִיק נְבוּאָתֵיהּ, וְנָהִיר, מַה דְּלָא הֲוָה כְּדֵין לְכֹלָּא, לְכָל שְׁאַר נְבִיאִין. אִינּוּן מָארֵיהוֹן דְּחֶלְמָא, מָארֵיהוֹן דְּמַרְאָה, כֻּלְּהוּ יַנְקֵי מֵאֲתָר דָּא לְתַתָּא, בְּלָא חִבּוּרָא דִּלְעֵילָּא, עַל יְדָא דְּדַרְגָּא אַחֲרָא תַּתָּאָה מִינֵּיהּ דְּאִיהוּ לְבַר.

534. Therefore, there are allegories in the sayings OF THE PROPHETS, because their prophecy is not completely polished, as was Moses's, whose prophecy was entirely polished because its light came from above, BINAH, where all the lights come from. It reached his grade, TIFERET OF ATZILUT, whence MOSES drew his prophecy, and shone. This no one else could do, not even the other prophets. And the visionaries and seers, all draw from the lower place, FROM THE CHAMBER OF HOD, without the connection OF NETZACH AND HOD OF ZEIR ANPIN above, and from another, lower grade, NAMELY MALCHUT, which is outside, IN THE FIRST CHAMBER.

535. כְּמָה דְּדַרְגָּא דִּנְבִיאִים דִּלְעֵילָּא, לָא הֲווֹ חָמָאן לֵיהּ נְבִיאִים, בַּר עַל יְדָא דְּדַרְגָּא אַחֲרָא תַּתָּאָה. הָכִי נָמֵי אִלֵּין, דַּרְגָּא דְּיַנְקוּ דִּילְהוֹן

אִיהוּ לְעֵילָּא, בְּהַאי דַּרְגָּא תַּתָּאָה, אֲבָל לָא אִתְגַּלְיָא לוֹן, אֶלָּא עַל יְדָא דְּדַרְגָּא אַחֲרָא לְבַר, דְּאִיהוּ תַּתָּאָה מִנֵּיהּ, בְּגִין דְּנָפְקָא מֵהַאי הֵיכָלָא, וּמָטָא מִלָּה עַד הַהוּא מְמָנָא דְּקַיְּימָא עַל תַּרְעָא דְּהֵיכָלָא דָּא, וּמִתַּמָּן לְהַהוּא מְמָנָא דִּתְחוֹת יְדֵיהּ, וְכֵן עַד כֻּלְּהוּ דְּכַמָּה אִינּוּן דְּנַטְלֵי הַהִיא מִלָּה, וְאִתְעָרְבוּ בַּהֲדָהּ. וְעַל דָּא כַּד מָטָא לְגַבֵּיהּ דְּבַר נָשׁ, כַּמָּה אִינּוּן דְּאִתְעַרְבֵי בַּהֲדָהּ, וע"ד לָא צַחְצְחָא מִלָּה כַּדְקָא יֵאוֹת.

535. The prophets RECEIVE FROM NETZACH AND HOD OF ZEIR ANPIN, but do not see the grade OF NETZACH AND HOD OF ZEIR ANPIN, only through another, lower grade, MALCHUT OF ATZILUT. In the same manner, THE VISIONARIES AND SEERS draw from this lower grade of above, FROM THE CHAMBER OF HOD, but it is revealed to them only through another grade outside THAT CHAMBER, MALCHUT OF THE FIRST CHAMBER, which is lower. For WHAT comes out of the chamber OF HOD, reaches the chieftain at the gate of the chamber, and thence to another chieftain beneath him, and so on, UNTIL IT COMES TO MALCHUT OF THE FIRST CHAMBER. How many are those who take part in passing it! So until it reaches men, many handled IT, and therefore it is not properly polished.

536. כַּד מִתְחַבְּרָן אִלֵּין אַרְבַּע גַּלְגַּלִּין, בְּאַרְבַּע אִינּוּן דִּי בְּאֶמְצָעִיתָא, כְּדֵין כֻּלְּהוּ אִקְרוּן חֲמוּדוֹת. וְאִינּוּן מָארֵיהוֹן, דְּמַרְאֶה. ובג"כ, הַאי חֵיוָתָא דְּקַאמְרָן, שַׁלְטָא עָלַיְיהוּ. ובג"כ, אִקְרֵי דָּנִיאֵל, אִישׁ חֲמוּדוֹת. דִּכְתִּיב, כִּי חֲמוּדוֹת אָתָּה. וְכֹלָּא רָזָא כַּדְקָא יֵאוֹת. זַכָּאִין אִינּוּן דְּיַדְעִין רָזֵי דְּמָארֵיהוֹן, לְמֵיהַךְ בְּאֹרַח קְשׁוֹט, בְּעָלְמָא דֵּין וּבְעָלְמָא דְּאָתֵי.

536. When the four wheels are connected to the four STRUTS in the middle, FOR EACH WHEEL HAS THREE STRUTS, RIGHT, LEFT, AND MIDDLE, they are called 'greatly beloved', men of vision, for the living creature we referred to, FLASH, has sway over them. For that reason Daniel was called "man greatly beloved" (Daniel 10:11), as it is written, "for you are greatly beloved" (Daniel 9:23). This is a mystery as ought to be. Happy are those who know the secrets of their Master, and walk in the path of truth in this world and in the World to Come.

48. The chamber of brightness – Netzach

A Synopsis

Rabbi Shimon describes the third chamber as the place where the verdicts of the souls are handed over to the chieftains, who hold the seal of life and the seal of death depending on the verdict. He tells us of the death of babies, and children, and young people and adults. We are told of the four gates, and of how the soul is anointed with the 22 letters of the Torah. He moves on to a discussion of war, and wrath and fury and the punishment of souls who sinned. The sinner still has a chance to repent, however, and he can be released from the reprimand that he stands under. Rabbi Shimon talks about the two-colored Seraphim that are mercy and judgment, and who always care for the sorrowful. They are also called 'windows,' and they watch over those who pray, taking their prayers up to the gate of the fourth chamber. We learn about the 'companions to the destroyer' and also about the 'angel friends' who save and protect good people. Four angels watch over Yisrael, one in each direction. They look after those who comfort the poor, those who wanted to sin but didn't, and those who study the Torah and look after the sick. Yisrael blows the Shofar to awaken God's compassion. Rabbi Shimon says that the 'windows' above are the reason for the windows in the Tabernacle below because the synagogue below is the counterpart of the one above.

537. הֵיכָלָא תְּלִיתָאָה. הֵיכָלָא דָּא, הֵיכָלָא דְּקַיְּימָא בִּנְהִירוּ עִלָּאָה, יַתִּיר עַל כָּל אִלֵּין קַדְמָאֵי. בְּהֵיכָלָא דָּא קַיְימִין אַרְבַּע פִּתְחִין, חַד לִסְטַר דָּרוֹם, וְחַד לִסְטַר מִזְרָח, וְחַד לִסְטַר צָפוֹן, וְחַד לִסְטַר מַעֲרָב. בְּכָל פִּתְחָא וּפִתְחָא אִית מְמָנָא חֲדָא, דְּקַיְּימָא מְמָנָא עַל כָּל פִּתְחָא וּפִתְחָא.

537. The third chamber OF NETZACH stands in the supernal light more than the first ones. There are four gates in this chamber, one to the south, one to the east, one to the north, and one to the west, CORRESPONDING TO CHOCHMAH AND BINAH, TIFERET AND MALCHUT. There is a chief to each gate, as ought to be.

538. פִּתְחָא קַדְמָאָה, דָּא פִּתְחָא דְּקַיְּימָא בֵּיהּ חַד מְמָנָא, מַלְכִּיאֵ"ל שְׁמֵיהּ. וְאִיהוּ שַׁלִּיטָא עַל כָּל אִינּוּן פִּתְקִין, דְּנַפְקֵי מִבֵּי דִּינָא דְּמַלְכָּא,

לְאִתְדְּנָא עָלְמָא. בְּגִין דְּהַאי אִיהוּ מְמָנָא לְאַשְׁגָּחָא בְּהוּ בְּאִינּוּן פִּתְקִין, וּתְרֵין סוֹפְרִין תְּחוֹת יְדֵיהּ, חַד מִימִינָא וְחַד מִשְּׂמָאלָא.

538. At the first gate stands the chief Malkiel, in charge over the notes, ON WHICH THE VERDICT IS WRITTEN, emerging from the King's court that judges the world. This chief supervises over these notes, with two scribes under him, one to the right and one to the left.

539. לְהַאי, אִתְיְיהִיבוּ תִּקּוּנֵי פִּתְקִין לְאַתְקְנָא, עַד לָא יִפְקוּן מֵהַאי תַּרְעָא לְבַר, וְיִתְמַסְרוּ בִּידָא דְּהַהוּא מְמָנָא, דִּי בְּהֵיכְלָא קַדְמָאָה. דְּהָא מִזְּמְנָא דְּאִתְמְסָרוּ בִּידָא דְּהַהוּא מְמָנָא דִּבְהֵיכְלָא קַדְמָאָה, הָא נַפְקֵי מִתַּמָּן, וְלֵית רְשׁוּ לְאָתָבָא לוֹן.

539. MALKIEL is given the notes to be corrected, before they leave the gate, to be handed to the chieftain of the first chamber. Once they are given to the chieftain of the first chamber, they leave the place, and there is no possibility to return them SO AS TO CORRECT THEM.

540. דְּהָא מִיַּד אִזְדְּמַן מְמָנָא דְּסִטְרָא אַחֲרָא מְסָאֲבָא, מָארֵיהּ דְּדִינָא קַשְׁיָא תַּקִּיפָא, דְּלָא מְרַחֵם, וְסַנְגַּדִיאֵ"ל שְׁמֵיהּ, וְאִיהוּ מְמָנָא עַל תַּרְעָא דְּהֵיכְלָא אַחֲרָא דִּי בְּסִטְרָא אַחֲרָא, דְּאִיהוּ גֵּיהִנָּם, וְכַמָּה אִינּוּן גַּרְדִּינֵי נִימוּסִין מִמַּנָן לְשַׁטְיָא בְּעָלְמָא, וּזְמִינִין לְמֶעְבַּד דִּינָא.

540. For immediately comes a chieftain of the unholy pitiless Other Side, of strict Judgment, Sangadiel by name. He is in charge over the gate of another chamber of the Other Side, Gehenom. Some complainants and accusers are sent to hover about the world, prepared to execute justice.

541. וּבְגִין כָּךְ, קַיְּימָא הַהוּא מְמָנָא לְעַיְינָא בְּפִתְקִין, וְאִינּוּן תְּרֵין סוֹפְרִין דְּקַיְימֵי תְּחוֹת מְמָנָא דָּא, שַׁמְּשִׁיאֵ"ל וְקָמוּאֵ"ל, אִלֵּין סוֹפְרִין לְאַתְקְנָא פִּתְקִין, וְהַהוּא מְמָנָא עֲלַיְיהוּ דְּאִיהוּ מַלְכִּיאֵ"ל. בְּגִין דְּבְאִינּוּן הֵיכָלִין דִּי בְּסִטַר אַחֲרָא מְסָאֲבָא, אִתְפְּקִידוּ מְמַנָן יְדִיעָאן, בְּהִפּוּכָא מֵאִלֵּין מְמַנָן דִּי בְּהֵיכָלִין אִלֵּין, וְכָל אִינּוּן רוּחִין וְכָל אִינּוּן מְמַנָן,

דְּתַמָּן, כֻּלְּהוּ לְאַבְאָשָׁא.

541. While the chief is leafing through the verdicts, the two scribes, Shamashiel and Kamuel, correct the scripts, under Malkiel. For in the chambers of the unholy Other Side, certain chieftains were appointed, the opposite of those appointed in the chambers OF HOLINESS, and all the spirits and the officers in charge on the Other Side, all do harm.

542. ת״ח, הַאי סַנְגַּדִיאֵ״ל כַּד נָטִיל פִּתְקָא, מִסִּטְרָא דְּהַהוּא מְמָנָא דְּקַיְּימָא לְפִתְחָא קַדְמָאָה, פָּתַח חַד פִּתְחָא, לְסִטְרָא דַּחֲשׁוֹכָא, דְּאִקְרֵי בְּאֵר שַׁחַת, וְתַמָּן מְמָנָן אֶלֶף וְרִבְבָן זְמִינִין לְנַטְלָא אִינּוּן פִּתְקִין, וְהַאי מְמָנָא עֲלַיְיהוּ. וּכְדֵין כָּרוֹזִין נָפְקִין, וְכַמָּה גַּרְדִּינֵי שַׁטְיָין בְּעָלְמָא, וְהַהוּא דִּינָא אִשְׁתְּלִים, וע״ד, מְמָנָא דָּא קַיְּימָא לְעַיְינָא בְּפִתְקִין, וּלְאַתְקְנָא נִימוּסֵי פִּתְקִין, עַד לָא נַפְקוּ מֵהַאי פִּתְחָא, וְהַאי פִּתְחָא אִיהוּ פִּתְחָא דְּדָרוֹם.

542. Come and see: When this Sangadiel takes the scrip from the chieftain standing at the first gate, he opens an entrance to the side of darkness called "pit of destruction" (Tehilim 55:24), THE TWO FIRST CHAMBERS OF THE OTHER SIDE, where thousands and tens of thousands of officers are ready to take the scripts, with the chieftain SANGADIEL over them. Then the criers come out, and the accusers hover about the world, and the judgment is executed. Therefore, the chieftain MALKIEL reads the scripts carefully to correct the verdicts before they leave the gate. This is the gate to the south.

543. פִּתְחָא תִּנְיָינָא, דָּא פִּתְחָא דְּחַיִּין וּמוֹתִין תַּלְיָין בֵּיהּ, בְּגִין דְּהַאי פִּתְחָא, חַתְמִין חֲתִימִין דְּכָל פִּתְקִין, דְּכֵיוָן דְּפִתְקִין אִתְקָנוּ כַּדְקָא יֵאוֹת, חַד שַׁמָּשָׁא זַמִּין, גַּזְרִיאֵ״ל שְׁמֵיהּ, וְנָטִיל פִּתְקִין בְּהַאי פִּתְחָא תִּנְיָינָא, וְתַמָּן חַתְמִין לְהוּ.

543. The second gate, life and death depend upon it, for in this gate are signed all the scripts COMING FROM THE COURT. When the scripts are corrected, an attendant named Gazriel takes them to the second gate to be signed.

544. מְמָנָא חֲדָא קַיְימָא עַל הַהוּא פִּתְחָא, וְעַזְרִיאֵ״ל שְׁמֵיהּ, וְכָל פִּתְחָא וּפִתְחָא אִתְקְרֵי עַל שְׁמָא דְּהַהוּא מְמָנָא דְּאִתְפַּקְדָא עָלֵיהּ. הַאי מְמָנָא תְּחוֹת שׁוּלְטָנֵיהּ, וּתְחוֹת יְדֵיהּ, תְּרֵין שַׁמָּשִׁין דִּי שְׁמָהוֹן סָנוּרִיָּ״א, עֲדִיאֵ״ל. חַד מִימִינָא וְחַד מִשְּׂמָאלָא. הַהוּא מִימִינָא, בֵּיהּ תַּלְיָין חַיִּין. וְהַהוּא דִּשְׂמָאלָא, בֵּיהּ תַּלְיָא מוֹתָא. וּתְרֵין חוֹתָמִין בִּידַיְיהוּ, חוֹתָם חַיִּים וְחוֹתָם מָוֶת. דָּא קָאֵים לְסִטְרָא דָּא, וְדָא קָאֵים לְסִטְרָא דָּא.

544. A chieftain stands at the gate, named Azriel. Each gate is named after the chieftain in charge of it. The chieftain AZRIEL has under him two attendants, Sanuriya and Adiel, one to the right and one to the left. Life depends upon him of the right, and death upon him of the left. They have two seals in their hands, a seal of life and a seal of death, one on this RIGHT side, the other on that LEFT side.

545. הַאי פִּתְחָא סָתִים כָּל יוֹמֵי שַׁתָּא, וּבְיוֹמָא דְּשַׁבְּתָא, וּבְיוֹמֵי דְּחָדְשָׁא אִתְפְּתַח, לְאַחֲזָאָה חַיִּים בְּהַהוּא חוֹתָמָא, דְּתַלְיָין בֵּיהּ חַיִּים, בְּגִין דְּשַׁבָּת וְחֹדֶשׁ חוֹתָמָא דְּחַיִּים אִתְקְיָּים בְּהוּ.

545. This gate is closed for six days, and open on Shabbat and new moons, as a sign of life in the seal, upon which life depends. For the seal thrives on Shabbatot and new moons.

546. בְּיוֹמָא דְּכִפּוּרֵי, דְּיִשְׂרָאֵל כֻּלְּהוּ קַיְימֵי בִּצְלוֹתִין וּבָעוּתִין, וּמִשְׁתַּדְּלֵי בְּפוּלְחָנָא דְּמָארֵיהוֹן, סָתִים הַהוּא פִּתְחָא, עַד שַׁעֲתָא דִּצְלוֹתָא, דְּמִנְחָה. כֵּיוָן דְּאַעְבַר הַאי צְלוֹתָא דְּמִנְחָה, מֵאֲתָר בֵּי דִּינָא דְּהֵיכָלָא דִּזְכוּתָא, חַד אֲוִירָא נָפְקָא, וּפִתְחָא דָּא אִתְפְּתַח, וְהַאי מְמָנָא דְּהֵיכָלָא דָּא קַיְימָא, וְאִינּוּן תְּרֵין שַׁמָּשִׁין חַד מִימִינָא וְחַד מִשְּׂמָאלָא, וְחוֹתָמֵי דְּחַיִּים וּמוֹתָא בִּידַיְיהוּ, וְכָל פִּתְקִין דְּעָלְמָא קַמַּיְיהוּ, וּכְדֵין אַחְתִימוּ הֵן לַחַיִּים הֵן לַמָּוֶת. וְדָא הוּא פִּתְחָא דְּמִזְרָח.

546. On Yom Kippur, when Yisrael are occupied with prayers and petitions, and strive to worship their Master, this gate is closed until the prayer of Minchah. When this prayer passes from the court house in the chamber of merit, an air comes out, the gate is opened, the chieftain stands with the two attendants, one on his right and one on his left, with seals of life and death in their hands, and all the scripts OF THE COURT of the world are before them. They then sign to life or death. This is the east gate, THE SECRET OF THE CENTRAL COLUMN.

547. פִּתְחָא תְּלִיתָאָה, דָּא פִּתְחָא דְּקַיְימָא בְּקִיּוּמָא, לְמִנְדַּע כָּל אִינּוּן דִּי דִּינָא יַעֲבַר עֲלַיְיהוּ, בֵּין לְמַרְעִין, בֵּין לְמַכְאוֹבִין, בֵּין לְמִסְכְּנוּ. דִּינָא דְּלָא קַיְּימָא לְמוֹתָא. כַּד תַּרְעָא דְּפִתְחָא דָּא סָגִיר, כְּדֵין דִּינָא אִתְרְשִׁים עַל ב"נ, דְּלָא תַּיְיבִין לֵיהּ, בַּר בְּחֵילָא דִּצְלוֹתָא תַּקִּיפָא, וְתִיּוּבְתָּא שְׁלִים. דִּכְתִיב יִסְגּוֹר עַל אִישׁ וְלֹא יִפָּתֵחַ.

547. The purpose of the third gate is to know all those upon whom judgment is executed, either sickness, pain, or poverty, NAMELY, not Judgment for death. When this gate is closed, the judgment is written upon man, and can not be repealed, save by intense prayer, and complete repentance, as it is written, "He shuts up a man, and there can be no opening" (Iyov 12:14).

548. חַד מְמָנָא קַיְּימָא עַל פִּתְחָא דָּא, וְקַפְצִיאֵ"ל שְׁמֵיהּ, וְהַאי מְמָנָא עַל פִּתְחָא דָּא, בְּגִין לְסַגְּרָא הַאי פִּתְחָא, עַל הַהוּא בַּר נָשׁ, דְּאִתְחֲזֵי לְאִתְעַנְשָׁא, בְּגִין דְּלָא יִתְקַבַּל בִּצְלוֹתָא, עַד דְּיֵיתוּב לְקָמֵי מָארֵיהּ.

548. There is one chieftain in charge over this gate, named Kaf'tziel. He is in charge over the gate, and closes it before a person worthy of punishment, so he may not be admitted by prayer, until he repents before his Master.

549. וּבְהַהוּא זִמְנָא דְּאִתְגְּזַר דִּינָא בִּבְנוֹי דְּלָא חָאבוּ, בְּאִינּוּן רַבְיָין זְעִירִין, חַד מְמָנָא שַׁמָּשָׁא תְּחוֹת יְדֵיהּ, עִירִיאֵ"ל שְׁמֵיהּ, וְנָפַק וְכָרִיז לְסְטַר שְׂמָאלָא, עַד דְּאִתְּעַר חַד רוּחָא, דְּאִיהוּ רוּחָא דִּפְגִימוּ, אִתְבְּרֵי בִּפְגִימוּ דְּסִיהֲרָא, וְאִקְרֵי אַסְכְּרָ"ה, וְהַאי אִיהוּ רוּחָא דְּקַיְּימָא עַל דַּרְגָּא רְבִיעָאָה, בְּהֵיכָלָא תְּלִיתָאָה, דִּי בִּסְטַר מְסָאֲבָא, וְדָא קַיְּימָא עַל קְטוּלָא

דִלְהוֹן, וְיִתְחֲזֵי לוֹן לְרַבְיֵי, כְּאִתְּתָא דִּרְבִיאַת לְרַבְיֵי, וַאֲחִידַת לוֹן, וְקָטְלַת לוֹן.

549. When sentence is pronounced on his children who committed no crime, NAMELY, small children, a chief under KAF'TZIEL, called 'Iriel', comes out and cries to the left side until a spirit is awakened, a flawed spirit, created when the moon was waning, called 'Askara'. He stands on the fourth grade of the third chamber of the side of defilement, in charge over babies death. He is seen before them in the guise of a woman raising children, but, seizes and kills them.

550. וּכְדֵין הַהִיא נִשְׁמְתָא, סַלְּקָא, וְאָחִיד לָהּ הַאי מְמָנָא, וְסַלְּקָא לָהּ לַמְמָנָא דְּקַיְימָא עַל הֵיכָלָא רְבִיעָאָה, וְהַהוּא מְמָנָא מְגַדְּלָא לוֹן, וְאִשְׁתַּעְשַׁע בְּהוּ, וְסָלִיק לוֹן לְאִתְחֲזָאָה קָמֵי מַלְכָּא קַדִּישָׁא, בְּכָל שַׁבָּת וְשַׁבָּת, וּבְכָל רֵישׁ יַרְחָא וְרֵישׁ יַרְחָא, וְאִתְחֲזוּן קַמֵּיהּ, וְאִתְבָּרְכוּן מִנֵּיהּ. וּבְשַׁעְתָּא דְּרוּגְזָא שַׁלְטָא, אִסְתַּכַּל בְּהוּ קוּדְשָׁא בְּרִיךְ הוּא, וְחָיֵיס עַל עָלְמָא.

550. This chief seizes the soul OF THE BABY, and raises it before the chieftain of the fourth chamber, who raises them and takes delight in them. He elevates them to be seen before the Holy King on each Shabbat and new moon. They are presented before Him and blessed by He. When fury has sway over the world, the Holy One, blessed be He looks at them and has compassion for the world.

551. וְכָל אִינּוּן רַבְיָין, דְּלָא אַשְׁלִימוּ שְׁנִין, עַד תְּלֵיסַר שְׁנִין וְיוֹמָא חַד, כֻּלְּהוּ אִתְמְסָרוּ בִּידָא דְּהַאי, מִתְּלֵיסַר שְׁנִין עַד עֶשְׂרִין, כֻּלְּהוּ אִתְמְסָרוּ עַל יְדָא דְּרוּחָא אַחֲרָא, דְּאִקְרֵי אָגִירִיסוֹ"ן, דְּנָפְקָא מֵהַאי נָחָשׁ עֲקִימָא, דְּגָרִים מוֹתָא לְכָל עָלְמָא, וְאִיהוּ יצה"ר. מֵעֶשְׂרִין שְׁנִין וּלְעֵילָּא, אִתְדָּן בְּ"נ מִבֵּי דִּינָא, אֲתָר דְּאִקְרֵי זְכוּתָא, אִיהוּ בְּגַרְמֵיהּ אָתָא, וּבְחוֹבוֹי אִתְדָּן, וְאִתְמְסַר בִּידָא דְּהַאי חִוְיָא דְּאִיהוּ מַלְאָךְ הַמָּוֶת.

551. All the children who did not reach thirteen years and a day, are all given into the hands of this chief IRIEL. Those from thirteen to twenty years of age are given to the spirit called 'Agirsion', issued from the subtle serpent, the Evil Inclination, who brought death to the world. A man over twenty years is sentenced by the court in the place called 'merit', THE FOURTH CHAMBER, and comes himself to the court. He is judged according to HIS OWN sins, and delivered to the hands of that serpent, the Angel of Death.

552. בְּגִין דְּהָא מֵעֶשְׂרִין שְׁנִין וּלְתַתָּא, עַד תְּלֵיסַר שְׁנִין, הַאי רוּחָא דְּקַיְימָא בֵּיהּ כְּנָחָשׁ, אָזִיל אֲבַתְרֵיהּ, דָּא אֲגִירִיסוֹ"ן דְּקָאָמַרָן. בְּגִין דְּלָא אִתְנְטִיר כַּד הֲוָה רַבְיָא דָּקִיק כִּדְקָא יֵאוֹת. וְחָמֵי בֵּיהּ סִימָן דְּיִתְפְּגִים לְבָתַר. וְהַאי אִתְנְטִיל בְּלָא רְשׁוּ, וְעַ"ד כְּתִיב, וְיֵשׁ נִסְפֶּה בְּלֹא מִשְׁפָּט. וְרָזָא דָּא כְּתִיב וְהִנֵּה טוֹב מְאֹד, וְתָנֵינָן, וְהִנֵּה טוֹב מְאֹד, דָּא מַלְאַךְ הַמָּוֶת, דְּאַקְדִּים לֵיהּ עַד לָא יִתְפְּגִים לְבָתַר. וְהַאי מְמָנָא דְּקָאֵים עַל הַאי פִּתְחָא, אָעִיל נִשְׁמָתֵיהּ וְסַלְקָא לָהּ לְעֵילָּא.

552. For when he is under twenty years of age, down to thirteen, the spirit Agirison, that is within him as a serpent, follows him, since he did not refrain from sinning when he was a little child, as he should have done. The spirit saw in him a sign that he will be corrupted later on. He is therefore taken without permission, as it is written, "but sometimes ruin comes for want of judgment" (Mishlei 13:23). This is the secret of the verse, "and, behold, it was very good" (Beresheet 1:31). We learned that this refers to the Angel of Death, who hastened TO TAKE HIS SOUL, before he will become a sinner. The chieftain over this gate, KAF'TZIEL, takes his soul and raises it upward.

553. מִתְּלֵיסַר שְׁנִין וּלְתַתָּא, אִתְדָּן עַל חוֹבוֹי דְּאָבוֹי, וְאִתְמְסַר בִּידָא דְּהַאי אַסְכָּרָא דְּקָאָמַרָן. וְכָל חַד וְחַד, הֵיכָלָא דָּא לָקֳבֵל הֵיכָלָא דָּא. דָּא בְּהִפּוּכָא מִן דָּא, כִּדְקָאָמַרָן, וְהַאי פִּתְחָא אִיהוּ לִסְטַר צָפוֹן.

553. Under thirteen years of age, he is judged for his father's sins, and delivered to the said Askara. Each chamber OF HOLINESS has a parallel chamber ON THE OTHER SIDE. One is opposite to the other, as we said. This is the gate to the north.

554. פִּתְחָא רְבִיעָאָה, פִּתְחָא דָּא קַיְימָא לְאַסְוָותָא, וְאִקְרֵי פִּתְחָא דְּאַסְוָותָא, בְּהַאי פִּתְחָא קַיְימָא חַד מְמָנָא, פְּדָיאֵ״ל שְׁמֵיהּ. וְהַאי קַיְימָא עַל כָּל אִינּוּן אַסְוָותִין דְּעָלְמָא, וּלְאַעֲלָא צְלוֹתִין דְּכָל אִינּוּן מָארֵי דְּמַכְאוֹבִין וּמַרְעִין וְצַעֲרִין, וְהַאי אִיהוּ סָלִיק בְּכָל אִינּוּן צְלוֹתִין, וְאָעִיל לוֹן קָמֵי קוּדְשָׁא בְּרִיךְ הוּא.

554. The fourth gate is for healing, called 'the gate of healing'. The chieftain of this gate is called 'Peda'el', DERIVED FROM REDEMPTION (HEB. *PIDYON*). He is in charge over all the remedies in the world, and brings in all the prayers of those in pain, sickness, and sorrow. He mounts together with these prayers, and presents them before the Holy One, blessed be He.

555. וְהַאי אִיהוּ מַלְאָךְ מֵלִיץ אֶחָד מִנִּי אָלֶף, בְּגִין דְּאִינּוּן אֶלֶף קַיְימִין בְּהַהוּא פִּתְחָא, וְהַאי חַד מִנַּיְיהוּ, וּכְתִיב וַיְחֻנֶּנּוּ וַיֹּאמֶר פְּדָעֵהוּ מֵרֶדֶת שַׁחַת מָצָאתִי כֹפֶר. בְּגִין דְּסָלִיק בְּהַאי צְלוֹתָא, וְקַיְימָא מֵלִיץ טוֹב עָלֵיהּ דְּבַר נָשׁ, וְאַדְכַּר זְכוּתֵיהּ דְּעָבֵד קָמֵי מַלְכָּא קַדִּישָׁא, בְּגִין דְּהַאי אִיהוּ דְּקַיְימָא תָּדִיר לְטָב, וע״ד, כָּל אַסְוָותָא קַיְימָא בְּהַאי פִּתְחָא דִּי פְּדָיאֵ״ל מְמָנָא בֵּיהּ. פִּתְחָא דָּא אִיהוּ לִסְטַר מַעֲרָב. וּבְגִין דָּא, אִלֵּין אַרְבַּע פִּתְחִין קַיְימִין בְּהֵיכָלָא דָּא.

555. This is "an angel over him, an interpreter, one among a thousand" (Iyov 33:23), for there are a thousand who stand at the gate, and PEDA'EL is one among them. It is also written, "then He is gracious to him, and says, 'Deliver him from going down to the pit. I have found a ransom'" (Ibid. 24), as this prayer mounts and becomes a good interpreter for that person, and speaks well of him before the Holy One, blessed be He. It is always for a good cause. Therefore, all the remedies are found in that gate, over which Peda'el is in charge. This is the gate to the west. There are four gates to this chamber, EACH HAVING A UNIQUE FUNCTION.

556. בְּהֵיכָלָא דָּא קַיְימָא רוּחָא חֲדָא דְּאִקְרֵי נֹגַהּ, הַאי אִיהוּ רוּחָא שַׁלִּיטָא בְּהַאי הֵיכָלָא, כָּל זִיוָא וְכָל תִּיאוּבְתָּא קַיְימָאן בֵּיהּ. הַאי רוּחָא

אִיהוּ קַיְּימָא לְכָל אִינּוּן דְּאִית לוֹן חוּלָקָא בְּעָלְמָא דְּאָתֵי, דָּא אַעְטָר לְאִינּוּן נִשְׁמָתִין בְּזִיוָא דִּיקָרָא, בְּגִין לְמִנְדַּע כָּל אִינּוּן רוּחִין דִּי בְּהֵיכָלִין אַחֲרָנִין, דְּדָא אִיהוּ בַּר עָלְמָא דְּאָתֵי, וְיַעְבַר בְּכֻלְּהוּ, וְלֵית מַאן דִּימְחֵי בִּידֵיהּ.

556. In this chamber there is another spirit called 'Nogah' (lit. 'brightness'). This spirit rules over this chamber, and every luster and desire are in it. This spirit is for those who have a portion in the World to Come. He bedecks the souls with precious luster, so all the other spirits in the other chambers know that this soul is worthy of the World to Come, and might pass through all the other chambers with no one to detain it.

557. הַאי רוּחָא, אִיהוּ רוּחָא דַּכְיָא, בָּרִיר מֵאִלֵּין תַּתָּאִין, זָהֲרִיאֵ״ל שְׁמֵיהּ, מֵהַהוּא מִשְׁחָא דִּרְבוּת קוּדְשָׁא דְּנָגִיד מֵעָלְמָא דְּאָתֵי, נָגִיד בֵּיהּ, וּמֵהַהוּא מִשְׁחָא אִתְרַבֵּי וְאִצְמַח. וְהַאי אִיהוּ נֵר, כְּמָה דְּאַתְּ אָמֵר עָרַכְתִּי נֵר לִמְשִׁיחִי. בְּגִין דְּהַאי אִיהוּ סִדּוּרָא לְאַדְלָקָא בּוּצִינִין מִתַּתָּא לְעֵילָּא, כַּד שָׁרָא עָלֵיהּ נְהִירוּ דְּנָגִיד מִלְּעֵילָּא, בְּגִין דְּהַאי אִתְסָדַר, כַּד אִתְכְּלִילוּ בֵּיהּ כָּל אִינּוּן תַּתָּאִין לְתַתָּא.

557. This spirit is purer and clearer than those below HIM. His name is Zahariel, anointed by the holy anointing oil drawn from the World to Come, BINAH, and it is nourished and grows by it. This alludes to a candle, as it is written, "I have set up a candle for My anointed" (Tehilim 132:17). For he is the set order of lighting candles from below upwards, when light from above, BINAH dwells upon him. Because he is set in order when all those below are included in him, NAMELY, THE CHAMBERS BELOW, MOUNT UP TO HIM, AND THEN "I HAVE SET UP A CANDLE..."

558. וְכַד אִתְסָדַר הַאי רוּחָא בְּכָל אִינּוּן תַּתָּאִין, וְנָהִיר, כְּדֵין אַפִּיק מִנֵּיהּ נְהוֹרָא חַד, דִּי שְׁמֵיהּ אַהֲדִיאֵ״ל וְהַאי כָּלִיל בְּרוּחָא דָּא, הַאי קַיְּימָא תְּחוֹת הַאי רוּחָא, לְאַמְשְׁחָא לְכָל אִינּוּן נִשְׁמָתִין דְּסַלְּקִין, דְּאִית לוֹן חוּלָקָא בְּעָלְמָא דְּאָתֵי, וְאִתְחָזוּן לְסַלְּקָא לְעֵילָּא.

558. When this spirit is set AND ARRANGED by all the lower beings who went up to him, and he shines, he emits one light by the name of Ahadiel, who is included in this spirit, ZAHARIEL. The spirit Ahadiel is underneath the spirit, ZAHARIEL, and anoints all the rising souls, who have a portion in the World to Come, and are worthy of ascending.

559. בְּגִין דְּכַד נִשְׁמְתָא סַלְקָא, וְעָאלַת בְּאִינּוּן הֵיכָלִין תַּתָּאִין, רְשִׁימָא אִיהִי בְּעֶשְׂרִין וּתְרֵין אַתְוָון דְּאוֹרַיְיתָא, דִּרְשִׁימִין בְּהַאי נִשְׁמְתָא. וְכַד נִשְׁמְתָא זַכָּאת וְקָמַת קַמֵּיהּ דְּהַהוּא רוּחָא, דָּא מְמָנָא אֲהַדִיאֵ״ל מָשַׁח לוֹן. וְסַלְקִין וְעָאלִין בְּהַהוּא נְהַר דִּינוּר וְסַלְקִין וְאִתְקְרִיבוּ לְקָרְבָּנָא.

559. For when a soul ascends, it first enters the lower chambers, THE CHAMBER OF THE SAPPHIRE STONE, AND THE CHAMBER OF THE VERY HEAVEN. The soul is engraved with the 22 letters of the Torah written upon it. And when the soul is found worthy OF ASCENDING TO THIS CHAMBER, it stands in front of this spirit, ZAHARIEL, and the chief Ahadiel anoints it. It rises and enters the river of fire, and goes up THENCE and is offered as sacrifice TO STAND ALWAYS BEFORE ATIK YOMIN.

560. הַאי נְהוֹרָא כָּלִיל בִּתְלַת נְהוֹרִין, בְּגִין דְּהַהוּא רְבוּת מִשְׁחָא, אִתְכְּלִיל בִּתְלַת גְּוָונִין. וְכַד נָצִיץ הַאי נְהוֹרָא, נָצִיץ מִנֵּיהּ עֶשְׂרִין וּתְרֵין נְהוֹרִין, לָקֳבֵל כ״ב אַתְוָון דְּאוֹרַיְיתָא, דִּרְשִׁימִין בְּהַאי נִשְׁמְתָא. וְאִלֵּין עֶשְׂרִין וּתְרֵין נְהוֹרִין, כֻּלְּהוּ מְמָנָן שַׁמָּשִׁין דְּקַיְימֵי עִמֵּיהּ, וְכֻלְּהוּ אִתְקְרוּן עַל שְׁמָא דְּהַאי נְהוֹרָא דְּעָלַיְיהוּ, וְכֻלְּהוּ אִתְכְּלִילוּ בֵּיהּ. הַאי נְהוֹרָא בְּכָל אִינּוּן נְהוֹרִין, אִתְכְּלִיל בְּהַאי רוּחָא, וְהַאי רוּחָא כָּלִיל בֵּיהּ, וְאִסְתַּכֵּי לְאִתְיַשְּׁבָא גּוֹ הֵיכָלָא רְבִיעָאָה.

560. This light, AHADIEL, comprises three lights, since the anointing oil, THE LIGHT OF BINAH, WHENCE IT CAME, comprises three colors, THE THREE COLUMNS. When this light glitters, 22 lights glitter by it, corresponding to the 22 letters of the Torah, written upon the soul. These 22 lights, are all chiefs and attendants standing WITH AHADIEL, named after the light above them, AHADIEL, and included in it. This light, AHADIEL, together with the 22 lights is included in the spirit ZAHARIEL, who is included in AHADIEL, and seeks to be settled in the fourth chamber.

561. רוּחָא דָא, כַּד אִתְכְּלִיל מִנְּהוֹרָא דָא, וּמִכֻּלְּהוּ נְהוֹרִין, כַּד דָּחֲקִין לְאִתְנַצְּצָא נָפְקָא מִנַּיְיהוּ חַד חֵיוָתָא קַדִּישָׁא, כְּלִילָא בִּתְרֵי גְּוָונֵי, אַרְיֵא וְנִשְׁרָא, וְאִיהִי חַד דְּיוּקְנָא, וְהַאי אִקְרֵי אֲהִיאֵ״ל.

561. When the spirit ZAHARIEL includes the light AHADIEL and the 22 letters, urging to glitter, one holy living creature comes out combined of two colors of a lion and an eagle. It has one shape, FOR THE SHAPES OF THE LION AND THE EAGLE MERGED INTO ONE, called 'Ahiel'.

562. וְהַאי חֵיוָתָא קַדִּישָׁא, נַפְקֵי מִנְּצִיצוּ דִּילָהּ, כַּד מָטֵי נְהִירוּ דְּהַאי רוּחָא עִלָּאָה בָּהּ, אַרְבַּע אוֹפַנִּים, כְּלִילָן בְּכָל גְּוָונִין, וְאִינּוּן הַדְרִיאֵ״ל, יְהַדְרִיאֵ״ל, אֲהַדוֹרְיָ״א, אָסִימוֹ״ן. כָּל אִלֵּין בִּתְמַנְיָא גַּדְפִּין, וְאִלֵּין אִינּוּן מְמֻנָּן, עַל כָּל חֵילֵי שְׁמַיָּא, מְגִיחֵי קְרָבָא. בְּגִין דְּלָא אִשְׁתְּכַח קְרָבָא בְּעָלְמָא, אוֹ עֲקִירוּ דְּמַלְכוּתָא מֵאַתְרַיְיהוּ, עַד דְּחֵילֵי שְׁמַיָּא, וְכֹכָבַיָּא דִּשְׁאַר רְקִיעִין, כֻּלְּהוּ אַחְזִיו קְרָבִין וְסִכְסוּכִין אִלֵּין בְּאִלֵּין. וְאִלֵּין אַרְבַּע אוֹפַנִּים, קַיְימֵי עֲלַיְיהוּ לְאַרְבַּע סִטְרִין דְּעָלְמָא.

562. From the glittering of this holy living creature, when light from the high spirit ZAHARIEL reaches it, four wheels come out, comprising all the colors, LION, OX, EAGLE AND MAN, called 'Had'riel, Yehad'riel, Ahadoriya, Asimon'. They all have eight wings, appointed over the heavenly armies who wage war, for there is no war in the world, nor a kingdom uprooted from its place, unless the heavenly armies and the stars of the rest of the firmaments wage war upon each other. The four wheels stand upon them in the four directions of the world.

563. אִלֵּין אַרְבַּע, כַּד נַטְלִין לְאַגָּחָא קְרָבִין, מֵרָזָא דְּהֵיכָלָא דִּלְעֵילָּא נַטְלִין, דְּאִיהוּ בֵּי דִּינָא, וְאִקְרֵי זְכוּתָא. מִזִּיעָא דִּלְהוֹן אַפִּיקוּ כַּמָּה חֵילִין וּמַשִׁרְיָין דְּלֵית לוֹן חוּשְׁבָּנָא. וְכֻלְּהוּ קַיְימֵי תְּחוֹת אִלֵּין אוֹפַנִּים.

563. When the four wheels go to wage wars, by the secret of the chamber of above, THE FOURTH CHAMBER, they depart, FOR THERE is a court house, named merit. From their sweat, countless armies and hosts OF ANGELS are issued. They all abide under these wheels.

564. מִנְּהוֹן קַיְימֵי עַל שִׁירָתָא, וּמִנְּהוֹן שְׁלִיחָן עַל עָלְמָא. לָקֳבֵל אִינּוּן שְׁלִיחָן דְּלִסְטַר מְסַאֲבָא, דְּנָפְקֵי מִגּוֹ הַהוּא הֵיכָלָא תְּלִיתָאָה דִּילָהּ, וְאִינּוּן מְקַטְרְגֵי עָלְמָא לְאַבְאָשָׁא. וְאִלֵּין אִשְׁתְּכָחוּ לָקֳבְלַיְיהוּ, דְּלָא יִשְׁלְטוּן לְגַבֵּי אִינּוּן דְּמִשְׁתַּדְּלֵי בְּאוֹרַיְיתָא, כד״א כִּי מַלְאָכָיו יְצַוֶּה לָּךְ וְגוֹ׳. וּכְתִיב עַל כַּפַּיִם יִשָּׂאוּנְךָ פֶּן תִּגּוֹף בָּאֶבֶן וְגוֹ׳. דָּא אֶבֶן נֶגֶף צוּר מִכְשׁוֹל. הַאי אִקְרֵי אֶבֶן נֶגֶף צוּר מִכְשׁוֹל. וְהַאי אִקְרֵי אֶבֶן בֹּחַן פִּנַּת יִקְרַת, צוּר יִשְׂרָאֵל. וְכֹלָּא קַיְימָא דָּא לָקֳבֵל דָּא.

564. Some of them recite poetry, and some are messengers to this world corresponding to the messengers of the side of defilement, coming out of its third chamber, and prosecute and cause harm in the world. THE MESSENGERS OF THIS CHAMBER are against them, so they would not have power over those occupied in the Torah, as it is written, "For He shall give His angels charge over you, to keep you in all your ways. They shall bear you up in their hands, lest you dash your foot against a stone…" (Tehilim 91:11-12). This is "a stone of stumbling and…a rock of offense" (Yeshayah 8:14). DEFILEMENT is called "a stone of stumbling," a rock of offense. HOLINESS is called "a tried stone, a precious corner stone" (Yeshayah 28:16), "the Rock of Yisrael" (Yeshayah 30:29). The one corresponds to the other.

565. מֵרָזָא דְּהֵיכָלָא תְּלִיתָאָה דִּי בְּסִטְרָא אַחֲרָא, נַפְקֵי תְּרֵין רוּחִין, דְּאִקְרוּן אַ״ף וְחֵמָ״ה, וּמִתְּרֵין אִלֵּין, נָפְקִין כָּל אִינּוּן שְׁלִיחָן דְּאָזְלִין לְאַסְטָאָה בְּנֵי נָשָׁא מֵאָרְחָא דִּקְשׁוֹט, וְאִלֵּין אִינּוּן דְּקַיְּימָאן, וְאַקְדִּימוּ עַל ב״נ, דְּקָא אָזִיל לְאוֹרְחָא דְּמִצְוָה. וְעַל דָּא אִלֵּין אוֹפַנִּים קַיְּימָן לָקֳבְלַיְיהוּ, בְּגִין לְאַגָּנָא עָלֵיהּ דב״נ דְּלָא יִתְנְזָקוּן. מֵאִלֵּין תְּרֵין רוּחִין דָּחִיל מֹשֶׁה, כַּד הֲוָה נָחִית מִן טוּרָא, דִּכְתִּיב כִּי יָגֹרְתִּי מִפְּנֵי הָאַף וְהַחֵמָה.

565. From the mystery of the third chamber of the Other Side, two spirits emerge, called 'wrath and fury'. From these two all the messengers come out, misleading men from the path of truth. They stand before a man on a righteous path TO DISTRACT HIM. For this reason these wheels oppose them, to protect the man from incurring damage by them. Moses was afraid of these two, when he went down the mountain, as it is written, "For I was afraid of the wrath and fury" (Devarim 9:19).

566. בְּאֶמְצָעִיתָא דְּהֵיכָלָא דָּא, אִית אַתְרָא אַחֲרָא, דְּקַיְּימָא לְעֵילָּא לְעֵילָּא, בְּאַרְבַּע פִּתְחִין, לְאַרְבַּע סִטְרֵי עָלְמָא, עֶשֶׂר מְמָנָן לְכָל פִּתְחָא וּפִתְחָא, וְחַד מְמָנָא עֲלַיְיהוּ. וְהַאי כָּלִיל בִּנְהוֹרָא דְּאִקְרֵי אֲהַדִּיאֵ״ל, וְהַאי אִיהוּ אוֹפָן בְּתוֹךְ הָאוֹפָן, מְשֻׁלָּבָן דָּא בְּדָא.

566. In the middle of this chamber, there is another place up above, with four gates to the four directions of the world. There are ten chiefs in charge over each gate, and one chieftain over them. THIS CHIEFTAIN comprises the light Ahadiel, they are wheel within wheel, combined with one another.

567. אִלֵּין אַרְבְּעִין, נַטְלֵי דִּינָא מִבֵּי זְכוּתָא, לְאַלְקָאָה לְהַאי נִשְׁמְתָא דְּחָבָאת וּבָעָאת לְאַלְקָאָה. וְאִלֵּין קַיְימֵי בְּשַׁלְהוֹבֵי נוּרָא לְגַבֵּי אִינּוּן נִשְׁמָתִין, וְטָאסִין לְבַר מֵהֵיכָלָא דָּא, וְאַלְקָאן לְנִשְׁמְתָא דָּא, וְקַיְּימָא נְזִיפָא לְבַר, כָּל אִינּוּן יוֹמִין דְּאִתְגְּזָרַת עָלָהּ, וְלָא עָאלַת לְפַרְגּוֹדָא.

567. The forty CHIEFS receive from the chamber of merit, the indictment, to strike the sinning soul, and they have to strike it. They stand within flames of fire facing the souls, then soar out of the chamber and strike that soul. The soul stands reprimanded all the days it was sentenced to, and does not cross the screen, TO ENTER THE CHAMBER.

568. וְאִלֵּין אַרְבָּעִים, אִינּוּן דְּקַיְימִין וַאֲנְזִיפוּ וּמְנַדִּין, לְכָל אִינּוּן דְּאַפִּיקוּ מִפּוּמַיְיהוּ מִלָּה דְּלָא אִצְטְרִיכָא, וּבָתַר דָּא אַפִּיקוּ מִפּוּמַיְיהוּ מִלָּה קַדִּישָׁא, מִלָּה דְּאוֹרַיְיתָא, וּמִטַּנְּפֵי פּוּמַיְיהוּ בָּהּ. וְאִלֵּין קַיְימֵי, וּמְנַדִּין לוֹן, וְקַיְימֵי בְּהַאי נִדּוּיָא אַרְבְּעִין יוֹמִין, דְּלָא אִשְׁתְּמַע צְלוֹתְהוֹן.

568. These forty CHIEFS reprimand and excommunicate all those who uttered something they should not have, and IMMEDIATELY after, pronounced a holy word of the Torah, and sully their mouths therein. The chiefs excommunicate them, and they are excommunicated for forty days, for their prayer is not accepted.

569. וְכֵן לְכָל אִינּוּן דְּחָאבוּ אִינּוּן חוֹבִין, דְּבַעְיָין לְנַזְפָא, עֲשָׂרָה כָּרוֹזִין נַפְקֵי בְּכָל יוֹמָא, וּמַכְרְזֵי בְּכָל אִינּוּן רְקִיעִין, וּבְכָל אִינּוּן חֵילִין וּמַשִׁרְיָין, אִזְדְּהָרוּ בִּפְלַנְיָא דְּאִיהוּ נְזִיפָא. נְזִיפָא אִיהוּ עַל חוֹבָא פְּלוֹנִי דַּעֲבַד, עַד דְּתָב קַמֵּי מָארֵיהּ, רַחֲמָנָא לִישֵׁזְבָן.

569. So for all sinners who deserve to be reprimanded, ten criers come out every day, and proclaim in all the firmaments, the armies and the hosts OF ANGELS, beware of so-and-so, for he is reprimanded for such-and-such a sin he committed, until he repents before his Master. May the Merciful One save us.

570. כַּד תָּב מֵהַהוּא חוֹבָא, מִתְכַּנְּפֵי אִלֵּין אַרְבְּעִין, וְשָׁרָאן לֵיהּ. וּכְדֵין אַכְרִיזוּ עָלֵיהּ, פְּלַנְיָא שָׁרָא נְזִיפָא. מִכָּאן וּלְהָלְאָה צְלוֹתָא עָאלַת. וְעַד לָא תָּב, נָזִיף אִיהוּ לְעֵילָּא וְתַתָּא, וּנְטִירוּ דְּמָארֵיהּ אִתְעֲדֵי מִנֵּיהּ. וַאֲפִילּוּ בְּלֵילְיָא נִשְׁמָתֵיהּ נְזִיפָא, דְּסָתְמִין לָהּ כָּל תַּרְעֵי שְׁמַיָּא וְלָא סַלְקָא, וְדַחְיָין לָהּ לְבַר.

570. When he repents his sin, the forty chiefs gather and release him FROM THE REPRIMAND. Then a proclamation resounds: ‘so-and-so is released from the reprimand.’ From now on the prayer enters. But before he repents, he is reprimanded above and below, and the protection of his Master is removed from him. Even at night, WHEN HIS SOUL DEPARTS AND WISHES TO RISE ABOVE, his soul is reprimanded, and the gates of heaven are closed before it. It does not mount, but is rejected outside.

571. הַאי אוֹפָן דְּקַיְּימָא עַל אִלֵּין אַרְבְּעִין, כַּד נָטִיל מָטָא לְהַהוּא אֲתָר דְּאִקְרֵי תָּא הָרָצִי״ם. וְכַד עָאל, עָאלוּ עִמֵּיהּ אִינּוּן אַרְבְּעִין, דִּי מְמָנָן בְּאַרְבַּע פִּתְחִין, וְסַלְקִין כָּל אִינּוּן מְגִינִּין דִּי דַּהֲבָא. וְאִלֵּין אִינּוּן

מַלְאֲכִין דְּאִקְרוּן חַשְׁמַלִי״ם. וְאִינּוּן מְגִינִּין וְסַיְיפִין וְרוּמְחִין, דְּרַהֲטֵי לְאַגָּנָא עֲלַיְיהוּ דְּיִשְׂרָאֵל מִשְּׁאַר עַמִּין, וּלְאַגָּחָא קְרָבָא בְּהוּ, וּלְנַקְמָא לוֹן כְּפוּם שַׁעֲתָא, בְּלָא אֲרִיכוּ.

571. There is a wheel in charge over the forty CHIEFS. He travels to the place called "the couriers' chamber" (I Melachim 14:28). He enters with the forty CHIEFS in charge over the four gates, and together they raise the golden shields. These are the angels called electrums, who hasten with shields, swords, and spears to protect Yisrael from the other nations, and wage war against them, to take revenge at once, without wasting TIME.

572. ובג״כ אִקְרֵי תָּא הָרָצִים, אֲתַר דְּאִינּוּן רָצִים רַהֲטֵי, וְאוּחוּ לְאַגָּחָא, וּלְנָקְמָא נוּקְמִין לָקֳבֵל רָצִים אַחֲרָנִין, דְּרַהֲטֵי לְאַבְאָשָׁא וּלְאַתְרְעָא מַזָּלִין, לְשַׁלְטָאָה עֲלַיְיהוּ. וְרָזָא דָּא, הָרָצִים יָצְאוּ דְּחוּפִים. רָצִים מִסִּטְרָא דָּא, וְרָצִים מִסִּטְרָא דָּא, וּבְגִינֵיהוֹן, וְהָעִיר שׁוּשָׁן צָהֲלָה וְשָׂמֵחָה, אוֹ נָבוֹכָה. אִי מְקַדְּמֵי אִלֵּין דְּהָכָא, הָעִיר שׁוּשָׁן שָׂמֵחָה. וְאִי מְקַדְּמֵי אִלֵּין דְּסִטְרָא אַחֲרָא, הָעִיר שׁוּשָׁן נָבוֹכָה.

572. It is therefore called "the couriers' chamber", REFERRING TO where they run from. They run and hasten to fight and take revenge, contrary to other couriers, running in haste to bring evil and weaken the fortune OF PEOPLE, thus to have power over them. This is the secret meaning of the verse, "the couriers went out in haste" (Ester 3:15). There are couriers on this side OF HOLINESS, and couriers on that side OF THE OTHER SIDE. And because of them "the city of Shushan rejoiced and was glad" (Ester 8:15), or "was in consternation" (Ester 3:15). If the couriers OF HOLINESS arrive earlier, the city of Shushan rejoices, and if the couriers of the Other Side come first, the city of Shushan is in consternation.

573. וְהָא אוּקִימְנָא, דִּבְכֹלָּא קַיְימִין אִלֵּין לָקֳבֵל אִלֵּין, סִטְרָא דָּא לָקֳבֵל סִטְרָא דָּא. ובג״כ, אִלֵּין אִינּוּן מְגִינִּין לְכֹלָּא. כַּד סַלְקִין אִלֵּין בְּאִלֵּין, נָפַק חַד אֲוִירָא דִּלְעֵילָּא, וְאִתְעָבֵידוּ כֻּלְּהוּ מָגֵן חַד. וְסִימָנָךְ, אָנֹכִי מָגֵן לָךְ.

573. We already explained that IN THE CHAMBER they stand facing each other, this side OF HOLINESS, against that side OF THE OTHER SIDE. And for that reason, THE COURIERS IN HERE defend all, and when they ascend, INCLUDED in each other, one air comes out from above, and they all become one shield, alluded to by "I am your shield" (Beresheet 15:1).

574. תְּרֵיסָר גַּלְגַּלִּין, אִינּוּן דְּסַחֲרָאן גּוֹ הֵיכָלָא דָּא, וְאִינּוּן אִקְרוּן שְׂרָפִים, דִּתְרֵין גַּוְונִין, חִוָּור וְסוּמָק, רַחֲמֵי וְדִינָא, אִלֵּין אִינּוּן קַיְימֵי לְאַשְׁגָּחָא תָּדִיר, עַל כָּל אִינּוּן מָארֵי דְּצַעֲרָא, דְּצַעֲרִין לוֹן שְׁאַר עַמִּין, וְדַחֲקִין לוֹן, וְאִקְרוּן חַלּוֹנוֹת. וְהַיְינוּ דִּכְתִּיב, מַשְׁגִּיחַ מִן הַחַלּוֹנוֹת.

574. Twelve wheels are turning at the chamber, called 'two-colored Seraphim', red and white, NAMELY, Mercy and Judgment. They always care for the sorrowful, to whom the other nations cause sorrow and oppression. They are called 'windows', as in the verse, "He looks in at the windows" (Shir Hashirim 2:9).

575. וְאִלֵּין קַיְימֵי לְאִסְתַּכְּלָא, כָּל אִינּוּן דִּמְצַלָּאן צְלוֹתַיְיהוּ, דִּמְקַדְּמֵי לְבֵי כְּנִישְׁתָּא, וְאִתְמְנוּן מֵאִינּוּן עֲשָׂרָה קַדְמָאֵי. כְּדֵין סַלְּקִין וְכַתְבִין לוֹן לְעֵילָּא, בְּגִין דְּאִלֵּין אִקְרוּן חֲבֵרִים לְגַבַּיְיהוּ. הה"ד חֲבֵרִים מַקְשִׁיבִים לְקוֹלֵךְ הַשְׁמִיעִנִי.

575. They are standing watchful over those who pray, early to come to the synagogue, to be counted among the first ten. THE SERAPHIM then mount and inscribe them above. For these FIRST TEN are called 'their friends'. This is the meaning of "the companions hearken for your voice; cause Me to hear it" (Shir Hashirim 8:13).

576. זַכָּאִין אִינּוּן צַדִּיקַיָּיא, דְּיַדְעֵי לְסַדְּרָא צְלוֹתְהוֹן כַּדְקָא יֵאוֹת, בְּגִין דְּכַד הַאי צְלוֹתָא שָׁרָאת לְאִסְתַּלְּקָא, אִלֵּין סַלְּקִין בְּהַאי צְלוֹתָא, וְעָאלִין בְּכָל אִינּוּן רְקִיעִין, וּבְכָל אִינּוּן הֵיכָלִין, עַד תַּרְעָא דִּפְתְחָא עִלָּאָה, וְעָאלַת הַהִיא צְלוֹתָא קָמֵי מַלְכָּא, לְאִתְעַטְּרָא. כְּמָה דְּאִתְּמַר.

576. Happy are the righteous who know how to properly arrange their prayer, because when this prayer begins to ascend, THE SERAPHIM mount with it. They enter throughout the firmaments and chambers, up to the gate of the supernal opening, where the prayer comes in to be adorned before the King, as we learned.

577. תָּא חֲזֵי, כָּל אִינּוּן דִּמְצַלָּאן צְלוֹתִין, וּמְקַדְּשֵׁי לְמָרֵיהוֹן בִּרְעוּתָא שְׁלִים, הַאי צְלוֹתָא בַּעְיָא לְאַפָּקָא לָהּ מִגּוֹ מַחֲשָׁבָה, וּבִרְעוּתָא דְּמִלּוּלָא וְרוּחָא, וּכְדֵין אִתְקַדָּשׁ שְׁמֵיהּ דְּקוּדְשָׁא בְּרִיךְ הוּא. וְכַד מָטָאת לְגַבֵּי אִלֵּין חֲבֵרִים, כֻּלְּהוּ נַטְלֵי לְהַהִיא צְלוֹתָא, וְאַזְלָן בַּהֲדָהּ עַד הֵיכָלָא רְבִיעָאָה, בְּהַהוּא פִּתְחָא. וְאִלֵּין מְשַׁבְּחִין בְּהַהוּא זִמְנָא דִּמְצַלָּאן צְלוֹתִין, וּמְקַדְּשֵׁי בְּהַהוּא זִמְנָא, אִלֵּין אִינּוּן דִּי מְמָנָן בִּימָמָא בְּהוּ בְּיִשְׂרָאֵל, לְמֶהֱוֵי עִמְּהוֹן חֲבֵרִים. וּבְלֵילְיָא, בְּאִינּוּן אַחֲרָנִין, דְּאַמְרֵי שִׁירָתָא בְּלֵילְיָא.

577. Come and see: Those who say prayers and sanctification before their Master with their whole will, their prayer should come straight from thought, with speech and spirit full of desire. Then the name of the Holy One, blessed be He is sanctified, and when prayer reaches THE ANGELS, the friends, they all take the prayer and walk with it to the gate of the fourth chamber. THERE THE ANGELS praise THE HOLY ONE, BLESSED BE HE, when YISRAEL say prayers and sanctifications TO THE HOLY ONE, BLESSED BE HE. At that time OF DAY, day-chiefs are appointed over PRAISING with Yisrael, and to be their companions. At night, THEY ARE FRIENDS with those who chant at night.

578. וְתָא חֲזֵי כְּתִיב, גּוֹזֵל אָבִיו וְאִמּוֹ וְאוֹמֵר אֵין פָּשַׁע חָבֵר הוּא לְאִישׁ מַשְׁחִית. וְהָא אוֹקְמוּהָ, בְּגִין דְּמָנַע בִּרְכָאן דְּקוּדְשָׁא בְּרִיךְ הוּא, דְּאִיהוּ אָבִיו. כְּמָה דִּכְתִּיב, שְׁאַל אָבִיךָ וְיַגֵּדְךָ. וּכְתִּיב יִשְׂמַח אָבִיךָ. וְאוּקְמוּהָ.

578. Come and see: It is written, "He who robs his father or his mother, and says, it is no transgression; he is companion of a destroyer" (Mishlei 28:24). We already explained that it is because he withheld blessings from the Holy One, blessed be He, his Father, as it is written, "ask your father, and he will recount it to you" (Devarim 32:7), and "let your father…be glad" (Mishlei 23:25). This was explained.

579. חָבֵר הוּא לְאִישׁ מַשְׁחִית, מַאן אִישׁ מַשְׁחִית. דָּא אִיהוּ הַהוּא אִישׁ, דְּפָגִים לְסִיהֲרָא. וְאִקְרֵי אִישׁ תַּהְפּוּכוֹת. אִישׁ לָשׁוֹן. אִישׁ יוֹדֵעַ צַיִד אִישׁ שָׂדֶה. וְהַאי אִיהוּ אִישׁ מַשְׁחִית, דְּהַאי אִיהוּ מָנַע בִּרְכָאן מֵעָלְמָא. אוּף הָכִי, מַאן דְּמָנַע בִּרְכָאן מֵעָלְמָא, חָבֵר הוּא לְהַאי אִישׁ מַשְׁחִית כִּדְקָאמְרָן. וְדָא הוּא רָזָא, בְּגִין דְּאִצְטְרִיךְ לֵיהּ לְבַ"נ לְבָרְכָא לְקוּדְשָׁא בְּרִיךְ הוּא, וּלְצַלָּאָה צְלוֹתָא כַּדְקָא יָאוֹת. בְּגִין דְּיִתְבָּרַךְ שְׁמֵיהּ קַדִּישָׁא, וְיִתְחַבַּר בְּאִלֵּין חֲבֵרִין קַדִּישִׁין, וְלָא יִפְגּוֹם צְלוֹתֵיהּ. בְּגִין דְּיִמְנַע בִּרְכָאן מֵעָלְמָא, וְיִתְחַבַּר בְּהַהוּא חָבֵר אִישׁ מַשְׁחִית דְּאִיהוּ מָנַע בִּרְכָאן מֵעָלְמָא, וְגָרִים מוֹתָא לְכֻלְּהוּ.

579. "He is companion of a destroyer": HE ASKS: Who is the destroyer? AND HE ANSWERS: He is a man who blemished the moon, MALCHUT, NAMELY, THE OTHER SIDE, called "a perverse man" (Mishlei 16:28), "a slanderer" (Tehilim 140:12), " a cunning hunter, a man of the field" (Beresheet 25:27). This is a destroyer, who withholds blessings from the world. Here also, whoever withholds blessings from the world is a companion of a destroyer, as we said. This is a mystery – It behooves a man to bless the Holy One, blessed be He and pray in a proper manner, so that His Holy Name be blessed, and he will join the holy companions, THE ANGELS, and not blemish his prayer. For IF HE BLEMISHES HIS PRAYER, blessings will be withheld from the world, and he will be considered a companion to the destroyer, who withholds blessings from the world, and brings death to all.

580. כְּתִיב וְחוֹבֵר חָבֶר, מַאי וְחוֹבֵר חָבֶר. הַהוּא מַאן דְּאָזִיל בָּתַר סִטְרָא אַחֲרָא, וְחָרָשׁ חַרְשִׁין, אִיהוּ מָשַׁךְ עָלֵיהּ רוּחָא אַחֲרָא מִסַּאֲבָא, וְאִתְחַבַּר בְּהַהוּא חַבְרוּתָא דְּהַהוּא חָבֵר רָע, וְשַׁאֲרֵי בְּחַבְרוּתָא בַּהֲדֵי, הַהוּא חָבֵר אִישׁ מַשְׁחִית. אֲמַאי אִקְרֵי חָבֵר. בְּגִין דִּבְשַׁעֲתָא דְּאִתְיְילִיד ב"נ אִתְחַבַּר עִמֵּיהּ. וְתָדִיר קַיְימָא בַּהֲדֵיהּ חָבֵר. לְבָתַר, אִתְהַפַּךְ לֵיהּ חָבֵר אִישׁ מַשְׁחִית.

580. HE ASKS: What is "a charmer (lit. 'a befriender')" (Devarim 18:11)? AND HE ANSWERS: He who follows the Other Side, charms, and thus draws to himself another, unholy spirit, and joins an evil friend. That friend, the destroyer, abides by him. Why is he called 'a friend'? Because when that man was born, THE OTHER SIDE, NAMELY, THE EVIL INCLINATION, befriended him, and is now always his friend. Later the friend turns into a destroyer.

581. וְהָכִי אִית בְּסִטְרָא דִּקְדוּשָּׁה, בְּסִטְרָא דִּימִינָא, חָבֵר טוֹב, דְּעָבֵיד טִיבוּ עִמֵּיהּ דְּבַר נָשׁ בְּעָלְמָא דֵּין וּבְעָלְמָא דְּאָתֵי. וְאִלֵּין חֲבֵרִים קַיְימֵי תָּדִיר עָלֵיהּ דב"נ, בְּחַבְרוּתָא חֲדָא, לְשֵׁיזָבָא לֵיהּ, וּלְאַגָּנָא עָלֵיהּ, וּלְמֶהֱוֵי עִמֵּיהּ חֲבֵרִים, לְקַדְּשָׁא שְׁמָא דְּמָארֵיהוֹן, וּלְזַמְּרָא וּלְשַׁבְּחָא קָמֵיהּ. תָּדִיר.

581. There is also a good friend on the side of holiness, the right side, who does good with men in this world and in the World to Come. These ANGELS friends, are always with him joined to save and protect him, and be his companions in sanctifying the Name of their Master, to chant and praise Him always.

582. מֵאִלֵּין נַפְקֵי אַרְבַּע סָמְכִין אַחֲרָנִין, לְאִינּוּן תְּרֵיסַר דְּקָאָמַרָן, הָנֵי חֲבֵרִים. וְאִלֵּין אִינּוּן קַיְימֵי לְגַבֵּי אִינּוּן דְּיָעֲטִין עֵיטָא לְאַבְאָשָׁא לְצַדִּיקַיָּיא. אע"ג דְּלָא עַבְדֵּי, וְסַלְקֵי וְאוֹדְעֵי מִלָּה לְעֵילָּא, וּבַטְלֵי לְהַהוּא עֵיטָא, וְאִלֵּין אִקְרוּן אֶרְאֶלִ"ים ואע"ג דְּכֻלְּהוּ אִתְמְנוּן לְדָא, כָּל חַד וְחַד אִתְמְנָא וְאִתְפְּקַד עַל מִלִּין יְדִיעָאן. וּתְחוֹת אִלֵּין לֵית לוֹן חוּשְׁבְּנָא.

582. From these TWELVE TWO-COLORED SERAPHIM come out four other pillars, SUPPORTING the twelve TWO-COLORED SERAPHIM, the friends, as said. The pillars are standing against those who give advice to harm the righteous. And before anything is done, they go up and announce what they heard, and the advice is canceled. They are called 'Er'elim' (Eng. 'angels'). And though all are appointed to that task, NEVERTHELESS each one is in charge over certain SPECIFIC matters. Under them there are countless ANGELS.

583. אִלֵּין אַרְבַּע, קַיְימֵי לְאַרְבַּע סִטְרֵי עָלְמָא, וְכָל חַד קָאֵים לְאַשְׁגָּחָא

עֲלַיְיהוּ דְּיִשְׂרָאֵל. וְאִלֵּין אִקְרוּן חֲרַכִּים, כְּמָה דְּאַתְּ אָמֵר מֵצִיץ מִן הַחֲרַכִּים. שְׁמָא דְּאִלֵּין אַרְבַּע דְּאִקְרוּן חֲרַכִּים, עִיגָאֵ״ל. עִירְיָ״ה. עָרִיאֵ״ל. יְהִירָאֵ״ל. עִיגָאֵ״ל אִיהוּ קָאִים לִסְטַר מִזְרָח, וְדָא קַיְּימָא לְאַשְׁגָּחָא עַל כָּל אִינּוּן דְּעַבְדִין עוֹבָדִין טָבִין, וְעַל כָּל אִינּוּן דִּמְחַשְּׁבֵי מַחֲשָׁבָה דְּמִצְוָה, אַף ע״ג דְּלָא יַכְלֵי לְמֶעְבַּד.

583. These four ER'ELIM stand to the four directions of the world, each standing watchful over Yisrael. They are called 'lattices', according to the verse, "He peers through the lattice" (Shir Hashirim 2:9), AND THE TWELVE ARE CALLED 'WINDOWS'. The names of the four lattices are Iga'el, Iriya, Ariel, Yehira'el. Iga'el stands to the east, looking after all those who do good deeds, and think righteous thoughts, though they are not able to perform.

584. עִירְיָ״ה, קַיְּימָא לִסְטַר דָּרוֹם. וְדָא קַיְּימָא לְאַשְׁגָּחָא, לְכָל אִינּוּן דִּמְנַחֲמֵי לְמִסְכְּנָא, אוֹ דצערי לִבַּיְיהוּ עָלֵיהּ, אַף ע״ג דְּלָא יַכְלֵי לְמֵיהַב לֵיהּ. וּלְאִינּוּן דְּאַזְלֵי לְאוֹרְחָא דְּמִצְוָה. וּלְאִינוּן דְּעָבְדֵי חֶסֶד עִם מֵתִים. וְאִיהוּ קַיְּימָא קִיּוּמָא דֶּאֱמֶת. וְהַאי אִתְמַנָּא לְאַדְכְּרָא לֵיהּ לְעֵילָּא, וּלְאַחֲקָא דְּיוּקְנֵיהּ לְעֵילָּא, לְאַעֲלָא לֵיהּ לְעָלְמָא דְּאָתֵי.

584. Iriya stands to the south. He is looking after all those who comfort the poor, or those whose heart is sorry for them, though they are not able to give anything to them; also those who walk in the path of righteousness. And those who do kindness to the dead, he supports true kindness. His duty is to mention them above, engrave their form above, and bring them to the World to Come.

585. עָרִיאֵ״ל, קַיְּימָא לִסְטַר צָפוֹן. וְדָא קַיְּימָא לְאַשְׁגָּחָא לְכָל אִינּוּן דַּחֲשִׁיבוּ לְמֶעְבַּד בִּישִׁין, וְלָא עַבְדֵי. אוֹ בָּעָאן לְמֶחֱטֵי, וְאָתוּ לְמֶעְבַּד, וְאִתָּקַף בְּיִצְרֵיהּ וְלָא עָבִיד.

585. Ariel stands to the north. He is watchful over those who planned to do evil, but did not, or wanted to sin, but when they came to commit TRANSGRESSION, they overcame their inclination and abstained from doing it.

586. יְהִירָאֵ"ל קַיְּימָא לְסִטַר מַעֲרָב. וְהַאי קַיְּימָא לְאַשְׁגָּחָא לְכָל אִינּוּן דְּלָעָאן בְּאוֹרַיְיתָא. וְעַיְילֵי בְּנַיְיהוּ לְמִלְעֵי בְּאוֹרַיְיתָא לְבֵי רַב. וּלְכָל אִינּוּן דְּמִסְתַּכְּלֵי עַל מְרַע, כַּד אִיהוּ בְּבֵי מַרְעֵיהּ. וְאַשְׁגָּחוּ עָלֵיהּ, וְאוֹדְעוּ לֵיהּ דְּיִסְתָּכַּל בְּחוֹבוֹי וּבְעוֹבָדוֹי, וְיֵתוּב מִנַּיְיהוּ לְמָארֵיהּ. בְּגִין דְּכָל מַאן דְּיִשְׁתָּדַּל בְּהַהוּא מְרַע, דְּיִסְתָּכַּל בְּעוֹבָדוֹי, וְיֵתוּב בְּתִיּוּבְתָּא קָמֵי קוּדְשָׁא בְּרִיךְ הוּא, אִיהוּ גָּרִים לֵיהּ לְאִשְׁתְּזָבָא, וּלְאָתָבָא לֵיהּ רוּחֵיהּ.

586. Yehira'el stands to the west. He is in charge over those who are occupied in the Torah, and bring their sons to study Torah in school, and over those who look after the sick in their sickbed. They watch over them and tell them to examine their sins and deeds, and repent before their Master. For whoever looks after the sick, let him look after his deeds and repent before the Holy One, blessed be He, who will cause him to be saved, and his spirit to return to Him.

587. וע"ד כְּתִיב אַשְׁרֵי מַשְׂכִּיל אֶל דָּל בְּיוֹם רָעָה יְמַלְּטֵהוּ יְיָ'. מַאי בְּיוֹם רָעָה, בְּיוֹם רַע מִבָּעֵי לֵיהּ. אֶלָּא בְּיוֹם רָעָה, בְּיוֹמָא דְּשַׁלְטָא הַהוּא רָעָה לְמֵיסַב נִשְׁמָתֵיהּ. אַשְׁרֵי מַשְׂכִּיל אֶל דָּל, דָּא הוּא מְרַע. כד"א, מַדּוּעַ אַתָּה כָּכָה דַּל בֶּן הַמֶּלֶךְ. ובג"כ, בְּיוֹם רָעָה יְמַלְּטֵהוּ יְיָ'. וְאִלֵּין אִינּוּן דְּמִסְתַּכְּלֵי בְּהַהוּא מְרַע, לְאָתָבָא לֵיהּ מֵחוֹבוֹי גַּבֵּי קוּדְשָׁא בְּרִיךְ הוּא, כְּמָה דְּאוּקִימְנָא. בְּהֵיכָלָא דָּא קַיְּימָא עָלֵיהּ, לְאַשְׁגָּחָא. וּבְיוֹמָא דְּשַׁרְיָא דִּינָא עַל עָלְמָא, יִשְׁתְּזִיב מִנֵּיהּ, כד"א בְּיוֹם רָעָה יְמַלְּטֵהוּ יְיָ'. יוֹמָא דְּאִתְמְסַר דִּינָא לְהַהִיא רָעָה לְשַׁלְטָאָה בֵּיהּ וְכֻלְּהוּ אִלֵּין קַיְּימֵי לְאַשְׁגָּחָא. וע"ד אִקְרוּן חֲרַכִּים.

587. Concerning that, it is written, "Blessed is he who considers the poor: Hashem will deliver him in the day of evil" (Tehilim 41:2). HE ASKS: What is a day of evil? It should have been written, 'an evil day.' AND HE ANSWERS: A "day of evil" REFERS TO the day when evil has sway to take his soul. "Blessed is he who considers the poor (Heb. *dal*)." This refers to the sick, as it is written, "Why are you, being the king's son, so wasted (Heb. *dal*)" (II Shmuel 13:4). For that reason, "Hashem will deliver him in the day of evil," referring to those who look after the sick, and cause them to repent their sins before the Holy One, blessed be He as we explained. In this chamber stands THE ANGEL YEHIRA'EL watchful over him, so when Judgment dwells over the world, he will be saved. Therefore, "Hashem will deliver him in the day of evil," and on the day when Judgment is given in the hands of evil, THE ANGEL OF DEATH, to have power over him, "HASHEM WILL DELIVER HIM." All THE FOUR ER'ELIM are standing watchful, and therefore they are called 'lattices'.

588. בְּיוֹמָא דְּרֹאשׁ הַשָּׁנָה, כַּד קוּדְשָׁא בְּרִיךְ הוּא קָאִים בְּדִינָא עַל עָלְמָא, וְהַהוּא סִטְרָא בִּישָׁא אָתֵי לְאַסְטָאָה, כְּדֵין מִתְכַּנְּפֵי כָּל הָנֵי, וְקַיְימָן קָמֵי קוּדְשָׁא בְּרִיךְ הוּא. וּכְדֵין מִתְעַטְּרָן כֻּלְּהוּ, וְקַיְימָן קָמֵי קוּדְשָׁא בְּרִיךְ הוּא. בְּהַהוּא זִמְנָא מַה כְּתִיב, מַשְׁגִּיחַ מִן הַחַלּוֹנוֹת מֵצִיץ מִן הַחֲרַכִּים. מֵצִיץ: כְּמַאן דְּאַשְׁגַּח מֵאֲתָר דָּקִיק, דְּחָמֵי וְלָא חָמֵי כָּל מַה דְּאִצְטְרִיךְ. וּלְבָתַר, מַשְׁגִּיחַ מִן הַחַלּוֹנוֹת, אֲתָר אַשְׁגָּחוּתָא יַתִּיר, דְּפָתַח פִּתְחִין לְרַחֲמָא עַל כֹּלָּא, וְכַד קוּדְשָׁא בְּרִיךְ הוּא אַשְׁגַּח עַל עָלְמָא, אִסְתָּכַּל בְּאִלֵּין חַלּוֹנוֹת, וּבְאִלֵּין חֲרַכִּים, וְחָיִיס עַל כֹּלָּא.

588. On the day of Rosh Hashanah (the Jewish New Year) when the Holy One, blessed be He stands in Judgment over the world, and the Other Side comes to prosecute, THE TWELVE SERAPHIM AND THE FOUR ER'ELIM gather and stand before the Holy One, blessed be He. They are all adorned and stand before Him. At that time it is written, "he looks in at the windows; he peers through the lattice" (Shir Hashirim 2:9). "He peers," looking through a slit, sees, but sees not all that needs seeing. Later, "He looks in at the windows," where He can look more closely, meaning that He opens openings to have pity over all. And when the Holy One, blessed be He looks at the world, He looks through these windows and the lattices, and has compassion over all.

589. וּכְדֵין כַּד יִשְׂרָאֵל תָּקְעִין בְּהַהוּא שׁוֹפָר וְאִתְּעַר מִתַּתָּא הַהוּא קוֹל דְּנָפִיק מִשּׁוֹפָר, כָּלִיל מֵאֶשָּׁא וּמַיָּא וְרוּחָא, וְאִתְעָבֵיד מִכֹּלָּא הַהוּא קוֹל, בְּגִין לְאִתְּעָרָא קוֹל עִלָּאָה, דְּנָפְקָא מִגּוֹ הַהוּא שׁוֹפָר, דְּאִיהוּ כְּגַוְונָא דָא, כָּלִיל בְּאֶשָּׁא וּבְמַיָּא וְרוּחָא. כְּדֵין כָּרוֹזָא נָפְקָא, וְאַכְרִיז בְּכֻלְּהוּ

רְקִיעִין, וְאָמַר קוֹל דּוֹדִי הִנֵּה זֶה בָּא וְגוֹ׳, מַשְׁגִּיחַ מִן הַחַלּוֹנוֹת מֵצִיץ מִן הַחֲרַכִּים.

589. When Yisrael blow the Shofar, a sound is raised, coming out of the Shofar included of fire, water, and wind. That sound is made of them all, to rouse a high sound, ZEIR ANPIN, coming out of the Shofar, BINAH, likewise included of fire, water, and wind, THE THREE COLUMNS. Then the crier goes out and proclaims through all the firmaments, "The voice of my beloved is come…he looks in at the windows; he peers through the lattice" (Ibid.).

590. וּכְדֵין יַדְעֵי כֻּלְּהוּ, דְּהָא קוּדְשָׁא בְּרִיךְ הוּא חָיִיס עֲלַיְיהוּ דְּיִשְׂרָאֵל, וְאָמְרֵי זַכָּאִין אִינּוּן יִשְׂרָאֵל, דְּאִית לוֹן עֵיטָא בְּאַרְעָא, בְּגִין לְאִתְּעָרָא רַחֲמֵי מִלְּעֵילָּא, כְּדֵין כְּתִיב אַשְׁרֵי הָעָם יוֹדְעֵי תְרוּעָה, יוֹדְעֵי תְּרוּעָה וַדַּאי, יוֹדְעֵי תְרוּעָה: מְתַבְּרֵי הַאי תְּרוּעָה, דְּאִיהוּ דִּינָא קַשְׁיָא, דְּכֹלָּא אִתְדָּנוּ בֵּהּ. זַכָּאִין אִינּוּן יִשְׂרָאֵל בְּעָלְמָא דֵּין, וּבְעָלְמָא דְּאָתֵי, בְּגִין דְּאִינּוּן יַדְעֵי אָרְחוֹי דקוּדְשָׁא בְּרִיךְ הוּא, וְיַדְעֵי לְמֵהַךְ בְּאָרְחוֹי, וּלְיַחֲדָא יִחוּדָא כַּדְקָא יֵאוֹת.

590. Then all know that the Holy One, blessed be He has compassion over Yisrael, and say, happy are Yisrael, to have the means on earth, BY BLOWING THE SHOFAR, to awaken compassion above. Then it is written, "happy are the people who know the joyful note" (Tehilim 89:16). Assuredly, they know the note, for they break the note, which is harsh Judgment, by which all are judged. Happy are Yisrael in this world and in the World to Come, for they know the ways of the Holy One, blessed be He, and know how to walk in His ways and properly bind the unity.

591. אִלֵּין חַלּוֹנוֹת, וְאִלֵּין חֲרַכִּים, קַיְימֵי כֻּלְּהוּ לְאַחֲדָא כָּל צְלוֹתִין, דְּסַלְקִין מִתַּתָּא לְעֵילָּא, וּלְאַשְׁגָּחָא בְּהוּ, לְאַעֲלָא לוֹן קָמֵי קוּדְשָׁא בְּרִיךְ הוּא. וְעַל דָּא כָּל בֵּית הַכְּנֶסֶת דְּלָאו בֵּיהּ חַלּוֹנוֹת, לָאו אֲתָר לְצַלָּאָה בֵּיהּ כַּדְקָא יֵאוֹת.

591. The windows, SERAPHIM, and the lattices, ER'ELIM, are all ready to unite all the prayers coming up from below, and watch over them to bring them before the Holy One, blessed be He. Therefore, every synagogue without windows is not a worthy place for prayer.

592. דְּהָא בֵּית הַכְּנֶסֶת לְתַתָּא, לָקֳבֵל בֵּית הַכְּנֶסֶת דִּלְעֵילָּא. בֵּית הַכְּנֶסֶת דִּלְעֵילָּא דְּאִית בֵּיהּ חַלּוֹנוֹת כְּמָה דְּאַמָרָן, הָכִי נָמֵי לְתַתָּא. לְעֵילָּא כְּנֶסֶת הַגְּדוֹלָה, אִית בֵּיהּ תְּרֵיסָר חַלּוֹנוֹת עִלָּאִין, הָכִי נָמֵי לְהַאי בֵּית הַכְּנֶסֶת תַּתָּאָה. וְכֹלָּא קַיְּימָאן דָּא לָקֳבֵל דָּא, בְּגִין דְּעָלְמִין קַיְּימִין אִלֵּין בְּגַוְונָא דְּאִלֵּין, וְקוּדְשָׁא בְּרִיךְ הוּא סָלִיק יְקָרֵיהּ בְּכֹלָּא. וע״ד בְּיוֹם רָעָה יְמַלְּטֵהוּ יְיָ׳, כַּד שַׁלְטָא הַהִיא סִטְרָא בִּישָׁא, יְמַלְּטֵהוּ יְיָ׳.

592. For the synagogue below is the counterpart of the synagogue above, in which there are windows as we said. So there are below. For as above, in the great synagogue, THE CHAMBER, there are twelve supernal windows, NAMELY, THE TWELVE SERAPHIM, they are also in the lower synagogue. The one faces the other, because the worlds stand the one facing the other, SEALED BY ONE ANOTHER, AND WHATEVER IS IN THE SEAL, IS FOUND IN THE INSIGNIA, and the glory of the Holy One, blessed be He is raised in every way. Therefore, "Hashem will deliver him in the day of evil" (Tehilim 41:2), MEANING THAT when the Evil Side has sway, Hashem will deliver him, THROUGH THE WINDOWS AND THE LATTICES.

593. כְּגַוְונָא דָּא, הַאי מְמָנָא יְהִירָאֵ״ל, קַיְּימָא עַל כָּל אִינּוּן דְּחַיְּיסֵי עַל מִסְכְּנֵי, כד״א אַשְׁרֵי מַשְׂכִּיל אֶל דָּל. וּבְגִין דָּא כֹּלָּא קַיְּימָא בְּהֵיכָלָא דָּא, וְהֵיכָלָא דָּא אִתְכְּלִיל בְּהֵיכָלָא אַחֲרָא רְבִיעָאָה, דְּתַמָּן הוּא גְּזֵרִין וְדִינִין לְכֹלָּא. זַכָּאָה חוּלָקֵיהּ מַאן דְּיָדַע גִּנְזֵי דְּמָארֵיהּ, לְיַחֲדָא לֵיהּ, וּלְקַדְּשָׁא שְׁמֵיהּ דְּמָארֵיהּ תְּדִירָא, לְמִזְכֵּי לֵיהּ בְּעָלְמָא דֵּין וּבְעָלְמָא דְּאָתֵי.

593. In the same manner, the chieftain Yehira'el stands over all those who feel compassion for the poor, as said, "Blessed is he who considers the poor" (Ibid.). Hence everything is in this chamber. And this chamber is included within another, fourth chamber, where the decrees and Judgments of everyone are found. Happy is the portion of him, who knows the treasures of his Master, to be devoted to him and sanctify the Name of his Master always, so he may have merit in this world and in the World to Come.

49. The chamber of merit – Gvurah

A Synopsis

We hear that the fourth chamber, 'merit,' is the one by which God becomes known on earth. This is the chamber where all the merits, debts, punishments and rewards are kept. Rabbi Shimon gives us a great amount of detail about the four chambers that are really all one chamber, and about the spirit who takes everything and who is called Zechut El. From him there issue seventy lights and then another two lights, and these lights are spoken of with much emphasis on the number 72. We hear about the three letters that are engraved on Zechut El. The chambers are for lawsuits and judgment, for verdicts and sentences. Rabbi Shimon tells us the names of the chieftains at the gates of the chambers. He reveals how information is sent from this chamber down to men of vision and dreams, down to prophets, with the knowledge descending from grade to grade. Some of the grades are appointed to watch people and keep them from evil, some to help people who have come to be purified, some to perform miracles and signs, and some to report back on peoples' actions. In the same way, the Other Side has grades that do various evil works in the world. Rabbi Shimon tells us of the chiefs who are variously in charge of merits, deliverance, judgment, transgressions and the scales of justice. Again we hear about the glowing living creature called Tumiel who is in charge of prayers and who reigns over four Seraphim. The Seraphim emit sparks of fire that create 72 wheels glowing with fire that create the river of fire in which spirits are burned after death. During Shabbat the river stops burning and the living creature enters the middle of the chamber, the place called 'Delight'. Here there are tens of thousands of chieftains who stand over the tables prepared on earth for Sabbath, ready to say 'Amen' to the blessings that Tumiel puts on those tables. There is a chamber opposite to the one called 'Delight', and it is called 'Pestilence' – it is reserved for those whose tables are not properly laid and who loved cursing. Everything is judged in the chamber of merit except for three things: children, life and sustenance. This is because all three flow down from above, from Yesod of Zeir Anpin.

594. הֵיכָלָא רְבִיעָאָה. הֵיכָלָא דָּא, דִּי קוּדְשָׁא בְּרִיךְ הוּא אִשְׁתְּמוֹדַע שׁוּלְטָנֵיהּ בְּאַרְעָא בְּגִינֵיהּ. וְדָא אִיהוּ הֵיכָלָא, דְּקַיְּימָא לְמֵטַר אָרְחוֹי דְּאוֹרַיְיתָא. דָּא הֵיכָלָא אִקְרֵי דִּזְכוּת, דְּבֵיהּ אִתְדָּנוּ כָּל דִּינִין דְּעָלְמָא,

וְכָל זַכְיָין, וְכָל חוֹבִין, וְכָל עוֹנָשִׁין, וְכָל אֲגַר טַב, לְאִינּוּן דְּנַטְרֵי פִּקּוּדֵי אוֹרַיְיתָא.

594. By the fourth chamber, the reign of the Holy One, blessed be He over the earth is made known. It stands guard to keep the ways of the Torah. This chamber is called 'merit', and in it are judged all the cases of the world. This is the chamber where are all the merits, debts, punishments, and rewards for those who keep the precepts of the Torah.

595. הֵיכָל דָּא דִּזְכוּת, מְשַׁנְיָיא מִכָּל שְׁאַר הֵיכָלִין, וְהַאי הֵיכָלָא, כְּלִילָן בֵּיהּ אַרְבַּע הֵיכָלִין, מְשַׁנְיָין דָּא מִן דָּא, וְכֻלְּהוּ חַד הֵיכָלָא. בְּהֵיכָלָא דָּא אִית רוּחָא חֲדָא, דְּאִקְרֵי זְכוּת אֵל. וְהֵיכָלָא דָּא אִקְרֵי עַל שְׁמֵיהּ זְכוּת, וְהַאי אִיהוּ אֵל. וְהָכָא אִתְדָּנוּ כָּל דִּינִין דְּעָלְמָא, וְהַאי אִיהוּ רָזָא דִּכְתִיב, וְאֵל זוֹעֵם בְּכָל יוֹם.

595. This chamber, of merit, is different than the rest of the chambers. It comprises four chambers, different from each other, and all of them are one. In this chamber there is a spirit called 'Zechut El', after whom the chamber is named merit (Heb. *zechut*), and El, because here all the lawsuits in the world are judged. This is the secret of "and El who has indignation every day" (Tehilim 7:12).

596. ד' הֵיכָלִין, ד' אִלֵּין דְּאִינּוּן בְּהֵיכָלָא דָּא, דָּא לְגוֹ מִן דָּא, כֻּלְּהוּ כְּלִילָן דָּא בְּדָא, וְכֻלְּהוּ חַד הֵיכָלָא, וְאִקְרֵי זְכוּתָא. אַרְבַּע הֵיכָלִין אִלֵּין, אִית לְהוּ פִּתְחִין. חַד מְמָנָא עִלָּאָה דְּקַיְימָא לְבַר לְפִתְחָא קַדְמָאָה דְּהֵיכָלָא דָּא, סַנְסָנִיָ"ה שְׁמֵיהּ, וְעַל שְׁמָא דָּא, אִית מְמָנָא אַחֲרָא לְסִטְרָא אַחֲרָא דִּשְׂמָאלָא, דְּנָטִל דִּינִין בְּהַהוּא הֵיכָלָא דִּילֵיהּ, לְאַתְעֲרָא לְמֶעְבַּד בְּעָלְמָא. וּבְגִין דְּנָטִיל מִנֵּיהּ, אִקְרֵי עַל שְׁמֵיהּ, סַנְסָנִיָ"ה. וְאִיהוּ שַׁלִּיט עַל הַהוּא אַסְכָּרָ"א דְּרַבְיֵי.

596. The four chambers within this chamber, are one inside the other, all included within one another, and are one chamber, merit. All the four chambers have gates. A high chieftain stands outside the first gate of this chamber, Sansaniya by name. By the same name there is another chieftain, on another side of the left, who takes the Judgments FROM SANSANIYA, to his chamber, with which to arouse and execute judgment upon the world. Since he takes from him, he too is named Sansaniya. He is in charge over Askara of the babies.

597. וְהַאי מְמָנָא עִלָּאָה סַנְסַנְיָ״ה, כַּד נָטִיל דִּינָא, אַכְרִיז לְאִינּוּן מְמָנָן דְּקַיְימִין עַל תְּרֵיסָר פִּתְחִין, וְאִינּוּן כָּרוֹזִין דְּמַכְרְזֵי כָּל אִינּוּן דִּינִין, דְּאִתְדָּנוּ מֵהֵיכָלָא דִּזְכוּתָא דָּא.

597. This high chieftain, STANDING OUTSIDE THE FIRST GATE OF THIS CHAMBER, CALLED 'Sansaniya', once Judgment is received, he proclaims to all the chiefs standing at the twelve openings OF THIS CHAMBER. These are the criers who announce all the lawsuits sentenced in this chamber of merit.

598. רוּחָא דָּא דְּנָטִיל כֹּלָּא, דְּאִקְרֵי זְכוּת אֵ״ל דְּקָאָמַרָן, כֹּלָּא כָּלִיל בֵּיהּ. מִנֵּיהּ נַפְקוּ שַׁבְעִין נְהוֹרִין נְצִיצִין, וְכֻלְּהוּ בְּעִגּוּלָא קַיְימֵי, בְּגִין לְאַחֲזָאָה דָּא בְּדָא דְּלָא אִתְכַּסֵּי דָּא מִן דָּא. כָּל זַכְיָין, וְכָל עוֹנָשִׁין, וְכָל דִּינִין, קָמֵי כֻּלְּהוּ נְהוֹרִין אִלֵּין קַיְימִין.

598. The spirit who receives everything, Zechut El, comprises everything. From him issue seventy glittering lights, all standing in a circle, so they may see each other, and not be covered by one another. All the merits, the punishments, the judgments, are standing before these lights.

599. מִנַּיְיהוּ נַפְקֵי תְּרֵין נְהוֹרִין, דְּקַיְימֵי קָמַיְיהוּ תָּדִיר. וְאִלֵּין ע' נְהוֹרִין, וּתְרֵין נְהוֹרִין דְּקַיְימֵי קָמַיְיהוּ, אִינּוּן לְגוֹ בְּאֶמְצָעִיתָא דְּהֵיכָלָא. וְעַל רָזָא דְּהֵיכָלָא דָּא כְּתִיב, שָׁרְרֵךְ אַגַּן הַסַּהַר אַל יֶחְסַר הַמָּזֶג.

599. From THE SEVENTY LIGHTS come out two lights, always standing before THE SEVENTY LIGHTS. The seventy lights, together with the two lights standing in front of them, are inside in the middle of the chamber. Of the secret of this chamber it is written, "Your navel is like a round goblet, that never lacks blended wine" (Shir Hashirim 7:3), FOR HERE ALL THE DEBTS AND MERITS MERGE.

600. לָקֳבֵל אִינּוּן נַפְקֵי שַׁבְעִין וּתְרֵין נְהוֹרִין אַחֲרָנִין, מִסִּטְרָא דִּימִינָא. וְשַׁבְעִין וּתְרֵין נְהוֹרִין אַחֲרָנִין, מִסִּטְרָא דִּשְׂמָאלָא. וְאִלֵּין קַדְמָאֵי אִינּוּן פְּנִימָאֵי לְגוֹ, בְּאֶמְצָעִיתָא דְּהֵיכָלָא. לְקַמֵּי נְהוֹרִין אִלֵּין, עָאלִין כָּל זַכְוָון וְכָל חוֹבִין לְאִתְדַּכָּאָה. כָּל עוֹבָדִין דְּעָלְמָא, מֵאִלֵּין פְּנִימָאֵי נַפְקֵי. אִשְׁתְּכָחוּ כָּל נְהוֹרִין דְּנָפְקֵי מֵרוּחָא דָּא עִלָּאָה, מָאתָן וְשִׁית סְרֵי נְהוֹרִין, וְכֻלְּהוּ כְּלִילָן בְּרוּחָא דָּא.

600. From these 72 LIGHTS come out other 72 of the right, and 72 of the left. The first 72 are inside in the middle of the chamber. Before the INTERNAL lights, come all the merits and debts to be purified. All the deeds in the world are come from these 72 internal lights. It is found then that all the lights issuing from this high spirit ZECHUT EL, are 216 lights, FOR 3 TIMES 72 ARE 216, and they are all included in this spirit.

601. אִינּוּן תְּרֵי נְהוֹרִין, דְּקַיְימֵי קָמֵי אִינּוּן שַׁבְעִין, אִינּוּן סַהֲדֵי סַהֲדוּתָא תָּדִיר, וְכָתְבֵי פִּתְקֵי דִּינָא דִּזְכוּ אוֹ דְּחוֹבָה. אִלֵּין שַׁבְעִין אִינּוּן גָּזְרִין גַּזְרֵי וְדַיְינִין דִּינִין. וְכָל דִּינִין דְּעָלְמָא הֵן לְטָב הֵן לְבִישׁ הָכָא אִיהוּ.

601. These two lights stand before the seventy, always testifying and recording verdicts, acquittals, or condemnations. The seventy decree and judge. All the judging in the world, for good or ill, is done here.

602. רוּחָא דָּא, דְּאִיהוּ זְכוּת אֵ"ל כִּדְקָאמְרָן, בֵּיהּ רְשִׁימִין תְּלַת אַתְוָון, דְּמִתְדַּבְּקָן בֵּיהּ מִלְעֵילָּא, דְּאִינּוּן יה"ו. וְהָא אוּקִימְנָא דְּכַד אִלֵּין אַתְוָון מִתְדַּבְּקָאן בְּהַאי אֲתַר, דְּאִתְדַּבְּקוּתָא דִּדְכוּרָא בְּנוּקְבָא. כְּדֵין אִתְרְשִׁימוּ בְּהַאי רוּחָא, אִינּוּן אַתְוָון. וְהָכָא אָמַר דָּוִד, וֵאלֹהֵי לְצוּר מַחְסִי. רָזָא דְּרוּחָא דָּא דְּאִקְרֵי אֵ"ל וְרָזָא דְּאִינּוּן אַתְוָון דִּרְשִׁימִין בֵּיהּ, דְּאִקְרוּן יה"ו, אִלֵּין תְּלַת סִטְרִין דִּנְהוֹרִין דְּקָאֲמַרָן.

602. Upon the spirit Zechut El three letters are engraved, joining him from above, *Yud-Hei-Vav*. We already explained that when these letters are joined together where there is unity between male and female, *YUD-HEI-VAV* BEING THE SECRET OF CHESED, GVURAH AND TIFERET AND ARE MALE, AND ZECHUT EL THE SECRET OF THE FEMALE, they are written upon this spirit, ZECHUT EL. Here David says, "and my Elohim (Heb. *v'elohai*), the rock of my refuge" (Tehilim 94:22). THE LETTERS OF V'ELOHAI ARE THE SAME AS OF EL *YUD-HEI-VAV*, the secret of the spirit called 'El', together with the letters *Yud-Hei-Vav* written upon him. These are the three sides of the lights we mentioned, NAMELY, THREE TIMES 72, TO THE RIGHT, LEFT AND CENTER; RIGHT AND LEFT CORRESPONDING TO THE SECRET OF *YUD-HEI*, AND THE MIDDLE ONE BEING *VAV*.

603. אִינּוּן תְּלַת בָּתֵּי דִּינִין, דְּמִתְפַּלְּגֵי בְּדִינִין אַחֲרָנִין, בְּמִילֵּי דְּעָלְמָא, בְּעוּתְרָא בְּמִסְכְּנוּ, בְּמַרְעִין בִּשְׁלִימוּ, דְּאִינּוּן אַרְבַּע הֵיכָלִין דְּאִינּוּן מְתַקְּנָן לְכָל אִינּוּן אַחֲרָנִין, תְּרֵין הֵיכָלִין לְאִלֵּין תְּרֵי סִטְרֵי נְהוֹרִין אַחֲרָנִין, וְחַד הֵיכָלָא לְכָל אִינּוּן מָארֵי דְּעַיְינִין, דְּעַבְדֵי חוּשְׁבָּנָא מִכָּל עוֹבָדִין דְּעָלְמָא. וְחַד הֵיכָלָא, לְסוֹפְרִין אַחֲרָנִין, דִּי תְּחוֹת אִלֵּין קַדְמָאֵי פְּנִימָאֵי. אִלֵּין אַרְבַּע הֵיכָלִין, כְּלִילָן בְּהֵיכָלָא דָּא, דְּאִקְרֵי עַל שְׁמָא דְּהַאי רוּחָא זְכוּתָא, כִּדְקָאמְרָן.

603. THIS PARAGRAPH IS WANTING, IT SHOULD HAVE SAID: AFTER THAT ONE LIGHT EMERGED TO FOUR SIDES, THE LIGHT PRODUCED THREE OTHERS, WHICH ARE THREE COURT HOUSES. These three courts differ FROM THE INTERNAL 72, and judge matters other THAN CRIMINAL LAWS, SUCH AS matters of the world, richness and poverty, sickness or perfect HEALTH. For the four chambers also deal with other LAWSUITS. These two chambers are to the two other sides of the light, NAMELY, THE TWO 72'S ON THE RIGHT AND LEFT SIDES, THE SECRET OF THE THREE COURTS, THAT SENTENCE OTHER CASES. There is one chamber for all the eyed ones who do the reckoning for the deeds of the world, NAMELY, INCLUDING CRIMINAL LAWS, THE SECRET OF THE MIDDLE, INTERNAL 72; another chamber is for the scribes under the first, internal ones. These four chambers are all included within this chamber named merit after the spirit, as we said.

604. בְּכָל פִּתְחָא וּפִתְחָא דְּאִלֵּין הֵיכָלִין, אִית מְמָנָא חַד, בְּפִתְחָא

קַדְמָאָה אִית מְמָנָא חֲדָא, דִּשְׁמֵיהּ אִקְרֵי גַּזְרִיאֵ״ל. הַהוּא מְמָנָא אִיהוּ לְגַלָּאָה דִּינִין, דְּאִתְדָּנוּ וְאִתְגְּזָרוּ לְהַהוּא מְמָנָא קַדְמָאָה, דִּשְׁמֵיהּ סַנְסָנְיָ״ה דִּמְנֵיהּ נָטִיל הַאי מְמָנָא אַחֲרָא, דְּקַיְּימָא עַל הֵיכָלָא דְּסִטְרָא אַחֲרָא, וְקַיְּימָא עַל אַסְכָּרָה דְּרַבְיֵי, כִּדְקָאמְרָן.

604. In each of the gates in these chambers, there is one chieftain. At the first gate, there is a chieftain named Gazriel. His duty is to make known the sentences and verdicts of the Judgments to the first chieftain STANDING OUT OF THE DOOR, whose name is Sansaniya, from whom receives another chieftain in charge over the chamber of the Other Side, in charge over the croup (Aramic *askara*) sickness in babies.

605. וְהַאי מְמָנָא גַּזְרִיאֵ״ל, נָטִיל מִלָּה דְּבֵי דִּינָא פְּנִימָאָה. דְּכֹלָּא, אִתְגְּזַר תַּמָּן, וּכְדֵין אוֹדִיעַ מִלָּה לְהַאי מְמָנָא דִּלְבַר, וְכָל אִינּוּן כָּרוֹזֵי מַכְרְזֵי וְאַמְרֵי בְּכָל רְקִיעִין, כָּךְ וְכָךְ אִתְגְּזַר מִבֵּי מַלְכָּא, עַד דְּנַטְלֵי הַהִיא מִלָּה בְּהֵיכָלָא דִּלְתַתָּא, וּמִתַּמָּן נַפְקֵי וּמַכְרְזֵי מִלָּה, עַד דְּאִשְׁתְּמַע בְּכֻלְּהוּ רְקִיעִין תַּתָּאִין, וְנַחְתֵּי וְאוֹדְעֵי מִלָּה, לְכֻלְּהוּ דִּלְתַתָּא.

605. The chieftain, Gazriel, takes the verdicts from the internal court, as everything is sentenced there, and notifies the chieftain outside THE DOOR, SANSANIYA. All the criers proclaim throughout the firmaments, such-and-such was decreed at the house of the King. Then the matter is taken by the chamber below, THE THIRD CHAMBER, where it resounds until it is heard in all the lower firmaments, and made known to everyone down below.

606. וְנַטְלֵי מִלָּה כֻּלְּהוּ תַּתָּאִין, מִדַּרְגָּא לְדַרְגָּא, אֲפִילּוּ צִפֳּרֵי שְׁמַיָּא, וְעוֹפֵי דְּאַרְעָא, כֻּלְּהוּ נַטְלֵי מִלָּה, וְאוֹדְעֵי לָהּ בְּעָלְמָא. עַד דְּנַטְלֵי מִלָּה כָּל אִינּוּן גַּרְדִּינֵי נִימוּסִין, וְאַחְזְיָין בְּחֶלְמָא לִבְנֵי נָשָׁא, וְאַתְיָא הַהִיא מִלָּה לִזְמַן קָרִיב.

606. The lower beings take the matter from grade to grade. Even the birds in the sky and the fowl on earth take it and make it known in the world, until the complainants and accusers take it, and appear before men in their dreams. Shortly afterward it comes to pass.

607. וּלְזִמְנִין דְּהַהִיא מִלָּה דְּאִצְטְרִיכָא לְמַלְכֵי אַרְעָא, דְּאִינּוּן מְמָנָן לְאַתְזְנָא, וּלְדַבְּרָא עַמִּין. דְּאוֹדְעִין הַהִיא מִלָּה עַד רְקִיעָא דְּשִׁמְשָׁא דִּלְתַתָּא, וְקַיְּימָא תַּמָּן. עַד דְּאִינּוּן מְמָנָן שִׁמְשָׁא, דְּאִתְמָנוּן עַל שִׁמְשָׁא, נַטְלֵי הַהִיא מִלָּה, וְאוֹדְעֵי לָהּ לְאִינּוּן מְמָנָן עִלָּאִין דִּי בְּסִטְרָא אַחֲרָא, וְאִינּוּן מוֹדִעִין הַהִיא מִלָּה לְמַלְכֵי אַרְעָא, דְּאִינּוּן בְּסִטְרָא דִּלְהוֹן.

607. Sometimes, when something has to be made known to the kings on earth, who sustain and lead nations, the matter is disclosed to the firmament of the lower sun, where IT stands, until the chiefs of the sun, appointed over the sun, take the matter and notify the supernal chieftains of the Other Side, who make it known to the kings of the earth on their side.

608. וְכַד הֲווֹ נְבִיאִים בְּהוּ בְּיִשְׂרָאֵל, הֲווֹ נַטְלִין נְבוּאָה דִּלְהוֹן, מִתְּרֵין עַמּוּדִין עִלָּאִין דְּאוֹרַיְיתָא סָמִיךְ עֲלַיְיהוּ. לְבָתַר דְּאִסְתַּלָּקוּ נְבִיאִים מֵעָלְמָא, וְאָתוּ מָארֵי דְּמַרְאָה, וּמָארֵי דְּחֶלְמָא, נַטְלֵי מִלָּה מֵאַתְרֵיהּ כִּדְקָאֲמָרָן. וְכַד מַלְכֵי הֲווֹ בֵּינַיְיהוּ דְּיִשְׂרָאֵל, וּנְבִיאִים אִסְתַּלָּקוּ, וּמָארֵי דְּחֶלְמָא וּמַרְאָה לָא אִשְׁתְּכָחוּ, אוֹדְעִין מִלָּה לְאִינּוּן מַלְכִין, מֵהַאי פִּתְחָא כִּדְקָאֲמָרָן.

608. When there were prophets in Yisrael, they used to draw their prophecy from the two supernal pillars, NETZACH AND HOD, upon which the Torah, ZEIR ANPIN, is supported. When the prophets were gone from the world, those who see in visions and in dreams came, who took everything from its place, as we said. And when there were kings in Yisrael but the prophets were gone, and no men who see in visions and in dreams were to be found, the matter was made known to the kings through this gate, THE FIRST GATE OF THIS CHAMBER.

609. וְאִי תֵּימָא הֵיךְ נָטִיל מִלָּה מֵהַאי אֲתָר. תָּא חֲזֵי, כָּל דַּרְגָּא וְדַרְגָּא, וְכָל פִּתְחָא וּפִתְחָא, כֻּלְּהוּ אִית לוֹן לְבַר, מְמָנָן יְדִיעָן, דְּאִתְמָנוּן בְּכָל אִינּוּן רְקִיעִין, עַד דְּנַחְתֵּי לְתַתָּא בִּרְקִיעִין תַּתָּאִין וְאוֹדְעִין מִלָּה לְאִינּוּן דְּאִצְטְרִיךְ בְּגִין דְּהָא מֵאִלֵּין הֵיכָלִין דְּאִינּוּן סִטְרָא דִּקְדוּשָׁה וְרָזָא

דִּמְהֵימְנוּתָא, אִתְפָּרְשׁוּ דַּרְגִּין לְתַתָּא, כֻּלְּהוּ בְּרָזָא דִּמְהֵימְנוּתָא, וְנַחְתּוּ דַּרְגִּין עַל דַּרְגִּין, עַד דְּפָרְחִין מֵהַאי עָלְמָא, וְאִתְמְנוּן בֵּיהּ.

609. And if you say: How could THE KINGS OF YISRAEL take from such a HIGH place, as this? Come and see: Each grade and every gate has certain chiefs outside, appointed over all those firmaments, all the way down to the lower firmaments. They notify the matters to those who should know. For from these chambers on the side of holiness and the secret of the Faith, grades are going down, all in the secret of the Faith. They descend until they soar into this world, and are appointed over it.

610. מִנְּהוֹן, לְנַטְרָא בְּנֵי נָשָׁא מִסִּטְרָא אַחֲרָא, וּמִנְּזִיקֵי עָלְמָא, וּבְאִינּוּן אָרְחֵי דְּקָא אָזְלֵי. וּמִנְּהוֹן, לְסַיְּיעָא לִבְנֵי נָשָׁא, כַּד אַתְיָן לְאִתְדַּכָּאָה. וּמִנְּהוֹן, לְמֶעְבַּד אָתִין וְנִסִּין בְּעָלְמָא. וּמִנְּהוֹן דְּקַיְימֵי לְאַשְׁגָּחָא בְּעוֹבָדִין דִּבְנֵי נָשָׁא, לְמִסְהַד סַהֲדוּתָא. וְכֵן מִתְפָּרְשִׁין כַּמָּה דַּרְגִּין לְסִטְרַיְיהוּ, וְכֻלְּהוּ בְּרָזָא דִּמְהֵימְנוּתָא עִלָּאָה, בִּקְדוּשָּׁה עִלָּאָה.

610. Some of them ARE APPOINTED to keep people from the Other Side, and the harms of the world, and watch their ways. Others help people who come to be purified. Some perform miracles and signs, and others watch the deeds of men, to testify ABOVE. So the grades differ according to their aspects. All this is in the secret of the supernal Faith, supernal holiness.

611. כְּגַוְונָא דָּא בְּסִטְרָא אַחֲרָא, סִטְרָא מִסָּאֲבָא, מִתְפָּרְשִׁין דַּרְגִּין מֵאִינּוּן הֵיכָלִין לְתַתָּא, כֻּלְּהוּ דַּרְגִּין לְאַבְאָשָׁא, וּלְאַסְטָאָה עָלְמָא: מִנְּהוֹן, קַיְימֵי לְאַסְטָאָה בְּנֵי נָשָׁא, מֵאֹרַח טַב לְאֹרַח בִּישָׁא. וּמִנְּהוֹן קַיְימֵי לְסָאֲבָא בְּנֵי נָשָׁא, לְאִינּוּן דְּאָתוּ לְאִסְתַּאֲבָא, כְּמָה דִּתְנֵינָן, אָתָא בַּר נָשׁ לְאִסְתַּאֲבָא, מְסָאֲבִין לֵיהּ בְּהַאי עָלְמָא, וּמְסָאֲבִין לֵיהּ בְּהַהוּא עָלְמָא, וְאִינּוּן אִקְרוּ צוֹאָה רוֹתַחַת. כד״א צֵא תֹּאמַר לוֹ. וְאִינּוּן דַּרְגִּין דְּקַיְימָן לְסָאֲבָא יַתִּיר, וּבְגִין כַּךְ, אִלֵּין תָּדִיר לְקָבֵל אִלֵּין, וְכֹלָּא אִיהוּ בְּדַרְגִּין יְדִיעָאן כִּדְקָא חֲזֵי.

611. The Other Side works in the same manner. In the side of defilement, from the chambers OF UNHOLINESS grades go down. These grades all do evil and seduce the world. Some lead men astray from the path of good into the evil way, others stand to defile people, who come to be defiled. We learned that when a man comes to be defiled, he is defiled in this world, and defiled in that world. They are called 'boiling excrement' (Heb. *tzoah*), as it is written, "You shall go (Heb. *tze*), and say to it" (Yeshayah 30:22). These grades defile even more, and are therefore always meant for those WHO COME TO BE DEFILED. All that happens in certain grades, in a proper manner.

612. פִּתְחָא תִּנְיָינָא. בְּהַאי פִּתְחָא אִית מְמָנָא, דַּהֲרִיאֵ"ל שְׁמֵיהּ. וְאִיהוּ לִסְטַר יְמִינָא, וְהַאי אִיהוּ מְמָנָא, לְאַעֲלָא כָּל זְכוּתִין דִּזָכוּ בְּהוּ בְּנֵי נָשָׁא, בְּגִין דְּיִתְדָּן בַּר נָשׁ לְטָב עֲלַיְיהוּ כַּד אִתְדָּן לְטָב, וְאִינּוּן זַכְיָין קַיְימָן סַגִּיאָן עַל חוֹבֵי בְּנֵי נָשָׁא, כְּדֵין הַאי מְמָנָא, פָּקִיד עַל אַגְרָא וְחוּלָקָא דְּאִינּוּן זַכְיָין וְאַגְרָן לְטָב.

612. Over the second gate there is a chief called 'Dahariel' of the right. He is in charge over all the merits won by men, so they will be acquitted. When a man has a good verdict, when there are more merits than sins in men, then this chief DAHARIEL is in charge over their due and the portion of the merits and their good reward.

613. וְאַפִּיק הַהוּא דִּינָא, וּמָנֵי לֵיהּ לְהַהוּא מְמָנָא, דְּאִקְרֵי פְּדָיאֵ"ל, דִּי בְּהֵיכָלָא תְּלִיתָאָה. וּכְדֵין א"ל, פְּדָעֵהוּ מֵרֶדֶת שַׁחַת. בְּגִין דְּכַד ב"נ קָאֵים בְּבֵי מַרְעֵיהּ, וְאִתְפַּס בְּתְפִיסוּ דְּמַלְכָּא, כְּדֵין אִתְדָּן ב"נ. וְכָל זְכוּ וְכָל חוֹבָה דְּעֲבַד בְּהַאי עָלְמָא, כֹּלָּא עָאל בְּהַאי הֵיכָלָא לְאִתְדָּנָא.

613. He takes out the GOOD sentence, and appoints a chief called 'Peda'el' of the third chamber, and tells him, "deliver (Heb. *pede*) him from going down to the pit" (Iyov 33:24). For when a man is on his deathbed, caught in the King's prison, then he is judged. All his merits and every debt he accumulated in this world come into the court to be judged.

614. וְכַד אִתְדָּן לְטָב, בְּהַאי פִּתְחָא נָפַק דִּינֵיהּ לְטָב, לִימִינָא דְּהַאי מְמָנָא דַּהֲרִיאֵ"ל, דְּקַיְּימָא בֵּיהּ, וְאוֹדְעִין דִּינֵיהּ לְטָב, עַד דְּאִשְׁתְּזִיב.

וְנַחְתָּא הַהוּא דִּינָא, בְּכָל אִינּוּן מְמָנָן, דַּרְגִּין דְּאִשְׁתְּמוֹדְעוּ לְטָב לְתַתָּא, כֻּלְּהוּ דַּרְגִּין עַל דַּרְגִּין, וְכֹלָּא, בֵּין לְטָב בֵּין לְבִישׁ, מִבֵּי מַלְכָּא אִתְדָּן הַהוּא ב״נ.

614. When his verdict is good, his good judgment comes out of this gate, to the right of the chief Dahariel, standing there AT THE GATE. His good sentence is announced until he is saved AND CURED FROM HIS ILLNESS. The judgment goes down through all the chieftains, the good grades, descending through all the grades, UNTIL IT REACHES THE MAN IN THIS WORLD. Man is judged for everything, for better for worse by the King's court.

615. פִּתְחָא תְּלִיתָאָה. בְּהַאי פִּתְחָא אִית מְמָנָא חַד, גַּדִיאֵ״ל שְׁמֵיהּ. וְאִיהוּ לִסְטַר שְׂמָאלָא, וְהַאי אִיהוּ מְמָנָא, לְאַעֲלָא כָּל חוֹבִין וְכָל בִּישִׁין, דב״נ אַסְטֵי אֲבַתְרַיְיהוּ בְּהַאי עָלְמָא. וְנָחִית לוֹן גּוֹ מַתְקְלָא לְאַתְקְלָא, בְּאִינּוּן זַכְוָן דְּעָאלוּ בִּידָא דְּהַהוּא מְמָנָא אַחֲרָא דְּקָאָמַרָן.

615. Over the third gate there is a chief named Gadiel. He is of the left side, in charge over all the transgressions and evil deeds a man goes after in this world. He puts them on the scales to weigh them against the merits put there by another chief, DAHARIEL we mentioned.

616. וְהַהוּא מַתְקְלָא קַיְּימָא גּוֹ פִּתְחָא רְבִיעָאָה, וְתַמָּן אִתְקָלוּ זַכְוָון וְחוֹבִין כַּחֲדָא. מַאן דְּנָצַח מִנַּיְיהוּ, הָכִי אִית לֵיהּ מְמָנָן בְּהַהוּא סִטְרָא. אִי נַצְחָן זַכְוָן, כַּמָּה מְמָנָן אִית בִּסְטַר דִּימִינָא, וְנַטְלֵי הַהוּא דִּינָא, וּמַעֲבְרִין בִּישִׁין וּמַרְעִין מֵהַהוּא ב״נ, עַד דְּאִשְׁתְּזִיב. אִי נַצְחָן חוֹבִין, כַּמָּה מְמָנָן אִית לֵיהּ בְּהַהוּא סִטְרָא דִּשְׂמָאלָא, עַד דְּנַטְלֵי מִלָּה הַהוּא סִטְרָא אַחֲרָא, וְכָל אִינּוּן גַּרְדִּינֵי נִמּוּסִין, עַד דְּאִתְרַע מַזָּלֵיהּ. וּכְדֵין נַחְתָּא הַהוּא סִטְרָא אַחֲרָא, וְנָטִיל נִשְׁמְתָא. זַכָּאָה חוּלָקֵיהוֹן דְּצַדִּיקַיָּיא בְּעָלְמָא דֵּין וּבְעָלְמָא דְּאָתֵי.

616. These scales stand within the fourth gate, where the good deeds and sins are weighed together. Whichever is in the ascendancy, has chiefs on its side. If the good deeds prevail, some chieftains of the right side take the sentence, and remove evils and diseases away from that man until he is saved. If transgressions prevail, its chieftains of the left side come, until the Other Side takes the matter, with all those who seek strict law, until the man's good fortune weakens, and that side comes down and takes away his soul. Happy is the portion of the righteous in this world and in the World to Come.

617. פִּתְחָא רְבִיעָאָה. בְּהַאי פִּתְחָא, קַיְימָא חַד מְמָנָא, מֹאזְנִיָ"ה שְׁמֵיהּ. וְהַאי אִיהוּ מַתְקְלָא, דְּנַטְלָא זַכְיָין וְחוֹבִין, וּבֵיהּ אִתְקָלוּ כֻּלְּהוּ כַּחֲדָא. וְדָא אִקְרֵי מֹאזְנֵי צֶדֶק. כְּדִכְתִּיב מֹאזְנֵי צֶדֶק. בְּהַאי אִתְקָלוּ כֻּלְּהוּ לְאִתְדְּנָא.

617. On the fourth gate stands a chief called 'Mozniya' (Eng. 'from scales'). These are the scales, where good and bad deeds are put and weighed together. They are called 'just scales', as it is written, "just balances" (Vayikra 19:36). Everyone is weighed by it to be judged.

618. תְּחוֹת הַאי מְמָנָא, אִית תְּרֵין מְמָנָן, חַד לִימִינָא וְחַד לִשְׂמָאלָא. חַד לִימִינָא, הֲרִיאֵ"ל שְׁמֵיהּ. חַד לִשְׂמָאלָא, גְּדוּדִיאֵ"ל שְׁמֵיהּ. וְכַד אִתְקָלוּ זַכְיָין וְחוֹבִין, דָּא אַכְרַע לְסְטַר יְמִינָא, וְדָא אַכְרַע לִסְטַר שְׂמָאלָא. וְכֻלְּהוּ אִתְכְּלִילוּ בְּהַאי רוּחָא דְּאִקְרֵי זְכוּ"ת אֵל.

618. Under this chief, MOZNIYA, there are two chiefs, one on the right and one on the left. The one on the right is called 'Hariel', and the one on the left is called 'Gedudiel'. When the merits and sins are weighed, the one ON THE RIGHT balances the scales to the right, and the one ON THE LEFT balances to the left. They are all included within the spirit called 'Zechut El'.

619. וְכַד אִתְכְּלִילָן כֻּלְּהוּ בֵּיהּ, אַפִּיק חַד חֵיוָתָא, קַדִּישָׁא, וְהַאי חֵיוָתָא מְלָהֲטָא, וְאִקְרֵי שְׁמֵיהּ, תּוּמִיאֵ"ל. הַאי חֵיוָתָא, אִיהִי חֵיוָתָא דְּקַיְימָא לְאַשְׁגָּחָא בְּעָלְמָא, בְּאִינּוּן עֵינֵי יְיָ', דְּאַזְלָן וְשַׁטְאן בְּעָלְמָא. וְאִינּוּן עֵינֵי

יְיָ׳, כֻּלְּהוּ נַטְלֵי אַשְׁגָּחוּתָא, מֵאִינּוּן עוֹבָדִין טָבִין דְּאִתְעֲבִידוּ בִּטְמִירוּ, וּלְאַשְׁגָּחָא בְּאִינּוּן עוֹבָדִין דְּאִינּוּן בִּשְׁלִימוּ דְּלִבָּא, ואע״ג דְּלָא אִתְעֲבִידוּ כַּדְקָא יָאוֹת.

619. When they are all comprised IN ZECHUT EL, he issues a living creature. This is a glowing living creature, called 'Tumiel'. It stands guard over the world by the eyes of Hashem, who hover and walk about the world. These eyes of Hashem are watchful over the good deeds done secretly, and watch over the deeds done with a whole heart, though not done properly.

620. הַאי חֵיוָתָא אִיהִי קַיְּימָא בְּאַשְׁגָּחוּתָא דִּצְלוֹתִין. בְּגִין דְּאִינּוּן שְׁאֶלְתִּין דְּשָׁאֲלֵי בְּנֵי נָשָׁא בִּצְלוֹתֵהוֹן, כֻּלְּהוּ קַיְימֵי בִּידָא דְּהַאי חֵיוָתָא, וְאָנַח לְהוּ בְּהַאי הֵיכָלָא, וְקַיְימִין אִינּוּן שְׁאֶלְתִּין בְּהַאי הֵיכָלָא עַד אַרְבְּעִין יוֹמִין, לְאַשְׁגָּחָא בְּהוּ.

620. This living creature stands watchful over the prayers, because the petitions, uttered by men in their prayers, are all in the hands of this living creature. It puts them in this chamber, where they are kept for forty days.

621. דְּהָא בְּכָל אַרְבְּעִין וְאַרְבְּעִין, נָפְקָא הַאי חֵיוָתָא, וְנָטִיל לְכָל אִינּוּן שְׁאֶלְתִּין, וְאָנַח לוֹן קָמַיְיהוּ דְּאִינּוּן שַׁבְעִין וּתְרֵין נְהוֹרִין, וְדַיְינִין לוֹן. וּכְדֵין הַאי רוּחָא דְּאִקְרֵי זְכוּ״ת אֵל, מְעַיֵּין בְּהוּ, אִי זָכֵי אִי לָא זָכֵי. אִי זָכֵי, נָפְקָא הַאי צְלוֹתָא, וּמִתְגַּלְגְּלָא הַאי שְׁאֶלְתָּא, וְנָפְקָן עִמָּהּ תְּרֵיסָר מְמָנָן, וְכָל חַד וְחַד תַּבְעִין מֵעִם הַהוּא רוּחָא, קִיוּמָא בְּהַאי שְׁאֶלְתָּא, וְאִתְקַיְּימָא בְּהוּ.

621. Every forty days, this living creature comes out, takes all the prayers and puts them before the 72 lights to be judged. Then the spirit, Zechut El looks at them carefully, to see whether that man is worthy or not. If he is worthy, the prayer goes out, and this petition rolls, and twelve chiefs with it, each demanding from that spirit that the prayer be accepted, and it is accepted by them.

622. תְּחוֹת הַאי חֵיוָתָא, אַרְבָּעָה שְׂרָפִין מְלַהֲטָן, שְׂרַפְאֵ״ל, בַּרְקִיאֵ״ל, קְרִישִׁיאֵ״ל קְדוּמְיָ״ה. וְאִלֵּין אַרְבַּע תְּחוֹת הַאי חֵיוָתָא קַיְימֵי לְאַרְבַּע סִטְרֵי עָלְמָא, אִלֵּין ד׳ קַיְימֵי לְד׳ סִטְרֵי עָלְמָא, וְאִינּוּן מְמָנָן לְאַשְׁגָּחָא בְּכָל אִינּוּן דְּנָטְרֵי יוֹמָא דְּשַׁבְּתָא, וּמְעַנְּגֵי שַׁבְּתָא כַּדְקָא יֵאוֹת.

622. Under the living creature, glow four Seraphim – Seraph’el, Barkiel, Krishiel, Kedumiyah. These four are under the living creature to the four directions of the world. They are appointed to watch over those who keep the Shabbat and delight it as they ought.

623. מֵאִלֵּין אַרְבַּע כַּד נָטְלֵי, נָפְקֵי שְׁבִיבִין דְּאֶשָּׁא, וּמֵאִלֵּין שְׁבִיבִין אִתְעָבִידוּ שַׁבְעִין וּתְרֵין גַּלְגַּלִּין, מְלַהֲטָן בְּאֶשָּׁא. מֵהָכָא אִתְעֲבֵיד נְהַר דִּינוּר. אֶלֶף אַלְפִין יְשַׁמְּשׁוּנֵיהּ לְהַהוּא נַהֲרָא, כָּל אִינּוּן דִּמְעַנְּגֵי שַׁבְּתָא, אִלֵּין אַרְבַּע מְמָנָן מַשְׁגְּחָן בְּכָל אִינּוּן דִּמְעַנְּגֵי שַׁבְּתָא, וְהַאי חֵיוָתָא קַיְּימָא עָלַיְיהוּ, וְנָטְלֵי בְּגִינָהּ תְּחוֹתָהּ.

623. When the four SERAPHIM travel, sparks of fire come out. From the sparks 72 wheels glowing with fire were made, whence the river of fire was made. Thousands will serve this river. All the four SERAPHIM watch over those who give pleasure to the Shabbat. The living creature TUMIEL is above them, and they travel according to it and under it.

624. בְּכָל יוֹמָא וְיוֹמָא, נָגִיד הַהוּא נְהַר דִּינוּר, וְאוֹקִיד לְכַמָּה רוּחִין, וּלְכַמָּה שַׁלִּיטִין. וְכַד עָיֵיל שַׁבְּתָא, כָּרוֹזָא נָפְקָא, וְשָׁכִיךְ הַהוּא נְהַר דִּינוּר, וְזַעְפִּין וְזִיקִין וּשְׁבִיבִין אִשְׁתְּכָכוּ. וְהַאי חֵיוָתָא אָזְלָא וְסָלְקָא עַל אַרְבָּעָה אִלֵּין שְׂרָפִים דְּקָאָמַרָן. וְעָאל גּוֹ אֶמְצָעִיתָא דְּהֵיכָלָא דָּא, בְּהַהוּא אֲתַר דְּאִקְרֵי עֹנֶג.

624. Every day the river of fire flows and burns spirits and rulers. When Shabbat arrives, a proclamation resounds, and the river is calmed. All the storms, glimmers, and sparks are calmed. This living creature stands on the four Seraphim, and enters the middle of the chamber, the place called ‘delight’.

625. בְּגִין דִּבְהַאי אֲתָר, כַּד עָיֵיל שַׁבְּתָא, מִתְסַדְּרָאן תַּמָּן כָּל פָּתוֹרֵי דִּבְנֵי עָלְמָא, דְּאִקְרוּ בְּנֵי הֵיכָלָא דְּמַלְכָּא, וְאֶלֶף אַלְפִין, וְרִבּוֹ רִבְוָון מְמָנָן, קַיְימֵי עַל אִינּוּן פָּתוֹרֵי. וְהַאי חֵיוָתָא עִלָּאָה עַל אִלֵּין אַרְבָּעָה שְׂרָפִים, וְעָאל בְּהַהוּא אֲתָר, וְחָמָא כָּל אִינּוּן פָּתוֹרֵי, וְאַשְׁגַּח בְּכָל פָּתוֹרָא וּפָתוֹרָא, וְהֵיךְ מְעַנְּגֵי לֵיהּ לְכָל פָּתוֹרָא וּפָתוֹרָא, וְקַיְימָא וּבָרִיךְ לֵיהּ לְהַהוּא פָּתוֹרָא. וְכָל אִינּוּן אֶלֶף אַלְפִין, וְרִבּוֹא רִבְבָן, כֻּלְּהוּ פַּתְחֵי וְאַמְרֵי אָמֵן.

625. In this place, DELIGHT, once Shabbat enters, all the tables are set of the people, called 'the children of the King's chamber'. Thousands and tens of thousands of chieftains stand at these tables. The supernal living creature above the four Seraphim, enters and looks at each table, how each of them is given pleasure, and it blesses that table. And the thousands and tens of thousands of chieftains, all open and say 'Amen'.

626. וּמַה בְּרָכָה הִיא דְּבָרִיךְ עַל הַאי פָּתוֹרָא דְּמִתְסַדָּר וְאִתְעַנְּגָא כַּדְקָא יֵאוֹת. אָז תִּתְעַנַּג עַל יְיָ׳ וְגוֹ׳ כִּי פִּי יְיָ׳ דִּבֵּר. וְכֻלְּהוּ אַמְרֵי, אָז תִּקְרָא וַיְיָ׳ יַעֲנֶה וְגוֹ׳. רוּחָא עִלָּאָה דְּאִקְרֵי זכו״ת אֵל, כַּד הַהוּא פָּתוֹרָא אִתְעַנָּג בְּכֻלְּהוּ סְעוּדָתֵי, בִּסְעוּדָתָא בַּתְרָאָה תְּלִיתָאָה מְסַיֵּים וְאָמַר, עַל כָּל אִינּוּן קַדְמָאֵי, וְאָמַר אָז יִבָּקַע כַּשַּׁחַר אוֹרֶךָ וְגוֹ׳, כְּבוֹד יְיָ׳ יַאַסְפֶךָ. כָּל אִינּוּן שַׁבְעִין נְהוֹרִין אַחֲרָנִין בְּכָל סִטְרִין, פַּתְחֵי וְאַמְרֵי, הִנֵּה כִּי כֵן יְבוֹרַךְ גָּבֶר יְרֵא יְיָ׳.

626. HE ASKS: What is the blessing it says over the table, pleasing and properly set? AND HE ANSWERS: It is, "then shall you delight yourself in Hashem…for the mouth of Hashem has spoken it" (Yeshayah 58:14). And everybody says, "Then shall you call, and Hashem shall answer…" (Ibid. 9). When the table has the pleasure of all the three meals, the supernal spirit Zechut El, at the last repast, finishes by saying about all the preceding ones, "Then shall your light break forth like the morning, the glory of Hashem shall be your rearguard" (Ibid. 8). All the seventy other lights on the three sides open and say, "Behold, thus shall the man be blessed who fears Hashem" (Tehilim 128:4).

627. וְכַד פָּתוֹרָא דְּבַר נָשׁ לָא קַיְּימָא בְּהַהוּא אֲתָר בְּסִדּוּרָא דְּעִנּוּגָא כַּדְקָא יֵאוֹת, כְּדֵין הַאי חֵיוָתָא, וְאִינּוּן אַרְבַּע דִּתְחוֹתָהּ, וְכָל אִינּוּן אֶלֶף אַלְפִין וְרִבּוֹ רִבְבָן, כֻּלְּהוּ דַּחְיָין לֵיהּ לְבַר, לְהַהוּא סִטְרָא אַחֲרָא, וּכְמָּה גַּרְדִּינֵי נִימוּסִין, כֻּלְּהוּ נַטְלֵי לֵיהּ וְעַיְילֵי לֵיהּ לְהַהוּא אֲתָר, דְּאִיהוּ בְּהִפּוּכָא מִן דָּא, וְאִקְרֵי נֶגַע. וְכַד עַיִיל לָהּ תַּמָּן, וְאַמְרֵי וַיֶּאֱהַב קְלָלָה וַתְּבוֹאֵהוּ וְלֹא חָפֵץ בִּבְרָכָה וַתִּרְחַק מִמֶּנּוּ. יְנַקֵּשׁ נוֹשֶׁה לְכָל אֲשֶׁר לוֹ וְגוֹ', אַל יְהִי לוֹ מוֹשֵׁךְ חָסֶד וְגוֹ'. רַחֲמָנָא לִשֵׁזְבָן.

627. When a man's table is not at the place CALLED 'DELIGHT', properly set to please, then this living creature with the four SERAPHIM underneath it, and the thousands and tens of thousands all reject it outside, to the Other Side. And the accusers take it and put it in a place opposite TO DELIGHT (HEB. *ONEG*, *AYIN-NUN-GIMEL*) called 'pestilence' (Heb. *nega*, *Nun-Gimel -Ayin*). When they put it there, they say, "for he loved cursing, and it came to him; and he delighted not in blessing, and it was far from him" (Tehilim 109:17), "Let the creditor seize everything that he has…let there be none to extend kindness to him" (Ibid. 11-12). May the Merciful One save us.

628. בְּגִין דְּעִנּוּגָא דְּשַׁבְּתָא, וּמְהֵימְנוּתָא דְּקוּדְשָׁא בְּרִיךְ הוּא אִיהוּ. ובג"ד, כָּל אִינּוּן דִּמְעַנְּגֵי עִנּוּגָא דְּשַׁבְּתָא וְזִמְנֵי וּמוֹעֲדֵי, אִלֵּין אַרְבַּע דְּקַיְימֵי תְּחוֹת הַאי חֵיוָתָא, קַיְימָא לָקֳבֵל הַהוּא נְהַר דִּינוּר, וְלָא שַׁבְקֵי לְאִתּוֹקְדָא בֵּיהּ, לְכָל אִינּוּן דְּמִתְעַנְּגֵי עִנּוּגַיְיהוּ כַּדְקָא יֵאוֹת.

628. Since the delight of Shabbat is the Faith in the Holy One, blessed be He, NAMELY, THE DELIGHT OF THE SHECHINAH CALLED 'FAITH', then all those who delight in Shabbat, and the holidays, the four SERAPHIM beneath the living creature, are standing in front of the river of fire, and do not let them burn in it, who enjoy their pleasure properly.

629. תְּחוֹת אִלֵּין אַרְבַּע, אִית מִמָּנָן אַחֲרָנִין, דְּקַיְימֵי לְבַר, דְּאִשְׁתְּמוֹדְעָאן מִסִּטְרָא דְּהֵיכָלָא דָּא וּמַכְרְזֵי לְכֹלָּא אִינּוּן דִּינִין, וְכָל אִינּוּן גְּזֵרִין דְּאִתְגְּזָרוּ בְּהַאי הֵיכָלָא.

629. Under the four SERAPHIM there are other officers standing outside, who convene on this side of this chamber, who proclaim all the sentences, and the decisions decreed in this chamber.

630. כֹּלָּא אִתְּדָן הָכָא, בַּר תְּלַת מִלִּין, דְּלָא אִתְיְיהִיב רְשׁוּ הָכָא בְּהֵיכָלָא דָּא דְּאִקְרֵי זְכוּתָא. וְאִלֵּין אִינּוּן: בְּנֵי, חַיֵּי, וּמְזוֹנֵי. דְּהָא אִלֵּין תְּלָתָא, לָא קַיְימֵי הָכָא, בְּגִין דְּהָא בְּמַזָּלָא תַּלְיָאן. דְּהָא הַהוּא נָהָר דְּנָגִיד וְנָפִיק, תַּמָּן תַּלְיָין חַיִּין דִּלְעֵילָּא, וְתַמָּן תַּלְיָין מְזוֹנֵי, וְתַמָּן תַּלְיָין בְּנֵי, דְּהָא אִלֵּין תְּלָתָא מִתַּמָּן נַפְקֵי, וְנַגְדֵּי וְאִתְמַשְׁכָאן לְתַתָּא. וּבְגִין כַּךְ, כֹּלָּא קַיְימָא בְּהֵיכָלָא דָּא, בַּר הָנֵי תְּלָתָא.

630. Everything is judged here, except three matters, over which there is no permission to give Judgment in the chamber called 'merit'. These are children, life and sustenance, because they are not here but depend upon Mazal. For the river which is drawn and flows, WHICH IS YESOD OF ZEIR ANPIN, WHOSE SOURCE IS THE BEARD OF ARICH ANPIN, comes from where there is life above. There is food there, and children. For all the three come out from there and flow downward. For that reason all is found in this chamber save these three.

631. בַּר נָשׁ כַּד אִיהוּ בְּבֵי מַרְעֵיהּ, הָכָא אִתְּדָן, וְכָל שְׁאַר דִּינִין דְּעָלְמָא. וְאִי תֵּימָא, בַּר נָשׁ בְּבֵי מַרְעֵיהּ, אִי אִתְּדָן לַחַיִּים יָהֲבִין לֵיהּ. לָאו דְּחַיִּין תַּלְיָין הָכָא, אֶלָּא כַּד אִתְּדָן הָכָא לְחַיִּים, כְּדֵין נַגְדִּין חַיִּים מִלְּעֵילָּא, וְיָהֲבֵי לֵיהּ. זַכָּאָה חוּלָקֵיהוֹן דְּצַדִּיקַיָּיא דְּיַדְעֵי אָרְחוֹי דְּאוֹרַיְיתָא, וְזַכָּאן בָּהּ לְחַיֵּי עָלְמָא, עֲלַיְיהוּ כְּתִיב וְעַמֵּךְ כּוּלָּם צַדִּיקִים לְעוֹלָם יִרְשׁוּ אָרֶץ.

631. When man is on his deathbed, he is judged here, also for all other laws of the world. If you say, why is it that when a man is on his death bed, if he is sentenced to have life, it is given him, YET CHILDREN, LIFE AND SUSTENANCE ARE NOT SUPPOSED TO DEPEND UPON THIS PLACE? HE ANSWERS: THE MEANING is not that life depends upon this place, but once he is judged here to life, then life is drawn from above FROM MAZAL and is given him. Happy is the portion of the righteous, who know the ways of the Torah, and by it merit life eternal. Of them it is written, "Your people also shall be all righteous; they shall inherit the land forever" (Yeshayah 60:21).

50. The fifth chamber of love – Chesed

A Synopsis

Rabbi Shimon says that the fifth chamber lights up the lower ones, shining in the secret of the faith. The spirit of 'Love' lives in the chamber – he is called 'Suriyah', and consists of four colors. He has been given all the secrets of his Master. In this chamber all the supernal treasures and the mystery of mysteries are kept. The four colors mentioned join to produce the holy living creature called 'splendor' (Zohar). The chamber holds all the souls and spirits that are still destined to descend into bodies; however, no new ones have come in since the destruction of the temple. Once they have all descended to be men, the chamber will be empty and Messiah will come. The spirit 'Love' and the living creature 'Splendor' mate to produce two lights that are included in each other and that are called 'El Shadai'. We are told how people are sent spiritual nourishment so they will not be starved by the Other Side, and how two officers in this chamber cause the love to flow between Yisrael below and God above. All the acts of kindness in the world go up to this chamber and then go further up to the supernal love. A verse about this chamber says: "Many waters cannot quench love, nor can the floods drown it..."

632. הֵיכָלָא חֲמִישָׁאָה, הֵיכָלָא דָּא קַיְימָא לְאַנְהָרָא לְאִלֵּין תַּתָּאֵי. וְהַאי אִיהוּ הֵיכָלָא דְּקַיְימָא לְאַנְהָרָא בְּרָזָא דִּמְהֵימְנוּתָא. פִּתְחָא חֲדָא קַיְימָא בְּהַאי הֵיכָלָא, וְחַד מְמָנָא עָלֵיהּ, וְהַהוּא מְמָנָא אִקְרֵי סָנֵיגוֹרְיָ"ה. הַאי מְמָנָא קַיְימָא עַל פִּתְחָא דָּא, בְּגִין לְמֵילַף סַנֵּיגוֹרָא דִּלְהוֹן, קַמֵּיהּ דְּמָארֵיהוֹן. וְלָא יִשְׁלוֹט עָלַיְיהוּ סִטְרָא אַחֲרָא.

632. The fifth chamber is for illuminating the lower beings. It shines in the secret of the Faith. There is an opening to this chamber, and a chief in charge over it, called 'Sanegoryah'. The chief stands at the gate to argue in favor (Heb. *sanegor*), NAMELY, TO GIVE GOOD RECOMMENDATION ON YISRAEL, before their Master, so the Other Side will not have sway over them.

633. בְּהֵיכָלָא דָּא, קַיְימָא חַד רוּחָא, דְּכָלִיל בְּאַרְבַּע, דְּהָא רוּחָא דָּא כָּלִיל בְּאַרְבַּע גְּוָונִין, חִוָּור וְאוּכָם יָרוֹק וְסוּמָק. וְהַאי אִיהוּ רוּחָא דְּקַיְימָא כָּלִיל בְּכֹלָּא, וְאִקְרֵי סוּרִיָ"ה, רַב עַל כָּל אִינּוּן חַיָּילִין תַּתָּאִין.

וְכֻלְּהוּ קַיְימִין תְּחוֹתֵיהּ, וּמְמֻנָּן תְּחוֹת יְדֵיהּ.

633. There is a spirit in this chamber, consisting of four, for this spirit comprises four colors: white, black, green and red, CHESED, GVURAH, TIFERET AND MALCHUT. This spirit, which consists of them all, is called 'Suriyah', a general of all the lower armies beneath him and appointed by him.

634. הַאי רוּחָא, דְּסָגִיר וּפָתַח. כָּל מַפְתְּחָאן עִלָּאִין כֻּלְּהוּ אִתְמַסְרָן בִּידֵיהּ. כָּל חַיָּילִין תַּתָּאִין, כֻּלְּהוּ אִתְכְּלִילָן וְקַיְימָן תְּחוֹתֵיהּ, וּמִנֵּיהּ אִתְזָנוּ הַאי קַיְּימָא בְּכָל רָזִין דְּמָארֵיהּ, כָּל גִּנְזִין עִלָּאִין כֻּלְּהוּ אִתְמַסְרָן בִּידֵיהּ.

634. This is the spirit who opens and closes, for all the higher keys were given into his hand. All the lower armies are included and stand beneath him, sustained by him. This spirit knows all the secrets of his Master, for they were all handed to him.

635. הַאי רוּחָא אִקְרֵי אַהֲבָה. ובג"ד, אִקְרֵי הֵיכָל דָּא, הֵיכַל אַהֲבָה. בְּגִין דְּהָכָא אִתְגְּנִיזוּ כָּל רָזָא דְּרָזִין, לְמַאן דְּאִצְטְרִיךְ לְאִתְדַּבְּקָא בֵּיהּ. וְהָכָא הוּא רָזָא דִּכְתִּיב, שָׁם אֶתֵּן אֶת דּוֹדַי לָךְ.

635. This spirit is called 'Love', and for that reason the chamber is called 'the chamber of love'. For here the mystery of mysteries were stored for whoever should conceive it. This is the secret of the verse, "there will I give you my love" (Shir Hashirim 7:13).

636. רוּחָא דָּא, אִיהוּ נָטִיר כָּל נְטִירוּ דִּלְעֵילָּא, וְדָא אִקְרֵי שׁוֹמֵר יִשְׂרָאֵל. שׁוֹמֵר הַבְּרִית. בְּגִין דְּהָכָא אִיהוּ נְטִירוּ דְּכָל גִּנְזִין עִלָּאִין, וְעַל דָּא גְּנִיזִין דְּמָארֵיהּ גְּנִיזִין בֵּיהּ. מֵהַאי נַפְקֵי שְׁבִילִין וְאָרְחִין לְאִינּוּן דִּלְתַתָּא, בְּגִין לְאִתְעֲרָא בְּהוּ רוּחָא דְּרְחִימוּתָא.

636. This spirit is in charge of the keeping above, called "He who keeps Yisrael" (Tehilim 121:3), "who keeps covenant" (Devarim 7:9). Here are kept all the supernal treasures, and the stores of his Master are there stored. From here start all the paths and ways to those below, to awaken in them the spirit of love.

637. אִלֵּין ד׳ גְּוָונִין דְּבֵיהּ, אִתְכְּלִילָן דָּא בְּדָא. וְכַד בָּעָאן לְאַכְלְלָא, בָּטַשׁ דָּא בְּדָא, וְנָפַק מִכֻּלְּהוּ חַד חֵיוָתָא קַדִּישָׁא, דְּאִקְרֵי זֹהַר. וְהַאי חֵיוָתָא עַל דָּא כְּתִיב, הִיא הַחַיָּה אֲשֶׁר רָאִיתִי עַל נְהַר כְּבָר.

637. The four said colors were included within one another. Whenever they wish to be included, they strike each other, and one holy living creature emerges, called 'splendor' (Heb. *zohar*). Of this living creature it is written, "This is the living creature that I saw…by the river K'var" (Yechezkel 10:20).

638. מֵהֵיכָלָא דָּא, נָפְקִין כָּל רוּחִין קַדִּישִׁין דְּקַיְּימִין בְּקִיּוּמָא דִּנְשִׁיקִין עִלָּאִין. דְּהָא מֵאִינּוּן נְשִׁיקִין, נָפְקָא אֲוִירָא דְּרוּחָא, לְקִיּוּמָא דְּנַפְשָׁא לְכָל אִינּוּן נִשְׁמָתִין עִלָּאִין, דְּאִתְיְיהִיבוּ בִּבְנֵי נָשָׁא. וְרָזָא הַהוּא דִּכְתִיב, כִּי עַל כָּל מוֹצָא פִּי יְיָ׳ יִחְיֶה הָאָדָם. בְּגִין דִּבְהַאי הֵיכָלָא קַיְּימִין כָּל נִשְׁמָתִין, וְכָל רוּחִין, דִּזְמִינִין לְנַחְתָּא בִּבְנֵי נָשָׁא, מִיּוֹמָא דְּאִתְבְּרֵי עָלְמָא. וְעַל דָּא, הֵיכָלָא דָּא נַקְטָא, כָּל אִינּוּן נִשְׁמָתִין דְּנָפְקִין מֵהַהוּא נָהָר דְּנָגִיד וְנָפִיק. וּבְגִין דָּא, הֵיכָלָא דָּא לָא קַיְּימָא לְעָלְמָא בְּרֵיקָנַיָּיא.

638. From this chamber come out all the holy spirits, sustained by the existence of the supernal kissing. For from these kisses an air of a spirit issues that sustains the ilfe of all the high souls given to men. This is the secret of the verse, "but by every word that proceeds out of the mouth of Hashem does man live" (Devarim 8:3). In this chamber you may find all the souls and spirits destined to descend to men since the world was created. Therefore, this chamber holds all the souls born of that river which is drawn and issuing, YESOD OF ZEIR ANPIN, and therefore is never empty.

639. וּמִיּוֹמָא דְּאִתְחָרַב בֵּי מַקְדְּשָׁא, לָא עָאלוּ הָכָא נִשְׁמָתִין אַחֲרָנִין. וְכַד יִסְתַּיְּימוּן אִלֵּין, הֵיכָלָא קַיְּימָא בְּרֵיקָנַיָּא, וְיִתְפְּקַד מִלְּעֵילָּא, וּכְדֵין יֵיתֵי מַלְכָּא מְשִׁיחָא. וְאַתְעַר הֵיכָלָא דָּא לְעֵילָּא, וְיִתְעַר הֵיכָלָא לְתַתָּא.

639. Since the destruction of the Temple no other souls came in here. And when there will be no more, NAMELY, ALL THE SOULS IN THIS CHAMBER WILL GO DOWN TO BE CLOTHED IN MEN, this chamber will be empty, and it will be visited from above, and King Messiah will come. Then the chamber above will be aroused – MALCHUT – and the chamber below, SO HIS KINGDOM WILL BE REVEALED IN THIS WORLD.

640. וּבְרָזָא דְּהֵיכָלָא דָּא כְּתִיב, שְׁנֵי שָׁדַיִךְ כִּשְׁנֵי עֳפָרִים וְגוֹ׳. בְּגִין דִּבְהֵיכָלָא דָּא הַהוּא רוּחָא דְּקָאָמַרָן, וְהַהוּא חֵיוָתָא, אַפִּיק תְּרֵין נְהוֹרִין כְּלִילָן דָּא בְּדָא, מִתְקַשְּׁרָן דָּא בְּדָא, וְאִקְרוּן אֵ״ל שַׁדַּ״י. אִלֵּין אִקְרוּן שַׁדַּ״י, וְאֵ״ל דִּלְתַּתָּא, מִתְחַבְּרָן דָּא בְּדָא, וְאָעִיל דָּא בְּדָא, וְאִקְרֵי אֵ״ל שַׁדַּ״י. בְּגִין דְּנָפַק מִכְּלָלָא דְּאִלֵּין שָׁדַיִם.

640. It is written of the secret of this chamber, "your two breasts are like two fawns…" (Shir Hashirim 4:5). For in this chamber there is the spirit we mentioned, LOVE, and that living creature, SPLENDOR, AND THEIR JOINING TOGETHER issued two lights, included in one another, and united together, to be called, 'El Shadai'. The two lights are called 'Shadai', and together with El of the chamber below called Zechut El, they join each other and intermingle to be called 'El Shadai', for they issued from the two breasts (Heb. *shadayim)*.

641. וְהַאי אֵ״ל דְּאִיהוּ מִסִּטְרָא דִּימִינָא, נָטִיל מֵאֲתַר דָּא, כָּל אִינּוּן רַחֲמִין, דְּקַיְימֵי לְאַתְזָנָא הַהוּא הֵיכָלָא דִּלְתַתָּא, דְּאִקְרֵי זְכוּתָ״א, עַל שְׁמָא דְּהַאי רוּחָא דְּבֵיהּ דְּקָאָמַרָן. הַאי שַׁדַּי, יָנִיק לְכָל אִינּוּן תַּתָּאִין, וּלְכָל אִינּוּן הֵיכָלִין, וּלְכָל אִינּוּן דִּלְבַר, דְּקַיְימֵי מִסִּטְרָא דָּא, דְּאִקְרוּן יִתְדוֹת הַמִּשְׁכָּן, כְּמָה דְּאוֹקִימְנָא. וְעַל דָּא אִקְרֵי שַׁדַּי, בְּגִין דִּמְסַפְּקָא מְזוֹנָא לְכֻלְּהוּ תַּתָּאֵי, כְּמָה דְּאִיהוּ מְקַבְּלָא, מִסִּטְרָא דִּימִינָא.

641. The name 'El' is of the right. It takes from this place all the compassion there that nourish the chamber below called 'merit', named after the spirit in it, as we said. The name 'Shadai' suckles all the lower beings and all the chambers, and those standing outside on this side, called 'the pegs of the Tabernacle', as we explained. It is therefore called 'Shadai', for giving plenty of food to the lower beings, that it receives from the right.

642. מֵהָכָא, נָפְקוּ אִינּוּן נְהוֹרִין, דְּאִקְרוּן לַהַט הַחֶרֶב הַמִּתְהַפֶּכֶת. בְּגִין דְּמִתְהַפְּכָא לְכַמָּה גְּוָונִין, וְהָא אוֹקִימְנָא, דְּאִלֵּין מִתְעָרֵי דִּינָא בִּשְׁלִיחוּתָא דִּלְעֵילָּא, וְאִינּוּן בְּעָלְמָא מִסְּטָר שְׂמָאלָא, כַּד אִתְפָּשַׁט רוּחָא דָּא, וּבָטַשׁ לְאַפָּקָא נְהוֹרִין לְכָל סְטְרִין, כְּאִינּוּן שָׁדַיִם דְּרָמָאן חֲלָבָא לְכָל סְטָר, הָכִי נָמֵי מֵהַאי רוּחָא, נַפְקֵי לְכָל סְטָר, וְאַפִּיקוּ חַד חֵיוָתָא אַחֲרָא, דִּי מְמָנָא עַל אִלֵּין, דְּאִקְרֵי לַהַט הַחֶרֶב הַמִּתְהַפֶּכֶת. וְדָא אִקְרֵי.

642. From here come out the lights called, "the bright blade of a revolving sword" (Beresheet 3:24), for they revolve and turn into several colors. We already explained that they are those aroused to accomplish a mission above. And in this world they are of the left. When this spirit expands, it strikes and emits lights on all sides, RIGHT AND LEFT, like breasts pouring milk on all sides. So from this spirit lights come out on every side, and issue another living creature in charge over those called 'the bright blade of a revolving sword'. This is called (A FEW LINES ARE MISSING).

643. וְהַהוּא וְהַאי דִּמְמָנָא עַל עָלְמָא. בִּזְמְנָא דִּי מְמָנָא כַּפְנָא עַל עָלְמָא וְאִתְדָּן בֵּיהּ, כְּדֵין הַאי חֵיוָתָא אִתְפַּקְדָא עַל עָלְמָא, וְאַפִּיק רוּחָא דִּמְזוֹנָא, לְכָל אִינּוּן בְּנֵי מְהֵימְנוּתָא, דְּלָא יְמוּתוּן בְּכַפְנָא, וְסָעִיד לְבַיְיהוּ. בְּגִין דְּהָא מִסִּטְרָא אַחֲרָא, כַּד שַׁלְטָא כַּפְנָא בְּעָלְמָא, נַפְקֵי מֵהַאי סִטְרָא תְּרֵין רוּחִין מְסָאֲבִין, וְאִקְרוּן שׁוֹד וְכָפָן. וְדָא אִיהוּ רָזָא, לְשׁוֹד וּלְכָפָן תִּשְׂחָק. בְּגִין דְּאִלֵּין קַיְימִין בְּעָלְמָא, וְעַבְדִין לוֹן לִבְנֵי נָשָׁא קִטְרוּגָא. חַד, הַהוּא דְּקָא מְשַׁדֵּר לְהוּ כַּפְנָא, וּמַיְיתֵי. וְחַד, דְּקָא אַכְלֵי בְּנֵי נָשָׁא וְלָא שַׂבְעִין, בְּגִין דְּהָא רוּחָא בִּישָׁא שַׁלְטָא בְּעָלְמָא.

643. (THE BEGINNING IS MISSING) he is in charge over the world. When there is hunger, and the world is sentenced to it, this living creature is appointed over the world. It issues a spirit of nourishment to the faithful, so they will not starve on account of the Other Side. While hunger has sway over the world, two spirits of defilement issue from that side, called "destruction and famine." This is the secret of the verse, "At destruction and famine you shall laugh" (Iyov 5:22). They abide in the world and denounce men. The one who sends them hunger and they die IS DESTRUCTION. When the other, FAMINE, has sway, people eat but are never satisfied, WHICH IS FAMINE because an evil spirit rules over the world.

644. חֵיוָתָא דָּא, אַפִּיק חַד נִיצוֹצָא, דְּקָא נָפִיק מִנְּצִיצוּ דִּתְרֵין נִיצוֹצִין דְּאַמָרָן, דְּאִינּוּן מִתְהַפְּכָאן לְכַמָּה גְּוָונִין. וְהַאי נִיצוֹצָא אִקְרֵי שְׂרָפִים, וְהַאי אָחִיד בְּהוֹן, וְלָהִיט לוֹן.

644. This is the living creature, which produced the spark coming out of the two glittering sparks, that revolve and turn into several colors, SOMETIMES FEMALE, SOMETIMES MALE. This spark is called 'Seraphim'. It grasps and inflames them.

645. בְּהֵיכָלָא דָּא אִית תְּרֵין מְמָנָן, נְהוֹרִין דְּקַיְימִין עַל אֶלֶף וְרִבּוֹא רִבְבָן דְּאִקְרוּן גְּפָנִים, וְאֶלֶף, וְרִבּוֹא רִבְבָן דְּאִקְרוּן רִמּוֹנִים, וְכֻלְּהוּ קַיְימִין בַּחֲבִיבוּתָא, וְאִלֵּין אִינּוּן דְּאַעֲלֵי רְחִימוּתָא בֵּין יִשְׂרָאֵל לְתַתָּא, וְקוּדְשָׁא בְּרִיךְ הוּא לְעֵילָּא. וְכֻלְּהוּ מִתְעָרֵי רְחִימוּתָא, וְקַיְימָן בִּרְחִימוּ. וְכַד אַתְעַר רְחִימוּ מִתַּתָּא לְעֵילָּא, וּמֵעֵילָּא לְתַתָּא, כְּדֵין אִתְמַלְיָא הֵיכָלָא, דָּא, מִכַּמָּה טָבִין, מִכַּמָּה חֲסָדִין, מִכַּמָּה רַחֲמִין וּכְדֵין רְחִימוּ דִּלְתַתָּא, גּוֹ רְחִימוּ עִלָּאָה, אִתְדַּבַּק דָּא בְּדָא.

645. In this chamber there are two officers, lights standing upon thousands and tens of thousands called 'vines', and thousands and tens of thousands called 'pomegranates'. They all exist through love, and bring love between Yisrael below, and the Holy One, blessed be He, above. They all arouse love and endure through love. When love is awakened from below upward, and from above downward, the chamber is filled with goodness, and charity, and mercy, and the love below and the love above join each other. *BET-HEI* BELOW ARE ATTACHED TO *ALEPH-HEI* ABOVE. (*ALEPH-HEI-BET-HEI* = AHAVEH, LIT. 'LOVE').

646. מֵהָכָא נַפְקֵי תְּרֵין מְמָנָן, וְאִקְרוּן אַהֲבָה, עַל שְׁמָא דְּהֵיכָלָא. וְאִלֵּין קַיְימִין לְאַשְׁגָּחָא עַל כָּל אִינּוּן דִּמְיַחֲדֵי יִחוּדָא דְּמָארֵיהוֹן

בִּרְחִימוּ, וּמַסְרֵי נַפְשַׁיְיהוּ עָלֵיהּ בִּרְחִימוּ, וְסַלְקֵי וְאַסְהִידוּ לְעֵילָּא וְכָל אִינּוּן דְּעַבְדֵּי חֶסֶד בְּעָלְמָא, אִינּוּן חֲסָדִין סַלְקִין וְעָאלִין גּוֹ הַאי הֵיכָלָא, וּמִתְעַטְּרֵי תַּמָּן, וְסַלְקֵי לְאִתְעַטְּרָא גּוֹ אַהֲבָה עִלָּאָה. וְעַל דָּא כְּתִיב, כִּי גָדוֹל מֵעַל שָׁמַיִם חַסְדֶּךָ. בְּהֵיכָלָא דָּא כְּתִיב, מַיִם רַבִּים לֹא יוּכְלוּ לְכַבּוֹת אֶת הָאַהֲבָה וּנְהָרוֹת לֹא יִשְׁטְפוּהָ וְגוֹ'.

646. From here come out two chiefs, called 'love' after the chamber. Their duty is to watch over those who proclaim the unison of the Master with love, sacrifice their lives with love, and ascend to testify above. All those who do an act of kindness in the world, these acts go up and enter this chamber to be adorned, then go further up to be adorned by the supernal love. Concerning this the verse says, "For Your kindness (Heb. *Chesed*) is great above the heavens" (Tehilim 108:5). Of this chamber it is written, "Many waters cannot quench love, nor can the floods drown it…" (Shir Hashirim 8:7).

51. The chamber of desire – Tiferet

A Synopsis

Rabbi Shimon tells us about the sixth chamber, the chamber of desire that is called: "word that proceeds out of the mouth of Hashem." Here all the wishes and petitions in the world are granted. This is the chamber where Moses was taken after death. We learn of the spirit in charge of this chamber who is named Raziel, and we learn of the roles of Michael, Gabriel, Raphael and Uriel, who are instrumental in defence, in healing, in bringing medicine and in carrying messages. Rabbi Shimon talks about water, fire, air and dust that are Chesed, Gvurah, Tiferet and Malchut. He tells us that Rabbi Akiva reached this chamber and died with complete love; he was not judged, because he drew the light of Wisdom from below upward, rather than from above downward. We learn about the ten martyrs, whose souls rose up to God but whose bodies were delivered to the Other Side. Rabbi Shimon comes to the conclusion that holiness is joy and that the Other Side is sadness. He talks about how all the lower chambers are included in this chamber, standing on pillars. The officers in charge of these chambers look after the marriage of males and females, all births, the speech of children who study the Torah, the declarations of judgment, and the gladdening of the world. We read about the supernal kisses that unite the lower and higher grades, and of what happened when Jacob reached this chamber. We hear of how Abraham and Isaac comprised Love and Judgment together, and how there is no justice without merit. This explains how the Sanhedrin began to develop the criminal laws. Then we are told about the prophets, and how the seers get their visions and dreams from the chambers of Brightness and Splendor. There is a description of the sixth chamber of the Other Side, where all the wicked pleasures are found. Rabbi Shimon says that there are things the body delights in, and things the soul delights in. He tells us that all the souls of the chambers below the sixth chamber are included in the sixth chamber, and there are two names that include all the other names – they are Yud Hei Vav Hei Elohim and Yud Hei Vav Hei Tzevaot. The first name is of Jacob, and the second of Joseph. These are the secret of the first temple and the second temple.

647. הֵיכָלָא שְׁתִיתָאָה. דָּא הוּא הֵיכָלָא דְּאִקְרֵי הֵיכָלָא דְּרָצוֹן, דְּאִיהוּ רַעֲוָא, דְּאִקְרֵי מוֹצָא פִּי יְיָ׳, חֶדְוָה דְּאִתְדַּבְּקוּתָא דְּכֹלָּא. וְהָכָא אִיהוּ

רַעֲוָא דְּרַעֲוִין, בְּרָזָא דִּכְתִיב, כְּחוּט הַשָּׁנִי שִׂפְתוֹתַיִךְ. רַעֲוָא דְּכָל נִשְׁמָתִין, דְּנָפְקֵי מֵהַהוּא מוֹצָא פִּי יְיָ׳.

647. The sixth chamber is called 'the chamber of desire'. This is the desire called, "word that proceeds out of the mouth of Hashem" (Devarim 8:3). It is the joy of everything joined. And here is the desire of all desires, according to the secret of the verse, "Your lips are like a thread of scarlet" (Shir Hashirim 4:3). It is the desire of all the souls coming out of the mouth of Hashem.

648. הַאי הֵיכָלָא, הֵיכָלָא דְּרַעֲוָא. דְּקַיְימָן הָכָא כָּל שְׁאֶלְתִּין, וְכָל בָּעוּתִין דְּעָלְמָא. בְּגִין דְּרַעֲוָא דְּכָל רַעֲוִין, כַּד נְשִׁיקִין אִשְׁתְּכָחוּ, בְּרָזָא דִּכְתִיב, וַיִּשַּׁק יַעֲקֹב לְרָחֵל. וּכְדֵין כַּד נָשִׁיק דָּא לְדָא, כְּדֵין אִקְרֵי עֵת רָצוֹן. בְּגִין דְּהָא כְּדֵין שְׁלִימוּ אִשְׁתְּכַח, וְכָל אַנְפִּין נְהִירִין. וְכַד צְלוֹתִין סַלְקִין, כְּדֵין אִיהוּ עֵת רָצוֹן לְאִשְׁתַּכְחָא, וע״ד כְּתִיב וַאֲנִי תְּפִלָּתִי לְךָ יְיָ׳ עֵת רָצוֹן. דְּאִיהוּ חִבּוּרָא דָּא עִם דָּא.

648. This chamber is the chamber of desire, where all the wishes and petitions in the world are granted. For it is the desire of all the desires, where they are kissing, according to the secret of the verse, "and Jacob kissed Rachel" (Beresheet 29:11). Then, when they kiss each other, it is time of favor, because then wholeness is found, and all faces illuminate. Whenever prayers rise, it is a time of goodwill. Therefore it is written, "But as for me, let my prayer be to You, O Hashem, in an acceptable time" (Tehilim 69:14), which refers to their joining each other.

649. בְּהֵיכָלָא דָּא קַיְימָן שִׁית פִּתְחִין, ד׳ פִּתְחִין לְד׳ סִטְרִין דְּעָלְמָא, וְחַד לְעֵילָא, וְחַד לְתַתָּא. בְּאִלֵּין פִּתְחִין אִתְמְנָא חַד רוּחָא, דְּאִיהוּ רַב עַל כֻּלְּהוּ דִּי מְמָנָן בְּכָל אִלֵּין פִּתְחִין, וְרָזִיאֵ״ל שְׁמֵיהּ. וְהַאי אִתְמָנָא וְאִתְפְּקַד בְּכָל אִינּוּן רָזִין עִלָּאִין, דְּפוּמָא לְפוּמָא מְמַלְּלָן, דְּנַשְׁקִין דָּא לְדָא בִּרְחִימוּ דִּרְחִימוּתָא.

649. There are six entrances to this chamber, four entrances to the four directions of the world, CHESED, GVURAH, TIFERET AND MALCHUT, one above and one below, NETZACH AND HOD. There is one spirit in charge over the entrances, greater than all the chieftains of the entrances, named Raziel. He is appointed to be in charge over the supernal secrets, that talk mouth to mouth, and kiss each other in loving love.

650. רָזִין אִלֵּין לָא קַיְימָן לְגַלָּאָה, אֲבָל כַּד תַּרְעִין אִתְפַּתְּחוּ, כְּדֵין יַדְעִין כֻּלְּהוּ הֵיכָלִין, וְכָל אִינּוּן רוּחִין, וְכָל אִינּוּן מַשִּׁרְיָין, דְּהָא תַּרְעֵי דִּרְצוֹן אִתְפַּתְּחוּ. וְלָא עָאלִין בְּאִלֵּין תַּרְעִין, אֶלָּא רַעֲוֵי דִּצְלוֹתִין, רַעֲוֵי דְּשִׁבְחָא, רַעֲוֵי דְּנִשְׁמָתִין קַדִּישִׁין עִלָּאִין.

650. These secrets are not meant to be revealed, but when the gates are opened, all the chambers know, and all the spirits and legions, that the gates of desire were opened. Through these gates no one enters, save the desire of the prayers, the desires of the praises, the desires of the holy high souls.

651. הַאי אִיהוּ הֵיכָלָא דְּמֹשֶׁה, בְּהַאי הֵיכָלָא אִתְכְּנִישׁ מֹשֶׁה בִּרְחִימוּ, וְנָשִׁיק נְשִׁיקִין. בְּהַאי הֵיכָלָא, מֹשֶׁה יְדַבֵּר וְהָאֱלֹהִים יַעֲנֶנּוּ בְקוֹל.

651. This is the chamber of Moses. To this chamber Moses was gathered in love, and with kisses, NAMELY, HE DIED BY THE KISS OF DEATH. In this chamber, "Moses speaks and the Elohim answers him by a voice" (Shemot 19:19).

652. כַּד אִתְדַּבְּקוּ נְשִׁיקִין בִּנְשִׁיקִין, דָּא עִם דָּא, וְעַל דָּא כְּתִיב, יִשָּׁקֵנִי מִנְּשִׁיקוֹת פִּיהוּ וְגוֹ'. לֵית נְשִׁיקִין דְּחֶדְוָה וּרְחִימוּתָא אֶלָּא כַּד מִתְדַּבְּקָן דָּא בְּדָא, פּוּמָא בְּפוּמָא, רוּחָא בְּרוּחָא, דִּכְדֵין רָוָואן דָּא עִם דָּא, בְּתַפְנוּקִין דְּכֹלָּא, וּבְחֶדְוָה, מִנְּהִירוּ עִלָּאָה.

652. When THE KISSERS are joined in kissing each other, it is written, "Let him kiss me with the kisses of his mouth..." (Shir Hashirim 1:1). There are no kisses of joy and love, save when they cling to each other, mouth to mouth, spirit to spirit, and saturate each other with pleasure and joy from the supernal illumination.

653. תָּא חֲזֵי, מֹשֶׁה יְדַבֵּר, דִּכְתִּיב הִנָּךְ יָפָה רַעְיָתִי, וּכְתִיב כְּחוּט הַשָּׁנִי שִׂפְתוֹתַיִךְ. וְהָאֱלֹהִים יַעֲנֶנּוּ בְקוֹל, דִּכְתִּיב הִנְּךָ יָפֶה דוֹדִי אַף נָעִים, וּכְתִיב שִׂפְתוֹתָיו שׁוֹשַׁנִּים נוֹטְפוֹת מוֹר עוֹבֵר.

653. Come and see: "Moses speaks" REFERS TO ZEIR ANPIN, as it is written, "Behold, you are fair, my love" (ibid. 15), and "your lips are a thread of scarlet" (Shir Hashirim 4:3). THESE ARE THE WORDS OF ZEIR ANPIN TO THE SHECHINAH. "And the Elohim answers him by a voice": THIS IS THE SHECHINAH TALKING TO ZEIR ANPIN, as it is written, "behold, you are fair, my beloved yea, pleasant" (Shir Hashirim 1:16), and, "His lips like lilies, dropping flowing myrrh" (Shir Hashirim 5:13). THESE ARE THE WORDS OF THE SHECHINAH TO ZEIR ANPIN.

654. הַאי רוּחָא, אִתְמְסָרוּ בִּידֵיהּ, כָּל רָזִין דְּאִינּוּן נִשְׁמָתִין עִלָּאִין, דְּמִתְעָרֵי תִּיאוּבְתָּא דִּרְחִימוּ דִּלְעֵילָּא וְתַתָּא כַּחֲדָא. אִינּוּן נִשְׁמָתִין עִלָּאִין, כְּגוֹן רַבִּי עֲקִיבָא וְחַבְרוֹי, דְּאִלֵּין לָא אִתְקְרִיבוּ לְאִסְתַּחֲאָה בִּנְהַר דִּינוּר, כְּמָה דִּשְׁאַר נִשְׁמָתִין אִסְתַּחְיָין תַּמָּן וְעָבְרוּ בֵּיהּ, וְהָא אוּקִימְנָא.

654. To the spirit, RAZIEL, were given all the secrets of the high souls, who awaken the need of love above and below together, NAMELY, MALE AND FEMALE, WHEN THEY RAISE MAYIN NUKVIN (FEMALE WATERS). These are the supernal souls, such as Rabbi Akiva and his companions, THE TEN MARTYRS, who did not bathe in the river of fire, like the rest of the souls who pass through it to bathe. THEY DID NOT NEED IT BECAUSE OF THEIR GREAT HOLINESS. We already explained that.

655. רוּחָא דָא, אַפִּיק תְּרֵיסַר נְהוֹרִין, וְכֻלְּהוּ קַיְימֵי בְּרָזָא דִּתְחוֹת הַאי רוּחָא. בְּאַרְבַּע סִטְרִין דְּעָלְמָא, קַיְימִין ד׳ נְהוֹרִין עִלָּאִין, דְּשַׁלְטִין לְאַרְבַּע סִטְרִין. בְּסִטְרָא דְּדָרוֹם, קַיְּימָא חַד נְהוֹרָא עִלָּאָה יְמִינָא דְּכָל עָלְמָא, דְּהָא מִנֵּיהּ שָׁרָאן יִשְׂרָאֵל לְאִתְאַחֲדָא בְּרָזָא דִּמְהֵימְנוּתָא, וְאִיהוּ מִיכָאֵל, רַב חֵילָא דִּנְהוֹרָא עִלָּאָה, דְּנַחְתָּא מִסִּטְרָא דְּדָרוֹם, דְּתַמָּן נְהוֹרָא קַיְּימָא בְּתוּקְפֵּיהּ.

655. The spirit RAZIEL let out twelve lights, that exist by the secret under that spirit. There are four high lights to the four directions, ruling over the four winds. To the south stands one supernal light, the right of the whole world, from which Yisrael begin to be united by the secret of the Faith. This is Michael, minister over the force of the supernal lights descending from the south, CHESED, where the light is strong.

656. הַאי מִיכָאֵל, נְהוֹרָא יְמִינָא, אַפַּטְרוֹפּוֹסָא רַבָּא דְּיִשְׂרָאֵל. בְּגִין, דְּכַד סִטְרָא אַחֲרָא קַיְּימָא לְאַסְטָאָה עֲלַיְיהוּ דְּיִשְׂרָאֵל, כְּדֵין מִיכָאֵל טָעַן עִמֵּיהּ, וְאִתְעָבֵיד סַנֵּיגוֹרְיָא עֲלַיְיהוּ דְּיִשְׂרָאֵל, וְאִשְׁתְּזִבְן מֵהַהוּא קַטֵּיגוֹרְיָא דְּמָארֵי בַּעֲלֵי דְּבָבוּ יִשְׂרָאֵל.

656. Michael, the light of the right, is the great guardian, THE CARETAKER, of Yisrael. When the Other Side accuses and prosecutes Yisrael, Michael stands against him as counsel for the defense, AN ADVOCATE IN FAVOR of Yisrael, and they are saved from prosecution of the chief enemy of Yisrael.

657. בַּר בִּזְמְנָא דְּאִתְחֲרַב יְרוּשָׁלַם, דְּהָא כְּדֵין אִתְגַּבָּרוּ חוֹבִין וּמִיכָאֵל לָא יָכִיל בַּהֲדֵיהּ דְּסִטְרָא אַחֲרָא, דְּטַעֲנָתֵיהּ דְּמִיכָאֵל תְּבִירָא עֲלַיְיהוּ דְּיִשְׂרָאֵל, וּכְדֵין הֵשִׁיב אָחוֹר יְמִינוֹ מִפְּנֵי אוֹיֵב.

657. Except at the time of the destruction of Jerusalem, when the sins multiplied, and Michael could not overcome the Other Side, because his pleadings were broken. Then, "He has drawn back His right hand from before the enemy" (Eichah 2:3).

658. בְּסִטְרָא דְּצָפוֹן, קַיְּימָא נְהוֹרָא אַחֲרָא, דְּהָא אִיהוּ קַיְּימָא לְבַטְּלָא דִּינָא מִבֵּי הֵיכָלָא רְבִיעָאָה. וְיָהַב לִמְמָנָא דְּפִתְחָא דִּבְהַהוּא פִּתְחָא קַיְּימָא מְמָנָן אַחֲרָן דְּאִינּוּן דִּבְסְטַר מְסָאֲבָא, מְחַכָּאן לְהַהוּא מְמָנָא וְנַטְלֵי דִּינָא. וּלְזִמְנִין דְּהַאי נְהוֹרָא דִּבְסִטְרָא דְּצָפוֹן, אִיהוּ עָבֵיד דִּינָא, וְלָא יִתְמְסָר בִּידָא דְּסִטְרָא אַחֲרָא. בְּגִין דְּכָל דִּינִין דְּאִתְעָבֵידוּ בֵּיהּ, אִית לוֹן אַסְוָותָא. וְקוּדְשָׁא בְּרִיךְ הוּא עָבֵיד חֶסֶד בְּאִינּוּן אַתְרֵי.

658. To the north stands another light, whose duty is to nullify sentences of the fourth chamber. It gives THE NULLIFICATION to the chief in charge over the gate, where stand other chieftains of the side of defilement, waiting to take the sentence from the chief. Sometimes, the light of the north side executes the judgment ITSELF, and it is not given to the Other Side. For all the judgments executed by it ITSELF, can be mended, and the Holy One, blessed be He does kindness in such places, THOUGH THEY ARE OF THE LEFT.

659. גַּבְרִיאֵ״ל אִיהוּ הַאי נְהוֹרָא דְּבִסְטְרָא דְּצָפוֹן, וּבְכָל אֲתַר דְּאִיהוּ מָחֵי, שָׁרֵי בֵּיהּ חֶסֶד. בְּגִין דְּגַבְרִיאֵ״ל בִּתְרֵין סִטְרִין, כָּלִיל בְּתַרְוַויְיהוּ, וְעַל דָּא, מַחְיָא וְאַסְוָותָא בֵּיהּ. בְּסִטְרָא דָּא קַיְּימָא רָזָא דִּכְתִּיב, כִּי כַּאֲשֶׁר יְיַסֵּר אִישׁ אֶת בְּנוֹ יְיָ׳ אֱלֹהֶיךָ מְיַסְּרֶךָּ. וְאִלֵּין יִסּוּרִין דִּרְחִימוּתָא, דִּכְלִילָן בְּסִטְרָא דָּא וּבְסִטְרָא דָּא.

659. HE EXPLAINS: Gabriel is the light of the north, and wherever he strikes there is Chesed, for Gabriel consists of two sides, and comprises both GVURAH AND CHESED. He therefore strikes, but with a healing effect. On this side there is the secret of the verse, "as a man chastens his son, so Hashem your Elohim chastens you" (Devarim 8:5). These are sufferings of love, including this and that side, GVURAH AND CHESED.

660. בְּסִטְרָא דְּמִזְרָח, קַיְּימָא נְהוֹרָא אַחֲרָא, דְּאִיהוּ קַיְּימָא בְּכָל מִלֵּי דְּאַסְוָותָא, לְמֵיעַל קַמֵּי מָארֵיהּ, כָּל אִינּוּן דְּאִתְנַשְׁיָין בְּבֵי מַרְעַיְיהוּ, וּלְקָרְבָא זִמְנִין וְקִצִּין לְאִינּוּן מַרְעִין דְּאִשְׁתְּלִימוּ מֵהֵימְנוּתַיְיהוּ. וְאַסְחַר עָלְמָא בְּכָל יוֹמָא וְיוֹמָא, בְּגִין לְאַשְׁלְמָא אַסְוָותָא בְּפִקּוּדָא דְּמָארֵיהּ, וְהַאי נְהוֹרָא רְפָאֵ״ל שְׁמֵיהּ. וְאַף עַל גַּב דְּהָא אוֹקִימְנָא לֵיהּ לְסִטְרָא אַחֲרָא. וְדָא אָחִיד לְסִטְרָא דָּא, וּלְסִטְרָא דָּא, לְסִטְרָא דְּמִיכָאֵל, וּלְסִטְרָא דְּגַבְרִיאֵל.

660. To the east side there is another light, found in all that pertains to healing. It presents before the Holy One, blessed be He all those who were forgotten in their beds of sickness, AND NOT HEALED IN TIME, in order to bring nearer the time and end of their illness, for they were perfected in their Faith, MEANING THAT THE SICKNESSES KEEP THE TIME ALLOTTED TO

THEM BY FAITH, AND DO NOT WANT TO LEAVE EARLIER. AND IT ASKS THEM TO LEAVE BEFORE THEIR TIME IS DUE. The light goes about the world every day to perfect the medicine at the command of its Master. This light is named Raphael. IT IS HIM, though we stated that RAPHAEL is of the west side, and grasps this and that side, the side of Michael and the side of Gabriel, BEING OF THE CENTRAL COLUMN, TIFERET, COMPRISING THE TWO COLUMNS, RIGHT AND LEFT, WHICH ARE MICHAEL AND GABRIEL.

661. וְהַאי אִיהוּ מְמָנָא, בְּשַׁעֲתָא דְּאִתְדָּן בַּר נָשׁ בְּהֵיכָלָא רְבִיעָאָה לַחַיִּים, כְּדֵין אִיהוּ אַקְדִּים בְּאַסְוָותָא. וְהַאי אַסְוָותָא מִגּוֹ דְּחִיקוּ נָפְקָא, בְּגִין דְּמִתְּרֵין סִטְרִין נָפְקָא, וְהַאי דְּחִיקוּ אַתְיָא מִגּוֹ סְטַר שְׂמָאלָא, וְאַסְוָותָא מִגּוֹ סְטַר יְמִינָא. וְעַל דָּא, הַהוּא מְרַע כַּד אַתְיָא לֵיהּ אַסְוָותָא, מִגּוֹ דְּחִיקוּ סַגִּיא אַתְיָא לֵיהּ.

661. This is the chieftain whose charge it is, when a man is sentenced to remain alive, in the fourth chamber, to hasten the medicine. This medicine comes through distress, FOR UNLESS HE WERE ILL, HE WOULD NOT HAVE NEEDED MEDICINE, and since it comes out of the two sides, CHESED AND JUDGMENT. This distress, THE ILLNESS, comes out of the left, and the medicine of the right side. Therefore the sick, when healing is sent to him, it comes out of great distress.

662. וְהָכִי הוּא מִסִּטְרָא דְּמַעֲרָב, וְאַף עַל גַּב דְּאַמָרָן דִּרְפָאֵל בִּסְטַר מִזְרָח, וְאוּקְמוּהָ בִּסְטַר דָּא דְּמַעֲרָב, אַסְוָותָא וְחַיִּין לָאו אִיהוּ אֶלָּא מִסְּטַר מִזְרָח, דְּהָא מִתַּמָּן אִתְמַשְׁכָאן חַיִּין לְתַתָּא.

662. So it is on the west side, THAT THE MEDICINE COMES ALSO FROM THE WEST SIDE, BECAUSE THE WEST IS MALCHUT INCLUDING ALL THE LIGHTS OF THE THREE COLUMNS, AS WAS SAID. Though we said that Raphael is of the east side, and we stated that he is ALSO of the west, NEVERTHELESS healing and life come only from the east side, but, thence life is drawn downward TOWARDS MALCHUT, WHICH IS THE WEST SIDE.

663. וּבְהַאי סִטְרָא דְּמַעֲרָב, נְהוֹרָא חַד וְנוּרִיאֵ״ל שְׁמֵיהּ, וְאִיהוּ אוּרִיאֵ״ל. וְדָא אִיהוּ כָּלִיל מִכֻּלְּהוּ, וְקַיְּימָא שְׁלִיחָא בְּכֹלָּא. וְאִית לֵיהּ ג׳

סְטְרִין, אֲבָל תְּרֵין אִינּוּן, בְּגִין דְּכָל חַד מֵאִלֵּין כָּלִיל בְּחַבְרֵיהּ, דְּאִינּוּן אַרְבַּע יְסוֹדִין תַּתָּאִין, מֵאִינּוּן אַרְבַּע יְסוֹדֵי עָלְמָא, עִלָּאִין עַל כֹּלָּא. וּבְגִין דְּכֻלְּהוּ מִתְקַשְּׁרָן דָּא בְּדָא, רָמֵז קְרָא וְאָמַר, אֶל גִּנַּת אֱגוֹז יָרַדְתִּי לִרְאוֹת.

663. On the side of the west, there is one light called 'Nuriel', which is Uriel. It consists of them all, and acts as a messenger on every matter. FOR WEST IS MALCHUT INCLUDING ALL THE THREE COLUMNS. It has three sides, NAMELY, THREE COLUMNS, but they are actually two, since each comprises the other, MEANING THAT THERE ARE MAINLY THE RIGHT COLUMN AND THE LEFT COLUMN, AND THE CENTRAL COLUMN IS BUT THE COMBINATION OF THE TWO COLUMNS AND DOESN'T ADD TO THEM. SO THERE ARE REALLY NOT MORE THAN TWO COLUMNS. They are the four foundations, THE THREE COLUMNS AND THE RECEIVING MALCHUT, lower than the four foundations of the world IN BINAH, which are superior to the rest. Since they are all connected to each other, the verse says, "I went down into the garden of nuts to see" (Shir Hashirim 6:11), ALLUDING TO THE FRUIT OF THE NUT, WHICH IS DIVIDED INTO FOUR INTERCONNECTED PARTS.

.664 אִינּוּן תְּרֵיסַר נְהוֹרִין, קַיְימִין בְּהַהוּא רוּחָא דְּקָאמְרָן, וְהַהוּא רוּחָא עֲלַיְיהוּ בִּשְׁלִימוּ, אִלֵּין אַרְבַּע נְהוֹרִין עִלָּאִין, אִית תְּחוֹתַיְיהוּ תְּמַנְיָא אַחֲרָנִין, לְמֶהֱוֵי בִּשְׁלִימוּ, וּבְכֻלְּהוּ שְׁלִימוּ חַד, וְכַד מִתְפָּרְשִׁין כֻּלְּהוּ, אִינּוּן תְּלַת לְכָל סְטָר.

664. These twelve lights are within the spirit RAZIEL, about whom we said he is in perfection above them. THE EXPLANATION IS THAT beneath the four supernal lights, IN THE FOUR RISING SPIRITS, MICHAEL, GABRIEL, RAPHAEL AND URIEL, there are eight other lights, in order to achieve perfection, for together they are one wholeness, and when they expand, they are three on each side.

.665 אִלֵּין אַרְבַּע סַמְכִין, קַיְימִין לְסַלְּקָא וּלְאִתְאַחֲדָא הַאי הֵיכָלָא לְעֵילָּא, בַּאֲתָר דְּאִקְרֵי שָׁמַיִם, לְאִתְחַבְּרָא נְשִׁיקִין אִלֵּין בְּאִלֵּין כַּחֲדָא. תְּחוֹת אִלֵּין, כַּמָּה דַּרְגִּין לְדַרְגִּין, כֻּלְּהוּ נַפְקֵי מִנַּיְיהוּ, מֵאִלֵּין יְסוֹדִין

תַּתָּאִין, מִנַּיְיהוּ מִסִּטְרָא דְּמַיָּא, וּמִנַּיְיהוּ מִסִּטְרָא דְּאֶשָּׁא, וּמִנַּיְיהוּ, מִסִּטְרָא דְּרוּחָא, וּמִנַּיְיהוּ מִסִּטְרָא דְּעַפְרָא.

665. The function of the four pillars, THE FOUR SAID LIGHTS, is to raise the chamber and unite it with a place called 'heaven', TIFERET OF ATZILUT, to connect the kissing together. Under them, many grades upon grades all come out of the four lower foundations, THE FOUR LIGHTS, MICHAEL, GABRIEL, RAPHAEL AND URIEL. Some go out from the aspect of water, WHICH IS CHESED, MICHAEL, others from the aspect of fire, WHICH IS GVURAH, GABRIEL, some from the aspect of air, WHICH IS TIFERET, RAPHAEL, and some from the aspect of earth, WHICH IS MALCHUT, URIEL.

666. כְּגַוְונָא דָּא תָּנֵינָן, אַרְבָּעָה נִכְנְסוּ לַפַּרְדֵּס, וְכֻלְּהוּ אִתְבְּרִירוּ לְדוּכְתָּא דָּא, לְאִלֵּין אַרְבַּע יְסוֹדֵי. וְכָל חַד וְחַד אִתְקְשַׁר בְּדוּכְתֵּיהּ, דָּא בְּסִטְרָא דְּאֶשָּׁא, וְדָא בְּסִטְרָא דְּמַיָּא, וְדָא בְּסִטְרָא דְּרוּחָא, וְדָא בְּסִטְרָא דְּעַפְרָא. וְכֻלְּהוּ אִטְבָּעוּ בִּיסוֹדָא דִּילֵיהּ, כְּמָה דְּעָאלוּ. בַּר הַהוּא שְׁלֵימָא חֲסִידָא, דְּאַתְיָא בְּסִטְרָא דִּימִינָא, וְאִתְדַּבַּק בִּימִינָא, וְסָלִיק לְעֵילָּא.

666. We also learned, in the same manner, about the four who entered the orchard. They were all chosen for this place, to the four elements, each was drawn to his own place, the one to the aspect of fire, one to the side of water, one to the aspect of air, and one to the aspect of earth. They were all engraved EACH by his own element, when they entered, except the pious and whole who came from the right side, CHESED, clung to the right and ascended, NAMELY, RABBI AKIVA.

667. וְכַד מָטָא לְהַאי אֲתַר דְּאִקְרֵי הֵיכָל אַהֲבָה, אִתְדָּבַק בֵּיהּ בִּרְעוּ דְּלִבָּא. אָמַר, הַאי הֵיכָלָא, צְרִיכָא אִיהוּ לְדַבְּקָא לֵיהּ, בְּהֵיכָלָא דִּלְעֵילָּא, בְּאַהֲבָה רַבָּה. כְּדֵין אִשְׁתְּלִים בְּרָזָא דִּמְהֵימְנוּתָא, וְאִיהוּ סָלִיק וְאַשְׁלִים אַהֲבָה זוּטָא בְּאַהֲבָה רַבָּא, כַּדְקָא חָזֵי. וע"ד מִית בְּאַהֲבָה, וְנָפַק נִשְׁמָתֵיהּ בְּהַאי קְרָא, וְאָהַבְתָּ. זַכָּאָה חוּלָקֵיהּ.

667. When he reached this place called 'the chamber of love', he clung to it with the desire of the heart. He said that this chamber should be joined with the chamber above, CHESED OF ATZILUT, with 'great love'. Then he became perfected in the secret of the Faith, and ascended to complete the small love, MALCHUT, by the great love, CHESED, properly. That is why he died with love, and his soul departed by that word, "And you shall love" (Devarim 6:5). Happy is his portion.

668. כָּל אִינּוּן אַחֲרָנִין, נַחְתּוּ לְתַתָּא כָּל חַד וְחַד, וְאִתְעֲנָשׁוּ בְּהַהוּא יְסוֹדָא דְּנָחַת לְתַתָּא. אֱלִישָׁע נָחַת לְתַתָּא בִּסְטַר שְׂמָאלָא, דְּאִיהוּ אֶשָּׁא, וְנָחִית בֵּיהּ וְלָא סָלִיק, וְאִעְרַע בְּהַהוּא סִטְרָא אַחֲרָא, דְּאִקְרֵי אֵל אַחֵר. וְאִתְמְנַע מִנֵּיהּ תְּשׁוּבָה, וְאִתְתָּרַךְ בְּגִין דְּאִתְדְּבַק בֵּיהּ, וְעַל דָּא אִקְרֵי אַחֵר, וְאוּקִימְנָא.

668. All the others went down, each and every one, and were punished by the element to which they descended. Elisha went down by the left side, THE ELEMENT OF fire, NAMELY, GVURAH. He descended and never went up, and met the Other Side called 'a strange El'. Repentance was withheld from him, and he was expelled, since he was attached to him. Therefore, he was called 'an other,' as we already explained.

669. בֶּן עֲזַאי, נָחִית בִּיסוֹדָא דְּעַפְרָא, וְעַד לָא מָטָא לְאוּקִידוּ דְּעַפְרָא, דְּמָטֵי לְהַהוּא סְטַר אַחֲרָא, אַטְבַע בְּהַהוּא עַפְרָא, וּמִית. וְעַל דָּא כְּתִיב, יָקָר בְּעֵינֵי יְיָ' הַמָּוְתָה לַחֲסִידָיו.

669. Ben Azai went down by the element of earth, WHICH CORRESPONDS TO MALCHUT. Before he reached the burning fire within the earth, NAMELY, THE JUDGMENT IN IT, which touches the Other Side, he was drowned by the earth and died. It is written about this, "Precious in the sight of Hashem is the death of His pious ones" (Tehilim 116:15), MEANING THAT HE DIED PIOUS, WITHOUT TOUCHING JUDGMENT.

670. בֶּן זוֹמָא, נָחִית בִּיסוֹדָא דְּרוּחָא, וְאִעְרַע בְּרוּחָא אַחֲרָא, דְּמָטָא לִסְטַר מְסָאֲבָא, דְּאִקְרֵי פֶּגַע רָע, וּבְגִין כַּךְ פָּגַע בֵּיהּ, וְלָא אִתְיַישָּׁב בֵּיהּ, וְכֻלְּהוּ לָא אִשְׁתֵּזָבַן מֵעוֹנְשָׁא. וְעַל דָּא אָמַר שְׁלֹמֹה, יֵשׁ הֶבֶל אֲשֶׁר

נַעֲשָׂה עַל הָאָרֶץ אֲשֶׁר יֵשׁ צַדִּיקִים שֶׁמַּגִּיעַ אֲלֵיהֶם כְּמַעֲשֵׂה הָרְשָׁעִים. בְּגִין דְּאִלֵּין נַחְתּוּ בְּדַרְגִּין אִלֵּין, וְאִתְעֲנָשׁוּ.

670. Ben Zoma descended by the element of air, CORRESPONDING TO TIFERET, and met a spirit that reaches the side of defilement, called "evil hindrance" (I Melachim 5:18). It therefore hurt him, but did not settle in him, AND HE WAS HURT. None was saved from punishment. Upon this said Solomon, "There is a vanity which is done upon the earth; that there are just men, to whom it happens according to the deeds of the wicked" (Kohelet 8:14). They were punished for going down these grades, MEANING THAT THEY DREW THE ILLUMINATION OF CHOCHMAH FROM ABOVE DOWNWARDS, WHICH IS CALLED 'DESCENT'.

671. תָּא חֲזֵי, בְּגִין דְּר׳ עֲקִיבָא סָלִיק לְעֵילָּא כַּדְקָא יָאוּת, עָאל בִּשְׁלָם וְנָפַק בִּשְׁלָם. דָּוִד שָׁאִיל שְׁאֶלְתָּא, וְלָא אִתְפְּרַשׁ, דִּכְתִיב מִמְתִים יָדְךָ יְיָ׳ מִמְתִים מֵחֶלֶד חֶלְקָם בַּחַיִּים. תּוֹהָא עַל מַה דָּא אִלֵּין דְּאִתְקְטָלוּ בְּקְטוּלֵי עָלְמָא צַדִּיקַיָּיא, זַכָּאִין דְּלָא חָאבוּ חוֹבָה בְּגִין דְּיִתְעָנְשׁוּן. ת״ח, מִמְתִים יָדְךָ יְיָ׳, מִמְתִים מֵחֶלֶד חֶלְקָם בַּחַיִּים, הָכָא אִיהוּ תְּרֵי סִטְרֵי, יָדְךָ יְיָ׳. וְחֶלֶד. יָדְךָ יְיָ׳, דָּא קוּדְשָׁא בְּרִיךְ הוּא, דְּנִשְׁמְתָא אִתְכְּנִישׁ לְגַבֵּיהּ. מִמְתִים מֵחֶלֶד, דָּא סִטְרָא אַחֲרָא, דְּגוּפָא אִיהוּ שַׁלְטָא עֲלוֹי, דִּכְתִיב לֹא אַבִּיט אָדָם עוֹד עִם יוֹשְׁבֵי חָלֶד.

671. Come and see: Since Rabbi Akiva went up, NAMELY, HE DREW THE ILLUMINATION OF CHOCHMAH FROM BELOW UPWARD, properly, therefore, he came in peace and left in peace. David asked a question, which remained unexplained. It is written, "from men, by Your hand, Hashem, from men whose portion in life is of the world" (Tehilim 17:14). He asked why there are righteous amongst those who were killed in the world. They were meritorious and never committed sin, to be punished for it. Come and see: The verse, "from men, by Your hand, Hashem, from men (Heb. *metim*) whose portion in life is of the world" points at two ways OF DEATH (HEB. *MITAH*); "by Your hand, Hashem" and "the world." The first one refers to the Holy One, blessed be He, to whom the soul is gathered. "From men…of the world (Heb. *cheled*)" refers to the Other Side, who has control over the body, as it is written, "I shall behold man no more with the inhabitants of the world (Heb. *cheled*)" (Yeshayah 38:11), REFERRING TO THOSE WHO DWELL UNDER THE OTHER SIDE CALLED GRAVE (HEB. *CHEDEL*).

672. תָּא חֲזִי, נִשְׁמָתָא דְּאִלֵּין, לְאַשְׁלְמוּתָא דְּרוּחָא קַדִּישָׁא, דִּלְהוֹן עֲשָׂרָה רוּחִין מִתַּתָּא כַּדְקָא יָאוּת, וְגוּפָא דִּלְהוֹן יִתְמְסַר לְמַלְכוּ חַיָּיבָא. כָּל חַד נָטִיל חוּלָקֵיהּ, בְּרָזָא דְּקָרְבְּנִין.

672. Come and see: The souls of THE TEN MARTYRS complemented the Holy Spirit, ZEIR ANPIN OF ATZILUT, for they had ten proper spirits from below, CORRESPONDING TO THE TEN SFIROT OF ZEIR ANPIN, and their bodies were given over to the evil kingdom. Each took his share, JUST AS in the mystery of the sacrifices.

673. וְתָא חֲזֵי, רֵישָׁא שֵׁירוּתָא דִּמְהֵימְנוּתָא, גּוֹ מַחֲשָׁבָה, בָּטַשׁ בּוּצִינָא דְּקַרְדִּינוּתָא, וְסָלִיק גּוֹ מַחֲשָׁבָה, וְאַפִּיק נִצוֹצִין, נְצִיצִין זָרִיק לִתְלַת מֵאָה וְעֶשְׂרִין עֵיבָר, וּבָרִיר פְּסוֹלֶת מִגּוֹ מַחֲשָׁבָה, וְאִתְבְּרִיר.

673. Come and see: The start of the beginning of the Faith, KETER, within thought, WHICH IS CHOCHMAH, struck the strong spark OF THE SECRET OF BINAH. There came up a thought, MEANING THAT BINAH WENT UP TO CHOCHMAH AND THEY JOINED, and they emitted sparks, THE ILLUMINATION OF CHOCHMAH FROM WITHIN THOUGHT. It threw sparks to 320 directions, and separated the refuse from thought, to be purified. And it was separated.

674. אוּף הָכִי, כְּגַוְונָא דָּא סָלִיק בְּמַחֲשָׁבָה, כְּמָה דְּאִתְבְּרַר בֵּיהּ פְּסוֹלֶת, וְיִתְבְּרַר אִלֵּין, בְּהוּ אִשְׁתְּלִים מַאן דְּאִצְטְרִיךְ, וַדָּאי כַּד סָלִיק, בְּמַחֲשָׁבָה סָלִיק וְכֹלָּא כְּמָה דְּאִצְטְרִיךְ. חִידוּ מִסִּטְרָא דָּא, וַעֲצִיבוּ מִסִּטְרָא דָּא.

674. In the same manner, CONCERNING THE TEN MARTYRS, it came up in thought, as the refuse was separated. NAMELY, THAT WAS SORT OF THE BREAKING OF THE VESSELS, AND THEREFORE THE SOULS, WHO ARE THE LIGHTS, WENT UP TO ZEIR ANPIN, AND THE VESSELS, THE BODIES, WERE DELIVERED TO THE OTHER SIDE, THE EVIL KINGDOM. Some were selected, with whom to complement whoever needed a complement, MEANING THAT THE SOULS WERE SELECTED AS MAYIN NUKVIN (FEMALE WATERS) TO ZEIR ANPIN, THAT IS COMPLEMENTED BY THEM. Assuredly, when it rose, it rose into thought, NAMELY, THEY DREW THE ILLUMINATION OF CHOCHMAH FROM THOUGHT WHICH IS CHOCHMAH. Everything is as it ought to be, joy on this side, FOR THE ASCENSION OF SOULS, and sadness on that side, FOR THE BODIES WERE DELIVERED TO THE OTHER SIDE.

675. כְּתִיב וְשִׁבַּחְתִּי אֲנִי אֶת הַשִּׂמְחָה אֲשֶׁר אֵין טוֹב לָאָדָם תַּחַת הַשֶּׁמֶשׁ כִּי אִם לֶאֱכוֹל וְלִשְׁתּוֹת וְלִשְׂמוֹחַ וְהוּא יִלְוֶנּוּ בַּעֲמָלוֹ יְמֵי חַיָּיו אֲשֶׁר נָתַן לוֹ הָאֱלֹהִים תַּחַת הַשָּׁמֶשׁ, וְשִׁבַּחְתִּי אֲנִי אֶת הַשִּׂמְחָה, וְכִי שְׁלֹמֹה מַלְכָּא מְשַׁבַּח דָּא. אֶלָּא וְשִׁבַּחְתִּי אֲנִי אֶת הַשִּׂמְחָה, דָּא חֶדְוָותָא דְּמַלְכָּא קַדִּישָׁא, בִּזְמְנָא דְּאִיהוּ שַׁלְטָא, בְּשַׁבְּתָא וּבְיוֹמִין טָבִין, דְּמִכָּל עוֹבָדִין טָבִין דב״נ עָבִיד, אֵין טוֹב לָאָדָם תַּחַת הַשֶּׁמֶשׁ, כִּי אִם לֶאֱכוֹל וְלִשְׁתּוֹת, וּלְאַחֲזָאָה חֶדְוָותָא בְּהַהוּא, סִטְרָא בְּגִין דִּיְהֵא לֵיהּ חוּלָקָא לְעָלְמָא דְּאָתֵי.

675. It is written, "So I commend mirth, because a man has no better thing under the sun, than to eat, and to drink, and to be merry, for that shall accompany him in his labor during the days of his life, which the Elohim gives him under the sun" (Kohelet 8:15). HE ASKS REGARDING "So I commend mirth," could it be that King Solomon praises that, NAMELY, TO EAT, DRINK, AND BE MERRY? HE ANSWERS: "So I commend mirth" refers to the rejoicing in the Holy King, while He rules, on Shabbat and holidays, in all the good deeds men do, "because a man has no better thing under the sun, than to eat, and to drink" and to demonstrate the joy of that side OF HOLINESS, so he will have a portion in the World to Come.

676. וְהוּא יִלְוֶנּוּ בַּעֲמָלוֹ. מַאן. דָּא קוּדְשָׁא בְּרִיךְ הוּא, הוּא יִלְוֶנּוּ, וְיֵהָךְ עִמֵּיהּ לְאַעֲלָא לֵיהּ לְעָלְמָא דְּאָתֵי. דָּבָר אַחֵר וְהוּא יִלְוֶנּוּ, מַאן הוּא. הַהוּא ב״נ דְּאָכִיל וְשָׁתֵי וְחָדֵי, כָּל מַאי דְּאַפִּיק לְמֵיכַל וּלְמִשְׁתֵּי, הוּא יִלְוֶנּוּ לְקוּדְשָׁא בְּרִיךְ הוּא בְּהַלְוָאָה, וְאִיהוּ יָהִיב לֵיהּ כִּפְלֵי כִּפְלַיִם, מִכָּל מַה דְּאַפִּיק בְּהַאי. בִּתְרֵין אִלֵּין, אוֹזִיף ב״נ לְקוּדְשָׁא בְּרִיךְ הוּא, כַּד

חַיִּיס לֵיהּ לְמִסְכְּנָא. וְכַד אַפִּיק בְּשַׁבָּתֵי וְזִמְנֵי. דְּהָא כֹּלָּא אוֹזִיף לְקוּדְשָׁא בְּרִיךְ הוּא, כד״א מַלְוֵה יְיָ׳ חוֹנֵן דָּל וּגְמוּלוֹ יְשַׁלֶּם לוֹ.

676. "For that shall accompany him in his labor" (Ibid.): HE ASKS: WHO WILL ACCOMPANY HIM? AND HE ANSWERS: The Holy One, blessed be He will accompany him and show him into the World to Come. Another explanation about the meaning of "accompany (Heb. *yilvenu*)." IT MEANS THAT when a man eats, drinks, and is merry, all his expenses for food and drink, he will lend (Heb. *yalvenu*) as a loan to the Holy One, blessed be He, AND THE HOLY ONE, BLESSED BE HE will give him twice his expenses FOR SHABBAT AND HOLIDAYS. With these, man lends two to the Holy One, blessed be He: ONE, his pity for the poor, TWO, his expenses for Shabbat and holidays, for he lends all to the Holy One, blessed be He, as said, "He that gives graciously to the poor, makes a loan to Hashem, and that which he has given He will pay him back" (Mishlei 19:17).

677. ובג״כ, דָּא שִׂמְחָה, וְדָא עֲצִיבוּ. דָּא חַיִּים וְדָא מָוֶת. דָּא טוֹב, וְדָא רָע, דָּא גַּן עֵדֶן, וְדָא גֵּיהִנָּם. וְכֹלָּא, דָּא בְּהִפּוּכָא דְּדָא, וע״ד גּוּפָא דִּלְהוֹן הֲוָה בַּעֲצִיבוּ, וְנִשְׁמְתָא בְּחֶדְוָה. וְכַד הֲווֹ אִלֵּין עֲשָׂרָה דְּאִקְרוּן הֲרוּגֵי מַלְכוּת, הֲרוּגִים הֲווֹ מִסִּטְרָא אַחֲרָא, וְאַשְׁלִימוּ אֲתָר אַחֲרָא דִּקְדוּשָּׁה. ובג״כ, כֹּלָּא גַּלְיָא קָמֵי קוּדְשָׁא בְּרִיךְ הוּא, וְאִתְעֲבֵיד כַּדְקָא יָאוֹת.

677. For that reason, this, HOLINESS is joy and that, THE OTHER SIDE is sadness. This is good and that is bad. This is the Garden of Eden and that is Gehenom. All this, HOLINESS, is the opposite of that, THE OTHER SIDE. Therefore, the body OF THE TEN MARTYRS was sad FOR IT WAS KILLED, and the soul rejoices, BECAUSE IT WENT TO CLEAVE TO THE HOLY ONE, BLESSED BE HE. When those called 'the ten martyrs' WERE KILLED, were killed by the Other Side, they complemented another place of holiness. For that reason, all is known before the Holy One, blessed be He, and is well done.

678. בְּהֵיכָלָא דָּא קַיְימִין אִינּוּן תְּרֵיסָר. אַרְבַּע אִלֵּין לְעֵילָּא, וּתְמַנְיָא עִמְּהוֹן. בְּגִין דְּכָל חַד, נָטִיל עִמֵּיהּ תְּרֵין, כְּמָה דְּאִיהוּ סִדּוּרָא דִּדְגָלִים וְכֵן בְּסִדּוּרָא דִּלְתַתָּא, עַד סוֹף דְּכָל דַּרְגִּין.

678. In this chamber there are twelve lights, four above, and eight with them. Each OF THE FOUR takes two with it, as in the arrangement of the standards. This arrangement goes on downward to the end of all the grades. IT IS CONSIDERED THAT THERE ARE THREE ASPECTS TO EACH OF THE FOUR SFIROT, CHESED, GVURAH, TIFERET AND MALCHUT.

679. בְּהֵיכָלָא דָא, עָאלִין כָּל אִינּוּן צְלוֹתִין, וְכָל אִינּוּן רַעֲוִין דִּשְׁבָחִין דְּאִתְעֲבִידוּ בִּרְחִימוּ, וְכַד עָאלִין בְּהַאי הֵיכָלָא, כֻּלְּהוּ מִתְדַּבְּקָן בֵּיהּ. וּבְכָל יוֹמָא, וּבְכָל זִמְנָא דִּנְשִׁיקִין אִתְחַבָּרוּ, כְּדֵין אִיהוּ זִמְנָא, דְּקוּדְשָׁא בְּרִיךְ הוּא אִשְׁתַּעְשַׁע בְּנִשְׁמָתִין דְּצַדִּיקַיָּיא, וּמַהוּ הַשַּׁעְשׁוּעַ דְּמִתְעָרִין אִינּוּן נְשִׁיקִין, וְאִינּוּן אַקְדִּימוּ לְהַהוּא עִנּוּגָא, וְעַ"ד כְּתִיב אָז תִּתְעַנַּג עַל יְיָ' וְאוֹקִימְנָא.

679. Into this chamber come all the prayers, and all the desires in the praises, uttered with love. When they enter this chamber, they all cleave to it. Every day, and when the kisses are united, it is the time when the Holy One, blessed be He takes delight in the souls of the righteous. The delight is that the kisses TO THE RIGHTEOUS are awakened, which preceded that delight, that is mentioned in, "then shall you delight yourself in Hashem" (Yeshayah 58:14), as we explained.

680. הֵיכָלָא דָא, כְּלָלָא דְּכָל אִינּוּן הֵיכָלִין תַּתָּאִין, כֻּלְּהוּ כְּלִילָן בְּהַאי הֵיכָלָא. הֵיכָלָא קַדְמָאָה, דְּתַמָּן קַיְּימָא הַהוּא רוּחָא דְּקָאמְרָן, וְכָל אִינּוּן חֵיוָון דְּבֵיהּ, אִסְתְּמִיךְ בִּתְרֵין סַמְכִין לִסְטַר מִזְרָח, וּבִתְרֵין סַמְכִין לִסְטַר דָּרוֹם, וּבִתְרֵין סַמְכִין לִסְטַר מַעֲרָב, וּבִתְרֵין סַמְכִין לִסְטַר צָפוֹן, וְאִינּוּן תְּמַנְיָא. וְאִלֵּין אִקְרוּן יְתֵדוֹת הַמִּשְׁכָּן, וְקַיְימֵי לְבַר.

680. This chamber comprises all the lower chambers, and they are included in it. The first chamber, THE SAPPHIRE STONE, where stands the spirit STAT'URIYAH that we mentioned and all the living creatures, is supported by two pillars on the east side, two pillars on the south side, two pillars on the west side, and two pillars on the north side. Altogether there are eight pillars, called 'the pegs of the Tabernacle'. They stand outside.

681. כַּד מַלְכָּא עִלָּאָה אָתֵי, נַטְלֵי אִינּוּן יְתֵדוֹת, וְאִתְעֲקָרָן מֵאַתְרַיְיהוּ

אִינּוּן מֵיתָרִים, דְּאִינּוּן תְּמַנְיָא אַחֲרָנִין, בַּר מֵאִינּוּן יְתֵדוֹת דְּקָא אֲמָרָן. וְהַהוּא רוּחָא קַדְמָאָה דִּי בְּגוֹ הֵיכָלָא דָּא, קָדִים וְעָאל, וְאִתְכְּלִיל בְּגוֹ הַהוּא רוּחָא תִּנְיָינָא דְּבֵיהּ.

681. When the Supernal King comes, these pegs travel, uprooted from their place, and from the strings TO WHICH THEY WERE BOUND, which are other eight beside the pegs. The first spirit in that chamber, STAT'URIYAH, hastens to come in and be included in that second spirit OF THE CHAMBER, ADIRIYAH.

682. אִינּוּן תְּרֵין סַמְכִין דְּלִסְטַר מִזְרָח, אִינּוּן קַרְעִיאֵ״ל, דְּאִתְמַנָּא לְבַר עַל תְּרֵיסַר אַלְפֵי מְמָנָן, דְּכֻלְּהוּ אִקְרוּן יְתֵדוֹת הַמִּשְׁכָּן, דָּא לִימִינָא לִשְׂמָאלָא שַׁמְעִיאֵ״ל, וְאִתְמַנָּא עַל תְּרֵיסַר אַלְפֵי מְמָנָן אַחֲרָנִין, וְכֻלְּהוּ יְתֵדוֹת כִּדְקָאמְרָן. סַמְכִין דְּאִתְמַנּוּן לִסְטַר דָּרוֹם, חַד סַעֲדִיאֵ״ל, וְחַד סְטָרִיאֵ״ל, כָּל חַד וְחַד, עַל תְּרֵיסַר אַלְפֵי מְמָנָן אַחֲרָנִין. אִלֵּין לָא אִתְעֲדוּן מִשּׁוּלְטָנֵהוֹן לְעָלְמִין.

682. The two pillars on the east side, the one is called 'Kar'iel', which is in charge outside over twelve thousand officers, all named the pegs of the Tabernacle. This is on the right. The one on the left is called 'Sham'iel', in charge over twelve thousand other officers, that are pegs as well. The pillars in charge over the south side, one of them is called 'Sa'adiel', and the other Stariel. Each is appointed over the twelve thousand other officers, who are always under their sway.

683. אִלֵּין כֻּלְּהוּ, מְמָנָן עַל קִיּוּמָא דְּעָלְמָא, אִלֵּין אִינּוּן דְּתַקְלֵי בְּמַתְקְלָא דְּכוּרִין וְנוּקְבִין, לְאִתְנַסְּבָא דָּא עִם דָּא. וְאִלֵּין אִקְרוּן מֹאזְנַיִם, עַל דָּא כְּתִיב, בְּמֹאזְנַיִם לַעֲלוֹת, וְלָא אִינּוּן דִּכְתִּיב בְּהוּ מֹאזְנֵי צֶדֶק, דְּקָאמְרָן. כָּל אִינּוּן דְּשָׁקְלִין דָּא עִם דָּא, וְלָא שָׁקִיל דָּא יַתִּיר מִן דָּא, סַלְּקִין וְאִתְחַבְּרָן כַּחֲדָא, וְאִינּוּן חִבּוּרָא דִּדְכַר וְנוּקְבָא כַּחֲדָא, וְעַל דָּא בְּמֹאזְנַיִם לַעֲלוֹת. וְאַע״ג דִּלְזִמְנִין מִסְתַּיְּיעָא מִלְּתָא, וְשָׁקִיל דָּא יַתִּיר מִן דָּא, סַלְּקִין וּמִתְחַבְּרָן כַּחֲדָא, וְהָא אוֹקִימְנָא.

683. They are all in charge over the maintenance of the world. They weigh upon the scales males and females, to marry them. They are called 'scales', upon which it is written, "to be laid in the balance" (Tehilim 62:10); it is not written of them "just balances" (Vayikra 19:36), of which we spoke before. All those who were weighed, unless the one weighs more than the other, mount and come together. This is the joining of male and female together. Upon this says the verse, "to be laid in the balance (lit. 'scales to mount')" though it sometimes happens that the one weighs more than the other, nevertheless they mount and become one, as we already explained.

684. אִינּוּן תְּרֵין סַמְכִין דִּלְסְטַר צָפוֹן, פַּתְחִיאֵ"ל, עֲטָרִיאֵ"ל. וּמְמָנָן כָּל חַד וְחַד, עַל תְּרֵיסַר אַלְפִין מְמָנָן אַחֲרָנִין, וְאִינּוּן יְתֵדוֹת הַמִּשְׁכָּן, וּבְאִלֵּין אַחֲרָנִין דְּקָאמְרָן. אִינּוּן מְמָנָן תְּרֵין סַמְכִין אַחֲרָנִין דִּלְסְטַר מַעֲרָב, אִינּוּן פְּדָתִיאֵ"ל תּוּמִיהָאֵ"ל, וְאִתְמְנוּן כָּל חַד עַל תְּרֵיסַר אַלְפֵי מְמָנָן אַחֲרָנִין, וְכֻלְּהוּ יְתֵדוֹת הַמִּשְׁכָּן כִּדְקָאמְרָן.

684. The two pillars on the north side ARE CALLED 'Pat'chiel and Atariel'. Each one is in charge over twelve thousand other officers, the pegs of the Tabernacle, LIKE THE OTHER ONES WE MENTIONED. These chieftains, the two pillars on the west side, are Pedatiel and Tumiha'el, each in charge over twelve thousand other officers, all pegs of the Tabernacle, like we said.

685. אִלֵּין אִינּוּן דְּאוֹשְׁדֵי דִּמְעִין, עַל כָּל אִינּוּן דִּמְתָרְכֵי נְשֵׁיהוֹן קַמַּיְיתָא. בְּגִין דְּאִינּוּן שֶׁבַע בִּרְכָאן דְּאִתְמְסָרוּ לָהּ, אִתְעֲדָן, וְלָא אִתְקַיָּימוּ, בְּגִין דְּאִתְתָּרְכָא, וְלָא אִתְדְּבָקוּ בַּעְלָהּ וְאִתְּתָא כַּחֲדָא. וְעַל דָּא כֻּלְּהוּ אוֹשְׁדֵי דִּמְעִין, דְּאַחְזֵי תֵּירוּכִין, דְּאִינּוּן שֶׁבַע בִּרְכָאן כְּמָה דְּאִתְעֲדָן מֵאֲתָר אַחֲרָא. כְּדֵין בְּהַהִיא שַׁעֲתָא קָלָא נָפַק וְאָמַר, אֵי זֶה סֵפֶר כְּרִיתוּת אִמְּכֶם אֲשֶׁר שִׁלַּחְתִּיהָ.

685. They shed tears over all those who divorce their first wives, because the Seven Benedictions UTTERED UNDER THE CHUPAH, which were given to her, were gone and did not endure since she was divorced, for husband and wife did not cleave together. Therefore, they all shed tears, for the divorce shows that these Seven Benedictions were as if gone from another place, NAMELY, FROM UPPER MALCHUT, TO WHICH THE WOMAN BELOW

CORRESPONDS. At that time a voice resounds, saying, "Where is the bill of your mother's divorcement, with which I have put her away?" (Yeshayah 50:1)

686. הֵיכָלָא תִּנְיָינָא, דְּקָא אַמָרָן דְּכָלִיל לְהֵיכָלָא קַדְמָאָה, לְאִתְיַיחֲדָא בֵּיהּ. וְכָל אִינּוּן חֵיוָון, הָכִי נָמֵי אִית לֵיהּ תְּמַנְיָא סַמְכִין כְּקַדְמָאֵי. וְכוּלְהוּ מְמָנָן, כָּל חַד וְחַד, עַל תְּרֵיסָר אַלְפֵי מְמָנָן אַחֲרָנִין, כְּאִלֵּין קַדְמָאֵי כִּדְקַאמְרָן. תְּרֵין סַמְכִין אִינּוּן לִסְטַר מִזְרָח, תְּרֵין סַמְכִין לִסְטַר דָּרוֹם, וּתְרֵין סַמְכִין לִסְטַר צָפוֹן, וּתְרֵין סַמְכִין לִסְטַר מַעֲרָב.

686. The second chamber we mentioned, THE VERY HEAVEN, includes the first chamber, THE SAPPHIRE STONE, to become one with it, together with all the living creatures THERE. It too has eight pillars like the first ones IN THE FIRST CHAMBER, each in charge over twelve thousand other officers, like the first ones. Two pillars are to the east, two pillars to the south, two pillars to the north, and two pillars to the west.

687. אִלֵּין תְּרֵין סַמְכִין דְּלִסְטַר מִזְרָח, יְהַדָּנִיאֵ"ל, גְּזוּרִיָּ"ה. תְּרֵיסָר אַלְפֵי מְמָנָן דְּכָל חַד, וְכֻלְּהוּ יְתֵדוֹת. אִינּוּן תְּרֵין סַמְכִין דְּלִסְטַר דָּרוֹם, אֲהַרִיאֵ"ל, בָּרְהִיאֵ"ל. כָּל חַד וְחַד, אִינּוּן עַל תְּרֵיסָר אַלְפִין כְּקַדְמָאֵי.

687. The two pillars to the east are called 'Yehadaniel' and 'Gezuriyah', and they have twelve thousand officers beneath them, all of them pegs. The two pillars to the south, Ahariel and Barhiel, each is in charge over twelve thousand like the first ones.

688. אִלֵּין מְמָנָן עַל מַשְׁבֵּר, וְנַטְלֵי אִינּוּן קַלֵי דְּנָשִׁין, וּמַנְחָן לוֹן קָמֵי הַהוּא הֵיכָלָא. וְכַד הַהוּא סִטְרָא אַחֲרָא אָתֵי לְקַטְרְגָא בְּהַאי שַׁעֲתָא, דְּאִיהוּ שַׁעֲתָא דְּסַכָּנָה, קַיְימֵי אִלֵּין, וְעָאלִין הָנֵי קָלֵי לַמְמָנָא דְּעַל פִּתְחָא, וְלָא יָכִיל הַהוּא סִטְרָא אַחֲרָא לְקַטְרְגָא. וּלְזִמְנִין דְּקָדִים הַהוּא סְטָר אַחֲרָא וְעָאל וְקַטְרִיג, וְיָכִיל לְנַזְקָאָה.

688. These are in charge over birth. They take the sounds uttered by women and put them in the entrance to the chamber. When the Other Side comes to denounce, it is a time of danger. They stand and usher in the sounds to the chief in charge over the gate, and the Other Side cannot prosecute. Sometimes, BECAUSE OF A WOMANS SINS, the Other Side hastens and comes in to accuse, then he might cause harm.

689. אִלֵּין תְּרֵין סַמְכִין דִּלְסְטַר צָפוֹן, חַלְחָלִיאֵ"ל, קַרְסְפִיהָאֵ"ל, אִינּוּן מְמָנָן כָּל חַד עַל תְּרֵיסָר אַלְפִין אַחֲרָנִין. דִּלְסְטַר מַעֲרָב אִינּוּן, סוּגַדְיָ"ה. גְּדַרְיָ"ה. וְאִלֵּין עַל תְּרֵיסָר אַלְפֵי אַחֲרָנִין.

689. The two pillars to the north, Chalchaliel and Kraspiha'el, are each appointed over twelve thousand others. On the west are Sugadyah and Gedaryah, appointed over twelve thousand other.

690. וְאִלֵּין מְמָנָן עַל הַהוּא דָּמָא דִּבְרִית, כַּד אִתְגְּזַר הַהוּא וַלְדָּא לִתְמַנְיָא יוֹמִין וְאִלֵּין נַטְלֵי הַהוּא דָּמָא, וּמַנְחָן לֵיהּ קָמֵי הַאי הֵיכָלָא. וְכַד רוּגְזָא אַתְעַר בְּעָלְמָא, אַשְׁגַּח קוּדְשָׁא בְּרִיךְ הוּא עַל הַהוּא דָּמָא, וְלָא אִתְיְיהִיב לְהַהוּא סִטְרָא אַחֲרָא רְשׁוּ לְאַעֲלָא תַּמָּן.

690. These are in charge over the blood of the covenant. When the baby is circumcised at the eighth day, they take the blood and put it in front of the chamber. When wrath is aroused over the world, the Holy One, blessed be He looks at that blood, and the Other Side is not given permission to enter there.

691. תָּא חֲזֵי, בִּזְמְנָא דְּאִתְגְּזַר הַהוּא בַּר נָשׁ לִתְמַנְיָא יוֹמִין, וְשָׁרַאת עָלֵיהּ שַׁבָּת, מַלְכוּת קַדִּישָׁא, הַהִיא עָרְלָה דְּגַזְרִין וְשָׁדָאן לֵיהּ לְבַר, כְּדֵין קַיְּימָא הַהוּא סִטְרָא אַחֲרָא, וְחָמָא דְּהַאי אִיהוּ חוּלָקֵיהּ מִקָּרְבְּנָא דָּא, כְּדֵין אִתְבַּר, וְלָא יָכִיל לְשַׁלְטָאָה וּלְקַטְרְגָא עֲלוֹי, וְסָלִיק וְאִתְעֲבָד סַנֵּיגוֹרְיָא עַל יִשְׂרָאֵל, קָמֵי קוּדְשָׁא בְּרִיךְ הוּא.

691. Come and see: When a man is circumcised at the eighth day, Shabbat has ALREADY dwelt upon him, WITHIN THE EIGHT DAYS. It is the holy Malchut. When the Other Side sees the foreskin, which is cut and thrown outside, his portion from that offering, THEN THE OTHER SIDE is broken and cannot have power over him or denounce him, and becomes an advocate of Yisrael before the Holy One, blessed be He.

692. הֵיכָלָא תְּלִיתָאָה. הֵיכָלָא דָא דְקַיְימָא לְאַכְלְלָא, וּלְיַחֲדָא בֵּיהּ הַהוּא הֵיכָלָא תִּנְיָינָא, וְהַהוּא רוּחָא, וְכָל אִינּוּן חֵיוָון דְּבֵיהּ, כֻּלְּהוּ כְּלִילָן וְאִתְיַיחֲדָן דָּא בְּדָא. וְאִינּוּן חַד רוּחָא דִּכְלִיל דָּא בְּדָא, הָכִי נָמֵי אִית לֵיהּ תְּמַנְיָא סַמְכִין, לְאַרְבַּע סִטְרִין דְּעָלְמָא, וְכֻלְּהוּ אִקְרוּן יְתֵדוֹת הַמִּשְׁכָּן. תְּרֵין סַמְכִין דִּלְסְטַר דָּרוֹם, אִינּוּן שַׁכְנִיאֵ"ל, עֲזוּזְיָ"ה. תְּרֵין סַמְכִין דִּלְסְטַר מִזְרָח, יְהוֹדִיָ"ה עַזְרִיאֵ"ל. וְאִלֵּין קַיְימֵי כָּל חַד וְחַד, עַל י"ב אַלְפֵי מְמָנָן אַחֲרָנִין, וְכֻלְּהוּ אִקְרוּן יְתֵדוֹת הַמִּשְׁכָּן.

692. The third chamber, BRIGHTNESS, awaits to be included and joined by the second chamber, THE VERY HEAVEN, and the spirit and all the living creatures in it are all united and joined together, and become one spirit which combines the one in the other. It too has eight pillars turned towards the four directions, all called 'the pegs of the Tabernacle'. Two pillars are to the south, Shachniel, Azuzyah. Two pillars are to the east, Yehodiyah, Azriel. Each stands upon twelve thousand other officers, all called 'the pegs of the Tabernacle'.

693. וְאִלֵּין אִתְמָנוּן עַל הַהוּא הֲבָל דְּתִינוֹקוֹת דְּלָעָאן בְּאוֹרַיְיתָא, לְקַיְימָא עָלְמָא. וְאִלֵּין נַטְלֵי הַהוּא הֲבָל, וְסַלְּקֵי לֵיהּ לְעֵילָּא. וְכָל הֲבָל וַהֲבָל דְּאִינּוּן תִּינוֹקוֹת דְּלָעָאן בְּאוֹרַיְיתָא לְקַיְימָא עָלְמָא, אִתְעָבֵיד מִנֵּיהּ רוּחָא חֲדָא, וְסַלְּקָא הַהוּא רוּחָא לְעֵילָּא, וְאִתְעַטַּר בְּעִטְרָא קַדִּישָׁא, וְאִתְמַנָּא נְטוּרָא דְּעָלְמָא, וְכֵן כֻּלְּהוּ.

693. They are in charge over the utterances of children who study the Torah, with which to sustain the world. They take the utterance and raise it up, and each utterance of the children who study the Torah, turns into one spirit, which rises upward to be bedecked by a holy crown, and is appointed a guardian of the world. And so the rest of them.

694. תְּרֵין סַמְכִין דְּאִינּוּן לִסְטַר צָפוֹן, עַזְפִּיאֵ"ל, קַטְטָרִיהָאֵ"ל. וְאִינּוּן מְמָנָן עַל תְּרֵיסַר אַלְפֵי מְמָנָן אַחֲרָנִין כָּל חַד וְחַד כִּדְקָאמְרָן. תְּרֵין

סַמְכִין דִּלְסְטַר מַעֲרָב, אִינּוּן עֲסִסְנִיָ״ה, אַדִירִירִיָ״ה. וְאִלֵּין מְמָנָן עַל תְּרֵיסַר אַלְפִין מְמָנָן אַחֲרָנִין, כָּל חַד וְחַד כִּדְקָאמְרָן.

694. The two pillars on the north side are Azpiel, Ktatariha'el. They are each in charge over twelve thousand officers. The two pillars on the west are Asisaniyah, Adiririyah, each appointed over twelve thousand other officers, as we said.

695. אִלֵּין אִתְמָנוּן לְאַכְרְזָא בְּכָל רְקִיעִין, לְכָל אִינּוּן דִּמְעַבְּרִין בְּנַיְיהוּ מֵאוֹרַיְיתָא, וְסַלְּקִין לוֹן דְּלָא יִלְעוּן בָּהּ, כְּדֵין נַפְקֵי כָּל הָנֵי מְמָנָן וּמַכְרְזֵי וְאַמְרֵי, וַוי לִפְלָנְיָא דְּאַעֲבַּר בְּרֵיהּ מֵאוֹרַיְיתָא, וַוי לֵיהּ דְּקָא אִתְאֲבִיד מֵעָלְמָא דֵּין, וּמֵעָלְמָא דְּאָתֵי.

695. Their duty is to announce throughout the firmaments the names of those who prevent their sons from studying the Torah, and detain them from being occupied in it. Then all the officers declare, 'Woe to so-and-so who prevented his son from studying the Torah. Woe to him, for he perishes in this world and in the World to Come'.

696. הֵיכָלָא רְבִיעָאָה. הֵיכָלָא דָּא הֵיכָלָא דְּקַיְּימָא בִּנְהִירוּ יַתִּיר. הֵיכָלָא דָּא, סַחֲרִין לֵיהּ תְּלָתִין וּתְרֵין יְתֵדוֹת עִלָּאִין, וְחָמֵשׁ מֵאָה אֶלֶף אַחֲרָנִין דִּמְמָנָן תְּחוֹת אִלֵּין. וְאַרְבַּע אַחֲרָנִין, עִלָּאִין עַל כֻּלְּהוּ, וְכֻלְּהוּ יְתֵדוֹת דְּהֵיכָלָא דָּא. אִלֵּין אַרְבַּע אִינּוּן: חַסְדִיהָאֵ״ל. קְסִירִיָ״ה. קְדוּמִיָ״ה. דַּהֲרִיאֵ״ל. אִלֵּין אַרְבַּע מְמָנָן עַל כֻּלְּהוּ, וְכֻלְּהוּ אַחֲרָנִין, כֻּלְּהוּ מְמָנָן תְּחוֹתַיְיהוּ.

696. The fourth chamber has much light. It is surrounded by 32 supernal pegs, and five hundred thousand other chiefs are under them. The other four are superior to them all, all of them pegs of this chamber. These four are Chasdiha'el, Kasiriyah, Kedum'iyah and Dahariel. They are in charge over the rest, and all the rest are appointed under them.

697. וְעַל יְדָא דְּאִלֵּין, אִתְיְדַע דִּינָא לְמֶעְבַּד בְּעָלְמָא, וְעַל אִלֵּין כְּתִיב וּמֵאמַר קַדִּישִׁין שְׁאֵלְתָּא. לְהָנֵי אַרְבַּע, אַתְיָין כָּל אִינּוּן חַיָּילִין, דִּי

מְמֻנָּן עַל דִּינָא, לְשָׁאֲלָא הֵיךְ אִתְגְּזַר דִּינָא בְּעָלְמָא. כָּל אִינּוּן דִּינִין דְּלָא אִתְיְיהִיבוּ בְּפִתְקִין, לְקִיּוּמָא דְּעָלְמָא, וְעַל דָּא כֻּלְּהוּ אַתְיָין לְשָׁאֲלָא. וּבְגִין כָּךְ כֻּלְּהוּ מְמֻנָּן עַל דָּא.

697. Through them Judgment is made known so it may be executed in the world. Of these says the verse, "the sentence by word of the holy ones" (Daniel 4:14). The armies in charge over Judgment come to these four, to ask how the world was sentenced. This refers to all the verdicts never committed to writing, which concern the survival of the world. FOR THAT REASON THEY DO NOT KNOW, and therefore come to ask them. That is why they are all appointed over that.

698. אִינּוּן תְּלָתִין וּתְרֵין אַחֲרָנִין, אִינּוּן מְמֻנָּן עַל כָּל אִינּוּן דְּלָעָאן בְּאוֹרַיְיתָא תָּדִיר, וְלָא פַּסְקֵי בִּימָמָא וּבְלֵילְיָא, וְאִלֵּין אַחֲרָנִין כֻּלְּהוּ דִּתְחוֹתַיְיהוּ, אִינּוּן מְמֻנָּן עַל כָּל אִינּוּן דְּקָבְעִין זִמְנִין יְדִיעָאן לְאוֹרַיְיתָא. וְעַל דָּא אִינּוּן מְמֻנָּן כֻּלְּהוּ, וּלְאַעַנְשָׁא כֻּלְּהוּ, לְכָל אִינּוּן דְּיָכְלֵי לְאִשְׁתַּדְּלָא בְּאוֹרַיְיתָא, וְלָא מִשְׁתַּדְּלֵי.

698. The other 32 are appointed over those who study the Torah incessantly, and never stop by day or by night. The others beneath them are in charge over those who set regular times for study of the Torah. The duty of them all is to punish those who could have studied the Torah but did not.

699. הֵיכָלָא חֲמִישָׁאָה. הֵיכָלָא דָּא, קַיְימִין בֵּיהּ תְּלַת מֵאָה וְשִׁתִּין וְחָמֵשׁ מְמֻנָּן, כְּחוּשְׁבַּן יְמֵי שַׁתָּא. וְעֵילָּא מִנַּיְיהוּ אַרְבַּע סַמְכִין עִלָּאִין עַל כֻּלְּהוּ. וְאִלֵּין אִינּוּן: קְרַשִׁיהָאֵ"ל. סַרְטִיהָאֵ"ל. עֲסִירִיָ"ה. קַדְמִיאֵ"ל. וְאִלֵּין אִקְרוּן יְתֵדוֹת דְּהֵיכָלָא דָּא.

699. In the chamber LOVE stand 365 chiefs like the number of days in a year. Above them there are four supernal pillars: Krashiha'el, Sartiha'el, Asiriyah and Kadmiel. They are called 'the pegs of this chamber'.

700. אִלֵּין אִתְמְנוּן לְבַדְּחָא עָלְמָא. כַּד נִשְׁמְתָא אִתּוֹסְפַת מֵעֶרֶב שַׁבָּת

לְעֶרֶב שַׁבָּת. וְאִיהִי נַפְקַת, כַּד אִיהִי נַפְקַת, נָפְקִין אִלֵּין עִמָּהּ, וּמְעַבְרֵי מִיִשְׂרָאֵל כָּל עֲצִיבוּ, וְכָל יְגִיעָא, וְכָל מְרִירוּ דְּנַפְשָׁא, וְכָל רוּגְזָא דְּעָלְמָא, וְאִלֵּין אִינּוּן בְּדִיחֵי עָלְמָא.

700. Their duty is to gladden the world. A soul is added from Shabbat eve to Shabbat eve, and when it comes out, they come out with it, and remove from Yisrael all sadness and labor, bitterness, and anger. These are those who gladden the world.

701. כָּל אִינּוּן דִּלְתַתָּא מֵאִלֵּין אַרְבָּעָה, כֻּלְּהוּ אִתְמָנוּן לְאַעְבְּרָא דִּינָא, מֵאִינּוּן מָארֵי דְּדִינָא, וּמֵאִינּוּן דְּטַרְדֵי לוֹן בְּגֵיהִנָּם, דְּיִסַּלְקוּן דִּינָא מִנַּיְיהוּ. וְעַל דָּא, כָּל אִלֵּין יְתֵדוֹת כֻּלְּהוּ קַיְימֵי בְּחֶדְוָה, וּמֵחֶדְוָה נַפְקֵי, וְכֻלְּהוּ הֵיכָלִין קַיְימֵי לְאִתְעַטְרָא לְעֵילָּא. כְּמָה דְּאִתְּמַר.

701. All those beneath those four, are all appointed to nullify the verdict of the accusers, and from those punished in Gehenom. Therefore, all the pegs rejoice, and are produced out of rejoicing, and all the chambers ascend and adorn themselves above, as we learned.

702. הֵיכָלָא שְׁתִיתָאָה. הֵיכָלָא דָּא, הֵיכָלָא דְּקַיְימָא עַל כָּל הֵיכָלִין תַּתָּאִין. בְּהַאי, מֵאָה אַחֲרָנִין דְּקַיְימָאן לְבַר, דְּאִקְרוּן יְתֵדוֹת כְּאִינּוּן אַחֲרָנִין. וְאִינּוּן מֵאָה לִסְטַר יְמִינָא, וּמֵאָה אַחֲרָנִין לִסְטַר שְׂמָאלָא.

702. The sixth chamber is over all the lower chambers. There are a hundred others standing outside THE CHAMBER, called 'pegs' like the others. There are a hundred to the right and a hundred to the left.

703. תְּרֵין מְמָנָן עִלָּאִין לִסְטַר יְמִינָא, וּתְרֵין מְמָנָן אַחֲרָנִין עִלָּאִין לִסְטַר שְׂמָאלָא. אִלֵּין דִּימִינָא אִינּוּן: מַלְכִּיאֵ"ל. שְׁמַעְיָהאֵ"ל. וְאִלֵּין דִּשְׂמָאלָא, אִקְרוּן מִסַרְסָנִיָּ"ה. צַפְצְפִיָּ"ה. אִלֵּין אִינּוּן יְתֵדוֹת עִלָּאִין, מִימִינָא וּמִשְּׂמָאלָא.

703. There are two supernal chiefs on the right side, and two other chiefs on the left side. Those of the right are Malkiel, Shmayah'el. Those of the left are called 'Misarsaniyah' and 'Tzaftzafiyah'. These are the supernal pegs, to the right and to the left.

704. וְאִלֵּין אִינּוּן קַיְימֵי וּזְמִינִין בְּעָלְמָא. בְּהַהוּא זִמְנָא, דְּצַדִּיקָא מָטָא זִמְנֵיהּ לְאִסְתַּלְּקָא מֵעָלְמָא, וְאִתְיְיהִיב רְשׁוּ לְסִטְרָא אַחֲרָא. אִלֵּין אַרְבַּע קַיְימֵי לְאִתְעַתְּדָא תַּמָּן, בְּגִין דְּתִפּוּק נִשְׁמָתֵיהּ בִּנְשִׁיקָה, וְלָא תִּצְטַעֵר בְּשׁוּלְטָנוּ דְּסִטְרָא אַחֲרָא. זַכָּאִין אִינּוּן צַדִּיקַיָּיא בְּעָלְמָא דֵּין, וּבְעָלְמָא דְּאָתֵי. דְּמָארֵיהוֹן אַקְדִּים עָלַיְיהוּ שׁוּלְטָנֵיהוֹן, לְמֶהֱוֵי נְטִירָן בְּעָלְמָא דֵּין, וּבְעָלְמָא דְּאָתֵי.

704. They stand ready in the world, and when it is time for a righteous man to pass away from the world, and the Other Side is given permission, they stand there, so his soul will leave with a kiss, and not be pained by the sway of the Other Side. Happy are the righteous in this world and in the World to Come, whose Master hastens to have them under the rule OF THE FOUR, so they will be watched in this world and in the World to Come.

705. מֵהֵיכָלָא דָּא, שָׁרָאן כָּל רָזִין, וְכָל דַּרְגִּין עִלָּאִין וְתַתָּאִין, לְאִתְחַבְּרָא. בְּגִין דְּיִשְׁתְּכַח כֹּלָּא עֵילָּא וְתַתָּא בִּשְׁלִימוּ, לְמֶהֱוֵי כֹּלָּא חַד, וְחִבּוּרָא חַד, לְאִתְיַיחֲדָא שְׁמָא קַדִּישָׁא כַּדְקָא יֵאוֹת, וּלְאִשְׁתַּלְמָא, לְאַנְהָרָא נְגִידוּ עִלָּאָה בְּתַתָּאָה, וּנְהִירוּ דְּבוּצִינִין כְּחַד, דְּלָא תַּעְדֵּי דָּא מִן דָּא. וּכְדֵין נָגִיד וְאִתְמְשַׁךְ מַאן דְּאִתְמְשַׁךְ, דְּלָא אִתְיְדַע וְלָא אִתְגַּלְיָיא, בְּגִין דְּיִתְקָרֵב וְיִתְיַיחֵד דָּא עִם דָּא, לְמֶהֱוֵי כֹּלָּא בְּיִחוּדָא שְׁלִים כַּדְקָא יֵאוֹת.

705. From this chamber all the mysteries and upper and lower grades begin to be united, so all will be complete above and below, and all will be one, in one unity, and the Holy Name will be united as it should be, so the supernal abundance will illuminate the lower one, and all the candles will burn as one, and not separately. Then abundance flows from the one, who is not known nor revealed, so that everything will get closer and join each other, and the whole will be united properly.

706. זַכָּאָה חוּלָקֵיהּ, מַאן דְּיָדַע בְּרָזִין דְּמָארֵיהּ, לְאִשְׁתְּמוֹדְעָא לֵיהּ

כַּדְקָא יֵאוֹת. דְּהָא אִינּוּן אַכְלִין חוּלָקֵיהוֹן בְּעָלְמָא דֵּין, וּבְעָלְמָא דְּאָתֵי. עַל דָּא כְּתִיב הִנֵּה עֲבָדַי יֹאכֵלוּ. זַכָּאִין אִינּוּן צַדִּיקַיָּיא דְּמִשְׁתַּדְּלֵי בְּאוֹרַיְיתָא יְמָמָא וְלֵילֵי. בְּגִין דְּאִינּוּן יַדְעֵי אוֹרְחוֹי דְּקוּדְשָׁא בְּרִיךְ הוּא, וְיַדְעֵי לְיַחֲדָא יְחוּדָא קַדִּישָׁא כַּדְקָא יֵאוֹת, דְּכָל דְּיָדַע לְיַחֲדָא שְׁמָא קַדִּישָׁא בִּשְׁלִימוּ כַּדְקָא חֲזֵי, זַכָּאָה אִיהוּ בְּעָלְמָא דֵּין, וּבְעָלְמָא דְּאָתֵי.

706. Happy is the portion of whoever knows the secret of his Master, to know Him properly. They eat their share of this world, and the World to Come. Of this says the verse, “Behold, My servants shall eat” (Yeshayah 65:13). Happy are the righteous who are occupied in the Torah day and night, for they know the ways of the Holy One, blessed be He, and know well how to effect the holy unison. For whoever knows how to unite the Holy Name wholly, as ought, happy is he in this world and in the World to Come.

707. קִשּׁוּרָא דְּכָל הָנֵי הֵיכָלִין, הָכָא מִתְקַשְּׁרָן. לְאִתְדַּבְּקָא רוּחָא בְּרוּחָא, תַּתָּאָה בְּעִלָּאָה. וּבְאִלֵּין נְשִׁיקִין אִסְתָּלַּק רוּחָא דִּלְתַתָּא לְאִתְדַּבְּקָא בְּרוּחָא דִּלְעֵילָּא. וְכַד מִתְדַּבְּקָן רוּחָא בְּרוּחָא, כְּדֵין רוּחָא עִלָּאָה סְתִימָאָה שָׁארֵי עַל הַאי רוּחָא דְּאֶמְצָעִיתָא. וְעַד לָא אִתְּעַר לְאִתְדַּבְּקָא רוּחָא בְּרוּחָא, רוּחָא עִלָּאָה. לָא שַׁרְיָא עַל רוּחָא דְּאֶמְצָעִיתָא.

707. The connection between all the chambers is made here, IN THIS CHAMBER, when one spirit clings to another, WHICH IS THE SECRET OF KISSING, the lower SPIRIT to the upper SPIRIT. By these kisses the spirit below rises to cleave to the spirit above, and when spirit cleaves to spirit, the supernal, concealed spirit, BINAH, hovers about the spirit in the middle, TIFERET, CALLED ‘JACOB’. As long as there is no arousal for the spirits to unite, the upper spirit, BINAH, does not dwell upon the middle spirit, TIFERET THAT IS CALLED ‘JACOB’.

708. וְרָזָא דָּא, כַּד אִתְאֲחִיד רוּחָא בְּרוּחָא, כְּדֵין שָׁרָאן נְשִׁיקִין לְאִתְחַבְּרָא וּמִתְעָרִין שְׁאַר שַׁיְיפִין בְּתִיאוּבְתָּא, וְרוּחָא דָּא מִתְדַּבְּקָא

בְּדָא. וּכְדֵין, שַׁיְיפִין כֻּלְּהוּ מִתְעָרֵי אִלֵּין בְּאִלֵּין, לְאִתְקַשְּׁרָא שַׁיְיפָא בְּשַׁיְיפֵיהּ.

708. The mystery is that when one spirit joins another, then there are kisses so they will be united, and the rest of the organs, NAMELY, THE OTHER ASPECTS OF THE CHAMBER, are awakened with longing. The spirits cling together and all the organs are aroused to be connected between them, to connect one organ with another.

709. וְאִי תֵּימָא, מַאן אַתְעַר שַׁיְיפֵי תַּתָּאֵי, אוֹ שַׁיְיפֵי עִלָּאֵי. שַׁיְיפֵי תַּתָּאֵי מִתְעָרֵי תָּדִיר לְגַבֵּי עִלָּאֵי, מַאן דְּאִיהוּ בַּחֲשׁוֹכָא, תָּאִיב תָּדִיר לְמֶהֱוֵי בִּנְהוֹרָא. שַׁלְהוֹבָא אוּכְמָא דִּלְתַתָּא, אַתְעַר תָּדִיר לְגַבֵּי שַׁלְהוֹבָא חִוְּורָא דִּלְעֵילָּא, בְּגִין לְאִתְדַּבְּקָא בֵּיהּ, וּלְמִשְׁרֵי תְּחוֹתֵיהּ, וְרָזָא דָּא, אֱלֹהִים אַל דֳּמִי לָךְ אַל תֶּחֱרַשׁ וְאַל תִּשְׁקוֹט אֵל.

709. You may ask, who bestirs the lower organs or the upper organs TO JOIN EACH OTHER? HE ANSWERS: The lower organs are always aroused to be with the upper ones. Whoever is in the dark, always longs to be in the light. The black flame below is always aroused to be with the white flame above, to cling to and dwell beneath it. This is the secret of the verse, "Do not keep silence, Elohim; do not hold Your peace, and be still, El" (Tehilim 83:2).

710. כַּד נָטִיל יַעֲקֹב הַאי הֵיכָלָא שְׁתִיתָאָה, כְּדֵין אִקְרֵי בִּשְׁמָא קַדִּישָׁא עִלָּאָה שְׁלֵימָא, וַיְיָ'. וְאִי תֵּימָא שְׁלֵימָא דְּכֹלָּא. לָאו הָכִי, אֶלָּא כַּד אִשְׁתְּלִימוּ כֻּלְּהוּ הֵיכָלִין אִלֵּין בְּאִלֵּין, כְּדֵין אִקְרֵי כֹּלָּא בִּשְׁמָא שְׁלִים, יְדֹוָ"ד אֱלֹהִים. וְדָא הוּא שְׁמָא שְׁלִים מִכֹּלָּא. וְעַד לָא אִתְחַבְּרוּ דָּא עִם דָּא, הֵיכָלִין בְּהֵיכָלִין, לָא אִקְרֵי בִּשְׁמָא שְׁלֵימָא דָּא. וְכַד מִתְחַבְּרָן כַּחֲדָא אִלֵּין בְּאִלֵּין, כְּדֵין אִשְׁתְּלִים כֹּלָּא מֵעֵילָּא וְתַתָּא. וּנְהִירוּ דְּעֵילָּא לְעֵילָּא, נַחְתָּא וְשַׁרְיָא עַל כֹּלָּא, וְאִתְקַשַּׁר כֹּלָּא כַּחֲדָא, לְמֶהֱוֵי כֹּלָּא חַד.

710. When Jacob, TIFERET, received the sixth chamber, he was named by the whole Holy Name *Vav*-Yud Hei Vav Hei. You may say, that this name is absolutely complete. This is not so. When all the chambers finish joining together, everything is called 'Yud Hei Vav Hei' Elohim, which is an absolutely complete name. This is a completely whole name. Before the chambers are united, it was not called by that complete name. When they join each other, everything is complete above and below, and the light high above, WHICH IS BINAH, flows down to dwell upon everything, and everything is bound together, to become one.

711. וְרָזָא דְּמִלָּה, יַעֲקֹב נָטִיל אַרְבַּע נָשִׁין, וְכָלִיל לוֹן בְּגַוֵּיהּ. וְאַף עַל גַּב דְּאוֹקִימְנָא לְהַאי מִלָּה בְּרָזָא אַחֲרָא, דְּאִיהוּ קַיְּימָא בֵּין תְּרֵין עָלְמִין. וְרָזָא דְּכֹלָּא, כַּד יַעֲקֹב נָטִיל הַאי הֵיכָלָא, דְּאִיהוּ שְׁתִיתָאָה, נָטִיל וְכָלִיל בְּגַוֵּיהּ כָּל אִינּוּן אַרְבַּע נָשִׁין, אַרְבַּע מַלְאָכִין, וְכֻלְּהוּ דַּבְקֵי בְּהֵיכָלָא דָּא. אִלֵּין אִינּוּן אַרְבַּע רֵישֵׁי נַהֲרִין, דִּכְתִּיב וּמִשָּׁם יִפָּרֵד וְהָיָה לְאַרְבָּעָה רָאשִׁים. אִלֵּין אַרְבַע רֵישִׁין, אִינּוּן אַרְבַּע נָשִׁין נָטִיל לוֹן יַעֲקֹב, נָטִיל הֵיכָלָא דָּא.

711. The secret of the matter: Jacob took four wives and included them within him. Though we explained it through another mystery, NAMELY, that he stands between two worlds OF ATZILUT, CALLED 'RACHEL AND LEAH'; NEVERTHELESS, the secret of the whole matter is that when Jacob took this chamber, the sixth one, he included in it these four women, who were four angels, all attached to this chamber. These are the four sources of the rivers, as it is written, "and from thence it was parted, and branched into four streams" (Beresheet 2:10). These four branches are the four women Jacob married, who took this chamber.

712. וּכְדֵין אִקְרֵי הַאי הֵיכָלָא וַיְיָ׳, כַּד אִיהוּ לְטָב כד״א וַיְיָ הוֹלֵךְ לִפְנֵיהֶם יוֹמָם. וַיְיָ׳ אָמַר הַמְכַסֶּה אֲנִי מֵאַבְרָהָם. וְכַד אִתְחֲבַּר יִצְחָק, בְּהֵיכָלָא דְּבֵי דִּינָא, דְּאִקְרֵי זְכוּתָ״א, כְּדֵין אִקְרֵי כֹּלָּא וַיְיָ׳, לְאַעֲנְשָׁא לְחַיָּיבַיָּא, כד״א וַיְיָ׳ הִמְטִיר עַל סְדוֹם וְגוֹ׳, וְכֹלָּא בְּרָזָא חֲדָא כַּדְקָא יָאוּת.

712. Then this chamber was named *Vav*-Yud Hei Vav Hei, when it is for the good, as it is written, "And Hashem went before them by day" (Shemot

13:21), "And Hashem said, 'Shall I hide from Abraham'" (Beresheet 18:17). When Isaac was united with the chamber of the court house, called 'the chamber of merit', then everything was called 'Vav-Yud Hei Vav Hei', so the wicked will be punished, as it is written, "And Hashem rained upon Sodom" (Beresheet 19:24). All that pertains to one mystery, as should be.

713. וְכַד יַעֲקֹב נָטִיל הֵיכָלָא דָּא, כְּדֵין אִקְרֵי כֹּלָּא רָצוֹן שָׁלוֹם. וְדָא הוּא עֵת רָצוֹן. וּמִכָּאן וּלְהָלְאָה, שָׁרָאן הֵיכָלִין לְאִתְחַבְּרָא וּלְאִתְקַשְּׁרָא אִלֵּין בְּאִלֵּין. וְאַף עַל גַּב דְּתָנֵינָן דְּרוֹמִית מִזְרָחִית. וְכֹלָּא אִיהוּ כַּחֲדָא, הָכָא אִיהוּ רוּחָא בְּרוּחָא, דְּבֵיקוּתָא חֲדָא.

713. When Jacob received this chamber, everything was considered a complete desire. This is a time of goodwill. From now on, the chambers start to join and unite with each other. And though we learned THAT THE ORDER OF UNISON IS south-east, MEANING THAT ONE DRAWS FROM SOUTH, CHESED, EASTWARD, TOWARD TIFERET, FOR SOUTH IS THE MAIN ONE. YET HERE IT IS SAID THAT TIFERET IS THE MAIN ONE, AND THAT IT PRECEDES CHESED, THE SIXTH CHAMBER. HE ANSWERS: All is one, because here one spirit is attached to the other, WHICH IS THE SECRET OF KISSING, IN WHICH TIFERET IS PRINCIPAL AND IS HIGHER THAN CHESED, YET THERE LIES THE SECRET OF EMBRACING; THEREFORE, CHESED IS MORE VALUABLE. THIS IS THE SECRET OF THE VERSE, "THE BLESSINGS OF YOUR FATHER (THE SECRET OF TIFERET) ARE POTENT ABOVE THE BLESSINGS OF MY PROGENITORS (WHICH ARE CHESED AND GVURAH)" (BERESHEET 49:26), FOR THROUGH MANY BLESSINGS AND KISSINGS IT BECAME MORE VALUABLE THAN CHESED AND GVURAH, AND WAS CONSIDERED ABOVE THEM.

714. מִכָּאן שָׁרֵי אַבְרָהָם, דְּאִיהוּ יְמִינָא, דְּאִקְרֵי אַהֲבָה רַבָּה דְּקָאמְרָן. וְאִיהוּ נָטִיל הֵיכָלָא דְּאִקְרֵי אַהֲבָ״ה. כְּדֵין, שָׁדַיִם נָכוֹנוּ, וְאִתְמַלְיָין מִכָּל טוּב, לְסַפָּקָא וּלְאַתְזְנָא כֹּלָּא מֵהָכָא. וְכַד אִלֵּין שָׁדַיִם נָכוֹנוּ וְאִתְמַלְיָין מִגוֹ רְחִימוּ עִלָּאָה, כְּדֵין אִקְרֵי הֵיכָלָא דָּא אֵל שַׁדַּ״י כְּדְקָאמְרָן. וּבְהַאי אִסְתַּפַּק כָּל עָלְמָא כַּד אִתְבְּרֵי, דְּהָא כַּד אִתְבְּרֵי עָלְמָא, לָא יָכִיל לְמֵיקָם בְּקִיּוּמָא, וְלָא הֲוָה קָאֵים, עַד דְּאִתְגְּלֵי הֵיכָלָא דָּא דְּנָטִיל אַבְרָהָם, וְכַד אִתְגְּלֵי אַבְרָהָם בְּהַאי הֵיכָלָא, כְּדֵין אָמַר לְעָלְמָא דַּי, הָא

סְפּוּקָא לְאַתְזָנָא מִנֵּיהּ עָלְמָא וּלְאִתְקַיְּימָא. ובג״כ, אֵל שַׁדַּי אִקְרֵי, אֵ״ל שַׁדַ״י לְכֹלָּא בֵּיהּ.

714. Here lies the beginning of Abraham, who is of the right, NAMELY, CHESED OF ZEIR ANPIN, called 'great love', as we said. And he received the chamber called 'love', NAMELY, THE FIFTH CHAMBER. Then, "your breasts (Heb. *shadayim*) were firm" (Yechezkel 16:7), REFERRING TO THE NAME 'SHADAI' and filled with goodness to sustain and nourish all from here. And when the breasts were firm and filled by the supernal love, then this chamber was called 'El Shadai', as we said. And by this the world found supply when it was created, because when the world was created, it could not exist, and did not endure, until this chamber was revealed, that Abraham took. When Abraham was seen in this chamber, the world said enough, (Heb. *dai*) for there is supply ENOUGH to sustain and nourish the world. It was therefore called 'El Shadai', WHICH MEANS El in whom there is enough (Heb. *shedai*).

715. וְזַמִּין קוּדְשָׁא בְּרִיךְ הוּא לְמַלְיָא לֵיהּ, וּלְאַתְקְנָא לֵיהּ לְזִמְנָא דְּאָתֵי דִּכְתִיב לְמַעַן תִּינְקוּ וּשְׂבַעְתֶּם מִשֹּׁד תַּנְחֻמֶיהָ לְמַעַן תָּמוֹצּוּ וְהִתְעַנַּגְתֶּם מִזִּיז כְּבוֹדָהּ. שֹׁד תַּנְחֻמֶיהָ וְזִיז כְּבוֹדָהּ, כֹּלָּא אִיהוּ בְּהַאי הֵיכָלָא. וּכְדֵין בְּהַהוּא זִמְנָא כְּתִיב, מִי מִלֵּל לְאַבְרָהָם הֵינִיקָה בָנִים שָׂרָה, דְּהָא יְנִיקָא תַּלְיָא בֵּיהּ בְּאַבְרָהָם.

715. The Holy One, blessed be He will fill and repair it in the future, as it is written, "that you may suck, and be satisfied with the breast of her consolations; that you may drink deeply, and be delighted with the abundance of her glory" (Yeshayah 66:11). "The breast of her consolations" and "the abundance of her glory" are all in this chamber. Then, at that time, it is written, "Who would have said to Abraham, that Sarah should give children suck?" (Beresheet 21:7), for sucking depends upon Abraham, WHO IS CHESED.

716. יִצְחָק דְּאִיהוּ שְׂמָאלָא, דְּקוּדְשָׁא בְּרִיךְ הוּא, אֲתָר דְּמִנֵּיהּ מִתְעָרִין כָּל דִּינִין דְּעָלְמָא, וְאִיהוּ דְּרוֹעָא דִּשְׂמָאלָא, שֵׁירוּתָא דְּכָל דִּינִין, וְכָל דִּינִין מִתְעָרֵי מִתַּמָּן, הַאי אִיהוּ נָטִיל וְאָחִיד הַהוּא הֵיכָלָא דְּאִקְרֵי

זְכוּתָא, לְאִתְחַבְּרָא דִּינָא בְּדִינָא, וּלְמֶהֱוֵי כֹּלָּא קְשׁוּרָא חֲדָא, בְּגִין דְּהַאי אִיהוּ דִּינָא דִּלְעֵילָּא, וּרְשִׁימִין דְּדִינִין קַיְימִין בֵּיהּ.

716. Isaac is at the left of the Holy One, blessed be He, whence all the Judgments in the world are awakened. He is the left arm, the source of every Judgment, whence they are awakened. From there he takes the Judgment called 'merit', WHICH IS THE FOURTH CHAMBER, to bind all the Judgments together so they will be in one knot, since Isaac is the Judgment above IN ZEIR ANPIN, where all the Judgments are listed.

717. וְהָכָא אִתְרְשִׁים שְׁמָא קַדִּישָׁא, דְּאִקְרֵי אֱלֹהִים. בְּגִין דְּאִית אֱלֹהִים חַיִּים, דְּאִיהוּ לְעֵילָּא לְעֵילָּא, סָתִים מִכֹּלָּא. וְאִית אֱלֹהִים, דְּאִיהוּ בֵּי דִּינָא דִּלְעֵילָּא. וֵאלֹהִים, דְּאִיהוּ בֵּי דִּינָא דִּלְתַתָּא. הה״ד אַךְ יֵשׁ אֱלֹהִים שׁוֹפְטִים בָּאָרֶץ. אֱלֹהִים עִלָּאָה, רָזָא דֶּאֱלֹהִים חַיִּים, כָּלִיל לְאִלֵּין דִּלְתַתָּא, וְכֹלָּא אִיהוּ חַד.

717. Here the Holy Name Elohim is written, for there is a living Elohim high above, concealed to all, WHICH IS BINAH, and there is Elohim, the celestial court, GVURAH OF ZEIR ANPIN, and there is Elohim, that is the terrestrial court, WHICH IS MALCHUT. This is the meaning of the verse, "verily there is Elohim who judges in the earth" (Tehilim 58:12). The upper Elohim, the secret of a living Elohim, BINAH, comprises the lower beings, so all is one.

718. בְּהַאי הֵיכָלָא, אִתְּעַר יִצְחָק, וְכֻלְּהוּ שַׁבְעִין וּתְרֵין נְהוֹרִין דִּכְלִילָן בֵּיהּ, דְּמִנַּיְיהוּ אִתְגְּזָרוּ כָּל דִּינִין דְּעָלְמָא דִּלְתַתָּא, דִּכְתִּיב בִּגְזֵרַת עִירִין פִּתְגָּמָא. וַאֲמַאי אִקְרוּן עִירִין. אֶלָּא בְּגִין דְּכֻלְּהוּ קַיְימִין בְּהַאי עִיר. עִיר יְיָ׳ צְבָאוֹת. עִיר אֱלֹהֵינוּ. כָּל אִינּוּן הֵיכָלִין לְעֵילָּא, כָּל חַד וְחַד אִקְרֵי עִיר, כד״א עִיר וְקַדִּישׁ. וְאִלֵּין אִינּוּן עִירִין, דְּקַיְימִין לְגוֹ בְּגוֹ דְּהֵיכָלָא, דְּקַיְימִן בְּעִיר, בג״כ אִקְרוּן עִירִי״ן.

718. In this chamber Isaac is awakened, GVURAH OF ZEIR ANPIN, together with the 72 lights included in him, for all the sentences in the world below were pronounced by him, as it is written, "This matter is by the decree of the watchers (Aramaic *irin*)" (Daniel 4:14). Why are ALL THE DECREES AND JUDGMENTS called 'irin'? Because they all dwell in this city, "the city (Heb. *ir*) of the Hashem Tzeva'ot…the city of our Elohim" (Tehilim 48:9). All the chambers above, each is called 'city', as it is written, "a watcher (Heb. *ir*) and a holy one" (Daniel 4:20). These cities stand inside the chamber CALLED 'IR'. SINCE they are in 'ir', they are called 'irin'.

719. הַאי הֵיכָלָא, אִתְכְּלִיל בְּיִצְחָק, וְכֹלָּא אִיהוּ בְּהֵיכָלָא דְּאַבְרָהָם, בְּגִין דִּימִינָא אַכְלִיל לִשְׂמָאלָא. וְתָא חֲזֵי, כָּל חַד וְחַד כָּלִיל לְחַבְרֵיהּ. וְהָא אוֹקִימְנָא, דבג"ד אַבְרָהָם עָקַד לְיִצְחָק, בְּגִין לְאַכְלְלָא בֵּיהּ דִּינָא, וּלְאִשְׁתַּכְחָא שְׂמָאלָא כָּלִיל בִּימִינָא וּלְאַשְׁלְטָא יְמִינָא עַל שְׂמָאלָא.

719. This chamber is included in Isaac. Everything is in the chamber of Abraham, THE FIFTH CHAMBER, because the right, CHESED, is included in the left, GVURAH. Come and see: Each comprises its fellow CHAMBER. We already explained that this is the reason why Abraham sacrificed Isaac, to make Judgment, ISAAC, a part of himself, and to include the left within the right, and cause the right to have power over the left.

720. וע"ד קוּדְשָׁא בְּרִיךְ הוּא פָּקִיד לֵיהּ לְאַבְרָהָם, לְקָרְבָא בְּרֵיהּ לְדִינָא, וּלְאַתְקְפָא עֲלוֹי, וְלָא פָּקִיד לְיִצְחָק, אֶלָּא לְאַבְרָהָם. וע"ד אִשְׁתְּכַח, דָּא בְּדִינָא, וְדָא בְּחֶסֶד, וְכֹלָּא חַד, וְאִתְכְּלִיל דָּא בְּדָא. וְהָכִי, אִתְכְּלִילוּ הֵיכָלִין תַּתָּאִין בְּעִלָּאִין.

720. Therefore, the Holy One, blessed be He commanded Abraham to offer his son as sacrifice to Judgment, and to overpower him. He did not command Isaac to be sacrificed, but commanded Abraham, SO THAT ABRAHAM, CHESED, WILL COMPRISE ISAAC, WHO IS JUDGMENT. Therefore, the one is found to consist of Judgment, and the other Chesed. And all is one, once they were included in each other. So the lower chambers were included in the upper.

721. כַּד נָטִיל יִצְחָק הֵיכָלָא דָּא, כְּדֵין כֹּלָּא אִיהוּ לְטָב. דִּינָא בִּזְכוּתָא. וע"ד, בָּעֵי ב"נ דְּדָאִין דִּינָא, לְמֵידַן דִּינָא בִּזְכוּתָא. בְּגִין דְּאִיהוּ רָזָא

עִלָּאָה, שְׁלִימוּ דְּדִינָא. בְּגִין דְּלֵית שְׁלִימוּ דְּדִינָא, אֶלָּא בִּזְכוּתָא, דָּא בְּלָא דָּא לָאו אִיהוּ שְׁלִימוּ. דִּינָא בִּזְכוּתָא, דָּא אִיהוּ שְׁלִימוּ דִּמְהֵימְנוּתָא, כְּגַוְונָא דִּלְעֵילָּא.

721. When Isaac received this chamber, everything was sentenced in a good way, NAMELY, Judgment tempered with merit. Therefore, a man who judges should give the verdict according to merit. This is the high secret of the wholeness of justice, for there is no wholeness to justice, only with merit. Without it there is no perfection. Judgment with merit conveys the wholeness of Faith, reflecting the upper one.

722. בְּיוֹמָא דר״ה, כַּד דִּינָא אִתְּעַר בְּעָלְמָא, בָּעָאן יִשְׂרָאֵל לְתַתָּא, לְאַתְעָרָא רַחֲמֵי מִגּוֹ שׁוֹפָר, כְּגַוְונָא דְּרָזָא עִלָּאָה. וְהָא אוֹקִימְנָא. וּבָעֵינָא לְחַבְּרָא דִּינָא לְקָבֵל זְכוּתָא, בְּגִין דְּכַד קַיְימָא דִּינָא בִּזְכוּתָא, כֹּלָּא אִיהוּ בְּחִבּוּרָא חֲדָא. וְעֵילָּא וְתַתָּא בִּשְׁלִימוּ. וּכְדֵין, וְעוֹלָתָה קָפְצָה פִּיהָ, דְּלֵית לָהּ רְשׁוּ לְאַסְטָאָה וּלְקַטְרְגָא בְּעָלְמָא. וּכְדֵין כֹּלָּא בְּיִחוּדָא חֲדָא כַּדְקָא יָאוֹת. וְדִינָא בְּלָא זְכוּ לָאו אִיהוּ דִּינָא.

722. On the day of Rosh Hashanah, when Judgment is aroused in the world, it behooves Yisrael below to awaken compassion through the Shofar, which reflects the high mystery, as already stated. And they should temper justice with merit, WHICH IS CHESED. For when Judgment is tempered with merit, all is in unison, and there is perfection above and below, and "iniquity stops her mouth" (Iyov 5:16), and has no permission to accuse or denounce in the world. Then all is in a proper unison. Judgment without merit is no Judgment.

723. וְדָא אִיהוּ דְּיִשְׂרָאֵל, דְּאִית לוֹן דִּינָא בִּזְכוּתָא. אֲבָל שְׁאַר עַמִּין, לָא אִית לוֹן דִּינָא בִּזְכוּתָא, וע״ד אָסִיר לָן, לְסַדְּרָא דִּינִין דִּילָן בְּעַרְכָּאֵי דְּעַמִּין עוֹבְדֵי עֲבוֹדָה זָרָה, דְּהָא לֵית לוֹן חוּלָקָא בְּסִטְר מְהֵימְנוּתָא דִּילָן. דִּכְתִיב, לֹא עָשָׂה כֵן לְכָל גּוֹי וּמִשְׁפָּטִים בַּל יְדָעוּם. וּמִסִּטְרָא דְּיִשְׂרָאֵל כָּל מַאן דְּדָאִין דִּינָא, וְלָא אַכְלִיל בֵּיהּ זְכוּת, דָּא אִיהוּ חָטֵי, דְּקָא גָּרַע רָזָא דִּמְהֵימְנוּתָא, וְאַסְטֵי גַּרְמֵיהּ לְהַהוּא סִטְרָא, דְּאִית בֵּיהּ דִּינָא בְּלָא זְכוּת.

723. This concerns Yisrael, who temper Judgment with merit. But the rest of the nations do not have Judgment of merit. Therefore, it is forbidden for us to administer justice in their courts, for they have no part in our side of the Faith, as it is written, "He has not dealt so with any other nation and as for His ordinances they have not known them" (Tehilim 147:20). On the side of Yisrael, whoever judges without taking merit into account is a sinner, because he lessens the secret of the Faith, and turns aside to the place where there is Judgment without merit, NAMELY, THE OTHER SIDE.

724. ות״ח, כַּד קַיְימֵי סַנְהֶדְרִין לְתַתָּא, לְמֵידָן דִּינֵי נְפָשׁוֹת, אִצְטְרִיכוּ לְמִפְתַּח בִּזְכוּתָא. בְּגִין לְאַכְלְלָא זְכוּתָא בְּדִינָא. וְתוּ, דְּהָא אִקְרוּן מְבֵּי זְכוּתָא. וע״ד, אִשְׁתַּדְּלוּתָא דִּילְהוֹן, לְמִפְתַּח בִּזְכוּתָא, וְשָׁרָאן בִּזְכוּתָא מִזְעֵירָא, וּלְבָתַר אִשְׁתְּלִים דִּינָא מֵעִלָּאָה. לְמֶהֱוֵי זְכוּתָא כָּלִיל בְּדִינָא. דָּא לְעֵילָּא, וְדָא לְתַתָּא. דִּינָא בִּזְכוּתָא, שְׁלִימוּ דְּדִינָא. דָּא בְּלָא דָּא, לָאו אִיהוּ שְׁלִימוּ. וּבְגִין כַּךְ, יִצְחָק וְרִבְקָה כַּחֲדָא אִינּוּן, דָּא דִּינָא, וְדָא זְכוּתָא, לְמֶהֱוֵי שְׁלִימוּ כַּחֲדָא. זַכָּאָה חוּלָקֵיהוֹן דְּיִשְׂרָאֵל, דְּקוּדְשָׁא ב״ה יָהַב לוֹן אוֹרַיְיתָא שְׁלֵימָתָא, לְמֵיהַךְ בְּאֹרַח קְשׁוֹט, כְּגַוְונָא דִּלְעֵילָּא.

724. Come and see: When the members of the Sanhedrin started to deal with criminal laws, they had to open with a merit, in order to temper Judgment with merit. Moreover, they were called to sentence from the house of merit, NAMELY, THE SECRET OF THE SANHEDRIN IS IN THE CHAMBER OF MERIT. Therefore, they tried to start with a merit, and when they so start with the lesser one OF THE SANHEDRIN, later the Judgment was completed by the most prominent OF THE SANHEDRIN, so merit will be included within justice. This one above, and that one below. Judgment with merit is the wholeness of justice, for without each other there is no wholeness. Therefore, Isaac and Rivkah were as one, the one Judgment, and the other mercy, and together they constitute wholeness. ISAAC IS JUDGMENT, AND RIVKAH IS MERIT. Happy is the portion of Yisrael, for the Holy One, blessed be He gave them a whole Torah, so they may walk in the path of truth, reflecting THE LIGHTS OF above.

725. תָּא חֲזֵי, דְּאִינּוּן לָא דַּיְינִין דִּינָא, אֶלָּא בִּזְכוּ, וּלְעַיְינָא זְכוּתָא בְּקַדְמֵיתָא, לְמֶהֱוֵי כָּלִיל דָּא בְּדָא. וְסַנְהֶדְרִין קָא מְהַפְּכֵי בִּזְכוּתָא

בְּדִינָא, לְאַכְלְלָא כֹּלָּא כַּחֲדָא, בְּגִין דְּלָא יִשְׁלוֹט סִטְרָא אַחֲרָא. דְּהָא כַּד זְכוּתָא לָא אִשְׁתְּכַח, סִטְרָא אַחֲרָא אִשְׁתְּכַח, דְּאִקְרֵי חוֹבָה, וְאִתְחַבְּרַת בְּדִינָא, וְאִתְתְּקֵפַת וְדָא הוּא דִּינָא בְּחוֹבָה.

725. Come and see: They did not judge, only with merit. They first looked at the good deeds, to include them together. The Sanhedrin looked well at the merits and at the prosecution, to combine them, so the Other Side will not rule. Wherever there is no merit, the Other Side abides, called 'guilt'. THE OTHER SIDE then joins the Judgment and gets stronger, this is called 'a sentence of guilt'.

726. וְעַל דָּא, בְּיוֹמָא דְּרֹאשׁ הַשָּׁנָה, בָּעֵינָא לְחַבְּרָא זְכוּתָא בְּדִינָא, וְלָא יִתְגַּבַּר חוֹבָה. וּבְגִין כָּךְ, בָּעֵינָא זְכוּתָא וְדִינָא לְמֶהֱוֵי כַּחֲדָא, בְּגִין דְּאִיהוּ שְׁלִים. דְּכַד סִטְרָא אַחֲרָא שַׁלְטָא, לָאו אִיהוּ שְׁלִים, אֶלָּא קִטְרוּגָא, כְּמָה דְּאִיהוּ קִטְרוּגָא, וְאִינּוּן אַרְבַּע מִיתוֹת, וְכַד סִטְרָא דְּאִיהוּ זְכוּת שַׁלְטָא, כֹּלָּא אִיהוּ שְׁלִים, שָׁלוֹם וֶאֱמֶת חֶסֶד וְרַחֲמִים.

726. Therefore, on Rosh Hashanah, we should temper Judgment with merit, so guilt will not have the upper hand. Hence, we must let Judgment and merit be together, so they may become one whole. For when the Other Side, WHICH IS GUILT, rules, there is no perfection, only accusation. This resembles the accusation FROM WHICH ARE DRAWN four deaths. But when the side of merit rules, all is wholeness, "peace and truth" (II Melachim 20: 19), "love and compassion" (Tehilim 103:4).

727. וְכַד אִתְחַבְּרַת סִטְרָא אַחֲרָא בְּדִינָא, שַׁלְטָא בְּקִטְרוּגָא, בְּאִינּוּן אַרְבַּע מִיתוֹת בֵּית דִּין: סְקִילָה, שְׂרֵיפָה, הֶרֶג, וְחֶנֶק. כֻּלְּהוּ שׁוּלְטָנוּתָא דְּקִטְרוּגָא בִּישָׁא. סְקִילָה, בְּגִין דְּאִיהוּ אֶבֶן נֶגֶף. שְׂרֵיפָה, בְּגִין דְּאִיהוּ צוּר מִכְשׁוֹל, אֶשָּׁא תַּקִּיפָא. הֶרֶג, דָּא חֶרֶב תֹּאכַל בָּשָׂר. תֹּאכַל בָּשָׂר וַדַּאי, דְּשַׁלְטָא בְּבִשְׂרָא, וְדָא הוּא קֵץ כָּל בָּשָׂר. חֶנֶק, בְּגִין דְּאִיהוּ קִלְלַת אֱלֹהִי"ם, הַהוּא דְּשַׁלְטָא עַל חֶנֶק, עַל צְלִיבוּ. וְאוֹקִימְנָא, בְּגִין דְּלָא יִשְׁתְּאַר אֶלָּא בִּשְׂרָא בִּלְחוֹדוֹי, וְהַהוּא קִלְלַת אֱלֹהִים, שַׁלְטָא בְּבִשְׂרָא, מָרָה חֲשׁוֹכָא. וּבְגִין כָּךְ, דָּא לְטָב וְדָא לְבִישׁ.

727. When the Other Side is connected with Judgment, it has power, by accusation, over the four capital punishments decreed by court: stoning, burning, decapitation, and strangulation. All of them are under the sway of the evil prosecutor: stoning, because THE OTHER SIDE is "a stone of stumbling" (Yeshayah 8:14); burning, because he is "a rock of offense" (Ibid.), a strong fire; decapitation is a "sword shall devour flesh" (Devarim 32:42). Assuredly it shall devour flesh, for it rules over flesh, it is THE OTHER SIDE, CALLED "the End of all Flesh" (Beresheet 6:13). Strangulation, for the curse of Elohim is upon the strangulation, upon the hanged, THE SECRET OF THE VERSE, "FOR HE THAT IS HANGED IS ACCURSED OF ELOHIM" (DEVARIM 21:23). We explained that nothing remained IN HIM, WHO IS HANGED, save the flesh, BECAUSE THE SOUL LEFT IT, and the curse of Elohim is upon the flesh, which is dark poison. Hence, HOLINESS brings good, AND THE OTHER SIDE brings evil.

728. וְאִצְטְרִיכוּ יִשְׂרָאֵל דְּרָזָא דִּמְהֵימְנוּתָא בְּהוּ, לְאִסְתַּמְרָא, בְּגִין דְּיִשְׁלוֹט סִטְרָא דִּמְהֵימְנוּתָא, וְלָא יַהֲבוּן דּוּכְתָּא לְסִטְרָא אַחֲרָא לְשַׁלְטָאָה זַכָּאִין אִינּוּן בְּעָלְמָא דֵּין, וּבְעָלְמָא דְּאָתֵי, עֲלַיְיהוּ כְּתִיב וְעַמֵּךְ כֻּלָּם צַדִּיקִים וְגוֹ'.

728. It behooves Yisrael, who have the secret of the Faith, to take heed that the side of the Faith will be in ascendancy, and that the Other Side will not be given place to exercise his power. They are happy in this world and in the World to Come. It is written of them, "your people also shall be all righteous…" (Yeshayah 60:21).

729. נְבִיאִין, דְּאִינּוּן סִטְרִין עִלָּאִין, תְּרֵין יַרְכִין דְּסַמְכִין לְאוֹרַיְיתָא קַדִּישָׁא, אִינּוּן נַטְלִין לְהֵיכָלָא דִּתְרֵין רוּחִין בֵּיהּ, דְּאִינּוּן נֹגַהּ וְזֹהַר. וְאִינּוּן תְּרֵין יַרְכִין לְתַתָּא, לְסַמְכָא לְאִינּוּן הֵיכָלִין דִּלְעֵילָּא, דְּאִקְרוּן תּוֹרָה שֶׁבְּעַל פֶּה. כְּמָה דְּאִית סַמְכִין לְאוֹרַיְיתָא דְּאִיהִי תּוֹרָה שֶׁבִּכְתָב, כַּךְ אִית סַמְכִין קַיְימִין לְאוֹרַיְיתָא דְּאִיהִי תּוֹרָה שֶׁבְּעַל פֶּה. וְאִתְכְּלִילוּ דָּא בְּדָא. כְּדֵין אִלֵּין תְּרֵין סַמְכִין דִּלְתַתָּא, כַּד מִתְחַבְּרָן בְּאִלֵּין עִלָּאִין, אִתְרְשִׁים בְּהוּ סִטְרָא דִּנְבוּאָה, וּמַאן אִיהוּ. מַרְאֶה, דְּאִיהוּ כְּגַוְונָא דִּנְבוּאָה.

729. The prophets, the supernal sides, the two thighs NETZACH AND HOD, who support the Holy Torah, TIFERET, receive the chambers where the two spirits, brightness and splendor, abide. THESE ARE THE THIRD CHAMBER, THE CHAMBER OF BRIGHTNESS, AND THE SECOND CHAMBER, THE VERY HEAVEN. These are the thighs below, IN BRIYAH, that support the chambers above called 'the Oral Law', NAMELY, MALCHUT OF ATZILUT. As there are struts to the Torah, the Written Law, so there are pillars supporting the Oral Law, MALCHUT, which include each other. When the two struts below, BRIGHTNESS AND SPLENDOR, are connected with the upper CHAMBERS, IN MALCHUT OF ATZILUT, the aspect of prophecy is impressed upon them. This is a vision, a sort of prophecy.

730. וְכָל אִינּוּן מָארֵיהוֹן דְּמַרְאֶה, מֵהָכָא יַנְקִין. לְעֵילָּא נְבוּאָה, הָכָא מַרְאֶה. וע"ד, אִיהוּ דָּא כְּגַוְונָא דָּא, וְדָא כְּגַוְונָא דָּא. וְכַד מִתְחַבְּרָן דָּא בְּדָא, כְּדֵין שַׁלִּיט עַל הַאי אֲתָר, שְׁמָא קַדִּישָׁא, דְּאִקְרֵי צְבָאוֹת. בְּגִין דְּכָל אִינּוּן חַיָּילִין קַדִּישִׁין, כֻּלְּהוּ קַיְימֵי הָכָא, וְכֻלְּהוּ אִקְרוּן מִסִּטְרָא דִּנְבוּאָה, מַרְאֶה וְחֶלְמָא מִסִּטְרָא דִּנְבוּאָה הֲווֹ.

730. All the seers are nourished from here, FROM THE CHAMBERS OF BRIGHTNESS AND SPLENDOR, INCLUDED IN THE CHAMBERS OF MALCHUT, from above IN NETZACH AND HOD OF ZEIR ANPIN, they suck prophecy, and from below, MALCHUT, vision. Therefore, high and low reflect each other, MEANING THAT PROPHECY IS LIKE A VISION, AND VISION IS LIKE PROPHECY. When NETZACH AND HOD, BRIGHTNESS AND SPLENDOR are united with each other, the Holy Name Tzevaot (lit. 'armies') rules over this place, since all the holy armies are here, all named after the aspect of prophecy, because visions and dreams are of the side of prophecy.

731. ואע"ג דְּקָא אַמְרֵינָן, דִּי בְּגוֹ הַהוּא אוֹת קַיָּימָא קַדִּישָׁא, שַׁרְיָא שְׁמָא דָּא. בְּגִין דְּכֻלְּהוּ חַיָּילִין נַפְקֵי מֵהַאי אוֹת. עִם כָּל דָּא, יַרְכִין דְּאִינּוּן קַיְימִין לְבַר, קָרֵינָן עַל שְׁמָא דָּא, וְאִלֵּין אִינּוּן דְּאִקְרוּן בַּרְיָיתֵי, דְּהָא בָּרַיְיתָא לְבַר מִמִּשְׁנָה. מַתְנִיתִין קַיְימָא לְגוֹ בַּרְיָיתֵי, וְאִקְרוּן יַרְכִין בָּתֵּי בָּרָאֵי, כְּגַוְונָא דִּי לְעֵילָּא.

731. We say that within the sign of the Holy Covenant, NAMELY, YESOD, the name TZEVAOT dwells, for all the armies come out of this sign, YESOD. Nevertheless, the thighs, which stand out OF THE BODY, are also named TZEVAOT. They are called 'Baraithas', WHICH MEANS 'EXTERNALS', because the Baraitha is outside the Mishnah, and the Mishnah stands upon the Baraitha, NAMELY, THE BARAITHA EXPLAINS THE MISHNAH, AND THE BARAITHAS are called 'the thighs OF THE MISHNAH', external chambers, the same as NETZACH AND HOD above, STANDING OUTSIDE THE BODY OF THE FACE.

732. מַתְנִיתִין אִיהוּ רָזָא דְקַיְּימָא לְגוֹ, דְּאוֹלְפֵי תַּמָּן עִקָּרָא דְּכֹלָּא, וְעַל תָּנָאֵי, וְרָזָא דְּהַךְ, אֶנְהָגֲךָ אֲבִיאֲךָ אֶל בֵּית אִמִּי תְּלַמְּדֵנִי. אֶל בֵּית אִמִּי: דָּא קה״ק. תְּלַמְּדֵנִי: דָּא הוּא רָזָא דְּמַתְנִיתִין. דְּכַד עָאל דָּא נָהָר דְּנָגִיד וְנָפִיק, בְּהַהוּא בֵּית קֹדֶשׁ הַקֳּדָשִׁים, כְּתִיב תְּלַמְּדֵנִי. וְדָא הוּא רָזָא, דְּאִקְרֵי מִשְׁנָה. כד״א אֶת מִשְׁנֵה הַתּוֹרָה הַזֹּאת.

732. The Mishnah is a mystery, found inside, because one learns the essence of things from there. So the Tannaim OF THE MISHNAH ARE OF THE INTERNAL PART. This is the secret meaning of the verse, "I would lead you, and bring you into the house of my mother, that you may instruct me" (Shir Hashirim 8:2). "The house of my mother" refers to the Holy of Holies, WHICH IS YESOD OF MALCHUT OF ATZILUT, CORRECTED BY THE ASPECT OF YESOD OF IMA, THEREFORE CALLED "THE HOUSE OF MY MOTHER", THE INNER PART OF MALCHUT. "That you may instruct me" refers to the secret of the Mishnah, NAMELY, when the river that is drawn and comes out, YESOD OF ZEIR ANPIN, from the Holy of Holies, then "you will instruct me," MEANING THAT YOU WILL GIVE FROM YOUR BOUNTY TO ME. This is the inner reason WHY MALCHUT is called 'Mishnah' (lit. 'second'), BECAUSE SHE IS SECOND TO ZEIR ANPIN, IN THE SECRET OF THE UNION, as it is written, "a copy of this Torah" (Devarim 17:18).

733. כַּד אִתְמַשְׁכָא לְבַר, אִקְרֵי בָּרַיְיתָא. תְּרֵין יַרְכִין אִינּוּן בָּרַיְיתֵי, רָזָא דְּרָזִין דְּלָא אִתְיְיהִיב לְאִתְגַּלָּאָה. בְּגִין דְּלָא אִתְמְסַר רָזָא בַּר לְחַכִּימֵי עֶלְיוֹנִין. וַוי אִי אִתְגְּלֵי, וַוי אִי לָא אִתְגְּלֵי, בְּגִין דְּאִיהוּ רָזָא מֵרָזִין עִלָּאִין דקוּדְשָׁא בְּרִיךְ הוּא אַנְהִיג בֵּיהּ עָלְמָא.

733. When she is drawn outside, she is called 'Baraitha', WHICH MEANS EXTERNAL. The two thighs are Baraithas, NAMELY, EXTERNALS. This mystery of mysteries is not to be revealed, because the secret is passed solely to most high wise men. Woe if it is revealed, BECAUSE THE WICKED WILL EXPLOIT IT, and woe if it is not revealed, BECAUSE THE RIGHTEOUS WILL LOSE IT, for this is one of the highest secrets, with which the Holy One, blessed be He leads the world.

734. בַּיִת רִאשׁוֹן קַיְימָא בִּימֵי שְׁלֹמֹה, לָקֳבֵל עָלְמָא עִלָּאָה, וְאִיהוּ אִקְרֵי בַּיִת רִאשׁוֹן, וְאִשְׁתַּמַּשׁ כֹּלָּא בְּבֵית קֹדֶשׁ הַקֳּדָשִׁים, אֲתָר דְּאִשְׁתַּמֵּשׁ בֵּיהּ שִׁמְשָׁא בְּסִיהֲרָא. וְרָזִין עִלָּאִין כֻּלְּהוּ בִּשְׁלִימוּ, וְקַיְימָא עָלְמָא בְּאַשְׁלְמוּתָא. וּלְבָתַר גָּרְמוּ חוֹבִין, וְאִתְמְשָׁכוּ רָזִין, וְאִתְדַּחְיָין מִבֵּית קֹדֶשׁ הַקֳּדָשִׁים לְבַר. כַּד אִתְדָּחוּ לְיַרְכִין, כְּדֵין קַיְימוּ לְבַר, דְּאִקְרוּן בָּתֵּי בָּרָאי, וְאִצְטְרִיכוּ לְבַרְיָיתֵי.

734. The first Temple stood at the time of Solomon, and corresponded to the Supernal World, WHICH IS BINAH, AND BINAH is called 'the first Temple'. Everything came together in the Holy of Holies, where the sun is united with the moon, NAMELY, ZEIR ANPIN WITH MALCHUT. The supernal secrets were all in perfection, and the world was perfected. Afterwards, because of transgressions, the mysteries were drawn out of and rejected from the Holy of Holies. Once they were rejected towards the thighs, NETZACH AND HOD, they stood outside, and were called 'external chambers', and the Baraithas were needed FOR PEOPLE COULD NOT NOURISH FROM THE MISHNAH.

735. בַּיִת שֵׁנִי קַיְימוּ בְּבָתֵּי בָּרָאי בְּיַרְכִין, וּמִנַּיְיהוּ אָהַדְרוּ וְשָׁאֲרוּ בְּבֵית קֹדֶשׁ הַקֳּדָשִׁים וְאִיהוּ בַּיִת שֵׁנִי. וְאִינּוּן אַחֲרָנִין אִשְׁתָּאֲרוּ בְּבָרַיְיתָא לְבַר, בֵּינֵי יַרְכִין. וַהֲווּ אוּלְפִין מִמַּתְנִיתִין, וְאִתְנְהִיגוּ מִינָּהּ, וְהַיְינוּ רָזָא דִּכְתִּיב, כִּי מִצִּיּוֹן תֵּצֵא תוֹרָה.

735. At the time of the second Temple, YISRAEL were at the external chambers in the thighs. Some of them returned to sing in the Holy of Holies, of the second Temple, MALCHUT, FOR THE FIRST TEMPLE IS BINAH. Others stayed in the Baraitha outside, between the thighs. THOSE WHO

RETURNED TO THE HOLY OF HOLIES, studied the Mishnah, and behaved according to its laws, NAMELY, ACCORDING TO THE TEACHING OF THE MISHNAH. This is the secret of the verse, "for out of Zion shall go forth Torah" (Yeshayah 2:3), ZION BEING THE INTERNAL PART OF MALCHUT, CALLED 'MISHNAH'.

736. וּלְבָתַר כַּד גָּרְמוּ חוֹבִין, אִתְעֲדֵי שׁוּלְטָנוּתָא דְּהַאי בַּיִת שֵׁנִי, ואע״ג דְּשׁוּלְטָנָא דִּילֵיהּ לָא הֲוָה כְּבַיִת רִאשׁוֹן, דַּהֲוָה בֵּיהּ שְׁלָמָא תָּדִיר, בְּגִין דְּמַלְכָּא דִּשְׁלָמָא דִּילֵיהּ תָּדִיר הֲוָה בְּגַוֵּויהּ, וע״ד הֲוָה בִּשְׁלָם. בַּיִת שֵׁנִי לָא הֲוָה בֵּיהּ שְׁלָם הָכִי, בְּגִין דְּעָרְלָה קִטְרוּגָא בֵּיהּ תָּדִיר, וע״ד הֲווֹ כַּהֲנֵי זְמִינִין בְּגַוֵּיהּ, לְקַטְרְגָא בְּהַאי עָרְלָה, וּלְהוּ אִצְטְרִיךְ מִלָּה, לְקַטְרְגָא בַּהֲדָהּ, וּלְאַגָּנָא עַל בַּיִת שֵׁנִי. וְכֹלָּא בְּרָזָא כַּדְקָא חֲזֵי.

736. Afterwards, because of transgressions, the second Temple was no more in ascendancy. It did not have the power of the first Temple, in which time there was always peace, because the King, who has peace, ZEIR ANPIN, was always in it, IN A NEVER ENDING UNION, and therefore there was peace. There was no such peace at the time of the second Temple, because the foreskin always brought accusations, and the priests were in readiness to denounce, NAMELY, TO CONDEMN this foreskin. And they needed that, in order to condemn through it THE OTHER SIDE, in order to protect the second Temple. All was in that secret properly.

737. לְבָתַר גָּרְמוּ חוֹבִין, וְשַׁלְטָא הַהִיא עָרְלָה, וְאִתְדַּחְיָין מִבַּיִת שֵׁנִי לְבַר, וְנַחְתּוּ מִתַּמָּן לְחַמּוּקֵי יַרְכִין, לְתַתָּא, עַד דִּי שָׁרוֹן לְתַתָּא בְּרַגְלִין. וְכַד יִתְבוּן בְּרַגְלִין, כְּדֵין, וְעָמְדוּ רַגְלָיו בַּיּוֹם הַהוּא, וְעָלְמָא בְּכֹלָּא יִתְנְהִיג בְּרָזָא עִלָּאָה כַּדְקָא חֲזֵי. וְאַף ע״ג דְּאִתְדַּחוּ וְלָא אִשְׁתְּבָקוּ מִנֵּיהּ, וּלְעָלְמִין אִתְאֲחִידוּ בֵּיהּ.

737. Due to more transgression, the foreskin came to power, and YISRAEL were driven out of the second Temple, and descended into the rounded thighs, NETZACH AND HOD, and down, THROUGH BRIYAH until they came to dwell at the feet, IN ASIYAH. When they sat at the feet, NAMELY, SO THEY

SHOULD CORRECT THEM, then "And His feet shall stand in that day..." (Zecharyah 14:4). And the world will behave in all matters according to the high mystery, as it should. And though they were rejected FROM THE INTERNAL PART, they were never left by it, and forever they will cling to it.

738. וּמַאן דְּיָדַע וּמָדִיד בְּשִׁיעוּרָא דְּקַו הַמִּדָּה, אַרְכָּא דִּמְשִׁיכוּ דְּיַרְכִּין עַד רַגְלִין, יָכִיל לְמִנְדַּע מְשִׁיחָא דְּגָלוּתָא דְּאִתְמְשַׁךְ. וְרָזָא אִיהוּ בֵּין מְחַצְּדֵי חַקְלָא, וְכֹלָּא בְּרָזָא עִלָּאָה. וּבְגִין דָּא, כֻּלְּהוּ בָּרַיְיתֵי, וְכֻלְּהוּ תָּנָאֵי, וְכֻלְּהוּ אָמוֹרָאֵי, קַיְימֵי בְּדוּכְתַּיְיהוּ כַּדְקָא חֲזֵי, אִלֵּין לְגוֹ, וְאִלֵּין לְבַר, בְּאִינּוּן חַמּוּקֵי יַרְכִין וּלְתַתָּא מִבָּרְכִין. וּבְכֻלְּהוּ אִקְרֵי תּוֹרָה שבע"פ. וּבְכֻלְּהוּ נַחְתֵּי יִשְׂרָאֵל וְאִתְגָּלוּ.

738. Whoever knows how to measure, by the measuring line, the distance between the thighs and the feet, may know the duration of the exile. This is a secret among the reapers of the field. All this is a high mystery. For that reason all the Baraithas, all the Tannaim and the Amoraim are in their proper places, the ones inside, and the others outside in the rounded thighs, WHICH ARE NETZACH AND HOD, and underneath the thighs. MALCHUT is called by all these, the Oral Law. Yisrael descended by them and were exiled AMONG THE NATIONS.

739 וּכְדֵין כַּד יִסְתַּיֵּים גָּלוּתָא, בִּמְשִׁיכוּ דְּרַגְלִין, כְּדֵין וְעָמְדוּ רַגְלָיו בַּיּוֹם הַהוּא, וְיִתְעֲבַר הַהוּא רוּחָא מְסַאֲבָא עָרְלָה מִן עָלְמָא, וְיִתְהַדְרוּן יִשְׂרָאֵל בִּלְחוֹדַיְיהוּ לְשַׁלְטָאָה כַּדְקָא יֵאוֹת, בְּגִין דְּהַהוּא עָרְלָה, נָחִית לוֹן לְתַתָּא, עַד הַשְׁתָּא. וּמִכָּאן וּלְהָלְאָה, דְּהַאי עָרְלָה אִתְקְצָץ וְאִתְעֲבָר מִגּוֹ עָלְמָא, כְּדֵין וַיִּשְׁכּוֹן יִשְׂרָאֵל בֶּטַח בָּדָד עֵין יַעֲקֹב. בְּהַהוּא עֵין יַעֲקֹב, וְלָא אִשְׁתְּכַח מְקַטְרְגָא עֲלַיְיהוּ. זַכָּאָה חוּלָקֵיהוֹן דְּיִשְׂרָאֵל בְּעָלְמָא דֵּין בְּעָלְמָא דְּאָתֵי.

739. Then, when exile will be over by stretching the feet, SO THEY WILL BE CORRECTED, then "His feet shall stand in that day" and the spirit of defilement, named foreskin, shall be removed from the world. And Yisrael alone shall rule, as ought. Because the foreskin drew them down until then, and from now on, after the foreskin shall be cut and removed from the world, "Yisrael then shall dwell in safety alone; the fountain (also: 'eyes') of Jacob" (Devarim 33:28), NAMELY, in the fountain of Jacob WHICH IS MALCHUT, WHERE CHOCHMAH DWELLS, CALLED 'EYES', and there will be no accuser to prosecute them. Happy is the portion of Yisrael in this world and in the World to Come.

740. יוֹסֵף הַצַּדִּיק, עַמּוּדָא דְּעָלְמָא, אִיהוּ נָטִיל בִּרְשׁוּתָא הֵיכָלָא טָמִיר וְגָנִיז, וּבִרְשׁוּתֵיהּ קַיְּימָא הֵיכָלָא שְׁבִיעָאָה. ואע״ג דְּקָא אַמָרָן דְּהֵיכָלָא דִּלְבְנַת הַסַּפִּיר בִּרְשׁוּתֵיהּ קַיְּימָא, הָכִי הוּא דְּבֵיהּ מִתְתָּקַן. אֲבָל ת״ח, נְבִיאִים דְּקָא אַמָרָן. כַּד מִתְחַבְּרֵי לְתַתָּא, תְּרֵין דַּרְגִּין מִתְפָּרְשִׁין מִנַּיְיהוּ, מַרְאֶה וַחֲלוֹם, וְקַיְימֵי בְּיַרְכִין. בְּאִינּוּן חַמּוּקִין קַיְימֵי מַרְאֶה, וְההוּא דְּאִקְרֵי נְבוּאָה קְטַנָּה. מִיַּרְכִין וּלְתַתָּא קָאֵים חֲלוֹם, עַד דְּמָאטוּ רַגְלִין בְּרַגְלִין. וְתַמָּן קָאֵים הֵיכָלָא תַּתָּאָה וְאִקְרֵי לִבְנַת הַסַּפִּיר.

740. Joseph the righteous, the pillar of the world, WHICH IS YESOD, took with permission the chamber that was hidden and treasured; the seventh chamber was under his authority. Though we said that the chamber of the sapphire stone was under his authority, and in it he is corrected, nevertheless, Come and see: From the prophets, whom we said to be united below, two grades are divided, vision and dream. They abide at the thighs, WHICH ARE NETZACH AND HOD. By the rounded thighs stands the vision, that which is called 'the little prophecy'. Underneath the thighs stands the dream, AT THE KNEES BELOW THE THIGHS; until feet will touch feet, NAMELY, THE FEET OF ATZILUT WILL BE ONE WITH THE FEET OF BRIYAH, YETZIRAH AND ASIYAH, FOR BRIYAH, YETZIRAH AND ASIYAH WILL RETURN TO BE ATZILUT AND BE UPLIFTED TO PROPHECY AND VISION, and there, BELOW THE THIGHS stands the lower chamber called 'the sapphire stone'.

741. כֹּלָּא יַרְכִין בְּיַרְכִין, לְאִשְׁתַּלְמָא חַד בְּחַד, וְכֻלְּהוּ דַּרְגִּין דִּנְבוּאָה, דְּהָא מִתַּמָּן נַפְקֵי וְשָׁרָאן, וְאִתְעֲבִידוּ מִנַּיְיהוּ מַרְאֶה, וְשָׁרָאן עַל הַאי אֲתָר, וְאִתְעֲבִיד מִנַּיְיהוּ חֲלוֹם. יוֹסֵף הַצַּדִּיק, אִיהוּ שְׁלֵימָא דְּכֹלָּא, אִיהוּ נָטִיל כֹּלָּא. בְּגִין דְּכֹלָּא אִתְקַן בְּגִינֵיהּ, כֹּלָּא תָּאִיב בְּתִיאוּבְתָּא בְּגִינֵיהּ.

741. All THE JOINING TOGETHER of the thighs is in order to perfect them by one with another. All grades of prophecy come out of there to hover, and vision is made of them; then they hover about this place, THE SAPPHIRE STONE, and a dream is made from them. Joseph the Righteous, WHO IS YESOD, is the perfection of all; he receives all. Since everything is corrected through him, they all desire and long for him.

742. תָּא חֲזֵי, בְּשַׁעְתָּא דְּיוֹסֵף הַצַּדִּיק קַיְּימָא לְאַתְקְנָא כֹּלָּא, כְּדֵין אִיהוּ נָטִיל כֹּלָּא. וְכַד אִתְחַבָּר בְּהֵיכָלֵיהּ, כְּדֵין מִתְעָרֵי כֻּלְּהוּ, לְנַטְלָא תִּיאוּבְתָּא וּרְעוּתָא, עִלָּאֵי וְתַתָּאֵי, וְכֹלָּא אִינּוּן בִּרְעוּתָא חֲדָא וּשְׁלִימוּ חַד, לְמֶחְדֵי עִלָּאֵי וְתַתָּאֵי, רְעוּתָא חֲדָא כִּדְקָא יָאוֹת. וְכֻלְּהוּ תַּתָּאֵי קַיְימֵי בְּקִיּוּמָא בְּגִינֵיהּ, וע״ד כְּתִיב, וְצַדִּיק יְסוֹד עוֹלָם. וְעַל הַאי יְסוֹדָא קָאִים הַאי עָלְמָא.

742. At the time when Joseph the Righteous, is ready to correct everything, he receives all, and joins his chamber. Then everybody above and below is awakened to receive the desire and wish, united by one desire and wholeness, that the higher and lower will rejoice by the one desire. All the lower beings are maintained by him. Therefore it is written, "but the righteous is an everlasting foundation" (Mishlei 10:25), for this is the foundation by which the world is sustained.

743. הַאי לִבְנַ״ת הַסַּפִּי״ר, לָא קָאִים בְּקִיּוּמֵיהּ, עַד דְּהַאי יוֹסֵף הַצַּדִּיק. אִתְתַּקָּן. וְכַד אִיהוּ אִתְתַּקָּן, כֹּלָּא מִתְתַּקְּנֵי דָּא הוּא יְסוֹדָא דְּכֻלְּהוּ בִּנְיָינָא. וְעַל דָּא כְּתִיב, וַיִּבֶן יְיָ׳ אֱלֹהִים אֶת הַצֵּלָע, וְלָא כְּתִיב וַיִּיצֶר, וְלָא כְּתִיב וַיִּבְרָא. בְּגִין דְּהַאי קַיְּימָא עַל יְסוֹדָא, וּלְבָתַר דִּיסוֹדָא אִתְקָּן, כֹּלָּא אִתְבְּנֵי עָלֵיהּ. ובג״ד, כֻּלְּהוּ קַיְימִין בְּהַאי, וְהָא אוּקִימְנָא.

743. The chamber of the sapphire stone does not come into existence until Joseph the Righteous, YESOD OF ZEIR ANPIN, is ready. Once he is corrected, everyone else is also corrected. This is the secret of the building, MALCHUT, and about this says the verse, "and of the side, which Hashem Elohim has taken…He built" (Beresheet 2:22). It is not written, 'and He created,' nor 'formed', BUT "BUILT," because it stands upon Yesod, and once the foundation is prepared, everything is built upon it. THEREFORE IT IS WRITTEN, "AND… HE BUILT." Thus everything is sustained BY YESOD, as we already explained.

744. ת״ח, כְּתִיב וַיִּבֶן יְיָ׳ אֱלֹהִים אֶת הַצֵּלָע, דַּהֲוַת מִסִּטְרָא דְּאֲחוֹרָא, וְאִתְקִין לָהּ לְאַהֲדְרָא אַנְפִּין בְּאַנְפִּין. הָכִי אוֹקִימְנָא. אֲבָל וַיִּבֶן, אִסְתָּכַּל לְסַלְּקָא לָהּ בְּהַהוּא דַּרְגָּא דְּעָלְמָא עִלָּאָה שַׁרְיָא בֵּיהּ, לְמֶהֱוֵי דָּא כְּגַוְונָא דְּדָא.

744. Come and see: It is written, "and of the side, which Hashem Elohim has taken…He built." THIS MEANS THAT MALCHUT was at the back side OF ZEIR ANPIN, and He put it so she will again be face to face WITH ZEIR ANPIN. This is how we explained it. Also, "He built" means that He kept it in mind to raise her to the same grade, where the Supernal World dwells, WHICH IS BINAH, so they will be alike.

745. תּוּ וַיִּבֶן, אִסְתָּכַּל בְּסִטְרוֹי, וְאִתְקִין וְכַוִּין כָּל רוּחוֹתֶיהָ, לְמִזְרַע וּלְאַשְׁקָאָה וּלְאוֹלְדָא, לְמֶעְבַּד לָהּ כָּל צָרְכוֹי, כְּמָה דְּאִצְטְרִיךְ. וּלְבָתַר וַיְבִיאֶהָ, בְּמָּה. בְּהַאי צַדִּיק. דִּכְתִּיב, וּבָזֶה הַנַּעֲרָה בָּאָה אֶל הַמֶּלֶךְ, דְּהַאי אַמְשִׁיךְ לְכֹלָּא, לְסַלְּקָא לְאִתְעַטְּרָא בִּשְׁלִימוּ. הָכָא מְנִיעוּ דְּכָל חוֹבִין, הָכָא מְנִיעוּ דְּכָל תִּיאוּבְתִּין בִּישִׁין.

745. We should explain more that "He built" means that THE EMANATOR looked to His sides and He made and directed the sides OF MALCHUT, so they would sow, and water, and beget offspring, and supply her with all her needs, as it ought to be. Then He "brought her" (Ibid.). HE ASKS: How DID HE BRING HER? AND HE ANSWERS: By this Righteous, NAMELY, YESOD, as it is written, "by this (REFERRING TO YESOD CALLED 'ZEH' – THIS) the girl would come to the king" (Ester 2:13). For He conducts everything, so it would rise, and be bedecked to perfection. From here comes THE STRENGTH TO prevent sins, from here comes the STRENGTH OF prevention of all unholy desires.

746. מַה דְּלָא אִיהוּ בְּהַהוּא הֵיכָלָא שְׁתִיתָאָה, בְּסִטְרָא אַחֲרָא, דְּתַמָּן כָּל עִנּוּגִין בִּישִׁין, וְכָל סִטְרִין דְּתִיאוּבְתִּין דְּעִנּוּגָא דְּהַאי עָלְמָא, וְכַד הַאי עָלְמָא אִתְנְהִיג בְּהוּ, בְּנֵי נָשָׁא כַּשְׁלֵי בְּהוּ לְהַהוּא עָלְמָא. דְּחָמָאן כַּמָּה עִנּוּגִין וְתִיאוּבְתִּין, דְּגוּפָא אִתְהֲנֵי וְאִתְעֲנִיג מִנַּיְיהוּ, וְטָעְיָין

אֲבַתְרַיְיהוּ. הֲדָא ה״ד, וַתֵּרֶא הָאִשָּׁה כִּי טוֹב הָעֵץ לְמַאֲכָל וְגוֹ׳. דְּהָא כָּל תִּיאוּבְתִּין וְכָל עִנּוּגִין דְּעָלְמָא בֵּיהּ תַּלְיָין.

746. This is not so at the sixth chamber of the Other Side, where are found all the wicked pleasures and all kinds of inclinations towards the pleasures of this world. When this world is led by them, people fail to merit the World to Come, for they see the pleasures and desires the body takes delight in, and go whoring after them. This is as it is written, "the woman saw that the tree was good for food" (Beresheet 3:6), as all the desires and the pleasures of the world depend on it.

747. וע״ד, כְּגַוְונָא דָּא, אִית מִלִּין דְּגוּפָא אִתְהֲנֵי בְּהוּ, וְעַיְילֵי לְגוּפָא, וְלָא לְנִשְׁמְתָא. וְאִית מִלִּין דְּנִשְׁמְתָא אִתְהֲנֵי מִנַּיְיהוּ, וְלָא גוּפָא. וְעַל דָּא, דַּרְגִּין פְּרִישִׁין דָּא מִן דָּא. זַכָּאִין אִינּוּן צַדִּיקַיָּיא, דְּנַטְלֵי אוֹרַח מֵישָׁר, וּמַנְעֵי גַּרְמַיְיהוּ מֵהַהוּא סִטְרָא, וּמִתְדַּבְּקָן בְּסִטְרָא דִּקְדוּשָּׁה.

747. In the same manner, there are things the body delights in. They enter the body and not the soul. Some things the soul delights in, and not the body. Therefore, the grades are different from each other. Happy are the righteous who take the path of truth and keep themselves from that side, and cleave to the side of holiness.

748. בְּהֵיכָלָא דָּא, כְּלִילָן כָּל שְׁאַר שְׁמָהָן, דְּכָל אִלֵּין הֵיכָלִין דִּלְתַתָּא. תְּרֵי שְׁמָהָן אִינּוּן דִּכְלִילוּ שְׁאַר שְׁמָהָן אַחֲרָנִין. חַד דְּכַד אִתְחַבַּר עֵילָּא בְּתַתָּא, וְיַעֲקֹב נָטִיל הֵיכָלֵיהּ, בְּאִינּוּן נְשִׁיקִין, בְּרָזָא עִלָּאָה. כְּדֵין כָּלִיל כָּל שְׁאַר שְׁמָהָן, וְאִקְרֵי יְהוָ״ה אֱלֹהִי״ם, וְדָא אִקְרֵי שֵׁם מָלֵא, כְּמָה דְּאוּקִימְנָא. וְחַד, כַּד אִתְחַבַּר יְסוֹדָא דְּעָלְמָא בְּהֵיכָלֵיהּ, וְכֻלְּהוּ מִתְעָרֵי בַּחֲבִיבוּתָא וּבְתִּיאוּבְתָּא לְגַבֵּיהּ, וְכֻלְּהוּ כְּלִילָן בֵּיהּ, כְּדֵין כָּלִיל שְׁאַר שְׁמָהָן, וְאִקְרֵי יְהוָ״ה צְבָאוֹת. וְדָא אִקְרֵי שְׁמָא קַדִּישָׁא שְׁלִים, וְלָאו אִיהוּ שְׁלִים כְּהַאי אַחֲרָא.

748. In this chamber all the rest of the souls in the other chambers below are included. There are two names, which include the rest of the names. One of them, when the upper is joined with the lower, and Jacob receives his chamber through the kissing, in the upper secret, includes then all the other names and is called 'Yud Hei Vav Hei' Elohim. This is considered a full name, as we established. The other, when the foundation of the world, JOSEPH, joins its chamber, all are aroused with love and passion for it, and are included in it. Then it includes all other names and is called 'Yud Hei Vav Hei Tzevaot'. It is considered the whole Holy Name, but not whole as the other, YUD HEI VAV HEI ELOHIM.

749. מַה בֵּין הַאי לְהַאי. דָּא שַׁלִּיט עִלָּאָה בְּתַתָּאָה, גּוּפָא בְּגוּפָא כִּדְקָאמְרָן. וְדָא שַׁלִּיט מֵאֲתַר דְּסִיּוּמָא דְגוּפָא וּלְתַתָּא, בְּאִינּוּן הֵיכָלִין וּבְכֹלָּא דִלְתַתָּא, וְרָזָא דָּא, בַּיִת רִאשׁוֹן וּבַיִת שֵׁנִי. ובג״ד, הֵיכָלָא דָּא כָּלִיל כָּל שְׁאַר שְׁמָהָן דִּלְתַתָּא, כְּמָה דְּאוּקִימְנָא. וע״ד, שְׁמָהָן אִלֵּין, דָּא סַלְקָא וְדָא נָחִית. זַכָּאִין אִינּוּן צַדִּיקַיָּיא, דְּיַדְעִין אָרְחוֹי דְּאוֹרַיְיתָא.

749. HE ASKS: What is the difference between them, BETWEEN JACOB AND JOSEPH? AND HE ANSWERS: The one, JACOB, WHO IS TIFERET CALLED 'BODY', the upper rules over the lower, body over body, AS TIFERET OF ATZILUT RULES OVER TIFERET OF THE CHAMBERS. BOTH ARE CONSIDERED THE PART OF THE BODY FROM THE CHEST UPWARD, BOTH ARE ASPECTS OF JACOB, as we said. And the other, JOSEPH, YESOD OF ATZILUT, rules from the final part of the body OF THE CHAMBERS, and downward, NAMELY, THEIR YESOD, THE CHAMBER OF THE SAPPHIRE STONE, and all that is underneath. This is the secret of the first Temple and the second Temple, THE FIRST CHAMBER IS THE SECRET OF MATING OF TIFERET AND MALCHUT FROM THE CHEST UP, AND THE SECOND CHAMBER IS THE SECRET OF MATING OF TIFERET AND MALCHUT FROM THE CHEST DOWN, THE ASPECT OF YESOD AND MALCHUT. For that reason, this chamber includes all the rest of the names below, as we explained. Therefore, these names, one goes up and the other goes down. THE LOWER GOES UP TO THE UPPER, AND THE UPPER DESCENDS TO THE LOWER. Happy are the righteous who know the ways of the Torah.

750. יְסוֹדָא דָּא, אִתְתַּקַּן לִתְרֵין סִטְרִין. חַד, לְאַתְקְנָא כָּל שְׁאַר דִּלְתַתָּא. וְחַד, לְאַתְקְנָא הֵיכָלָא שְׁבִיעָאָה, וּלְאַתְקְנָא דָּא בְּדָא, לְמֶהֱוֵי כֹּלָּא רְעוּ חֲדָא כַּדְקָא יֵאוֹת. עַד הָכָא יְחוּדָא דִּתְרֵין סִטְרִין, דִּלְעֵילָּא

וְתַתָּא, לְאִתְיַיחֲדָא כַּחֲדָא בִּשְׁלִימוּ, לְמֵיהַךְ בְּאֹרַח מֵישָׁר.

750. Yesod is corrected on two sides, the one IN THE FIRST CHAMBER, in order to fix whatever is down below, and the other to correct the seventh chamber, so all will be corrected by each other, and become one proper desire. So far the unison of both sides, one above and one below, to be united to perfection, so as to walk the way of truth.

751. זַכָּאָה חוּלָקֵיהּ, מַאן דְּיָדַע לְיַחֲדָא יִחוּדָא, וּלְסַדּוּרֵי סִדּוּרָא דִּמְהֵימְנוּתָא, לְמֵיהַךְ בְּאֹרַח מֵישָׁר. זַכָּאָה אִיהוּ בְּהַאי עָלְמָא, וּבְעָלְמָא דְּאָתֵי. וע״ד כְּתִיב, חֶסֶד וֶאֱמֶת נִפְגָּשׁוּ צֶדֶק וְשָׁלוֹם נָשָׁקוּ. וּכְדֵין אֱמֶת מֵאֶרֶץ תִּצְמָח וְצֶדֶק מִשָּׁמַיִם נִשְׁקָף. גַּם יְיָ׳ יִתֵּן הַטּוֹב וְאַרְצֵנוּ תִּתֵּן יְבוּלָהּ.

751. Happy is the portion of whoever knows how to create the unison and arrange the order of the Faith, to walk the right path. Happy is he in this world and in the World to Come. Of this says the verse, "Love and truth are met together; righteousness and peace have kissed each other," then "Truth will spring out of the earth and righteousness will look down from heaven. Hashem moreover shall give that which is good, and our land shall yield its produce" (Tehilim 85:11-13).

52. The chamber of the Holy of Holies

A Synopsis

Rabbi Shimon says that the seventh chamber is the innermost chamber where the secret of all secrets is hidden. The spirit of life from Binah is found in this chamber, the desire to unite everything. The chamber is called 'the house of the Holy of Holies', a place for the supernal soul, Binah, through which the World to Come will awaken. We learn that 'world' means ascent, the ascension of the lower world to the upper world, meaning the ascension of Malchut and the chambers to hide within the supernal hiding place. The 'Supernal World' means the ascension of Binah to disappear within the supreme desire that is completely unknowable, Arich Anpin. Rabbi Shimon shows us how the innermost secret of the Ark is like the seventh chamber. The chamber receives all the spirits who are about to descend into the world before they have received their bodies, and it receives them again when they are finished with the world. The spirits wait in this chamber until the time when Messiah will come and the world will rejoice like it did before the sin of the Tree of Knowledge. This seventh chamber is the chamber of passion, the chamber of delight, the chamber of pleasure above and below. All the souls here receive the light of Binah; therefore it is more hidden and more treasured than the rest of the chambers. Rabbi Shimon says that this chamber is called 'the Ark of the Covenant', and explains that it receives the souls from the first chamber where they are united, male with female and female with male. He talks about Jacob and Joseph, saying that the Ark of the Covenant took the spirit of life above from Jacob and that from Joseph it took spirits and souls to pour the life into. Jacob sustains the angels above, and Joseph sustains the human souls below, but both are in Zeir Anpin. When the priest sends up the offering to cause union through desire and through song, then the highest soul of all, Binah of Atzilut, wakes and enters into all the chambers and shines on them all. The higher light, the soul, is united with the hidden light, Eve – and this hidden light is included in the light that is even more hidden, Arich Anpin. Rabbi Shimon explains how Moses knew when to pray at length and when to pray briefly. Whoever prays at length will have a longer life, and yet whoever prays at length when he should be brief will have heartache. We are told that within the seventh chamber there is a hidden point, a spirit that receives a supernal male spirit – they enter into each other and become one. Rabbi Shimon warns against those who would graft one species onto another, but says that those who graft one kind onto its own kind have a stake in the World to Come. In this way the left is perfected by the right, the male by the female and everything is derived from the perfection that is called 'the act of the Divine Chariot,' because the Merkabah is achieved by grafting. This is the secret of the verse: "And Hashem Elohim formed man," because the formation of man comes from the Chariot, Yud Hei Vav Hei Elohim that grafted them together. After being completed by one another they were called 'Zeir Anpin and Malchut'. Rabbi Shimon speaks of the four Chariots Michael, Gabriel, Uriel and Raphael and of two spirits called 'the brass mountains'. The discussion turns to: "And they had the hands of a man under their wings," where 'the hands of a man' means places and receptacles that receive men with their prayers, that open gates to let them in, that unite, and that fulfill their wishes. They are also the Holy Names through which men send their prayers and enter the supernal gates. In the chambers the secret of the faith is that all the living creatures and Chariots are different from one another, and when they join together they are better because they include and complement one another. Rabbi Shimon explains the parts of the prayer from 'Who forms' up to Amidah and how the prayer corresponds to the order of the seven chambers. After the prayer one must confess one's sins and transgressions in order to receive the blessings and avoid the accusations of the Other Side. Just as the Other Side takes a portion of the burnt offering, the Other Side takes the confession as his portion of the prayer service. Rabbi Shimon says that in prayer the true path consists of thought, desire, voice and speech, these tie the knots so that the Shechinah can be supported by them. He adds that thought produces desire, desire produces a voice, and the sound that is heard ascends to connect the lower and upper chambers. The sound draws blessings from high above and is secretly supported by the pillars of thought, desire, voice and speech. He concludes by saying that this description of the seventh chamber is the last of the chambers on the side of holiness.

752. הֵיכָלָא שְׁבִיעָאָה. הֵיכָלָא דָּא, הֵיכָלָא פְּנִימָאָה מִכָּל הָנֵי הֵיכָלִין. הַאי הֵיכָלָא אִיהוּ סְתִימוּ, דְּלָאו בֵּיהּ דְּיוּקְנָא מַמָּשׁ, וְלֵית גּוּפָא כְּלַל. הָכָא סְתִימוּ דְּגוֹ רָזָא דְּרָזִין, הַאי אִיהוּ רָזָא, דְּאִיהוּ אֲתָר, לְאַעֲלָא תַּמָּן בְּגוֹ אִינּוּן צִנּוֹרִין דִּלְעֵילָּא. רוּחָא דְּכָל רוּחִין, רַעֲוָון דְּכָל רַעֲוִין, לְאִתְחַבְּרָא כֹּלָּא כַּחֲדָא. רוּחָא דְּחַיֵּי בְּהַאי, לְמֶהֱוֵי כֹּלָּא תִּקּוּנָא חֲדָא.

752. The seventh chamber is the innermost chamber. It is concealed, has no substantial form, and no body at all, IT IS CONSIDERED TO HAVE A HEAD

ONLY. Here the secret of all secrets is hidden. It is a secret, a place where all the upper channels, FROM ATZILUT, are gathered. HERE lies the spirit which comprises all the spirits OF ALL THE CHAMBERS, a will, which includes every will, to unite all the chambers as one. The spirit of life FROM BINAH is in this chamber, so that all will be one correction.

753. הֵיכָלָא דָא, אִקְרֵי בֵּית קֹדֶשׁ הַקֳּדָשִׁים. אֲתָר לְקַבְּלָא הַאי נִשְׁמְתָא עִלָּאָה, דְּאִקְרֵי הָכִי, לְאִתְעֲרָא עָלְמָא דְּאָתֵי לְגַבֵּיהּ.

753. This chamber is called 'the house of the Holy of Holies', a place to receive the supernal soul, BINAH, which is so called so as to awaken in it the World to Come, WHICH IS BINAH.

754. הַאי עָלְמָא עוֹלָם אִקְרֵי. עוֹלָם: סְלִיקָא, דְּסָלִיק עָלְמָא תַּתָּאָה לְגַבֵּי עָלְמָא עִלָּאָה, וְאִסְתַּתַּר בְּגַוֵּוהּ, וְאִתְעַלָּם בֵּיהּ, אִתְגַּלְיָיא בִּסְתִּירָה. עוֹלָם: דְּסָלִיק אִיהוּ, בְּכָל אִינּוּן דְּקָרְבִין בֵּיהּ, וְאִסְתַּתְּרָן גּוֹ סְתִירוּ עִלָּאָה. עוֹלָם עִלָּאָה: סָלִיק וְאִסְתַּתַּר בִּרְעוּתָא עִלָּאָה, גּוֹ טְמִירוּ דְּכָל טְמִירִין דְּלָא אִתְיְידַע כְּלַל, וְלָא אִתְגְּלֵי, וְלֵית מַאן דְּיָדַע לֵיהּ.

754. This world WHICH IS MALCHUT is named World. World MEANS ascent, the ascension of the lower world, WHICH IS MALCHUT, to the upper world, WHICH IS BINAH, in which she hides and disappears, only to be revealed in secret. World MEANS the ascension OF MALCHUT with all her familiars, NAMELY, THE CHAMBERS, to hide within the supernal hiding place, BINAH. The Supernal World, WHICH IS CALLED 'BINAH', MEANS the ascension OF BINAH to disappear within the supreme will, the most hidden of all, that is never known, nor revealed, and there is no one to know it, ARICH ANPIN.

755. פָּרוֹכְתָּא דְּפַרְסָא פְּרִיסָא, חַפְיָא גּוֹ טְמִירוּ סָתִים. כַּפּוֹרְתָא פְּרִיסָא גּוֹ טְמִירִין עִלָּאִין, לְאַסְתְּמָא סְתִימִין דְּהָא טְמִירִין וּסְתִימִין.

755. The curtain is a veil BETWEEN THE SIXTH CHAMBER, HOLY, AND THE SEVENTH CHAMBER, THE HOLY OF HOLIES, that is spread to cover and hide what is hidden, THE SEVENTH CHAMBER. The cover of the Ark is spread with high secrets UPON THE ARK OF THE TESTIMONY WITHIN THE HOLY OF HOLIES, THE SECRET OF YESOD OF MALCHUT OF ATZILUT, WRAPPED BY THE SEVENTH CHAMBER, in order to hide that which are not revealed IN THE INNER PART OF THE ARK OF THE TESTIMONY, because they are hidden and unrevealed.

756. לְגוֹ מִן כַּפּוֹרְתָּא, אִית אֲתַר סָתִים וְטָמִיר וְגָנִיז, לְאַכְנָשָׁא לֵיהּ בְּגַוֵּיהּ. מְשַׁח רְבוּת עִלָּאָה, רוּחָא דְּחַיֵּי, עַל יְדָא דְּהַהוּא נָהָר דְּנָגִיד וְנָפִיק, וְהַהוּא נָהָר אִקְרֵי מַבּוּעָא דְּבֵירָא, דְּלָא פַּסְקִין מֵימוֹי לְעָלְמִין. וְכַד הַאי עָיֵיל וְנָגִיד כָּל הַהוּא רְבוּת קוּדְשָׁא מִלְּעֵילָּא, מֵאֲתַר דקה"ק. נְהִירוּ נְגִידוּ נָחִית וְאָתֵי, גּוֹ אִינּוּן צִנּוֹרִין. הַאי אִתְמַלְיָיא מִתַּמָּן, כְּנוּקְבָא דְּמִתְעַבְּרָא וְאִתְמַלְיָא מִן דְּכוּרָא. אוּף הָכִי נָמֵי הַאי הֵיכָלָא, מִתְתַּקְנָא תָּדִיר לְקַבְּלָא, כְּנוּקְבָא דִּמְקַבְּלָא מִן דְּכוּרָא. קַבִּילוּ דְּקַבִּילוּ, כָּל אִינּוּן רוּחִין וְנִשְׁמָתִין קַדִּישִׁין דְּנַחְתִּין לְעָלְמָא, וְאִתְעַכְּבוּ תַּמָּן. כָּל הַהוּא זִמְנָא דְּאִצְטְרִיךְ.

756. Inside the cover, THE SECRET OF THE ARK, there is a place that is hidden, concealed and stored, where the supreme anointing oil is gathered, the spirit of life, by the river that flows and goes out FROM EDEN, YESOD OF ZEIR ANPIN OF ATZILUT. This river is called 'the spring of the well', MALCHUT, whose water never stops flowing. And when YESOD brings and draws in the holy anointing oil from the Holy of Holies above, WHICH IS BINAH OF ATZILUT, then illumination is drawn and comes into the channels OF YESOD OF MALCHUT OF ATZILUT. And MALCHUT OF ATZILUT is filled from there, as a female conceives and is filled by the male. So the SEVENTH chamber is prepared to receive THE LIGHTS OF YESOD OF ZEIR ANPIN OF ATZILUT THROUGH MALCHUT OF ATZILUT THAT IT DONS, as a female receives from the male. It receives all the spirits and holy souls who descend into the world, TO BE CLOTHED IN PEOPLE, they are detained there for as long as is necessary, NAMELY, UNTIL THEY DESCEND TO BE DRESSED IN PEOPLE. SIMILARLY, AFTER DEPARTING FROM THIS WORLD, THEY RETURN TO THE SEVENTH CHAMBER.

757. יִתְעַכְּבוּן עַד דְּיֵיתֵי מַלְכָּא מְשִׁיחָא, וְיִסְתַּפְּקוּן כָּל אִינּוּן נִשְׁמָתִין,

וְיֵיתוּן וְיַחְדֵי עָלְמָא כְּמִלְּקַדְמִין. וּכְדֵין, יַחְדֵי קוּדְשָׁא בְּרִיךְ הוּא כְּמִלְּקַדְמִין, כד"א יִשְׂמַח יְיָ' בְּמַעֲשָׂיו.

757. They wait IN THE SEVENTH CHAMBER until King Messiah will come, and all the souls will be satisfied, AND COME TO THEIR PLACE IN ATZILUT, and the world will rejoice as before THE DIMINUTION OF THE MOON, AND THE SIN OF THE TREE OF KNOWLEDGE OF GOOD AND EVIL, as it is written, "let Hashem rejoice in His works" (Tehilim 104:31).

758. בְּהַאי הֵיכָלָא, קַיְימִין עִנּוּגִין וְתַפְנוּקִין דְּרוּחֵי, וְאִשְׁתַּעְשְׁעוּתָא דְּאִשְׁתַּעֲשָׁע קוּדְשָׁא בְּרִיךְ הוּא בְּגִנְתָּא דְּעֵדֶן. הָכָא אִיהוּ תִּיאוּבְתָּא דְּכֹלָּא, וְעִנּוּגָא דְּכֹלָּא, לְאִתְחַבְּרָא כֹּלָּא כַּחֲדָא, וּלְמֶהֱוֵי כֹּלָּא חַד, קִשּׁוּרָא דְּכֹלָּא בְּיִחוּדָא חֲדָא הָכָא קַיְימָא.

758. In this chamber are the delights and enjoyments of the spirits, and the pleasure that the Holy One, blessed be He is delighted with in the Garden of Eden. Here lies the desire of all, the delight of all, to unite all the chambers as one, and turn them all into one. Here lies the bond of all in one unity.

759. דְּכַד שַׁיְיפֵי כֻּלְּהוּ מִתְחַבְּרָאן בְּשַׁיְיפִין עִלָּאִין, כָּל חַד וְחַד כַּדְקָא חֲזֵי לֵיהּ, לֵית לוֹן תִּיאוּבְתָּא, וְלֵית לוֹן עִנּוּגָא, בַּר בְּיִחוּדָא דְּהַאי הֵיכָלָא, כֹּלָּא הָכָא תַּלְיָא. כַּד אִתְחַבְּרוּתָא דְּהָכָא אִתְיְיחָד בְּיִחוּדָא חֲדָא, כְּדֵין כָּל נְהִירוּ דְּשַׁיְיפִין, וְכָל נְהִירוּ דְּאַנְפִּין, וְכָל חֶדְוָון, כֻּלְּהוּ נְהִירִין וְחַדָאן.

759. When all the organs, ALL THE ASPECTS OF THE CHAMBERS, join the higher organs OF THE SEVENTH CHAMBER, each according to its worth, they have no passion, no pleasure, only that of being united in that chamber. Everything depends upon this place. And when the joining here becomes a union, all the illuminations in the organs and the illumination in the face, and all the joys, shine and rejoice.

760. זַכָּאָה חוּלָקֵיהּ, מַאן דְּיָדַע לְסַדְּרָא סִדּוּרִין, וּלְאַתְקְנָא תִּקּוּנֵי אִשְׁתַּלְמוּתָא כַּדְקָא יֵאוּת, רְחִימוּ דְקוּדְשָׁא בְּרִיךְ הוּא בְּהַאי עָלְמָא,

וּבְעָלְמָא דְּאָתֵי. וּכְדֵין, כָּל דִּינִין, וְכָל גְּזָרִין בִּישִׁין, מִתְעַבְּרִין וּמִתְבַּטְּלִין מֵעָלְמָא.

760. Happy is the portion of he who knows how to establish orders, and to properly arrange the corrections of perfection. He is beloved by the Holy One, blessed be He, in this world and in the World to Come. Then all Judgments, accusations, and evil decrees are removed from the world.

761. הֵיכָלָא דָּא, הֵיכָלָא דְּתִיאוּבְתָּא, הֵיכָלָא דְּעִנּוּגָא, הֵיכָלָא לְאִשְׁתַּעְשְׁעָא עֵילָּא וְתַתָּא כַּחֲדָא. וּמְקַבְּלָא כֹּלָּא נְהִירוּ דְּבוּצִינָא עִלָּאָה דְּנָהִיר לְכֹלָּא, וּלְאִתְיַיחֲדָא כֹּלָּא כַּדְקָא יָאוּת. בְּיִחוּדָא שְׁלִים. וְעַל דָּא, הֵיכָלָא דָּא קָאִים בִּטְמִירוּ דְּכֹלָּא, גָּנִיז מִכֹּלָּא. אע״ג דְּכֻלְּהוּ טְמִירִין. דָּא טָמִיר וְגָנִיז יַתִּיר. לְמֶהֱוֵי בְּרִית קַיְימָא כֹּלָּא כַּחֲדָא, דְּכַר וְנוּקְבָּא לְמֶהֱוֵי שְׁלִים.

761. This chamber is the chamber of passion, the chamber of delight, the chamber in which to have pleasure above and below as one. NAMELY, THE HOLY ONE, BLESSED BE HE HAS PLEASURE WITH THE SOULS HERE, AND IN THE LOWER GARDEN OF EDEN, AT THE SAME TIME. All receive the light of the upper light, that shines upon all, NAMELY, THE LIGHT OF BINAH, so that all will be properly united in complete unison. Therefore, this chamber is more hidden, more treasured than the rest. Though all of them are hidden, this one is more so, and more treasured, BECAUSE IT IS THE PLACE OF YESOD, so the sign of the covenant will be as one, male and female, in perfection.

762. הֵיכָל דָּא אִקְרֵי אֲרוֹן הַבְּרִית, דְּאִיהוּ אֲדוֹן כָּל הָאָרֶץ. בְּגִין דְּהַאי אִיהוּ אֲתָר, דְּנַפְקוּ מִנֵּיהּ כָּל נִשְׁמָתִין דְּעָלְמָא, לְיַחֲדָא יִחוּדָא לְתַתָּא, וּלְאַמְשָׁכָא יִחוּדָא דְקוּדְשָׁא בְּרִיךְ הוּא מֵעֵילָּא לְתַתָּא, לְיָהֲבָא לַצַּדִּיק, בְּגִין דְּנַפְקוּ מִצַּדִּיק, וְעַיְילֵי בְּצַדִּיק. וּלְבָתַר נַפְקֵי מִצַּדִּיק, וְעַיְילֵי בַּאֲתָר דְּנַפְקֵי מִתַּמָּן.

762. This chamber is called 'the Ark of the Covenant'. It is the master of all the earth, because it is the place whence all the souls of the world come, to create unity below, and draw the unison of the Holy One, blessed be He from above downward and give it to the righteous, NAMELY, TO THE FIRST CHAMBER WHICH IS YESOD, CALLED 'RIGHTEOUS', since all souls come out of the Righteous, FROM YESOD OF ZEIR ANPIN, and enter the Righteous, THE CHAMBER OF YESOD. Then they come out of the Righteous, THE CHAMBER OF YESOD, TO BE CLOTHED BY PEOPLE. AND AFTER THEIR DEMISE FROM THIS WORLD, they enter where they came from, NAMELY, THE SEVENTH CHAMBER.

763. הַאי אֲרוֹן הַבְּרִית, נָקִיט כֹּלָּא מִצַּדִּיק. וּלְבָתַר, נַפְקֵי מִנֵּיהּ, וְעַיְילֵי בְּצַדִּיק לְתַתָּא. לְבָתַר נַפְקֵי מִצַּדִּיק דִּלְתַתָּא, וְעַיְילֵי בְּהַאי אֲרוֹן הַבְּרִית. לְמֶהֱוֵי כָּל נִשְׁמָתִין כְּלִילָן מֵעֵילָּא וּמִתַּתָּא. לְמֶהֱוֵי שְׁלִים מִכָּל סִטְרִין. וְהַאי אֲרוֹן הַבְּרִית, נָקִיט מִצַּדִּיק אִינּוּן נִשְׁמָתִין, מִתְּרֵין סִטְרִין.

763. HE EXPLAINS HIS WORDS: The Ark of the Covenant IN THE SEVENTH CHAMBER receives everything from the Righteous, YESOD OF ZEIR ANPIN OF ATZILUT. Then they come out of THE ARK OF THE COVENANT, and enter the lower Righteous, THE FIRST CHAMBER WHICH IS YESOD. Afterwards they come out of the lower Righteous TO BE CLOTHED IN PEOPLE, AND AFTER THEIR DEMISE, they enter the Ark of the Covenant IN THE SEVENTH CHAMBER, so all the souls will be included above IN BINAH, THE SEVENTH CHAMBER, and below, YESOD OF THE CHAMBERS, to be whole on all sides. The Ark of the Covenant, WHICH IS THE SEVENTH CHAMBER, receives the souls from the Righteous, THE FIRST CHAMBER, that comprises two sides, MALE AND FEMALE, FOR IN THE FIRST CHAMBER, THE MALE SOULS ARE UNITED WITH THE FEMALE SOULS.

764. ת"ח, מַבּוּעָא דְּבֵירָא לָא מִתְפָּרְשָׁא מִבֵּירָא לְעָלְמִין, וְעַל דָּא, הַאי אֲתָר, שִׁכְלוּלָא דְּכֹלָּא, קִיּוּמָא דְּכָל גּוּפָא, לְמֶהֱוֵי שְׁלִים בְּכֹלָּא כַּדְקָא יֵאוֹת. הָכָא, הוּא יִחוּדָא וְקִשּׁוּרָא כַּחֲדָא, לְמֶהֱוֵי עֵילָּא וְתַתָּא חַד, בְּקִשּׁוּרָא חֲדָא, דְּלָא מִתְפָּרְשָׁן כָּל שַׁיְיפִין דָּא מִן דָּא, וּלְאִשְׁתַּכְּחָא כֹּלָּא אַנְפִּין בְּאַנְפִּין.

764. Come and see: The spring of the well, YESOD, is never separated from the well, WHICH IS MALCHUT OF ATZILUT CLOTHED BY THE SEVENTH

CHAMBER. This place, therefore, is the completion of all, it maintains the body, so as to make everything into one whole, as ought to be. Here, IN THE SEVENTH CHAMBER, is the bond and unity that make everything as one, and high and low are all in one bond, so the organs, THE ASPECTS AND GRADES OF THE CHAMBERS, will not be separated from each other, and so all will be TOGETHER face to face.

765. וְעַל דָּא תָּנֵינָן, מַאן דְּשַׁמִּישׁ עַרְסֵיהּ מֵאַחוֹרָא, אַכְחִישׁ תִּקּוּנָא דְּאִסְתַּכְּלוּתָא אַנְפִּין בְּאַנְפִּין, לְאַנְהָרָא כֹּלָּא כַּחֲדָא, וּלְאִשְׁתַּכְּחָא כֹּלָּא אַנְפִּין בְּאַנְפִּין, בִּדְבֵקוּתָא כַּדְקָא יָאוּת, כְּמָה דְּאַתְּ אָמֵר וְדָבַק בְּאִשְׁתּוֹ, בְּאִשְׁתּוֹ דַּיְיקָא, וְלָא אֲחוֹרֵי אִשְׁתּוֹ.

765. Therefore, we learned that whoever performs his marital duties from the back, rejects the correction of looking face to face, WHICH IS THE CUSTOM OF THE HIGHER ONES, that illuminates everything equally, so all will properly cleave face to face, as it is written, "and cleaves to his wife" (Beresheet 2:24), which evidently refers to his wife, not his wife's back.

766. תְּרֵין אִינּוּן, יַעֲקֹב אִיהוּ לְעֵילָּא, יוֹסֵף לְתַתָּא. תְּרֵין תִּיאוּבְתִּין אִינּוּן. חַד הֵיכָלָא שְׁתִיתָאָה. וְחַד הַאי הֵיכָלָא שְׁבִיעָאָה. תִּיאוּבְתָּא לְעֵילָּא, בְּאִינּוּן נְשִׁיקִין דְּנָטִיל יַעֲקֹב. תִּיאוּבְתָּא לְתַתָּא, בְּהַאי שִׁמּוּשָׁא דְּנָטִיל יוֹסֵף. מִתְּרֵין סִטְרִין אִלֵּין, נָטִיל אֲרוֹן הַבְּרִית רוּחָא דְּחַיֵּי. מִסִּטְרָא דְּיַעֲקֹב, נָטִיל רוּחָא דְּחַיֵּי דִּלְעֵילָּא, דְּאִתְדָּבַק בֵּיהּ בְּאִינּוּן נְשִׁיקִין, וְאָעִיל רוּחָא דְּחַיֵּי דִּלְעֵילָּא בֵּיהּ, לְאִתְזָנָא מִנֵּיהּ. מִסִּטְרָא דְּיוֹסֵף, דְּאִיהוּ לְתַתָּא, בְּסִיּוּמָא דְּגוּפָא, בְּהַאי הֵיכָלָא. נָטִיל רוּחִין וְנִשְׁמָתִין לְאַרְקָא לְתַתָּא, לְהַאי עָלְמָא.

766. There are two: Jacob above, FROM THE CHEST UPWARD, THE SECRET OF TIFERET, and Joseph below, FROM THE CHEST DOWNWARD, YESOD. There are two passions: the one is the sixth chamber, WHICH JACOB RECEIVED, and the other is the seventh chamber, THE CHAMBER OF THE HOLY OF HOLIES, WHERE YESOD OF ZEIR ANPIN MINISTERS, THAT IS JOSEPH. The passion above, FROM CHEST UPWARD, is of the kissing that Jacob took IN THE SIXTH CHAMBER. The passion below is of the service that Joseph took upon himself, IN THE SEVENTH CHAMBER, HOLY OF

HOLIES. The Ark of the Covenant, THE SECRET OF THE CHAMBER OF HOLY OF HOLIES, received from these two aspects, JACOB AND JOSEPH. 1) From the side of Jacob it took the spirit of life of above, that JACOB cleft to through the kisses. This spirit of life of above entered THE ARK OF THE COVENANT, WHICH IS THE SEVENTH CHAMBER, to be nourished by it. 2) From the side of Joseph, down below at the final part of the body, YESOD, this chamber, THE SEVENTH took from him spirits and souls to pour them into this world.

767. אִלֵּין תְּרֵין סִטְרִין, מִתְפָּרְשָׁן לִתְרֵין סִטְרִין. סִטְרָא דְּיַעֲקֹב, אִתְפָּשַׁט וְיָהִיב תּוּקְפָּא, לְנַבְעָא בְּאִינּוּן שָׁדַיִם, דְּאִתְמַלְיָין מֵהַהוּא רוּחָא דְּחַיֵּי, וְיָנִיק בְּהוּ לְאִינּוּן מַלְאֲכִין קַדִּישִׁין, דְּאִינּוּן חַיִּין וְקַיְימִין לְעָלְמִין, וְקַיְימִין בְּקִיּוּמָא בֵּיהּ, סִטְרָא דְּיוֹסֵף, עָיֵיל בְּתִיאוּבְתָּא וְיָהֵב תּוּקְפָּא לְגוֹ, וְעָבֵיד נִשְׁמָתִין וְרוּחִין, לְנַחְתָּא לְתַתָּא, וּלְאַתְזָנָא בְּהוּ בְּנֵי עָלְמָא.

767. These two aspects, Jacob and Joseph, are divided into two sides. The aspect of Jacob, Tiferet, expands and gives strength of flowing to the breasts (Heb. *shadayim*), the secret of El Shadai, that were filled by the spirit of life. He suckles the holy angels, who live and endure forever, for by sucking they achieve perfection. The aspect of Joseph, Yesod, enters with passion into the Ark of the covenant, and empowers it inside, producing souls and spirits that will go down and sustain the inhabitants of the world.

768. וְעַל דָּא, קַיְימִין תְּרֵין סִטְרִין אִלֵּין, דָּא לְעֵילָּא, וְדָא לְתַתָּא. דָּא לְאַתְזָנָא לְעֵילָּא, וְדָא לְמֵיזָן לְתַתָּא. כָּל חַד וְחַד כַּדְקָא חֲזֵי לֵיהּ, וְכֹלָּא אִיהוּ חַד, וְחַד רָזָא אִיהוּ. וְעִם כָּל דָּא, יוֹסֵף זָן לְכָל גּוּפָא, וְאַשְׁקֵי לֵיהּ. דְּמֵהַאי רוּחָא דְּחַיֵּי דְּאִתְדַּבְּקוּתָא דְּיַעֲקֹב, נָחִית לְתַתָּא, וּבֵיהּ אִתְדָּבַק הַאי אֲרוֹן הַבְּרִית, בִּרְעוּתָא לְעֵילָּא, וְנָחִית הַהוּא רוּחָא דְּחַיֵּי לְתַתָּא, בְּהַהוּא אִתְדַּבְּקוּתָא דְּיוֹסֵף, וְכַד אִתְחֲבָּר כֹּלָּא כַּחֲדָא, אִתְמַלְיָין אִינּוּן שָׁדַיִם לְיָנְקָא לְכֹלָּא, וּבְגִין כַּךְ כֹּלָּא אִיהִי חַד, זַכָּאָה חוּלָקֵיהּ, מַאן דְּיָדַע לְקַשְּׁרָא קִשְׁרִין, וּלְיַחֲדָא יִחוּדָא בִּצְלוֹתָא בִּרְעוּתָא דְּלִבָּא כַּדְקָא יֵאוֹת, בְּגִין לְדַבְּקָא שַׁיְיפָא בְּשַׁיְיפָא, רוּחָא בְּרוּחָא, כֹּלָּא בִּכְלָלָא חֲדָא, לְמֶהֱוֵי כֹּלָּא חַד כַּדְקָא חֲזֵי.

768. Therefore, these two sides, JACOB AND JOSEPH, abide, JACOB above, and JOSEPH below. JACOB sustains THE ANGELS above, and JOSEPH sustains THE HUMAN SOULS below, each one according to his task. All is one, and of the same secret, FOR BOTH ARE IN ZEIR ANPIN, JACOB ABOVE THE CHEST, AND JOSEPH BELOW THE CHEST. Nevertheless, Joseph sustains the whole body, NAMELY, HE DRAWS THE LIGHT OF LIFE ALSO FROM THE UNION OF KISSING, WHICH IS THE ASPECT OF THE CHEST AND ABOVE OF THE BODY and waters it. For from the spirit of life, to which Jacob cleaves, IN THE SECRET OF KISSING, it comes down TO JOSEPH, THE SECRET OF THE CHEST DOWNWARD. The Ark of the Covenant OF THE SEVENTH CHAMBER higher will of above, FROM THE UNION OF KISSING, and the spirit of life comes down INTO HUMAN SOULS, by the clinging of Joseph TO THE ARK OF THE COVENANT. When all becomes one, NAMELY, WHEN JOSEPH IS ALSO INCLUDED IN THE LIGHT OF THE UNION OF KISSING, the breasts are filled and give suck to all, EVEN HUMAN SOULS, and for that reason all is one. Happy is the portion of he, who knows how to properly bind knots and create unity by his prayer, through his heart's desire, so the organs will cleave together, spirit with spirit, all under one unity, so all will become one, as it should be.

769. תָּא חֲזֵי, הַאי הֵיכָלָא, כַּד אִלֵּין רוּחִין קַדִּישִׁין, וְכָל אִינּוּן הֵיכָלִין וּרְתִיכִין, כֻּלְּהוּ מִתְיַיחֲדֵי כַּחֲדָא, וְאִשְׁתְּכָחוּ בְּקִשּׁוּרָא חֲדָא, כְּדֵין הַאי רוּחָא עִלָּאָה דְּכֻלְּהוּ, דְּאִיהוּ נְקוּדָה חֲדָא, אַסְתִּים בְּהוּ, וְלָא אִתְגַּלְיָיא, וְאִתְעֲבֵיד רוּחָא סָתִים כְּגַוְונָא עִלָּאָה. וְסִימָנֵיךְ אֱגוֹזָא, יְחוּדָא בְּקִשּׁוּרָא דְּכֹלָּא כִּדְקָאמְרָן, לְאִתְקַשְּׁרָא דָּא בְּדָא, לְמֶהֱוֵי כֹּלָּא שְׁלִים, בִּשְׁלִימוּ כַּחֲדָא.

769. Come and see: In this chamber, when the holy spirits, chambers and Chariots, all unite to become bound together as one, a spirit superior to all those IN THIS CHAMBER, which is a point, NAMELY, THE ASPECT OF YESOD, CALLED 'POINT', becomes concealed within them and is not revealed. This concealed spirit reflects the upper one IN ATZILUT. You can see that in THE INSIDE PART OF a nut, WHICH RESEMBLES A BRAIN DIVIDED INTO FOUR LOBES, CORRESPONDING TO CHESED, GVURAH, TIFERET AND MALCHUT, ALL CONNECTED IN THE MIDDLE TO BE ONE. Here also one unity connects them all, as we said, that they are connected together and complete in one wholeness.

770. והא אוקימנא כגוונא דא, קרבנא סלקא ליחדא יחודא ולאסתפקא כל חד וחד כדקא חזי ליה מההוא תננא דסליק, כהנא דאיהו ימינא, בקשורא דיחודא ברעותא, וליואי בשירתא. כליל דא בדא. היכלא בהיכלא, רוחא ברוחא, עד דמתחברן באתרייהו, שייפא בשייפא, למהוי כלא כליל כחדא כדקא יאות.

770. In the same manner, we explained that when the offering goes up to cause unison and to supply each with its needs, from that smoke that the priest, who is of the right, raises the bond of unity by desire, and the Levites by a song, FOR THEY ARE OF THE LEFT; ALSO HERE are included in one another, one chamber in another, one spirit in another, until they are connected to their places, MALE AND FEMALE OF ATZILUT, member within member, so all will properly become one.

771. והא אוקימנא דכד אשתלים כלא כחדא, שייפין עלאין בתתאין, כדין, נשמתא עלאה דכלא, אתערת, ועאלת בכלהו, ונהיר לכלא, וכלהו מתברכאן עלאין ותתאין. וההוא דלא אתיידע, ולא עאל בחושבנא, רעותא דלא אתפס לעלמין, כדין כלא סליק עד אין סוף, ואתקשר כלא בקשורא חדא, ובסים, ההוא רעותא לגו בגו בסתימו.

771. Here we explained that when they were all perfected together, NAMELY, ALL THE CHAMBERS WERE INCLUDED WITHIN THE SEVENTH CHAMBER, and the supernal organs, MALE AND FEMALE OF ATZILUT, ILLUMINATE upon the lower CHAMBERS, then the highest soul of all, BINAH OF ATZILUT is awakened and enters into them and shines upon them all. All are blessed: the higher beings, MALE AND FEMALE OF ATZILUT, and the lower beings, THE CHAMBERS AND ALL THAT IS INSIDE THEM. The one that is not known, nor numbered, the will that is never grasped, ATIK, IS CLOTHED BY THEIR INTERNAL PART. Everything then rises up to the Endless World and gathers into one bond, and the will, WHICH IS NEVER GRASPED, ATIK, is sweetened in the innermost part, in secret.

772. נהירו דנשמתא עלאה, סלקא לגו בגו, ונהיר לכלא. בגו דהאי

נְהִירוּ, אָעִיל סְתִימוּ דְּמַחֲשָׁבָה, דְּאִיהוּ כָּלִיל כֹּלָּא, וּבְגוֹ לְגוֹ, בְּהַהוּא רְעוּ דְּמַחֲשָׁבָה, אַנְהִיר וְאִתְבְּסָם וְתָפִיס וְלָא תָּפִיס, וְסַלְקָא רְעוּ דְּמַחֲשָׁבָה לְתַפְשָׂא בֵּיהּ, וְכַד הַאי סָלִיק, נְהִירוּ דִּלְתַתָּא תָּפִיס בֵּיהּ.

772. HE EXPLAINS HIS WORDS: The light of the supernal soul, BINAH, rises to the innermost part, there to shine upon all. Within this light OF THE SOUL, a concealed thought comes in TO BE CLOTHED. It includes all, BEING THE SUPERNAL ABA AND IMA, THE LIGHT OF CHAYAH. At the innermost of will of thought, ABA AND IMA, it illuminates and perfumes itself, grasps yet grasps not ARICH ANPIN. The will of thought rises to grasps ARICH ANPIN, and when it does, WHEN ABA AND IMA RISE TO CLOTHE ARICH ANPIN, the light below, YISRAEL-SABA AND TEVUNAH, grasps ARICH ANPIN.

773. וְכֵן כֹּלָּא, לְאִתְקַשְּׁרָא וּלְאִתְמַלְּיָא וּלְאִתְבָּרְכָא כֹּלָּא כַּחֲדָא, כַּדְקָא יֵאוֹת. וּכְדֵין אִתְקַשַּׁר דָּא בְּדָא כַּדְקָא אֲמָרָן, הֵיכָלִין בְּהֵיכָלִין, תַּתָּאִין בְּעִלָּאִין, רָזָא דְּכַר וְנוּקְבָא כַּחֲדָא, נְהִירוּ עִלָּאָה, בִּנְהִירוּ דִּסְתִים וְגָנִיז יַתִּיר בֵּיהּ. וְהַהוּא דְּגָנִיז, כָּלִיל בְּמָה דִּגְנִיז יַתִּיר, עַד דְּאִשְׁתְּכַח כֹּלָּא כַּדְקָא יֵאוֹת, בְּיִחוּדָא חֲדָא.

773. Everyone should also be joined together, so that all will be connected, filled and blessed properly, as one. Then the chambers are connected with each other, lower and higher, the secret of male and female together. The higher light, THE SOUL, is united with the light, which is more concealed and hidden, CHAYAH, and that which is more hidden is included in that which is hidden even more, ARICH ANPIN, until all will be found to be in one proper unison.

774. וְעַל דָּא, מֹשֶׁה הֲוָה יָדַע לְסַדְּרָא סִדּוּרָא דְּמָארֵיהּ מִכָּל בְּנֵי עָלְמָא, כַּד אִצְטְרִיךְ לְאַרְכָא, אָרִיךְ. לְקַצְרָא, קָצַר. כְּמָה דְּאוֹקִימְנָא, אֵל נָא רְפָא נָא לָהּ. תָּנֵינָן, מַאן דְּאָרִיךְ בִּצְלוֹתֵיהּ וְיִסְתַּכַּל בֵּיהּ, לְסוֹף אָתָא לִידֵי כְּאֵב לֵב. וְתָנֵינָן, מַאן דְּאוֹרִיךְ בִּצְלוֹתֵיהּ, יוֹרְכוּן יוֹמוֹי.

774. Therefore, Moses knew how to act according to the laws of his Master better than all the inhabitants of the world. When he had to lengthen, he did so, and when he had to be brief, he was brief, as we explained that he said, "Heal her now, O El, I pray You" (Bemidbar 12:13). We learned that whoever prays at length and then watches it will have heartache. But we also learned the opposite, that whoever prays at length, the number of his days is increased.

775. וְרָזָא דְּמִלָּה, מַאן דְּאָרִיךְ בַּאֲתָר דְּבָעֵי לְקַצְּרָא, אָתֵי לִידֵי כְּאֵב לֵב, מַאן לֵב. דָּא הוּא דִּכְתִּיב, וְטוֹב לֵב מִשְׁתֶּה תָּמִיד. בְּגִין דְּאִיהוּ אֲתָר דְּבָעֵי לְקַצְּרָא, וְלָא לְאַרְכָא בֵּיהּ, דְּהָא כֹּלָּא קָאִים לְעֵילָּא, וּבָעֵי דְּלָא לְאַמְשָׁכָא לֵיהּ, לְקַשְּׁרָא לֵיהּ בְּקִשּׁוּרָא דִּלְעֵילָּא, בְּלָא אֲרִיכוּ לְמֶהֱוֵי כֹּלָּא חַד בְּיִחוּדָא חַד. וְכֵיוָן דְּאִתְקָשַּׁר כַּחֲדָא, כְּדֵין לָא בָּעֵי לְאַרְכָא בְּאָרִיכוּ, וּלְאִתְחַנְּנָא בְּתַחֲנוּנֵי. וְכַד אָרִיךְ בַּאֲרִיכוּ, בַּאֲתָר דְּאִצְטְרִיךְ, קוּדְשָׁא בְּרִיךְ הוּא קַבִּיל צְלוֹתֵיהּ, וְדָא הוּא יְקָרָא דְּקוּדְשָׁא בְּרִיךְ הוּא, בְּגִין דְּיִחוּדָא דִּצְלוֹתָא קָא מְקַשֵּׁר קִשְׁרִין, וְאַסְגֵּי בִּרְכָאן לְעֵילָּא וְתַתָּא.

775. HE ANSWERS: The mystery of the matter is that whoever lengthens where he should be brief, will have heartache. What is the meaning of heart? It is according to the verse, "but he that is of a merry heart has a continual feast" (Mishlei 15:15). THIS IS THE SECRET OF MALCHUT CALLED "HEART," THAT DRAWS MOCHIN OF CHOCHMAH, CALLED "FEAST," IN THE SECRET OF THE VERSE, "EAT, O DEAR ONES, AND DRINK" (SHIR HASHIRIM 5:1). This place is in need of being brief, not of prolonging, because all is found above, and must not be drawn downward, BUT to be bound upward, without lengthening, until all will be as one. Once everything is connected, there is no need of prolonging and begging. When one prolongs where it is needed, NAMELY, AT THE GRADE OF ZEIR ANPIN, THE SECRET OF CHASSADIM COVERED BY CHOCHMAH, the Holy One, blessed be He receives his prayer. This is the glory of the Holy One, blessed be He, ZEIR ANPIN, that in order to unite prayer, He binds and multiplies blessings above and below, AS BLESSINGS ARE DRAWN FROM ABOVE DOWNWARD.

776. גּוֹ הֵיכָלָא דָּא, קַיְּימָא נְקוּדָה חֲדָא טְמִירְתָּא, וְהַאי נְקוּדָה אִיהִי

רוּחָא, לְקַבְּלָא רוּחָא אַחֲרָא עִלָּאָה. וְכַד שַׁרְיָא רוּחָא בְּרוּחָא, כְּדֵין עָאל דָּא בְּדָא וְאִיהוּ חַד, וּדְבֵקוּתָא חֲדָא. וְאִתְרְכִיב דָּא בְּדָא לְמֶהֱוֵי חַד, כְּהַאי אִילָנָא דְּאַרְכִּיב דָּא בְּדָא וְאִיהוּ חַד, זִינָא בְּזִינֵיהּ. וַוי מַאן דְּאַרְכִּיב זִינָא בְּלָא זִינֵיהּ, כְּאִינּוּן בְּנֵי אַהֲרֹן, דְּבָעוּ לְאַרְכָּבָא אִילָנָא בְּאַחֲרָא דְּלָאו אִיהוּ זִינֵיהּ.

776. Within this chamber there is a hidden point. This point is a spirit, that receives UPON IT another supernal spirit, WHICH IS MALE. When spirit dwells within spirit, they enter each other, cleave and become one. They comprise each other to become one, as a tree that is grafted with its own kind. Woe to him who makes a crossbreed, and grafts together different species, like the sons of Aaron did, who wanted to crossbreed another kind upon the tree.

777. וּמַאן דְּאַרְכִּיב זִינָא בְּזִינֵיהּ, וְיָדַע לְקַשְּׁרָא קִשְׁרָא בְּקִשְׁרֵיהּ, הֵיכָלָא בְּהֵיכָלֵיהּ, דַּרְגָּא בְּדַרְגֵּיהּ, דָּא אִית לֵיהּ חוּלָקָא בְּעָלְמָא דְּאָתֵי, כְּמָה דְּאוּקִימְנָא. וְעַל דָּא, הַאי אִיהוּ שְׁלִימוּ דְּכֹלָּא. וְכַד אִשְׁתְּלִים דָּא בְּדָא, וְאִיהוּ כֹּלָּא חַד עוֹבָדָא זִינָא בְּזִינֵיהּ דְּנָפִיק מֵהַאי שְׁלִימוּ הַהוּא אִקְרֵי מַעֲשֵׂה מֶרְכָּבָה.

777. Whoever makes a graft of one kind with its own kind, and knows how to bind knot with knot, chamber with chamber, grade with grade, he has a portion in the World to Come, as we explained. Therefore, it is the overall perfection, when they are perfected by one another, THE LEFT BY THE RIGHT, THE MALE BY THE FEMALE, AND ALSO THE CHAMBERS, and everything becomes one act of a kind with its own kind, derived from that perfection, called 'the act of the Divine Chariot', FOR CHARIOT (HEB. *MERKAVAH*) IS DERIVED FROM GRAFTING (HEB. *MARKIV*).

778. וְרָזָא דָּא וַיִּיצֶר יְיָ' אֱלֹהִים אֶת הָאָדָם, שֵׁם מָלֵא. וְאָדָם אִיהוּ עוֹבָדָא דְּהַאי מֶרְכָּבָה, דְּאַרְכִּיב דָּא בְּדָא, עוֹבָדָא דִּשְׁלִימוּ דְּכֹלָּא, וְכַד אִשְׁתְּלִים דָּא בְּדָא, כְּדֵין יְיָ' אֱלֹהִים, שֵׁם מָלֵא. זַכָּאָה אִיהוּ מַאן דְּיָדַע לְקַשְּׁרָא קִשְׁרֵי מְהֵימְנוּתָא. וּלְיַחֲדָא יִחוּדָא כַּדְקָא חָזֵי.

778. This is the secret of the verse, "And Hashem Elohim formed man" (Beresheet 2:7). The whole name YUD HEI VAV HEI ELOHIM IS WRITTEN THERE, because the formation of man is an act coming from this Chariot, YUD HEI VAV HEI ELOHIM, that made the graft of the one and the other, A KIND WITH ITS OWN KIND, an act of overall perfection, FOR RIGHT WAS PERFECTED BY THE LEFT, AND THE LEFT PERFECTED BY THE RIGHT, AND THE SAME HAPPENED WITH MALE AND FEMALE. When they were completed by one another, they were called 'ZEIR ANPIN AND MALCHUT', Yud Hei Vav Hei Elohim, which is a whole name. Happy is he, who knows how to tie the knots of Faith and to make the unison in a proper manner.

779. ת"ח, כְּמָה דְּאִיתְנְהוּ שְׁמָהָן קַדִּישִׁין עִלָּאִין, מִתְחַבְּרִין אִלֵּין בְּאִלֵּין, הָכִי אִיהוּ שְׁמָא קַדִּישָׁא. אִתְפְּרַשׁ לְעֵילָּא, וְאִתְפְּרַשׁ לְתַתָּא. שְׁמָא דָּא אִיהוּ לְעֵילָּא, שְׁמָא דָּא אִיהוּ בְּאֶמְצָעִיתָא, שְׁמָא דָּא אִיהוּ לְתַתָּא. יְהוָ"ה דְּאִיהוּ רָזָא דִּשְׁמָא קַדִּישָׁא, אִיהוּ חַד. רָזָא דְּכֹלָּא. עָלְמָא עִלָּאָה, בִּסְתִימוּ דִּסְתִימוּתָא דְּעָלֵיהּ, דְּאִשְׁתַּתֵּף בַּהֲדֵיהּ, וְאִיהוּ חַד. עָלְמָא תַּתָּאָה, בִּסְתִימוּ דְּאֶמְצָעִיתָא, רָזָא רְתִיכָא קַדִּישָׁא עִלָּאָה דְּעָלֵיהּ, וְאוּקִימְנָא.

779. Come and see: The same as the Holy Supernal Names, SUCH AS THE NAME OF 42 LETTERS, that join each other, the Holy Name YUD HEI VAV HEI too is spelled above, IN BINAH, and below, IN MALCHUT. This name YUD HEI VAV HEI is above, IN THE FIRST THREE SFIROT, IN THE UNISON OF YUD HEI VAV HEI, ALEPH HEI YUD HEI; name is in the middle, IN CHESED, GVURAH AND TIFERET, IT IS IN THE UNISON YUD HEI VAV HEI ELOHIM, and this name is below, IN NETZACH, HOD, YESOD AND MALCHUT, IS IN THE UNISON YUD HEI VAV HEI ADONAI. Yud Hei Vav Hei is the secret of the Holy Name, which is One, the secret of all, INCLUDING ALL NAMES. The Supernal World, BINAH, AND THE FIRST THREE SFIROT CALLED 'ALEPH HEI YUD HEI' IS UNITED with the most concealed that is above it, CHOCHMAH CALLED 'YUD HEI VAV HEI', TO BECOME THE UNITY YUD HEI VAV HEI, ALEPH-HEI-YUD-HEI, that joins it to be one. The lower world, MALCHUT CALLED 'ADONAI', IS UNITED with the concealed one, ZEIR ANPIN CALLED 'YUD HEI VAV HEI', TO FORM THE UNITY YUD HEI VAV HEI ADONAI. That which is "In the middle" THE SECRET OF MALCHUT ABOVE THE CHEST OF ZEIR ANPIN

CALLED 'ELOHIM' IS COMBINED with the secret of the Holy Supernal Chariot above it, WHICH IS CHESED, GVURAH AND TIFERET CALLED 'YUD HEI VAV HEI', TO MAKE THE UNITY YUD HEI VAV HEI ELOHIM, WHICH IS THE ACT OF THE DIVINE CHARIOT, as we explained.

780. מֵהַאי גִּיסָא, ד׳ רְתִיכִין נָפְקִין, וּמֵהַאי גִּיסָא אַרְבַּע רְתִיכִין נָפְקִין, בְּגִין דְּכָל חַד וְחַד מִתְפָּרַשׁ לְאַרְבַּע, כָּל רְתִיכָא אַרְבַּע אִינּוּן, כַּד מִסְתַּכְּלִין דַּרְגִּין. וְכֵן כֻּלְּהוּ אַרְבַּע בְּאַרְבַּע, עַד דְּנַחְתִּין דַּרְגָּא לְתַתָּא בְּהַהוּא אֲתַר דְּאִקְרֵי בְּרָזָא דִּשְׁמָא קַדִּישָׁא דְּאִיהוּ אֲדֹנָ״י, בְּאִינּוּן רְתִיכִין דְּקַיְימֵי וְנַטְלֵי בִּשְׁמָא דָּא, וְאִינּוּן אִקְרוּן הָרֵי נְחֹשֶׁת, בְּגִין דְּאִית הָרִים וְאִית הָרִים. אִית הָרִים עִלָּאִין, וְהָרִים תַּתָּאִין. וְאִינּוּן בִּתְלַת סִטְרִין קַיְימֵי, וְנַפְקֵי מִגּוֹ זָהָב וָכֶסֶף וּנְחֹשֶׁת.

780. From this side, BINAH, come out four Chariots, THE FOUR SFIROT CHESED, GVURAH, TIFERET AND MALCHUT ABOVE THE CHEST; from that side, MALCHUT FROM THE CHEST DOWNWARD OF ZEIR ANPIN CALLED 'ADONAI', come out four Chariots, THE SECRET OF THE FOUR ANGELS, MICHAEL, GABRIEL, URIEL AND RAPHAEL, because each is separated into four, and each Chariot is four. And when the grades watch, THE THREE COLUMNS AND THE RECEIVING MALCHUT, they all go by quartets, until the grades go down to the place called by the holy name Adonai, after the Chariots that stand and travel by that name ADONAI. They are called "mountains of brass" (Zecharyah 6:1), for there are mountains and mountains, the upper mountains, CHESED, GVURAH AND TIFERET OF ZEIR ANPIN, and the lower mountains, NETZACH, HOD AND YESOD OF ZEIR ANPIN, THAT SHINE UPON MALCHUT. They stand on three sides, RIGHT, LEFT, AND CENTRAL, and come out of gold, silver, and brass, AS NETZACH, HOD AND YESOD OF ZEIR ANPIN COME OUT OF CHESED, GVURAH AND TIFERET OF ZEIR ANPIN CALLED 'GOLD, SILVER, AND BRASS'.

781. נְחֹשֶׁת לְתַתָּא, בְּגִין דְּאִינּוּן רְתִיכִין דְּנַפְקֵי מִגּוֹ אָלֶ״ף דָּלֶ״ת נוּ״ן יוֹ״ד דִּי בְּגוֹ הֵיכָלָא קַדְמָאָה, דְּאִינּוּן אַרְבַּע רְתִיכִין דְּנָפְקִין מִגּוֹ אִינּוּן תְּרֵין רוּחִין יְמִינָא וּשְׂמָאלָא, מִגּוֹ לִבְנַת הַסַּפִּיר, כִּדְקָאמְרָן. אִלֵּין תְּרֵין רוּחִין דְּקָאָמְרֵינָן הָתָם, אִינּוּן אִקְרוּן תְּרֵי טוּרִים, וְאִינּוּן הָרֵי נְחֹשֶׁת.

781. There is brass down below, IN BRIYAH, for the Chariots, coming out of the name Adonai of the first chamber, are four Chariots that emerge from two spirits, right and left of the sapphire stone. These two spirits are called 'two mountains', the brass mountains.

782. מֵאִינּוּן תְּרֵי רוּחִין דְּאִקְרוּן הָרֵי נְחֹשֶׁת, נַפְקֵי אִינּוּן ד' רְתִיכִין, דְּמִשְׁתַּמְּשֵׁי בְּהַהוּא שְׁמָא דְּאָלֶ"ף דָּלֶ"ת, דְּאִשְׁתְּקַע בְּסַנְדַּלְפוֹ"ן, מָארֵיהּ דְּאַפַּיָּא. וְכֻלְּהוּ שְׁלִיחָן עַל אִלֵּין בְּעָלְמָא, בְּרָזָא דְּסוּסְוָון וּרְתִיכִין, בְּגִין דְּאִית רְתִיכָא עַל סוּסְוָון, דְּנַטְלֵי לָהּ.

782. From the two spirits called 'brass mountains', four Chariots are issued, THE SECRET OF THE FOUR WHEELS, that use the name OF ADONAI, engraved upon the archangel Sandalphon. All THE CHARIOTS are messengers to the world, these on those, in the mystery of horses and Chariots, for each Chariot has horses to drive it.

783. וְדָא שְׁמָא קַדִּישָׁא, אִתְכְּלִיל בְּיוֹ"ד הֵ"א, כְּמָה דְּאוֹקִימְנָא, דְּאִתְכְּלִיל אָלֶ"ף דָּלֶ"ת בְּיוֹ"ד הֵ"א, וְאִיהוּ יְאֲהַדוֹנָהִ"י. וְהָא אִתְּמַר, אֱלֹהִים לָא אִתְכְּלִיל בִּשְׁמָא אַחֲרָא, בְּגִין דְּאִית אֱלֹהִים חַיִּים, וּמֵהַאי, אִתְפָּשַׁט לְכַמָּה סִטְרִין, וְלָא אִתְכְּנִישׁ, אֶלָּא אִתְפָּשַׁט.

783. The holy hame ADONAI is included in Yud Hei VAV HEI, as we said that Adonai is included within Yud Hei Vav Hei to form *Yud-Aleph-Hei-Dalet-Vav-Nun-Hei-Yud*. We already learned that. THE NAME Elohim is not included in any other name, LIKE ADONAI THAT IS INCLUDED WITHIN YUD HEI VAV HEI, AND ITS OWN ASPECTS IS NULLIFIED IN YUD HEI VAV HEI. BUT THE NAME ELOHIM IS NOT ANNULLED AND INCLUDED WITHIN ANOTHER NAME. For there is a living Elohim IN BINAH, whence IT, ELOHIM OF BINAH is extended into several sides, NAMELY GVURAH OF ZEIR ANPIN, AND MALCHUT, BOTH CALLED 'ELOHIM'. IT ALSO EXPANDS INTO BRIYAH, YETZIRAH AND ASIYAH, AND ITS ILLUMINATION is not gathered ANYWHERE but keeps on expanding. THEREFORE, IT IS NOT INCLUDED AND ANNULLED WITHIN ANY OTHER NAME.

784. שְׁמָא דְּכָלִיל כָּל שְׁמָהָן, יוֹ"ד הֵ"א וָא"ו הֵ"א, בְּרָזָא דְּאַתְוָון

צֵרוּפָא דִשְׁמָא קַדִישָׁא, דְבֵיהּ הֲוָה יָדַע כַּהֲנָא, לְצָרְפָא בְּכָל סִטְרוֹי, עַד דְסַלְקֵי שְׁמָהָן בְּכַמָּה סִטְרִין, בְּאַרְבְּעִין וּתְרֵין גַּוְונִין, בְּאִשְׁתְּטָחוּ דְבוּצִינָא דְקַרְדִינוּתָא, דְהַאי אִיהוּ כָּלִיל כָּל שְׁמָהָן.

784. The name, which includes all other names, IS YUD HEI VAV HEI FULLY SPELLED, *Yud-Vav-Dalet*, *Hei-Aleph*, *Vav-Aleph-Vav*, *Hei-Aleph*, of the secret of the permutation of letters of the Holy Name. The priest knew how to permute it on all sides, until the names appear on several sides, in 42 manners of the expansion of the hard spark IN BINAH, which includes all the names.

785. וּשְׁמָא דָא, כָּלִיל כָּל שְׁמָהָן. אהיו״ל דינ״ם סִימָן. בְּאִלֵּין אַתְוָון כְּלִילָן אַחֲרָנִין מִתְחַבְּרָן. וְנַפְקֵי אִלֵּין, וְעַיְילֵי אִלֵּין. לְבָתַר כַּד אִתְנְטֵי וְאִתְפָּשַׁט בּוּצִינָא דְקַרְדִינוּתָא, מִצְטָרְפֵי אַתְוָון בְּגַוֵּוהּ, וְעָאלֵי אַתְוָון, וְנַפְקֵי אַתְוָון, בְּרָזָא דְאִלֵּין תֵּשַׁע אַתְוָון. וְאִלֵּין אִתְמְסָרוּ לְקַדִישֵׁי עֶלְיוֹנִין, לְמֵהַךְ בְּאוֹרְחָא דְרָזָא דְאַתְוָון. לְצָרְפָא יִחוּדָא דִשְׁמָהָן דְאַתְוָון, כְּמָה דַהֲוָה יָדַע כַּהֲנָא לְצָרְפָא שְׁמָהָן, בְּאַתְוָון רְשִׁימָן.

785. HE EXPLAINS FURTHER THAT this Name YUD HEI VAV HEI includes all the names OF THE COMBINATION *Aleph-Hei-Yud-Vav-Lamed-Dalet-Yud-Nun-Mem* as a sign, that within these letters are included the other NAMES that join THE NAME YUD HEI VAV HEI. THESE ARE THE THREE NAMES, ALEPH HEI YUD HEI, ELOHIM, ADONAI. Some come in, some come out. Afterwards, when the hard spark OF BINAH bent and expanded, the letters joined BINAH, and the letters came in and out in the secret of these nine letters, which were given to the highest holy men, with which to walk in the path of the secret permutation of the letters of unison, made of the letters that form the names, as the priest knew how to permute the names of the written letters.

786. וִידֵי אָדָם מִתַּחַת כַּנְפֵיהֶם. כֻּלְּהוּ יְדֵי אָדָם, הָא אוֹקִימְנָא, דְאִינּוּן רוּחִין וְחֵיוָון וְאוֹפַנִּים. כֻּלְּהוּ בְּגַדְפִּין, וִידִין תְּחוֹת גַּדְפַּיְיהוּ, לְקַבְּלָא צְלוֹתִין, וּלְקַבְּלָא מָארֵי דִתְיוּבְתָּא. יְדֵי אָדָם אַתְרִין וְדוּכְתִּין, לְקַבְּלָא בְּנֵי נָשָׁא, בִּצְלוֹתְהוֹן וּבָעוּתְהוֹן, וּלְאַפְתְּחָא פִּתְחִין לְקַבְּלָא לוֹן, לְיַחֲדָא

וּלְקַשְׁרָא קִשְׁרִין, וּלְמֶעְבַּד רְעוּתֵהוֹן.

786. “And they had the hands of a man under their wings” (Yechezkel 1:8). We already explained that the hands of a man are winged spirits, living creatures and wheels, with hands under their wings, with which to receive prayers, and the contrite. “The hands of a man” means places and receptacles that receive men, with their prayers and petitions, open gates to let them in, unite and tie knots, and abide by their wishes.

787. וְאִלֵּין אַתְרִין וְדוּכְתִּין דְּאִקְרוּן יְדֵי אָדָם, דְּקַיְימֵי לִבְנֵי נָשָׁא, אִלֵּין אִינּוּן שְׁמָהָן קַדִּישִׁין, דְּשַׁלִּיטִין בְּכָל דַּרְגָּא וְדַרְגָּא, דִּבְהוֹן עָאלִין בְּנֵי נָשָׁא, בִּצְלוֹתְהוֹן וּבָעוּתְהוֹן, בְּכָל תַּרְעִין עִלָּאִין. וּבְדָא שַׁלְטִין תַּתָּאִין לְעֵילָּא. וְרָזָא דָּא, יָדֶיךָ עָשׂוּנִי וַיְכוֹנְנוּנִי, וְאִלֵּין שְׁמָהָן קַדִּישִׁין.

787. These places and receptacles are called ‘the hands of men’, since they are there for men. They are the Holy Names that rule over each grade, through which men enter by their prayer and petition and into all the supernal gates. By this the lower beings rule above. This is the secret of the verse, “Your hands have made me and fashioned me” (Tehilim 119:73), referring to the Holy Names CALLED “HANDS”.

788. וַיֹּאמֶר יְיָ' אֶל מֹשֶׁה נְטֵה אֶת יָדְךָ עַל הַשָּׁמַיִם. וְכִי הֵיךְ יָכִיל לְאָרָמָא יְדֵיהּ עַל שְׁמַיָּא. אֶלָּא נְטֵה: אַרְכִּין. כד"א, וַיֵּט שָׁמַיִם וַיֵּרַד, מְשִׁיכוּ מִלְּעֵילָּא לְתַתָּא. יָדְךָ: אַתְרָךְ. אַתְרָא דְּדַרְגָּא דִּילָךְ, דְּאַתְּ שָׁארֵי בְּגַוֵּיהּ, וְדָא בְּרָזָא דִּשְׁמָא קַדִּישָׁא. וְכֹלָּא עִלָּאֵי וְתַתָּאֵי, בְּרָזָא דִּשְׁמָהָן נַטְלֵי וְקַיְימֵי. וּבְהוּ עָאלִין בְּנֵי נָשָׁא לְהֵיכָלִין עִלָּאִין, וְלֵית מַאן דְּיִמְחֵי בִּידַיְיהוּ. זַכָּאִין אִינּוּן דְּיַדְעִין לְסַדְּרָא יִחוּדָא דְּמָארֵיהוֹן כַּדְקָא יָאוּת, וּלְמֵיהַךְ בְּאֹרַח קְשׁוֹט, בְּגִין דְּלָא יִטְעוּן בְּרָזָא דִּמְהֵימְנוּתָא.

788. “And Hashem said to Moses, ‘Stretch out your hand towards (lit. ‘on’) heaven’” (Shemot 9:22). HE ASKS: How could he lift his hands upon the heaven? AND HE ANSWERS: ‘Stretch’ MEANS to bow, as it is written, “He bowed the heavens also, and came down” (Tehilim 18:10), WHICH MEANS THAT he drew from above downward. “Your hand” means your place,

NAMELY, where your grade is, in which you dwell, TIFERET. This DRAWING is in the secret of the Holy Name. Everyone, upper and lower, is moved and sustained by the secret of the names. Through them men enter the upper chambers, and no one detains them. Happy are those who know how to properly established the unison of their Master, to walk in the path of truth, so they will not misunderstand the secret of the Faith.

789. ת"ח, בְּהֵיכָלִין אִלֵּין, אִית רָזָא עִלָּאָה גּוֹ מְהֵימְנוּתָא. וְכֻלְּהוּ חֵיוָון רְתִיכִין, כֻּלְּהוּ מְשַׁנְיָין דָּא מִן דָּא, לְאִתְכַּלְלָא אִלֵּין בְּאִלֵּין לְטַב, לְאִתְתַּקְּנָא. וְסִימָנִיךְ וַיְשַׁנֶּהָ וְאֶת נַעֲרוֹתֶיהָ לְטוֹב. בְּשִׁבְעָה הֵיכָלִין אִלֵּין, שְׁלִימוּ דְּעֵילָּא. כַּד אִשְׁתְּלִים דָּא בְּדָא, וְעָאלוּ צְלוֹתִין וּבָעוּתִין. דְּמַאן דְּיָדַע לְסַדְּרָא לוֹן, לְאַתְקְנָא לוֹן לְעֵילָּא. כד"א וְאֵת שֶׁבַע הַנְּעָרוֹת הָרְאוּיוֹת לָתֶת לָהּ מִבֵּית הַמֶּלֶךְ.

789. Come and see: In these chambers there is a supernal secret within the Faith, WHICH IS MALCHUT OF ATZILUT CLOTHED IN THEM, CALLED 'FAITH'. All the living creatures and Chariots are different than each other, and by their combining together they are mended for the better. This is understood from the verse, "and he advanced her and her maids to the best place in the house" (Ester 2:9). Within these seven chambers is found the perfection of above, when THEY ARE INCLUDED AND complemented by one another. And prayers and petitions enter them, of those who know how to set them in order, and mend them above, as it is written, "and the seven maids chosen to be given her, out of the king's house" (Ibid.).

790. הֵיכָלָא קַדְמָאָה. יוֹצֵר אוֹר וּבוֹרֵא חֹשֶׁךְ. נְהִירוּ דְּאֶבֶן טָבָא סְפִּירוּ, דְּאֶבֶן טָבָא נָצִיץ לִתְרֵין סִטְרִין, כְּמָה דְּאוּקִימְנָא לִימִינָא וְלִשְׂמָאלָא, אוֹר וְחֹשֶׁךְ. מָה רַבּוּ מַעֲשֶׂיךָ יְיָ׳ כֻּלָּם בְּחָכְמָה עָשִׂיתָ, כֻּלְּהוּ אוֹפַנִּים וְגַלְגַּלִּים, מָלְאָה הָאָרֶץ קִנְיָנֶיךָ וְגוֹ׳. הַמֶּלֶךְ הַמְרוֹמָם לְבַדּוֹ מֵאָז שְׁמָא קַדִּישָׁא יְאַהֲדוֹנָהִ"י, כְּלָלָא דִּשְׁמָא קַדִּישָׁא, שְׁלִים בִּתְרֵי שְׁמָהָן, וְדָא הוּא סָלִיק בַּאֲוִירָא, וּמִתְנַשֵּׂא מִימוֹת עוֹלָם.

790. HE NOW GOES ON TO EXPLAIN THE ORDER OF THE SEVEN CHAMBERS WITHIN THE PRAYER FROM 'WHO FORMS' UP TO AMIDAH. HE SAYS: The first chamber, THE SAPPHIRE STONE, IS THE SECRET OF "I form the light, and create darkness" (Yeshayah 45:7), being the precious sapphire stone, a jewel that glitters on two sides, right and left, that are light and darkness, as we explained, BECAUSE BEFORE THE LEFT COLUMN JOINS THE RIGHT, IT IS DARKNESS, FOR THEN CHOCHMAH IS WITHOUT CHASSADIM. THE NEXT PHRASE "Hashem, how manifold are Your works! In Wisdom have You made them all" (Tehilim 104:24) REFERS TO all the spheres and wheels IN THE FIRST CHAMBER, OF WHICH HE SAYS "IN WISDOM HAVE YOU MADE THEM ALL, the earth is full of Your creatures..." It continues with "O king! who are sublime alone for ever," WHO REVOLVES AROUND the Holy Name, *Yud-Aleph-Hei-Dalet-Vav-Nun-Hei-Yud* OF THE FIRST CHAMBER, the entirety of the Holy Name, complete with the two names YUD HEI VAV HEI AND ADONAI. This name rises in the air, AND OF THIS IT IS SAID, 'and self-exalted from the days of everlasting'. 'EXALTED' MEANS UP IN THE AIR. SO FAR, THE MEDITATIONS FOR THE FIRST CHAMBER.

791. הֵיכָלָא תִּנְיָינָא, אֵל בָּרוּךְ גְּדוֹל דֵּעָה, אוֹרְפָנִיאֵ"ל, דְּכָלִיל רָזִין דְּאַתְוָון זְעִירִין דְּאַלְפָא בֵּיתָא. הָכָא אִינּוּן דְּקָאמְרֵי קָדוֹשׁ וּבָרוּךְ. וְהָכָא אִיהוּ קְדוּשָּׁה, וּבָרוּךְ כְּבוֹד יְיָ'. הֵיכָלָא תְּלִיתָאָה, לָאֵל בָּרוּךְ נְעִימוֹת יִתֵּנוּ.

791. The second chamber, THE VERY HEAVEN, IS THE SECRET OF THE PRAYER "The blessed El, great in Wisdom," WRITTEN IN ALPHABETICAL HEBREW ORDER. THIS IS THE SECRET OF THE ANGEL Urfaniel, who GOVERNS THE SECOND CHAMBER, AND includes the mystery of the small letters of the alphabet. THE ORDER OF THE LETTERS IN THIS PRAYER ARE THE SECRET OF THE SMALL LETTERS. Here ARE ANGELS who say sanctification and "blessed be," for here they recite sanctification, NAMELY, THEY SAY, 'HOLY, HOLY, HOLY', and 'blessed be the glory of Hashem FROM HIS DWELLING PLACE'. In the third chamber THEY RECITE, "to the blessed El they will sound songs…"

792. הֵיכָלָא רְבִיעָאָה הַמְחַדֵּשׁ בְּטוּבוֹ בְּכָל יוֹם תָּמִיד מַעֲשֵׂה בְרֵאשִׁית. בְּגִין דְּהָכָא מִתְגַּלְגְּלִין נְהוֹרִין, וְדִינִין דְּעָלְמָא. מַאן דְּאִיהוּ לְחַיִּים, מִתְחַדֵּשׁ כְּמִלְקַדְמִין, לְאִתְקַיְּימָא בְּעָלְמָא, בִּנְהוֹרָא דִּימִינָא, דְּאִקְרֵי אֵל כִּדְקָאמְרָן.

792. In the fourth chamber, THE CHAMBER OF MERIT, they say, 'Who renews, in His goodness, day by day in perpetuity the works of Creation,' for here IN THE FOURTH CHAMBER, the lights and Judgments of the world are spinning, and whoever merits life is renewed as before, and sustained by the light of the right called 'El' as we said.

793. הֵיכָלָא חֲמִישָׁאָה. הֵיכָלָא דָּא אִקְרֵי אַהֲבַת עוֹלָם. וְדָא אִיהוּ מְשִׁיכוּ דִּרְחִימוּתָא דְּהֵיכָלָא דְּאִקְרֵי אַהֲבָה, וְדָא הִיא אַהֲבַת עוֹלָם אֲהַבְתָּנוּ יְיָ' אֱלֹהֵינוּ, בא"י הַבּוֹחֵר בְּעַמּוֹ יִשְׂרָאֵל בְּאַהֲבָה, בְּרָזָא דְּאֵ"ל שַׁדַּ"י.

793. The fifth chamber, WHICH IS THE CHAMBER OF LOVE, is called 'everlasting love'. It causes love to flow from the chamber called 'love'. For this reason IT IS SAID, 'With everlasting love have You loved us, Hashem, our Elohim,' and 'blessed are You, Hashem, who has chosen His people Yisrael with love', in the secret of El Shadai.

794. הֵיכָלָא שְׁתִיתָאָה, אֱמֶת וְיַצִּיב וְנָכוֹן וְקַיָּים. וּבָעֵינָן דְּלָא לְאַפְסְקָא בֵּין הֵיכָלִין אִלֵּין. דְּהָא בִּמְשִׁיכוּ דִּצְלוֹתָא וּרְעוּתָא מִתְחַבְּרָאן כַּחֲדָא, וְאִתְקַשְּׁרָאן אִלֵּין בְּאִלֵּין, בְּרָזָא דִּשְׁמָהָן קַדִּישִׁין דְּשָׁלִיטִין בְּכָל חַד וְחַד.

794. In the sixth chamber, THE CHAMBER OF DESIRE, the prayer continues with 'True and valid, firmly fixed and all-enduring'. The prayer must not be interrupted here, for in the continuation of the prayer and desire, the chambers are connected and tied to each other, in the secret of the Holy Names, governing in each of them.

795. הֵיכָלָא שְׁבִיעָאָה, אֲדֹנָי שְׂפָתַי תִּפְתָּח, רָזָא דְּרָזִין בִּלְחִישׁוּ, וְלָא אִשְׁתְּמַע קָלָא. הָכָא אִיהוּ רְעוּתָא דְּלִבָּא, לְאִתְכַּוְּונָא וּלְסַלְּקָא רְעוּתָא מִתַּתָּא לְעֵילָּא, עַד אֵין סוֹף, וּלְקַשְּׁרָא שְׁבִיעָאָה בִּשְׁבִיעָאָה, דָּא בְּדָא מִתַּתָּא לְעֵילָּא וּלְבָתַר, מֵעֵילָּא לְתַתָּא, לְאַמְשָׁכָא בִּרְכָאן בְּכֻלְּהוּ עָלְמִין, מִמְּקוֹרָא דְּחַיֵּי, דְּאִיהוּ הֵיכָלָא שְׁבִיעָאָה עִלָּאָה בִּרְעוּתָא דְּלִבָּא, וּבִסְתִימוּ דְּעַיְינִין, דְּרָזָא דְּאַתְוָון דְּשֶׁבַע שְׁמָהָן עִלָּאִין קַדִּישִׁין.

795. In the seventh chamber, THE CHAMBER OF HOLY OF HOLIES, IT IS SAID, "Hashem, open my lips" (Tehilim 51:17). It is a most secret mystery that SHOULD BE whispered, so that no sound shall be heard. Here lies the heart's desire to direct the sound upward from below up to the Endless World, and tie the seventh CHAMBER, THE HOLY OF HOLIES, to the seventh, WITHIN BINAH OF ATZILUT, one with another from below upward, and then from up above downward, to draw blessings from the source of life, the seventh supernal chamber, with the heart willing, and the eyes closed, in the mystery of the seven superior Holy Names.

796. הֵיכָלָא שְׁבִיעָאָה עִלָּאָה דָּא, דְּאִיהוּ מְקוֹרָא דְּחַיֵּי, דָּא אִיהוּ בִּרְכָתָא קַמַּיְיתָא. וְדָא אִיהוּ הֵיכָלָא קַדְמָאָה, שֵׁירוּתָא דְּכֹלָּא מֵעֵילָּא לְתַתָּא, וּלְנַטְלָא שְׁבִיעָאָה מִתַּתָּא, לְאִתְחַבְּרָא דָּא בְּדָא, שְׁבִיעָאָה בִּשְׁבִיעָאָה. דְּהָא מֵהַאי דִּלְתַתָּא, עָיֵיל מַאן דְּעָיֵיל, לְהֵיכָלָא עִלָּאָה.

796. This supernal seventh chamber, NAMELY, BINAH, which is the source of life, is the first blessing, FOR BY THIS BLESSING MALCHUT ASCENDS, WITH ALL THAT IS INCLUDED WITHIN HER, TO BINAH. This is the first chamber, the beginning of all from above downward, FOR ALL MOCHIN OF MALE AND FEMALE AND BRIYAH, YETZIRAH AND ASIYAH ORIGINATE IN BINAH. It receives the seventh chamber from below, NAMELY, THE CHAMBER OF THE HOLY OF HOLIES WHICH WENT UP TO BE INCLUDED WITHIN MALCHUT OF ATZILUT, to connect seventh to seventh, because from the one below, THE CHAMBER OF THE HOLY OF HOLIES, one ascends to the supernal chamber, BINAH.

797. וְדָא הוּא רָזָא, בָּרוּךְ, רִבּוּיָא דְּכֻלְּהוּ תַּתָּאֵי, כְּלִילָא בְּחֵיוָון וּשְׂרָפִים וְאוֹפַנִּים, וְכֻלְּהוּ הֵיכָלִין רִבּוּיָא דְּרָזָא דְּקֹדֶשׁ הַקֳּדָשִׁים, דְּשַׁרְיָא בְּגַוֵּיהּ בִּגְנִיזוּ, וּכְדֵין אִקְרֵי בָּרוּ״ךְ, בְּכָל אִלֵּין רִבּוּיִין וּבִרְכָאן, וְרָזִין דְּאִשְׁתְּלִימוּ בָּהּ.

797. This is the secret of 'blessed' OF THE FIRST BLESSING OF AMIDAH, WHICH REFERS TO the many lower beings which were included within the living creatures, Seraphim and wheels, and all the chambers in the manifold secret of the chamber of the Holy of Holies, FOR ALL THESE WERE INCLUDED and dwell treasured within MALCHUT OF ATZILUT. Then

MALCHUT OF ATZILUT is called 'blessed', FOR SHE IS NOW BLESSED BY the manifold blessings and secrets perfected within her.

798. אַתָּ"ה, עִטּוּרָא דִּסְתִימוּ דְּאַתְוָון, כְּלָלָא דְּכֻלְּהוּ כ"ב אַתְוָון. וְדָא הוּא אָ"ת. ה' דְּכָלִיל לוֹן מֵעֵילָּא, בְּהַאי ה', וְכָנִישׁ לוֹן בְּגַוָּיהּ, וְדָא אִיהוּ אָ"ת ה'. וְכַד אִיהִי בִּשְׁלִימוּ בְּהַהוּא נָהָר דְּאָחִיד בָּהּ, סַלְקָא לְאִתְעַטְּרָא לְעֵילָּא, וְדָא אִיהוּ רָזָא דִּכְתִיב, וּבָזֶה הַנַּעֲרָה בָּאָה אֶל הַמֶּלֶךְ, וּכְדֵין אֵת כָּל אֲשֶׁר תֹּאמַר יִנָּתֵן לָהּ. וְדָא אִיהוּ רָזָא בָּרוּךְ אַתָּה, וּבָעֵי לְאִתְכַּוְּונָא בְּהַאי רָזָא, וּלְקַשְּׁרָא רְעוּתָא בְּהַאי רָזָא.

798. 'You' (Heb. *atah*) INDICATES the wreathed concealed letters THAT SHINE UPON MALCHUT, 'YOU', which is the entirety of the 22 letters from *Aleph* to *Tav*. This is the *Aleph-Tav* OF THE WORD 'ATAH' (*ALEPH-TAV-HEI*). The *Hei* OF ATAH INDICATES THE *HEI* OF MALCHUT, which includes THE 22 LETTERS from above, YESOD OF ZEIR ANPIN, and gathers them within her. This is the *Aleph-Tav-Hei* OF THE WORD ATAH. When she is perfected in that river, YESOD OF ZEIR ANPIN, that seizes her, she goes up to be decorated above, IN ZEIR ANPIN. This is the secret of the verse, "by this (NAMELY, YESOD CALLED 'THIS') the girl (MALCHUT) would come to the king (YESOD)" (Ester 2:13). Then, "whatever she desires would be given her" (Ibid.). This is the mystery of 'blessed are You'. One should meditate upon this mystery, and tie his will with this mystery, WHEN UTTERING THE WORDS 'BLESSED ARE YOU'.

799. יְיָ' אֱלֹהֵינוּ: דָּא אִיהוּ קִשּׁוּרָא וְיִחוּדָא דְּמַלְכָּא עִלָּאָה לְעֵילָּא, בְּהַאי, כַּד הַנַּעֲרָה בָּאָה אֶל הַמֶּלֶךְ אֵת כָּל אֲשֶׁר תֹּאמַר יִנָּתֵן לָהּ.

799. THE INTENTION OF 'Hashem our Elohim' is the knot and unison of the Holy King above, NAMELY, THE UNISON OF CHOCHMAH AND BINAH, FOR 'HASHEM' IS CHOCHMAH, AND 'OUR ELOHIM' IS BINAH. With that, when, "the girl would come to the king," TO ZEIR ANPIN, "whatever she desires would be given her," REFERRING TO THE ILLUMINATION OF CHOCHMAH AND BINAH, THAT WILL BE GIVEN TO HER.

800. וֵאלֹהֵי אֲבוֹתֵינוּ: דָּא רָזָא דַּאֲבָהָן, לְבָרְכָא לָהּ. וְדָא אִיהוּ רָזָא,

אֱלֹהֵי אַבְרָהָם אֱלֹהֵי יִצְחָק וֵאלֹהֵי יַעֲקֹב. כְּמָה דְּהַאי נַעֲרָה לָא אִשְׁתְּבָקַת מִתַּתָּאֵי, הָכִי נָמֵי לָא אִשְׁתְּבָקַת מֵאֲבָהָן לְעָלְמִין. אִיהוּ אֲחִידַת בְּהוֹן לְעַטְרָא לָהּ.

800. 'And the Elohim of our fathers' is the secret of the patriarchs, WHO ARE CHESED, GVURAH AND TIFERET OF ZEIR ANPIN, that bless her, MALCHUT. This is the secret of 'the Elohim of Abraham', CHESED; 'the Elohim of Isaac', GVURAH; and 'the Elohim of Jacob', TIFERET. As this girl, NAMELY, MALCHUT, is not abandoned by the lower beings, FOR ALL OF THEM WERE INCLUDED WITHIN HER, so was she never abandoned by the patriarchs, WHO ARE CHESED, GVURAH AND TIFERET OF ZEIR ANPIN, whom she clings to, to be adorned.

801. וּבְגִין דְּאִתְבָּרְכָא מִכָּל חַד מִנְּהוֹן, בָּעֵי לְאַדְכְּרָא לָהּ עַל כָּל חַד וְחַד. וּלְבָתַר יִתְכַּנְּשׁוּן כֻּלְּהוּ בְּחִבּוּרָא חֲדָא, וּמִתְעַטְּרֵי בַּהֲדָהּ, הָאֵל הַגָּדוֹל הַגִּבּוֹר וְהַנּוֹרָא, הָא כֻּלְּהוּ כַּחֲדָא, לְסַלְּקָא לְעֵילָּא בְּקַדְמִיתָא מֵעֵילָּא לְתַתָּא וְהַשְׁתָּא מִתַּתָּא לְעֵילָּא. לְאַכְלְלָא לוֹן בַּהֲדֵיהּ דְּכֵיוָן דְּאָמַר הָאֵל הַגָּדוֹל הַגִּבּוֹר וְהַנּוֹרָא כֻּלְּהוּ כְּלִילָן בָּהּ. וּכְדֵין, אֵל עֶלְיוֹן גּוֹמֵל חֲסָדִים טוֹבִים קוֹנֵה הַכֹּל. וְדָא כְּלָלָא דְּכֹלָּא.

801. Since MALCHUT is blessed by each OF CHESED, GVURAH AND TIFERET OF ZEIR ANPIN, she should be mentioned in connection with each of them, NAMELY, 'THE ELOHIM OF ABRAHAM, THE ELOHIM OF ISAAC, AND THE ELOHIM OF JACOB' MEANING 'THE ELOHIM OF', WHICH IS MALCHUT OF, EACH OF THE FATHERS. Then they are all gathered together, to be bedecked with her, NAMELY, by 'the El that is great, mighty, and tremendous,' for they all gather to raise her up TO CHESED, GVURAH AND TIFERET. FOR 'THE EL' IS MALCHUT, ' THAT IS GREAT' IS CHESED, 'THE MIGHTY' IS GVURAH, AND 'THE TREMENDOUS' IS TIFERET. AND THE NAME OF THE EL, WHICH IS MALCHUT, IS SPOKEN, SO SHE WILL RISE TO ALL OF CHESED, GVURAH AND TIFERET TOGETHER. First, BY 'THE ELOHIM OF ABRAHAM'...SHE RECEIVES FROM THEM from above downward, FROM CHESED, GVURAH AND TIFERET TO MALCHUT, and now, IN 'THE EL THAT IS GREAT'...SHE IS INCLUDED WITHIN THEM from below upward, so they may be comprised within her. For that reason it is written, 'the El that is great, mighty, and tremendous,' MEANING THAT they were all included within her, AND THEN SHE MAY ASCEND WITH CHESED, GVURAH AND TIFERET UP TO BINAH. It continues with 'the most high El, who bestows gracious favors, possessor of all', IN WHICH 'THE MOST HIGH EL' IS THE RIGHT COLUMN OF BINAH, 'WHO BESTOWS GRACIOUS FAVORS' THE LEFT OF BINAH, AND THE 'POSSESSOR OF ALL', IS THE CENTRAL COLUMN OF BINAH, WHICH POSSESSES THE TWO COLUMNS TOGETHER. This is the total of all, SINCE ALL MOCHIN AND ALL THE GRADES COME FROM THE THREE COLUMNS WITHIN BINAH.

802. וְזוֹכֵר חַסְדֵי אָבוֹת, דְּאִשְׁתָּהוּ בַּהֲדָהּ וְעָאלוּ בִּמְעָהָא, וְאִתְבָּרְכוּן תַּמָּן. וּלְבָתַר שָׁארֵי לוֹן וְאַפִּיק לוֹן כַּד אִינּוּן אִתְבָּרְכָאן מִגַּוָּוהּ. וּבְהַהִיא הִשְׁתַּחֲוָאָה דְּאָמַר בא״י מָגֵן אַבְרָהָם, הָכָא נַפְקֵי כֻּלְּהוּ בִּכְלָלָא, דְּהָא בִּימִינָא כֻּלְּהוּ מִתְבָּרְכָאן כַּדְקָא חָזֵי.

802. 'Who remembers the pious deeds of the patriarchs' MEANS THAT CHESED, GVURAH, TIFERET AND MALCHUT stayed with BINAH and entered its bowels, NAMELY, THEY WERE INCLUDED WITHIN THE INTERNAL PART OF BINAH CALLED 'BOWELS', where they are blessed. Later, BINAH releases them FROM THE INTEGRATION and extracts them out when they are blessed, and by bowing, with the words, 'Blessed are You, O Hashem! The Shield of Abraham,' they all come out together FROM BINAH AND TO THEIR PLACES. FOR 'THE SHIELD OF ABRAHAM' IS CHESED AND OF THE RIGHT, and everyone is properly blessed by the right.

803. ת״ח, הֵיכָלָא שְׁבִיעָאָה דָּא, רָזָא דְּמַלְכָּא עִלָּאָה, וּמִתְעַטְּרָן בֵּיהּ אֲבָהָן כִּדְקָאמְרָן, וְאִתְכְּלִילוּ בֵּיהּ. וְעַד הַשְׁתָּא אִתְכְּלִילוּ, וּבָעֵי לְאַפָּקָא לוֹן, אִיהוּ הֵיכָלָא דָּא, וְכַד אַפִּיק לוֹן מְבָרְכָאן, בְּגִין הַאי נְעָרָה, כְּדֵין אִיהִי אֲחִידַת בְּהוּ, בְּכָל אִינּוּן בִּרְכָאן. וְאַף ע״ג דְּהָא אִתְכְּלִילוּ הֵיכָלִין בְּהֵיכָלִין, הַשְׁתָּא אִתְאֲחִידוּ בְּאִינּוּן בִּרְכָאן כַּחֲדָא, וְכַד אָמַר מֶלֶךְ עוֹזֵר וּמוֹשִׁיעַ וּמָגֵן, כְּדֵין אַפִּיק לוֹן מְבָרְכָאן.

803. Come and see: The seventh chamber is the secret of the Supernal King, WHO IS BINAH, and the patriarchs, CHESED, GVURAH AND TIFERET, are bedecked by Him as we said, NAMELY, THEY ASCEND TO HIM, to become a part of Him. Up to now, BEFORE THE WORDS, 'KING, HELPER, SAVIOR

AND SHIELD...' they are part OF BINAH, which chamber, BINAH, has to issue them from its inside. And now that it extracts them from the blessings IN ORDER THAT THEY WILL SUPPLY THIS to this girl, MALCHUT, then THE GIRL holds on to THE FATHERS, and to all the blessings CHESED, GVURAH AND TIFERET RECEIVED WHILE STILL IN BINAH. And though chambers were already included together, AND SO MALCHUT WITHIN CHESED, GVURAH, TIFERET AND BINAH, NEVERTHELESS – now THAT CHESED, GVURAH AND TIFERET COME OUT OF BINAH – CHESED, GVURAH, TIFERET AND MALCHUT hold on to those blessings, together. And with the words 'King, Helper, Savior and Shield', BINAH extracts them from ITS blessings, AND THEY GO EACH TO HIS PLACE.

804. וְהַאי, אִיהוּ חַד הֵיכָלָא שְׁבִיעָאָה, בְּרָזָא דִּשְׁמָא קַדִּישָׁא עִלָּאָה, בוכ"ו. 'בְּרָכָה 'וָחֶסֶד 'כֹּחַ 'וּמִשְׁפָּט, כְּלָלָא כֹּלָּא וְרָזָא דָּא, הוּא רָזָא דְּאֶהְיֶ"ה כְּלָלָא דְּכֹלָּא. בְּגִין דְּאִלֵּין אַתְוָון כְּלָלָא דְּכֹלָּא. בְּגִין דְּאִלֵּין אַתְוָון, אַפִּיקוּ אִלֵּין דְּנַפְקוּ מִנַּיְיהוּ, כְּלָלָא דַּאֲבָהָן, וְדָא אִיהוּ דְּמִתְחַבְּרָא בַּהֲדַיְיהוּ, דְּאִקְרֵי בְּרָכָה.

804. This MENTIONED SEVENTH CHAMBER is a seventh chamber in the secret of the Holy Supernal Name, *Bet-Vav-Caf-Vav*, THE HEBREW INITIALS OF 'Blessing, and Chesed, Strength and Justice,' a name which comprises everything. THIS IS THE SECRET OF MALCHUT AND CHESED, GVURAH AND TIFERET WITHIN BINAH, BECAUSE 'BLESSING' IS MALCHUT; 'CHESED' IS THE RIGHT COLUMN; 'STRENGTH' IS THE LEFT COLUMN, GVURAH; AND 'JUSTICE' IS THE CENTRAL COLUMN, TIFERET. This is the secret of *Aleph-Hei-Yud-Hei*, which includes all MOCHIN, FOR THE LETTERS OF THE NAME *BET-VAV-CAF-VAV* ARE PRECEDED BY THOSE OF THE NAME *ALEPH-HEI-YUD-HEI*. AFTER *ALEPH* OF *ALEPH-HEI-YUD-HEI* COMES *BET* OF *BET-VAV-CAF-VAV*; AFTER *HEI* – *VAV*, AFTER *YUD* – CAF, AND AFTER THE LAST *HEI* – THE LAST *VAV*. For these letters comprise everything, since the letters OF THE NAME *BET-VAV-CAF-VAV* issued those who issued from them, NAMELY, CHESED, GVURAH AND TIFERET AND MALCHUT, all of the fathers, WHO ARE CHESED, STRENGTH, AND JUSTICE, HINTED AT IN THESE INITIALS. The one to be united with them is called 'Blessing', ALSO HINTED AT IN THESE INITIALS.

805. כֵּיוָן דְּאָמַר בא"י מָגֵן אַבְרָהָם, הָא אֲחִידַת בִּרְכָאן מִנַּיְיהוּ, בְּרָזָא

דְּהֵיכָלָא חֲמִישָׁאָה אַהֲבָה, דְּאִיהוּ יְמִינָא, וְאִיהוּ חֲמִישָׁאָה, לְאִתְקַשְּׁרָא בִּרְחִימוּ דְּבִרְכָאן דִּימִינָא. וְהָכִי אִצְטְרִיךְ, מֵעֵילָּא לְתַתָּא לְאִתְבָּרְכָא. בְּקַדְמֵיתָא אִתְכְּלָלוּ הֵיכָלָא בְּהֵיכָלָא כִּדְקָאמְרָן, וְהַשְׁתָּא נַטְלֵי בִּרְכָאן לְאִשְׁתַּכְּחָא אִלֵּין מִקַּדְמַת אִלֵּין. ואע״ג דְּאִית דְּנָטִיל בְּקַדְמֵיתָא. כֵּיוָן דְּאִשְׁתְּכָחוּ מִסִּטְרָא דִּימִינָא בִּרְכָאן, בְּהֵיכָלָא חֲמִישָׁאָה שָׁארֵי לְאַחֲדָא.

805. Once the words 'Blessed are You, O Hashem! The Shield of Abraham' are uttered, AND THE FATHERS AND MALCHUT COME OUT OF BINAH INTO THEIR PLACES, MALCHUT grasps the blessings, THAT ARE DRAWN from THE FATHERS in the secret of the fifth chamber, THE CHAMBER of love, which is right, NAMELY, CHESED, so the fifth chamber will be united with love to the blessings of the right, DRAWN BY 'THE SHIELD OF ABRAHAM' WHICH IS RIGHT. This is the way to be blessed, WHEN THE BLESSINGS DESCEND from above downward, NAMELY, WHEN THEY COME OUT FROM BINAH AND INTO THEIR PLACES, THE FIFTH CHAMBER RECEIVES THE BLESSINGS BEFORE THE SIXTH CHAMBER. First the chambers were joined together like we said, but now the blessings are taken to be here before they are there. Though one comes first, BEFORE THE FIFTH CHAMBER, NAMELY THE SIXTH CHAMBER, THE CHAMBER OF DESIRE, NEVERTHELESS since the blessings are of the right, WHICH IS CHESED, they take hold of the fifth chamber, WHICH IS CHESED, AND NOT THE SIXTH CHAMBER WHICH IS TIFERET.

806. וּלְבָתַר בְּסִטְר שְׂמָאלָא, בְּרָזָא דָּא אַתָּה גִּבּוֹר. וְהַאי אִיהוּ חִבּוּרָא אַתָּה וְגִבּוֹר, תְּרֵין דִּינִין. וְכֵיוָן דְּאִתְמַשְׁכָאן בִּרְכָאן, אִתְכְּלִיל בְּרַחֲמֵי, וְאִשְׁתְּכַח בְּהַהוּא סִטְרָא כֹּלָּא כַּחֲדָא, וְדָא הוּא מְחַיֵּה מֵתִים סוֹמֵךְ נוֹפְלִים וְרוֹפֵא חוֹלִים וְכוּ'.

806. After that comes the left side, WHICH IS GVURAH. In this mystery are the words 'You are mighty,' the combination of two Judgments, 'You' and 'mighty', FOR 'YOU' IS THE NAME OF MALCHUT, WHICH IS JUDGMENT, AND 'MIGHTY' IS THE LEFT COLUMN, WHICH IS JUDGMENT. Since the blessings were drawn FROM WHAT THE FATHERS RECEIVED WHILE STAYING WITHIN BINAH, JUDGMENT was tempered with Mercy, and MERCY was found in that side to make it as one. This is the meaning of the words 'resurrects the dead...supports the fallen, and heals the sick...' WHICH SHOWS MERCY.

807. וְדָא אִיהוּ בְּרָזָא דִשְׁמָא קַדִישָׁא דְאִקְרֵי אֲכַדְטַ"ם, רָזָא אִיהוּ בְּאַתְוָון דִשְׁמָא דְאִקְרֵי אֱלֹהִי"ם. בְּגִין דְּאִלֵּין אַתְוָון סַלְּקִין לְאִתְעַטְּרָא לְעֵילָּא, וְאַפִּיקוּ לְהוּ אִלֵּין לְאִתְקְרֵי בְּהוֹן, וְסַלְּקִין לְאִתְעַטְּרָא לְעֵילָּא אֱלֹהִים חַיִּים, וְגָרַע בְּאַתְוָון, לְאַחֲדָא בִּגְרִיעוּ. וּמֵהָכָא אִתְפְּשַׁט לְתַתָּא, לְנַטְלָא מִגּוֹ אִלֵּין אַתְוָון אַחֲרָנִין, וּלְסַלְּקָא מֵאִלֵּין אַתְוָון, לִשְׁמָא דֶאֱלֹהִים.

807. MERCY is in the secret of the holy name *Aleph-Caf-Dalet-Tet-Mem*, which is the secret of the letters of the name Elohim. FOR THE LETTERS OF *ALEPH-CAF-DALET-TET-MEM* PRECEDE THOSE OF ELOHIM, EXCEPT *ALEPH* WHICH IS THE FIRST LETTER, AND FINAL *MEM*, WHICH HAS NO LETTER PRECEDING IT, AS IT IS ALSO *MEM*. THE *CAF* OF *ALEPH-CAF-DALET-TET-MEM* PRECEDES *LAMED* OF ELOHIM, THE *DALET* PRECEDES *CAF*, AND THE *TET* PRECEDES *YUD*. For the letters OF ELOHIM, A NAME OF GVURAH AND THE LEFT COLUMN, went up to be bedecked above IN BINAH, where they issued THE LETTERS OF *ALEPH-CAF-DALET-TET-MEM* to be called by them. FOR WHEN THE LETTERS OF ELOHIM went up to be bedecked above IN BINAH CALLED 'a living Elohim', CHESED WITHIN BINAH diminished THE JUDGMENTS within the letters OF ELOHIM, THAT WENT UP, so they would join a lesser JUDGMENT. From here, BINAH, THE NAME *ALEPH-CAF-DALET-TET-MEM* is spread downward INTO THE CHAMBER OF GVURAH through the other letters, THOSE OF THE name *ALEPH-CAF-DALET-TET-MEM* OF A LESSER JUDGMENT, and ascends through these letters to the name Elohim WITHIN THE CHAMBER OF GVURAH, SO AS TO MITIGATE THE JUDGMENTS IN IT.

808. כֵּיוָן דְּאִתְמַשְׁכָאן אַתְוָון בְּחַמִישָׁאָה וּרְבִיעָאָה מֵעֵילָּא כִּדְקָאמְרָן, שָׁארֵי וְאָחִיד בִּרְכָאן מֵאֶמְצָעִיתָא דְכֹלָּא, מֵהֵיכָלָא שְׁתִיתָאָה, וְאָחִיד בִּרְכָאן בְּהַאי וּבְהַאי. וּבג"כ אַתָּה קָדוֹשׁ, אִתְכְּלִיל אַתָּה בְּקָדוֹשׁ.

808. Since the letters OF *BET-VAV-CAF-VAV* AND *ALEPH-CAF-DALET-TET -MEM* flowed into the fifth chamber, CHESED, and the fourth chamber,

GVURAH, from above, BINAH, as we said, the blessings started to hold on to the middle part of all, NAMELY, THE CENTRAL COLUMN WHICH IS TIFERET within the sixth chamber, THE CHAMBER OF DESIRE, TIFERET. The blessings hold on to this and that, RIGHT AND LEFT, WHICH TIFERET COMPRISES. For that reason it is said 'You are holy,' for 'You' WHICH IS MALCHUT THAT IS GVURAH, is part of 'holy' WHICH IS TIFERET THAT IS CHESED. THUS, TIFERET IS INCLUDED WITHIN BOTH CHESED AND GVURAH.

809. וְשִׁמְךָ קָדוֹשׁ, כֵּיוָן דְּאָמַר אַתָּה קָדוֹשׁ, אֲמַאי וְשִׁמְךָ קָדוֹשׁ, הַיְינוּ שֵׁם, הַיְינוּ אַתָּה. אֶלָּא הָא תָּנֵינָן, בְּכָל אֲתָר דְּאִשְׁתְּכַח יִחוּדָא וְקִשּׁוּרָא, בָּעֵינָן קְדוּשָּׁה, וְתוֹסֶפֶת קְדוּשָּׁה, וְהַהוּא תּוֹסֶפֶת עִקָּרָא הוּא יַתִּיר מִכֹּלָּא. ובג"כ, בְּכֻלְּהוּ כְּתִיב אַתָּה, וְלָא יַתִּיר, וְהָכָא בְּהַאי אֲתָר, אָמַר קְדוּשָּׁה, וְתוֹסֶפֶת קְדוּשָּׁה. אַתָּה קָדוֹשׁ קְדוּשָּׁה, וְשִׁמְךָ קָדוֹשׁ תּוֹסֶפֶת קְדוּשָּׁה. וּקְדוֹשִׁים בְּכָל יוֹם: אִלּוּ שְׁאַר קְדוּשִׁין עִלָּאִין, דִּי בְּכָל הֵיכָלָא וְהֵיכָלָא, דְּמִתְקַדְּשֵׁי מֵהַאי תּוֹסֶפֶת. בְּגִין דִּקְדוּשָּׁה קַמַּיְיתָא אִיהִי לָהּ, וְתוֹסֶפֶת קְדוּשָּׁה, לְאִתְקַדְּשָׁא כָּל אִינּוּן שְׁאַר דְּקַאמְרָן.

809. "...and Your Name is holy." HE ASKS: IT IS WRITTEN, "You are holy." Why add 'and Your Name is holy'. This is 'Name' and 'You', MEANING THAT MALCHUT IS CALLED BOTH 'NAME' AND 'YOU'. HE ANSWERS: We have learned that wherever there is unity and contact BETWEEN THE SFIROT, holiness and additional holiness must be drawn, and the addition is the most important part. Hence in them all, THE FIRST AND SECOND BLESSINGS, it is written 'You', and no more. Here, IN THE THIRD BLESSING, TIFERET, THAT COMBINES AND TIES THE SFIROT – CHESED AND GVURAH TOGETHER, in this place, there is holiness and additional holiness. 'You are holy' is holiness, and so is 'and Your Name is holy'. 'And they who are holy' are the rest of superior sanctifications in each and every chamber, that become more sacred by the addition OF HOLINESS, since the first sanctification is FOR MALCHUT PROPER, and the additional sanctification is for the rest, NAMELY, THE SANCTIFICATIONS IN EACH OF THE OTHER CHAMBERS.

810. וּלְבָתַר אִתְקַדְּשָׁא כֹּלָּא מֵעֵילָּא, וּמִכֻּלְּהוּ אֲבָהָן, אִתְקְשַׁר בְּקִשּׁוּרָא

חֲדָא, וְהַיְינוּ בָּרוּךְ אַתָּה יְיָ׳ הָאֵל הַקָּדוֹשׁ. הָכָא כֹּלָּא קְשׁוּרָא חֲדָא, בְּגִין דְּאָמַר בא״י הָאֵל הַקָּדוֹשׁ. וְעַל דָּא אִקְרֵי צְרוֹרָא וְקִשׁוּרָא דְּכֹלָּא בְּיִחוּדָא חַד. זַכָּאָה חוּלָקֵיהּ, מַאן דְּיָדַע לְסַדְּרָא שְׁבָחֵי דְּמָארֵיהּ בַּאֲתַר דְּאִצְטְרִיךְ. עַד הָכָא, דְּבֵקוּתָא וּבִרְכָּאן וּקְדוּשָׁה כַּחֲדָא בַּאֲבָהָן.

810. Then all became more sacred from above, BY BINAH, and by the patriarchs, CHESED, GVURAH AND TIFERET, FOR ALL was tied into one bond by the words 'Blessed are You, O Eternal, holy El'. Here all becomes bound together due to the words 'Blessed are you, O Eternal, holy El'. Therefore it is called 'TIFERET', the knot and unity of all in one unison. Happy is the portion of whoever knows how to arrange the praises of his Master in the proper place. Up to this place, IN THE FIRST THREE BLESSINGS, there is devotion, blessings, and sanctification together with the fathers, WHO ARE CHESED, GVURAH AND TIFERET, FOR THE FIRST BLESSING IS CHESED, THE SECOND IS GVURAH, AND THE THIRD TIFERET.

811. מִכָּאן וּלְהָלְאָה, קַיְימִין שְׁאֶלְתִּין וּבָעוּתִין. שֵׁירוּתָא דְּבָעֵי בַּר נָשׁ לְמִשְׁאַל, לְמִנְדַּע בְּמִלִּין דְּמָארֵיהּ, בְּגִין לְמֶחֱזֵי תִּיאוּבְתֵּיהּ לְגַבֵּיהּ, וְלָא אִתְפְּרַשׁ מִנֵּיהּ. בְּגִין דְּבָעֵי ב״נ לְאִשְׁתַּתְּפָא בִּקְדוּשָׁה דִּשְׁמָא קַדִּישָׁא עִלָּאָה, לְאִתְעַטְּרָא בֵּיהּ, וְאִיהוּ שְׁמָא דְּבִרְכָּאן וְקִדּוּשִׁין, כוז״ו. רָזָא דִּשְׁמָא קַדִּישָׁא יְדֹוָ״ד דְּאִיהוּ קַדִּישׁ בִּקְדוּשָׁה. וְאִלֵּין אַתְוָון אַפִּיקוּ מִנֵּיהּ הָנֵי אַתְוָון אַחֲרָנִין, חִבּוּרָא דְּהָנֵי, כְּחִבּוּרָא דִּדְכַר בְּנוּקְבָּא. וְהָנֵי קַדִּישִׁין עִלָּאִין, רָזָא דִּקְדוּשָׁה.

811. From this place onward IN THE AMIDAH, there are entreaties and petitions. First it behooves a man to ask to know the words of his Master, to show his passion for Him, and not to be separated from Him. THIS IS THE SECRET OF THE PRAYER, 'DO YOU GRACIOUSLY BESTOW UPON US FROM YOUR KNOWLEDGE, UNDERSTANDING, AND DISCERNMENT'. For a man should take part in the sanctification of the high and Holy Name, to be adorned by it. And the name of the blessings and sanctifications is *Caf-Vav-Zayin-Vav*, which is the secret of the Holy Name Yud Hei Vav Hei, which is most sacred, and these letters, YUD HEI VAV HEI, produced the other letters, *CAF-VAV-ZAYIN-VAV*. FOR THESE LETTERS PRECEDE

THOSE OF YUD HEI VAV HEI, FOR AFTER *YUD* OF YUD HEI VAV HEI COMES *CAF* OF *CAF-VAV-ZAYIN-VAV*, AFTER *HEI* COMES *VAV*, AFTER *VAV* COMES *ZAYIN*, AND AFTER THE LAST *HEI* COMES THE LAST *VAV*. The combination of these NAMES, YUD HEI VAV HEI AND *CAF-VAV-ZAYIN-VAV* resembles the joining of male and female, FOR THE NAME YUD HEI VAV HEI, WHICH SHINES UPON ZEIR ANPIN, IS MALE, AND THE NAME *CAF-VAV-ZAYIN-VAV*, WHICH SHINES UPON THE CHAMBERS, IS FEMALE. These holy supernal names are the secret of sanctification.

812. אִלֵּין אַתְוָון אַחֲרָנִין אִקְרוּן טַ״ל. טַל הַשָּׁמַיִם. רָזָא דְּחוּשְׁבְּנָא דְּאַתְוָון דִּילֵיהּ, בְּגִין דְּהָכָא לְתַתָּא, קַיְימָן כָּל מִלִּין בְּחוּשְׁבְּנָא, וְלָא חוּשְׁבְּנָא, אֶלָּא לְסִיהֲרָא. ובג״כ בָּעֵי לְאִתְקַשְּׁרָא בִּקְדוּשָּׁה דְּמָארֵיהּ, וְלָא יִתְפְּרַשׁ ב״נ מִנֵּיהּ. וְכַד שָׁאִיל, שֵׁירוּתָא דִּשְׁאֶלְתִּין לְמִנְדַּע לְמָארֵיהּ, לְאַחֲזָאָה דְּתִיאוּבְתֵּיהּ לְגַבֵּיהּ. מִכָּאן וּלְהָלְאָה, יִתְפְּרַשׁ זְעֵיר זְעֵיר, וַיִשְׁאַל שְׁאֶלְתּוֹי מַה דְּאִצְטְרִיךְ לְשָׁאֲלָא.

812. The other letters, *CAF-VAV-ZAYIN-VAV*, are called 'dew', the dew of heaven, which is the reckoning of its letters, THAT HAS THE SAME NUMERICAL VALUE AS THAT OF DEW (HEB. *TAL*), for down below, IN MALCHUT, all words are counted, IN THE SECRET OF THE ILLUMINATION OF CHOCHMAH CALLED 'RECKONING' AND 'NUMBER'. There is no reckoning save that of the moon, WHICH IS MALCHUT, FOR CHOCHMAH IS NOT REVEALED IN ANY SFIRAH BUT MALCHUT, SO THERE IS NO RECKONING BUT IN MALCHUT. For that reason one needs to be connected with the sanctification of his Master, and not to be separated from Him. When one asks, one should ask first to know one's Master, and show that his passion is turned towards Him. THIS IS THE SECRET OF THE FIRST PETITION 'DO GRACIOUSLY BESTOW UPON US FROM YOUR KNOWLEDGE, UNDERSTANDING, AND DISCERNMENT'. From now on, one may be separated little by little, and request whatever is needed.

813. וְכָל שְׁאֶלְתּוֹי יֵהוֹן, לְבָתַר דִּיסַדֵּר סִדּוּרָא דָּא דְּקָאמְרָן. כְּגַוְונָא דָּא, כָּל שְׁאֶלְתּוֹי יֵהוֹן בְּתַחֲנוּנִים וּבָעוּתִין לְקַמֵּי מָארֵיהּ, וְלָא יַרְחִיק גַּרְמֵיהּ מִנֵּיהּ. זַכָּאָה חוּלָקֵיהּ, מַאן דְּיָדַע לְסַדְּרָא סִדּוּרָא דָּא, לְמֵהַךְ בְּאֹרַח מֵישָׁר, כַּדְקָא חָזֵי.

813. All his asking should be requested after he arranges this order that we said. In the same manner, all his petitions should be by way of entreating and beseeching before his Master and he must not separate himself from Him, NAMELY HEAVEN FORBID THAT HE MIGHT NOT COMPLAIN ABOUT HIM. Happy is whoever knows this sequence by which to go in the path of truth properly.

814. כְּגַוְונָא דְּאִתְאַחֲדָא אֶשָּׁא בְּמַיָּא, וּמַיָּא בְּאֶשָּׁא. דָּרוֹם בְּצָפוֹן, וְצָפוֹן בְּדָרוֹם. מִזְרָח בְּמַעֲרָב, וּמַעֲרָב בְּמִזְרָח. הָכִי נָמֵי אִתְקָשַּׁר כֹּלָּא כַּחֲדָא, וְיִחוּדָא אִשְׁתְּלִים דָּא בְּדָא.

814. As fire is united with water, and water with fire, south with north, and north with south, AS FIRE AND WATER ARE THE INNER PART OF CHESED AND GVURAH, AND SOUTH AND NORTH ARE THE OUTER SIDE OF CHESED AND GVURAH, as east and west, west and east, TIFERET AND MALCHUT, so all are together and the unison is completed by each other.

815. וְכָל אִינּוּן דְּיַדְעִין לְסַדְּרָא צְלוֹתְהוֹן כַּדְקָא יֵאוֹת, לְאִתְכַּלְּלָא הָנֵי הֵיכָלִין אִלֵּין בְּאִלֵּין, וּלְאִתְקַשְּׁרָא דָּא בְּדָא. הַאי ב"נ אִתְקָשַּׁר בְּהוּ, וְקָרִיב לֵיהּ לְאִתְכַּלְּלָא בְּהוּ. שְׁאֶלְתָּא שָׁאִיל וְיָהִיב לֵיהּ. זַכָּאָה חוּלָקֵיהּ בְּהַאי עָלְמָא, וּבְעָלְמָא דְּאָתֵי.

815. All those who know how to arrange their prayer properly, to include all the chambers within each other and connect them to each other, such a man is joined with them, and approaches them to be included within them. He asks and his petition is granted. Happy he is in this world and in the World to Come.

816. בָּתַר דְּסִיֵּים שְׁאֶלְתִּין וְגוּפָא שְׁלִים בְּכָל סִטְרִין בְּחֶדְוָה דְּלִבָּא וְאִיהוּ שָׁאִיל וְסִיֵּים שְׁאֶלְתִּין. יֶהְדָּר לְאַמְשָׁכָא בִּרְכָאן וְחֶדְוָואן לְתַתָּא, בְּרָזָא דְּהֵיכָלָא תְּלִיתָאָה, לְאַמְשָׁכָא לְתַתָּא, וְדָא הוּא רְצֵה יְיָ' אֱלֹהֵינוּ בְּעַמְּ"ךָ יִשְׂרָאֵ"ל. וּבְגִין דְּמַעֲמָדוֹת אִינּוּן סַמְכִין דְּגוּפָא. שֵׁירוּתָא לְתַתָּא מִן גּוּפָא תְּרֵין יַרְכִין, עַד דְּמָטֵי לְבִרְכִּין.

816. After his petitions are all said, and the body is whole on all sides to the heart's rejoicing and he asked and finished asking, a man must again draw blessings and joys downward in the secret of the third chamber, NETZACH, to draw downward. This is the meaning of 'Accept, O Hashem our Elohim, Your people Yisrael'. For the Daily Selections, NAMELY, THE LEGS, NETZACH AND HOD, uphold the body, TIFERET. They start beneath the body and are called 'the two thighs down to the knees', FOR NETZACH AND HOD ARE DIVIDED INTO: FROM THE THIGH TO THE KNEES, THE SECRET OF THE BLESSING 'ACCEPT', AND FROM THE KNEES DOWNWARD, THE SECRET 'WHO RESTORES HIS DIVINE GLORY TO ZION', AND 'WE GRATEFULLY ACKNOWLEDGE'.

817. וְאִלֵּין אִינּוּן רָזָא דְּמַעֲמָדוֹת, דְּקַיְימֵי עַל קָרְבְּנָא. וְהָכָא אִיהוּ רָזָא שֵׁירוּתָא דִּתְרֵין יַרְכִין מִלְּעֵילָּא, עַד בִּרְכִין, חִבּוּרָא דִּנְבִיאִים. וּמַרְאוֹת, בְּרָזָא דְּאַתְוָון דִּשְׁמָא קַדִּישָׁא, דְּאִקְרֵי הַשְׁתָּפָ"א. דְּאִיהוּ רָזָא דִּשְׁמָא דְּאִקְרֵי צְבָאוֹת. דָּא סָלִיק, וְדָא נָחִית. דָּא נְבִיאִים, וְדָא מַרְאוֹת.

817. This is the secret of the daily selections about the sacrifices, CORRESPONDING TO THE TWO THIGHS, NETZACH AND HOD. Here, IN THE THIRD CHAMBER, is the secret of the starting point of the two thighs above IN THE BODY, down to the knees, where the prophets are connected, AS PROPHECY IS DRAWN FROM NETZACH AND HOD OF ATZILUT, and the visions FROM NETZACH AND HOD OF THE CHAMBERS, in the secret of the holy name *Hei-Shin-Tav-Pe-Aleph*, which is the secret of the name Tzevaot, ACCORDING TO THE ATBASH CIPHER, when this one, THE FIRST LETTERS OF THE ATBASH CIPHER ascend, while the other LETTERS OF THE ATBASH CIPHER descend. THE NAME TZEVAOT is for the prophets and THE NAME *HEI-SHIN-TAV-PE-ALEPH* is for the visions. AND NETZACH AND HOD ARE CALLED 'TZEVAOT'.

818. וְהָכָא אִיהוּ רָזָא עִלָּאָה דִּבְרַיְיתֵי דְּקַאמְרָן, וְכַד מָטֵי אִינִישׁ לְבִרְכִּין, יִכְרַע בָּרוּךְ א"י הַמַּחֲזִיר שְׁכִינָתוֹ לְצִיּוֹן, וְהָא הָכָא אַהַדְרוּ בְּרַיְיתֵי לְמַתְנִיתִין וְאִתְבָּרְכָאן כַּחֲדָא.

818. Here, IN THE THIRD CHAMBER, is the high secret called 'Baraitha', as we said ABOVE, FOR BARAITHA MEANS EXTERNAL, AND NETZACH AND HOD ARE OUTSIDE THE BODY, WHICH IS TIFERET, and when a man reaches the knees, WHICH ARE HOD, he should kneel. 'Blessed are You, O Hashem, who restores His divine glory to Zion': In this verse the Baraithas are restored to be Mishnah and they are blessed together. FOR HERE NETZACH AND HOD OF THE CHAMBERS WERE INCLUDED WITHIN THE HOLY OF HOLIES IN THE SECRET OF MALCHUT, WHICH IS THE SECRET OF MISHNAH, THE INNER MEANING OF THE VERSE 'BLESSED ARE YOU, O HASHEM, WHO RESTORES HIS DIVINE GLORY TO ZION', FOR ZION IS YESOD OF MALCHUT.

819. הֵיכָלָא תִּנְיָינָא לְתַתָּא, דְּאִתְפְּקָדוּ בֵּיהּ נִשְׁמָתִין לְסַלְּקָא, לְאִתְחֲזָאָה בְּחֵיזוּ דְּחֶלְמָא. מוֹדִים, לְאַכְרְעָה בִּרְכִּין, לְאוֹדָאָה עַל נִשְׁמָתִין, כִּדְקַאמְרָן עַל נִשְׁמוֹתֵינוּ הַפְּקוּדוֹת, עַד דְּמָטֵי לְהַטּוֹב שִׁמְךָ וּלְךָ נָאֶה לְהוֹדוֹת.

819. The second chamber below, THE CHAMBER OF THE VERY HEAVEN, is where the souls are entrusted to go up to see the visions of the dream, WHICH IS BENEATH THE THIGHS, WHERE THE KNEES ARE, FOR THE DREAM IS DRAWN FROM BELOW THE THIGHS. THIS IS WHERE WE SAY 'we gratefully acknowledge,' and kneel to give thanks for the souls, from 'and the souls that are entrusted to you,' up to 'All beneficent is Your Name, to whom it is fitting to render thanks'.

820. וְדָא הוּא גּוֹ רָזָא דִּשְׁמָא קַדִּישָׁא, דְּאִקְרֵי בָּ"ם בְּמוּכָ"ן. דָּא אִקְרֵי אֵל אֱלֹהִים, דְּאִיהוּ בְּרָזָא עִלָּאָה. אֵל אֱלֹהִי"ם יְהֹוָ"ה הוּא יוֹדֵעַ. כְּלָלָא דְּאִלֵּין אַתְוָון אַחֲרָנִין דְּנַפְקֵי מִנַּיְיהוּ, וּלְתַתָּא, רָזָא דְּחֶלְמָא. רָזָא לְהַהוּא אֲתָר לְאַעֲלָא בְּהוּ נִשְׁמָתִין. וּבָעֵינָן לְאַמְשָׁכָא בְּהָנֵי בִּרְכָאן, בְּגִין לְאַשְׁכְּחָא נַיְיחָא בְּהַאי עָלְמָא, וּבְעָלְמָא דְּאָתֵי.

820. This is the inner mystery of the Holy Name called *Bet-final Mem*, *Bet-Mem-Vav-Caf-final Nun*, WHICH CONSISTS OF THE LETTERS COMING AFTER THE LETTERS OF THE NAMES EL ELOHIM. It is called 'El Elohim', through a supernal mystery OF CHESED AND GVURAH OF ATZILUT, as it is written, "El Elohim Hashem, He knows" (Yehoshua 22:22). The entirety of the other letters *BET-FINAL MEM, BET-MEM-VAV-CAF-FINAL NUN*, that come OUT OF EL ELOHIM, and downward, IN THE SECOND CHAMBER, is the secret of the dream, the secret of putting souls in this place TO LOOK AT

THE VISION OF THE DREAM. We should go on with the benedictions, in order to find rest in this world and in the World to Come.

821. הֵיכָלָא תַּתָּאָה לְתַתָּא, שִׂים שָׁלוֹם טוֹבָה וּבְרָכָה. הָכָא אִיהוּ כְּלָלָא דְשָׁלוֹם. שָׁלוֹם לְעֵילָא, שָׁלוֹם לְתַתָּא, שָׁלוֹם לְכָל סִטְרִין, שָׁלוֹם בְּפַמַלְיָא דִלְעֵילָא, שָׁלוֹם בְּפַמַלְיָא דִלְתַתָּא, וְהֵיכָלָא דָא אִיהוּ פַּמַלְיָא דִלְתַתָּא. בְּחִבּוּרָא חֲדָא בְּפַמַלְיָא דִלְעֵילָא. וּמֵהָכָא נָגִיד לְכָל אִינּוּן תַּתָּאֵי דִלְבַר.

821. The chamber down below, THE CHAMBER OF THE SAPPHIRE STONE, THE MYSTERY OF YESOD AND MALCHUT, IS THE SECRET MEANING OF 'bestow peace, happiness, and blessing'. Here peace is perfected, peace above, IN YESOD OF ZEIR ANPIN, and peace below, IN YESOD OF MALCHUT, peace on all sides, BOTH IN RIGHT AND LEFT, peace in the celestial retinue, YESOD AND MALCHUT OF THE CHAMBERS OF ATZILUT, and peace in the terrestrial retinue. For this chamber OF THE SAPPHIRE STONE, AND YESOD AND MALCHUT OF THE CHAMBERS OF BRIYAH WITHIN IT the terrestrial retinue is united with the celestial retinue, whence PEACE flows down to all the lower beings, outside THE CHAMBERS OF BRIYAH.

822. וְהָכָא אִתְכְּלִיל וְאִשְׁתְּלִים כֹּלָּא כַּחֲדָא, עֵילָא וְתַתָּא, בִּנְהִירוּ חֲדָא, לְאִשְׁתַּלְמָא שֵׁם מָלֵא, יְיָ' אֱלֹהִים. שֵׁם דָּא דְאִיהוּ שָׁלֵם, בְּכָל אִינּוּן הֵיכָלִין, בְּכָל אִינּוּן נְהוֹרִין עִלָּאִין, לְמֶהֱוֵי כֻּלְּהוּ חַד.

822. Here everything is joined to be perfected together, above IN ZEIR ANPIN, and below IN MALCHUT, by one illumination, NAMELY, BY UNION that completes the full name Yud Hei Vav Hei Elohim, YUD HEI VAV HEI BEING ZEIR ANPIN AND ELOHIM BEING MALCHUT. This name is complete in all the chambers INCLUDED WITHIN MALCHUT, and in all the supernal lights, INCLUDED WITHIN ZEIR ANPIN, to make them one.

823. הַאי ב"נ, כַּד אִשְׁתְּאִיל מֵהֵיכָלָא דָא לְנָפְקָא לְבַר. יְשַׁוֵּי גַּרְמֵיהּ, כְּמַאן דְּנָפִיק מֵחַבְרוּתָא דְמַלְכָּא, וּמִגּוֹ הֵיכָלֵיהּ, וְיַמְאִיךְ גַּרְמֵיהּ קָמֵיהּ.

אֲבָל יֶחֱדֵי גַּרְמֵיהּ, דְּהָא קַדְמָאָה אִיהוּ, לְנַטְלָא עִטְרָא דִּמְשִׁיכוּ דְּבִרְכָּאָן דְּנַגְדִּין מִיִּחוּדָא דְּמָארֵיהּ. דָּא אִיהוּ בַּר, דְּאִיהוּ מֵהֵיכָלָא דְּמַלְכָּא. דְּהָא בְּהַאי שַׁעֲתָא דְּקָא נָפִיק מִקַּמֵּי מַלְכָּא, וְכֹלָּא קָשִׁיר בְּכָל הָנֵי סִטְרִין, בְּקִשּׁוּרָא דְּיִחוּדָא, וּבִרְכָּאן, וּקְדוּשָּׁה, וְתוֹסֶפֶת קְדוּשָּׁה. קוּדְשָׁא בְּרִיךְ הוּא קָרֵי לְפָמַלְיָא דִּלְעֵילָּא, וְאָמַר לוֹן, כְּתוֹבוּ לְהַאי ב״נ פְּלַנְיָא, מֵאִינּוּן דְּאִקְרוּן חוֹשְׁבֵי שְׁמוֹ.

823. A man, WHO MEDITATES UPON ALL THESE MEDITATIONS, when he is asked to leave the chamber and go out, should behave as if he is withdrawing from the presence of the King, and from His palace, and should lower himself before Him. But it also behooves him to rejoice in being the first to receive the crown of continuation of the blessings drawn from the unison of his Master. He is a son, AMONG THE CHILDREN of the King's chamber. For when he withdraws from the company of the King, all is united in all respects, by the tie of unity, the blessings and sanctification, and the additional holiness. The Holy One, blessed be He calls the celestial retinue, WHICH ARE THE GRADES JOINED BY HIM, and tells them, write the name of so-and-so, amongst those, who are called "those who thought upon His Name" (Malachi 3:16).

824. מַאן חוֹשְׁבֵי שְׁמוֹ. אִינּוּן דִּמְחַשְּׁבֵי וּמְכַוְּונִין בְּרָזָא דִּשְׁמֵיהּ, לְיַחֲדָא הֵיכָלִין בְּהֵיכָלִין, לְקַשְּׁרָא קִשְׁרִין, וּלְיַחֲדָא כֻּלְּהוּ בְּיִחוּדָא חֲדָא. וְאִלֵּין אִינּוּן חוֹשְׁבֵי שְׁמוֹ, כד״א וּלְחוֹשְׁבֵי שְׁמוֹ. כְּדֵין אַכְתִּיבוּ לֵיהּ, וְאִתְרְשִׁים וְאִשְׁתְּמוֹדַע לְעֵילָּא, וְאִשְׁתְּלִים אִיהוּ לְעֵילָּא וְתַתָּא.

824. HE ASKS, who are "those who thought upon His name"? AND HE ANSWERS: They are those who think and who meditate on the secret of His name, in order to unite the chambers together, tie knots, and unite everything into one union. These are those who "thought upon His Name." This man is then written AMONGST THOSE WHO THOUGHT UPON HIS NAME, to be distinguished and known above, and be perfected above and below.

825. וּמַאן דְּקָרִיב קָמֵי מָארֵיהּ, וְצַלֵּי צְלוֹתֵיהּ, וְלָא אַשְׁלִים יִחוּדָא, וְלָא חָיִישׁ עַל יְקָרָא דְּמָארֵיהּ, לְקַשְּׁרָא קִשְׁרִין כִּדְקָאמְרָן, טַב לֵיהּ דְּלָא

אִבְרֵי. וְקוּדְשָׁא בְּרִיךְ הוּא אָמַר כִּתְבוּ אֶת הָאִישׁ הַזֶּה עֲרִירִי גֶּבֶר לָא יִצְלַח בְּיָמָיו. וְדָא אִיהוּ גּוֹזֵל אָבִיו וְאִמּוֹ.

825. Whoever approaches his Master, and prays without perfecting the unison, and without caring for the glory of his Master to tie knots as said, it were better for him not to have been born, and the Holy One, blessed be He says, "write this man childless, a man that shall not prosper in his days" (Yirmeyah 22:30). This man "robs his father or his mother" (Mishlei 28:24), NAMELY, THE HOLY ONE, BLESSED BE HE AND HIS SHECHINAH, THAT ARE HIS FATHER AND MOTHER.

826. הָכָא אִשְׁתְּלִים כֹּלָּא לְעֵילָּא וְתַתָּא, רָזָא דִּשְׁמָא קַדִּישָׁא שַׁלִּיטָא לְעֵילָּא. מְצַפֵּ"ץ מְצַפֵּ"ץ. יְיָ' יְיָ' אֵל רַחוּם וְחַנּוּן. הָכָא אִיהוּ רָזָא דִּשְׁמָא קַדִּישָׁא דָּא, לְאִתְקַדְּשָׁא בְּאַתְווֹי בְּבֵי עֲשָׂרָה, וְאַתְוָון אַחֲרָנִין בִּקְדוּשָּׁה דִּיחִידָאי בִּצְלוֹתָא. בָּתַר דְּסִיֵּים, קָאֵים עַל רַגְלוֹי, לְאוֹדָאֵי עַל חוֹבוֹי, בְּגִין דְּלָא יְהֵא פִּטְרָא דְּפוּמָא לְסִטְרָא אַחֲרָא, לְאַסְטָאָה לֵיהּ, וְאִתְכַּפְיָא קָמֵיהּ. וְיֵיקוּם בְּקִיּוּמֵיהּ לְאִתְבָּרְכָא מִבֵּי מַלְכָּא.

826. Here is perfected high and low the secret of the Holy Name that rules above, *Mem-Tzadi-Pe-Tzadi, Mem-Tzadi-Pe-Tzadi*, DERIVED FROM "Hashem, Hashem, El merciful and gracious" (Shemot 34:6), FOR YUD HEI VAV HEI INTERCHANGED BY THE METHOD OF ATBASH CIPHER, TURNS INTO *MEM-TZADI-PE-TZADI.* Here the secret of the Holy Name YUD HEI VAV HEI, YUD HEI VAV HEI is consecrated by a public of ten, and the other letters, *MEM-TZADI-PE-TZADI, MEM-TZADI-PE-TZADI,* in a solitary sanctification in prayer. THE THIRTEEN DIVINE ATTRIBUTES ARE SAID ONLY IN PUBLIC, AND WHEN ALONE, THE THIRTEEN DIVINE ATTRIBUTES ARE SAID WITH THE PERMUTATION OF ATBASH CIPHER, *MEM-TZADI-PE-TZADI, MEM-TZADI-PE-TZADI.* After finishing THE THIRTEEN DIVINE ATTRIBUTES, it behooves man to stand up and confess his sins, so there will be no pretext for the Other Side to accuse him, and so he is subjugated before him. Now he stands firm, blessed from the King's house.

827. וְזַכָּאָה חוּלָקֵיהּ מַאן דְּאִתְקַדָּשׁ בְּהַאי גַּוְונָא בִּצְלוֹתָא כִּדְקָאַמְרָן, וְקָשַׁר קִשְׁרִין, וְיִיחֵד יִחוּדִין, וְיִתְכַּוֵּון בְּכֹלָּא כַּדְקָא יֵאוֹת, וְלָא יִסְטֵי

לִימִינָא וְלִשְׂמָאלָא. צְלוֹתֵיהּ לָא אַהְדַּר בְּרֵיקָנַיָּא. קוּדְשָׁא בְּרִיךְ הוּא גָּזִיר וְאִיהוּ מְבַטֵּל. עַל דָּא כְּתִיב יִשְׂמַח אָבִיךָ וְאִמֶּךָ וְתָגֵל יוֹלַדְתֶּךָ. אִית לֵיהּ חוּלָקָא בְּעָלְמָא דֵּין, וּבְעָלְמָא דְּאָתֵי.

827. Happy is the portion of whoever is consecrated in this manner by his prayer, as we said, who ties the knots and makes unisons, with proper meditation, not deviating right or left. His prayer then will not be returned empty handed; the Holy One, blessed be He decrees, yet he annuls it. Of him it is written, "Let your father and your mother be glad, and let she who bore you rejoice" (Mishlei 23:25), he has a portion in this world and in the World to Come.

828. כְּתִיב וַתָּקָם בְּעוֹד לַיְלָה וַתִּתֵּן טֶרֶף לְבֵיתָהּ וְגוֹ׳ מֵהַהוּא רִבּוּיָא דְּבִרְכָּאָן, וּקְדוּשָּׁה, וְתוֹסֶפֶת קְדוּשָּׁה דְּקָא נַטְלָא. כד״א וְלָעֶרֶב יְחַלֵּק שָׁלָל, דִּפְלִיגַת חוּלָקָא לְכֹלָּא, וַאֲפִילּוּ לְסִטְרָא אַחֲרָא חוּלָקָא בִּלְחוּדָהָא.

828. It is written, "She rises also while it is yet night, and gives food to her household, and a portion to her maidens" (Mishlei 31:15), MEANING THAT MALCHUT GIVES OF THE manifold blessings, sanctification and additional sanctification, which she receives, as it is said, "and at night he shall divide the spoil" (Beresheet 49:27), AS MALCHUT divides portion to everyone, and even to the Other Side she gives a portion.

829. וְרָזָא דָּא, רָזָא לִבְנֵי מְהֵימְנוּתָא. חוּלָקָא דְּסִטְרָא אַחֲרָא מִסְאֲבָא, כָּל אִינּוּן חוֹבִין, וְכָל אִינּוּן חֲטָאִין, דְּהַהוּא ב״נ דְּקָשַׁר קִשְׁרִין דְּיִחוּדָא, דְּאִתְוַדָּה עֲלַיְיהוּ, כֻּלְּהוּ שַׁרְיָין עָלֵיהּ דסט״א. וְאִינּוּן חוּלָקָא וְאַחֲסַנְתָּא דְּסִטְרָא אַחֲרָא מִסְאֲבָא. וְאִי לָא אוֹדֵי עָלֵיהּ, אִשְׁתְּכַח מְקַטְרְגָא וְיָכִיל לֵיהּ.

829. This is a mystery for those of the Faith: the part of the unholy Other Side is all the sins and transgressions of the man who tied the bonds of unison, and confessed them. They all dwell upon the Other Side, to be the part and portion of the unholy Other Side. But if he did not confess them, then the accuser comes TO DENOUNCE HIM, and prevails.

830. וְאִי אוֹדֵי עַל כָּל חוֹבוֹי, בְּהַהִיא צְלוֹתָא, דְּקָשִׁיר קִשְׁרִין דְּיִחוּדָא, וְאִתְבָּרְכָאן עִלָּאֵי וְתַתָּאֵי. וּמֵהַהוּא חוּלָקָא דְּסִטְרָא אַחֲרָא, כָּל אִינּוּן חוֹבִין וְחַטָּאִין דְּאוֹדֵי עָלַיְיהוּ, נַטְלָא לוֹן לְחוּלָקֵיהּ. וְרָזָא דָּא שָׂעִיר. דִּכְתִּיב וְהִתְוַדָּה עָלָיו אֶת כָּל עֲוֹנוֹת וְגוֹ׳, וּכְתִיב וְנָשָׂא הַשָּׂעִיר וְגוֹ׳, דָּא הוּא חוּלָקֵיהּ וְעַדְבֵיהּ וְאַחֲסָנְתֵּיהּ. וְאִי הַהוּא ב״נ תָּב לְסָרְחָנֵי דְּחוֹבוֹי, וַוי לֵיהּ, דְּכֻלְּהוּ נָטִיל לוֹן מֵהַהוּא סִטְרָא, בְּעַל כָּרְחֵיהּ דְּהַהוּא סִטְרָא. וּמִגּוֹ דְּנָטִיל לוֹן מֵהַאי סִטְרָא בְּעַל כָּרְחֵיהּ דְּהַהוּא סִטְרָא, כְּדֵין אַבְאִישׁ לֵיהּ, וְאִתְהַפֵּךְ עָלֵיהּ מְקַטְרְגָא, וְקַטְרִיג לֵיהּ. וְכַד אוֹדֵי עֲלוֹי, נָטִיל לוֹן הַהוּא סִטְרָא אַחֲרָא, וְאִיהוּ עַדְבֵיהּ וְחוּלָקֵיהּ.

830. If he confessed his sins in that prayer by connecting the bonds of unison, the upper and lower are blessed. And it is of the part of the Other Side, that all the sins and transgressions he confessed, he takes as his own portion. This is the secret of the goat, as it is written, "and confess over him all the iniquities of the children of Yisrael…and the goat shall bear upon it" (Vayikra 16:21-22). This is his part, portion and property. And if man reverts to corrupt ways, woe to him, for he takes back the transgressions from that side against the will of that side, which harms him, and becomes his accuser to speak ill of him. But when he confesses them, that Other Side takes them to be its allotted part.

831. וְרָזָא דָּא, הָכִי נָמֵי קָרְבְּנָא, דְּבָעֵי לְאוֹדָאָה עַל הַהוּא קָרְבְּנָא, כָּל חוֹבוֹי וְחֶטְאוֹי, לְמֵיהַב חוּלָקָא לְמַאן דְּאִצְטְרִיךְ. קָרְבְּנָא כֹּלָּא לְסִטְרָא דָּא חוּלָקָא דְּקוּדְשָׁא, וּרְעוּתָא דְּקוּדְשָׁא. וּלְסִטְרָא דָּא, הַהוּא חוּלָקָא דְּאִינּוּן חוֹבִין, וְחַטָּאִין דְּאִתְיְיהִיבוּ בְּהוֹדָאָה עַל הַהוּא בִּשְׂרָא דְּקָרְבְּנָא. כְּמָה דִּכְתִּיב, אִם רָעֵב שׂוֹנַאֲךָ הַאֲכִילֵהוּ לֶחֶם וְגוֹ׳. כִּי גֶחָלִים אַתָּה חוֹתֶה וְגוֹ׳, וְסִימָנִיךְ יָבֹא הַמֶּלֶךְ וְהָמָן אֶל הַמִּשְׁתֶּה. זַכָּאָה אִיהוּ מַאן דְּיָדַע אָרְחֵיהּ לְמֵהַךְ בְּאֹרַח קְשׁוֹט.

831. This is also a secret of the offering: one has to confess over it all his sins and iniquities, in order to give a portion to him who needs it, NAMELY, THE OTHER SIDE. The whole sacrifice goes to the side of holiness, which is the part of holiness and its desire. The OTHER Side receives the portion of all the sins and iniquities given by the confession over the flesh of the offering, as it is written, "If your enemy be hungry, give him bread…for you shall heap coals of fire…" (Mishlei 25:21-22). This may be understood from the verse, "let the king and Haman come this day to the banquet" (Esther 5:4). Happy is he who knows His ways, to walk the path of truth.

832. וְכָל מַאן דְּלָא יָדַע לְסַדְּרָא שְׁבָחָא דְּמָארֵיהּ, טַב לֵיהּ דְּלָא אִבְרֵי. בְּגִין דְּאִצְטְרִיךְ צְלוֹתָא דְּאִיהוּ שְׁלָמָא לְעֵילָּא. מִגּוֹ מַחֲשָׁבָה, וּרְעוּתָא דְּלִבָּא, וְקָלָא, וּמִלָּה דִּשְׂפְוָון. לְמֶעְבַּד שְׁלִימוּ וְקִשּׁוּרָא וְיִחוּדָא לְעֵילָּא, כְּגַוְונָא דְּאִיהוּ לְעֵילָּא. כְּגַוְונָא דְּנָפְקָא שְׁלִימוּ מֵעֵילָּא לְתַתָּא, הָכִי אִצְטְרִיךְ מִתַּתָּא לְעֵילָּא, לְקַשְּׁרָא קִשְׁרָא כַּדְקָא יֵאוֹת.

832. Whoever knows not how to arrange the praise of his Master, it is better for him not to have been born. The prayer should be whole above, by thought, heart's desire, voice and words of mouth, all to create perfection, connection and unison above. As perfection comes from above downward, so the connection should be properly made, from below upward.

833. רָזָא לְחַבְרַיָּיא דְּיֵהַכוּן בְּאֹרַח מֵישַׁר, מַחֲשָׁבָה. וּרְעוּתָא. וְקָלָא. וּמִלָּה. אִלֵּין אַרְבַּע מְקַשְּׁרִין קִשְׁרִין. לְבָתַר קְשִׁירוּ קִשְׁרִין כֻּלְּהוּ כַּחֲדָא, אִתְעֲבִידוּ כֻּלְּהוּ רְתִיכָא חֲדָא, לְאַשְׁרָאָה עֲלַיְיהוּ שְׁכִינְתָּא, וְאִתְעֲבֵידוּ כֻּלְּהוּ לְבָתַר אַרְבָּעָה סַמְכִין לְאִתְעַטְּרָא בְּהוּ, וּשְׁכִינְתָּא אִסְתְּמִיךְ עֲלַיְיהוּ, בְּכָל אִינּוּן קִשְׁרִין עִלָּאִין.

833. This mystery is for the friends, so they may walk the true path. Thought, will, voice, and speech are the four that tie the knots, CORRESPONDING TO CHOCHMAH AND BINAH, TIFERET AND MALCHUT. THOUGHT AND WILL ARE CHOCHMAH AND BINAH, VOICE AND SPEECH ARE TIFERET AND MALCHUT. After they tied the knots together, they became one Chariot, so the Shechinah, THE SECRET OF SPEECH, may dwell upon them. They then turned into four pillars to be bedecked by, and the Shechinah is supported by them with all the high knots.

834. מַחֲשָׁבָה אַפִּיק רְעוּתָא, רְעוּתָא דְּנָפִיק מִגּוֹ מַחֲשָׁבָה, אַפִּיק קָלָא דְּאִשְׁתְּמַע, וְהַהוּא קָלָא דְּאִשְׁתְּמַע, סָלִיק לְקַשְּׁרָא קִשְׁרִין מִתַּתָּא

לְעֵילָּא, הֵיכָלִין תַּתָּאִין בְּעִלָּאִין. קָלָא דְּאִיהוּ קָשִׁיר קִשְׁרִין וּמָשִׁיךְ בִּרְכָאן מֵעֵילָּא לְתַתָּא בִּלְחִישׁוּ, סָמִיךְ אִלֵּין אַרְבָּעָה סַמְכִין: מַחֲשָׁבָה. וּרְעוּתָא. קָלָא. וּמִלָּה. סְמִיכוּ בְּסִיוּמָא דְּקִשׁוּרָא, אֲתָר דְּכֹלָּא אִתְקָשַׁר בֵּיהּ כַּחֲדָא, וְאִתְעֲבִידוּ כֻּלְּהוּ חַד.

834. HE EXPLAINS FURTHER: Thought, THE SECRET OF CHOCHMAH, produces AND BEGETS will, THE SECRET OF BINAH. Will, which came out of thought, BEGETS AND produces a sounding voice THE SECRET OF ZEIR ANPIN. The sound that is heard ascends and binds knots from below upwards, connects the lower and upper chambers. The sound, which connects BETWEEN THE TWO COLUMNS OF BINAH, and draws blessings from high above, FROM BINAH, is secretly supported TOO by those four pillars, thought, will, voice, and speech, THE SECRET OF CHOCHMAH AND BINAH, TIFERET AND MALCHUT. The support comes at the end of the knot, NAMELY AT SPEECH, MALCHUT, where everything is bound together and becomes one, AS MALCHUT RECEIVES ALL OF THEM INTO HER.

835. זַכָּאָה אִיהוּ בַּר נָשׁ דְּקָשַׁר קִשְׁרִין דְּמָארֵיהּ, וְסָמִיךְ סְמִיכִין כַּדְקָא יָאוֹת, וְאִתְכַּוַּון בְּכָל הָנֵי מִלִּין דְּקָאמְרָן. זַכָּאָה אִיהוּ בְּהַאי עָלְמָא, וּבְעָלְמָא דְּאָתֵי. עַד הָכָא אִשְׁתַּכְלָלוּ הֵיכָלִין בְּסִטְרָא דִּקְדוּשָּׁה.

835. Happy is the man who ties the knots of his Master and produces proper struts, who is intent upon all the things we said. Happy is he in this world and in the World to Come. So far is the construction of the chambers on the side of holiness.

53. The seven chambers of the Other Side

A Synopsis

Rabbi Shimon opens with: "But they, like Adam have transgressed the covenant." He speaks to Adam, saying that he was only asked to keep one precept, and yet he could not keep it and was seduced by the serpent. Next he talks about David, who ran away from Saul and was rejected from the Holy Land. Nevertheless, he says, David did not turn to evil. He describes the grades of the evil inclination, the seven names it is called by, and the seven names of Gehenom. These correspond to the seven chambers of the Other Side. Just as there are grades and chambers on the side of holiness there are grades and chambers on the side of defilement. Many grades and chieftains stand ready to purify people who worship God, and many grades and chieftains stand ready to defile people who sin. Rabbi Shimon tells us that everyone sees the Angel of Death when his time of reckoning comes.

836. רִבִּי שִׁמְעוֹן פָּתַח וְאָמַר, וְהֵמָּה כְּאָדָם עָבְרוּ בְרִית שָׁם בָּגְדוּ בִי. מַאן יְגַלֶּה עָפָר מֵעֵינֶיךָ אָדָם קַדְמָאָה, דְקוּדְשָׁא בְּרִיךְ הוּא פָּקִיד לָךְ פִּקּוּדָא חֲדָא, וְלָא יָכִילַת לְקַיְּימָא בָּהּ. בְּגִין דְּאִתְפַּתִּית עַל מִלִּין בִּישִׁין, דְּאַסְטֵי לָךְ הַהוּא חִוְיָא בִּישָׁא, דִּכְתִּיב וְהַנָּחָשׁ הָיָה עָרוּם. וּבְגִין כָּךְ, אִתְפַּתִּית אֲבַתְרֵיהּ, וְגַרְמַת מִיתָה לְגַרְמָךְ, וּלְכָל אִינּוּן תּוֹלְדִין דְּנַפְקוּ מִינָּךְ. תָּא חֲזֵי, דְּכָל מַאן דְּאִתְפַּתָּא אֲבַתְרֵיהּ וְנָחִית לְגַבֵּיהּ בְּרִגְעָא חֲדָא, יִתְאֲבִיד לְגַבֵּיהּ.

836. Rabbi Shimon opened the discussion with the verse: "But they, like Adam have transgressed the covenant" (Hoshea 6:7). Who will remove dust from your eyes, Adam, if the Holy One, blessed be He gave you one precept and you could not keep it, for you were enticed by the wicked things with which the evil serpent seduced you, as is written, "the serpent was craftier" (Beresheet 3:1). Hence you were seduced by it, and brought death to you and all your offspring. Come and see: Whoever is seduced by it, and goes down to it, he will be lost in an instant, NAMELY, FALL UNDER ITS DOMINION.

837. תָּא חֲזֵי, דָּוִד הֲוָה קִיּוּמָא נָעִיץ בִּמְקוֹרָא דְּמַיִין נַבְעִין, וְכַד אִתְדַּחְיָא לְאַרְעָא אַחֲרָא, וְצַעֲרִין לֵיהּ, וּלְפוּם צַעֲרֵיהּ אִתְדַּחְיָא מֵאַרְעָא

קַדִּישָׁא. אַף עַל גַּב דְּנָחִית מִדַּרְגּוֹי לְדַרְגָּא תַּתָּאָה, קָם בְּקִיּוּמֵיהּ, וְלָא עָאל לְסִטְרָא אַחֲרָא, וְאִסְתְּמַר מִנֵּיהּ. מַה כְּתִיב וְאוּלָם חַי יְיָ' וְחֵי נַפְשֶׁךָ כִּי כְפֶשַׂע בֵּינִי וּבֵין הַמָּוֶת. דְּהָא נָחִית בְּדַרְגּוֹי, עַד דַּהֲוָה בֵּיהּ הַאי שִׁיעוּרָא. וְזַכָּאָה חוּלָקֵיהּ, מַאן דְּאִסְתְּמַר מֵהַהוּא סִטְרָא בִּישָׁא, וּמִכָּל דַּרְגִּין דְּהַהוּא סִטְרָא, דְּמִשְׁתַּכְּחֵי בְּעָלְמָא.

837. Come and see: David, whose existence depended upon the source of running water, NAMELY, BINAH, FOR DAVID IS THE SECRET OF MALCHUT ABOVE THE CHEST, THE PLACE OF BINAH, WHENCE HE TAKES HIS LIFE AND EXISTENCE. When he was chased into another land, WHEN HE RAN AWAY FROM SAUL, he was grieved, and for his grief, he was rejected from the Holy Land, NAMELY, HE FELL FROM HIS GRADE, WHICH IS THE HOLY LAND. Though he descended through his grades to the last one, he nevertheless resisted and did not enter the Other Side, but kept away from it, as it is written, "but truly as Hashem lives, and as your soul lives, there is but a step between me and death" (I Shmuel 20:3). For he went down the grades until there was but a step between him AND DEATH, WHICH IS THE OTHER SIDE CALLED 'DEATH'. Happy is the portion of he who is kept from that evil, and from all the grades of that side that abide in the world.

838. דְּכַמָּה סִטְרִין וְדַרְגִּין אִית לְיֵצֶר הָרָע: נָחָשׁ עֲקַלָּתוֹן. שָׂטָן. מַלְאַךְ הַמָּוֶת. יֵצֶר הָרָע. וְהָא אוּקְמוּהָ. דאע"ג דִּבְשְׁמָהָן אִלֵּין אִקְרֵי, שֶׁבַע שְׁמָהָן אִינּוּן לֵיהּ: שָׂטָן. טָמֵא. שׂוֹנֵא. אֶבֶן מִכְשׁוֹל. עָרֵל. רָע. צְפוֹנִי. אִלֵּין אִינּוּן שֶׁבַע שְׁמָהָן, לָקֳבֵל שֶׁבַע דַּרְגִּין דְּהֵיכָלִין דִּילֵיהּ, דְּכֻלְּהוּ מִסִּטְרָא מִסְאֲבָא כִּדְקָאמְרָן. לָקֳבֵל אִלֵּין שִׁבְעָה שְׁמָהָן, אִינּוּן דְּאִקְרֵי בְּהוּ גֵּיהִנָּם, אֲתָר דְּאִתְדָּנוּ בֵּיהּ חַיָּיבַיָּא דְּעָלְמָא. וְאִלֵּין אִינּוּן: בּוֹר. שַׁחַת. דּוּמָה. טִיט הַיָּוֵן. שְׁאוֹל. צַלְמָוֶת. אֶרֶץ תַּחְתִּית. כָּל אִלֵּין שִׁבְעָה מָדוֹרִין דְּגֵיהִנָּם, לָקֳבֵל אִלֵּין שֶׁבַע שְׁמָהָן, דְּאִית לֵיהּ לְיֵצֶר הָרָע.

838. There are several aspects and grades to the Evil Inclination, which are the Satan, the Angel of Death, and the Evil Inclination. And we explained that though it is called by those names, it has seven names IN PARTICULAR: the Satan, unholy, foe, a stone of stumbling, uncircumcised, evil, northern.

These seven names correspond to the seven grades of its chambers, all of them on the side of defilement, as we said, and to the seven names given to Gehenom, NAMELY where the wicked are condemned. These are: pit, grave, Dumah, gruesome mud, Sheol, shadow of death, a nether land. These are the seven departments of Gehenom corresponding to the seven names of the Evil Inclination. AND THE SEVEN CHAMBERS OF THE OTHER SIDE ARE CALLED BY THE SAME NAMES AS THE SEVEN DEPARTMENTS OF GEHENOM.

839. וְהָא אוֹקִימְנָא, דִּכְמָּה דְּאִית דַּרְגִּין וְהֵיכָלִין לְסִטַר קְדוּשָּׁה, הָכִי נָמֵי לְסִטַר מִסְאֲבָא. וְכֻלְּהוּ מִשְׁתַּכְּחֵי וְשָׁלְטֵי בְּעָלְמָא, בְּסִטַר מִסְאֲבָא. שִׁבְעָה הֵיכָלִין אִינּוּן , דְּאִינּוּן לָקֳבֵל שִׁבְעָה שְׁמָהָן, דְּאִקְרֵי בְּהוּ גֵּיהִנָּם. וְכֻלְּהוּ קַיְימֵי לְדַיְינָא, וּלְסָאֲבָא, לְאִינּוּן חַיָּיבֵי עָלְמָא דְּדַבְקֵי בְּהוּ, וְלָא אִסְתַּמְּרָן אָרְחַיְיהוּ מִנֵּיהּ, כַּד אִינּוּן בְּהַאי עָלְמָא.

839. Here we explained that as there are grades and chambers on the side of holiness, so there are on the side of defilement, all of which abide in and rule the world on the side of unholiness. THEREFORE, THERE ARE seven chambers, corresponding to the seven names of Gehenom, NAMELY, CALLED BY THE SAME NAMES AS THE SEVEN DEPARTMENTS OF GEHENOM. All of them stand ready to condemn and defile the wicked of the world who clove to them, and did not keep away from them, while in this world.

840. דְּהָא מַאן דְּאָתֵי לְאִתְדַּכְּאָה בְּהַאי עָלְמָא, בְּסִטְרָא דְּדַכְיָא, מְדַכְּאִין לֵיהּ, בְּהַהוּא אֲתָר דְּאִקְרֵי רָזָא דִּמְהֵימְנוּתָא. דִּכְמָּה דַּרְגִּין אִינּוּן, וְכַמָּה מְמָנָן, דְּכֻלְּהוּ קַיְימִן לְקָרְבָא לִבְנֵי נָשָׁא לְפוּלְחָנֵיהּ דְּקוּדְשָׁא בְּרִיךְ הוּא, וּלְדַכְּאָה לֵיהּ. וּמַאן דְּאָתֵי לְאִסְתַּאֲבָא, מְסָאֲבִין לֵיהּ בְּהַאי סִטְרָא אַחֲרָא דְּאִיהוּ מִסְאֲבָא. דְּהָא כַּמָּה דַּרְגִּין, וְכַמָּה מְמָנָן, כֻּלְּהוּ קַיְימֵי לְסָאֲבָא לוֹן לִבְנֵי נָשָׁא.

840. Whoever comes to be purified in this world, on the side of purity, he is cleansed in the place called 'the secret of the Faith', NAMELY, MALCHUT OF HOLINESS. How many are the grades and chieftains all ready to draw people nearer to the worship of the Holy One, blessed be He, and purify them. And whoever comes to be defiled, he is defiled on the Other Side, which is unholy, where many grades and chieftains stand ready to defile people.

841. מַאן דְיִקְרַב בְּהוּ, וְאָתֵי לְאִתְמַשְׁכָא בָּתַר הַהוּא סִטְרָא בִישָׁא, עָלֵיהּ כְּתִיב, מִי גֶבֶר יִחְיֶה וְלֹא יִרְאֶה מָוֶת יְמַלֵּט נַפְשׁוֹ וְגוֹ׳. מַאן אִיהוּ בַּר נָשׁ דְּאִתְבְּרֵי בְּעָלְמָא דְּלָא יֶחֱמֵי מוֹתָא, הַהוּא דְּכָל עָלְמָא אִתְמַשְׁכָאן אֲבַתְרֵיהּ. דְּהָא בְּהַהוּא זִמְנָא דְּאָתֵי ב״נ לְמֵיהַב חוּשְׁבָנָא קָמֵי מָארֵיהּ, עַד לָא יִפּוּק מֵהַאי עָלְמָא, חָמֵי לֵיהּ, וְהָא אוּקִימְנָא.

841. He who comes near them, and is drawn after that Evil Side, of him it is written, “What man is he that lives, and shall not see death, but shall deliver his soul…” (Tehilim 89:49). Who is the man who was born into this world, and does not see death, to which all the world is drawn, NAMELY, THE ANGEL OF DEATH. For when the time comes to do reckoning before his Master, HIS TIME TO PASS AWAY FROM THE WORLD, before he does depart he sees him, THE ANGEL OF DEATH, as we already explained.

842. וְאִלֵּין שִׁבְעָה הֵיכָלִין, דְּאִינּוּן שִׁבְעָה מָדוֹרִין לַגֵּיהִנָּם. תְּרֵיסַר יַרְחִין אִקְרוּן, בְּגִין דְּהָא כְּמָה דְּאִית לְסְטַר מְהֵימְנוּתָא תְּרֵיסָר יַרְחִין, דַּרְגִּין קַדִּישִׁין, הָכִי נָמֵי אִית לְסִטְרָא אַחֲרָא דָא תְּרֵיסַר יַרְחִין, דְּחַיָּיבַיָּא אִתְדָּנוּ בְּהוּ, וְנִשְׁמָתָא דִלְהוֹן אִתְדָּנַת בְּהוּ. זַכָּאָה חוּלָקֵיהוֹן דְּצַדִּיקַיָּיא, דְּאִתְמְנְעָן רַגְלַיְיהוּ מִנַּיְיהוּ בְּהַאי עָלְמָא, וְלָא מִתְקָרְבֵי לְתַרְעַיְיהוּ, בְּגִין לְאִשְׁתְּזָבָא מִנַּיְיהוּ בְּהַהוּא עָלְמָא.

842. These seven chambers, the seven departments of Gehenom, are called ‘twelve months’. As there are twelve months of holy grades on the side of the Faith, MALCHUT, so the Other Side has twelve months, to which the wicked are condemned, and their souls are sentenced to. Happy is the portion of the righteous who keep their feet in this world away from their gates, to be saved from them in that world, SO THEY WILL NOT BE CONDEMNED BY THEM IN GEHENOM.

54. The first chamber of the Other Side, Empty Pit – the Satan of the Evil Inclination

A Synopsis

We hear that the first chamber is called 'a pit empty of everything'. Whoever enters it has nothing to cling to, nothing to stop him from falling. Rabbi Shimon describes the pit and all the chieftains and other spirits of unholiness who judge and torment the condemned soul. This chamber is prepared for those who cursed and who threw things in anger.

843. הֵיכָלָא קַדְמָאָה. שֵׁירוּתָא דְּסִטְרָא דיצה״ר. הַאי הֵיכָלָא קַדְמָאָה, אִקְרֵי בּוֹר רֵיקָא מִכֹּלָּא. מַאן דְּאָתֵי לְאַעֲלָא בֵּיהּ, לֵית מַאן דְּאָחִיד בֵּיהּ. כֻּלְּהוּ דַּחְיָין לֵיהּ לְמִנְפַּל דְּלָא יְקוּם, לֵית בֵּיהּ סָמָךְ לְטָב.

843. The first chamber is the beginning of the Evil Inclination. The first chamber is called 'a pit empty of everything'. Whoever enters it, has nothing to cling to, TO KEEP HIM FROM FALLING. Everyone pushes so he will fall and will not rise. There is no support for the good in it.

844. בְּהַאי הֵיכָלָא, קַיְּימָא חַד מְמָנָא, וְדוּמָה שְׁמֵיהּ. וְהַאי אִיהוּ קַיְּימָא לְעֵילָּא וְתַתָּא. דָּא אִיהוּ אָחִיד בְּנִשְׁמְתָא, כַּד אִתְדַּחְיָא מֵהֵיכָלָא קַדִּישָׁא, עַל יְדָא דְּהַהוּא מְמָנָא טָהֳרִיאֵ״ל, וְהַאי אִיהוּ קָאִים לְגַבֵּי הַהוּא תַּרְעָא דְּהַהוּא סִטְרָא קַדִּישָׁא, וּבְגִין כָּךְ קַיְּימָא הַאי דוּמָה, לְאַחֲדָא לָהּ לְנִשְׁמְתָא, וְכַמָּה גַּרְדִּינֵי נִימוּסִין בַּהֲדֵיהּ.

844. One chieftain called 'Dumah' stands in this chamber,. He stands above IN THE THIRD CHAMBER OF THE OTHER SIDE, and below, HERE IN THE FIRST CHAMBER. He seizes the soul when it is turned down from the holy chamber by the chieftain Tahariel. DUMAH stands by the gate of the holy side, NAMELY, BY THE GATE OF THE FIRST CHAMBER OF HOLINESS. Dumah stands there in order to take hold of the soul, AND DRAW IT INTO THE CHAMBERS OF DEFILEMENT, and several complainants and accusers stand with him.

845. וּתְחוֹת הַאי מְמָנָא, קַיְּימָא חַד מְמָנָא אַחֲרָא, דִּי אֶלֶף וְרִבְבָן

תְּחוֹתֵיהּ. וְהַאי מְמָנָא אִקְרֵי פִּתּוּ״ת. דָּא הוּא דְּאִיהוּ קַיְּימָא לְפַתָּאָה בְּנֵי נָשָׁא. וְהַאי אִיהוּ דְּשָׁרֵי לְגַבֵּיהּ, וְאַסְטֵי לֵיהּ, לְאִסְתַּכְּלָא וּלְעַיְּינָא בְּמָה דְּלָא אִצְטְרִיךְ בְּכַמָּה זְנוּנִין וּבְכַמָּה נִאוּפִין. וְכָל אִינּוּן דְּעִמֵּיהּ, כֻּלְּהוּ קַיְימָן לְגַבֵּיהּ, וְאָזְלִין קַמֵּיהּ, וְאַכְרִיחָן לֵיהּ לְאַסְטָאָה עֵינוֹי, לְאִסְתַּכְּלָא בְּמָה דְּלָא אִצְטְרִיךְ.

845. Under the chieftain DUMAH there is another chief, and thousands and tens of thousands beneath him. This chief is called ‘Pitut’. His job is to seduce (Heb. *lefatot*) people. He hovers by THE SOUL, and entices it to look closely at what it must not see, of much whoring and lechery. And all the angels with him stand by it and walk before it, and force it to avert it eyes to look at what it must not see.

846. וְהַאי אִיהוּ סַרְסוּרָא בִּישָׁא, לְכָל אִינּוּן בִּישִׁין, הַאי קָאֵים עַל קִבְרָא בְּזִמְנָא דְּאִתְדָּן הַהוּא גּוּפָא, וְתָבַר לֵיהּ עֵינוֹי. בְּגִין דְּאִיהוּ רָוַוח לוֹן, כַּד אִיהוּ בְּהַאי עָלְמָא, וְדִילֵיהּ אִינּוּן.

846. PITUT is an evil mediator, who entices to all those evils. He stands by the grave, once the body is sentenced, and crushes the eyes. For he earned them while the body was his in this world, and so they are his.

847. וּבְהַאי אֲתָר אִתְדָּנַת נִשְׁמְתָא, עַד דְּעָאלַת לְהַאי אֲתָר דְּאִקְרֵי בּוֹר, וְכַמָּה נְחָשִׁים וְעַקְרַבִּים אִית בֵּיהּ, דְּכֻלְּהוּ עָקְצֵי לָהּ לְהַאי נִשְׁמְתָא, וְאַחְדֵי בָּהּ, וְדַיְינִין לָהּ.

847. In this place, THE GRAVE, the soul is sentenced, until it is put in the place called ‘pit’, where there are some serpents and scorpions, WHICH ARE DEMONS. They all bite the soul, grasp and punish it.

848. לְגוֹ מִן דָּא, אִית חַד רוּחָא אַחֲרָא מְסָאֲבָא, דְּאִיהוּ עִלָּאָה עַל כֹּלָּא. וְדָא קַיְּימָא עַל כָּל הֵיכָלָא דָּא, וְכֻלְּהוּ נַטְלֵי בְּגִינֵיהּ, וְהַאי אִקְרֵי גַּמְגִימָ״א. הַאי הוּא סוּמָקָא כְּוַורְדָּא, אִיהוּ קָאֵים לְאַבְאָשָׁא תָּדִיר, דְּהָא כַּד צְלוֹתָא דב״נ אִתְדַּחְיָא, וְלָא זָכֵי בָּהּ הַהוּא ב״נ, הַאי רוּחָא

קַיְּימָא, וְסַלְקָא וְאִשְׁתַּתַּף בְּרוּחָא מְסָאֲבָא עִלָּאָה עַל כֹּלָּא, וְאַסְטֵי לְעֵילָּא, וְאַדְכִּיר חוֹבוֹי דְּבַר נָשׁ קָמֵי קוּדְשָׁא בְּרִיךְ הוּא, וְסִימָנִיךְ וַיָּבֹא גַּ״ם הַשָּׂטָ״ן בְּתוֹכָם, וְלָא כְּתִיב וַיָּבֹא הַשָּׂטָן אֶלָּא גַּם.

848. In front of THE SPIRIT PITUT, there is another spirit of unholiness, above them all. He is in charge over this chamber, and all therein travel by his prompting. He is called 'Gamgima', red as a rose, always ready to cause evil. When the prayer of man is turned down, and he gets no merit for it, then the spirit GAMGIMA rises to join the highest spirit of defilement, the SATAN. He then blames from above, and remembers the sins of men before the Holy One, blessed be He. This is known from the verse, "and the adversary came also among them" (Iyov 1:6). It is not written, "and the adversary came," but, "and the adversary came also (Heb. *gam*)," REFERRING TO THE SPIRIT GAMGIMA, THAT SHARED THE SATAN'S ACCUSATIONS.

849. וּמֵהַאי רוּחָא בִּישָׁא, תַּלְיָין כַּמָּה גַּרְדִּינִין אַחֲרָנִין, דְּאִינּוּן מְמָנָן לְאַחֲדָא מִלָּה בִּישָׁא, אוֹ מִלָּה טִנּוּפָא דְּאַפִּיק בַּר נָשׁ מִפּוּמֵיהּ, וּלְבָתַר אַפִּיק מִלִּין קַדִּישִׁין. וַוי לוֹן, וַוי לְחַיֵּיהוֹן, אִלֵּין אִינּוּן בְּנֵי נָשָׁא דְּגַרְמֵי לְאִלֵּין גַּרְדִּינִין אַחֲרָנִין לְשַׁלְטָאָה, לְמִפְגַּם אֲתָר קַדִּישָׁא. וַוי לוֹן בְּהַאי עָלְמָא, וַוי לוֹן לְעָלְמָא דְּאָתֵי. בְּגִין, דְּאִלֵּין רוּחִין מְסָאֲבִין, נַטְלִין הַאי מִלָּה מְסָאֲבָא, וְכַד אַפִּיק בַּר נָשׁ לְבָתַר מִלָּה קַדִּישָׁא, אַקְדִּימוּ אִלֵּין רוּחֵי מְסָאֲבֵי, וְנַטְלֵי הַהִיא מִלָּה מְסָאֲבָא, וּמְסָאֲבֵי לְהַהִיא מִלָּה קַדִּישָׁא, וְלָא זָכֵי בֵּיהּ ב״נ, וְכִבְיָכוֹל תָּשַׁשׁ חֵילָא קַדִּישָׁא.

849. Several other complainants depend upon this evil spirit. Their duty is to grasp the evil words or filth uttered by man, and afterwards holy words. Woe to them, woe to their lives, for these men enable these complainants to rule over the holy place and render it defective. Woe to them in this world, woe to them in the World to Come. For these spirits of defilement take the unholy word UTTERED, and when he afterwards says something that pertains to holiness, the evil spirits hasten to take the unholy word and with it defile the holy word. And so man does not merit HOLINESS, and the power of holiness weakens.

850. וְעֵילָּא מֵאִלֵּין אִית חַד מְמָנָא סַפְסִירִיט״א שְׁמֵיהּ. וְכַמָּה גַּרְדִּינֵי נִימוּסִין, וְהַאי מְמָנָא דְּעֲלַיְיהוּ, נַטְלֵי אִינּוּן מִלִּין בִּישִׁין, וְהָכִי נָמֵי נַטְלֵי כָּל אִלֵּין מִלִּין דְּזָרִיק ב״נ בִּידוֹי, כַּד רוּגְזָא שַׁרְיָא עָלוֹי, דְּהָא כְּדֵין הַאי מְמָנָא סַפְסִירִיטָ״א נָקִיט הַאי מִלָּה, דְּזָרִיק ב״נ בְּרוּגְזֵיהּ, וְסָלִיק וְאָמַר, דָּא הוּא קָרְבְּנָא דִּפְלַנְיָא, דְּקָרִיב לְסִטְרָא דִּילָן.

850. Over these there is a chief called ‘Safsirita’. Together with complainants, they take the evil things THE MAN SAID and also what he threw when he was angry. The chieftain Safsirita then holds the object the man threw in his anger, ascends and says, ‘This is the offering of so-and-so who sacrificed to our side’.

851. בְּגִין דְּכָל סִטְרָא דְּנַיְיחָא, אִיהוּ מִסִּטְרָא דִּימִינָא, וּמִסִּטְרָא דִּמְהֵימְנוּתָא. וְכָל סִטְרָא דְּרוּגְזָא, אִיהוּ מִסִּטְרָא אַחֲרָא בִּישָׁא, סִטְרָא מִסְאֲבָא. וְעַל דָּא מַאן דְּאַשְׁדֵי מִן יְדוֹי מִדִּי בְּרוּגְזָא, כָּל אִלֵּין נַטְלִין לָהּ לְהַאי מִלָּה דְּאִזְדְּרִיק, וְסַלְקֵי לָהּ לְעֵילָּא, וְאִתְקְרִיב לְהַהוּא סִטְרָא, וְאָמְרֵי דָּא קָרְבְּנָא דִּפְלַנְיָא.

851. For as the side of rest is of the right side, and of the side of Faith, so the side of anger is of the other, evil and unholy side. Therefore, whoever throws something in his anger, all those OF THE EVIL SIDE take what was thrown, raise it as an offering to that side, and say, ‘this is the offering of so- and-so’.

852. וְכָרוֹזָא קָארֵי בְּכָל אִינּוּן רְקִיעִין וְאָמְרֵי, וַוי לִפְלַנְיָא דְּאַסְטֵי בָּתַר אֵל זָר, וּפָלַח לְאֵל אַחֵר. וְכָרוֹזָא קָארֵי זִמְנָא תִּנְיָנָא וְאָמַר, אוֹי לָהֶם כִּי נָדְדוּ מִמֶּנִּי וְגוֹ׳. זַכָּאָה אִיהוּ בַּר נָשׁ, דְּאִסְתְּמַר מֵאָרְחוֹי, וְלָא יִסְטֵי לִימִינָא וְלִשְׂמָאלָא. וְלָא יִנְפּוֹל בְּגוֹ בֵּירָא עֲמִיקָא, דְּלָא יָכִיל לְסַלְקָא מִנֵּיהּ.

852. The crier resounds in all these firmaments: Woe to so-and-so who went after a strange El, and worshipped another El. The crier resounds again, saying, “Woe to them! for they have fled from Me” (Hoshea 7:13). Happy is the man who is careful in his ways not to turn aside to right or left, to fall into a deep pit from which he cannot ascend.

55. Second chamber of the Other Side, grave – unholy of the Evil Inclination

A Synopsis

The second chamber is darker than the first one, and is called 'grave'. Rabbi Shimon talks about the chiefs in charge of the three openings in the chamber and the fiends under them. This chamber is prepared for those who have done sexual crimes during their lives. Two spirits called 'evil' and 'plague' come out of this chamber and hover over the world, they are called the 'lower spirits' and they come out of the flame of fire.

853. הֵיכָלָא תִּנְיָינָא, הֵיכָלָא דָּא, אִיהוּ חָשׁוּךְ יַתִּיר עַל הֵיכָלָא קַדְמָאָה, הַאי אִקְרֵי שָׁחַת, לָקֳבֵל שְׁמָא דְּאִקְרֵי טָמֵא. בְּגִין דְּהֵיכָלָא קַדְמָאָה אִקְרֵי בּוֹר, לָקֳבֵל שְׁמָא דְּאִקְרֵי שָׂטָן. וְהַאי אִקְרֵי שָׁחַת, לָקֳבֵל שְׁמָא דְּאִקְרֵי טָמֵא. בְּהֵיכָלָא דָּא קַיְימִין תְּלַת פִּתְחִין, לִתְלַת סִטְרִין.

853. The second chamber OF THE OTHER SIDE is darker than the first chamber. It is called 'grave', corresponding to the name OF THE EVIL INCLINATION 'unholy', just as the first chamber is called 'pit' corresponding to the name OF THE EVIL INCLINATION 'the Satan'. And this one is called 'grave' in relation to the name OF THE EVIL INCLINATION THAT 'unholy'. This chamber has three openings.

854. פִּתְחָא קַדְמָאָה. בֵּיהּ קַיְימָא חַד מְמָנָא, עַסְטִירִיָ"א שְׁמֵיהּ. וְכַמָּה אֶלֶף וְרִבְבָן מְמָנָן תְּחוֹתֵיהּ, וְהַאי אִיהוּ קַיְימָא עַל כָּל אִינּוּן דִּמְחַבְּלֵי אָרְחַיְיהוּ, לְאוֹשְׁדָא זַרְעָא עַל אַרְעָא. אוֹ דְּמַפְקֵי זַרְעָא, דְּלָא כְּאָרְחָא. אוֹ לְכָל אִינּוּן דִּמְזָנוּ בִּידַיְיהוּ. אִלֵּין אִינּוּן דְּלָא חָמָאן אַנְפֵּי שְׁכִינְתָּא כְּלַל. אֶלָּא הַאי מְמָנָא דְּבִסְטַר מִסְאֲבָא דְּקַאמְרָן, נָפִיק בְּהַהוּא זִמְנָא, וְכַמָּה אִינּוּן אֶלֶף וְרִבְבָן, כֻּלְּהוּ מִתְכַּנְּפֵי עַל הַהוּא ב"נ, וּמְסָאֲבֵי לֵיהּ בְּהַאי עָלְמָא. וּלְבָתַר כַּד נָפַק נִשְׁמָתֵיהּ מִנֵּיהּ מֵהַאי עָלְמָא, הַאי מְמָנָא וְכָל אִינּוּן דְּעִמֵּיהּ, מְסָאֲבִין לֵיהּ לְנִשְׁמָתֵיהּ, וְאַחֲדִין בָּהּ, וְאָעִילוּ לָהּ לְאִתְדָּנָא בְּהוּ.

854. There is a chief in charge over the first opening, called 'Astiriya', and there are several thousands and tens of thousands OF FIENDS under him. He is in charge over all those who became corrupted in their ways, and spill semen on the ground, emit semen unnaturally, or play harlot with their hands, and do not see the Shechinah at all. At that time the chief on the side of defilement, whom we mentioned, comes out, with the thousands and tens of thousands WITH HIM. They all gather upon the man, to defile him in this world. This chief and his retinue defile his soul, seize it, and bring it to be judged by them.

855. וְאִלֵּין אִקְרוּן שִׁכְבַת זֶרַע רוֹתַחַת. דְּכֻלְּהוּ רוּגְזִין מְסָאֲבִין קַיְימִין כֻּלְּהוּ עַל דָּא, בְּגִין דְּכֻלְּהוּ קַיְימִין וְשָׁרָאן עָלֵיהּ דְּבַר נָשׁ, בְּהַהוּא זִמְנָא דְּאַרְתַּח גַּרְמֵיהּ, וְחָמִים לֵיהּ לְתִיאוּבְתָּא דָּא. וּכְדֵין נַטְלִין לֵיהּ לְהַהוּא תִּיאוּבְתָּא. וְהַהוּא זַרְעָא דְּאִתּוֹשַׁד בְּאַרְעָא. וְאִתְתָּקָפוּ בֵּיהּ, וְנַטְלֵי לֵיהּ. וְסַלְקֵי לֵיהּ לְעֵילָּא, וְגָרְמוּ דִּבְרִית דָּא דְּיִשְׁתַּעְבֵּד בְּסִטְרָא מְסָאֲבָא.

855. These FIENDS are called 'steaming emission of sperm', for all the angry and defiled live on it, to hover about the man in heat. They increase his passion, then take it, together with the semen that was spilt to the ground, which strengthens them, and raise it above. They cause the covenant ABOVE, WHICH IS YESOD, to be enslaved by the side of unholiness TO GIVE THEM ENJOYMENT AND STRENGTH.

856. פִּתְחָא תִּנְיָינָא, בֵּיהּ קַיְּימָא מְמָנָא אַחֲרָא, טַסְקִיפָ"ה שְׁמֵיהּ, וְהַאי אִיהוּ מְמָנָא, עַל כָּל אִינּוּן דִּמְחַבְּלֵי אָרְחַיְיהוּ, דְּלָא אוֹשְׁדֵי זַרְעָא עַל אַרְעָא, אֶלָּא דְּאוֹשְׁדֵי זַרְעָא בִּבְעִירֵי, אוֹ בְּאִיסּוּרִין חֲמוּרִין דְּאוֹרַיְיתָא, בְּאִינּוּן עֲרָיוֹת, הַאי מְמָנָא וְכַמָּה אֶלֶף וְרִבְבָן דְּעִמֵּיהּ, כֻּלְּהוּ קַיְימֵי עָלֵיהּ, לְאִתְדָּנָא לֵיהּ כְּמָה דְּאִתְּמַר בְּאִינּוּן אַחֲרָנִין.

856. Over the second opening there is another chief, Taskifa by name. He is in charge over all those who corrupt their way, and do not spill their sperm upon the ground but in beasts, or through the strict prohibitions of the Torah, such as sexual transgressions. This chief and his retinue of several thousands and tens of thousands are all in readiness to judge him, in the same way as we said concerning the other CONDEMNED IN THE FIRST OPENING.

857. ת״ח, מַאי מְמָנָא בִּידֵיהּ כַּסָּא חֲדָא, וְאִקְרֵי כּוֹס הַתַּרְעֵלָה כּוֹס חֲמָתוֹ, וְכָל אִינּוּן קְטוּלֵי בֵּית דִּין, דְּאִתְקְטָלוּ, אוֹ אִתְעֲנָשׁוּ עַל חוֹבִין אִלֵּין, כֻּלְּהוּ אִתְעֲקָרוּ מֵאִלֵּין סִטְרִין מִסְאֲבִין, וְלָא אִית לוֹן חוּלָקָא בְּהוֹן, וּבְהַאי כַּסָּא דְּאִקְרֵי כּוֹס הַתַּרְעֵלָה, בְּגִין כַּסָּא אַחֲרָא דְּשָׁתוּ בְּקַדְמֵיתָא.

857. Come and see: This chief has a cup in his hand called "the cup of poison," "the cup of His fury" (Yeshayah 51:17). Those who were killed by court or punished for these transgressions are torn from the sides of unholiness, and have no portion in them, or in the cup called "the cup of poison," because they first drank of another cup, BY THE COURT, PRIOR TO THEIR DEATHS. AND DEATH BY COURT IS THEIR ATONEMENT.

858. וְכָל אִינּוּן דְּלָא שָׁתוּ הַהוּא כַּסָּא דב״ד, לְאִתְעַקְרָא מֵהַאי כּוֹס הַתַּרְעֵלָה, לְבָתַר כַּד נָפִיק נִשְׁמָתֵיהּ מֵהַאי עָלְמָא, הַאי מְמָנָא וְכָל אִינּוּן דְּעִמֵּיהּ, אֲחִידָן בֵּיהּ וְדָא הוּא יוֹם הַמָּר, וְרַוֵּי לָהּ לְהַאי נִשְׁמְתָא, מִכַּמָּה דִּינִין מְשַׁנְיָין אִלֵּין מֵאִלֵּין.

858. All those who have not drunk of the cup of the court, NAMELY, WERE NOT EXECUTED BY COURT, so that the cup of poison will be torn from them, later, when the soul leaves this world, that chieftain and those with him seize it. This is, "a bitter day" (Amos 8:10), and the soul is filled with all those punishments that are different than each other.

859. בְּהֵיכָלָא דָא, קַיְימָא חַד רוּחָא, דְּאִלֵּין מְמָנָן תְּחוֹתֵיהּ, וְדָא הוּא נִיאֲצִירִיאֵ״ל. מֵהַאי רוּחָא תַּקִּיפָא, נַפְקֵי תְּלַת טִיפִּין, מְרִירָן, דְּנַפְלֵי בְּהַאי כּוֹס הַתַּרְעֵלָה. חַד אִקְרֵי חָצָ״ץ. וְחַד, אִקְרֵי מַר הַמָּוֶת וְחַד אִקְרֵי קוּבַּעַ״ת, וְאִלֵּין תְּלַת טִיפִּין נָפְלוּ לְבָתַר מֵהַאי כּוֹס, בְּהַהִיא חַרְבָּא דְּקַטְלָא בְּנֵי נָשָׁא, כְּמָה דְּאוּקְמוּהָ.

859. In this chamber there is a spirit in charge over those WE MENTIONED. He is Niatziriel. From this fierce spirit come out three bitter drops, that fall into the cup of poison. One is called 'division' (Heb. *chatzatz*), WHICH IS DERIVED FROM EXCISION AND ANNIHILATION, AS IN "WHEN THE

NUMBER OF HIS MONTHS IS ALREADY COMPLETE (HEB. *CHUTZATZU*)" (IYOV 21:21); the second is called "the bitterness of death," AS IS WRITTEN, "SURELY THE BITTERNESS OF DEATH IS PAST" (I SHMUEL 15:32); the third is called "dregs," AS IS WRITTEN, "THE DREGS, THE CUP OF POISON" (YESHAYAH 51:17). These three drops afterwards fall from the cup to the sword OF THE ANGEL OF DEATH, who kills people, as we said.

860. פִּתְחָא תְּלִיתָאָה, בֵּיהּ קַיְּימָא מְמָנָא חַד סַנְגַּדִיאֵ״ל שְׁמֵיהּ, וְהַאי אִיהוּ מְמָנָא, עַל כָּל אִינּוּן דְּעַיְילֵי הַאי בְּרִית קַדִּישָׁא, בְּאִינְתּוּ אַחֲרָא, דְּאִיהוּ מֵהַהוּא סִטְרָא דְּאֵל נֵכָר. וְכָל אִינּוּן דִּמְחַבְּלֵי אָרְחַיְיהוּ בְּדָא, וּמְשַׁקְּרֵי בְּאָת קַיָּימָא קַדִּישָׁא, הַאי מְמָנָא, וְכָל אִינּוּן מְמָנָן דְּעִמֵּיהּ, כֻּלְּהוּ מְצַיְּירֵי בְּגַוְוייְהוּ, צִיּוּרִין דְּאִינּוּן נָשִׁין מְסָאֲבִין, דְּאִסְתְּאָב בְּהוּ הַהוּא קַיָּימָא קַדִּישָׁא, וְכֻלְּהוּ אִתְרְשִׁימוּ קַמֵּיהּ, כַּד נָפִיק בַּר נָשׁ מֵהַאי עָלְמָא, וּמְסָאֲבֵי לֵיהּ לְבָתַר לְהַהוּא רוּחָא.

860. In the third opening stands a chief called 'Sangadiel'. He is in charge over all those who put the member of the Holy Covenant in a woman on the side of a strange El, and all those who corrupt their ways by being false to the sign of the Holy Covenant. This chief and all the chiefs with him paint on them pictures of these unholy women, by whom their holy member was defiled. All these are recorded before him, and when the man leaves this world, they defile the spirit.

861. וְהֵיכָלָא דָּא, תַּלְיָין כָּל רָזֵי דְּחַרְשִׁין, לְקַטְלָא בְּנֵי נָשָׁא עַד לָא יִמְטֵי זִמְנַיְיהוּ, וְכֻלְּהוּ חַרְשִׁין דְּאִצְטְרִיכוּ בְּנֵי נָשָׁא. אִינּוּן דְּחָרְשֵׁי חַרְשַׁיְיהוּ לְאִסְתַּאֲבָא בְּהוּ, כְּגוֹן דַּהֲוָה בִּלְעָם, חָרֵשׁ בְּחַרְשׁוֹי, וְאִסְתְּאַב בְּקַדְמֵיתָא בְּמִסָאֲבוּ דְּזַרְעָא רוּתַחַת דְּאַשְׁדֵּי בִּבְעִירֵי, וּבְגִין דָּא, בֵּיהּ אִתְּדָן, בְּהַהוּא שִׁכְבַת זֶרַע רוֹתַחַת דְּקָאמְרָן. וע״ד, הַאי הֵיכָלָא אִקְרֵי, שַׁחַת טָמֵא.

861. In this chamber are all the secrets of sorcery of killing people before their time and all the magic rhat people use IS STORED HERE. All the sorcerers, who practice magic to be defiled by them, like Bilaam who cast spells, were first defiled by the steaming semen they spilled in beasts. For that Bilaam was sentenced to the steaming emission of sperm, as we said. Therefore, this chamber is called 'unholy grave'.

862. וּבְהַאי הֵיכָלָא, אִית רוּחָא אַחֲרָא, דִּי מְמָנָא תְּחוֹת הַהוּא רוּחָא דִּלְעֵילָּא, וְהַאי אִקְרֵי סַרְטַיָ״א, וְכַמָּה אֶלֶף וְרִבְבָן תְּחוֹתֵיהּ. וְכֻלְּהוּ קַיְימֵי עַל הַהִיא מִלָּה, דְּנָפִיק בַּהֲדֵי רוּחָא דב״נ בְּחֶלְמָא, מִגּוֹ סִטְרָא קַדִּישָׁא. הַאי רוּחָא מִסְאֲבָא, וְכָל אִינּוּן גַּרְדִּינִין דְּעִמֵּיהּ, כֻּלְּהוּ נַפְקֵי וּמִתְחַבְּרָאן בְּהַהִיא מִלָּה, וְנַחְתֵּי בָּהּ, וּמִתְעָרְבֵי בַּהֲדָהּ, בְּגִין לְאַכְחֲשָׁא לָהּ מִנֵּיהּ, וְאוֹדְעִין לֵיהּ לב״נ מִלִּין אַחֲרָנִין, מִילִין כְּדִיבִין, בְּמִלָּה דִּקְשׁוֹט.

862. There is another spirit in that chamber, in charge under the higher spirit. He is called 'Sartaya', and has many thousands and tens of thousands under him. They all are sustained by and wait for the word, which comes out with the spirit of man, in his dream that comes from the holy side. This defiled spirit and all the complainants with him come out to join that word. They descend upon it to join it, to disprove the matter to him, and let him know other things instead, some of them false and some true.

863. דְּכַךְ אָרְחוֹי דִּכְדִיבָא, דְּאִלְמָלֵא לָא נָטִיל מִלָּה דִּקְשׁוֹט, לָא יָכִיל לְתַקְנָא כְּדִיבוֹי. אוּף הָכָא אִלֵּין, כֵּיוָן דְּמִתְעָרֵי בְּמִלֵּי קְשׁוֹט, וּמַכְחִישֵׁי לוֹן מִנֵּיהּ, מוֹדָעֵי לֵיהּ מִלָּה דִּקְשׁוֹט, בְּגִין לְקַיְּימָא כְּדִיבוֹי. לְבָתַר מִתְפַּשְּׁטָא הַהִיא מִלָּה, בְּאִינּוּן תַּתָּאֵי לְתַתָּא, דְּלֵית לוֹן קִיּוּמָא. וְלָא מִתְקַיְּימֵי, וְאוֹדְעֵי מִילִין בְּעָלְמָא, לְכַמָּה סִטְרִין לְכַמָּה זַיְינִין.

863. This is the way of a liar, that if he does not speak some truth, he cannot tell lies SO PEOPLE WOULD BELIEVE HIM. Here also, since they are mingled with truthful words HE SAW IN HIS DREAM, they disprove them, but LATER they tell him some truth to establish the false notions THEY GAVE HIM. Afterwards, it is spread to the lower SPIRITS below, who have no existence, nor validity. They announce the matter in the world to several sides and to some species.

864. מֵהֵיכָלָא דָא, נָפְקִין תְּרֵין רוּחִין, דְּמִתְהַפְּכָאן, לִזְמְנִין גּוּבְרִין, לִזְמְנִין נָשִׁין, וְאִלֵּין אָזְלִין וְשָׁטָאן בְּעָלְמָא בַּאֲוִירָא, וְחַיְיכָאן בִּבְנֵי נָשָׁא בְּגוֹ חֶלְמָא, וְאִתְחָזוּן לוֹן לְגוּבְרִין, כְּנָשִׁין שְׁפִירָן בְּחֵיזוּ דְּחֶלְמָא, וְנַטְלֵי תֵּיאוּבְתָּא דְּבַר נָשׁ. אוּף הָכִי לְנָשִׁין, אִתְחָזוּן כְּגוּבְרִין, וְאִלֵּין אִקְרוּן רָעָה וְנֶגַע, כד״א לֹא תְאוּנֶּה אֵלֶיךָ רָעָה וְנֶגַע לֹא יִקְרַב בְּאָהֳלֶךָ.

864. From this chamber come out two spirits – now they are men, and now they turn into women. They go about the world in the air, and laugh at men in their dreams, appearing in the guise of pretty women in their dreams, and so take the passion of men. Also, to women they seem like men. They are called 'evil' and 'plague', as it is written, "No evil shall befall you, nor shall any plague come near your dwelling" (Tehilim 91:10).

865. וְאִלֵּין אִקְרוּן רוּחֵי תַּתָּאֵי לְתַתָּא. דְּנַפְקֵי מִגּוֹ שַׁלְהוֹבָא דְּאֶשָּׁא. דְּכַד נַטְלִין אִלֵּין רוּחִין דִּלְעֵילָּא, דִּי בְּגוֹ הֵיכָלָא דָא, נַפְקוּ תְּרֵי שַׁלְהוֹבֵי דְּאֶשָּׁא, וְאִלֵּין טָסָאן בְּעָלְמָא, וְאִתְעֲבִידוּ אִלֵּין תְּרֵין רוּחִין כִּדְקָא אֲמָרָן, וְכֹלָּא בְּסִטְרָא דָא מְסָאֲבָא. זַכָּאִין אִינּוּן צַדִּיקַיָּיא דְּאִתְמְנָעָן מִסִּטְרִין אִלֵּין וְאִסְתְּמָרוּ מִנַּיְיהוּ. וְעַל דָּא כְּתִיב, לִשְׁמָרְךָ מֵאִשָּׁה זָרָה וְגוֹ'.

865. These EVIL AND PLAGUE are called 'the lower spirits', who come out of the flame of the fire, for when the spirits above within the chamber travel, two flames of fire come out to hover about the world, and from them these two spirits, EVIL AND PLAGUE, were made. All this is on the side of defilement. Happy are the righteous who stayed away from these sides, and kept themselves from them. Of this it is written, "that they may keep you from the strange woman..." (Mishlei 7:5).

56. The third chamber of the Other Side, Dumah, corresponding to the name 'foe' of the Evil Inclination

A Synopsis

Rabbi Shimon says that the third chamber has no light in it at all. It is called 'Dumah', and has four openings with a chief in charge of each opening. He describes the openings, the procedures where the verdict is passed, the spirits in charge of deaths, the spirits called 'wrath and fury'. He says that thousands of spirits come out of 'wrath' and 'fury' and make people who are studying the Torah sad instead of joyful. We learn that Moses was afraid of these spirits when Yisrael sinned by making the golden calf, as we read in: "for I was afraid of the wrath and fury." We read about the spirit appointed over the 'evil tongued', the serpent that sheds its skin. Rabbi Shimon says that when the serpents below shed their skin this arouses serpents in the 'pit', and all of this is caused by people speaking evil. In the same way when people study the Torah, many angels called 'the holy tongue' are united and join with holiness above.

866. הֵיכָלָא תְּלִיתָאָה. הֵיכָלָא דָּא, אִיהוּ הֵיכָלָא דְּאָפִיל וְחָשִׁיךְ, וְלֵית בֵּיהּ נְהוֹרָא כְּלַל, וְאִיהוּ אָפִיל יַתִּיר מִן קַדְמָאֵי. וְהַאי אִיהוּ דְּאִקְרֵי דוּמָ"ה, לָקֳבֵל שְׁמָא דְּאִקְרֵי שׂוֹנֵ"א. בְּהֵיכָלָא דָּא קָיְימֵי אַרְבַּע פִּתְחִין, חַד קַיְימָא לְסִטְרָא דָּא, וְחַד לְסִטְרָא דָּא, וְכֵן לְאַרְבַּע סִטְרִין.

866. The third chamber is dark and somber, for there is no light in it whatsoever. It is darker than the first CHAMBERS. It is called 'Dumah', corresponding to the name OF THE EVIL INCLINATION foe. There are four openings to this chamber, one on this side, another on that side, and so on.

867. חַד מְמָנָא קַיְימָא עַל הַאי פִּתְחָא קַדְמָאָה, וְהַאי מְמָנָא קַיְימָא בְּהַהוּא תַּקִּיפוּ דְּרוּגְזָא דְּעָלְמָא. כַּד דִּינָא שַׁרְיָא בְּעָלְמָא, הַאי מְמָנָא דְּשָׁרֵי בְּהַאי פִּתְחָא, נָטִיל זַיְינִין, וְאָנַח לוֹן לְאִינּוּן תַּרְעִין דְּבֵי כְּנִישְׁתָּא, וְהַאי אִקְרֵי סַקְפּוֹרְטַיָ"א וְדָא הוּא כִּשְׁלוֹנָא דְּעָלְמָא, וְעַל דָּא כְּתִיב דֶּרֶךְ רְשָׁעִים כָּאֲפֵלָה לֹא יָדְעוּ בַּמֶּה יִכָּשֵׁלוּ, בְּהַהוּא זִמְנָא דְּאִיהוּ שַׁלִּיט, וְשַׁרְיָא דִּינָא בְּעָלְמָא, אִיהוּ קַיְימָא לְמֶחֱמֵי בְּמַאן דְּאָזִיל יְחִידָאי

בְּשׁוּקָא, וְאִי הוּא אִעֲרַע בַּהֲדֵיהּ, יָכִיל לְנַזְקָא לֵיהּ, וּלְאַתְרַע מַזָּלֵיהּ.

867. There is a chief in charge of the first opening, sustained by the anger in the world, and when Judgment is upon the world, this chief that dwells in that gate takes weapons and puts them at the entrance to the synagogue. He is called 'Sakafortaya', and is the stumbling of the world. Of this it is written, "The way of the wicked is like darkness: they know not at what they stumble" (Mishlei 4:19). When he is in power, and there is Judgment upon the world, he goes to see who walks alone in a public place, and if he sees him, he may cause him harm and weaken his fortune.

868. פִּתְחָא תִּנְיָנָא, בֵּיהּ קַיְימָא חַד מְמָנָא אַחֲרִינָא, וְדָא אִיהוּ קַיְימָא לְנַטְלָא פִּתְקִין דְּדִינָא, וְדָא אִיהוּ סַנְגַּדְיאֵ״ל. וּתְחוֹת יְדֵיהּ, כַּמָּה גַּרְדִּינֵי נִמּוּסִין, דְּשַׁלְטָאן, דְּקַיְימִין לְקַבְּלָא אִינּוּן פִּתְקִין דְּדִינָא, וְהַאי קַיְימָא עַל פִּתְחָא דָּא.

868. On the second opening there is another chief, ready to receive the verdicts, NAMELY, THE NOTES UPON WHICH THE VERDICTS ARE WRITTEN. This is Sangadiel, under whom there are complainants and accusers in power, ready to receive these verdicts. THIS CHIEF stands at the SECOND opening.

869. וְכַד נָטִיל פִּתְקָא דְּדִינָא, הַאי קַיְימָא עַל פִּתְחָא דָּא, וְנָחִית לְתַתָּא, לְאִינּוּן פִּתְחִין חֲשׁוֹכָאן דִּלְתַתָּא. חַד לְהַהוּא דְּאִקְרֵי שָׁחַת. וְחַד לְהַהוּא דְּאִקְרֵי בּוֹר, דְּאִינּוּן לְתַתָּא. וְתַמָּן, כַּמָּה אֶלֶף, וְכַמָּה רִבְּבָן, מְמָנָן דְּשַׁלְטֵי בְּעָלְמָא לְמֶעְבַּד דִּינָא, וְאִשְׁתְּלִים דִּינָא בְּהַהוּא פִּתְקָא.

869. When he receives the verdict FROM THE CHIEFTAIN MALKIEL, OF THE FIRST OPENING OF THE THIRD CHAMBER OF HOLINESS, he stands at this opening, then descends into the dark gates below, to the one called 'grave', NAMELY, TO THE SECOND CHAMBER OF THE OTHER SIDE, and to the one called 'pit', WHICH IS THE FIRST CHAMBER OF THE OTHER SIDE, that are below. There are several thousands and tens of thousands of officers, whose duty it is to execute judgment in the world. Justice is concluded by verdict.

56. The third chamber of the Other Side, Dumah, corresponding to the name 'foe' of the Evil Inclination

870. פִּתְחָא תְּלִיתָאָה. בְּהַאי פִּתְחָא, אִית מְמָנָא אַחֲרָא, אַנְגְּרַיוֹ"ן שְׁמֵיהּ וְדָא אִיהוּ קַיְּימָא, עַל כָּל אִינּוּן מַרְעִין וּמַכְאוֹבִין, וְחִלְחוּלִין וְאֶשָּׁא דְּגַרְמֵי. דְּהָא מִנֵּיהּ נַפְקֵי כַּמָּה וְכַמָּה אֶלֶף וְרִבְבָן דִּמְמָנָן עִמֵּיהּ, עַל כָּל אִינּוּן מַרְעִין וּמַכְאוֹבִין כְּמָה דְּאִתְּמַר.

870. A chief named Angerayon is over the third opening. He is in charge over all illness and pains, trembling and the fire within the bones, NAMELY, WHICH DO NOT CAUSE DEATH, DRAWN FROM THE JUDGMENTS OF THE LEFT. Many thousands and tens of thousands of officers come out from him, in charge together with him over all the illnesses and pains, as we learned.

871. פִּתְחָא רְבִיעָאָה, הָכָא אִיהוּ חַד רוּחָא, דְּאִתְבְּרֵי בִּפְגִימוּ דְּסִיהֲרָא, וְאִקְרֵי אַסְכָּרָ"א. וְהַאי קַיְּימָא עַל קְטוּלֵי דְּרַבְיֵי, וְדָא אִתְחָזֵי לוֹן, וְחַיִיךְ בְּהוֹן, עַד דְּקָטִיל לוֹן, וְאִדְמֵי לוֹן כְּאִתְּתָא אִמֵּיהּ דְּרַבְיָא, וּמְנִיקָא לוֹן, וְחַיְיכָא בְּהוּ, וַאֲחִידַת לוֹן, וְקַטְלַת לוֹן.

871. In the fourth opening there is a spirit born when the moon was in diminution. He is called 'Askara', in charge over the death of children. He comes before CHILDREN, laughs with them until eventually he kills them. He is seen before them in the guise of a woman, like the child's mother, suckles them, laughs at them, grabs them and kills them.

872. בְּאֶמְצָעִיתָא דְּהַאי הֵיכָלָא, קַיְּימָא חַד רוּחָא, דְּאִקְרֵי אֲגִירִיסוֹ"ן. הַאי אִתְמַנָּא, עַל כָּל אִינּוּן דְּמֵתִין מִבַּר תְּלֵיסַר שְׁנִין, עַד עֶשְׂרִין שְׁנִין. הַאי אִיהוּ קְטוֹלָא דִּלְהוֹן, כְּמָה דְּאוֹקִימְנָא, וְדָא אִיהוּ בְּחַבְרוּתָא דְּהַהוּא נָחָשׁ כִּדְקָאמְרָן וְקַיְּימָא בַּהֲדֵיהּ, וְאָזִיל אֲבַתְרֵיהּ. וְעַל דָּא אִקְרֵי מַלְאַךְ הַמָּוֶת טוֹב מְאֹד, דִּכְתִּיב וְהִנֵּה טוֹב מְאֹד, וְאוֹקִימְנָא.

872. In the middle of this chamber stands a spirit called 'Agirison', in charge over those who died when they were between thirteen and twenty years of age. Their death COMES BY THE HAND OF THAT CHIEF, as we explained, by his joining the serpent we mentioned, which abides by him and follows him. For that reason the Angel of Death is called 'very good', as it is written, "and, behold, it was very good" (Beresheet 1:31), which we explained TO BE THE ANGEL OF DEATH.

873. מֵהָכָא מִתְפַּשְּׁטִין וְנָפְקִין תְּרֵין רוּחִין, אַ״ף וְחֵמָ״ה. וְאִלֵּין אִתְמְנוּן, עַל כָּל אִינּוּן דְּשַׁמְעֵי נְזִיפָא מִמָּאן דְּלָעֵי בְּאוֹרַיְיתָא, וְאִתְרַחְצָן בֵּיהּ, וְלָא חַיְישֵׁי עָלֵיהּ. וְכֵן עַל כָּל אִינּוּן דְּחַיְיכָאן מִמִּלֵּי דְּאוֹרַיְיתָא, אוֹ מִמִּלֵּי דְּרַבָּנָן.

873. From this place come and spread out two spirits called 'wrath' and 'fury', appointed over all those who are rebuked by someone who is occupied in the Torah, NAMELY, THAT HE WHO STUDIES THE TORAH SCOLDS THEM FOR NOT WALKING THE PATH OF TRUTH. They trust him, HIS GOODNESS, and are unaffected by that; also those who laugh and mock at the words of the Torah and of the words of the sages.

874. מֵאַף וְחֵמָה אִלֵּין, נָפְקִין כַּמָּה אֲלַף, וְכַמָּה רִבְבָן, וְכֻלְּהוּ נַפְקֵי וְשָׁארָן עֲלַיְיהוּ דִּבְנֵי נָשָׁא, אִינּוּן דְּמִשְׁתַּדְּלִין בְּאוֹרַיְיתָא, אוֹ דְּמִשְׁתַּדְּלֵי בְּמִלֵּי דְּמִצְוָה, וְאָזְלֵי בְּאָרְחָא דְּמִצְוָה. בְּגִין דְּיִתְעַצְּבוּן, וְלָא יֶחֱדוּן בָּהּ. וּמִתְּרֵין אִלֵּין דָּחִיל מֹשֶׁה, כַּד חָאבוּ יִשְׂרָאֵל, וְנָחִית מִן טוּרָא דִּכְתִּיב, כִּי יָגֹרְתִּי מִפְּנֵי הָאַף וְהַחֵמָה.

874. From wrath and fury come out some thousands and tens of thousands. They all come out and hover above people who study the Torah, or are occupied in the precepts, and walk in their ways, to make them sad instead of rejoicing IN THE TORAH AND THE PRECEPTS THEY ARE OCCUPIED WITH. Moses was afraid of these two when Yisrael sinned BY THE MAKING OF THE CALF, and he descended from the mountain, as it is written, "for I was afraid of the wrath and fury" (Devarim 9:19).

875. תְּחוֹת אִלֵּין, אִית רוּחָא חֲדָא, דְּקַיְּימָא עַל כָּל אִינּוּן מָארֵי דְּלִישָׁנָא בִּישָׁא, דְּכַד מִתְעָרֵי בְּנֵי נָשָׁא בְּלִישָׁנָא בִּישָׁא, אוֹ הַהוּא ב״נ דְּאִתְעָרֵי בְּלִישָׁנָא בִּישָׁא, כְּדֵין אִתְעַר הַאי רוּחָא בִּישָׁא מְסָאֲבָא דִּלְעֵילָּא, דְּאִקְרֵי סַכְסִיכָ״א. וְאִיהוּ שָׁארֵי עַל הַהוּא אִתְעֲרוּתָא דְּלִישָׁנָא

בִּישָׁא, דְּשָׁארֵי בֵּיהּ בְּנֵי נָשָׁא, וְאִיהוּ עָאל לְעֵילָּא, וְגָרִים בְּהַהוּא אִתְעֲרוּ דְּלִישָׁנָא בִּישָׁא, מוֹתָא וְחַרְבָּא וְקָטוֹלָא בְּעָלְמָא. וַוי לְאִינּוּן דְּמִתְעָרֵי לְהַאי סִטְרָא בִּישָׁא, וְלָא נַטְרֵי פּוּמַיְיהוּ וְלִישָׁנֵהוֹן, וְלָא חַשְׁשֵׁי עַל דָּא, וְלָא יַדְעֵי דְּהָא בְּאִתְעֲרוּ דִּלְתַתָּא, תַּלְיָא אִתְעֲרוּ דִּלְעֵילָּא, בֵּין לְטָב בֵּין לְבִישׁ.

875. Under these, WRATH AND FURY, there is a spirit appointed over the evil tongued. For when men start to slander, the evil unholy spirit above, called 'Sachsicha', is bestirred, dwells upon this stirring of the evil tongue that men let loose, and causes, by that arousal of the evil tongue, death, sword, and killing in the world. Woe to those who awaken this Evil Side and do not guard their mouth and tongue, nor care for this. They do not know that awakening above depends upon a awakening below, either good or bad.

876. תָּא חֲזֵי, כַּד הַאי אִתְעֲרוּ דְּלִישָׁנָא בִּישָׁא אִתְעַר לְתַתָּא, כְּדֵין הַאי נָחָשׁ עֲקַלָּתוֹן, סָלִיק קַשְׂקְשׂוֹי, וְאוֹקִים לוֹן בִּסְלִיקוּ, וְאִתְעַר מֵרֵישָׁא עַד רַגְלוֹי. וְכַד קַשְׂקְשׂוֹי סְלִיקוּ וּמִתְעָרֵי, כְּדֵין כָּל גּוּפָא אִתְעַר. קַשְׂקְשׂוֹי, אִלֵּין אִינּוּן כָּל גַּרְדִּינֵי נִימוּסִין דִּלְבַר.

876. Come and see: When the evil tongue is awakened below, a slant serpent above raises its scales TO STAND UPRIGHT, and stirs from head to toe. The scales are all those who transgress the law and justice outside.

877. וְכֻלְּהוּ מִתְעָרֵי וְאַחֲדִין בְּהַהוּא מִלָּה בִּישָׁא, וּמִתְעָרֵי לְגַבֵּי הַהוּא נָחָשׁ בָּרִיחַ, כְּדֵין כָּל גּוּפָא בִּישָׁא, אִתְעַר מֵרֵישֵׁיהּ וְעַד רַגְלוֹי, בְּכָל הָנֵי הֵיכָלִין דְּקָאמְרָן. וְכָל אִינּוּן קַשְׂקְשִׂין בְּהַהוּא גִּלְדָא, נַחְתִּין לְתַתָּא, וְהַהוּא גִּלְדָא אִתְפְּשַׁט מִנֵּיהּ וְנָחִית לְתַתָּא. וְגוּפָא סָלִיק, וְאִתְעַר לְמֶהֱוֵי דַּלְטוֹרָא לְעֵילָּא.

877. They bestir to grab that evil word THE MAN SAID, and awaken the "piercing serpent" (Yeshayah 27:1), THE MALE SERPENT. Then the whole evil body of that serpent bestirs, from head to toe, to damage all the chambers of which we talked. Then all the scales on the skin come off, and the skin is shed and comes down. The body, WITHOUT SKIN AND SCALES, comes up aroused to be an accuser above.

878. תָּא חֲזֵי, אַף עַל גַּב דִּזְמְנָא קְבִיעָא אִיהוּ, לְכָל חִוְיָין דְּעָלְמָא, לְאִתְפַּשְׁטָא מַשְׁכָּא דִּלְהוֹן, לָא מִתְפַּשְּׁטֵי, אֶלָּא בִּזְמְנָא דְּמִתְעָרֵי בְּלִישָׁנָא בִּישָׁא לְתַתָּא, וּכְדֵין אִתְעַר הַהוּא חִוְיָא בִּישָׁא לְעֵילָּא, וּפָשַׁט מַשְׁכֵיהּ וְקַשְׂקַשּׂוֹי מִנֵּיהּ. דָּא סָלִיק, וְדָא נָחִית, וְקַשְׁיָא עָלֵיהּ הַהוּא אִתְפַּשְׁטוּתָא דְּקַשְׂקַשּׂוֹי בְּמַשְׁכֵיהּ מִכֹּלָּא. מַאי טַעֲמָא. בְּגִין דְּאִתְפְּרַשׁ מִזִּוּוּגֵיהּ. דְּאַלְמָלֵא הֲוָה כֹּלָּא בְּחִבּוּרָא חֲדָא, לָא יַכְלִין עָלְמִין לְמִסְבַּל לוֹן, וְכֹלָּא בְּגִין אִתְעֲרוּתָא דְּלִישָׁנָא בִּישָׁא דִּלְתַתָּא.

878. Come and see: Though there is a set time for all the serpents in the world to shed their skin, NAMELY, EVERY SEVEN YEARS, NEVERTHELESS, they shed it only when the evil tongue is stirred below. Then the evil serpent above is aroused, and sheds its skin and scales. This goes up and that goes down, MEANING THAT THE BODY GOES UP AGAINST BINAH, AND THE SKIN AND SCALES COME OFF IT AND GO DOWN. This sloughing OF SKIN AND SCALES is difficult for the serpent, because it is separated from its spouse, NAMELY, THE SKIN AND SCALES ARE THE ASPECT OF MALCHUT OF THE SERPENT, THE SPOUSE OF THE SERPENT. WHY WOULD IT DO THIS – BE SEPARATED FROM ITS MALCHUT? BECAUSE if all were united, NAMELY, WITH MALCHUT, THE SKIN AND SCALES WHICH ARE THE ASPECT OF FIERCE JUDGMENT, the world would not have been able to bear it. IT IS THEREFORE THE CORRECTION OF THE WORLD. WITH ALL THAT, all this is caused by the arousal of the evil tongue below. THIS MEANS THAT THOUGH IT IS THE CORRECTION OF THE WORLD, IT IS NOT DONE OF ITS OWN, BUT CAUSED BY THE SIN OF SLANDER.

879. וְכַד חִוְיָין דִּלְתַתָּא מִתְפַּשְּׁטֵי מֵהַהוּא מַשְׁכָּא, כְּדֵין כָּל חַד וְחַד יָהִיב קָלָא, וְאִתְּעַר לְכַמָּה חִוְיָין דְּקַיְימֵי בְּהַהוּא אֲתָר, דְּאִקְרֵי בּוֹר, דְּתַמָּן כַּמָּה נְחָשִׁין קַיְימִין. וְכֻלְּהוּ דִּלְטוֹרִין, לְאַתְעֲרָא לְהַאי חִוְיָא רַבָּא, לְמֶהֱוֵי דִּלְטוֹרָא עַל עָלְמָא. וְכֹלָּא בְּגִין הַאי אִתְעֲרוּ דְּלִישָׁנָא בִּישָׁא, כַּד קַיְימָא אִתְעֲרוּתָא דִּילֵיהּ לְתַתָּא.

56. The third chamber of the Other Side, Dumah, corresponding to the name 'foe' of the Evil Inclination

879. When the serpents below shed their skin, each one raises its voice, and arouses several serpents in that place called 'pit', where there are snakes. All of them gossip ABOUT THE WORLD, to arouse the great serpent to gossip about the world. All this is caused by the awakening of the evil tongue, which happens below.

880. כְּגַוְונָא דָּא, מַאן דְּלָעֵי בְּאוֹרַיְיתָא, כַּמָּה אִינּוּן דְּאִקְרוּן לְשׁוֹן הַקֹּדֶשׁ, דְּמִתְחַבְּרָן וְאַתְעֲרֵי אַתְעֲרוּתָא, לְהַהוּא אֲתָר דְּאִקְרֵי לָשׁוֹן הַקֹּדֶשׁ. לָשׁוֹן מֵהַהוּא קֹדֶשׁ דִּלְעֵילָּא. וְכַמָּה קְדוּשׁוֹת וְקִדּוּשִׁין מִתְעָרִין מִכָּל סִטְרִין. זַכָּאָה חוּלָקֵיהוֹן דְּצַדִּיקַיָּיא, אִינּוּן דְּגַרְמֵי לְאַתְעֲרָא קִדּוּשִׁין לְעֵילָּא וּלְתַתָּא, קְדוּשָּׁה דִּלְעֵילָּא וּקְדוּשָּׁה דִּלְתַתָּא.

880. In the same manner, whoever studies the Torah, many ANGELS called 'the holy tongue', are united and arouse that place called 'the holy tongue', NAMELY, the tongue that comes from holiness above, WHICH IS THE SECRET OF THE CENTRAL COLUMN, WHICH IS THE TIP (TONGUE) OF THE SCALES, THAT JOINS TOGETHER RIGHT AND LEFT, SO THAT HOLINESS WILL BE REVEALED IN THEM. Many sanctifications and holy beings are bestirred on all sides. Happy is the portion of the righteous, who caused sanctifications to be stirred above and below, the sanctification above, IN BINAH, and sanctification below, IN MALCHUT.

881. וְעַל דָּא כְּתִיב, וְהִתְקַדִּשְׁתֶּם וִהְיִיתֶם קְדוֹשִׁים. וְהִתְקַדִּשְׁתֶּם: אֵלּוּ מַיִם רִאשׁוֹנִים. וְאִינּוּן אִתְקְרוּן מַיִין עִלָּאִין. וִהְיִיתֶם קְדוֹשִׁים: אִלֵּין מַיִין תַּתָּאִין, וְאִקְרוּן מַיִם אַחֲרוֹנִים. וּמָזוֹן בְּאֶמְצַע, בֵּין מַיִם רִאשׁוֹנִים לְמַיִם אַחֲרוֹנִים. וְעַל דָּא מָזוֹן, לָאו אִיהוּ בְּמַיִם אַחֲרוֹנִים, אֶלָּא בְּמַיִם רִאשׁוֹנִים. מַיִם רִאשׁוֹנִים מֵעֵילָּא דִּמְזוֹנָא תַּלְיָא בֵּיהּ. וְלָא בְּמַיִם אַחֲרוֹנִים. וְרָזָא לְקַדִּישֵׁי עֶלְיוֹנִין אִתְיְיהִיב. זַכָּאָה חוּלָקֵיהוֹן בְּעָלְמָא דֵּין, וּבְעָלְמָא דְּאָתֵי.

881. Of this it is written, "You shall therefore sanctify yourselves, and you shall be holy" (Vayikra 11:44). "You shall…sanctify yourselves" refers to the first water, called 'supernal water', NAMELY, THE SANCTIFICATION

ABOVE, IN BINAH. And "you shall be holy" refers to the last water (fingerbowl water), NAMELY, THE SANCTIFICATION BELOW, WHICH IS MALCHUT. The food comes between the first and last water. Therefore, the food is not in the last water, MALCHUT, but in the first water, BINAH, because the first water comes from above, FROM BINAH, where food abides, AS ALL MOCHIN ARE FROM BINAH, but it is not in the last water, WHICH IS MALCHUT RECEIVING FROM BINAH, WHICH HAS NOTHING ON HER OWN. This secret was handed to the high holy men, happy is their portion in this world and in the World to Come.

57. The fourth chamber of the Other Side, Debt, corresponding to the gruesome mud and a stone of stumbling

57. The fourth chamber of the Other Side, Debt, corresponding to the gruesome mud and a stone of stumbling

A Synopsis

We learn that this chamber has to do with balancing the merits and sins of a person. The fourth chamber on the holy side is called 'merit' and holds a man's precepts or good deeds; the fourth chamber on the Other Side is called 'debt' and holds his sins. Then the scales are balanced on Rosh Hashanah, and one side or the other wins. If the scales tip to 'merit', the person is given life. If the scales tip to 'debt', he is delivered to death. If he is on the side of holiness God answers when he calls to Him. If he is on the side of defilement he has no one to answer him and he is far away from God. In this fourth chamber of the Other Side the 'strange Elohim' are found, and also everyone who incites men to prostitution and adultery. Rabbi Shimon tells us about the spirits called 'plague' and 'plague and pestilence'. He talks about how the unholy side is strengthened if the tables are not prepared properly on Shabbat eve. We learn that in this fourth chamber there are no children, no longevity and no sustenance. Rabbi Shimon reveals that those who curse arouse the serpent called "Leviathan, the crooked serpent," who brings curses on the world.

882. הֵיכָלָא רְבִיעָאָה. הֵיכָלָא דָּא, אִיהוּ דְּאִקְרֵי חוֹבָ"ה. וְדָא אִיהוּ טִיט הַיָּוֵן, לָקֳבֵל שְׁמָא אַחֲרָא דְּאִקְרֵי אֶבֶן מִכְשׁוֹל, וְכֹלָּא חַד. אִיהוּ חוֹבָ"ה, בְּגִין דְּתַמָּן קַיְימֵי כָּל חוֹבֵי דְּעָלְמָא, אַכְרָעוּתָא דְּחוֹבִין.

882. The fourth chamber is called 'debt'. This is the gruesome mud, corresponding to another name OF THE EVIL INCLINATION, a stumbling stone, and all is one. It is CALLED 'debt', BECAUSE all the sins of the world ARE THERE, NAMELY, the balancing of the sins, AS WILL BE EXPLAINED.

883. בְּגִין דְּכַד חָבָאן בְּנֵי נָשָׁא, כָּל אִינּוּן גַּרְדִּינֵי נִימוּסִין, נַטְלִין אִינּוּן חוֹבִין, וּמַנְחֵי לוֹן בְּהַאי הֵיכָלָא דְּאִקְרֵי חוֹבָה. וְכָל זַכְיָין דְּעָלְמָא, כֻּלְּהוּ מַלְאֲכִין קַדִּישִׁין דִּמְמָנָן עַל זַכְוָון דְּעָלְמָא, כֻּלְּהוּ נַטְלֵי לְאִינּוּן זַכְוָון, וְאוֹקְמֵי לוֹן בְּהֵיכָלָא רְבִיעָאָה דְּאִקְרֵי זְכוּת, וְתַמָּן קַיְימֵי זַכְוָון דִּבְנֵי נָשָׁא. וְחוֹבִין קַיְימֵי בְּהֵיכָלָא אַחֲרָא, דְּאִקְרֵי חוֹבָה. וְאַתְקָלוּ כַּחֲדָא

בְּיוֹמָא דְּרֹאשׁ הַשָּׁנָה כִּי גַּם אֶת זֶה לְעֻמַּת זֶה עָשָׂה הָאֱלֹהִים. וּלְבָתַר דְּאַכְרָעוּ זַכְיָין, אוֹ חוֹבִין, לְסִטְרָא דָּא, אוֹ לְסִטְרָא דָּא, הָכִי נָצַח.

883. For when men sin, all the complainants take the sins to put them in this chamber called 'debt'. As for all the precepts in the world, the holy angels, appointed over the merits in the world, take them and put them in the fourth chamber OF HOLINESS called 'merit', where the precepts of men abide. And the sins are in the other chamber called 'debt'. They are balanced on Rosh Hashanah, for "the Elohim has made the one as well as the other" (Kohelet 7:14), and according to the tipping of the scales by the precepts or sins, this or that side wins. IF THERE ARE MORE SINS, THE OTHER SIDE WINS, AND IF THERE ARE MORE PRECEPTS, THE HOLINESS WINS.

884. וע״ד, בְּיוֹמָא דְּרֹאשׁ הַשָּׁנָה, כַּד מִתְעָרִין אִלֵּין תְּרֵין סִטְרִין, זְכוּת וְחוֹבָה. וּבְהוּ תַּלְיָין חַיִּים וּמָוֶת. אִי זַכְיָין אַכְרָעוּ, לְסִטְרָא דָּא דְּאִקְרֵי זְכוּת, אִכְתּוּב בַּר נָשׁ בְּהַהוּא סִטְרָא דְּאִקְרֵי חַיִּים. בְּגִין, דְּהָנֵי תְּרֵין סִטְרִין קַיְימֵי בְּהַהוּא יוֹמָא, דָּא בְּסִטְרָא דָּא, וְדָא בְּסִטְרָא דָּא. אִי זָכֵי הַהוּא בַּר נָשׁ, וְנִצְחִין אִינּוּן זַכְיָין, הָא אִכְתּוּב הַהוּא ב״נ לְחַיִּים. בְּגִין דְּאָחִיד בֵּיהּ הַאי סִטְרָא קַדִּישָׁא, דְּאִקְרֵי זְכוּת, וְחַיִּים אָחִיד בֵּיהּ, וְאָמַר דָּא דִּילִי הוּא, וְדִידִי הֲוָה, וּכְדֵין אִכְתּוּב הַהוּא ב״נ לְחַיִּים.

884. Therefore, on the day of Rosh Hashanah, life and death depend upon these two sides, merit and debt. If the merits tip the scale to the side called 'merit', man is written on the side called 'life', since these two sides stand on that day, the one on that side, and the other on another side. If a man deserves it, and the merits win, he is written to life, as the holy side called 'merit' grasps him, and life grasps him and says: 'This one is mine, and was mine'. Then Man is written into life.

885. וְאִי נַצְחָן חוֹבִין, הַאי סִטְרָא אַחֲרָא מְסָאֲבָא, דְּאִקְרֵי חוֹבָה וּמָוֶת, אָחִיד בֵּיהּ, אָמַר הַאי דִּידִי הוּא, וְדִידִי הֲוֵי, וּכְדֵין אִכְתּוּב דְּאִיהוּ דִּילֵיהּ. וְדָא הוּא דְּתָנֵינָן, דְּהָא בְּיוֹמָא דָּא דר״ה, אִכְתּוּב ב״נ, אוֹ לְחַיִּים אוֹ לְמִיתָה. אִי אִכְתּוּב בְּסִטְרָא דִּקְדוּשָׁה, אִכְתּוּב לְחַיִּים,

וְאִתְקַיָּים תַּמָּן, וְאִתְדְבַק בֵּיהּ. וְאִי אִכְתּוּב בְּסִטְרָא אַחֲרָא, אִתְקְיָּים בְּסִטְרָא דִּמְסָאֲבוּתָא, וְדָבִיק בֵּיהּ, וְדָא הוּא הֵן לְחַיִּים הֵן לַמָּוֶת. וְאִתְמְשַׁךְ בְּהַאי סִטְרָא אוֹ בְּהַאי סִטְרָא.

885. If the sins win, the unholy Other Side – called 'debt and death' – grasps him and says: 'This is mine, and was mine'. And then it is written that the man is his. This is what we learned, that on the day of Rosh Hashanah, a man is written to life or death. If he is written to the side of holiness, he is written to life. He abides there and cleaves to it. If he is written upon the Other Side, he abides by the side of defilement, and clings to it, WHICH IS DEATH. It is either to life or death, NAMELY, it is drawn from either this or that side.

886. כָּל זִמְנָא דְּאִיהוּ קַיְּימָא בְּסִטְרָא דָּא דִּקְדוּשָּׁה, כָּל קִדּוּשִׁין וְכָל דַּכְיָין מִתְדַּבְּקִין בֵּיהּ. יִקְרָא וְקוּדְשָׁא בְּרִיךְ הוּא יָתִיב וְיִשְׁמַע לֵיהּ, עָלֵיהּ כְּתִיב יִקְרָאֵנִי וְאֶעֱנֵהוּ עִמּוֹ אָנֹכִי בְצָרָה אֲחַלְּצֵהוּ וַאֲכַבְּדֵהוּ אוֹרֶךְ יָמִים אַשְׂבִּיעֵהוּ וְאַרְאֵהוּ בִּישׁוּעָתִי. וְכָל זִמְנָא דְּאִיהוּ קַיְּימָא בְּסִטְרָא אַחֲרָא דִּמְסָאֲבָא, כָּל מִסְאֲבוּ, וְכָל חוֹבָה, וְכָל בִּישִׁין מִתְדַּבְּקָן בֵּיהּ. יִקְרָא, וְלֵית מַאן דְּיִשְׁמַע לֵיהּ. מְרַחֲקָא אִיהוּ מִקּוּדְשָׁא בְּרִיךְ הוּא, עָלֵיהּ כְּתִיב רָחוֹק מֵרְשָׁעִים יְשׁוּעָה וּכְתִיב גַּם כִּי תַרְבּוּ תְפִלָּה אֵינֶנִּי שׁוֹמֵעַ.

886. Whenever he is on the side of holiness, all sacredness and purity cleave to him. He calls and the Holy One, blessed be He, sits and listens. Of him says the verse, "He shall call upon Me, and I will answer him; I will be with him in trouble; I will deliver him, and honor him. With long life I will satisfy him, and show him My salvation" (Tehilim 91:15). As long as he is on the unholy Other Side, all defilement, all sins and evils cling to him. He calls and there is no one to listen to him. He is far away from the Holy One, blessed be He. Of him it is written, "Salvation is far from the wicked" (Tehilim 119:155), and "even when you make many prayers, I will not hear" (Yeshayah 1:15).

887. הֵיכָלָא דָּא, אִיהוּ אֲתָר דְּכָל אִינּוּן דְּאִקְרוּן אֱלֹהִים אֲחֵרִים, בְּגִין דְּאִתְגַּלְיָין הָכָא. וְכָל אִינּוּן דִּמְפַתּוּ לְהוּ לִבְנֵי נָשָׁא בְּעִנּוּגִין דְּהַאי

עָלְמָא, לְאַזְנָאָה לְאִתְעַנְּגָא בְּעִנּוּגֵי נִאוּפִין דְּעָלְמָא, וּמַשְׁכֵי לְהוּ בָּתַר עִנּוּגִין וְנִאוּפִין דְּהַאי עָלְמָא, כִּדְקַאמְרָן.

887. This chamber is the dwelling place of all those called 'strange Elohim', because they are revealed here. ALSO, HERE ARE FOUND all those who incite men to the pleasures of this world, to prostitution, to delight in the pleasures of fornication. They pull them toward the pleasures and adulteries of the world, as we said.

888. בְּהַאי הֵיכָלָא, אִתְחָזֵי חַד רוּחָא שַׁלִּיט תַּקִּיפָא, דְּאִיהוּ עַל כֻּלְּהוּ, וְדָא אִקְרֵי אוּף הָכִי אֵל, כְּגַוְונָא דְּאַחֲרָא דְּבִסְטַר קְדוּשָּׁה. הַאי אִיהוּ אֵ"ל נֵכָ"ר. וְדָא אִיהוּ דִּמְפַתֵּי לְבַר נָשׁ דְּלָעֵי בְּאוֹרַיְיתָא, אוֹ דְּקָאֵים בְּבֵי מִדְרָשָׁא. הַאי רוּחָא תַּקִּיפָא מְפַתֵּי לֵיהּ, וְחָשִׁיב כַּמָּה הִרְהוּרִין, וְאָמַר מַה אַתְּ קָאֵים הָכָא, טַב לָךְ לְמֵהַךְ בְּחִבּוּרַת אִינּוּן דְּגָאוּ עַל בְּנֵי נָשָׁא, וְאִינּוּן דְּאָזְלִין בָּתַר נָשִׁין שְׁפִירָאן, וּמִתְעַנְּגֵי בְּעִנּוּגֵי עָלְמָא. כֵּיוָן דב"נ אִתְפַּתֵּי אֲבַתְרֵיהּ, כְּדֵין כֻּלְּהוּ שַׁטְיָין וְאָזְלֵי וְאִתְמַשְׁכָאן אֲבַתְרֵיהּ.

888. In this chamber there is a powerful spirit, who has control over everyone. He, too, is called 'El', like the other SPIRIT OF THE FOURTH CHAMBER on the side of holiness. This is a strange El. He seduces the man who is occupied in the Torah, or stands in the synagogue. This powerful spirit seduces him, and THE MAN is thoughtful. THE SPIRIT says to him, 'Why are you standing here, it is better for you to go wherever people boast in front of others, go after pretty women, and take delight in the pleasures of the world'. Once a man is incited by him, all THE SPIRITS hover and follow him.

889. וְכַמָּה אִינּוּן אַחֲרָנִין דְּקַיְימִין תְּחוֹתֵיהּ, וְכֻלְּהוּ מְסָאֲבֵי לֵיהּ בְּהַאי עָלְמָא, וּמְסָאֲבֵי לֵיהּ בְּהַהוּא עָלְמָא. וְאִינּוּן אִקְרוּן צוֹאָה רוֹתַחַת דִּכְתִּיב צֵא תֹּאמַר לוֹ. אִינּוּן דַּרְגִּין דְּקַיְימִין לְסָאֲבָא תָּדִיר, וְהָא אִתְּמַר.

889. There are some other spirits under THE SAID SPIRIT. They all defile him in this world, and defile him in that world. These spirits are called 'steaming filth' (Heb. *tzoa*), as it is written, "go you (Heb. *tze*), say to it" (Yeshayah 30:22), FOR THEY TEMPT MAN TO GO OUT (HEB. *LATZET*) FROM

THE SYNAGOGUE AND FROM HOLINESS, AND INTO THE PLEASURES OF THE WORLD. These are the grades that are always ready to defile, as we learned.

890. בְּאֶמְצָעִיתָא דְּהַאי הֵיכָלָא, אִית רוּחָא אַחֲרָא, דְּאִקְרֵי נֶגַע. וּמֵהַאי נָפְקָא רוּחָא אַחֲרָא דְּאִקְרֵי נֶגַע צָרַעַת. וְאִיהוּ קַיְּימָא תָּדִיר, לְסָאֲבָא לְכָל אִינּוּן מָארֵיהוֹן דְּלִישָּׁנָא בִּישָׁא, יַתִּיר עַל כָּל מַה דְּמִסְאֲבִין לֵיהּ. וְהַאי נֶגַע עִלָּאָה, אִיהוּ מְמָנָא עַל כָּל אִינּוּן פָּתוֹרֵי דְּשַׁבְּתָא, דְּכַד עָיֵיל שַׁבְּתָא, וְלָא אִתְסְדָרוּ בְּעִנּוּגָא דְּשַׁבְּתָא כַּדְקָא יֵאוֹת, וְאִינּוּן קָא מְבַזֵּי עִנּוּגָא דְּשַׁבְּתָא, הַאי נֶגַע נָטִיל לְאִינּוּן פָּתוֹרֵי דְּלָאו אִינּוּן בְּעִנּוּגָא דְּשַׁבְּתָא כִּדְקָאמְרָן.

890. In the middle of the chamber there is another spirit called 'plague', from which comes out another spirit called 'plague of pestilence', ready to defile those of evil tongue more than they were defiled BY THE THIRD CHAMBER. This high plague is in charge over all the tables of Shabbat, for when Shabbat enters and THE TABLE is not properly set with the delights of Shabbat, thus slighting Shabbat, this plague receives these tables, empty of the delights of Shabbat, as we already said.

891. וְכַד הַאי נָטִיל לְאִינּוּן פָּתוֹרֵי, כָּל אִינּוּן גַּרְדִּינֵי נִימוּסִין דְּקַיְימֵי בֵּיהּ, כֻּלְּהוּ פָּתְחֵי וְאָמְרֵי, וַיֶּאֱהַב קְלָלָה וַתְּבוֹאֵהוּ וְלֹא חָפֵץ בִּבְרָכָה וַתִּרְחַק מִמֶּנּוּ. וַיִּלְבַּשׁ וְגו'. יְנַקֵּשׁ נוֹשֶׁה לְכָל אֲשֶׁר לוֹ וְגו'. אַל יְהִי לוֹ מוֹשֵׁךְ חָסֶד וְגו'.

891. When the plague receives these tables, the complainants and accusers standing there all open and say, "For he loved cursing, and it came to him, and he delighted not in blessing, and it was far from him. And he clothed himself with cursing like his garment..." (Tehilim 109:17-18), "Let the creditor seize everything that he has...Let there be none to extend kindness to him..." (Ibid. 11-12).

892. וְהָא אוֹקִימְנָא, בְּהַהוּא לֵילְיָא דְּשַׁבְּתָא, כַּד פָּתוֹרֵי אִתְיְיהִיבוּ

לְהַהוּא סִטְרָא בִּישָׁא, כְּדֵין אִתְתַּקַּף הַהוּא סִטְרָא בִּישָׁא, מִסְּאֲבָא, וְהַהוּא ב"נ אִתְמְסַר לְהַהוּא סִטְרָא. וַוי לֵיהּ דְּאִתְגְּרַע מֵהַהוּא סִטְרָא קַדִּישָׁא, דִּמְהֵימְנוּתָא. וְאִתְפְּקַד בְּסִטְרָא אַחֲרָא מִסְּאֲבָא. כְּגַוְונָא דָּא בְּכָל אִינּוּן סְעוּדָתֵי דִי"ט.

892. We have established that on Shabbat eve, when the tables were given to the Evil Side, that evil unholy side strengthens, and that man is delivered to the OTHER Side. Woe to him, for being reduced from the side of holiness and given to the other unholy side. It is the same for the holiday meals.

893. הָכָא בְּהַאי הֵיכָלָא, בְּנֵי חַיֵּי וּמְזוֹנֵי בְּהִפּוּכָא אִיהוּ. וּבְהַהוּא הֵיכָלָא אַחֲרָא קַדִּישָׁא, לָא קַיְימֵי תְּלַת אִלֵּין, וְתַלְיָין לְעֵילָּא, וְהָכָא קַיְימִין לְבִישׁ. דְּכַד מָטֵי ב"נ לְהַאי הֵיכָלָא, הָא תַּמָּן קַיְימִין חַיִּין לְשֵׁיצָאָה לוֹן. וְהָא תַּמָּן בְּנִין כַּד אִינּוּן זְעִירִין, מֵהָכָא נָפְקָא, בְּגִין לְאִתְמַנָּאָה קַטֵיגוֹרָא עֲלַיְיהוּ. וְהָא תַּמָּן קַיְימִין מְזוֹנֵי, לְאַעְבְּרָא לוֹן מִנֵּיהּ. וְכֹלָּא תַּלְיָא בְּחוֹבָה. וְעַל דָּא אִקְרֵי הַאי הֵיכָלָא חוֹבָה. כְּמָה דְּאִתְּמַר.

893. Here, in this chamber, is the opposite of children, longevity, and sustenance, MEANING THAT THESE THREE ARE WITHHELD FROM MEN. There are no CHILDREN, LONGEVITY, AND SUSTENANCE on the other, the holy fourth chamber, for they are extended from above. But here there are for evil, for when a man reaches this chamber, there is life to be consumed and children that are small, for from here comes the spirit that is appointed to be their accuser. There is food there, to be taken away from man. NAMELY, ALL THIS IS FOR THE WORSE. All depends on debt, NAMELY, SINS. Therefore, this chamber is called 'debt', as we learned.

894. וּמֵהָכָא נָפְקָא חַד רוּחָא מִסְּאֲבָא, דְּאִקְרֵי אֲרִירִ"א. וְכַמָּה אֲלַף וְרִבְבָן עִמֵּיהּ, וְכֻלְּהוּ אִקְרוּן אוֹרְרֵי יוֹם, כד"א יִקְּבוּהוּ אוֹרְרֵי יוֹם. וְהַאי רוּחָא וְכָל אִינּוּן דְּעִמֵּיהּ, כֻּלְּהוּ קַיְימֵי לְנַטְלָא הַהִיא מִלָּה דְּלָיֵיט בַּר נָשׁ גַּרְמֵיהּ בְּרוּגְזֵיהּ, וְאִלֵּין מִתְעָרֵי לְהַאי חִוְיָא, דְּאִקְרֵי לִוְיָתָן נָחָשׁ עֲקַלָּתוֹן, בְּגִין לְאַיְיתָאָה וּלְאַתְעָרָא לְוָוטִין עַל עָלְמָא, הה"ד יִקְּבוּהוּ אוֹרְרֵי יוֹם וְגוֹ'.

57. The fourth chamber of the Other Side, Debt, corresponding to the gruesome mud and a stone of stumbling

894. From here emerges an unholy spirit called 'Aririya', together with thousands and tens of thousands, all called "who curse (Heb. *orerei*) the day," according to the verse, "let them curse it (him) who curse the day" (Iyov 3:8). This spirit and those with him are ready to take the word of a man who curses himself in anger. They arouse the serpent called, "Leviatan, the crooked serpent" (Yeshayah 27:1), so it would bring and awaken curses upon the world. This is the meaning of, "let them curse it who curse the day…"

895. וְאִלֵּין אוֹרְרֵי יוֹם, שַׁלְטִין עַל רִגְעֵי וְשַׁעְתֵּי דְּיוֹמָא, וְנַטְלֵי אִינּוּן מִילִין דְּלָיִיט בַּר נָשׁ גַּרְמֵיהּ, בֵּין בְּרוּגְזָא, בֵּין בְּאוֹמָאָה, וּבְהַהִיא מִלָּה, מִתְעָרֵי לְהַאי נָחָשׁ עֲקַלָּתוֹן, דְּאִקְרֵי לִוְיָתָן, בְּגִין לְקַיְּימָא לֵיהּ לְחַבְּלָא לְעָלְמָא. וְעַל דָּא לָיִיט אִיּוֹב יוֹמֵיהּ בְּצַעֲרֵיהּ, וְלָא גּוּפֵיהּ. דִּכְתִיב וַיְקַלֵּל אֶת יוֹמוֹ בַּתְחִלָּה, וּלְבָתַר יִקְּבוּהוּ אוֹרְרֵי יוֹם. רַחֲמָנָא לִישֵׁזְבָן מִסִּטְרָא בִּישָׁא, וּמִתּוּקְפוֹי. וּמִכָּל מִלָּה בִּישָׁא.

895. Those who curse the day rule over the minutes and hours of the day, AND THEREFORE THEY ARE CALLED "WHO CURSE THE DAY." They take the words the man cursed himself by, whether in anger, or by oath, and with that word they arouse the slant serpent called 'Leviatan', to make him harm the world. Therefore, Job, in his grief, cursed his day, not his body, SO THEY WOULD NOT GRAB HIS WORDS, as it is written, "and cursed his day" (Iyov 3:1), and afterwards "let them curse it (him) who curse the day." May the Merciful One save us from the Evil Side and its Judgments, and from all that is evil.

58. The fifth chamber of the Other Side, Sheol, corresponding to the name 'uncircumcised'

A Synopsis

Rabbi Shimon tells us that the chief in charge of the fifth chamber, named 'enmity,' has a duty to stir up accusations in the world. There is another spirit in this chamber called 'robber'. All those who rob, who corrupt and destroy, and who kill by sword and spear emerge from this chamber and take their nourishment from it. We learn of spirits called 'spoilage' and 'famine'. As long as people do acts of kindness and give others food and drink these spirits are pushed away, but when Yisrael does not do acts of kindness the two spirits attack Yisrael. Rabbi Shimon tells how these spirits are also called 'foreskin', and are under the command of the spirit called 'Gezar Dinaya', or 'verdict'. 'Verdict' puts people in Sheol when they do not observe the sign of the holy covenant by having their sons circumcised. We are told of another spirit, 'Afrira', ashes of dust, who seduces people to stray from the path of truth. Lastly Rabbi Shimon explains the difference between 'first water' and 'last water,' or 'precept' and 'debt'. He says that Yisrael is blessed when God purifies them with supernal clean water.

896. הֵיכָלָא חֲמִישָׁאָה. הֵיכָלָא דָּא, אִיהוּ הֵיכָלָא דְּאִקְרֵי שְׁאוֹ״ל, לָקֳבֵל הַהוּא שְׁמָא דְּאִקְרֵי עָרֵל, וְהָא אוֹקִימְנָא דְּדָא אִיהוּ רָזָא דְּעָרְלָה. בְּהַאי הֵיכָלָא, אִית חַד פִּתְחָא, וְחַד מְמָנָא עָלֵיהּ. וְדָא אִיהוּ מְמָנָא לְאַתְעֲרָא תָּדִיר קִטְרוּגָא עַל עָלְמָא, וְהַאי רוּחָא אִקְרֵי אֵיבָ״ה, בְּגִין דִּשְׁמָא דְּהַאי פִּתְחָא אֵיבָ״ה שְׁמֵיהּ, וְסִימָנֵיךְ וְאֵיבָה אָשִׁית בֵּינְךָ וּבֵין הָאִשָּׁה וְגוֹ׳.

896. The fifth chamber is called 'Sheol', corresponding to the name of the Evil Inclination, uncircumcised, which we explained to be the secret of the foreskin. In this chamber there is one opening, and a chief in charge over it. The duty of this chief is to stir up accusations upon the world. This spirit is called 'enmity', after the name of the opening, enmity. This is understood from the verse, "and I will put enmity between you and the woman…" (Beresheet 3:15).

58. The fifth chamber of the Other Side, Sheol, corresponding to the name 'uncircumcised'

897. בְּהַאי הֵיכָלָא קַיְּימָא חַד רוּחָא דְּשַׁלִּיט עַל כֹּלָּא, וְהַאי אִקְרֵי שׁוֹדֵ"ד. וְאִיהוּ שׁוֹד וָשֶׁבֶר. וְדָא הוּא שׁוֹדֵד בְּטוּרֵי רָמָאֵי, גּוֹ טִנָּרִין וְטוּרִין. מֵהֵיכָלָא דָּא יַנְקֵי כָּל אִינּוּן מְשַׁדְּדֵי וּמְשַׁצֵּי בְּחָרְבְּנִין. וּמֵהָכָא נָפְקִין, כָּל אִינּוּן דְּקַטְלֵי בְּסַיְיפִין וְרוֹמְחִין, וְאַזְלִין בָּתַר לַהַט הַחֶרֶב הַמִּתְהַפֶּכֶת לְשֵׁיצָאָה כֹּלָּא.

897. There is a spirit in this chamber who rules everything. He is called 'robber' (Heb. *shoded*), and is a "wasting (Heb. *shod*) and destruction" (Yeshayah 59:7). This robber abides in the high mountains between rocks and mountains. From this chamber all the robbers suck, who corrupt and destroy; from here emerge those who kill by sword and spear, who go after "the bright blade of a revolving sword" (Beresheet 3:24), to exterminate everything.

898. מֵהַאי נָפִיק רוּחָא אַחֲרָא, וְאִקְרֵי שׁוֹד. וְכַד שַׁלִּיט כַּפְנָא עַל עָלְמָא, הַאי רוּחָא דְּאִקְרֵי שׁוֹ"ד, אִיהוּ אִשְׁתְּכַח. וְרוּחָא אַחֲרָא אִשְׁתַּתַּף עִמֵּיהּ, דְּאִקְרֵי כָּפָ"ן. וְאִלֵּין אַזְלֵי בְּעָלְמָא, וּמִשְׁתַּכְּחֵי לְקַבֵּל בְּנֵי נָשָׁא, וְהַיְינוּ דִּכְתִיב, לְשֹׁד וּלְכָפָן תִּשְׂחָק. וְאִלֵּין עָבְדִין קִטְרוּגָא לִבְנֵי נָשָׁא, וּמְשַׁדְּדֵי לְכֹלָּא. חַד דְּאִקְרֵי שׁוֹד, דְּבָתַר דְּאָזִיל בְּגוֹ טוּרִין רָמָאִין, וְשָׁדִיד וְחָרִיב וְשֵׁצֵי כֹּלָּא. כְּדֵין תָּב וְשָׁדַד לִבְנֵי נָשָׁא, וּמֵתִין בְּחוּלְשָׁא דִּילֵיהּ. וְכַד אַכְלֵי בְּנֵי נָשָׁא, לָא שַׂבְעִין, בְּגִין דְּאִיהוּ שַׁלְטָא בְּעָלְמָא.

898. From this spirit comes out another spirit called 'spoilage'. When famine has sway in the world, the spirit called 'spoilage' joins another spirit called 'famine'. They go about the world, as adversaries to men. This is the meaning of the verse, "at destruction and famine you shall laugh" (Iyov 5:24). They accuse men and rob all. The one is called 'spoilage', for haunting the high mountains, and robbing, destroying and wasting everything. Then he comes back to rob men, and they die of weakness, THAT HE CAUSES THEM. When people eat but are not satiated, it is due to him.

899. וּבְהַהוּא זִמְנָא, מַאן דְּעָבֵיד חֶסֶד עִם בְּנֵי נָשָׁא, וְיָהִיב לוֹן לְמֵיכַל

וּלְמִשְׁתֵּי, כְּדַאי אִיהוּ לְדַחְיָיא לוֹן לְאִלֵּין תְּרֵין רוּחִין לְבַר, דְּלָא שַׁלְטֵי בְּעָלְמָא. וְכַד יִשְׂרָאֵל לָא עַבְדֵּי חֶסֶד עִם בְּנֵי נָשָׁא, וּשְׁאָר עַמִּין עַבְדֵּי חֶסֶד בְּעָלְמָא. כְּדֵין אִלֵּין תְּרֵין רוּחִין מִתְבַּסְּמִין מִלַּיְיהוּ, וּמִתְקְפֵי עָלַיְיהוּ דְּיִשְׂרָאֵל. בְּגִין דְּהָא כְּדֵין אִתְקַף הַהוּא סִטְרָא אַחֲרָא, וְיִשְׂרָאֵל אִתְכַּפְיָין.

899. At that time, whoever does an act of kindness by men, and gives them food and drink, he is worthy of pushing these two spirits out, so they will have no power over the world. But when Yisrael do no kindness by men, and the other nations do kindness in the world, then these two spirits temper their business WITH THE NATIONS, and attack Yisrael, since then the Other Side becomes stronger and Yisrael are subjugated.

900. וְכַד יִשְׂרָאֵל עַבְדֵּי חֶסֶד, אִתְכַּפְיָא הַהוּא סִטְרָא אַחֲרָא וְאִתְחַלָּשׁ, וְסִטְרָא דִּקְדוּשָּׁה אִתְקַף. וְכַד יִשְׂרָאֵל לָא מִתְעָרֵי בְּחֶסֶד, אִינּוּן תְּרֵין רוּחִין מִתְהַפְּכֵי לְאַכְפְּיָיא לוֹן לְיִשְׂרָאֵל, וּכְדֵין אִינּוּן בִּרְכָאן דְּנַחְתֵּי מִלְּעֵילָּא, מִסְּטַר יְמִינָא, יַנְקֵי לוֹן שְׁאַר עַמִּין. וְהה"ד שָׂמוּנִי נוֹטֵרָה אֶת הַכְּרָמִים, אִלֵּין שְׁאַר עַמִּין. כַּרְמִי שֶׁלִּי לֹא נָטַרְתִּי, אִלֵּין יִשְׂרָאֵל. בְּגִין דִּשְׁאַר עַמִּין מַשְׁכֵי לֵיהּ בְּגַוַּויְיהוּ, בְּאִינּוּן חֲסָדִים דְּעַבְדִּין עִם בְּנֵי נָשָׁא. וְיִשְׂרָאֵל מְרַחֲקָן לֵיהּ מִגַּווַיְיהוּ, בְּגִין דְּלָא מִשְׁתַּדְּלֵי בְּאִינּוּן חֲסָדִים כִּשְׁאַר עַמִּין.

900. When Yisrael are kind, the Other Side is subdued and weakens, and the side of holiness gathers strength. But when Yisrael are not aroused to do kindness, the two spirits turn to subdue Yisrael and all the blessings flowing from the right side above, the other nations suckle them. This is WHAT THE SHECHINAH SAID: "they made me keeper of the vineyards" (Shir Hashirim 1:6), which are the other nations. "But my own vineyard I have not kept" (Ibid.), which is Yisrael, CALLED 'THE SHECHINAH'S VINEYARD', for the other nations took THE SHECHINAH in their midst, by the kindness they do by men. And Yisrael keep her away, for they are not kind as the rest of the nations.

58. The fifth chamber of the Other Side, Sheol, corresponding to the name 'uncircumcised'

901. וּתְחוֹת אִלֵּין רוּחִין, קַיְימִין כָּל אִינּוּן דְּאִקְרוּן עָרְלָה. זְמוֹרֵי עָרְלָה, עַנְפֵי עָרְלָה. וְעֵילָּא מִנְּהוֹן חַד מְמָנָא, דְּאִקְרֵי גְּזַר דִּינַיָּ"א. וְהַאי אִיהוּ קַיְימָא עַל כָּל אִינּוּן דְּלָא נַטְרֵי שְׁנֵי עָרְלָה דְּאִילָנָא. וְעַל כָּל אִינּוּן, דִּמְעַכְּבֵי אֶת קַיָּימָא לִבְרַיְיהוּ. וְעַל דָּא, בָּעָא חִוְיָא לְקָטְלָא לִבְרֵיהּ דְּמֹשֶׁה. עַד דְּגַזְרַת לֵיהּ צִפּוֹרָה, דִּכְתִּיב וַתִּקַּח צִפּוֹרָה צֹר וַתִּכְרֹת אֶת עָרְלַת בְּנָהּ וְגוֹ'.

901. Under these spirits are those called 'foreskin', the foreskin of the shoot, the foreskin of the branch. Above them there is a chieftain called 'Gezar Dinaya' (Eng. 'verdict'). He is appointed over those who do not observe the years of foreskin of trees, and those who delay the circumcision of their sons. For that the serpent wanted to kill the son of Moses, until Tziporah circumcised him, as it is written, "and cut off the foreskin of her son…" (Shemot 4:25).

902. וְהַאי רוּחָא, מְמָנָא עַל בְּנֵי נָשָׁא דִּמְחַבְּלֵי אָרְחַיְיהוּ, וְלָא חַיְישֵׁי לִיקָרָא דְּמָארֵיהוֹן, לְמֵיטַר אֶת קַיָּימָא קַדִּישָׁא. וְהַאי אָעִיל לוֹן לַגֵּיהִנָּם, לְהַהוּא אֲתָר דְּאִקְרֵי שְׁאוֹל וַאֲבַדּוֹן, וְאִתְדָּן תַּמָּן, כְּמָה דְּאוֹקִימְנָא הָכָא.

902. This spirit is in charge over men who corrupt their ways, and do not care for the glory of their Master, by observing the sign of the Holy Covenant. THIS SPIRIT puts them in Gehenom, in the place called 'Sheol' and perdition (Heb. *Avadon*), where they are sentenced, as we explained here.

903. בְּהַאי הֵיכָלָא לְגוֹ בְּאֶמְצָעִיתָא, קַיְימָא חַד רוּחָא, דְּאִיהוּ קַיְימָא וְכָמִין עַל אוֹרְחִין וּשְׁבִילִין, לְמֶחֱמֵי לְכָל אִינּוּן דְּעַבְרִין עַל פִּתְגָּמֵי אוֹרַיְיתָא. כְּדֵי לְמֵיעַל דְּבָבוּ, בֵּין תַּתָּא לְעֵילָּא. בְּגִין דְּכָל הַאי הֵיכָלָא אֵיבָה אִיהוּ.

903. In the middle of this chamber there is another spirit, standing and lurking by the ways and paths, to look for those who transgress the words of the Torah, and to bring hatred between MEN below and above, for the whole chamber is enmity.

904. הַאי וְכָל אִינּוּן אַחֲרָנִין, כֻּלְּהוּ קַיְימִין לְאַחֲזָאָה אַנְפִּין נְהִירִין לִבְנֵי נָשָׁא, וּלְמִפְתֵּי לְהוּ, בְּגִין דְּיִסְטוּן מֵאֹרַח קְשׁוֹט, וּלְאַמְשָׁכָא לוֹן אֲבַתְרַיְיהוּ, וּלְבָתַר אִינּוּן קַטְלֵי לוֹן, וִימוּתוּן בִּתְרֵין עָלְמִין. דִּכְתִּיב, וְאַחֲרִיתָהּ מָרָה כַלַּעֲנָה חַדָּה כְּחֶרֶב פִּיּוֹת.

904. This one and all the others are in the habit of being friendly toward people and seducing them to stray from the path of truth and follow them. Then they kill them, and they are dead in both worlds, as it is written, "but her end is bitter as wormwood, sharp as a two-edged sword" (Mishlei 5:4).

905. הַאי רוּחָא, אִיהוּ אִקְרֵי אַפְרִירָ"א. עַפְרָא דְּקִיטְמָא. דְּלָא עָבֵיד תּוֹלְדִין וְאֵיבִין לְעָלְמִין, בְּגִין דְּהַאי אִיהוּ עַפְרָא דְּקִיטְמָא. ואע"ג דְּאִקְרֵי עָפָר, לָאו אִיהוּ עַפְרָא קַדִּישָׁא, דְּעָבֵיד אֵיבִין, וְאִקְרֵי עַפְרוֹת זָהָב. אֶלָּא כְּמָה דְּאַתְּ אָמֵר, מֵעֲפַר שְׂרֵפַת הַחַטָּאת. וְדָא הוּא עֲפַר שְׂרֵפַת הַחַטָּאת, וְסִימָנָא דָּא אַתְיָא בִּתְרֵין סִטְרִין. חַד, בְּגִין דְּאִיהוּ כְּלִיל בְּהַאי חַטָּאת, רָזָא דְּהַהוּא חִוְיָא תַּקִּיפָא. וְחַד, דְּכַד ב"נ עָבֵיד חַטָּאת, אִיהוּ אַתְקִיף לְהַאי עָפָר, וְשַׁלְטָא בְּעָלְמָא.

905. This spirit is called 'Afrira', ashes of dust. He has no offspring, nor fruit in the world, since he is made of ashes of dust. Though he is called by that name, he is not of the holy soil which bears fruit, called "dust (Heb. *afrot*) of gold" (Iyov 28:6), but of "the ashes (Heb. *afar*) of the burnt purification" (Bemidbar 19:17), FOR ASHES ARE CALLED 'DUST'. He is "the ashes of the burnt purification," the indication IN THIS VERSE, comes in two versions, the one because that spirit is included within the purification (Heb. *chatat*) of sin, which is the secret of the powerful serpent CALLED BY THAT NAME. The other is when the man commits sin (Heb. *chatat*) and strengthens the dust, so it rules the world.

906. וְהַאי אִיהוּ כָּלִיל בְּמֵי הַמָּרִים הַמְאָרֲרִים, וע"ד, אִצְטְרִיךְ לְאַנְתּוּ

דְּאַסְטִיאַת תְּחוֹת בַּעְלָהּ, וְעַבְדַּת עוֹבָדָא דְּאֵשֶׁת זְנוּנִים, לְאַשְׁקָאָה לָהּ מַיָּא כְּלִילָן בְּעַפְרָא, דְּאִיהוּ מִקַּרְקַע הַמִּשְׁכָּן. וְהַאי עָפָר אִיהוּ מֵהַהוּא אֲתָר דְּאִקְרֵי קַרְקַע וְהַהוּא אִקְרֵי קַרְקַע דְּהַהוּא מִשְׁכָּן. וְהַאי עָפָר מֵהַהוּא קַרְקַע אִיהוּ. ובג״כ, אִצְטְרִיךְ כַּהֲנָא לְאַשְׁקָאָה לְהַאי אִתְּתָא, כְּגַוְונָא דָּא. וְכֹלָּא אִיהוּ בִּרְמִיזָא עִלָּאָה.

906. This SPIRIT CALLED 'DUST', is included within "the bitter water that causes the curse" (Bemidbar 5:18). Therefore the woman, who has gone astray from her husband and behaved as a harlot, should be given a drink of the water that comprises the dust of the ground of the Tabernacle. That dust comes from the place called 'ground', WHICH IS THE ASPECT OF BRIYAH, AND BRIYAH is called 'the ground of the Tabernacle', WHICH IS MALCHUT OF ATZILUT CALLED 'TABERNACLE'. The dust, WHICH IS THIS SPIRIT, comes of the same ground. For that reason the priest should give the woman a drink in that manner, TO PUT DUST OF THE GROUND INSIDE THE WATER. All that is a supernal allusion.

907. זַכָּאָה חוּלָקֵהוֹן דְּיִשְׂרָאֵל, דְּקוּדְשָׁא בְּרִיךְ הוּא מַדְכֵּי לוֹן בְּמַיִין דַּכְיָין עִלָּאִין דִּכְתִּיב וְזָרַקְתִּי עֲלֵיכֶם מַיִם טְהוֹרִים וּטְהַרְתֶּם. מַיִם טְהוֹרִים הָא אַמָרָן, בֵּין מַיִם רִאשׁוֹנִים לְמַיִם אַחֲרוֹנִים. ואע״ג דְּהָא אוֹקִימְנָא, מַיִם רִאשׁוֹנִים מִצְוָה, הָכִי אִתְקְרוּן. וּמַיִם אַחֲרוֹנִים חוֹבָה הָכִי נָמֵי אִתְקְרוּן, וְהָא אוֹקִימְנָא עַל תְּרֵין סִטְרִין אִלֵּין, דָּא סִטְרָא דִּקְדוּשָּׁה אִתְקְרֵי מִצְוָה. וְדָא סִטְרָא אַחֲרָא, אִתְקְרֵי חוֹבָה. ובג״כ חוּלָקֵיהּ נָטַל בְּהַהוּא מַיָּא, וע״ד כְּתִיב, וְזָרַקְתִּי עֲלֵיכֶם מַיִם טְהוֹרִים וּטְהַרְתֶּם.

907. Happy is the portion of Yisrael, for the Holy One, blessed be He, purifies them with supernal, clean water, NAMELY, THE WATER OF BINAH, as it is written, "Then will I sprinkle clean water upon you, and you shall be clean" (Yechezkel 36:25). We explained about clean water, when we talked OF THE DIFFERENCE between first water and last water. And though we explained there, THAT FIRST WATER IS OF BINAH AND LAST WATER FROM MALCHUT, SO first water is considered a precept, WHICH IS MALCHUT, and last water a debt. We expounded upon the two sides, that THE SUPERNAL

WATER is of the side of holiness called 'precept', and the LAST WATER is called 'debt', which is the Other Side IN THIS CHAMBER. For that reason the Other Side takes its share of that water. Of this the verse says, "Then will I sprinkle clean water upon you, and you shall be clean."

59. The sixth chamber, evil, corresponding to the name 'shadow of death'

A Synopsis

Rabbi Shimon describes the openings to the sixth chamber: 'death', 'evil', 'shadow of death' and 'somber'. These four openings cause evil, and this particular chamber comprises all the other chambers of defilement as well. Here all the evil lusts are found that cause people to be denied the World to Come. The chamber also includes all the pleasure of the fools, the heartless and the witless. Rabbi Shimon describes the meaning of: "but her end is bitter as wormwood," telling us that when a man succumbs to temptation he is punished by 'the harlot' who spills bitter drops into his mouth that then rip the soul away, cause his death and make his face become green and putrid. We learn next of the results of vanity. Rabbi Shimon offers two explanations of the verse: "I have had to sacrifice peace offerings," and talks about the fate of adulterers. He concludes by saying that when men take their pleasures in the world the good inclination stays away from them and eventually they are judged. The righteous are happy in this world and in the World to Come.

908. הֵיכָלָא שְׁתִיתָאָה. הֵיכָלָא דָּא, קַיְּימָא עִלָּאָה, עַל כָּל אִינּוּן שְׁאַר הֵיכָלִין תַּתָּאִין. אַרְבַּע פִּתְחִין, אִית לְהֵיכָלָא דָּא. חַד, אִקְרֵי מָוֶת. וְחַד, אִקְרֵי רָע. וְחַד, אִקְרֵי צַלְמָוֶ"ת. וְחַד, אִקְרֵי אֹפֶ"ל. אִלֵּין אַרְבַּע פִּתְחִין, קַיְימִין תָּדִיר לְאַבְאָשָׁא. אִלֵּין אִינּוּן כְּלָלָא דְּכֹלָּא.

908. The sixth chamber stands above the rest of the lower chambers. There are four openings to this chamber: one is called 'death', one 'evil', one 'shadow of death' and the last one 'somber'. These four openings are there to cause evil, and comprise everything, FOR SINCE IT CORRESPONDS TO THE HOLY CHAMBER OF TIFERET, WHICH INCLUDES ALL THE OTHER SIX CHAMBERS CHESED, GVURAH, TIFERET, NETZACH, HOD AND YESOD, SO THIS CHAMBER OF DEFILEMENT INCLUDES ALL THE CHAMBERS OF DEFILEMENT.

909. כְּמָה דְּאִית בְּסִטְרָא דִּקְדוּשָּׁה, בְּרָזָא דִּמְהֵימְנוּתָא, אַרְבַּע פִּתְחִין לְאַרְבַּע סִטְרִין, דְּמִתְקַשְּׁרָן דָּא בְּדָא, וְכֻלְּהוּ קַדִּישִׁין. הָכִי נָמֵי לְתַתָּא, הָכָא. וְכַד אִלֵּין מִתְקַשְּׁרָן וּמִתְחַבְּרָן דָּא עִם דָּא כַּחֲדָא, בְּהֵיכָלָא דָּא,

כְּדֵין אִקְרֵי בֵּית חָבֵר. כְּמָה דְּאַתְּ אָמֵר, מֵאֵשֶׁת מִדְיָנִים וּבֵית חָבֵר. וְהַאי הֵיכָלָא, קַיְימָא לְאַבְאָשָׁא תָּדִיר.

909. As there are on the side of holiness, in the secret of the Faith, four openings to the four sides, connected to each other, all of them holy, so it is down here. When they are united and joined with each other in this chamber, then this chamber is called 'a roomy house', as it is written, "a brawling woman in a roomy house" (Mishlei 21:9). This chamber is there to cause evil always.

910. עַל הַאי הֵיכָלָא כְּתִיב, וְנַעְתָּרוֹת נְשִׁיקוֹת שׂוֹנֵא, בְּגִין דְּהָכָא קַיְימָן, כָּל אִינּוּן נְשִׁיקִין בִּישִׁין, וְתִיאוּבְתִּין בִּישִׁין, וְכָל עִדּוּנִין דְּגוּפָא דְּהַאי עָלְמָא, דִּי בְּאִינּוּן עִדּוּנִין אִתְתָּרַךְ בַּר נָשׁ מֵהַאי עָלְמָא, וּמֵעָלְמָא דְּאָתֵי. וְעַל הַאי הֵיכָלָא כְּתִיב, כִּי נֹפֶת תִּטֹּפְנָה שִׂפְתֵי זָרָה וְגוֹ'.

910. It is written of this chamber, "but the kisses of the enemy are profuse" (Mishlei 27:6), for here abide all the evil kisses and evil lusts, and all the pleasures of the body in this world, for which delights man is driven from this world and the World to Come. Of this chamber the verse says, "For the lips of a strange woman drip honey..." (Mishlei 5:3). THESE DEFILED KISSES AND PLEASURES HERE CORRESPOND TO THE KISSES AND DELIGHTS OF THE SIXTH CHAMBER OF HOLINESS.

911. בְּהַאי הֵיכָלָא, קַיְימָא חַד רוּחָא, דְּאִיהוּ מְמָנָא עַל כָּל אִלֵּין דִּלְתַתָּא, וְאִיהוּ כְּלָלָא עַל כָּל שְׁאַר רוּחִין. הַאי הֵיכָלָא, מִתְקַשְּׁטָא בְּקִשּׁוּטוֹי דִּשְׁפִירוּ, עַל כָּל אִינּוּן הֵיכָלִין. בְּהֵיכָלָא דָּא, מִתְלַכְּדֵי רַגְלַיְיהוּ דְּטִפְּשָׁאֵי. עַל הַאי הֵיכָלָא כְּתִיב, אַל תַּחְמוֹד יָפְיָהּ בִּלְבָבֶךָ וְאַל תִּקָּחֲךָ בְּעַפְעַפֶּיהָ.

911. There is a spirit in this chamber in charge of all those below, that adornments of beauty more than the chambers BENEATH IT. The feet of fools are trapped in this chamber, of which the verse says, "Lust not after her beauty in your heart, nor let her take you with her eyelids" (Mishlei 6:25).

912. בְּהַאי הֵיכָלָא, תַּלְיָין כָּל תִּיאוּבְתִּין דְּעָלְמָא. וְכָל אִינּוּן עִנּוּגִין

דְּטִפְּשָׁאֵי, חַסְרֵי לִבָּא, חַסְרֵי דַּעְתָּא. כד"א וָאֵרֶא בַּפְּתָאִים אָבִינָה בַבָּנִים נַעַר. חֲסַר לֵב. עוֹבֵר בַּשּׁוּק אֵצֶל פִּנָּה וְגוֹ'. בְּנֶשֶׁף בְּעֶרֶב יוֹם וְגוֹ'. וּכְדֵין אִתְקְרִיבוּ רַגְלוֹי לְהַאי הֵיכָלָא, דְּאִיהוּ כְּלָלָא דְּכֻלְּהוּ תַּתָּאִין. כְּדֵין, וְהִנֵּה אִשָּׁה לִקְרָאתוֹ שִׁית זוֹנָה וּנְצוּרַת לֵב. שִׁית, דָּא אִיהוּ הַאי הֵיכָלָא, דְּאִיהוּ שְׁתִיתָאֵי לְכָל שְׁאַר הֵיכָלִין. וְהָכָא קַיְּימָא זוֹנָה, לְאַפְתְּאָה לְטִפְּשָׁאִין.

912. All the lusts in the world are from this chamber, and all the pleasure of the fools, the heartless and the witless, as it is written, "and beheld among the simple ones, I discerned among the youths, a young man void of understanding, passing through the street near her corner… in the twilight, in the evening" (Mishlei 7:7-8). Then his feet approach this chamber, which comprises all those below it, BEING THE CHAMBER OF TIFERET OF DEFILEMENT, WHICH INCLUDES ALL THE SIX DIRECTIONS. Then "behold, there met him a woman with the attire (Heb. *sheett*) of a harlot, and wily of heart" (Ibid. 10). The word '*sheett'* refers to this sixth (Heb. *shtit*) chamber in number. Here stands the harlot to seduce the fools.

913. בְּהַאי הֵיכָלָא קַיְּימָא וְלָא קַיְּימָא. נַחְתָּא וּמְפַתָּא, סַלְּקָא וְאַסְטִיאַת. כד"א בְּבֵיתָהּ לֹא יִשְׁכְּנוּ רַגְלֶיהָ. פַּעַם בַּחוּץ פַּעַם בָּרְחוֹבוֹת, כַּד סַלְּקָא לְעֵילָּא. וְאֵצֶל כָּל פִּנָּה תֶּאֱרוֹב כַּד נָטִיל נִשְׁמְתָא.

913. In this chamber THE HARLOT resides yet resides not, for she comes down to seduce, then goes up and blames, as it is written, "her feet do not remain in her house: now she is outside," WHEN SHE COMES DOWN TO SEDUCE, "now in the streets" when she goes up TO BLAME, "and she lies in wait at every corner" (Ibid. 11-12) , to take his soul away, NAMELY, TO KILL HIM.

914. מַה כְּתִיב, וְהֶחֱזִיקָה בּוֹ וְנָשְׁקָה לוֹ. אִלֵּין אִינּוּן נְשִׁיקִין, לְסָאֳבָא, וּלְאַטְעָאָה בְּנֵי נָשָׁא אֲבַתְרָהּ. בְּגִין דְּהָכָא, אִיהוּ אֲתַר דְּכָל אִינּוּן נְשִׁיקִין בִּישִׁין, וּמִכָּל זְנוּנִים נוּכְרָאִין, דְּאִינּוּן מְתִיקִין לְפוּם שַׁעֲתָא. וַוי לְסוֹפֵיְיהוּ, כְּמָה דִּכְתִיב וְחָלָק מִשֶּׁמֶן חִכָּהּ.

914. It is further written, "So she caught hold of him, and kissed him" (Ibid. 13). These are defiling kisses, to mislead people to follow her, for here is the place of all the evil kisses and strange harlotries, which are sweet for the moment, and woe to their ending, as it is written, "and her mouth is smoother than oil" (Mishlei 5:3).

915. וּכְתִיב וְאַחֲרִיתָהּ מָרָה כַלַּעֲנָה. מַאי מָרָה כַלַּעֲנָה. אֶלָּא, כַּד ב"נ אִתְפַּתָּא אֲבַתְרָהּ בְּהַאי עָלְמָא, וּמָטָא זִמְנֵיהּ לְאִסְתַּלְּקָא מֵהַאי עָלְמָא, אִיהִי קַיְּימָא עָלֵיהּ דב"נ, וְאִתְגְּלִימַת קַמֵּיהּ בִּגְלִימָא דְגוּפָא דְאֶשָּׁא וְחַרְבָּא שִׁינָנָא בְּיָדָהּ, וּתְלַת טִיפִּין בָּהּ.

915. It is also written, "but her end is bitter as wormwood" (Ibid. 4). HE ASKS: What is the meaning of "bitter as wormwood"? HE ANSWERS: When a man is tempted by her in this world, when his time arrives to pass away from this world, she is upon him, arrayed before him in a garment of a body of fire, a sharp sword in her hand, with three drops in it.

916. וְאוּקְמוּהָ, וּבָהּ טִפָּה חֲדָא, מֵאִינּוּן טִיפִּין דְּאִיהִי מְרִירָא, וּבְשַׁעֲתָא דְּאָטִיל לָהּ לְפוּמֵיהּ דב"נ, עָאל בְּמֵעוֹי. וּכְדֵין נִשְׁמָתָא אִתְבַּלְבְּלָא, וְהַהִיא טִיפָּה שַׁטְיָא וְאָזְלַת בְּגוֹ גוּפָא, וְאַעְקָרַת לָהּ לְנִשְׁמָתָא מֵאַתְרָהּ, וְלָא שָׁבִיק לָהּ לְנִשְׁמָתָא אֲתָר לְמֵיתַב, וְאִיהִי מָרָה כַלַּעֲנָה, וְאַטְעִים לָהּ ב"נ בִּמְרִירוּ, חֲלָף הַהוּא מְתִיקָא, דְּטָעֲמוּ בָּהּ בְּהַאי עָלְמָא, כַּד אִתְמְשָׁכוּ בַּתְרָהּ, לְבָתַר אַשְׁדֵּי טִפָּה אַחֲרָא, וְנִשְׁמָתָא נָפְקָאת, וּמִית ב"נ. וּלְבָתַר אַשְׁדֵּי טִיפָּה אַחֲרָא, וִירוֹקִין אַנְפּוֹי, וְאַבְאִישׁ. בְּגִין דְּנִשְׁמָתָא הִיא קַדִּישָׁא, וְכַד שַׁלְטָא עָלָהּ דָּא סִטְרָא אַחֲרָא מִסְאֲבָא, עַקְרַת מִקַּמֵּיהּ, וְלָא אִתְיַשְׁבָא כַּחֲדָא.

916. We explained that one of the drops OF THE SWORD is bitter, and when she spills it in a man's mouth, it enters his bowels, and the soul is confused. The drop travels within the body and plucks the soul from its place, and does not let it return. THE DROP is bitter as wormwood, and man tastes bitterness instead of the sweetness he savored in this world when he was attracted to her. She throws at him another drop, and the soul leaves, and the man dies. She then tosses yet another drop and his face becomes green and putrid. THE REASON THE SOUL LEAVES IS because the soul is sacred, and when the Other Side has power over it, it runs away from it, not to be with it.

917. בְּגִין כַּךְ, כְּמָה דְּאִתְדְּבַק בְּאִינּוּן נְשִׁיקִין בִּישִׁין בְּהַאי עָלְמָא, אוּף הָכִי נָמֵי בְּהַאי שַׁעֲתָא. דְּאִי ב״נ אִתְמְשַׁךְ אֲבַתְרָהּ בְּהַאי עָלְמָא, וְשָׁבַק סִטְרָא קַדִּישָׁא, כְּדֵין נִשְׁמְתָא לָא אָהַדְרַת לְהַהוּא אֲתָר קַדִּישָׁא. וּכְמָה דְּאִתְמְשַׁךְ אֲבַתְרָהּ בְּהַאי עָלְמָא, הָכִי נָמֵי שַׁלְטָא עַל נִשְׁמָתֵיהּ, וּכְדֵין נִשְׁמָתֵיהּ נַפְקַת בְּפִטּוּרֵי, וְאוּקְמוּהָ. וְכָל דָּא, בְּגִין אִינּוּן נְשִׁיקִין דְּנַשְׁקָא לֵיהּ בְּהַאי עָלְמָא, דְּאִינּוּן מְתִיקִין. וּלְבָתַר, מְרִירָן לֵיהּ בְּהַאי שַׁעֲתָא. וע״ד, וְהֶחֱזִיקָה בּוֹ וְנָשְׁקָה לוֹ, בְּהַאי עָלְמָא, כְּמָה דְּאוּקִימְנָא.

917. For that reason, as man clings with evil kisses in this world, also at this time, if he followed her in this world and left the holy side, the soul does not come back to the holy place, for since he went after her in this world, she now has control over his soul, and the soul leaves the body by ropes, as we explained. All that is caused by the sweet kisses she gave him in this world, and later, at that hour, he finds them bitter. Of this IT IS WRITTEN, "So she caught hold of him, and kissed him" (Mishlei 7:13) in this world, as we explained.

918. הֵעֵזָה פָנֶיהָ וַתֹּאמַר לוֹ, בְּגִין דִּבְהַאי הֵיכָלָא קַיְימִין כָּל קַטֵּיגוֹרִין, וְכָל שְׁלִיחָאן בִּישִׁין דְּמִשְׁתַּכְחֵי לְגַבֵּי דְּבַר נָשׁ, וְעָבְדֵי לֵיהּ דְּיִתַּקַּן בְּתִקּוּנוֹי, וִיסַלְסֵל בְּשַׂעְרֵיהּ, וְיִתְסְחֵי, וְיִתְתַּקַּן בְּגִין דְּיִסְתַּכְּלוּן בֵּיהּ. הָכָא קַיְימָא רוּחָא חֲדָא, דְּאִקְרֵי סְקַטוּפָ״ה. וְדָא הוּא מְמָנָא עַל כָּל תִּקּוּנָא וְסִלְסוּלָא דִּבְנֵי נָשָׁא.

918. "And with an impudent face said to him" (Ibid.), for in this chamber are all the accusers, THOSE WHO SPEAK ILL OF MEN, and the evil messengers that abide by man, and cause him to adorn himself and curl his hair, bathe and bedeck himself so he would be looked at. Here stands a spirit called 'Skatufa', in charge of the adornment and coiffure of men.

919. לְגוֹ דְּהַאי הֵיכָלָא, קַיְימָא חַד מְמָנָא אַחֲרָא, דְּהַאי מְמָנָא אַחֲרָא,

אִיהוּ אַתְעַר לֵיהּ לב״נ לְבָתַר, לְאַתְעֲרָא לוֹן, דְּהָא אִיהוּ מְתַקֵּן גַּרְמֵיהּ, וּמְסַלְסֵל בְּשַׂעֲרֵיהּ, דְּיִטּוֹל בִּידֵיהּ חַד מַרְאָה לְאִסְתַּכְּלָא בֵּיהּ, וְשַׁוֵּי לֵיהּ בִּידֵיהּ, וְאִסְתָּכַּל בֵּיהּ, וְחָמֵי דִּיוּקְנֵיהּ בְּהַהוּא חֵיזוּ. וּבְהַאי אַתְעַר לְהַהוּא רוּחָא חֵילָא אַחֲרָא. דְּאִקְרֵי עֲסִירְטָ״א, וּמֵהָכָא נַפְקֵי, כָּל אִינּוּן דְּאַחְזְיוּ כְּדִיבִין לִבְנֵי נָשָׁא בְּחֶלְמַיְיהוּ. וְכָל אִינּוּן דְּאַחְזְיָין מִלִּין וְלָא מִתְקַיְּימֵי בְּהוּ, אֶלָּא לְעַרְבְּבָא לוֹן.

919. Inside this chamber stands another chieftain, who arouses man and then arouses them, THE SPIRITS – NAMELY, HE STRENGTHENS THEM. After the man has adorned himself and done his hair, IT ENTICES HIM to take a mirror in his hand, and puts it in his hands. AND THE MAN looks at it, and sees his form in that mirror. By this another force stirs the spirit. It is called 'Asirta', whence come all those who show false visions to men in their dreams, and those who show things TO MEN, which do not happen, but are confused.

920. וּלְבָתַר, כַּד אִינּוּן בְּנֵי נָשָׁא אִתְמַשְׁכָאן בְּהַהוּא חֵיזוּ, דְּאִקְרֵי מַרְאָה. כְּדֵין כֻּלְּהוּ בְּגַסוּתָא דְּרוּחָא דִּילְהוֹן, וְהַאי רוּחָא דְּאִקְרֵי עֲסִירְטָ״א, אִיהוּ אַתְעַר לְחַד רוּחָא מְמָנָא דְּאִיהוּ תְּחוֹת יְדֵיהּ, וְעָאל בְּנוּקְבָא דִּלְתַתָּא דְּכָל נוּקְבִין, וְסָלִיק מִתַּמָּן חַד רוּחָא אַחֲרָא, דְּאִיהוּ מְמָנָא עִם הַהוּא רוּחָא דְּאִקְרֵי אַסְכָּרָא כִּדְקָאמְרָן. וְדָא אִיהוּ לִילִית אִימָּא דְּשֵׁדִין. וְכַד הַהוּא ב״נ אַתְעַר לְהַאי רוּחָא אַחֲרָא דְּאִקְרֵי עֲסִירְטָ״א, כְּדֵין אִתְחַבַּר עִמֵּיהּ דְּהַהוּא ב״נ, וְאִתְקַשַּׁר עִמֵּיהּ תָּדִיר. וּכְדֵין בְּכָל רֵישׁ יַרְחָא וְיַרְחָא, אַתְעַר הַהוּא רוּחָא, דְּחֵיזוּ בִּישָׁא בַּהֲדָהּ דְּלִילִית, וּלְזִמְנִין דְּאִתְּזַק מִנַּיְיהוּ הַהוּא בַּר נָשׁ, וַיִּפּוֹל לְאַרְעָא, וְלָא יָכִיל לְמֵיקָם, אוֹ יָמוּת. וְכָל דָּא גָּרִים, הַהוּא חֵיזוּ דְּמַרְאָה, דְּאִיהוּ מִסְתַּכֵּל בֵּיהּ. דְּהָא כְּמָה דְּאַחְזֵי גַּסוּתָא דְּרוּחָא בְּלִבֵּיהּ, הָכִי נָמֵי אַסְגֵּי רוּחָא בִּישָׁא לְגַבֵּיהּ. וְעַל דָּא כֹּלָּא קַיְּימָא בְּהַהוּא אִתְעֲרוּ דִּלְתַתָּא.

920. Then, when men are drawn TO LOOK at this vision called 'mirror', they become haughty. The spirit Asirta bestirs another spirit chief under him, who enters the lowest of the holes to raise another spirit from there, who shares his duties with the spirit Askara, whom we spoken of, who is Lilit, the mother of demons. When man arouses the other spirit, Asirta, BY LOOKING AT THE MIRROR, man is united with him and connected with him always. Then, on each new moon, this evil spirit of the mirror is awakened together with Lilit, WHO IS ASKARA. Sometimes the man is hurt by them and falls to the ground, not able to rise, or he dies. This is caused by looking at the mirror he looked at, for as the haughtiness in his heart is seen, when he looks at the mirror, so he draws more the evil spirit to him. For that reason everything depends on the awakening down below.

921. זִבְחֵי שְׁלָמִים עָלָי. תָּא חֲזֵי, שְׁלָמִים לָא אַתְיָין עַל חוֹבָה, וְלָא עַל חַטָּאת, אֶלָּא עַל שָׁלוֹם. מַאי שְׁלָמִים. אֶלָּא שְׁלָמִים מִתְּרֵין סִטְרִין, דְּלָא אִשְׁתְּכַח מְקַטְרְגָא עָלֵיהּ, לָא לְעֵילָּא, וְלָא לְתַתָּא. מַאן אִיהוּ מְקַטְרְגָא. אֶלָּא הַהוּא סִטְרָא דִּשְׂמָאלָא דְּיֵצֶר הָרָע, דְּיִשְׁתְּכַח בִּשְׁלָמָא דִּימִינָא. וע״ד, זִבְחֵי שְׁלָמִים עָלָי.

921. "I have had to sacrifice peace offerings" (Mishlei 7:14). Come and see: Peace offerings are not offered for a debt or for purification, but for peace. What is the meaning of peace offerings? Peace offerings are of two sides, AND THANKS TO THEM no one blames him above or below. The accuser is the left side of the Evil Inclination, AND BY THE PEACE OFFERINGS there is peace in the right. Therefore it is written, "I have had to sacrifice peace offerings," IN THE PLURAL FORM.

922. ד״א זִבְחֵי שְׁלָמִים עָלָי. הָא אֲנָא בִּשְׁלֵוָה לְגַבָּךְ, לְאַחֲזָאָה לָךְ שְׁלָם. ובג״כ, הַיּוֹם שִׁלַּמְתִּי נְדָרָי, לְאַפְתָּאָה בְּנֵי עָלְמָא תָּדִיר. עַל כֵּן יָצָאתִי לִקְרָאתֶךָ וְגוֹ׳, דְּיָדַעְנָא דְּאַנְתְּ חָסֵר לְבָּא, חָסֵר טוֹבָה. לְשַׁחֵר פָּנֶיךָ, לְאִתְחַבְּרָא בַּהֲדָךְ בְּכָל בִּישִׁין דְּעָלְמָא. וְיֵאוֹת לָךְ לְאַהֲנָאָה, וּלְמִטְעֵי בָּתַר תִּיאוּבְתִּין דְּהַאי עָלְמָא. וְדָחֵי לֵיהּ מִמִּלָּה לְמִלָּה, וּמִבִּישׁ לְבִישׁ. אַהֲדַרְנָא בְּאִינּוּן טִפְּשָׁאִין, וְשַׁחִירְנָא פָּנֶיךָ, וָאֶמְצָאֶךָּ, כְּבַר אַשְׁכַּחְנָא לָךְ לְאִתְדַּבְּקָא בָּךְ.

922. Another explanation for, "I have had to sacrifice peace offerings": SHE

SAYS TO HIM, I am come in tranquility, to offer you peace, and for that reason "this day have I paid my vows" (Ibid.), of seducing men always. "So I came out to meet you…" (Ibid. 15), for I know you are heartless and ungrateful, and "diligently to seek your face" (Ibid.) and come together with you in all the evil in the world. It is worthy of you to have pleasure and go after the lust of this world. She pushes him from one thing to another, from evil to evil, AND SAYS TO HIM, I have searched amongst the fools and have found you. Now I found you, to cling to you.

923. לְכָה נִרְוֶה דוֹדִים עַד הַבֹּקֶר, הה"ד, וְעֵין נוֹאֵף שָׁמְרָה נֶשֶׁף. דְּהָא כְּדֵין אִיהוּ זִמְנָא לְשַׁלְטָאָה. לְכָה נִרְוֶה דוֹדִים, נְהַךְ כַּחֲדָא, הָא אֲנָא עִמָּךְ, דְּהָא עַל כְּעַן אַתְּ רַבְיָא אַנְתְּ בְּחֵילָךְ, אִי הַשְׁתָּא לָא תִּתְעַנַּג גַּרְמָךְ, אֵימָתַי, כַּד תְּהֵא סִיב, הַשְׁתָּא הוּא זִמְנָא. מ"ט. כִּי אֵין הָאִישׁ בְּבֵיתוֹ, דָּא יֵצֶר טוֹב, דְּלָא שַׁרְיָא הָכָא בְּגַוָּוךְ, וְלָאו אִיהוּ זִמְנָא, הָלַךְ בְּדֶרֶךְ מֵרָחוֹק, דְּלָא שַׁרְיָא בב"נ, אֶלָּא בְּדֶרֶךְ מֵרָחוֹק, כַּד אִיהוּ מִתְּלֵיסַר שְׁנִין וּלְהָלְאָה. וְלָאו בְּכָל ב"נ, וַאֲנָא קָאִים עִמָּךְ מִיּוֹמָא דְּאִתְיְלִידַת, הה"ד לַפֶּתַח חַטָּאת רוֹבֵץ. וְהַשְׁתָּא דְּאַנְתְּ רַוָּוק, הַשְׁתָּא זִמְנָא לָךְ לְאִתְעַנְּגָא גַּרְמָךְ.

923. "Come, let us take our fill of love until the morning" (Ibid. 18). This is the meaning of "The eye also of the adulterer waits for the twilight" (Iyov 24:15), for this is the time of reign, AS THE KLIPOT ONLY RULE AT NIGHT. "let us take our fill of love": we shall go together, for I am with you. For until now you were a boy in your strength, and if you do not please yourself now, when then? When you are old SHALL YOU HAVE PLEASURE? Now is the time. Why? "For my husband (lit. 'the man') is not at home" (Mishlei 7:18). This is the Good Inclination, who is not here inside you, nor is this its time, "he is gone a long journey" (Ibid.). FOR THE GOOD INCLINATION does not abide by man, only from afar, when he is thirteen years of age or more, AND EVEN THEN not in every man. But I stay with you since the day you were born, as it is written, "sin crouches at the door" (Beresheet 4:7), NAMELY, WHEN HE CAME FROM HIS MOTHER'S WOMB. And now that you have no wife is the time to have pleasure.

924. צְרוֹר הַכֶּסֶף לָקַח בְּיָדוֹ, לְסַלְּקָא לְעֵילָא, וּלְאִתְעַכְּבָא תַּמָּן

וּלְאִתְעַנְּגָא. לְיוֹם הַכֶּסֶא יָבוֹא בֵּיתוֹ, אֵימַת יָבֹא לְקַבְלֵיהּ, לְיוֹם הַכֶּסֶא דְּאִיהוּ יוֹמָא דְּדִינָא, לְאַשְׁגָּחָא בְּדִינָא, דִּכְתִּיב בַּכֶּסֶה לְיוֹם חַגֵּנוּ. בִּזְמְנָא דְּאִצְטְרִיךְ ב״נ לְאִתְעַנְּגָא בְּעָלְמָא, וּלְאִתְהֲנֵי בֵּיהּ, אִתְרַחֲקָא מִנֵּיהּ. וּבִזְמְנָא דְּשַׁרְיָא דִּינָא בְּעָלְמָא, כְּדֵין אָתֵי לְגַבֵּיהּ לְמֶעְבַּד עַמֵּיהּ דִּינָא, וע״ד הִטַּתּוּ בְּרֹב לִקְחָהּ וְגוֹ׳. עַד יְפַלַּח חֵץ כְּבֵדוֹ. זַכָּאִין אִינּוּן צַדִּיקַיָּיא, דְּיָדְעִין אָרְחִין קַדִּישִׁין, לְמֵהַךְ בְּהוּ, וְלָא יִסְטוּן לִימִינָא וְלִשְׂמָאלָא, זַכָּאִין אִינּוּן בְּעָלְמָא דֵּין, וּבְעָלְמָא דְּאָתֵי.

924. "He has taken a bag of silver" (Mishlei 7:20). THESE ARE THE LIGHTS CALLED 'SILVER'. HE TOOK THE GOOD INCLINATION BY HAND, to raise above, and stay there to have pleasure. "And will come home at the new moon" (Ibid.), namely, when will THE GOOD INCLINATION cross his path? On the day of the new moon, Judgment Day, to oversee the trial, as it is written, "at the full (also: 'covered') moon on our feast day" (Tehilim 81:4), WHICH ALLUDES TO THE JUDGMENT DAY, ROSH HASHANAH. For when a man delights in the pleasure of the world, and takes his fill of pleasure, THE GOOD INCLINATION stays away from him, and when Judgment is upon the world, it comes back to do justice by him. Therefore, "with her much fair speech she causes him to yield…till a dart strike through his liver" (Mishlei 7:21-23). Happy are the righteous, who know the holy ways to walk by them, and stray neither right nor left. They are happy in this world and in the World to Come.

60. The seventh chamber of the Other Side, the dregs of wine

A Synopsis

We learn that the seventh chamber is the chamber of the dregs of wine, the dregs produced by the pressing of the bad grapes. Rabbi Shimon says that Eve gave Adam a drink of the dregs of wine and thus sent him to this seventh chamber. This is explained as meaning that she brought death to Adam and to all the generations after him. We are told of those who come to this chamber, defiled spirits, those who frequented prostitutes, and bastards. The seventh chamber corresponds to Gehenom, and in it there is a point from that all the other evil spirits come out and roam around the world. Rabbi Shimon also talks about the spirits ruled by 'Nesira' ('sowing') who weaken the unholy side and perform miracles for people who are not evil. From the seventh chamber the 'fire of a strong wind' emerges that judges the wicked of the world. We hear of the blazing spirit of fire and snow called 'Tzalmon' who also comes from here. Rabbi Shimon tells about four openings in the seventh chamber that face outside; in each opening the kings of other nations who did not oppress Yisrael are allowed to stand sometimes and see the light from the side of holiness. Rabbi Shimon concludes this description of the seven chambers by saying that we should remain on guard against the aspect of the serpent manifested by these seven chambers, and remember that even if we are saved from the head we are not necessarily saved from the tail. It is wise for men to avoid sinning so that the serpent will not bite and kill them.

925. הֵיכָלָא שְׁבִיעָאָה. הָדָא הוּא הֵיכָלָא דִּשְׁמָרֵי דְּחַמְרָא, לְאִתְרַוָּואָה בֵּיהּ. כד"א וַיֵּשְׁתְּ מִן הַיַּיִן וַיִּשְׁכָּר וַיִּתְגַּל. סְחִיטָא דְּכָל אִינּוּן עֲנָבִין, כֻּלְּהוּ עֲנָבִין בִּישִׁין, הָכָא אִיהוּ סְחִיטָא דִּלְהוֹן. וְדָא אִיהוּ יַיִן חֲמַר. שְׁמָרִים דְּחָמָר דְּלֵית מַאן דְּשָׁתֵי מִנֵּיהּ, דְּלָא גָּרִים מוֹתָא לְגַרְמֵיהּ. מִיֵּינָא דָּא, אַטְעִימַת חַוָּה לְבַעְלָהּ, וְעָאלַת לֵיהּ בְּהֵיכָלָא דָּא, דְּתָנֵינָן, סָחֲטָה עֲנָבִין, וְיָהִיבַת לֵיהּ, וְגָרִימַת מוֹתָא לֵיהּ, וּלְכָל עָלְמָא אֲבַתְרֵיהּ.

925. The seventh chamber is the chamber of the dregs of wine, to drink one's fill, NAMELY, TO GET DRUNK BY, as it is written, "and he drank of the wine, and was drunk, and he was uncovered" (Beresheet 9:21). The pressing of the grapes, the bad grapes, is done here, and it becomes foaming wine, AS

IT IS WRITTEN, "FOAMING WINE; IT IS FULL OF MIXTURE...BUT ITS DREGS, SHALL ALL THE WICKED OF THE EARTH...DRINK" (TEHILIM 75:9). FOAMING WINE MEANS the dregs of the wine. There is no one who drinks of them without bringing death to himself. Of this wine Eve gave her husband a drink, thus putting him in this chamber, as we learned that she pressed grapes and gave him to drink, thus bringing death to him, and to the whole world after him.

926. בְּהֵיכָלָא דָא, קַיְימִן כָּל אִינּוּן נִשְׁמָתִין מְסָאֲבִין, דְּנַחְתֵּי לְכָל אִינּוּן דִּי בְּסִטְרָא דָא מִתְדַּבְּקֵי, וְהַהוּא רוּחָא דְּנַחְתָּא לְכָל אִינּוּן דִּי מִסִּטְרָהָא, מֵהָכָא נַפְקֵי. כְּגַוְונָא דְּאִינּוּן סָטוּ אָרְחַיְיהוּ בְּהַאי עָלְמָא, וְאִשְׁתַּדָּלוּ בִּזְנוּתָא, בַּאֲתַר דְּלָא אִצְטְרִיךְ, לְאִתְרַחֲקָא מֵאֹרַח קְשׁוֹט. כְּדֵין, כְּמָה דְּאִיהוּ אִתְדַּבַּק בְּהַהוּא סִטְרָא דְּיֵצֶר הָרָע בִּזְנוּתָא, הָכִי נָמֵי נָפִיק מֵהֵיכָלָא דָא רוּחָא מְסָאֲבָא, לְסָאֲבָא לֵיהּ, וְלִבְרָא דְּנָפִיק מִתַּמָּן.

926. In this chamber are the unholy souls, who descend upon all those who cleave to this DEFILED side. The defiled spirit, who descends upon those of this side, comes from here. As for those who strayed from their way in the world and practiced prostitution where they should not have, and shunned the way of truth, when one cleaves to the side of the Evil Inclination by harlotry, a spirit of defilement comes out of this chamber to defile him and the child he begot BY PROSTITUTION.

927. וְהַהוּא בְּרָא אִקְרֵי מַמְזֵר, דְּאָתֵי מִסִּטְרָא דְּאֵל זָר. כְּמָה דְּאִיהוּ אִשְׁתְּכַח בְּהַהוּא תֵּיאוּבְתָּא, וּבְהַהוּא זְנוּתָא בְּהַהוּא סִטְרָא דְּיֵצֶר הָרָע, הָכִי נָמֵי מָשִׁיךְ לְגַבֵּיהּ דְּהַהוּא בְּרָא רוּחָא אַחֲרָא מְסָאֲבָא, דְּסָאִיב, וְכֹלָּא סָהֲדִין עָלֵיהּ דְּאִיהוּ מַמְזֵר, וְהָכִי כָּל עוֹבָדוֹי וְסִטְרוֹי בְּהַהוּא גַּוְונָא מַמָּשׁ.

927. That child is called 'a bastard', for he came from the side of a strange El. As a man is on the side of the Evil Inclination by that passion and harlotry, so he draws to that child another unholy spirit who defiles, and everyone testifies about him that he is a bastard, as happens to all his deeds and sides.

928. מְהֵיכָלָא דָּא נָפִיק חַד רוּחָא, דִּי מְמָנָא עַל אִינּוּן רוּחִין דְּאִקְרֵי צְפוֹנִי. וְסִמָּנִיךְ, צֹפְנֶיהָ צָפַן רוּחַ. וְהַאי אִיהוּ מְמָנָא עַל דָּא. וְהַאי הֵיכָלָא שְׁבִיעָאָה, לָקֳבֵל הַהוּא שְׁמָא דְּאִקְרֵי אֶרֶץ תַּחְתִּית. וְעַל דָּא כְּתִיב, וְאֶת הַצְּפוֹנִי אַרְחִיק מֵעֲלֵיכֶם.

928. From this chamber comes a spirit in charge of the spirits, called 'northern' (Heb. *tzefoni*), THE SEVENTH NAME OF THE EVIL INCLINATION. This is derived from the verse, "Whoever who hides her hides (Heb. *tzafan*) the wind (spirit)" (Mishlei 27:16). This spirit is in charge of THE NORTHERN. And the seventh chamber corresponds to the name OF GEHENOM, called "the nether parts of the earth" (Yechezkel 31:16). Of this, THE SAID NORTHERN, it is written, "and I will remove far off from you the northern one" (Yoel 2:20).

929. הָכָא אִיהוּ נְקוּדָה חֲדָא, דְּקַיְימָא לְגוֹ בְּגוֹ, וּמֵהָכָא נַפְקֵי כָּל אִינּוּן רוּחִין אַחֲרָנִין דְּשָׁטָאן בְּעָלְמָא, וְשַׁלְטִין בְּהַאי עָלְמָא, בְּכָל אִינּוּן מִלִּין וְעוֹבָדִין, דְּאִתְמְסָרוּ בְּסִטְרָא דִּשְׂמָאלָא. וּמֵהָכָא נַפְקֵי כָּל אִינּוּן זִיקִין נְצִיצִין, דְּמִתְדַּעֲכֵי לְאַלְתָּר, לַהֲטֵי וּמִתְדַּעֲכֵי. וּמֵאִלֵּין נָפְקִין רוּחִין אַחֲרָנִין, דְּשָׁטְיָין בְּעָלְמָא, וּמִשְׁתַּתְּפֵי לְאִינּוּן דְּנַפְקוּ מִגּוֹ תְּהוֹמָא רַבָּא. וְאִיהוּ הַאי הֵיכָלָא, כד"א מִשְׁפָּטֶיךָ תְּהוֹם רַבָּה. וְאִינּוּן רוּחִין דְּלָא אִתְמְסָרוּ לְמִגְלַם בְּעָלְמִין, וְאִתְחָזוּן וְלָא אִתְחָזוּן כְּמָה דְּאִתְּמָר.

929. Here there is a point standing in the innermost part. From here come out all the other spirits, who roam about the world, and rule over the world, by the things and deeds delivered on the left side. From here come out glitters and sparks, that are quenched immediately, burn and IMMEDIATELY are extinguished. From these are issued other spirits who hover about the world, and join THE SPIRITS that come from the great deep, as it is written, "Your Judgments are a great deep" (Tehilim 36:7). These are the spirits not destined to be clothed in this world, WITH THE GARMENT OF THE WORLD; they are seen and seen not, as we learned.

930. וּלְבָתַר אִינּוּן רוּחִין דְּשַׁטְיָין בְּעָלְמָא, וְאִלֵּין קַיְימֵי לְמֶרְחָשׁ נִסִּין לִבְנֵי נָשָׁא. בְּגִין דְּאִלֵּין לָא קַיְימִין בְּטִנּוּפָא דִּמְסָאֲבָא כָּל כָּךְ כְּאַחֲרָנִין. וְחַד רוּחָא מְמָנָא עֲלַיְיהוּ, וְאִקְרֵי נְסִירָ"א, דְּאִיהוּ אִתְנְסַר מֵאִינּוּן סִטְרִין

דִּמְסָאֲבוּ יַתִּיר, וְאִלֵּין פָּרְחֵי בַּאֲוִירָא, וְאַבְאִישׁוּ לְסִטְרָא דִּלְהוֹן, בְּגִין לְמֶעְבַּד נִסִּין לְאִינּוּן דִּי בְּסִטְרָא דִּקְדוּשָּׁה.

930. Also, THERE ARE spirits who roam about the world. They perform miracles to people who are not much steeped in the filth of defilement like others. There is a spirit appointed over them, called 'Nesira' (Eng. 'sowing'), because he is sowed AND SEPARATED from the most unholy sides, and they soar up in the air, and weaken their unholy side, so miracles may be performed to those of the holy side.

931. וּמֵרוּחָא דָּא דְּאִתְנְסַר, דְּאִקְרֵי נְסִירָ"א, מִנֵּיהּ נַפְקֵי כַּמָּה סִטְרִין אַחֲרָנִין, מִתְפָּרְשָׁן לִזְנַיְיהוּ, וְכֻלְּהוּ קַיְימָאן שְׁלִיחָאן בְּעָלְמָא, כָּל חַד כְּדְקָא חֲזֵי לֵיהּ, עַד דְּאִתְמְנוּן לְתַתָּא מַלְכִין וְסָרְכִין. וְלֵית לוֹן קִיּוּמָא תָּדִיר, כְּאִינּוּן אַחֲרָנִין דִּלְעֵילָּא.

931. From the spirit that was sowed AND SEPARATED FROM THE UNHOLY SIDE, called 'Nesira', come out some other sides divided to several kinds. All of them do errands in the world, each according to his worthiness. And so kings and ministers are appointed below. Yet, their existence is not continuous like that of the other ones above.

932. בְּהֵיכָלָא דָּא אִתְדַּבְּקוּתָא דְּסְטַר מִסְאֲבָא, וְכָל תִּיאוּבְתִּין מִסְאֲבִין, וּמְסָאֲבֵי לְעָלְמָא. הַאי אִיהוּ זַמִּין לְאַפָּקָא בְּכָל רִגְעָא וְשַׁעֲתָא אֶשָּׁא, וְלֵית מַאן דְּקָאִים קָמֵיהּ. מֵהָכָא נָפִיק אֶשָּׁא דְּרוּחָא תַּקִּיפָא לְתַתָּא, לְאִתְדְּנָא בְּיָהּ חַיָּיבֵי עָלְמָא. וּמֵהָכָא נָפְקָא רוּחָא מְלָהֲטָא, דְּאִיהוּ אֶשָּׁא וְתַלְגָּא, דְּאִקְרֵי צַלְמוֹן. כְּמָה דְּאַתְּ אָמֵר תַּשְׁלֵג בְּצַלְמוֹן.

932. This chamber is the unity of the unholy side, and all unholy lusts, which defile the world. It is destined to put forth fire at any time, and no one will prevail against it. From here comes fire of a strong wind, with which to judge below the wicked of the world; from here comes out a blazing spirit, of fire and snow, called 'Tzalmon', as it is written, "snow falls in Tzalmon" (Tehilim 68:15).

933. בְּהֵיכָלָא דָּא, קַיְימָאן אַרְבָּעָה פִּתְחִין, דְּמִתְפָּרְשָׁן לְאַרְבַּע סִטְרִין

לְבַר. וְאִלֵּין אַחֲדִין וְלָא אַחֲדִין בְּסִטְרָא דִּקְדוּשָּׁה. לָא אִתְאֲחָד, אֶלָּא דְּאִתְחָזֵי בְּאִינּוּן פִּתְחִין נְהוֹרָא דְּנָהִיר, וְאִיהוּ אֲתַר דְּמִתְתַּקַּן בְּכָל פִּתְחָא וּפִתְחָא, לְאִינּוּן חֲסִידֵי דִּשְׁאַר עַמִּין, אִינּוּן דְּלָא אַבְאִישׁוּ לוֹן לְיִשְׂרָאֵל, וְאִשְׁתַּדָּלוּ עִמְּהוֹן בְּקְשׁוֹט. אִלֵּין קַיְימֵי בְּאִלֵּין פִּתְחִין, וְנַיְיחֵי תַּמָּן.

933. There are four openings in this chamber, divided into four sides facing outside. They are united and not united on the side of holiness. They are not REALLY united, but through these openings a light is seen, shining FROM THE SIDE OF HOLINESS. There is a place prepared in every opening to the righteous of the nations, who did not oppress Yisrael, and strove to do them right. They stand in these openings and rest there.

934. בְּפִתְחָא דְּהַאי הֵיכָלָא בְּאֶמְצָעִיתָא, לְבַר, שִׁית פִּתְחִין דְּמִתְאַחֲדֵי בְּהַאי הֵיכָלָא, וְכֻלְּהוּ אַחֲדִין בֵּיהּ. הָכָא אִית כַּוִּין פְּתִיחָן, לְסִטְרָא דִּנְהוֹרָא קַדִּישָׁא, וְאִינּוּן דּוּכְתִּין מִתְתַּקְּנֵי לְמַלְכֵי שְׁאַר עַמִּין, אִינּוּן דְּלָא עָאקוּ לוֹן לְיִשְׂרָאֵל, וְאַגִּינוּ עֲלַיְיהוּ תָּדִיר. אִלֵּין אִית לוֹן יְקָר בְּגִינֵיהוֹן דְּיִשְׂרָאֵל, וְאִתְהֲנוּ בְּהַהוּא אֲפֵלָה דְּאִינּוּן יַתְבִין, מִגּוֹ נְהוֹרָא דְּנָהִיר מִסִּטְרָא דִּקְדוּשָּׁה. כְּמָה דְּאַתְּ אָמֵר, כָּל מַלְכֵי גוֹיִם כֻּלָּם שָׁכְבוּ בְכָבוֹד.

934. In the opening in the middle of the chamber, on the outer side, there are six openings connected with the chamber. They all hold on to it. Here there are windows open on the side of the holy light. These places are made for the kings of the other nations, who did not oppress Yisrael and always protected them. They are honored because of Yisrael, and enjoy, in the darkness where they sit, the light shining from the side of holiness, as it is written, "All the kings of the nations, even all of them, lie in glory" (Yeshayah 14:18).

935. וְאִי עָבְדוּ עָאקוּ לְיִשְׂרָאֵל, אוֹ דְּחִיקוּ לוֹן. כַּמָּה אִינּוּן דְּאַחְדִּין בְּהוּ, וְדַיְינִין לְהוּ לְתַתָּא תְּלַת זִמְנִין בְּיוֹמָא, מִכַּמָּה דִּינִין מְשַׁנְיָין אִלֵּין מֵאִלֵּין, לְאִינּוּן מַלְכִין דְּעָאקוּ לְהוּ, דְּאִתְדָּנוּ בְּהַהוּא עָלְמָא בְּכַמָּה

דִינִין. וְכָל יוֹמָא וְיוֹמָא סָהֲדִין סַהֲדוּתָא עֲלַיְיהוּ דְיִשְׂרָאֵל, וְעַל מְהֵימְנוּתָא דִלְהוֹן, וְנַחְתֵּי לְתַתָּא וְאִתְדָּנוּ תַּמָּן. זַכָּאִין אִינּוּן יִשְׂרָאֵל בְּעָלְמָא דֵין, וּבְעָלְמָא דְאָתֵי.

935. If they did wicked things to Yisrael or oppressed them, they are seized and sentenced below three times a day, by several different punishments for the oppressing kings. They are sentenced in that world to several punishments, and every day they have to give testimony about Yisrael, and their Faith, then they descend to be judged below. Happy are Yisrael in this world and in the World to Come.

936. עַד הָכָא שֶׁבַע הֵיכָלִין, מָדוֹרֵי דְסִטְרָא מְסָאֲבָא, מִסִּטְרָא דְנָחָשׁ. זַכָּאָה חוּלָקֵיהּ מַאן דְּאִשְׁתְּזִיב מִנֵּיהּ, וּמִלְּחִישׁוּתֵיהּ, דְּלָא יִתְנְשִׁיךְ מִנֵּיהּ, וְלָא יָטִיל בֵּיהּ אַרְסָא, דְּיֵמוּת בֵּיהּ. מִכָּל סִטְרִין אִית לְאִסְתַּמְּרָא מִינֵּיהּ, מֵעֵילָּא וּמִתַּתָּא. מַאן דְּיִשְׁתְּזִיב מֵרֵישָׁא, לָא יִשְׁתְּזִיב מִזַּנְבָא. כַּד אָכִיף רֵישָׁא, זָקִיף זַנְבָא, מָחֵי וְקָטִיל.

936. So far the seven chambers, the departments of the side of defilement of the aspect of the serpent WERE EXPOUNDED UPON. Happy is whoever is saved from it and its incantations THAT ARE GIVEN TO IT FROM ABOVE, so it would not bite him, nor inject poison in him until he is dead. We should be guarded from it on all sides, above and below. Whoever is saved from the head, is not saved from the tail, for when it bows his head, it lifts up its tail, strikes and kills.

937. וְעִם כָּל דָּא, אִם יִשּׁוֹךְ הַנָּחָשׁ בְּלֹא לָחַשׁ. כְּמָה דְּתָנֵינָן, נָטִיל רְשׁוּ וְאַפִּיק נִשְׁמְתָא. בג״כ אִצְטְרִיךְ לֵיהּ לב״נ לְאִסְתַּמְּרָא, דְּלָא יְחוּב קָמֵי קוּדְשָׁא בְּרִיךְ הוּא, בְּגִין דְּלָא יַלְחִישׁוּ לֵיהּ לְהַהוּא חִוְיָא דְּיִנְשׁוֹךְ וְיִקְטֹל.

937. With all that, "if the serpent bites and cannot be charmed (also 'without a charm')" (Kohelet 10:11). We learned that it is given permission and takes away the soul. For that reason it behooves a man to beware of sinning before the Holy One, blessed be He, so that the serpent may not be charmed to bite and kill.

61. "dust of the ground'

A Synopsis

Rabbi Shimon begins with: "And Hashem Elohim formed man of the dust of the ground," saying that man is made of dust, not clay. He interprets "dust shall be the serpent's food" and "He will destroy death forever" and "awake and sing, you that dwell in dust..." to mean that until the resurrection the serpent will have the power to rule, seduce and mock mankind. He speaks of the male and the female sides of the serpent and the male sun and the female moon, saying that darkness and somberness never separate, as written in: "and there was a thick darkness."

938. וַיִּיצֶר יְיָ' אֱלֹהִים אֶת הָאָדָם עָפָר מִן הָאֲדָמָה. עָפָר אִיהוּ, וְלָא חוֹמֶר. עָפָר אִיהוּ, וְיֵתוּב לְעַפְרָא. כד"א, כִּי עָפָר אַתָּה וְאֶל עָפָר תָּשׁוּב. לְבָתַר דְּחָטָא, ובג"כ כְּתִיב בֵּיהּ בְּנָחָשׁ, וְעָפָר תֹּאכַל כָּל יְמֵי חַיֶּיךָ. עָפָר דָּא הוּא אָדָם, דִּכְתִּיב כִּי עָפָר אַתָּה וְגוֹ'. ובג"כ כְּתִיב עָפָר, וְלָא כְּתִיב אֲדָמָה, וְלָא חוֹמֶר, וּכְתִיב וְנָחָשׁ עָפָר לַחְמוֹ.

938. "And Hashem Elohim formed man of the dust of the ground" (Beresheet 2:7), of dust, not of clay. He is dust and to dust shall he return, as it is written, "for dust you are, and to dust shall you return" (Beresheet 3:19). After he sinned, it is said of the serpent, "and dust shall you eat all the days of your life" (Beresheet 2:14). This dust is man, of whom it is written, "for dust you are." Therefore it is written, "dust," not earth or clay, and "dust shall be the serpent's food" (Yeshayah 65:25).

939. עַד דְּיִתְעַר קוּדְשָׁא בְּרִיךְ הוּא, וִיבָעֵר לְהַהוּא רוּחָא מִסְאֲבָא מֵעָלְמָא, דִּכְתִיב, בִּלַּע הַמָּוֶת לָנֶצַח וְגוֹ', וְיָקִים לְהַהוּא עָפָר, וְיִתְעַר לֵיהּ לְמֶחְדֵי בְּעָלְמָא, דִּכְתִיב הָקִיצוּ וְרַנְּנוּ שׁוֹכְנֵי עָפָר וְגוֹ'.

939. Until the Holy One, blessed be He, will arouse, and put away the spirit of defilement from the world, as it is written, "He will destroy death forever" (Yeshayah 25:8). And the dust will be resurrected, and will be roused to rejoice in the world, as it is written, "awake and sing, you that dwell in dust…" (Yeshayah 26:19).

940. כְּתִיב וְהַנָּחָשׁ הָיָה עָרוּם, וְהָא אוֹקִימְנָא. אֲבָל סִטְרָא דְּרָכִיב עָלֵיהּ, יָהִיב לֵיהּ חֵילָא לְשַׁלְטָאָה, וּלְמִפְתֵּי, וּלְאַסְטָאָה. וְדָא הוּא רָזָא דִּדְכוּרָא, דְּהָא דְּכוּרָא שַׁלִּיט עַל נוּקְבָּא, וְיָהִיב בָּהּ חֵילָא. שִׁמְשָׁא וְסִיהֲרָא מְשַׁמְּשִׁין כַּחֲדָא, וְלָא מִתְפָּרְשִׁין לְעָלְמִין, חֹשֶׁךְ וַאֲפֵילָה מְשַׁמְּשִׁין כַּחֲדָא. אִיהוּ חֹשֶׁךְ, וְאִיהִי אֲפֵילָה. כד"א וַיְהִי חֹשֶׁךְ אֲפֵלָה. חֹשֶׁךְ וַעֲרָפֶל. בְּגִין דְּאִית חֹשֶׁךְ, וְאִית חֹשֶׁךְ.

940. It is written, "the serpent was craftier than all the beasts of the field" (Beresheet 3:1), we already explained this verse. Nevertheless, that which rode ON THE SERPENT gave it power to rule, seduce and deviate from the path. He, WHICH RIDES UPON IT, is the secret of the male side OF THE SERPENT, for the male rules over the female and gives her power. The sun and moon, MALE AND FEMALE, officiate as one, and never separate. SO, darkness and somberness officiate together; he, THE MALE SERPENT is darkness, and she, THE FEMALE IS somber, as it is written, "and there was a thick darkness" (Shemot 10:22), darkness and mist. There is MALE darkness and FEMALE darkness.

62. "the End of all Flesh"

A Synopsis

Rabbi Shimon explains to Rabbi Elazar about "the End of all Flesh." He talks about the sacrifice on the altar where the priest, the Levites and Yisrael officiate respectively through their service, their singing and their prayers. Before the offering people should confess all their sins and transgressions and also the evil thoughts they had. The offerings awaken the Holy Spirit so that the three Columns Right, Left and Central are joined and raised up to the illumination of Chochmah and then upwards to infinity.

941. תְּנָן, מַאן דְּחָמָא גָּמָל בְּחֶלְמֵיהּ, מִיתָה אִתְגְּזָרַת עָלֵיהּ, וְאִשְׁתְּזִיב מִינָּהּ. בְּגִין דְּאִיהוּ סִטְרָא מִסְאֲבָא, וְהַאי אִיהוּ קֵץ כָּל בָּשָׂר.

941. We learned that whoever sees a camel in his dream, was sentenced to death, but was saved. This is the side of defilement called "the End of all Flesh" (Beresheet 6:13).

942. יוֹמָא חַד הֲוָה יָתִיב ר׳ אֶלְעָזָר קָמֵיהּ דְּרִבִּי שִׁמְעוֹן, אָמַר רִבִּי אֶלְעָזָר, הַאי קֵץ כָּל בָּשָׂר אִתְהֲנֵי מֵאִינּוּן קָרְבְּנִין דַּהֲווֹ יִשְׂרָאֵל מְקָרְבִין עַל גַּבֵּי מַדְבְּחָא, אוֹ לָא. אָמַר לֵיהּ, כֹּלָּא הֲווֹ מִסְתַּפְּקֵי כַּחֲדָא, לְעֵילָּא וּלְתַתָּא.

942. One day Rabbi Elazar was sitting before Rabbi Shimon. Rabbi Elazar said: This End of all Flesh, does it get enjoyment from the offerings Yisrael sacrifice upon the altar, or does it not? He said to him: All got their satisfaction as one, above and below.

943. וְתָא חֲזֵי, כַּהֲנֵי וְלֵיוָאֵי וְיִשְׂרָאֵל, אִינּוּן אִקְרוּן אָדָם, בְּחִבּוּרָא דְּאִינּוּן רְעוּתִין קַדִּישִׁין, דְּסַלְּקָא מִגַּוַּויְיהוּ. וְהַהוּא אִמְּרָא, אוֹ כִּבְשָׂא, אוֹ הַהוּא בְּהֵמָה, הַאי דְּקָרְבִין, אִצְטְרִיךְ עַד לָא אִתְקְרִיב עַל מַדְבְּחָא, לְפָרְשָׁא עָלֵהּ כָּל חֲטָאִין, וְכָל חוֹבִין, וְכָל הִרְהוּרִין בִּישִׁין דְּעֲבַד. וּכְדֵין הַהִיא, אִתְקְרֵי בְּהֵמָה בְּכֹלָּא, בְּגוֹ אִינּוּן חֲטָאִין וּבִישִׁין וְהִרְהוּרִין.

943. Come and see: The priest, Levites, and Yisrael, THE SECRET OF THE

THREE COLUMNS, RIGHT, LEFT AND CENTRAL, are called 'man together', by joining all the sacred desires ascending from them TO MAYIN NUKVIN (FEMALE WATERS), THE PRIESTS BY THEIR SERVICE, THE LEVITES BY THEIR SINGING, AND YISRAEL BY THEIR PRAYERS. Before offering the ewe lamb, ram, or cattle upon the altar, a man should confess over it all the sins, transgressions and evil thoughts he contemplated. Then this offering is called 'a beast in every respect', completed by sins, evils, and thoughts.

944. כְּגַוְונָא דְקָרְבְּנָא דַעֲזָאזֵל, דִּכְתִּיב וְהִתְוַדָּה עָלָיו אֶת כָּל עֲונוֹת בְּנֵי יִשְׂרָאֵל וְגוֹ', הָכִי נָמֵי הָכָא. וְכַד סַלְקָא עַל גַּבֵּי מַדְבְּחָא, מָטוּ לָהּ עַל חַד תְּרֵין. ובג"כ, דָּא סַלְקָא לְאַתְרֵיהּ, וְדָא סַלְקָא לְאַתְרֵיהּ, דָּא בְּרָזָא דְּאָדָם, וְדָא בְּרָזָא דִּבְהֵמָה, כְּמָה דְּאַתְּ אָמֵר אָדָם וּבְהֵמָה תּוֹשִׁיעַ יְיָ'.

944. Like the goat to Azazel, of which says the verse, "and confess over him all the iniquities of the children of Yisrael..." (Vayikra 16:21), here too, THE CUSTOM OF CONFESSING SINS SHOULD BE PRACTICED, for when the sacrifice is offered upon the altar, this goes to its place, and that goes to its place, the one in the secret of man, and the other in the secret of beast, as it is written, "Hashem, You preserve man and beast" (Tehilim 36:7).

945. חֲבִיתִּין וְכָל שְׁאַר מְנָחוֹת, לְאִתְּעָרָא רוּחָא דְקוּדְשָׁא, בִּרְעוּתָא דְּכַהֲנָא, וְשִׁירָתָא דְּלֵיוָאֵי, וּצְלוֹתָא דְּיִשְׂרָאֵל. וּבְהַהוּא תְּנָנָא, וְשַׁמְנָא וְקִמְחָא דְּסָלִיק, מִתְרַוְון וּמִסְתַּפְּקֵי כָּל שְׁאַר מָארֵי דְּדִינִין, דְּלָא יַכְלֵי לְשַׁלְטָאָה בְּהַהוּא דִּינָא דְּאִתְמְסַר לוֹן, וְכֹלָּא בְּזִמְנָא חֲדָא. תָּא חֲזֵי, כֹּלָּא אִתְעָבֵיד בְּרָזָא דִּמְהֵימְנוּתָא, לְאִסְתַּפְּקָא דָּא בְּדָא, וּלְאִסְתַּלְּקָא לְעֵילָּא מַאן דְּאִצְטְרִיךְ, עַד אֵין סוֹף.

945. The offering of fine flour, and the rest of the offerings, should awaken the Holy Spirit with the service of the priests, the song of the Levites and the prayer of Yisrael. By the smoke, oil, and flour that rise UPON THE ALTAR, the other claimants take their fill and are satiated, who cannot have control over the Judgment given them. All is done at the same time. Come and see: All is done in the secret of the Faith, to give abundance, the one to the other, NAMELY, THAT RIGHT AND LEFT WILL GIVE TO EACH OTHER

AND BE PERFECTED BY EACH OTHER, and to raise what needs to be raised, NAMELY, THE ILLUMINATION OF CHOCHMAH, WHICH SHOULD BE ELEVATED UPWARD FROM BELOW up to the Endless Light.

63. The chamber of the secret of sacrifice

A Synopsis

Rabbi Shimon prays that revealing the mysteries as he has done will please God. This leads into an interpretation of the mystery of 'thought'. He explains it this way: The supernal thought desires above all to pursue the source of illumination and to illuminate it with its own light, but there is a veil between them. Light pursues the supernal thought but can reach only as far as the veil, not beneath it. The supernal thought itself is considered unknown, its illumination strikes the illumination of the veil so that they shine together. This causes nine chambers to be formed, that are described only by what they are not. All nine lights that stand in the thought of Arich Anpin desire only to pursue the nine chambers in which are found all the secrets of the faith. The lights of the mystery of the supernal thought above and below are all called 'infinity' – here neither desire nor thought are found. When thought shines it is not known by whose light, but it is concealed in Binah and shines upon whoever it shines. The thought and the person enter each other until they are joined as a complete whole. During the sacrifice on the altar all grades are moving up, and thought is then 'bedecked by infinity,' since the illumination by which the supernal thought shines is called 'infinity'. Everything takes its existence from this completely unknown illumination. Rabbi Shimon speaks again about 'the End of all Flesh,' or the Other Side. He says that there is a joyful bond between Binah and Arich Anpin, on earth between male and female, and between Briyah, Yetzirah and Asiyah. He talks again about the sacrifice of the goat during each new moon, and about how the 'End of all Flesh' desires only flesh; the soul goes up to another place. Rabbi Shimon tells us that a righteous man is in himself a sacrifice for atonement, therefore he atones for the whole world. He turns to "Then a cloud covered the Tent of Meeting," telling us that when the cloud covered the Tabernacle the Shechinah dwelled on the earth and the spirit of defilement, the End of all Flesh, was removed from the world. If the wicked did not draw the spirit of defilement back into the world, it would stay away. Lastly, we learn that in the future God will remove the spirit of defilement, as in: "He will destroy death for ever." Rabbi Shimon ends Pequdei with a blessing to Hashem.

946 אָמַר רִבִּי שִׁמְעוֹן, אֲרֵימִית יְדַי בִּצְלוֹתִין לְעֵילָּא, דְּכַד רְעוּתָא עִלָּאָה, לְעֵילָּא לְעֵילָּא, קַיְּימָא עַל הַהוּא רְעוּתָא דְּלָא אִתְיְידַיע, וְלָא

אִתְפַּס לְעָלְמִין, רֵישָׁא דִּסְתִּים יַתִּיר לְעֵילָּא, וְהַהוּא רֵישָׁא אַפִּיק מַה דְּאַפִּיק, וְלָא יְדִיעַ. וְנָהִיר מַה דְּנָהִיר, כֹּלָּא בִּסְתִּימוּ.

946. Rabbi Shimon said: I have raised my hands high in prayer. HE PRAYED THAT REVEALING THESE MYSTERIES WOULD PLEASE THE HOLY ONE, BLESSED BE HE. When supernal desire up above, THE SECRET OF KETER OF ARICH ANPIN, is supported by the desire that is not known, nor ever conceived, the head, which conceals more the higher ones, emanates whatever it emanates, and is not known. It illuminates whatever it illuminates, all of it concealed.

947. רְעוּ דְּמַחֲשָׁבָה עִלָּאָה, לְמִרְדַּף אֲבַתְרֵיהּ, וּלְאִתְנַהֲרָא מִנֵּיהּ, חַד פְּרִיסוּ אִתְפְּרַס, וּמִגּוֹ הַהוּא פְּרִיסָא בִּרְדִיפוּ דְּהַהִיא מַחֲשָׁבָה עִלָּאָה, מָטֵי וְלָא מָטֵי, עַד הַהוּא פְּרִיסָא נָהִיר מַה דְּנָהִיר. וּכְדֵין הַהוּא מַחֲשָׁבָה עִלָּאָה, נָהִיר בִּנְהִירוּ סָתִים דְּלָא יְדִיעַ. וְהַאי מַחֲשָׁבָה לָא יָדַע.

947. The desire of the supernal thought, KETER OF ARICH ANPIN, is to pursue it and to illuminate with its light, BUT a veil is spread BETWEEN THEM, through which, by the pursuing after the supernal thought, light reaches and reaches not, BECAUSE OF THE VEIL. It illuminates up to the veil whatever it illuminates, BUT NOT BENEATH THE VEIL. Then a supernal thought illuminates with a concealed illumination, which is not known. The thought itself is considered unknown.

948. כְּדֵין בָּטַשׁ הַאי נְהִירוּ דְּמַחֲשָׁבָה דְּלָא אִתְיְידַע, בִּנְהִירוּ דִּפְרִסָא, דְּקַיְּימָא דְּנָהִיר מִמָּה, דְּלָא יְדִיעַ, וְלָא אִתְיְידַע, וְלָא אִתְגַּלְיָא. וּכְדֵין, דָּא נְהִירוּ דְּמַחֲשָׁבָה דְּלָא אִתְיְידַע, בָּטַשׁ בִּנְהִירוּ דִּפְרִיסָא, וְנָהֲרִין כַּחֲדָא.

948. Then the illumination of the unknown thought strikes the illumination of the veil, which IS SUPPORTED AND shines by what is not known and unknown, and what is not revealed. Thus the illumination of unknown thought strikes the light of the veil and they illuminate together.

949. וְאִתְעֲבִידוּ תִּשְׁעָה הֵיכָלִין, וְהֵיכָלִין לָאו אִינּוּן נְהוֹרִין, וְלָאו אִינּוּן

רוּחִין, וְלָאו אִינּוּן נִשְׁמָתִין, וְלָא אִית מַאן דְּקַיְּימָא בְּהוּ. רְעוּתָא דְּכָל תֵּשַׁע נְהוֹרִין, קַיְימֵי כֻּלְּהוּ בְּמַחֲשָׁבָה, דְּאִיהִי חַד מִנַּיְיהוּ בְּחוּשְׁבָּנָא, כֻּלְּהוּ לְמִרְדַּף אֲבַתְרַיְיהוּ. בְּשַׁעֲתָא דְּקַיְימֵי בְּמַחֲשָׁבָה, וְלָא מִתְדַּבְּקָן וְלָא אִתְיְידִיעוּ. וְאִלֵּין לָא קַיְימֵי, לָאו בִּרְעוּתָא, וְלָאו בְּמַחֲשָׁבָה עִלָּאָה, תַּפְסִין בָּהּ וְלָא תַּפְסִין. בְּאִלֵּין קַיְימִין כָּל רָזִין דִּמְהֵימְנוּתָא, וְכָל אִינּוּן נְהוֹרִין, מֵרָזָא דְּמַחֲשָׁבָה עִלָּאָה וּלְתַתָּא, כֻּלְּהוּ אִקְרוּן אֵין סוֹף. עַד הָכָא מָטוּן נְהוֹרִין, וְלָא מָטוּן, וְלָא אִתְיְידִיעוּ לָאו הָכָא רְעוּתָא, וְלָא מַחֲשָׁבָה.

949. Nine chambers are thereby formed. THESE chambers are not lights, spirits, nor souls, and no one can conceive them. The desire of all nine lights standing within thought OF ARICH ANPIN, each of THE NINE numbered, is to pursue THE NINE CHAMBERS, while THE NINE LIGHTS still are in thought OF ARICH ANPIN, BUT THE NINE CHAMBERS are not conceived or known. FOR these NINE CHAMBERS are not considered of THE ASPECT OF desire, nor of THE ASPECT OF the supernal thought, ARICH ANPIN, which they grasp yet grasp not. In these NINE CHAMBERS are all the secrets of the Faith. And the lights of the mystery of the supernal thought above and below, are all called 'the Endless World', FOR the lights reach here and reach not, nor are they known. Here abides neither desire nor thought.

950. כַּד נָהִיר מַחֲשָׁבָה, וְלָא אִתְיְדַע מִמַּאן דְּנָהִיר, כְּדֵין אִתְלְבַּשׁ וְאִסְתִּים גּוֹ בִּינָה, וְנָהִיר מַאן דְּנָהִיר, וְעָאיל דָּא בְּדָא, עַד דְּאִתְכְּלִילוּ כֻּלְּהוּ כַּחֲדָא.

950. When thought shines, though it is not known by whose light, it is clothed and concealed within Binah, and shines upon whoever it shines upon. They enter each other until they are joined as a complete whole.

951. וּבְרָזָא דְּקָרְבְּנָא כַּד סָלִיק, כֹּלָּא אִתְקַשַּׁר דָּא בְּדָא, וְנָהִיר דָּא בְּדָא, כְּדֵין קַיְימֵי כֻּלְּהוּ בִּסְלִיקוּ, וּמַחֲשָׁבָה אִתְעֲטַּר בְּאֵין סוֹף. הַהוּא נְהִירוּ דְּנָהִיר מִנֵּיהּ מַחֲשָׁבָה עִלָּאָה, דְּלָא יָדַע אִיהִי בָּהּ כְּלַל, אִקְרֵי אֵין סוֹף, דְּמִנֵּיהּ אִשְׁתְּכַח וְקַיְּימָא וְנָהִיר לְמַאן דְּנָהִיר, וְעַל דָּא כֹּלָּא קָאֵים.

זַכָּאָה חוּלָקֵיהוֹן דְּצַדִּיקַיָּיא בְּעָלְמָא דֵּין, וּבְעָלְמָא דְּאָתֵי.

951. In the secret of the sacrifice, when it is offered (lit. 'ascends'), everything is connected and shines upon each other. Then all grades are on the ascent, and thought is bedecked by the Endless World. For the illumination, by which the supernal thought illuminates, which is completely unknown, is called 'the Endless World', from which everything takes its existence, and which shines upon that which it shines on. HAPPY IS THE PORTION OF THE RIGHTEOUS IN THIS WORLD AND IN THE WORLD TO COME.

952. תָּא חֲזֵי, הַאי סִטְרָא אַחֲרָא, דְּאִקְרֵי קֵץ כָּל בָּשָׂר, כְּמָה דְּקִשּׁוּרָא אִשְׁתְּכַח לְעֵילָּא בְּחִדוּ, אוּף הָכִי נָמֵי לְתַתָּא, בְּחֶדְוָותָא, וּרְעוּתָא לְאִסְתַּפְּקָא כֹּלָּא לְעֵילָּא וְתַתָּא, וְאִימָא קַיְימָא עֲלַיְיהוּ דְּיִשְׂרָאֵל, כַּדְקָא יֵאוֹת.

952. Come and see: The Other Side, which is called 'the End of all Flesh'. As there is a bond above, BETWEEN BINAH AND ARICH ANPIN, in joy, so beneath, IN MALE AND FEMALE, AND BRIYAH, YETZIRAH AND ASIYAH, THERE IS A CONNECTION BETWEEN THEM in happiness and desire to give satisfaction to all, high and low, and Ima stands properly by Yisrael.

953. ת"ח, בְּכָל רֵישׁ יַרְחָא וְיַרְחָא, כַּד סִיהֲרָא אִתְחַדְשָׁא, יָהֲבִין לֵיהּ לְהַאי קֵץ כָּל בָּשָׂר, חוּלָקָא חֲדָא יַתִּיר עַל קָרְבְּנִין, לְאִתְעַסְּקָא בֵּיהּ, וְאִשְׁתַּמַּשׁ בְּחוּלָקֵיהּ, וִיהֵא סִטְרָא דְּיִשְׂרָאֵל בִּלְחוֹדַיְיהוּ, בְּגִין דְּיִתְאַחֲדוּן בְּמַלְכֵּיהוֹן.

953. Come and see: In each new moon, when the moon starts to wax, NAMELY, WHEN MALCHUT RENEWS ITS UNION WITH ZEIR ANPIN, the End of all Flesh is given another portion, A GOAT OF THE NEW MOON, in addition to THE USUAL sacrifices, so it may busy itself with it and attend to its own portion, and the side of Yisrael will stay for them alone, so they will be united with their King.

954. וְדָא אִיהוּ שָׂעִיר, בְּגִין דְּאִיהוּ חוּלָקָא דְּעֵשָׂו, דִּכְתִּיב בֵּיהּ שָׂעִיר.

הֵן עֵשָׂו אָחִי אִישׁ שָׂעִיר. וע״ד אִיהוּ אִשְׁתַּמַּשׁ בְּחוּלָקֵיהּ, וְיִשְׂרָאֵל אִינּוּן מִשְׁתַּמְּשֵׁי בְּחוּלָקֵיהוֹן. בג״כ כְּתִיב, כִּי יַעֲקֹב בָּחַר לוֹ יָהּ יִשְׂרָאֵל לִסְגֻלָּתוֹ.

954. This is the reason for sacrificing a goat (lit. 'hairy'), being the portion of Esau, of whom it is written, 'hairy', "Esau my brother is a hairy man" (Beresheet 27:11). Therefore, he attends to his own share, and Yisrael to theirs. This is the reason for the verse, "For Hashem has chosen Jacob to Himself, Yisrael for His peculiar possession" (Tehilim 135:4).

955. ות״ח, הַאי קֵץ כָּל בָּשָׂר, כָּל רְעוּתֵיהּ לָאו אִיהוּ אֶלָּא בְּבִשְׂרָא תָּדִיר. ובג״כ, תִּקּוּנָא דְּבִשְׂרָא תָּדִיר לְגַבֵּיהּ, וע״ד אִקְרֵי קֵץ כָּל בָּשָׂר. וְכַד אִיהוּ שַׁלִּיט, שַׁלִּיט עַל גּוּפָא, וְלָאו עַל נִשְׁמְתָא, נִשְׁמְתָא סַלְּקָא לְאַתְרָהּ, וּבִשְׂרָא אִתְיְיהִיב לְאֲתַר דָּא, כְּגַוְונָא דְּקָרְבְּנָא, דִּרְעוּתָא סַלְּקָא לַאֲתַר חַד, וּבִשְׂרָא לַאֲתַר חַד.

955. Come and see: All that 'End of all Flesh' ever desires is flesh. Therefore, the correction of flesh is always by it. Hence, it is called 'the End of all Flesh', yet he is in control over the body, but not over the soul. The soul ascends to its place, and the body is given to this place, THE END OF ALL FLESH, like a sacrifice; when the desire goes up one place else, TO MALE AND FEMALE, the flesh goes up to another place, THE END OF ALL FLESH.

956. וב״נ דְּאִיהוּ זַכָּאָה, אִיהוּ קָרְבְּנָא מַמָּשׁ לְכַפָּרָא, וְאַחֲרָא דְּלָאו אִיהוּ זַכָּאָה, לָא. בְּגִין דְּבֵיהּ מוּמָא, דִּכְתִּיב כִּי לֹא לְרָצוֹן יִהְיֶה לָכֶם. וע״ד צַדִּיקָא כַּפָּרָה אִיהוּ בְּעָלְמָא, וְקָרְבְּנָא מַמָּשׁ. זַכָּאִין אִינּוּן צַדִּיקַיָּיא בְּעָלְמָא דֵּין, וּבְעָלְמָא דְּאָתֵי.

956. A righteous man is in himself a sacrifice for atonement. This is not so for he who is not righteous, because he is blemished, as it is written, "for it shall not be acceptable for you" (Vayikra 22:20). Therefore, a righteous man atones for the world, a real sacrifice. Happy are the righteous in this